COMMUNIST SYSTEMS
IN COMPARATIVE PERSPECTIVE

ANCHOR PRESS · DOUBLEDAY

LENARD J. COHEN is Lecturer in the Department of Political Science, Queens College, CUNY.

JANE P. SHAPIRO is Associate Professor and Chairman of the Political Science Department at Manhattanville College.

COMMUNIST SYSTEMS IN COMPARATIVE PERSPECTIVE

Edited by
LENARD J. COHEN and JANE P. SHAPIRO

ANCHOR BOOKS
Anchor Press/Doubleday
Garden City, New York
1974

Library of Congress Cataloging in Publication Data

Cohen, Lenard J comp.

Communist Systems in Comparative Perspective.

Bibliography: p. 527

1. Communist state—Addresses, essays, lectures.
2. Communist countries—Politics and government—Addresses, essays, lectures. 3. Comparative government—Addresses, essays, lectures. I. Shapiro, Jane P., joint comp. II. Title.

JC474.C624 320.3'09171'1

ISBN 0-385-07993-1

Library of Congress Catalog Card Number 73–81456

Anchor Books Edition: 1974

Printed in the United States of America

First Edition

THIS BOOK IS FOR

Joan,
Jeanette, and
David Cohen

Alan,
Leslie, and
Peter Shapiro

PREFACE

COMPARATIVE Communism is the outgrowth of the study of Soviet politics in particular and of comparative politics in general. It is thus an attempt to blend the particular with the general—a task both difficult and elusive. How to strike a balance between these two central tasks, without excessively abstract generalization and without becoming absorbed in the specifics of one particular kind of communism, is a question that has already perplexed countless teachers and students of Comparative Communism.

There is an inherent tension in the study of Comparative Communism. This tension is the natural outcome of the manner in which Comparative Communism emerged as an accepted and recognized part of the study of politics. Its natural antecedent was the study of Soviet politics. At first, before World War II, that study involved essentially the application of concepts and approaches developed more broadly in the study of Western political systems: The emphasis was heavily on institutions, constitutions, and political history. It soon became clear that such an approach could not do justice to the specifics of the Leninist-Stalinist experience or adequately deal with a political system in which the political process was, to put it mildly, somewhat divorced from the formal constitutional structure.

In response to this recognition an altogether novel approach to the study of Soviet politics emerged after World War II. It focused more on the uniqueness and particularities of the Soviet experience; it concentrated its attention on the varieties of informal, indirect and even covert systems of party controls; it stressed the importance of political coercion both in the maintenance of the political system and especially in the effort to effect a far-reaching and ideologically influenced reconstruction of society; and it emphasized the ideological rather than the historical dimension in its broader generalizations about the Soviet political system. The study of the Soviet political system thus became almost autonomous in the wider study of politics: it operated with its own categories in response to an intellectual challenge that was perceived as almost unique.

The expansion of Soviet power westward, the appearance of new Communist systems in Eastern Europe and in the Far East, did mean —especially in the initial phases—the multiplication of political systems patterned largely on the Soviet model. As a result, the initial tendency was to view the other Communist systems essentially as an extension of the Soviet, with only some secondary adjustments to local particularities. The paradox here was that this involved the generalization of the particular: the superimposition of categories and concepts learned through the intensive and—it must be said in due justice—often innovative and perceptive study of Soviet politics.

It did not take long for scholars to realize that generalizing the particular—i.e., applying the Soviet experience to the other Communist states—was simply not good enough. The expansion of the Communist system to eight nations of Eastern Europe and to China, Korea, and Vietnam meant that what was initially a peculiar Soviet-Russian political product was now being adapted to a variety of societies with rich and distinctive political traditions of their own. Indeed, within Eastern Europe alone one can differentiate several alternative patterns of political tradition and behavior. The consequence was the inevitable fragmentation not only of Communist unity—a subject that has commanded scholarly attention now for almost two decades—but of the Communist political system as a single, relatively homogeneous type.

It was then that the study of Soviet politics and comparative politics came to be merged into what is now called Comparative Communism. Comparative Communism is an effort to retain from the study of Soviet experience what is relevant to the study of other Communist systems, while recognizing that the Communist form of government has developed many distinctive varieties even in the key aspects of the political system and the political process. In other words, we are not forgetting that communism is a novel experiment in social and political organization, which requires new insights and concepts, many of which were initially developed in the study of Soviet politics. At the same time, we recognize that the study of Soviet politics provides only the source of partial insights into other Communist systems and that comparative politics has in the meantime developed concepts and methods that can be creatively applied to the several Communist systems.

This volume represents a happy blend of these two approaches, and it is designed to give the student a balanced appreciation of both the unique and the general. Organized around several key categories derived from contemporary political science, it seeks to give the student a grasp of how the specific political context of several different countries has interacted with the more general manifestation of communism as a new form of social-political organization. The introductory essays to various chapters focus, in a perceptive and stimulating fashion, the student's attention on the most significant questions in need of further discussion and debate. The volume is thus both informative and heuristic, with the latter representing the more significant contribution.

It is important to stress the heuristic contribution of this volume because in any attempt to study Comparative Communism some imbalance is inevitable. One is either drawn to the challenge of the unique and becomes absorbed by the study of a political system, fascinated by the subtle interaction of the historical, the cultural, the political, and the ideological or, alternatively, one may be challenged by the very complexity of the undertaking to formulate broader and more sweeping generalizations, cutting across many different societies, cultures, and levels of economic development. A successful teacher, and a successful text, should try to give the student the opportunity to follow either path on his own—but also to tempt him to experiment with both, seeking to understand the relationship between the specific and the general. This volume does precisely that.

In addition, this volume strives to focus the student's attention on the question of change within Communist systems. This issue has commanded widespread attention in recent years, and the argument has swung back and forth between those who essentially emphasize the peculiarities of political change within the Communist systems and those who lean to the view that the eventual path that the Communist systems will follow has already in part been charted by Western political systems. As a participant in that debate who is inclined to emphasize more the immanent and the inherent dynamics of the several Communist systems, let me merely note that the use of the terms "pluralism" and "liberalization" by itself conveys a meaning and a message associated with the experience of Western-type political systems. The student of Comparative Communism will have to judge for himself the extent to which the patterns of change within Communist political systems can be fitted into these specifically Western and historically conditioned categories of analysis. My own view is that, either in "degenerating" or in "transforming" themselves, the several Communist systems will develop political processes and forms which will not duplicate the Western "pluralist" or "liberal" experience but which more likely will borrow from the administrative and technological experience of modern large-scale economic organization—and that their success or failure in so doing (i.e., transforming or degenerating) will be very much conditioned by the specific political settings of the several countries concerned. It is to be hoped that by reflecting on the various contributions to this volume, and by responding to the challenge posed in the introductory essays prepared by the editors, the student will be stimulated to formulate his own answers to this central question concerning change in Communist systems, and that in so doing he will advance further the study of Comparative Communism.

Finally, let me merely note my personal satisfaction that this volume has been prepared by two colleagues who have been closely associated with the study of Comparative Communism at Columbia University. Their creative work, including not only the preparation of this volume but also other important scholarly contributions to the study of several Communist political systems, is part of a dialogue on Communist affairs nurtured at Columbia University for more than a decade, a dialogue in which there are no students or teachers but in which we all learn from one another.

ZBIGNIEW BRZEZINSKI
July 5, 1973

CONTENTS

All nations will arrive at socialism—this is inevitable—but not all will do so in exactly the same way. Each will contribute something of its own in one or another form of democracy, one or another variety of the dictatorship of the proletariat, one or another rate at which socialist transformations will be effected in the various aspects of social life. There is nothing more primitive from the viewpoint of theory or more ridiculous from that of practice than to paint *this* aspect of the future in a monotonous gray "in the name of historical materialism."

—V. I. Lenin, 1918

In order to turn our country into an industrial power, we must learn conscientiously from the advanced experience of the Soviet Union. The Soviet Union has been building socialism for forty years, and its experience is very valuable to us. . . . Now, there are two different attitudes towards learning from others. One is the dogmatic attitude of transplanting everything, whether or not it is suited to our conditions. This is no good. The other attitude is to use our heads and learn those things which suit our conditions, that is, to absorb whatever experience is useful to us. That is the attitude we should adopt.

—Mao Tse-tung, 1957

. . . as a Socialist country we have felt and feel today that sovereignty under Socialism assumes the full independence and the responsibility of the revolutionary movement in each country for the selection of its own road of socio-economic development in keeping with specific conditions and the requirements of the people. Only such relationships among Socialist countries and Communist parties can promote the strengthening of the international revolutionary workers' and progressive movement generally . . . those who do not respect their own country and their own people in the first place cannot respect others either.

—Josip Broz Tito, 1968

INTRODUCTION: COMMUNIST SYSTEMS IN COMPARATIVE PERSPECTIVE*

COMMUNIST STUDIES IN FLUX

THE study of Communist political systems has been undergoing a major transformation. Initially composed of a small group of scholars seeking to describe and explain what was considered to be the unique nature of the Bolshevik regime during its first quarter century of rule, and later the complex relationship between the Soviet Union and its clientele states in Eastern Europe after World War II, Communist studies has recently burgeoned into a major subfield of contemporary political science. The traditional area-studies approach (Russian, Russian/East European, Chinese/East Asian), which focused predominantly on the geographical or cultural similarities among Communist states, has given way to new methods of political analysis. Variously referred to as "the behavioral revolution in Communist studies," "the post area studies perspective," or "comparative Communist studies," this new orientation has involved an effort to adapt innovations in the discipline of political science, and particularly the field of comparative politics, to the study of Communist regimes.[1]

* The Authors wish to express their appreciation to Professors Donald W. Klein, Robert Sharlet, Richard Sorich, Jan F. Triska, Zbigniew Brzezinski, Seweryn Bialer, William Brigman, and Michelle Boyer for their generous assistance and encouragement in the preparation of this volume.

[1] For the evolution in Communist studies, see Ghita Ionescu, *Comparative Communist Politics* (London: Macmillan, 1972); Robert Sharlet, "Comparative Communism and Methodological Pluralism," *Polity,* III, 3 (Spring 1971), pp. 427–41; Frederic J. Fleron, ed., *Communist Studies and the Social Sciences* (Chicago: Rand McNally, 1969); Roger E. Kanet, ed., *The Behavioral Revolution and Communist Studies* (New York: The Free Press, 1971), especially pp. 1–10; Chalmers Johnson, "The Role of Social Science in China Scholarship," *World Politics,* XVII, 2 (January 1965), pp. 256–71; and Richard W. Wilson, "Chinese Studies in Crisis," ibid., XXIII, 2 (January 1971).

The growing obsolescence of traditional modes of thinking and analysis with respect to Communist political systems has been motivated in large part by the proliferation of Communist regimes between 1945 and 1959 (from one to fourteen), and by the major political changes that have taken place in these states within the two decades since Stalin's death. In addition, the advent to power of Communist parties in Yugoslavia, Albania, China, and North Vietnam, largely as a consequence of their own revolutionary struggles and sacrifices, provided the context for the phenomenon of "national communism," the attempt by Communist leaders to formulate and pursue their own "separate roads in the construction of socialism."[2] Communist leaders who had become accustomed to interpreting the "correct" course of policy according to their own local circumstances during years of underground and partisan military activity were extremely reluctant, on assuming political power, to defer obediently to the dictates of the Soviet Union and to accept blindly the Stalinist pattern of socialist development. Yugoslavia and China provide the most clear-cut examples of autonomous political development. Hungary in 1956 and Czechoslovakia in 1968 represent the least successful sustained efforts to effect independent development.

The heterogeneous pattern of development among the Communist states clearly demonstrated that the study of these regimes could no longer simply be coterminous with Russian and Soviet area studies. Many of the conventional concepts and tools of research that were useful during the Stalinist era no longer served to explain Soviet politics in the post-Stalin era or the complex nature and functioning of fourteen different ruling Communist parties, operating within a wide variety of geographical and cultural settings, and in countries at various stages of socioeconomic development. It was not surprising, therefore, that a new generation of political scientists, recognizing the differences among Communist systems during the 1950s and early 1960s, turned to the new concepts and techniques being developed by their colleagues in other subfields of the discipline. These developments include: an expansion in the scope of political studies to encompass the experience of countries outside of the Western, or "Atlantic," area; an emphasis on the observable behavior of individuals and groups as the basic units of political analysis; an increased concern with the precision of methodological procedures and the selection of evidence when conducting political research; and an attempt to formulate empirically derived concepts, propositions, and theories that can help explain and predict political behavior beyond the confines of a single country or geographi-

[2] See Edmund Demaitre, "The Great Debate on National Communism," *Studies in Comparative Communism,* V, 2/3 (Summer/Autumn 1972), pp. 234–57; and Paul Zinner, ed., *National Communism and Popular Revolt in Eastern Europe* (New York: Columbia University Press, 1956).

cal area. It was hoped that studies carried out in a comparative framework would link the analysis of Communist regimes to the work being done on other types of political systems, as well as contribute to the quest for genuine cross-national propositions about the nature of political activity.[3]

Approaches to the Study of Communist Systems

As the above discussion suggests, the changing character of Communist studies has produced a variety of different approaches to the analysis of Communist regimes. By "approach" we mean a general strategy for the study of political phenomena. An approach usually involves a set of assumptions or an organizing concept employed by the political analyst, either explicitly or implicitly, to guide his research and coordinate the selection of material.[4] In the following pages, we will briefly survey the major approaches that have been utilized, describe their essential features, and suggest some of their principal strengths and weaknesses. Several of these approaches have constituted the intel-

[3] For an introduction to the changes which have taken place in Political Science, see, *inter alia,* William A. Welsh, *Studying Politics* (New York: Praeger, 1973); Heinz Eulau, ed., *Behavioralism in Political Science* (New York: Atherton Press, 1969); and James C. Charlesworth, *Contemporary Political Analysis* (New York: The Free Press, 1967).

[4] Alan C. Isak, *Scope and Methods of Political Science* (Homewood: Dorsey, 1969), pp. 157–59. William A. Welsh makes a distinction between "concept-based approaches" (system, function, communication, development) and "approaches based on techniques" (simulation, game theory) in his *Studying Politics,* op. cit., pp. 50–97.

Studies of Communist regimes, and political analyses in general, are not characterized by definitional precision in the use of terms such as "approach," "perspective," "conceptual framework," "model," or "paradigm." At the risk of perpetuating this problem, we have not sought to make any rigorous methodological distinctions between these terms but have used them somewhat interchangeably, as they are used in most of the studies discussed and included in this volume. For the nature of the problem and some insights into penetrating this terminological jungle, see Frederic J. Fleron, "Soviet Area Studies and the Social Sciences: Some Methodological Problems in Communist Studies," in Fleron, op. cit., pp. 1–33; James A. Bill and Robert L. Hardgrave, Jr., *Comparative Politics: The Quest for Theory* (Columbus: Charles E. Merrill, 1973), pp. 1–42; Lawrence C. Mayer, *Comparative Political Inquiry: A Methodological Survey* (Homewood: Dorsey, 1972); and George J. Graham, *Methodological Foundations for Political Analysis* (Waltham: Ginn, 1971).

lectual framework of Communist studies for a number of years but have only recently become subject to criticism and controversy. Other approaches, although widely advocated and discussed in recent years, are still in the initial stages of application by researchers. While many of the approaches overlap and are often combined in a single study, each of them represents a distinctive strategy for analysis. It is important for the student to bear in mind that the use of any one or any combination of the following approaches has had a significant effect on the nature of research and analysis of Communist regimes. As is the case in all research work, the particular approach and values employed by the student of communism will have considerable influence on the outcome of his work.

1. THE HISTORICAL-CULTURAL APPROACH

The configuration of common experiences and traditions that constitute the historical legacy of any society has an important influence on its political development. Advocates of the historical-cultural approach are particularly concerned with the ways in which the formation, operation, and development of Communist regimes may be influenced by traditional practices and experiences that preceded the Communist party's acquisition of power. To what extent, for example, has the political history of Czechoslovakia, including the particular form of subtle resistance to foreign subjugation demonstrated by its people before World War I and its democratic experience in the interwar years, affected that country's receptivity to Communist rule? How have Yugoslavia's heterogeneous population and the conflicts that have existed for centuries among the various ethnic groups of the Balkans affected the ability of the Communist regime to establish a new basis for political stability or carry out its highly innovative policies? In what way have historical patterns of political autocracy and administrative centralization in both Russia and China provided a congenial climate for the emergence and maintenance of Communist rule in these societies? These are the kinds of questions posed by proponents of the historical-cultural approach. A recent introductory text on Chinese politics, which considers the relationship between "communism and tradition," provides a good example of this type of argument:

> Historically the Chinese have always preferred a single, unambiguous authority. Two thousand years of Confucian government was an uninterrupted era of authoritarian rule. . . . For the Chinese the ideal condition was one in which there was no confusion

about the structure of the hierarchy. They have always thought of their evil days when there was open competition for power and when there was political pluralism. Historically they idealized the periods of dynastic stability and decried those when there was uncertainty about who was supreme. In modern times this attitude resulted in widespread distress over the complex balance of power that characterized the early Republic and warlord period. A ceaseless craving for one-party rule contributed to an exaggerated faith in the Kuomintang and then in the Communist regime.[5]

One of the major advantages of this approach is that it recognizes the important admixture of tradition and modernity in every society. It thus avoids the tendency to limit one's study of a political system to a static profile of political events that occurred only after the Communist party came to power. It seeks to demonstrate that historical patterns do have an influence on the contemporary political process and its probable development.[6] This approach also provides a useful antidote

[5] Lucian W. Pye, *China: An Introduction* (Boston: Little, Brown, 1972), pp. 344–45. Other examples include: Adam B. Ulam, "The Russian Political System," in Samuel H. Beer, et al., *Patterns of Government*, 3rd ed. (New York: Random House, 1973); Hugh Seton-Watson, *The East European Revolution*, 3rd ed. (New York: Praeger, 1956); Robert Lee Wolff, *The Balkans in Our Time* (New York: W. W. Norton, 1956); H. Gordon Skilling, "Communism and Czechoslovak Traditions," *Journal of International Affairs*, XX, 1 (1966), pp. 118–36, as well as many of the other articles included in this special issue, entitled "East Central Europe: Continuity and Change"; Ernest J. Simmons, ed., *Continuity and Change in Russian and Soviet Thought* (Cambridge: Harvard University Press, 1955); James H. Billington, *The Icon and the Axe* (New York: Alfred A. Knopf, 1966); Nicholas Berdyaev, *The Origin of Russian Communism* (London: Geoffrey Blos, 1948); Cyril E. Black, ed., *The Transformation of Russian Society* (Cambridge: Harvard University Press, 1967); C. P. Fitzgerald, *The Birth of Communist China* (New York: Praeger, 1964); and Karl A. Wittfogel, *Oriental Despotism: A Comparative Study of Total Power* (New Haven: Yale University Press, 1957).

The footnotes in this section outlining the various approaches do not provide an exhaustive survey of the available literature, but rather are intended to draw the reader's attention to some of the major studies which either utilize or critically examine the approaches discussed by the editors. The Bibliography at the end of the volume provides a guide to the large and rapidly growing body of work on Communist political systems.

[6] Robert E. Ward recently observed that social scientists trained as area specialists "share a high regard for the importance and relevance of history as a determinant of political outcomes. This is really a subcategory and a consequence of their concern with the cultural context of politics. One does not study culture in an historical vacuum. The same should be true

to those works which casually accept the claims of Communist leaders that their party successfully overturned the old regime and created a completely new society populated with "new men."

The danger of this approach, as one might expect, is to assume that little has changed, that communism is simply a contemporary manifestation of certain historical patterns and forces, and that it has had a relatively minor impact of its own on politics and society. It also tends to overemphasize the uniqueness of each Communist system, and has little regard for the importance of ideological kinship, structural features, and long-term goals shared by all of these regimes in varying degrees.

One recent mode of research on Communist systems that may be considered a variant of the historical-cultural approach, while avoiding many of its pitfalls, is the work being done on political culture.[7] Starting with the assumption that the pattern of attitudes and values toward political authority is an important component of the broader cultural makeup of every society, studies of political culture attempt to determine the nature of these attitudes and the most important factors that account for them. An outgrowth of earlier studies of "national character," this approach devotes considerable attention to the impact of historical factors and traditions on contemporary political attitudes, while simultaneously emphasizing the social and psychological bases of cultural patterns and the important cross-cultural similarities and differ-

---

of politics. It is a conceit born of the Enlightenment and reinforced by certain trends in current social science theorizing that political attitudes, behavior or institutions can be explained or understood that do not involve a substantial historical element. Professional exposure to societies where the so-called pre-modern stages of history are chronologically so much closer to the present, where nation-states have emerged well within the reach of living memories, and where people still live and strive to cope with problems that seem by our standards archaic, imbues one with a particularly keen sense of the contemporary relevance of history."

See his "Culture and the Comparative Study of Politics or the Constipated Dialectic," Presidential Address delivered at the Sixty-ninth Annual Meeting of the American Political Science Association (New Orleans, September 6, 1973), p. 12.

[7] See, *inter alia,* Robert C. Tucker, "Culture, Political Culture, and Communist Society," *Political Science Quarterly,* 88, 2 (June 1973), pp. 173–90; Alfred G. Meyer, "Communist Revolutions and Cultural Change," *Studies in Comparative Communism,* V, 4 (Winter 1972), pp. 345–70; Robert C. Tucker, "Communism and Political Culture," *Newsletter on Comparative Studies in Communism,* IV, 3 (May 1971), pp. 3–11; Dorothy Knapp, David W. Paul, and Gerson Sher, "Digest of the Conference on Political Culture and Comparative Communist Studies," ibid., V, 3 (May 1972), pp. 2–17.

ences that exist in this respect. The most prominent examples of this type of political science research have been of a comparative nature, although work on political culture in Communist societies has thus far been limited to single-country studies.[8]

2. THE TOTALITARIAN APPROACH

The appearance of dictatorial regimes in the Soviet Union, Italy, and Nazi Germany, as well as in a number of other European states during the 1920s and 1930s, prompted many observers to search for some theoretical explanation or framework that would account for the common features of these political systems. The concept of totalitarianism or the "totalitarian state" was elaborated by several writers as a means of characterizing the operation of modern dictatorial regimes. In the opinion of most scholars who consider this approach useful, the most striking characteristic of these regimes has been their attempt to exercise "total" political control over all spheres of society. Professors Friedrich and Brzezinski, probably the most influential advocates of this approach, delineated six "interrelated traits," or a "syndrome" of factors typically displayed by the totalitarian dictatorship: (1) an elaborated official ideology; (2) a single mass party, typically led by one man, "the dictator"; (3) a system of terror; (4) a monopoly of control over the means of mass communications; (5) a monopoly of control over the armed forces; and (6) a centrally directed economy. Friedrich and Brzezinski emphasize that the historical uniqueness of totalitarian dictatorship as a form of political control "could have arisen only within the context of mass democracy and modern technology," thus distinguishing it from earlier forms of autocracy and despotism.[9]

[8] See, for example, Richard H. Solomon, *Mao's Revolution and the Chinese Political Culture* (Berkeley: University of California Press, 1971); Frederick C. Barghoorn, *Politics in the USSR,* 2nd ed. (Boston: Little, Brown, 1972); M. George Zaninovich, "The Case of Yugoslavia: Delineating Political Culture in a Multi-ethnic Society," *Studies in Comparative Communism,* IV, 2 (April 1971), pp. 58–70; Joseph R. Fiszman, *Revolution and Tradition in People's Poland* (Princeton: Princeton University Press, 1972); Richard Fagen, *The Transformation of Political Culture in Cuba* (Stanford: Stanford University Press, 1969). For a review of some of the early postwar work on the psycho-cultural basis of Soviet political behavior, see John S. Reshetar, *Problems of Analyzing and Predicting Soviet Behavior* (Garden City: Doubleday & Company, 1955), espec. pp. 14–30; and his *The Soviet Polity* (New York: Dodd, Mead, 1971), pp. 38–71.

[9] Carl J. Friedrich and Zbigniew Brzezinski, *Totalitarian Dictatorship and*

Building upon their work, other scholars have used the term totalitarianism in different ways, accepting or rejecting various points of the six-trait syndrome and emphasizing what they consider to be additional features of modern autocratic rule. Leonard Schapiro, for example, makes a distinction between the "contours" and the "pillars" of a totalitarian polity. The *contours,* or "characteristic features," of a totalitarian regime include: the "Leader"; subjugation of the legal organs; control over private morality; continuous mobilization; and a claim to legitimacy based on moral support. The *pillars* include: "a so-called ideology"; a single, well-organized political party; the administrative machinery of the state; and the "instruments of rule," such as the military and the police. For Schapiro, it is the single "Leader," more than the party or the ideology, that is the pivotal element of the totalitarian polity.[10]

However defined, the concept of totalitarianism has been under attack for a variety of reasons.[11] Some social scientists feel that it has been subject to so many different interpretations that it can no longer serve as a useful analytical tool. Others object to the normative implications or "value-loaded" character of the concept, since it has frequently been used to support or deride the virtues of particular types of political systems (e.g., Mussolini's exhortation of the totalitarian state, or the pejorative use of "totalitarian Communism" in the West). Indeed, in recent years, many scholars have expressed concern that because the term totalitarian has been so closely associated with the

---

Autocracy, 2nd ed. (revised by C. J. Friedrich) (Cambridge: Harvard University Press, 1965), p. 27.

[10] Leonard Schapiro, *Totalitarianism* (New York: Praeger, 1972), pp. 18–72 See also Hannah Arendt, *The Origins of Totalitarianism,* 2nd enl. ed. (New York: Meridian Books, 1958); J. L. Talmon, *The Origins of Totalitarian Democracy* (New York: Praeger, 1960); Carl J. Friedrich, ed., *Totalitarianism* (Cambridge: Harvard University Press, 1954); and Richard Lowenthal, "The Model of the Totalitarian State," in Royal Institute of International Affairs, *The Impact of the Russian Revolution 1917–1967* (London: Oxford University Press, 1967), pp. 274–351.

[11] See Carl J. Friedrich, Michael Curtis, and Benjamin R. Barber, *Totalitarianism in Perspective: Three Views* (New York: Praeger, 1969); Alex Inkeles, "Models and Issues in the Analysis of Soviet Society," *Survey,* No. 60 (July 1966), pp. 3–17, but especially pp. 3–5; Alfred G. Meyer, "USSR, Incorporated," and Robert C. Tucker, "The Question of Totalitarianism," in Donald W. Treadgold, ed., *The Development of the USSR: An Exchange of Views* (Seattle: University of Washington Press, 1964), pp. 21–34; A. J. Groth, "The 'Isms' in Totalitarianism," *The American Political Science Review,* LVII, 4 (December 1964), pp. 888–901; and William Welch, "Totalitarianism: The Standard Critique Revised," *Rocky Mountain Social Science Journal,* 10, 2 (April 1973), pp. 57–69.

rhetoric and propaganda of the Cold War, it can no longer serve as a viable category for "objective" political analysis.

Perhaps the most frequent and important critique of the totalitarian approach has been based on methodological considerations. The description of a variety of both Fascist and Communist regimes as totalitarian, it is argued, tends to obscure the important differences that exist among these regimes. While these political systems may share certain common elements, the use of an all-encompassing term such as totalitarianism tends to encourage dichotomous and simplistic thinking, such as "we and they," "good and evil," "totalitarian dictatorship" versus "democracy." In fact, as many authors point out, there are important features of both "totalitarianism" and "democracy" in all political systems. While the totalitarian approach may have been useful at a particular point in time during the political development of Communist states, the major changes these states have undergone during the past decade or more have invalidated many of the features considered essential to the totalitarian approach. By stressing the monolithic and blatantly coercive elements of Communist regimes, which are characteristic of the initial postrevolutionary or mobilization stage of political development (e.g., arbitrary physical terror, coercion, purges, the attempted total monopoly of political control by the Communist party apparatus, etc.), the totalitarian approach overemphasizes the stability and institutionalization of Communist regimes and does not permit adequate consideration of the significant changes that have occurred within them.[12] These changes include a restriction of terror and its instrument, the secret police; the substitution of collective oligarchic leadership for one-man dictatorial rule; the limited decentralization of economic policy-making; and the emergence of functionally specialized elite groups and various other forms of political pluralism that affect the policy-making process. Indeed, these changes have prompted some scholars to suggest that totalitarianism is no longer a useful approach for the analysis of Communist regimes, although typically it was a stage through which all of them passed.[13]

These criticisms do not exhaust the arguments that seek to refute the utility of the totalitarian approach in describing contemporary Com-

[12] On the changing role of terror and coercion in Communist systems, see, for example, Alexander Dallin and George W. Breslauer, *Political Terror in Communist Systems* (Stanford: Stanford University Press, 1970), especially chapters 7 and 8.

[13] Richard Lowenthal suggests that, while the totalitarian framework generally has been preserved, the political system now has to respond to the "pressures generated by an increasingly advanced society." See his "Development vs. Utopia in Communist Policy," in Chalmers Johnson, ed., *Change in Communist Systems* (Stanford: Stanford University Press, 1970), especially pp. 108–16.

munist systems. Despite such criticisms, however, the initial advocates of the approach continue to defend it. Brzezinski, for example, while conceding that not all the features of the model are still fully applicable to the Soviet Union today and that many of its features have become "dysfunctional to Communist leaders," nevertheless advocates its utility "as an analytical category for a political system that establishes a relationship of total control of a society in the process of enforced and intense social transformation. . . . Without the concept of totalitarianism, we would simply not be able to examine the unique features of the Soviet system. . . ."[14]

There is no doubt that the features of the totalitarian approach, despite all their shortcomings, do describe various key aspects of Communist systems throughout at least one stage of their political development. In fact, the recent controversy surrounding the adequacy of the approach is in some respects a testimony to its utility as a heuristic tool. Some authors have suggested that the model can be extremely useful if it is considered either as a hypothetical set of interrelated characteristics, which may or may not approximate the features of a particular political system at a given point in time, or as one point on a spectrum of variables that may be used to classify and describe different types of political systems (including such factors as the degree of political centralization, the extent of ideological commitment, the tempo of mobilization, etc.).[15] Moreover, as long as the central political institutions and leadership continue to exercise a significantly higher degree of control over society than do most other political regimes, the concept of totalitarianism will continue to enjoy a certain degree of appeal and discussion.

3. THE COMPLEX-ORGANIZATIONS APPROACH

As in other modern political systems, bureaucratic organizations play a very significant role in Communist regimes. The importance of the party apparatus and a host of state administrative agencies in the formulation and execution of political decisions has been seen by many observers in recent years as the most distinctive feature of Communist

[14] Zbigniew Brzezinski, "Dysfunctional Totalitarianism," in Klaus von Beyme, ed., *Theorie und Politik* (The Hague: Nijhoff, 1971), p. 389. See also Patrick O'Brien, "On the Adequacy of the Concept of Totalitarianism," *Studies in Comparative Communism,* III, 1 (January 1970), pp. 55–60, and Carl J. Friedrich, "In Defence of a Concept," *Government and Opposition* (Spring 1969), pp. 249–54.

[15] Schapiro, op. cit., p. 124; see also Fleron, op. cit., pp. 11–19; and Welch, op. cit., pp. 61–69.

systems.[16] According to these authors, the tenuous distinction made between politics and administration in Western pluralistic systems completely disappears in Communist polities. In their opinion, the political process of Communist states can best be understood by a consideration of the same kinds of issues and problems that are evident in all highly bureaucratized states: informal bargaining between various administrative institutions and functionaries for prestige and limited resources; the difficulty of ensuring an accurate flow of information within the organizational hierarchy; the inherent tension in all complex organizations between line and professional staff employees; the conservative outlook and lack of innovative behavior among bureaucratic personnel who have become committed to routine procedures over a period of many years; the need of top-level officials to elicit compliance and efficiency from their subordinates, etc. Such factors are presumed to be at the heart of the political process in Communist regimes. Indeed, the record in virtually all these states of both periodic purges among high-level bureaucratic functionaries and a high frequency of institutional reorganization (decentralization, recentralization, bifurcation) suggests

[16] Alfred G. Meyer, "USSR, Incorporated," in Treadgold, ed., op. cit., pp. 21–28; Meyer, *The Soviet Political System* (New York: Random House, 1965), pp. 467–76; Allen Kassof, "The Administered Society: Totalitarianism without Terror," *World Politics,* XVI, 4 (July 1964), pp. 558–75; Paul Hollander, "Observations on Bureaucracy, Totalitarianism and the Study of Communism," *Slavic Review,* XXVI, 2 (June 1967), pp. 302–7; Hollander, "Politicized Bureaucracy: The Soviet Case," *Newsletter on Comparative Studies of Communism,* IV, 3 (May 1971), pp. 12–22; T. H. Rigby, "Traditional, Market, and Organizational Societies and the USSR," *World Politics,* XVI, 4 (July 1964), pp. 539–57; Rigby, "'Totalitarianism' and Change in Communist Systems," *Comparative Politics,* IV, 3 (April 1972), pp. 433–53; Jerry F. Hough, *The Soviet Prefects: The Local Party Organs in Industrial Decision-Making* (Cambridge: Harvard University Press, 1969); Erik P. Hoffmann, "Social Science and Soviet Administrative Behavior," *World Politics,* XXIV, 3 (April 1972), pp. 444–71 [a critical review of Hough's book, including a discussion of the problems and potentialities of this approach]; Hough, "The Bureaucratic Model and the Nature of the Soviet System," *Journal of Comparative Administration,* 5, 2 (August 1973), pp. 134–67; John A. Armstrong, "Sources of Administrative Behavior: Some Soviet and Western European Comparisons," *The American Political Science Review,* LIX, 3 (September 1965), pp. 643–55; Carl Beck, "Bureaucracy and Political Development in Eastern Europe," in Joseph LaPalombara, ed., *Bureaucracy and Political Development* (Princeton: Princeton University Press, 1963), pp. 268–300; A. Doak Barnett, *Cadres, Bureaucracy, and Political Power in Communist China* (New York: Columbia University Press, 1967); Franz Schurmann, *Ideology and Organization in Communist China,* 2nd ed. (Berkeley: University of California Press, 1968); and the article by Ezra Vogel reprinted in this volume, pp. 160–70.

the political significance of seemingly administrative matters. The hallmark of a Communist regime, it is suggested, is that it is an "administered society," a "modern bureaucracy writ large," or, as an Australian political scientist recently observed, a "mono-organizational system":

> The most salient feature of communist systems is the attempt to run the whole society as a single organization in which almost no socially significant activities are left to autonomously interacting individuals or groups, but instead are managed by centralized, hierarchical agencies themselves subject to close coordination, principally by the apparatus of the party. . . . Societies with these characteristics might be called mono-organizational, and the communist countries (except for Yugoslavia in recent years) display these characteristics in the "purest" form yet known . . . although they have been approached in varying degrees by several Western countries at war, by Nazi Germany, Fascist Italy, and by several "modernizing" single-party states.[17]

The complex-organizations approach, like the thrust of many studies on totalitarianism, is vitally concerned with various aspects of control and command by the party and state apparatus. This approach, however, stresses the points of similarity rather than the differences between Communist regimes and other highly bureaucratized systems, and indeed has attempted to characterize what is conceived to be the post-totalitarian society. While totalitarianism emphasizes the "nearly complete monopoly" of political power by a single leader utilizing various instruments of rule, the complex-organizations approach draws attention to the considerable amount of "crypto-bureaucratic" competition and conflict that exist beneath the surface of the political process. As Jerry Hough has observed recently, "We should recognize that many Soviet complaints about such phenomena as departmentalism or localism are evidence not simply of bureaucratic pathology, but of the politics of

[17] Rigby, " 'Totalitarianism' . . ." pp. 451–52. The tendency to view Communist systems primarily as large-scale organizational structures is increasingly popular among Western political leaders and journalists. In November 1973 a group of American politicians on a trip to Moscow dubbed the Communist Youth League (Komsomol), "USSR, Inc." "They turn out their leaders like General Motors puts out an automobile," one American commented. "It is a careful process that gives them stability in the system." A leading American journalist has described Mao Tse-tung as "Chairman of the Board" and Chou En-lai as "Managing Director of the Firm." Chou, it has been observed, "applies on a practical basis the revolutionary theories worked out by the top leadership in accordance with Maoist doctrine." See *The New York Times,* November 21, 1973, pp. 7, 37; and November 18, p. 17.

goal and policy formulation. We should understand that the complex system of checking and counter-checking involves a good deal of citizen participation in administrative life—participation that, to be sure, has the same relatively narrow class base it has in the West."[18] The process of bargaining and infighting which exists among institutional sectors and groups even during periods of allegedly "total" control by the dictatorial regime often eludes the analyst who assumes the omnipotence of central political authority.

A major criticism that has been leveled against the complex-organizations approach is that it exaggerates the notion that all modern industrial societies are "converging," based on apparent similarities in their institutional structures, and minimizes the distinctive characteristics of bureaucracy in Communist states. Thus, some critics of this approach point out that the role of governmental administration and private corporations in the direction and management of non-Communist societies cannot be compared to the efforts of a highly politicized revolutionary elite to transform radically the very fabric of society in accordance with its interpretation of a highly elaborate messianic ideology. While the ideological commitment and utopian pretensions of Communist-party elites may have waned considerably in recent years, the particular focus and scale of bureaucratic organizations in Communist systems would seem to preclude any superficial comparison with other societies.

4. THE MODERNIZATION, OR DEVELOPMENTAL APPROACH

Advocates of this approach[19] suggest that communism has served essentially as a vehicle for the industrialization and modernization of un-

[18] Jerry F. Hough, "The Bureaucratic Model . . . ," op. cit., pp. 164–65. See also his article included in Part IV of this volume, pp. 459–86.

[19] See, *inter alia,* Robert Sharlet, "The Soviet Union as a Developing Country: A Review Essay," *Journal of Developing Areas,* II, 2 (January 1968), pp. 270–76; Dennis Pirages, *Modernization and Political-Tension Management: A Socialist Society in Perspective; Case Study of Poland* (New York: Praeger, 1972); Francis A. Botchway, ed., *Modernization: Economic and Political Transformation of Society* (Berkeley: McCutchan, 1970), chapter 2; Charles K. Wilber, *The Soviet Model and Underdeveloped Countries* (Chapel Hill: University of North Carolina Press, 1969); John A. Armstrong, "Communist Political Systems as Vehicles for Modernization," in Monte Palmer and Larry Stern, eds., *Political Development in Changing Societies* (Lexington: D. C. Heath, 1971); pp. 127–58; J. M. Montias, "Modernization in Communist Countries: Some Questions of Methodology," *Studies in Comparative Communism,* V, 4 (Winter 1972), pp. 413–27; Benjamin Schwartz, "Modernization and the Maoist Vision, Some Reflections on

derdeveloped societies. The Soviet pattern of industrialization (formed, after a decade of experimentation, during the 1920s) was characterized by enforced social mobilization, centralized economic planning by governmental agencies, emphasis on rapid heavy-industrial development, collectivization of agriculture despite massive peasant resistance, and minimal concern for consumer needs. This pattern resulted from the search for a way to overcome Russia's chronic economic backwardness among the European powers. Having succeeded in transforming the country into a major industrial power, although at great human cost, the Soviet regime deemed its model of development an absolute law of socialist construction for all states in which Communist parties came to power, regardless of their extant natural resources, level of prior industrialization, and particular pre-Communist traditions. While the East European and Asian Communist leaders recognized that the Soviet pattern was not totally relevant for their countries, they nevertheless initially adopted the essential elements of the Stalinist model as the most efficient method of achieving industrialization. It was not until the decline of Soviet hegemony in the 1950s that a marked divergence in internal developments occurred (e.g., Yugoslavia after 1952, Poland after 1956, China after 1960–61).

The modernization approach often ignores the fact that Communist systems have not adopted a uniform strategy of modernization. East Germany and Czechoslovakia, for example, were essentially modernized when the Communists came to power, and although Communist parties in these states adopted Soviet techniques of political and so-

---

Chinese Communist Goals," *The China Quarterly,* No. 21 (January–March 1965), pp. 3–19; Schwartz, "China's Developmental Experience, 1949–72," in Michel Oksenberg, ed., *China's Developmental Experience,* Proceedings of the Academy of Political Science, XXXI, 1 (March 1973), pp. 17–26; Roger W. Benjamin and John H. Kautsky, "Communism and Political Development," *The American Political Science Review,* LXII, 1 (March 1968), pp. 110–23; John H. Kautsky, *The Political Consequences of Modernization,* (New York: John Wiley & Sons, 1971); Morris Watnick, "The Appeal of Communism to the Peoples of Underdeveloped Areas," reprinted in Reinhard Bendix and Seymour Martin Lipset, *Class, Status, Power,* 2nd ed. (New York: The Free Press, 1966), pp. 428–36; Kenneth Jowitt, *Revolutionary Breakthroughs and National Development: The Case of Romania, 1944–1965* (Berkeley: University of California Press, 1971); Charles Gati, "Modernization and Communist Power in Hungary," *East European Quarterly,* V, 3 (September 1971), pp. 425–59; Alec Nove and J. A. Newth, *The Soviet Middle East: A Model for Development?* (London: George Allen & Unwin, 1967); and Mark G. Field, "Symposium on the Social Consequences of Modernization in Socialist Countries," *Newsletter on Comparative Communist Studies,* VI, 3 (May 1973), pp. 36–51.

cial control, the Stalinist model of rapid economic development was not only irrelevant for both countries but also dysfunctional. The Soviets based their strategy on the rapid expansion of heavy industry throughout the period of their economic development. The Chinese initially copied the Soviet model but rejected it as untenable in the early 1960s, when they began to emphasize agriculture as the foundation of the economy and adopted policies that advanced the thesis of "walking on two legs," that is, coupling achievements in heavy industry with rapid development of the agricultural sector. As a consequence of its rift with the Soviet Union, the Yugoslav leadership, although initially embracing the Soviet model, pursued yet a third path of socioeconomic development. In each instance, Communist leaders have endeavored to endow their particular developmental model with the stamp of ideological orthodoxy. Even the Yugoslavs, who have been the most tolerant of the legitimacy of separate strategies of development, have attempted to elevate their unique experience in worker self-management to the status of a law "governing the development of socialism."[20] Given these varied patterns, one might ask whether it is possible to identify a distinctive Communist model of modernization. Or, should Communist regimes be categorized with other revolutionary, future-oriented political systems that share an appreciation of dictatorial or authoritarian methods of achieving rapid socioeconomic change at the expense of popular participation, private concerns, and individual needs.

A further drawback to the modernization approach, as noted above with respect to the complex-organizations approach, is that it encourages the observer to assume that, as industrial development and social change proceed, the political system will inevitably undergo significant change, that because all modernized societies confront similar problems, they are all likely to respond similarly.[21] Convergence theorists argue that

[20] Edward Kardelj, "Self-Management—A Law Governing the Development of Socialism," *Socialist Thought and Practice*, 51 (March–April 1973), pp. 26–39.

[21] This has led some observers to hypothesize about the possibilities of convergence of Communist and Western-democratic societies. See, *inter alia*, Inkeles, op. cit., pp. 6–12; Alfred G. Meyer, "Theories of Convergence," in Johnson, ed., op. cit., pp. 313–41; and E. I. Hopper, "Industrialization and the Problem of Convergence: A Critical Note," *The Sociological Review*, XIV, 2 (July 1966), pp. 163–96. Zbigniew Brzezinski and Samuel P. Huntington, *Political Power: USA/USSR* (New York: Viking, 1964), argue against the convergence theory because of the importance of political-cultural traditions in each society, as well as each regime's stated societal goals. See especially pp. 3–14, 419–36. Raymond Aron, in *The Industrial Society* (New York: Praeger, 1967), argues similarly. For the Soviet response, see Leon Gouré, et al., *Convergence of Communism and Capitalism: The Soviet View* (Miami: Center for Advanced International Studies, 1973).

once the Communist party has fulfilled its role as the vanguard for economic development, then its position in society must necessarily decline. The growing pluralization of modernized Communist systems, it is argued, will be accompanied by the increasingly important role of functional specialists and interest-group elites, which is already a prominent feature of Western industrialized societies. This view is most prevalent among those authors who envision the emergence of technocratic rule in industrialized societies.[22]

5. THE GROUP-CONFLICT APPROACH

Many of the scholars who argue that the totalitarian approach has become too static suggest that the "group theory of politics," which has enjoyed considerable popularity for the analysis of Western political systems, provides the most useful framework for investigating the nature of post-Stalin Communist systems.[23] According to these authors, the political process in Communist states comprises essentially a contest or struggle between various groups, competing "vectors" of influence, or "tendencies of opinion," each pressuring for the realization of their separate interests and goals. Even the totalitarian approach recognized the existence of various interest groups which exercised some influence on the policy-making process. Friedrich and Brzezinski, for example, identified institutions and categories of the population that resisted totalitarian control, "islands of separateness," including the family, the church, scholars, and highly trained technicians. In contrast to the well-organized and highly specialized interest associations found in plural-

[22] For the general argument, see "Post-Industrial Society—A Symposium," *Survey,* XVI, 1 (Winter 1971), pp. 1–77.

[23] See, *inter alia,* H. Gordon Skilling, "Interest Groups and Communist Politics," *World Politics,* XVIII, 3 (April 1966), pp. 435–51; Skilling and Franklyn Griffiths, eds., *Interest Groups in Soviet Politics* (Princeton: Princeton University Press, 1971); Jeremy Azrael, *Managerial Power and Soviet Politics* (Cambridge: Harvard University Press, 1966), espec. Chapter 6; Joel J. Schwartz and William R. Keech, "Group Influence and the Policy Process in the Soviet Union," *The American Political Science Review,* LXII, 3 (September 1968), pp. 840–51; Milton R. Lodge, *Soviet Elite Attitudes Since Stalin* (Columbus: Charles E. Merrill, 1969); Michael P. Gehlen, "Group Theory and the Study of Soviet Politics," in Sidney I. Ploss, ed., *The Soviet Political Process* (Waltham: Ginn, 1971), pp. 35–54; Ploss, "Interest Groups," in Allen Kassof, ed., *Prospects for Soviet Society* (New York: Praeger, 1968), pp. 76–103; and David E. Langsam and David W. Paul, "Soviet Politics and the Group Approach: A Conceptual Note," *Slavic Review,* XXXI, 1 (March 1972), pp. 136–41.

istic systems, however, group activity in Communist states has been analyzed in terms of broad social categories (e.g., peasants, manual workers, particular ethnic groups) or institutional and functional groups (e.g., the military, police, economic managers). In fact, while almost all Communist regimes claim to have eliminated the sources of intergroup conflict, categorizing the varying interests of different groups as basically "non-antagonistic contradictions," they nonetheless provide for group representation within high party organs. Typically, each Communist party's Central Committee has long been composed of party members who hold important positions in a variety of institutional and functional sectors within the society.

Some critics of the group-conflict approach question whether a framework for inquiry that has been applied primarily to Western systems can be transferred to the analysis of Communist systems. In these states, there is a dearth of detailed information about group structure and activity, including size and composition of membership, shared values and attitudes, and internal dynamics. Due to the paucity of available data, proponents of the group-conflict approach have typically ascribed the attributes of an interest group to broad institutional and social sectors without giving adequate consideration to whether or not the members of a "group" acually share a common set of beliefs; to what extent, if any, they seek to advance them politically; and whether the "group" is recognized by other actors in the political process.[24] Any satisfactory analysis of group activity must consider not only broad interest groupings, such as the party apparatus, security police, or the military, but also more limited "opinion groups" (the term is Skilling's) within these larger categories. For example, within the military establishment, there are likely to be competing branches and subgroups, such as navy versus air force, ground versus rocket forces, as well as generational conflicts and varying career experiences, which act to differentiate military personnel. Moreover, within each of these hypothetical opinion groups, there are undoubtedly spokesmen for diverse political persuasions that act to undermine further the cohesiveness of the group as it is broadly defined.

The general difficulty of obtaining data regarding the actual policymaking process presents a major obstacle to the analysis of interest-group behavior. While it is known that major policy decisions are typically made at the top of the party hierarchy, it is far from clear how these decisions are arrived at, except in rare cases when information becomes public as a result of intraparty factionalism. The handful of case

[24] On this and related points, see Andrew C. Janos, "Group Politics in Communist Society: A Second Look at the Pluralist Model," in Samuel P. Huntington and Clement H. Moore, *Authoritarian Politics in Modern Society* (New York: Basic Books, 1970), pp. 437–51.

studies that have examined group activity in Communist systems to date have demonstrated that group influence is directly related to the technicality of the policy issue under consideration. Thus, on issues such as educational policy or family law, representatives from various specialized groups apparently exercise considerable influence on the political decision makers.[25] Moreover, when there is disagreement among top party leaders regarding the policy to be adopted, there is much greater opportunity for group influence than when there is unanimity within the political leadership. In cases of major policy change such as, for example, the Soviet invasion of Czechoslovakia, the recent Chinese détente with the United States, or the impetus toward economic reform in several East European states, very little is known of the respective impact of various groups, if any, on decision-making.

A related difficulty of this approach is whether or not group conflict is an accurate description of the political pluralization that now characterizes Communist systems. Thus, what has frequently been termed group activity may be better understood as elite behavior, that is, individual leaders or "elite interest groups" from various societal sectors playing a role in the decision-making process. The relationship between these leaders and the groups they allegedly represent is rarely supported by empirical evidence. It is much easier to demonstrate that a given Communist leader has certain group attributes or affiliations than to establish that he actually serves as the political representative of a specific group. For example, did Anastas Mikoyan, a long-standing member of the Soviet party politbureau, represent the interests of his Armenian ethnic group, or was he simply a highly successful Armenian member of the central party apparatus? Does the early coal-mining experience of Edward Gierek, Polish Communist leader, suggest that he is likely to be particularly attentive to coal interests? Whether or not a given leader can be regarded as a representative of a particular group's interests depends on both his own role orientation and the group's perception of him as a political actor.[26]

[25] See A. H. Brown's review article of particular case studies, "Policy-making in the Soviet Union," *Soviet Studies,* XXIII, 1 (July 1971), pp. 120–48) and Peter H. Juviler and Henry W. Morton, eds., *Soviet Policy-Making* (New York: Praeger, 1967).

[26] The study of Communist elites has been an extremely popular and fruitful area of research in recent years. We have not included elite studies as a distinct approach, because almost all of the approaches outlined above focus on top leaders and political decision-makers to a significant extent. Some authors begin the study of "the elite" with the assumption that it is composed of various functional and institutional *groups,* while others view the officials who occupy positions in the top echelon of various Party, state, and economic hierarchies as unified members of a *bureaucratic* class or stratum. Most studies concerned with elites, however, devote more attention

Despite the difficulties and hazards of the group-conflict approach, it does seek to probe the dynamics of the policy-making process, which most other approaches have tended to ignore or dismiss. It suggests that Communist leaders are not insulated from group demands, which they must take into account in formulating policy, and that they are often compelled to satisfy at least some of them. The group-conflict approach also helps account for those instances when the political leadership is either reluctant or unable to formulate and issue clear policy directives, and for the frequent reversals of policies observed. Given the continued pluralization of Communist societies, with its attendant increase of interest-group activity in the political process, this approach is likely to become a more important tool of analysis in the future.

PROBLEMS OF RESEARCH AND ANALYSIS

One of the major obstacles to research on Communist systems is that of data collection. This problem is a consequence of a variety of factors, some of which may continue to plague scholars for years to come. Even the review of governmental acts and statutes, a routine method of political inquiry, is a difficult task, because many of these regulations remain unpublished or are published only years after enactment. Social scientists in Communist states are also hampered by problems of data collection, and, to date, the published results of their research and analysis have added little to the general store of knowledge about these countries.[27] With limited exceptions in recent years (Yugoslavia,

---

to the association between the social background characteristics, attitudes, and behavior of political leaders, unlike explicitly group-oriented studies, which are more concerned with the policy-making process. For recent surveys of the literature on Communist elites (which include extensive bibliographies and notes), see William A. Welch, "Introduction: The Comparative Study of Political Leadership in Communist Systems," in Carl Beck, et al., eds., *Comparative Communist Political Leadership* (New York: David McKay Co., 1973), pp. 1–42; and Gordon Bennett, "Elites and Society in China: A Summary of Research and Interpretation," in Robert A. Scalapino, ed., *Elites in the People's Republic of China* (Seattle: University of Washington Press, 1972), pp. 3–37.

[27] See the discussion by John S. Shippee, "Empirical Sociology in the Eastern European Communist Party-States," in Jan F. Triska, ed., *Communist Party-States: Comparative and International Studies* (Indianapolis: Bobbs-Merrill, 1969), pp. 282–336; Alexander Matejko, "Sociologists in Between," *Studies in Comparative Communism,* V, 2/3 (Summer/Autumn 1972), pp. 277–304; Bogdan Denitch, "Sociology in Eastern Europe," *Slavic Review,* XXX,

Czechoslovakia prior to 1969, Poland),[28] scholars have not been permitted the use of field observation or survey/interview techniques to collect data on important aspects of the political process. Even if such surveys were possible, there would still be problems associated with the language barrier, cultural and ideological differences, and the reluctance of the interviewees to respond candidly. Public-opinion data collected and published by social scientists or party-controlled institutions in Communist states has been of only limited value for scholars, because there is generally no opportunity to evaluate their validity or accuracy. (In any case, such data are provided for very few states.)

Indeed, even very basic data, essential for the political analysis of these systems, are often difficult to obtain.[29] For example, Table IV of this volume indicates that no statistical breakdown of the current occupational composition of the Czechoslovak Communist Party has been published, although detailed statistics regarding size and growth of party membership over the past several decades are published frequently in the Czechoslovak press. In the case of the Chinese Communist Party the regime has not published statistics regarding total party membership or its composition (including occupational breakdown, urban/rural ratio, sex ratio, age distribution, and length of party membership) in more than a decade. Even when statistics are available, ideological biases creep in. For example, in order to emphasize the "proletarian nature" of party membership, blue- and white-collar work-

---

2 (June 1971), pp. 316–39; Jerzy J. Wiatr, ed., *The State of Sociology in Eastern Europe Today* (Carbondale: Southern Illinois University Press, 1971); and Seymour Martin Lipset and Richard B. Dalson, "Social Stratification and Sociology in the Soviet Union," *Survey,* 3 (88), (Summer 1973), pp. 114–85. Two very critical but extremely interesting accounts of the interplay between political power and social science research in Communist states are Alexei Yakushev, "Are the Techniques of Sociological Surveys Applicable Under the Conditions of Soviet Society?" *European Journal of Sociology,* XIII (1972), pp. 139–58; and Szymon Chodak, "How was Political Sociology Possible in Poland?" *International Journal of Contemporary Sociology,* 10, 1 (January 1972), pp. 53–65.

[28] See particularly the volume produced by the British Inter-university, interdisciplinary comparative study project of political and social processes in Eastern Europe, co-ordinated by Ghita Ionescu; and Allen H. Barton, Bogdan Denitch, and Charles Kadushin, *Opinion-Making Elites in Yugoslavia* (New York: Praeger, 1973). See also Ellen Mickiewicz, "Policy Applications of Public Opinion Research in the Soviet Union," *Public Opinion Quarterly,* XXXVI, 4 (Winter 1972–73), pp. 566–78.

[29] Ellen Mickiewicz, ed., *Handbook of Soviet Social Science Data* (New York: The Free Press, 1973), offers the first collection of such data for the Soviet Union.

ers are not differentiated, but are typically grouped together as "workers and employees."

Biases in data collection and interpretation hamper all scholars seeking to analyze Communist systems.[30] Many Western scholars are emotionally caught up in the study of Communist states and are unmistakably sympathetic or antipathetic to these systems; accordingly, they tend to conduct research in a way that explicitly reinforces their particular biases. Indeed, a number of scholars seem to have assigned themselves the task of disproving Communist claims to social and economic reform in an effort to revoke the legitimacy of the Communist system itself. As the Cold War adversary nature of Communism versus Western democracy has declined in the 1970s, Western social science study of Communist regimes has become more objective and unemotional than in previous decades. For their part, scholars in Communist states have also become more objective and sophisticated in the analysis of their own societies, and their research has been less colored by ideological considerations than in earlier years.

As a consequence of the greater ease of data collection and research in the Soviet/East European states in recent years, scholars are no longer compelled to rely almost exclusively on the detailed examination of published materials and visible behavior of Communist leaders, or what has generally been referred to as the "art of Kremlinology."[31]

[30] See the interesting discussion by Alexander Dallin, "Bias and Blunders in American Studies on the USSR," *Slavic Review,* 32, 3 (September 1973), pp. 560–76; and the comments by John A. Armstrong, ibid., pp. 577–87; Michel Oksenberg, "Sources and Methodological Problems in the Study of Contemporary China," in A. Doak Barnett, ed., *Chinese Communist Politics in Action* (Seattle: University of Washington Press, 1969), pp. 577–606; Leigh and Richard Kagan, "Oh, Say Can You See? American Cultural Blunders on China," and John Gittings, "The Great Asian Conspiracy," in Edward Friedman and Mark Selden, eds., *America's Asia* (New York: Vintage Books, 1971), pp. 3–39, 108–45; and Harold R. Isaacs, "Sources for Images of Foreign Countries," in Melvin Small, ed., *Public Opinion and Historians: Interdisciplinary Perspectives* (Detroit: Wayne State University Press, 1970), pp. 91–105.

[31] Sidney I. Ploss argues that "the empirical data for study and interpretation of Soviet politics are neither meager nor prohibitively incomplete. A proved reliability attaches to the jargon of Communist discourse, which a Soviet historian has rightfully deplored as 'the cement-like language.' If this language is carefully examined over periods of time, in conjunction with the career patterns of Party leaders, issues and leadership alignments can be reasonably established." See his *Conflict and Decision-Making in Soviet Russia* (Princeton: Princeton University Press, 1965), p. 23. See also Ploss, *The Soviet Political Process: Aims, Techniques, and Examples of Analysis* (Waltham: Ginn, 1971). Other useful discussions include Robert Conquest,

Developed in the early postwar years in order to gain some insight into the Byzantine nature of political development in Communist states, a major feature of Kremlinological analysis involved the deciphering of Communist terminology, for it was recognized that much of the esoteric language used had very precise meanings to the highly selective audience for which it was intended.[32] Kremlinological techniques, however, continue to be important especially in studying the less accessible Asian Communist states. Despite China's more co-operative international posture since the Cultural Revolution, reliable data from that country are less available now than they were ten or fifteen years ago. Western scholars find that they must continue to rely on many of the tools of research developed during the 1950s, including the detailed analysis of published materials as well as interviews with POWs[33] and political emigrees.

Yet, there is a bright side to all this. Academic and cultural exchanges, begun almost fifteen years ago between the United States and the Soviet/East European states, now appear to be in the offing for China. Such programs provide possibilities for firsthand observation and

---

Power and Policy in the USSR (New York: Harper & Row, 1967), Part I; Donald S. Zagoria, *The Sino-Soviet Conflict 1956–1961* (Princeton: Princeton University Press, 1962), pp. 24–35; and Erik P. Hoffmann, "Methodological Problems of Kremlinology," in Fleron, op. cit., pp. 129–51.

[32] William E. Griffith, "On Esoteric Communications," *Studies in Comparative Communism,* III, 1 (January 1970), pp. 47–54.

[33] The Harvard-Air Force interview project yielded some very valuable data regarding Soviet POWs who managed to avoid repatriation after World War II. See the general discussion of the project in Alex Inkeles and Raymond A. Bauer, *The Soviet Citizen* (Cambridge: Harvard University Press, 1959), Part One. Other useful studies to emerge from the project include: H. Kent Geiger, *The Family in Soviet Russia* (Cambridge: Harvard University Press, 1968); Mark G. Field, *Doctor and Patient in Soviet Russia* (Cambridge: Harvard University Press, 1957); Joseph S. Berliner, *Factory and Manager in the USSR* (Cambridge: Harvard University Press, 1957). The utility of the project for the contemporary study of the Soviet system is limited, because it relies on data from the pre-1945 period, although several of the studies have also included postwar data gleaned from published sources. For a defense of the continuing value of the project's results, see Stephen White, "Communist Political Culture: An Empirical Note," *Newsletter on Comparative Studies of Communism,* VI, 2 (February 1973). See also studies based on interviews with Chinese refugees, including A. Doak Barnett, *Cadres, Bureaucracy and Political Power in Communist China,* supra; and Ezra F. Vogel, *Canton Under Communism* (Cambridge: Harvard University Press, 1969). A recent discussion of new source material for the study of China is in Karl Li, "Methodology and Data in the Study of The Chinese Political System," *Asian Forum,* V, 1 (January–March 1973), pp. 82–89.

study of Communist systems, as well as for an ongoing dialogue between participating professors and students. Exchange of hitherto unavailable materials between libraries involved in these programs has been especially valuable for Western scholars. In the atmosphere of international détente between Communist and non-Communist nations that has emerged during the 1970s, these exchanges may be expected to continue and even expand. Already, Soviet, East European, and Western scholars have engaged in some collaborative research.[34] Soviet and East European scholars often participate in professional conferences organized by Western social scientists, and they meet their Western counterparts regularly at international meetings of various disciplines within the social sciences. These recent collaborative efforts have yielded particularly fruitful results, helping to overcome the mutual skepticism and distrust that had earlier characterized such contacts and encouraging scholars in Communist societies to insist upon greater independence from governmental intervention in their professional activity. Thus, the possibilities for the study and analysis of Communist systems appear greater now than at any time in the past.

Communist Systems in Comparative Perspective

It is clear that, despite the handicaps noted above, Western scholars have succeeded in applying a variety of contemporary political science research approaches and techniques to the study of Communist systems. Scholars agree that these systems are not all alike, nor is any particular regime unique. Therefore, it is not surprising that in recent years a growing number of authors have proposed that a better understanding of Communist systems can be achieved through a comparative study of their similarities and differences. The comparative method seeks to identify those common elements (ideological predilection, institutional structure, policy priorities and long-term goals, etc.) and those sources of variation (cultural tradition, political history, demographic features, mode of revolutionary take-over, level of economic development, etc.) that account for the diverse nature of political behavior and development in these states.[35]

[34] See the relevant comments by Jan F. Triska in his Foreword to Pirages, op. cit., especially pp. vii–viii; and Paul Shoup, "Comparing Communist Nations: Prospects for an Empirical Approach," *The American Political Science Review,* LXII, 1 (March 1968), pp. 194–204.

[35] See, *inter alia,* Robert Sharlet, ed., "Symposium: Comparative Politics and Communist Systems," *Slavic Review,* XXVI, 1 (March 1967), pp. 1–28; Robert C. Tucker, "On the Comparative Study of Communism," *World Politics,* XIX, 4 (January 1967), pp. 242–57; Carl A. Linden, "Comparative

The comparative framework raises a number of questions that cannot be treated by the study of a single Communist regime. What type of socioeconomic and political environment is most favorable for the success of Communist revolutionary elites? Do Communist parties acquire and maintain political authority in societies with similar internal conditions and levels of economic development? Have Communist parties acquired power primarily in societies that are industrialized or developing, ethnically homogeneous or heterogeneous, in countries having a history of representative government or of authoritarian rule, in a period of relative international calm or within the context of global warfare, with external military and financial assistance or through independent struggle? Are there distinct European and Asian models of Communist rule? To what extent can a particular leader shape the institutional arrangements, ideology, and policies in these states? Would the pattern of Soviet development have been markedly different if Lenin had lived until World War II? How has the continued political leadership of Mao and Tito for more than a quarter of a century affected the development of their respective societies? Does the presence of a charismatic leader have a measurable influence upon the particular development of a Communist society? In this regard, would the East German experience have been different if a more charismatic figure than Walter Ulbricht had been at the apex of power for two decades? What impact does the fact of an artificially divided nation have

---

Communist Studies: Some Problems of Teaching and Approach," *Newsletter on Comparative Studies of Communism,* IV, 4 (August 1971); Chalmers Johnson, "Comparing Communist Systems," in Johnson, op. cit.; Ionescu, *Comparative Communist Politics,* supra; Donald W. Treadgold, ed., *Soviet and Chinese Communism: Similarities and Differences* (Seattle: University of Washington Press, 1967); Richard Cornell, "Comparative Analysis of Communist Movements," *Journal of Politics,* XXX, 1 (February 1968), pp. 66–89; Richard C. Gripp, *The Political System of Communism* (New York: Dodd, Mead, 1973), pp. 1–18; Jan F. Triska and Paul M. Johnson, "Political Development and Political Change in Eastern Europe: A Comparative Study," unpublished paper, Department of Political Science, Stanford University, 1973; John N. Hazard, *Communists and Their Law: A Search for the Common Core of the Legal Systems of the Marxian Socialist States* (Chicago: University of Chicago Press, 1969); and Richard T. De George, "The Meaning and Function of Communism: A Study in Comparative Method," *Newsletter on Comparative Studies of Communism,* V, 2 (February 1972), pp. 4–22. For an interesting discussion of the relative advantages and limitations which currently derive from the comparative technique, see B. Michael Frolic, "Noncomparative Communism: Soviet and Chinese Cities," and Jerry F. Hough, "Soviet Urban Politics and Comparative Urban Theory," both in *Journal of Comparative Administration,* 4, 3 (November 1972), pp. 279–310, and 311–34.

upon the portion under Communist rule? Three of the fourteen Communist states have been in this situation (Korea, Vietnam, Germany) for two decades or more (some observers have described China as divided, because of the Nationalist regime on Taiwan, but we do not subscribe to this view). These and a multitude of related questions derive from the comparative method of analysis.

The comparative perspective is a useful device for assessing the validity of any one of the conceptual approaches outlined earlier. While a close examination of the Soviet system during the Stalin era may reveal the essential elements of what can be labeled a totalitarian state, the presence or absence of these elements in other Communist states affects any general statement about the totalitarian features of Communist systems. Research on the Soviet system alone, and the a priori assumption that other Communist regimes have patterned themselves on the Soviet model with minor variations, cannot support any conclusive propositions about totalitarianism and communism. While the impact of political culture and tradition was particularly evident in the 1968 Czechoslovak reform movement, other Communist regimes have been more successful in erasing the influence of their pre-Communist heritage. Thus, any general conclusion about the effects of political culture and traditional practices on contemporary Communist regimes benefits from a comparative analysis. Indeed, one of the main reasons for the decline of the area-studies approach as the most useful means of studying Communist systems has been the widespread recognition among social scientists that a comparative analysis yields a clearer understanding of the nature of these systems and how they operate.

This volume is predicated on the belief that a better understanding of Communist societies can be achieved through the application of comparative methods than by studying them either individually or as a single monolithic bloc. The use of any one or a combination of the various approaches outlined above to explain particular problems or answer questions with respect to Communist political systems can usually yield more fruitful results when the experience of more than one country is taken into account. While the Soviet, Chinese, and Yugoslav cases continue to be the most diverse and, therefore, the most interesting to compare, the varied development of each of the fourteen Communist states needs to be considered in evaluating the Communist experience. The existence and likely increase of such variation would seem to preclude the rigid application of any single approach or model, limited to any one geographic area. Indeed, efforts to answer some of the most challenging questions of political inquiry concerning Communist regimes have, by their very nature, required social scientists to be rather eclectic in terms of the selection of approaches and the geographic areas of research.

With this in mind, we have attempted to include a broadly representative selection of articles, focusing on those aspects of political structure and process that we consider most essential in understanding the diversity of Communist rule in the 1970s.

COMMUNIST SYSTEMS IN COMPARATIVE PERSPECTIVE

I

The Emergence of Communist Political Systems

THERE have been two major patterns by which Communist parties have succeeded in acquiring political authority: (1) an indigenous revolutionary movement that gained political power after a prolonged armed struggle with relatively little or no external assistance and with a significant measure of popular support; and (2) a primarily foreign-engineered and militarily supported conspiratorial effort leading to the gradual erosion of the old regime and the expansion of domestic Commuinst power, the latter usually enjoying very minimal popular support. In both cases, the Communists' acquisition of power has been invaluably aided, perhaps indispensably, by the global and internal dislocations produced by a world war (Cuba is the single exception).

The Soviet, Chinese, Yugoslav, and, with some qualification, the Albanian, North Vietnamese, and Cuban cases exemplify the first pattern. It should be noted, however, that in the Soviet case, the demise of the existing government occurred first, by means of an urban-centered insurrection; this was *followed* by a protracted civil war and the gradual consolidation of political power by the Communist party. In the other instances of indigenous revolutionary activity, civil war over a broad territorial expanse and concentrated in largely rural areas *preceded* the Communist accession to power. Significantly, all the Communist political victories adhering to the pattern of indigenous revolutionary take-over occurred in societies completely lacking the requisite proletarian occupational structure and level of economic development envisioned by the orthodox Marxian revolutionary paradigm. The remaining East European and Asian parties came to power by means of the second pattern. As Hugh Seton-Watson carefully outlined a number of years ago, this pattern typically involved some combination of a three-stage process: genuine coalition, bogus coalition, and finally, a monolithic regime.[1]

Generally, the Communist parties that have come to power have been historically rather weak organizations. They have operated on the periphery of the political process and have almost always been

[1] *The East European Revolution* (New York: Praeger, 1956), pp. 167–71.

banned by their non-Communist predecessors as a real or imagined threat to the existing political system, hence usually being compelled to operate clandestinely and at great risk to their members (the Communist party in interwar Czechoslovakia is an important exception in this respect). In the first pattern of Communist take-over, the parties were able to gain strength and mobilize popular support for their struggle only when, under the direction of brilliant revolutionary strategists, they managed to combine a drive for autonomy and national liberation from foreign domination with demands for long-ignored socioeconomic reforms, eventually forming a broad-based movement (the "National Front," "the Fatherland Front," etc.). In the second pattern of take-over, the Communist parties gained strength largely through terrorist tactics and electoral manipulation, having been unable to inspire significant popular sympathy or support. These parties rarely produced a charismatic leader or mass following capable of establishing the party in power without Soviet military assistance.

The means by which each party acquired power have had major implications for its subsequent domestic role, its ability or motivation to deviate from the Soviet pattern of socialist development, and its relationship with the USSR. The articles in this section of the volume describe in some detail each pattern for the acquisition of political power, from a historical and political perspective. The Soviet and Chinese strategies, worked out largely by Lenin and Mao respectively, demonstrate the ability of each party to capitalize on existing economic conditions and situational factors, as well as the inertia and policy failures of their political rivals. The studies included here also illustrate the leadership roles exercised by Lenin and Mao within their respective parties, and their masterful understanding of the existing revolutionary possibilities. As Geyer's article indicates, Lenin faced far greater internal party opposition prior to the October coup than Mao seemed to have faced in the years immediately preceding the Chinese Communist victory. The Burks article provides a survey of the Communist seizure of power in Eastern Europe, indicating similarities and differences among the various countries. The author pays particular attention to Soviet party policy and military activities in the East European states. His case studies of the Yugoslav and Czechoslovak Communist parties offer the most diverse examples of the Communist acquisition of power in this region.

THE BOLSHEVIK INSURRECTION IN PETROGRAD

Dietrich Geyer

THE subject to be discussed bears many names, none of which entirely covers it: coup d'état, uprising, insurrection, the Great October Socialist Revolution, conspiracy of a minority (*zagovor*), "ten days that shook the world," *action directe,* carried out by a group of determined men. These terms differ widely and can no longer be employed as equivalents. Fifty years after the event, its history resides in the nuances, and the interest of the historian transcends the bare facts that seem to tell "how it really was."

The October days of 1917 have often been described,[1] and yet we never cease to reexamine them. This probably would not be the case if these events had been no more than a mere coup d'état of which it could be simply said: "The Bolsheviks did not seize power. They picked it up."[2] Without doubt more was at stake: the history of Russia and much of our own history as well. This may explain why we can no longer separate the consequences of the revolution from its mere chronology. The events and their historical results have merged, and our controversies possess a history of their own.

It is perhaps possible to say that there is agreement on at least one point: no one will deny that the transfer of power during October was

[1] This paper does not attempt to give a bibliographical review of the sources now available or an account of research done on the subject by Soviet and Western historians. Footnotes are confined to a minimum. All dates are given in Old Style.

[2] Adam B. Ulam, *Lenin and the Bolsheviks: The Intellectual and Political History of the Triumph of Communism in Russia* (London 1966), p. 314. The fullest narrative of the events published so far is S. Melguov's *Kak bol'sheviki zakhvatili vlast': Oktiabr'skii perevorot 1917 goda* (Paris, 1953).

the result of an uprising, of a violent effort to overthrow the Provisional Government—an action relying on the support of the armed forces of the Petrograd garrison, of the Baltic Fleet, and of the working class—organized and directed by the Bolshevik Party. But if we go but one step beyond this simple assertion, the event quickly ceases to be unequivocal. The term "uprising" (*vosstanie*) is ambivalent, and no description of it is possible that is not at the same time an evaluation. It raises the question of the character of the insurrection, and it is at this point that opinions begin to diverge.

It is well known that controversy over the uprising did not originate with historians. Among the first to doubt the rationality of the uprising were the men who eventually made the revolution. Lenin, as we know, first mentioned the controversial subject in two letters written from Finland in the middle of September 1917 after the defeat of the so-called "Kornilov Revolt."[3] "The Bolsheviks," he declared, "must take power at this very moment." In his opinion, only an "armed uprising" in Petrograd and Moscow, "an insurrection . . . treated as an art," would assure victory.[4] The laconic minutes of the meeting of the Central Committee on September 15 reflect the embarrassment of those who had to deal with Lenin's demands: Stalin pleaded for consultations with the most important party organizations; other participants wanted to make sure that no copies of the letters would be allowed to circulate; and Kamenev requested a rejection of Lenin's proposals and tried to persuade the Central Committee to pass a resolution "declaring all street actions to be for the moment inadmissible." The Committee finally decided to take measures "to prevent any actions in the barracks and in the factories."[5] This thinly veiled rejection of his proposals caused Lenin two weeks later to tender his resignation from the Central Committee, reserving for himself "freedom to campaign among the rank and file of the party and at the Party Congress."[6] Not until October 10, after Lenin had moved back to Petrograd from Finland, did the Central Committee consent (against the votes of Zinoviev and Kamenev) to place "the armed uprising on the order of the day," considering "that an armed uprising is inevitable and that the time for it is fully ripe."[7] But even

[3] "Bol'sheviki dolzhny vziat' vlast'. Pis'mo Tsentral'nomu Komitetu, Petrogradskomu i Moskovskomu komitetam RSDRP (b)" (September 12–14, 1917), *Polnoe sobranie sochinenii,* 5th ed. (Moscow, 1962), XXXIV, pp. 239–41; "Marksizm i vosstanie. Pis'mo Tsentral'nomu Komitetu RSDRP (b)" (September 13–14, 1917), ibid., pp. 242–47.

[4] Ibid., pp. 240, 246–47.

[5] *Protokoly Tsentral'nogo Komiteta RSDRP (b). Avgust 1917–fevral' 1918* (Moscow, 1958), p. 55.

[6] "Krizis nazrel" (September 29, 1917), *Polnoe sobranie sochinenii,* XXXIV, p. 282.

[7] *Protokoly Tsentral'nogo Komiteta,* p. 86.

then opposition persisted within the innermost circle of the party. The conflict had not been resolved.

The review of these facts, the correctness of which is not denied by Soviet historians, leads us to the core of the problem. Until October, the concept of an "armed uprising" or "insurrection" had been extremely vague and ill-defined for all. Those who spoke of an insurrection, whether to support it or reject it, saw before their eyes the scenes of the July 1917 days in Petrograd: street demonstrations by workers and soldiers, meetings with banners and placards, strikes and bloody clashes, the incitement of the masses against legal authority. These were the fruits of agitation in which organization and planning had played no major part. The Bolshevik leadership had shown itself incapable of channeling the underlying force of the movement, and instead of being a prelude to the seizure of power, the uprising had ended in defeat. Nevertheless, it corresponded to that classical type of insurrection that, since 1789, had been firmly established in the tradition of the European revolutions. Barricade fighting in 1848, the 1871 Paris Commune, the December 1905 revolt in Moscow, all followed the same basic pattern, which lost nothing of its fascination despite invariable failures.

In 1905, not even the Mensheviks had managed to avoid the prospect of an uprising.[8] In *Iskra,* their military experts discussed the best methods of erecting barricades, the place of artillery in street fighting, and the pros and cons of armed mass demonstrations. The insurrectionary formula was in no way binding. It committed the Social Democrats neither to a certain course of action nor to a conspiratorial activism. The term *vseobshchee narodnoe vosstanie* (general mass insurrection) had by 1905 become a substitute for everything that seemed to denote the climax of the revolution, even in the ranks of the liberal Kadets. The insurrection presupposed the action of the masses, of the overwhelming majority of the people. It was understood as a kind of revolutionary plebiscite, as an elementary event in the revolutionary process, as unpredictable as the processes of nature. Consequently, the legitimacy of the popular uprising could never be questioned.

As a matter of fact, as long as the tsarist regime remained firmly in the saddle, the controversies within the socialist camp centered on other issues. The debate was not whether a mass uprising should be welcomed or not but over the role of the party in the revolution. It is over this question that the well-known conflict between the Mensheviks and the Bolsheviks became irreconcilable. The Mensheviks had always rejected the idea that the rebellion, as they conceived it, could be planned, organized, let alone "made" by the Social Democrats. Not the party but the masses would have to launch it. The party, with its agitational ap-

[8] For a recent analysis of the discussions in 1905 see Alexander Fischer, *Russische Sozialdemokratie und bewaffneter Aufstand* (Wiesbaden, 1967).

paratus, should serve only as a regulating force. To contemplate planning or directing the uprising was considered adventurism, conspiratorial mentality, a betrayal of the revolution. Certainly, Lenin, too, had never thought of an armed insurrection in any other way than in connection with an uprising of large parts of the population, of the proletariat as well as of the peasantry. But unlike his Menshevik opponents, he considered insurrection a central part of the revolutionary strategy of his party. Since 1901, he had demanded again and again that preparations be made for a popular uprising. To prepare an uprising meant to organize the party. The task was to arm the party for the hour when the mass uprising had broken out. This was the basis of the conspiratorial organization of the Bolsheviks.[9] The professional revolutionaries were to assume the hegemony, the leadership of the movement, they were to fight as the advance guard of the rebellious masses, they were to determine the political aims of the uprising and to deliver the decisive blow. Should the party falter when the people were ready for the insurrection, it would lose, in Lenin's view, its right to exist. By the beginning of 1905, this policy had long been formulated. The London Congress of the Russian Social Democratic Party held in 1905 had discussed the practical aspects of this idea,[10] but the events of 1905 proved that the revolutionary situation as anticipated by Lenin would not come about unaided. The seizure of power, the victory of the "revolutionary democracy" could not be achieved by the barricade fights of Presnia in December 1905.

In September 1917, when Lenin demanded that armed insurrection be treated as an art, the political scene had changed completely, but the idea of the uprising occupied the same position in his revolutionary thought:

To be successful, insurrection must rely not upon conspiracy and not upon a party, but on the advanced class. *That is the first point. Insurrection must rely upon a revolutionary* upsurge of the people. *That is the second point. Insurrection must rely upon that* turning point *in the history of the growing revolution when the activity of the advanced ranks of the people is at its height, and when the* vacillations *in the ranks of the enemy and* in the ranks of the weak, half-hearted and irresolute friends of the revolution *are strongest. That is the third point . . . Once these conditions exist, however, to refuse to treat the insurrection as an* art *is a betrayal of Marxism and a betrayal of the revolution.*[11]

[9] See Dietrich Geyer, *Lenin in der Russischen Sozialdemokratie* (Cologne, 1962), pp. 318–46.

[10] *Tretti s"ezd RSDRP (b). Aprel'–Mai 1905: Protokoly* (Moscow, 1959), pp. 98–160; 450–51.

[11] "Marksizm i vosstanie," *Polnoe sobranie sochinenii*, XXXIV, pp. 242–43.

The controversies in the Central Committee of the party were not primarily concerned with whether such an interpretation of the uprising was compatible with the principles of Marxism, or whether by adopting Lenin's definition the party would become guilty of "Blanquism." The argument lay elsewhere: it was over the analysis of the revolutionary situation as given by Lenin and over the question whether the political course of the party and the struggle for power should really be tied to an insurrection. Lenin's first thesis stated that now (September 1917), as a result of the defeat of Kornilov, all the conditions he had mentioned as necessary for the uprising were at hand: the support of the class representing "the vanguard of the revolution," "a countrywide revolutionary upsurge of the masses," "vacillation on a serious political scale among our enemies and among the irresolute petty bourgeoisie," and "the turning point in the history of the revolution." There were, of course, no real guarantees that these assertions were correct. But Lenin went even further: "It would be naive," he declared, "to wait for a 'formal' majority for the Bolsheviks. No revolution ever waits for that."[12] Lenin's view of what a majority was had a quality of its own, for it had nothing to do with elections or votes. From the fact that the Bolsheviks had obtained a majority in the soviets of Petrograd and Moscow, he drew the conclusion that "we have the following of a class, the vanguard of the revolution"; because the Mensheviks and the Socialist-Revolutionaries had rejected a coalition with the Kadets after the Kornilov revolt, he inferred that they "clearly lost their majority among the people"; since Chernov proved incapable of solving the agrarian question, he saw a confirmation of the statement that "We have the following of the majority of the people. Our victory is assured, for the people are close to desperation, and we show the people a sure way out."[13] It is obvious that Lenin's deductions (a majority in the soviets of both capitals equals a majority of the vanguard of the people equals a majority of the people equals victory in revolution) were not immediately intelligible to his comrades. The degree of reality inherent in this optimism remained questionable. Not until the very moment of armed action did the top echelons of the party become convinced that the insurrection would succeed. These doubts persisted as late as the meeting of the Central Committee on October 16.[14]

Apart from Lenin's assertion that "the time for the insurrection is fully ripe," it was undoubtedly the political consequences of his theses that met with strong opposition. In September 1917, for the first time since the fiasco of the July days, the party saw itself fully rehabilitated in the eyes of "revolutionary democracy." During the fight against the

[12] Ibid., p. 241.
[13] Ibid., p. 244.
[14] *Protokoly Tsentral'nogo Komiteta RSDRP*, pp. 93–104.

Kornilov Revolt, its following had grown, and its political program, promising the masses peace and land, met with an increasing response among soldiers and workers. The Bolshevik majority in the soviets of Moscow and Petrograd and the catastrophic losses of the Mensheviks in the municipal elections were unmistakable signs of the dynamic growth of the Bolshevik party. From the beginning of September, the party had, with Lenin's approval, again taken up its old slogan: "All power to the Soviets"—the appeal with which they now planned to confront the Democratic Conference during its meeting in Petrograd. Chances for a radicalization of soviet democracy seemed not too bad during those days, and it was not absurd to hope that the pressure of the masses would in the foreseeable future compel the replacement of the Provisional Government by a Soviet government, that is, by a coalition in which the Bolsheviks would assume a decisive role. In accord with these views, the Bolsheviks declared to the Democratic Conference: "Our party . . . has never striven and does not now strive for the seizure of power against the will of the organized majority of the working masses."[15] Seizure of power on the basis of the Soviet democracy—compared to this, the course advocated by Lenin had to appear as risky, even adventurous.

It is worth noting that Lenin in his contributions to the September issues of *Rabochii Put'* did not preclude alternatives to insurrection and civil war. In the event that power should be transferred to the soviets one should not rule out "a peaceful development of the revolution," compromises with the Mensheviks and the SR's, and a non-Bolshevik Soviet government with a Bolshevik opposition party—"under a really complete democracy." On September 16 appeared an article by Lenin that stated, "Only an alliance of the Bolsheviks with the SR's and the Mensheviks, and an immediate transfer of all power to the Soviets would prevent civil war in Russia."[16] Even as late as September 27, two days before Lenin had tendered his resignation, the party organ carried the following lines by him: "By seizing full power the Soviets could still today—and this is probably their last chance—ensure the peaceful development of the revolution, peaceful elections of deputies by the people, a peaceful struggle in the Soviets . . . and power should pass peacefully from one party to another."[17]

What is hinted at here is only superficially inconsistent with Lenin's demand that preparations be made for an insurrection. The alternative between civil war and a peaceful revolution presupposed the fall of the

[15] "Deklaratsiia fraktsii bol'shevikov, oglashennaia na Vserossiiskom Demokraticheskom Soveshchanii" (September 18, 1917), ibid., p. 51.

[16] "Russkaia revoliutsiia i grazhdanskaia voina," *Polnoe sobranie sochinenii,* XXXIV, p. 222.

[17] "Zadachi revoliutsii," ibid., p. 237.

Provisional Government; it was valid only under the condition that power was transferred to the soviets. But in Lenin's mind, the method by which this power was to be gained was irrevocably linked with an armed insurrection. In this respect, the perspectives of a "Soviet democracy" that Lenin drew up had an agitational function only in the struggle for power. Last but not least, his reflections also had the aim of forcing the Bolshevik party into his line of thinking. He had to deal with a party whose top echelons did not concentrate their energies on an insurrection, but on political activities: on September 21 the Central Committee acquiesced to the vote of the Bolshevik faction at the Democratic Conference favoring participation in the Pre-Parliament.[18] This "peaceful" and "parliamentary" procedure Lenin violently attacked. There can be no doubt that compromises had become unacceptable to him.

It is probably correct to say that from September 1917 Lenin's position rested on the dialetic combination of three axioms: (1) those who support the Bolshevik slogan "All power to the soviets" must break with the parties which up to then had been the pillars of "revolutionary democracy"; (2) those who want a Soviet regime in this sense have to decide in favor of the insurrection; (3) those who decide in favor of the insurrection pronounce themselves for a Bolshevik Soviet regime.

Already in his first letters dealing with the uprising, Lenin had demanded that the Bolsheviks confront the Democratic Conference with a sharply worded ultimatum and demand the unconditional adoption of the Bolshevik program. Without waiting for an answer, the Bolsheviks were then to leave the Conference, and appeal immediately to the masses, to the factories and barracks: "*There* we must explain in passionate speeches our program and put the alternative: either the Conference adopts it in its entirety or else insurrection. There is no middle course. Delay is impossible . . . In putting the question in this way . . . we shall be able to determine the right moment to start the insurrection."[19] The passion with which Lenin strove to induce the party to act is clearly reflected in his brusque letters to the Central Committee and in his energetic appeals to party organizations and conferences. With growing aggressiveness, he pursued the boycott of the Pre-Parliament and condemned the "utter idiocy," the "sheer treachery" of those who wanted to wait for the All-Russian Congress of Soviets to convene. With arguments that acquired an emotional coloring he demanded again and again that the insurrection be treated as an art, as a problem drew on the experiences recorded in Engels' pamphlet, *Revolution and Counterrevolution in Germany,* and he never wearied in presenting

[18] *Protokoly Tsentral'nogo Komiteta RSDRP,* p. 65.
[19] *Polnoe sobranie sochinenii,* XXXIV, p. 247.

these terse reflections on the insurrection as Danton's and Marx's great legacy to which the party had to conform.[20]

It is impressive to see how unshakable Lenin was in his belief that no time must be lost. Now or never, he thought, was the moment to seize power and to assure its permanent possession. "It is my profound conviction that if we wait . . . and let the present moment pass, we shall ruin the revolution" (September 29).[21] Success seemed a certainty. His analysis of the revolutionary and military situations assured victory. The attack was to be opened simultaneously in three places: Moscow, Petrograd, and Finland. This time, he said, the army would not march against the insurgents; the wavering attitude of the government, the disintegration of the Mensheviks and the SR's, the agitation for peace and the distribution of land would assure the Bolsheviks of a majority in the country.[22] These judgments, however, should not be considered in isolation. The battle Lenin had to fight within his own party ranks became the driving force behind his argumentation and his analysis of the situation became a function of his polemics. This explains the excessive exaggeration of Lenin's political diagnoses. The fact of agrarian unrest led him to the prognosis that an enormous uprising of the peasants was at hand and that the Bolsheviks would betray democracy and the idea of liberty if they failed to take action in support of the peasants. By repeated references to symptoms of crises in the belligerent countries, Lenin placed the insurrection within the context of an international revolution. He interpreted reports about mass arrests of socialist party leaders in Italy and about the beginning of mutinies in the German navy as "indisputable symptoms," and as proof of the fact "that a turning point is at hand, that we are on the eve of a worldwide revolution."[23] Here reemerged the old idea that it was the destiny of the Bolsheviks to act as the vanguard of the international proletariat: "They will save the world revolution . . . and the lives of hundreds of thousands of people at the front."[24]

The basis of Lenin's astonishing assurance, the question of how he gained such unswerving confidence in the validity of his theses cannot be discussed here in full. Any answers have to take into account the psychological constitution of this man. But even psychology does not excuse us from looking for a rational explanation. It is certain that Lenin saw the military problems of the insurrection in closest connection with

[20] "Sovety postoronnego" (October 8, 1917), ibid., p. 383; Lenin's quotations are from Engels' brochure, which he mistook for a work written by Marx: ibid., p. 335.

[21] "Krizis nazrel," ibid., p. 283.

[22] Ibid., p. 282.

[23] Ibid., pp. 272, 275.

[24] "Pis'mo v Tsk, MK, PK i chlenam Sovetov Pitera i Moskvy-Bol'shevikam" (October 1, 1917), ibid., pp. 340–41.

the political problems of the revolution. "Events compel us . . . History has made the military question now the fundamental *political* question" (September 27).[25] The insight implied here Lenin may have found in Clausewitz: "Armed uprising," he wrote, "is a special form of political struggle," that is, "politics with other means." Added to this was (with reference to Marx), "Insurrection is an art quite as much as war."[26] Everything that was military or technical became incorporated into the political strategy of the revolution. Thus, Lenin's thesis that "to wait is a crime" could be detached from the specific moment and continually absorb new arguments from the changing situation. These were: that a separate peace among the imperialists was impending, that Kerensky schemed to deliver revolutionary Petrograd into the hands of the Germans, that a second Kornilov coup was at hand, and that "the success of both the Russian and the world revolution depends on two or three days' fighting."[27]

By October 10, Lenin had, as we know, succeeded in his attempt to secure within the top committee of the party a majority for his policy of insurrection. The decision of the Bolshevik faction to walk out on the Pre-Parliament during its opening session on October 7 was an important step in that direction. On the same day, Lenin returned from Finland and took lodgings on Vasilevskii Ostrov in Petrograd. Three days later the Central Committee voted in favor of his thesis that the time was ripe for an insurrection. The situation justified this resolution. At the beginning of October, the government was undoubtedly headed for a new and serious crisis; it rapidly lost authority. The military situation on the northern front was catastrophic. In the capital, one had every reason to doubt the loyalty of the strong garrison stationed there. Because of the continuous shortages of fuel and food, prices soared uncontrollably.[28] The lethargic attitude of the working people in the suburbs and in the factories could easily turn into unrest and riots. The pathos of the speakers at the Council of the Republic could not conceal the general misery. The Executive Committee of the All-Russian Congress of Soviets, consisting of prominent Mensheviks and SR's, was no less isolated than the Provisional Government. It was to be expected that the Second All-Russian Congress of Soviets, scheduled for October 20, would consolidate the Bolsheviks' gains. The Soviet

25 "Pis'mo I. T. Smilge," ibid., p. 264.

26 "Sovety postoronnego," ibid., pp. 382–83. See Werner Hahlweg, "Lenin und Clausewitz," *Archiv für Kulturgeschichte,* XXXVI (1954), pp. 30–59, 357–87.

27 *Polnoe sobranie sochinenii,* XXXIV, p. 384.

28 New information, based on archival sources, is given by Z. V. Stepanov, *Rabochie Petrograda v period podgotovki i provedeniia Oktiabr'skogo vooruzhennogo vosstaniia* (Moscow-Leningrad, 1965).

of Petrograd was dominated by Trotsky, the exponent of the Bolshevik majority. The Left SR's seemed ready to support the Bolsheviks. At a Congress of the Soviet Deputies of the Northern Region, held on October 11 at the Smolny Institute, the animosity toward the government led to manifestations approaching a formal declaration of civil war. Lenin hoped that this congress could be transformed into an organ of the uprising and that the Finnish troops and the Baltic fleet could be induced to march on Petrograd.[29] It appeared that the Central Committee had chosen the right moment for its decision to prepare the insurrection.

Upon closer inspection, however, it appears that on October 10 the Bolshevik Central Committee still avoided making a clear commitment. The technique of the uprising and the strategy of the power seizure had not been discussed. Instead, the old controversies flared up again because of Kamenev and Zinoviev, who protested that the insurrection would end in defeat and force the petty bourgeoisie into the camp of the Kadets, that a proletarian government would be unable to carry on a revolutionary war against the German imperialists, and that the mass of the soldiers would turn away from the Bolsheviks. They rejected Lenin's thesis that the majority of the people and the international proletariat had already been won over. In their view, the best chances for the party lay not in an insurrection but in the utilization of the impending All-Russian Congress of Soviets and in concentrating the party's efforts on elections for the Constituent Assembly.[30] In view of this opposition, Lenin was compelled to intensify his struggle for the acceptance of his strategy.[31] The polemics of his opponents became entangled in arguments that, no doubt, carried a certain historical dignity, but had little practical relevance. Lenin's opponents had difficulty keeping in touch with the actual situation.

As a matter of fact, the controversy had little effect on the course of events in Petrograd. The call for an insurrection could be dispensed with as soon as a method for the overthrow of the Provisional Government had been found. There is much evidence to indicate that Trotsky, the chairman of the Petrograd Soviet, had a large share in the solution of this problem. On October 6, a rumor concerning a "counterrevolutionary conspiracy" was discussed in the Soldiers' Section of the So-

[29] "Pis'mo k tovarishcham bol'shevikam, uchastvuiushchim na Oblastnom S"ezde Sovetov Severnoi Oblasti" (October 8, 1917), *Polnoe sobranie sochinenii,* XXXIV, pp. 385–90.

[30] G. Zinoviev, Iu. Kamenev, "K tekushchemu momentu" (October 11, 1917), *Protokoly Tsentral'nogo Komiteta RSDRP (b)* (Moscow, 1958), pp. 87–92.

[31] See Lenin's "Pis'mo k tovarishcham" (October 17), "Pis'mo k chlenam partii bol'shevikov" (October 19), "Pis'mo v Tsentral'nyi Komitet RSDRP (b)" (October 19, 1917), *Polnoe sobranie sochinenii,* XXXIV, pp. 398–427.

viet.[32] The rumor was that the government was preparing its flight from Petrograd and intended to abandon the "citadel of the revolution" to the approaching Germans. Trotsky made a momentous decision when he resolved immediately to take advantage of this rumor. In the Bolshevik declaration to the Pre-Parliament he painted a grim picture of the "deadly danger" that now threatened the capital. Kerensky, he wrote, planned the transfer of the government to Moscow with the view of transforming that city into a stronghold of the counterrevolution and breaking up the Constituent Assembly. The garrison, he continued, was soon to be evacuated, which meant the abandonment of the city to the Germany army and the smothering of the revolution.[33] Trotsky had obviously recognized the usefulness of this charge. If the alleged danger could be rendered credible, the Soviet of Petrograd would obtain a powerful and highly effective instrument for the organization of a broad line of resistance. It could also determine the nature of the appeal that was to be addressed to the garrison and to the workers. These were to be called upon to protect the capital from its external and internal enemies; to defend it against the counterrevolution, personified by Miliukov and the Kaiser. This strategy made the appeal for an insurrection superfluous. In the slogan "Petrograd in danger" the Bolsheviks had a formula capable of affecting the masses in a very fundamental way. Their agitation received a uniform direction, and the practical measures were given a concrete aim. The object was to paralyze the authority of the Military Staff of the Petrograd garrison, to put the troops under the command of the Soviet, and to enable the workers to arm themselves and to support the troops.

The Petrograd Soviet lost no time in realizing the chances thus offered. Already on October 9 the regiments were asked to increase their combat readiness.[34] Two days later, Trotsky's addresses before the Congress of Soviets of the Northern Region gave the appeal for the active defense of the capital wide resonance, far beyond Petrograd itself.[35] The immediate concern of the Bolshevik leaders was to incorporate the forces on the periphery of the city into the general plan for action, especially the troops of the northern front and of the Baltic fleet.[36] It was to the advantage of the Bolsheviks that they could oper-

[32] "Rezoliutsiia Soldatskoi Sektsii Petrogradskogo Soveta" (October 6, 1917), L. Trotsky, *Sochineniia* (Moscow, n.d.), vol. III, pt. 1, p. 321.

[33] "Deklaratsiia fraktsii bol'shevikov na zasedanii Demokraticheskogo Soveshchaniia" (October 7, 1917), ibid., pp. 321–23. See also *Protokoly Tsentral'nogo Komiteta RSDRP* (*b*), pp. 77–79.

[34] "Rezoliutsiia Petrogradskogo Soveta o vyvode voisk iz Petrograda" (October 9, 1917), L. Trotsky, *Sochineniia,* vol. III, pt. 1, p. 327.

[35] Ibid., vol III, pt. 2, pp. 5–14.

[36] On the role of the Baltic fleet in October 1917 see recent Soviet documentations sponsored by the Historical Institute of the Academy of Sciences

ate behind Soviet legitimacy. They carried out their preparations publicly and in an orderly manner. Already on October 15, the readers learned from their Sunday papers that the Bolsheviks planned action against the Provisional Government.[37] On the following day Trotsky declared before the plenum of the Soviet: "We are told that we prepare a staff for the seizure of power. We make no secret of it."[38] The Military-Revolutionary Committee, founded on October 11 as an operational center,[39] was, as a matter of fact, not a club of conspirators, but a formally elected institution of the Petrograd Soviet. This meant that it had many channels open: it had its own press and official contacts with the soviets in all districts of the city,[40] with the trade unions and the factory committees, the workers' militia and the Red Guards as well.[41] The government saw its sphere of power systematically diminished without being able to arrest the process of its isolation.

The wisdom of this tactical concept was proved by the fact that the Bolshevik Central Committee now began to concern itself with practical questions connected with the planned power seizure as well. On October 16 the Bolsheviks resolved to attach a permanent delegation to the Military-Revolutionary Committee.[42] Long discussions had again given rise to a multitude of doubts. Many members still tended to recall the fiasco of July whenever talk of an insurrection came up. The reports

---

and the Central Archives of the Soviet fleet: *Baltiiskie moriaki v podgotovke i provedenii Velikoi Oktiabr'skoi revoliutsii* (Moscow-Leningrad, 1957); *Protokoly i postanovleniia Tsentral'nogo Komiteta Baltiiskogo flota, 1917–1918* (Moscow-Leningrad, 1963).

[37] *Delo Naroda,* no. 181, October 15, 1917, quoted in R. P. Browder and A. F. Kerensky, eds., *The Russian Provisional Government 1917: Documents* (Stanford, 1961), III, pp. 1764–65. On October 14, the Menshevik leader Dan drew attention to the Bolshevik preparations for an uprising during a session of the Central Executive Committee of the All-Russian Soviets. See *Izvestiia TsIK,* no. 198, October 15, 1917, quoted in *Velikaia Oktiabr'skaia Socialisticheskaia Revoliutsiia. Khronika sobytii,* IV (Moscow, 1961), p. 429.

[38] L. Trotsky, *Sochineniia,* vol. III, pt. 2, p. 15.

[39] Important material has been collected in *Petrogradskii Voenno-Revoliutsionnyi Komitet: Dokumenty i materialy,* 3 vols., (Moscow, 1966–67); compare, *Velikaia Oktiabr'skaia Sotsialisticheskaia revoliutsiia. Dokumenty i materialy: Oktiabr'skoe vooruzhennoe vosstanie v Petrograde* (Moscow, 1957).

[40] See *Raionnye Sovety Petrograda v 1917 godu: Protokoly, rezoliutsii, postanovleniia obshchikh sobranii i zasedanii ispolnitelnykh komitetov,* I–III (Moscow-Leningrad, 1964–66).

[41] V. I. Startsev, "Voenno-revoliutsionnyi Komitet i Krasnaia gvardia v Oktiabr'skom vooruzhennom vosstanii," in *Oktiabr'skoe vooruzhennoe vosstanie v Petrograde: Sbornik statei* (Moscow-Leningrad, 1957), pp. 106–41.

[42] *Protokoly Tsentral'nogo Komiteta RSDRP (b),* p. 104.

of local Bolshevik representatives gave no basis for any definite opinions concerning the chances for success. In the end, the impression that gained hold was that the seizure of power was conceivable only if it developed from active resistance of the garrison, as a defensive action against measures of the government directly affecting the fate of the troops. This corresponded to the course chosen by the Soviet. Thus, Trotsky found himself justified even before achieving any success. The seizure of power had to start with the seizure of the garrison, with the gradual emasculation by the Military-Revolutionary Committee of the Military Headquarters. In the days that followed, the task became one of provoking the enemy, as a means of setting off the process of the transfer of power.

There was so little resemblance between these tactics and the common idea of an insurrection, that Trotsky could exploit the general confusion to conceal the further preparations. The government, the bourgeois press, and even the Mensheviks expected that, as in July, the action of the Bolsheviks would again erupt into armed mass demonstrations. On October 18 Maxim Gorky expressed his fears, "An organized mob will pour out into the streets, . . . and adventurers, thieves, and professional murders . . . will begin to 'make the history of the Russian revolution.' "[43] Trotsky declared on the same day that no decisions had been taken which were not publicly known: If the Soviet—"this revolutionary parliament finds it necessary to call a demonstration, then it will do so . . . We have still not set a date for the attack."[44] All the actions of the Military-Revolutionary Committee, including the arming of the workers' militia, were still declared to be purely defensive measures. Not the Soviet, Trotsky continued, but the bourgeoisie provoked the conflict; the counterrevolution was about "to mobilize all forces against the workers and soldiers." Trotsky announced that any plot against the forthcoming Second All-Russian Congress of Soviets and any attempt to clear Petrograd of its garrison would be answered "with a ruthless counteroffensive carried to its end."[45] Declarations of this kind seemed to leave it to the enemy to begin hostilities.

Bolshevik agitation was now entirely concentrated on the slogan: "The All-Russian Congress is in danger." Trotsky could not dispense with this formula if he wanted his concept of the gradual seizure of power to succeed. He declared that the deputies to the Congress must be enabled to fulfill their task without hindrance. This task was "to pass

[43] Novaia zhizn', no. 156, October 18, 1917, quoted in Browder and Kerensky, *The Russian Provisional Government,* III, p. 1766.
[44] L. Trotsky, *Sochineniia,* vol. III, pt. 2, pp. 31–33, for a second version of Trotsky's speech, see Browder and Kerensky, *The Russian Provisional Government,* III, p. 1767.
[45] Ibid.

resolutions transferring power to the All-Russian Congress of Soviets, concluding an immediate armistice on all fronts, and transferring all land to the peasants."[46] The procedure of having the organization of the coup d'état sanctioned by the soviet institutions of Petrograd remained unaltered. The Bolsheviks were thus obliged to observe the rules of the Soviet. Success was assured by the steady increase of the authority of the Petrograd Soviet, rather than by pressure on the Bolsheviks to start an insurrection. For Trotsky "insurrection as an art" meant treating Soviet legality as an art. Even some members of the Military-Revolutionary Committee may have believed that they worked exclusively to safeguard the forthcoming Congress of Soviets and to defend the garrison against counterrevolutionary pogroms. As late as October 24, Trotsky, Kamenev, and Balashev entered into negotiations with the Socialist-Revolutionaries on the basis of this formula.[47]

We know that even Lenin was deceived by the rationality of these moves and misinterpreted Trotsky's intentions. It was unacceptable to him that the seizure of power should be tied to the resolutions of the Congress; this seemed "a disaster, a sheer formality." The Congress had interest to him only if the insurrection anticipated its resolutions, thus reducing the function of the deputies to applauding the Bolshevik triumph. On the evening of October 24, shortly before taking the streetcar to the Smolny, he wrote in a state of extreme excitement: "We are confronted with problems which are not to be solved by conferences or congresses . . . , but exclusively by peoples, by the masses, by the struggle of the armed people." He categorically demanded a decision "at any cost, this very evening, this very night."[48] Little remained to be done in this respect. The Provisional Government had become a mere shadow; practically speaking, it had already lost its power. Its security depended on a few hundred rifles; its hope rested with the fiction that troops were marching to its relief. On October 21 the Petrograd Soviet had already set off the mechanism of the transfer of power. Consistently with the general tactics, the first move was to confront the District Headquarters under Colonel Polkovnikov with an ultimatum.[49] The Soviet demanded that the commissars it had appointed should be recognized and that henceforth all military orders obtain the sanction of the Revolutionary-Military Committee. The capitulation act thus had already been formulated. It was realized on October 23 when the Soviet claimed for itself the sole power of command over the garrison.[50] The

[46] Ibid.
[47] *Golos soldata,* October 25, 1917, reprinted in *Petrogradskii Voenno-revoliutsionnyi Komitet,* I, p. 99.
[48] *Polnoe sobranie sochinenii,* XXXIV, pp. 435–36.
[49] *Petrogradskii Voenno-revoliutsionnyi Komitet,* I, p. 59.
[50] Ibid., pp. 67, 97–98.

bulk of the regiments placed themselves under the command of Smolny; the Cossacks remained neutral; the citizens of the capital were asked to maintain a state of absolute calm and self-control.

What followed resembled a mere police action. The insurrection was not formally proclaimed, nor were the people called out into the streets, nor was the fighting quality of the workers put to test. The decisive signal for the seizure of power was finally given by the government itself when it tried to shut down the Bolshevik press on the morning of October 24. The final episode was insignificant. Macabre scenes took place in the Mariinskii Theater when Kerensky informed the Council of the Republic of the insurrection in the capital.[51] Before the sailors of Kronstadt went ashore on the following day and before the cruiser "Aurora" had readied its guns, the victors had already advertised their success: "The Provisional Government has been deposed. State power has passed into the hands of . . . the Revolutionary-Military Committee which heads the Petrograd proletariat and garrison."[52] The martial impressions left by the event of October 25 were mainly due to the simple fact that the cabinet continued its session in the Malachite Room of the Winter Palace, although the Prime Minister had left.

Kerensky's fall was undoubtedly a result of the brilliant technique of power seizure as developed by Trotsky. But the very fact that this could be performed so easily points to something beyond the mere technical aspects. The regiments of the garrison that followed the Bolshevik slogans formed no potential capable of sustaining the burden of a military contest. The military effectiveness of the workers' militia and the Red Guards is also doubtful. It became evident that the secret for success did not lie in the military means that the Military-Revolutionary Committee had at its disposal. The transfer of power in Petrograd was rather the result of the victory that the Bolsheviks previously achieved in the *political* sphere on the basis of that very Soviet Democracy whose principles they rejected, but whose apparatus they could not dispense with.[53] The coup d'état in Petrograd could be organized only after the Soviet had been conquered. It was possible to disarm the enemy physically because he was already disarmed politically. Power could not have been captured as long as it was not secured politically. The art of insurrection was a product of the art of politics; it was the result of a policy whose plebiscitary quality can hardly be contested. At the last moment even the Mensheviks and SR's seized Bolshevik formulas in

[51] *Rech'*, no 251, October 25, 1917, in Browder and Kerensky, *The Russian Provisional Government,* III, pp. 1772–74.

[52] "K grazhdanam Rossii" (October 25, 10:00 A.M.), *Petrogradskii Voenno-revoliutsionnyi Komitet,* I, p. 106.

[53] Oskar Anweiler, *Die Rätebewegung in Russland 1905–1921* (Leiden, 1958), pp. 180–241.

order to avoid being crushed between the Scylla of the counterrevolution and the Charybdis of a Bolshevik dictatorship.[54] Armistice and distribution of land—there was, in October, no plausible political alternative to this emergency program. This situation had a compelling force and not only the Provisional Government fell a victim to it, but soviet democracy as well. Lenin remained in power because he dared to do what had become a necessity.

[54] See Browder and Kerensky, *The Russian Provisional Government,* III, pp. 1778–84.

ORIGINS OF THE CHINESE REVOLUTION 1915–49

Lucien Bianco

THE importance of nationalism to China's Communist revolution is by now a commonplace. Since the Communists' triumph in 1949 the newspapers have reminded us of it constantly; before that, China specialists repeatedly made the same point. In a sense the whole history of modern China can be seen as a reaction to imperialism, to an outside force that threatened the country's very existence. Modern Chinese history in this view culminates in the birth—after an extraordinarily painful labor—of the Chinese nation. Never was the pain greater, or delivery closer, than during the Sino-Japanese War of 1937–45. It was with these eight years, the period of the Second World War in Asia, that this chapter is primarily concerned.

COMMUNISM AND NATIONALISM

One place after another in China fell with almost ridiculous ease before the Japanese *Blitzkrieg* (if we may use a term that had not yet been coined). But like Napoleon's army in Russia over a century before, the Japanese Imperial Army never took possession of the land it had conquered. It was swallowed up in the vastness of China, holding nothing but cities and connecting roads and railways. There were only two real campaigns in eight years of war, of which the second was just a

Reprinted from *Origins of the Chinese Revolution, 1915–1949* by Lucien Bianco, pp. 148–166, translated from the French by Muriel Bell. Stanford: Stanford University Press; London: Oxford University Press with the per-

continuation of the first. What was left to conquer in 1938, after the first campaign? Everything in China that counted was in Japanese hands: the great ports, the industrial and commercial centers, and the capital. In theory Japan occupied everything east of the line joining Peking to Canton via Hankow, the richest and most populous part of the country. Between the fall of 1938 and the spring of 1944, when the Japanese army launched another major campaign, the front was more or less stabilized along the Peking-Canton axis.

But the real war went on behind the front. Against an opponent of overwhelming economic and military superiority, China had two great assets. One was her enormous population and its morale; Chinese patriotism, so long considered a joke by skeptical Western residents, had at last under the pressure of extreme and desperate conditions become a force to be reckoned with. The other was the foreign assistance that was bound to come once Japan's imperialist designs finally impinged on countries more powerful than China. China's problem was to hold out until this assistance came; her assets were exploitable only in a protracted war because a short war meant the victory of the stronger. This was perfectly understood by Chiang Kai-shek, who announced his intention of "trading space for time." He did so with his habitual resoluteness, abandoning the important centers of the East and taking refuge in the underdeveloped and inaccessible interior.[1] But he failed to do the one thing that would have given his strategy of local war maximum effectiveness—namely, to conduct guerrilla warfare behind the Japanese lines.[2]

The social implications of guerrilla warfare are obvious. Mobilizing the rural masses would have required transforming the Chinese countryside and limiting the power of large landowners; hence Chiang's aversion to the idea. The same consideration explains why the Communists were the first to urge a strategy of protracted war, and why they were the most active, if not the only, leaders of guerrilla resistance efforts. Guerrilla activities benefited the Communists even more than the nation as a whole. From their stronghold in Shensi, they gradually infiltrated much of North China, occupying most of Shansi, Hopei, and Shantung behind the Japanese lines. In January 1938 they were among

---

[1] His wartime capital, Chungking, was in railroadless Szechwan province; moreover, the fog that shrouded the city for six months of the year made air attacks impossible during that period. The reasons for Chiang's choice were similar to the Communists' reasons for choosing Kiangsi as their soviet base area.

[2] There were in fact some Nationalist, i.e. Kuomintang, guerrilla forces, but in most cases they were formed on local initiative.

the founders of a local anti-Japanese government, the so-called Border Region Government, that coordinated the activities of the first guerrilla base area.[3] When Japan surrendered in 1945, there were nineteen Communist base areas, most of them in North China. There were 80,000 men in the Red Army in 1937; in 1945 there were 900,000, plus a militia force of 2.2 million men.[4] In 1937 the CCP governed 1.5 million peasants in desolate Shensi; in 1945 there were 90 million peasants under Communist rule, which extended across the whole North China Plain. In 1936 the Communists had their backs to the wall; their position was far more precarious than at the time of the Kiangsi soviets, and at times downright desperate. In 1945 the party had 1.2 million members and was a serious contender for power. So great was the CCP's growth during the war that by 1944 some informed observers were asking themselves if the Communists had not already won the impending civil war.

How did such an extraordinary change come about? In the first place, the CCP played the card of united front and national resistance for all it was worth. At the cost of relatively minor concessions, the party won official status for the first time, and was thus in a position to exploit the new possibilities created by a state of war. It all but abandoned its program of social revolution, including the confiscation of large landholdings (there were in any case fewer large landowners in North China than in Central or South China), and was content instead with strict enforcement of the law limiting land rent. This was enough to win over the tenant farmers without jeopardizing the party's official moderate image. For the peasant majority—the huge class of small owners—the party enacted and enforced a decrease in interest rates, which it fixed at 10 per cent a year, and a reduction in taxes, which it made progressive. That was all—and as many observers noted, it was reform, not revolution.

With social concerns relegated to the background, the accent was on national resistance. The CCP constantly invoked the necessity of "national salvation" (*chiu-kuo*). In *On New Democracy,* published in 1940, Mao unblinkingly presented himself as the faithful follower and rightful successor of Sun Yat-sen. Sun's doctrine, Mao asserted, was correct and well-suited to his time, and lacked only one thing to make it

[3] The Border Region Government of Hopei, Shansi, and Chahar was set up as a rival to the puppet government installed in Peking a month earlier by the Japanese. At first the Border Region Government had only two Communist members out of nine, but Communist influence spread rapidly throughout the region under its control.

[4] These are the official figures, and they are probably inflated. The Kuomintang, whose figures are distorted in the opposite direction, estimated Communist regulars in 1945 at 600,000 and Communist militiamen at 400,000.

equally applicable to the modern era: a concern with mobilizing the masses. The CCP's mobilization of the peasants, along with its emphasis on national resistance, was the second reason for its growth during the war. Patriotic propaganda was much more successful in winning over the peasants than agrarian revolution had been several years before. The peasantry supported the Border Region Government and actively assisted the Red Army, supplying among other things the best part of its troops.[5]

Why were the Communists so successful? First of all, because the anti-Japanese Border Region Government, which was dominated by the CCP, filled an important void; many Kuomintang officials fled or resigned their government posts at the first sign of danger. Second, because under the new government the peasantry served an apprenticeship in mass-style democracy, including public assemblies and meetings of associations of poor peasants, women, youth, militiamen. Far removed though it may have been from Western-style democracy, this was something altogether new in the peasant world and was in itself revolutionary. Last and most important, because the inhabitants of North China had no choice. The CCP's greatest ally was the Japanese army, whose atrocities left the peasantry in such desperate straits that it had no recourse but to seek the Red Army's protection. The Japanese response to guerilla warfare, assassination, and sabotage was systematic destruction and the indiscriminate slaughter of peasant villagers. The Japanese army launched "mopping-up" campaigns against "infested areas" (the term has a familiar ring today), guided by the

[5] The army was renamed the Eighth Route Army (*pa-lu-chün*) after the accord with the Kuomintang. During the civil war, its name was changed again, but it continued to be popularly known as the Eighth Route Army. In order not to confuse the reader, the term Red Army is used whenever the specific context does not require greater precision. In fact, the Eighth Route Army was only the most important and most celebrated of the Communist armies. Of the 86 members of one Eighth Route Army unit fighting in western Hopei in 1940, 70 were poor peasants and none were intellectuals. Only eleven had been to school, but only two of the other 75 were illiterate: 73 had learned to read thanks to the Red Army. Of the 29 who were members of the CCP, 28 had joined since the beginning of the war with Japan—eloquent testimony to the effect of patriotism on party membership. Similar evidence comes from northern Kiangsu in February 1941. Of 197 officers of the New Fourth Army (the most important Communist army outside North China), only 25 had joined the Red Army by 1936; the others had joined since 1937—to fight the Japanese. These examples are taken from Chalmers Johnson, *Peasant Nationalism and Communist Power: The Emergence of Revolutionary China, 1937–1945* (Stanford, Calif.: Stanford University Press, 1962), pp. 103, 155. This important book will be discussed shortly.

"three-all" policy ("burn all, kill all, loot all" within a given area, so as to make it uninhabitable). Poisonous fumes were pumped into tunnels in which the local population had taken refuge (800 inhabitants of one Hopei village were asphyxiated in this manner one sunny day in the summer of 1942); rapes in which fathers and brothers were forced at bayonet point to participate, and more—the war in Asia awaits its Malaparte.[6] The thing to remember is that the peasant was often safer if he joined a guerrilla detachment: since his life was in constant danger anyway, he was better off if he at least had a weapon. This was all the more true since the North China front was at once nowhere and everywhere; it was not a geographic front like the one between Kuomintang-ruled China to the Southwest and occupied China in the Southeast, but, in Fairbank's words, "the omnipresent social front of popular resistance."

The peasants of North China in wartime took orders from two sets of authorities, one by day, the other by night. On the orders of the Japanese, trenches were filled in by day that had been dug the night before on the orders of the guerrillas—another practice familiar to us from the Algerian and Vietnamese wars. The peasants paid two sets of taxes, organized two different sets of village leaders to deal with their daytime and nightime masters, and suffered reprisals from each side for carrying out the orders of the other. Though the Communists often were intruders in a village and though they sometimes took control by force,[7] they soon came to symbolize the nationalism to which the war they were waging had given birth. Left to themselves, the peasants certainly would not have resisted the Japanese army.[8] They would simply have lain low, in their customary fashion, in the hope of escaping notice. But once the Communists' guerrilla tactics had thrown the Japanese off balance and provoked them into retaliating with a wave of raids and massacres, the villagers came to hate the invaders with all their heart and soul. Hatred, it seems, is the most powerful agent of national self-consciousness.

[6] [In *Kaputt*, Malaparte gives a vivid and grisly account of his experiences as a war correspondent accompanying the German army in Russia during the Second World War.—Trans.]

[7] In relatively peaceful areas (along the Yangtze, for example, where the pro-Japanese Nanking government offered the peasants relative security), the New Fourth Army made little headway and even resorted to destroying the *pao-chia* registers and residence certificates to force peasant villages to oppose the Japanese.

[8] They probably would have killed a few Japanese here and there, out of the same kind of xenophobia that led to the murder of missionaries in the nineteenth century. But such incidents would have been no more than a petty nuisance to the Japanese.

War and Revolution

The foregoing analysis is much indebted to Chalmers Johnson's bold and intelligent study *Peasant Nationalism and Communist Power: The Emergence of Revolutionary China, 1937–1945,* one of the indispensable books on contemporary China. In fairness to Professor Johnson, be it noted that my presentation of his thesis includes examples and observations with which he might not agree. Since *Peasant Nationalism* goes straight to the central issues of the Chinese Revolution, it seems useful to begin by summarizing and discussing its main conclusions.

In Johnson's view, the Communist revolution succeeded not because of peasant misery but because of the Second World War. The cause of the revolution was not social or economic, but political. The war, in his judgment, contributed to the Communist triumph in two ways. First, it created peasant nationalism, a mass nationalism that differed fundamentally from the nationalism of the intellectuals so clearly in evidence before the outbreak of war. The nationalism of the intellectuals resembled that of the nineteenth-century European bourgeoisie; peasant nationalism, by contrast, more primitive but in the end decisive, was a nationalism of despair. Second, the war allowed the Communists to present themselves as nationalists and thus to win the peasantry's support as the natural leaders of patriotic resistance to the Japanese. In effect, Johnson concludes, during the war Communism came to be identified with nationalism. It was presented to the peasants as just another variety of nationalism, "a species of nationalist movement," and it was as such that it came to power.

Furthermore, the breaches in the united front, which became more numerous and more serious with every passing year of the war, tended to leave the Communists with a monopoly on patriotic resistance. The two camps were equally responsible for these breaches, but episodes like the New Fourth Army Incident, in which a Communist force of 9,000 men were encircled and destroyed by a Kuomintang division in January 1941, did much to confer on the Reds the halo of martyrs. Japanese anti-Communist propaganda, which tried to drive a wedge in the Chinese national front and justify Japan's invasion as an anti-Bolshevik crusade ("The Communists are our No. 1 enemies"), had the same result.[9] Judiciously exploited by written and verbal propaganda emanating from Yenan, the Communist capital, the Japanese propa-

[9] The collaborationist Nanking government headed by Wang Ching-wei called for an anti-Communist front uniting the Nanking and Chungking governments.

ganda efforts ended up persuading many peasants that the meaning of this new term "Communist" was simply "patriot."[10] This mistake was the more natural because the identity of names led many peasants to confuse the Kuomintang in Chungking with the collaborationist Kuomintang in Nanking.

For purposes of comparison and generalization, Johnson concludes by pointing to the similarities between the Chinese and Yugoslav experiences in the Second World War. In particular, he shows how Tito paved the way for the triumph of the revolution by coming to represent, as opposed to Drasha Mihailović, the principle of resistance to the Nazis. A "national Communism," inclined to independence from Moscow, became the practice, if not the ideology, of the only two people's democracies whose leaders had come to power without the help of the Russian army.

All this is very stimulating and seems to me for the most part well-founded. In what follows, my purpose is not so much to criticize Johnson's thesis as to qualify and supplement it. Some of his fundamental conclusions seem to me to be irrefutable. There can be no question, first of all, about the decisive importance of the Second World War. It was the war that brought the Chinese peasantry and China to revolution; at the very least, it considerably accelerated the CCP's rise to power. Second, it is clear that economic reasons alone were not enough to mobilize the peasantry. This point is implicit in the conclusion to Chapter Four, which is based on my own research; indeed, I tend to think that before the outbreak of war the peasantry was not in fact ripe for revolution. Finally, on a more general level, the importance of nationalism in the play of forces that led to the Chinese Revolution is beyond dispute.

Now let us return briefly to peasant nationalism and to the influence of the war as such. Johnson's study deals primarily with North China, the China of the Communist guerrilla armies. In the parts of China under Kuomintang control, what was the relationship between the peasantry and the Nationalist army, and how did the peasants regard the war?

Neither question can be answered without reference to how the army treated its recruits and how it behaved toward the peasant population. In fact, if not in theory, conscription affected only the poor and middle peasants; prosperous families either paid for a substitute or bribed the recruiting officer. Kuomintang soldiers were so badly fed that some actually died of starvation. A greater number were lost in epidemics, made the more disastrous by a total lack of hygiene, or died of tuberculosis, which they gave one another by eating from a common plate

[10] Along with reminders of the contacts taking place between men close to the Chungking government and representatives of Japan.

or bowl in the customary Chinese fashion. Since most soldiers could not read or write and their pitifully low pay put the services of a public scribe beyond their reach, they completely lost touch with their families. "For his family, a conscript's life usually ended on the day he disappeared down the road, shackled to his fellows"[11]—except when he managed to desert before his unit had gone too far. And the army was all too alert to the possibility of desertion: in one case, 200 conscripts were burned to death in a train bombed by the Japanese when their officers decided not to risk opening the train's locked doors.[12]

As for civilians, requisitions and pillaging were so frequent an occurrence that most peasants hated their own army more than the Japanese.[13] In some cases starving Chinese soldiers killed peasants who resisted their efforts to steal grain; in at least one case fleeing soldiers killed peasants for their clothing, with which they hoped to disguise themselves from their Japanese pursuers.[14] In 1938, to slow down the Japanese advance and protect the city of Chengchow, the government opened the dikes on the Yellow River, causing it to return to the course it had followed almost a hundred years before—a "heroic" decision that resulted in the death by drowning or starvation of thousands of peasants in eastern Honan.

One can easily imagine the peasants' reaction to the way the army behaved and carried on the war: they tried to defend themselves and to survive. They mixed sand in the rice requisitioned by the Kuomintang army, sent their idiot and invalid sons to fill their conscription quotas, and emigrated en masse to occupied areas when the Japanese offered good wages for peasant labor on their strategic connecting roads.[15]

[11] Graham Peck, *Two Kinds of Time,* p. 226. A good many of the examples and concrete details given below come from this book, which is just as indispensable for this period as Johnson's *Peasant Nationalism* and Edgar Snow's famous *Red Star over China.*

[12] This incident occurred in western Honan in 1941 on the Lunghai railroad, the major rail route from the East to the Northwest.

[13] "Their own" is of course misleading, since they never thought in such terms. Japanese soldiers, Kuomintang soldiers—they were the same plague, something inflicted from outside. And the Japanese army, being better fed, did not steal as much.

[14] This happened in the mountains on the Honan-Shansi border in 1941.

[15] Here is another vignette, one that tells more than any abstract discussion about the peasants' attitude toward conscription, one of those brutal facts that defies being reduced to a statistic. A poor, middle-aged peasant couple of Kunghsien, in Honan province, were dependent for their subsistence on the wages of their only son, who worked in a coal mine. When the couple, who were in their forties, unexpectedly had a second son, the conscription officers informed them that their older son would have to serve in the army, since the law exempted only one son per family. The wife pleaded with them, explaining that they would starve to death if the older boy left. When

Sometimes peasants formed bands that attacked isolated Kuomintang soldiers or killed recruiting agents. In Honan province, the indifference, incompetence, grain hoarding, and speculation of government officials greatly aggravated the famine of 1942–43, which according to unverified estimates left two million dead. When the Japanese reinvaded Honan in 1944,[16] they met next to no resistance; as their advance progressed, the peasants attacked, disarmed, and in some cases murdered the Nationalist soldiers.

What did the villagers know about the war's progress? Less than Stendhal's Fabrice at Waterloo. They never knew the invaders were near until they saw the Japanese soldiers' rifles on the horizon. Imperturbably they went about their daily rounds in the midst of danger; death would strike in any case if the planting and harvesting were not done on time. One May evening in 1941 the road running west from the western suburbs of Loyang, the capital of Honan, offered an unusual spectacle. A great crowd of townspeople fleeing the bombed city for the mountains kept having its progress impeded by another great crowd, made up of peaceable, tired peasants who were returning to their villages after harvesting grain all day. Although bombs were falling on Loyang, the city was not deserted; red banners aloft, delegations of old peasants were heading for the city's main temples as fast as their bound feet allowed. They wanted to burn incense in order to bring rain. The townspeople hoped the clouded sky would bring them protection against air raids; the peasants watched it with the same impatience, hoping for rainfall to save their drought-threatened crops.

But all these various grounds for caution in discussing the birth of peasant nationalism refer to the part of China under Kuomintang control, whereas the Johnson analysis refers to the guerrilla bases of North China, where the rural masses were mobilized in the fight against the Japanese. Do the data from the Kuomintang areas amount to a proof by converse of the Johnson thesis? Not exactly. Indeed, the attitude of the Nationalist army and local Kuomintang officials suggests to me that the upsurge of popular support for the Communists, over and above its obvious debt to the party's organizational and mass mobilization techniques, owed less to national than to social considerations; that its explanation lies less in the anti-Japanese activities of the party's cadres and the Red Army's officers and men than in their unprecedented conduct and responsiveness to the people's needs. True, the Communists were on the whole more determined and effective than the Kuomintang against the Japanese; but more important, they were a government and

---

the local authorities dismissed her pleas, "she went home and beat her baby on the ground until it was dead." Peck, *Two Kinds of Time,* pp. 266–67.

[16] They had occupied it previously at the outbreak of the war.

an army of the people. The peasantry had always regarded government as evil, and the military as the quintessence of evil. Now along came a new government, calling itself Communist, which on the whole treated the peasants rather well; even if this government had renounced agrarian revolution and the confiscation of large landholdings, it forced local despots and their men to accept its authority and to change their ways, just as it constrained mothers-in-law to be considerate toward their daughters-in-law, husbands to stop beating their wives, etc. The high-and-mighty district magistrate before whom one prostrated oneself gave way to a "delegate" who brought his camp bed with him and could hardly be distinguished from the local villagers. Above all, the way the Eighth Route Army behaved toward the peasants contradicted their entire previous experience of the military. What strange soldiers these were, who paid for what they bought, cleaned up the rooms they stayed in, mingled socially with the villagers, and were not above lending a hand in the fields![17]

Why did the Communists succeed in winning over the peasant masses? Because in addition to being authentic patriots they were genuine revolutionaries, men who understood the needs of the people, knew what changes had to be made, and set about making them. It need hardly be said that they were insincere in their dealings with the Kuomintang, subordinating even national resistance to their ultimate aims[18]; but they were always close to the people, the masses that they alone addressed with understanding. Seen in this way, the successive stages and tactical shifts in the CCP's history have an underlying principle of continuity: the Communists' fidelity to their calling and their past.

It was during the Second World War that the Communists won the civil war; this is true—but it is not the whole truth. We must add a further point: it was during the Second World War that the Kuomintang *lost* the civil war. War puts every belligerent power to the test and shows up outmoded regimes for what they are. As Lenin remarked on hearing

[17] "Support our army, the people's army that is really our own" (*yung-hu tsa-men lao-pai-hsing tzu-t'i ti chün-tui*) read the legend on a war poster showing peasants welcoming Red Army soldiers, sending recruits, bringing soldiers hot water, caring for the wounded, donating farm animals for food and transportation, etc. From J. K. Fairbank, E. O. Reischauer, and A. M. Craig, *East Asia: The Modern Transformation* (Boston: Houghton Mifflin, 1965), p. 856.

[18] In this connection, one must make distinctions not only of place (North China as opposed to Southwest China) but also of time. During the last two years of the war, when it had become clear that civil war was inevitable and that the United States would defeat Japan, both the Communists and the Kuomintang took care not to risk against the Japanese the crack troops they were counting on to win the postwar battle for China.

of the first Japanese victories over Nicholas II's naval squadron in 1905: "Tsushima is the Japanese bourgeoisie's critique of tsarism." In China, the war hastened the collapse of a weak regime. It stripped bare the Kuomintang's ineffectuality and rendered its contradictions more acute; chaos and negligence are the two words that constantly recur in the descriptions of neutral and even sympathetic observers. At the same time the war exposed the weakness of China's military force, and particularly its faction-ridden and incompetent command structure; an American general summed up the situation with the words "We are allied to a corpse." Once again we come back to the conclusions of the two preceding chapters: the gravity and complexity of China's social problems on the one hand, the inadequacy of the Kuomintang on the other. In short, we come back to the real tensions of Chinese society, tensions that could not be conjured away by the mere advent of a state of war.

Indeed, the war aggravated these tensions in at least two ways. First, it made the regime even more conservative; once the government was installed in the back country and thus cut off from the merchant bourgeoisie of the eastern ports and great cities, its social base consisted almost exclusively of that most conservative of classes, the large landowners. Second, and more important, the war touched off one of the greatest inflations of all time. The roots of this inflation undeniably lay in prewar financial and fiscal practices,[19] but its direct causes were war-related: the loss of major sources of revenue (customs duties were now collected by the Japanese), the need to finance the increased expenditures of wartime with the resources of a few poor provinces in the interior, and the unremitting efforts of the Japanese (who knew their enemy's weak point) to undermine price stability in Kuomintang-ruled China.[20] During the war the inflationary trend never reached the spectacular heights of the postwar years 1945 to 1949.[21] Even so,

[19] Before the war there was a large and chronic deficit: more than a fifth of the government's expenditures were financed by loans. Interest on the national debt absorbed one-third of the state's revenues year in and year out. The main problem may have been the government's excessive dependence on customs duties, which alone accounted for 53 per cent of its total revenues (excluding loans). The Kuomintang regime was only partly responsible for this state of affairs, which was inherited from an earlier period: in efficient foreign hands, customs collections brought a better return than other sources of revenue. Moreover, many other sources of income were in the hands of the warlords.

[20] In 1941 the government's income amounted to 15 per cent of its expenditures. But we must also take into account American aid, which was substantial even before Pearl Harbor.

[21] The following figures show the wartime rise in prices in Kuomintang-ruled China, with one *fapi* (a Chinese monetary unit) in June 1937 as the

things were bad enough; to take just one example, businessmen making the most trivial purchases had to be accompanied by coolies carrying enormous sacks of banknotes. No serious steps were taken to correct this sorry state of affairs, which as in the Weimar Republic hit the white-collar workers particularly hard. Government officials and clerks with fixed salaries saw their income shrink steadily; their very survival came to depend on monthly rice allotments, graft, and odd jobs the tax collector would not hear about. Thus it was some of the most modern elements of Chinese society, people indispensable to the war effort, who suffered most from inflation.

Inflation had the usual consequences—widespread financial speculation and corruption. To be sure, both speculation and corruption were ingrained in certain deep-seated practices of traditional Chinese society; among the many opportunities wartime offered the speculator, inflation was only a secondary consideration. That a 1940 investigation uncovered exorbitant profiteering by Szechwanese grain merchants is hardly surprising,[22] and has no direct relation to the war. The same cannot be said of the traffic in contraband Japanese goods, for which the Nationalist army furnished an important outlet and its high-ranking officers the major middlemen.[23] For members of the ruling class who were close to both the central government and provincial administrators, the American presence created opportunities for all kinds of fruitful deals, few of them honest. Whether the United States Army undertook to build an airstrip or simply to rent a building for offices and personnel, the fabulous sums at the disposal of the Quartermaster Corps were an irresistible invitation to the ingenious swindler. The effects of this particular kind of windfall on the morale of an impoverished country we can readily infer from the present-day example of South Vietnam.

Two other factors further undermined the country's morale: the gradual erosion produced by a protracted war and the feeling that the outcome of the war was no longer in China's hands. After the heroism of the early years (notably in Nanking in 1937 and in Chungking during the air raids of 1939 and 1940), patriotic fervor subsided. In the years following Pearl Harbor, the will to resist was replaced by feverish individual efforts to escape the worst consequences of the war, and amidst the collective torment to salvage and if possible promote personal and family interests. The last Japanese campaign, in the spring of 1944, led

base: 1938, 1.25 fapi; 1939, 2 fapi; 1940, 5 fapi; 1941, 13 fapi; 1942, 40 fapi; 1943, 140 fapi; 1944, 500 fapi. On the postwar inflation, see Chapter Seven.

22 The portion of their profit deemed excessive by the investigators (once the "normal" return had been deducted) was in itself more than the price paid to the farmer.

23 Which made it easy for enemy spies to operate in the guise of black marketeers.

to apocalyptic scenes that were not so much a matter of the invaders' cruelty, though that was real enough, as a consequence of their opponents' confused scramble for safety, a fierce *sauve-qui-peut* that took the place of Chinese resistance.

These, however, were not the most profound effects of the war. Just as brutal and generally more lasting were certain major changes in urban and rural life that occurred within a very short time. Chungking's response to aerial bombardment has just been mentioned; let us briefly compare this little-known case with the justly celebrated example of London. In the Chinese capital, the panic to be overcome was of an entirely different order. What remedy could a people who prayed for rain imagine against mechanical monsters that spat fire from the sky?[24] How dramatic the story of wartime Chungking is: the sudden elevation of a great rural market town, filled with the stench and the squealing of pigs, the cackling of chickens, the chanting of coolies, and the morning cry of the night soil collector, to the rank of a great Allied capital![25] Except for a rare trip up the Yangtze by steamer, the twentieth century had scarcely made contact with the city by the winter of 1938[26]; in the short time between then and the summer of 1939 its population of 200,000 quintupled. The newcomers assumed they were there only temporarily; they stayed six years. No one felt at home in this hybrid metropolis (an appropriate symbol of China herself, or rather of a moment in her history when great changes were taking place, when conflicting forces were colliding at every turn)—neither the refugees from the coast, who were disconcerted to find themselves back in medieval China, nor the native residents, who regarded the people "from below the river" as foreigners[27] and blamed them for bringing bombs and

[24] During the first air attack, on May 3, 1939, a dozen fires started by Japanese incendiary bombs swallowed up large slum areas of the city in less than two hours, and thousands of slum-dwellers along with them. The next night, as every Szechwanese can tell you, a lunar eclipse showed the Great Dog of the Heavens preparing to devour the moon. Throughout the night, gongs loud enough to frighten away the giant dog were sounded to help the moon—and to drown out the groans of people wounded the night before. At dawn the next day, Chungking was bombed again. Theodore H. White and Annalee Jacoby, *Thunder Out of China* (New York: William Sloane, 1946), p. 11.

[25] The American embassy in Chungking ranked immediately below those in London and Moscow.

[26] On the toil of the boat haulers in the gorges of the Yangtze, see Han Suyin, *The Crippled Tree*, pp. 150–57. Chungking became China's capital only seven years after its first telephone was installed and three years after round-the-clock electricity became available.

[27] And as such, fair game for exploitation. The newcomers, for their part, acted as if they were in a foreign land; they had nothing but scorn for the native Szechwanese, who did not know what a trolley car was and wore such

rising prices in their wake. Six years was perhaps not long enough to unify a community divided by such incomprehension and animosity. It was long enough, however, to shatter the mental universe of both parties. This spiritual upheaval was duly reflected in the city itself, which swallowed in one gulp the rice fields formerly outside its walls and saw its familiar landmarks altered: a People's Welfare Street ran through the Seven Stars Ravine, a Third Central Street across the Cliff of the Compassionate Buddha.

Even if prewar Chungking was nothing but a great market center that brought clothing and lamp-oil to thousands of villages in exchange for rice, meat, and opium, it was still a city. Yunnan, southwest of Szechwan, was a wholly rural province, where the Chinese farmers who worked the plain lived at several thousand years' remove from their closest neighbors, mountain tribesmen descended from the aboriginal peoples uprooted by the first Han settlers.[28] Into this universe, or rather these distinct universes, the war suddenly brought not only refugees, but highways, airports, a university, and American G.I.'s. The sociologist Fei Hsiao-tung, who did fieldwork in Yunnan in 1942, discovered there "the whole process of cultural development, from primitive headhunters to sophisticated and individualized city-dwellers." In Kunming, the neon-lit capital of Yunnan, students discussed Plato's *Republic* and Einstein's theory of relativity. In the suburbs, munitions plants surrounded the Flying Tigers' bases. Just outside the Valley of Kunming, an observer could watch rituals intended to ward off both air attacks and the evil spirits that spread epidemics. Should a traveler fall in with mountain tribesmen returning from the market to their native villages, he might be the honored guest that night at a "bachelor house," an establishment that Fei (a student of Malinowski) describes as comparable in every way to the similar establishments of the Trobriand Islands. "In a single day," Fei concludes, such a visitor "will have traveled from Polynesia to New York."[29]

The contact between these two worlds could not help but be explosive. With the upheavals and suffering that followed in its wake, the war opened up new possibilities for action and at the same time made such action seem necessary and even urgent to the masses. Like the Algerian fellahin before independence, tens of millions of Chinese sped past several historical stages, thinking the unthinkable and preparing themselves for the most radical changes.[30] Everyone today knows that war

---

dirty turbans. The river in question was the Yangtze, which some thousand miles downstream from Chungking flowed into Nanking and Shanghai.

[28] Han means Chinese. Non-Han minorities account for 6 per cent of China's population.

[29] See Fei Hsiao-tung and Chang Chih-i, *Earthbound China,* p. 9.

[30] On the Algerian experience, see Pierre Bourdieu and Abdelmalek Sayad,

has no equal as a catalyst of revolution. Our experience, or that of our parents, encompasses two world wars; in one generation they led to the two greatest revolutions in history. Martin du Gard's Meynestrel was at least consistent when he busied himself to bring about the fertile mass slaughter of the First World War.[31]

The Triumph of Chinese Nationalism

The triumph of Chinese nationalism was born of the extremity of the threat to China. The Japanese invasion not only helped China attain self-conscious nationhood, but also constrained the Allies, as reformed imperialists, to accord China the equal status that until then they had resolutely denied her. In 1943 the Americans and British renounced the extraterritorial privileges that Chinese nationalists had been inveighing against for a century.[32] In the same year Churchill and Roosevelt conferred with their colleague Chiang Kai-shek in Cairo, thus seemingly according equality to a country that for so long had had little more than colonial status in the white world. The end of the war in 1945 brought even more striking recognition: China was officially proclaimed one of the victorious Big Four.

But did Chinese nationalism triumph in 1945 or in 1949? To ask the question this way is to answer it. Despite the official celebrations, 1945 was too obviously someone else's victory, with Hiroshima bringing to a close an air and sea struggle in which China had had little part. The war itself had already shown the illusory character of the diplomatic success China had been allowed to win. The abolition of extraterritoriality was followed almost immediately by an agreement between Chungking and Washington removing American servicemen from the jurisdiction of Chinese courts. The American presence in Kuomintang-ruled China was far greater than it had ever been in the era of "unequal treaties." And the author of *China's Destiny,* who had attributed all the ills of modern China to imperialism, was reduced to making constant requests for the reinforcement and extension of this detested presence.[33]

Le Déracinement: La Crise de l'agriculture traditionelle en Algérie (Paris: Editions de Minuit, 1964).

[31] Roger Martin du Gard, *Summer, 1914* (volume II of *The World of the Thibaults*).

[32] Even France returned the French Concession in Shanghai to China—that is, to the pro-Japanese Nanking government, for the Vichy regime bowed to pressure from Tokyo in this matter.

[33] The hostile reactions of the Chinese populace were a clear indication of how unpopular this heaven-sent ally was.

With the Nationalists,[34] Chinese nationalism came to be recognized, but not to be taken seriously.

The Communists, for their part, after shedding the theoretical internationalism that had hampered their early efforts,[35] could plausibly claim to be more nationalist than the Nationalists, and indeed the only real nationalists. Whatever may have been the hidden thoughts and real feelings of the two parties during the war with Japan and the civil war, the evidence is beyond dispute: it was the Chinese Revolution, and only the Chinese Revolution, that brought Chinese nationalism to fruition.[36] Did the Communists exploit nationalism for their own ends? Of course they did. But it was through Communism that nationalism triumphed. True Chinese nationalists, far from reproaching the Communists for their sleight of hand, welcomed their contribution to the nationalist cause. Most of the Chinese émigré intellectuals in France, for example, who come largely from the landowning and literati families that were the ruling class of the old regime and are today "enemies of the people," prefer Peking to Taiwan, the China of today to that of yesterday; the People's Republic is their pride.[37] Not a man or woman among them was not gratified by the nuclear explosions in Sinkiang.[38] For the first time since they were children, China is strong, independent, respected, and feared. Such considerations weigh more heavily in their preference for Peking than the regime's social and ideological orientation.

In actual fact, Chinese Communism is first and foremost the triumphant assertion of Chinese nationalism. It is a nationalism of explosive

[34] We should not forget that this term designates the Kuomintang (Kuomintang is often translated as Nationalist Party), and that nationalism was the first and most important of Sun Yat-sen's Three Principles.

[35] Especially during the first phase of the CCP's history (1921–27), when many of its influential opponents reproached it with being more Russian than Chinese.

[36] It seems clear that "donning a nationalist guise" did no more violence to the real feelings of many of the Red Army's officers than to those of their commander-in-chief, Chu Teh. During the civil war the CCP continued to brandish the nationalist flag, noting among other things that its adversary was being equipped by "American imperialists."

[37] And sometimes, as the disorders of the Cultural Revolution make it necessary to add, their torment. But we can safely predict that they will absorb this setback as they have so many others. (A newly published work seems to confirm the accuracy of this prediction, originally made at the height of the Cultural Revolution: Tsien Tche-hao, *La République Populaire de Chine: Droit constitutionnel et institutions* [Paris: R. Pichon et R. Durand-Auzias, 1970]. See especially pp. 531–79 and 593–607.)

[38] Whereas a Frenchman can in good conscience come out against the nuclear establishment at Pierrelatte, to oppose China's bomb is a luxury no Chinese allows himself.

vitality, as aggressive as it is vigorous, as often ill-considered as profound. And this is as it must be. After all, whether we are dealing with classes or with peoples, how else can we imagine the triumph of the oppressed?

EASTERN EUROPE

R. V. Burks

EASTERN Europe, with a population of some 140 million souls inhabiting an area roughly the size of the Southern Confederacy, is one of the world's most complex and differentiated areas with a long history of ethnic intermixture and conflict. While at the time of the Communist seizures the area was preponderantly agrarian, with the most rugged mountains and the greatest poverty in the south, the provinces which bordered on Germany in the north and west were industrial, some of them heavily so. The politics of the area was to a considerable extent determined by the fact that it was in effect landlocked and, moreover sandwiched in between the major Teutonic power to the northwest and the Russian colossus to the northeast.

Thus, despite the geographic compactness of the area and its historic identity, the Communists had to apply a variety of tactics in widely differing situations in seizing power. To make clear just what transpired, and what the Communists may have learned therefrom, requires an involved and multifaceted presentation. In the first section of this chapter we attempt to evaluate the role of Soviet military occupation in the Communist seizure of power. In the second we discuss some divergencies of view which appear to have arisen among the Communists as to the how and where of seizure. In section three we present a rough classification of the different types of seizure: guerrilla war, pseudo-parliamentary procedure, and the imposition of baggage-train governments. In the next two sections we deal in some detail with a guerrilla type seizure (the case of the Yugoslav Partisans) and a "peaceful transiton" (the case of Czechoslovakia). . . . Finally, we try to discover what general

From R. V. Burks, "Eastern Europe," in Cyril E. Black and Thomas P. Thornton, *Communism and Revolution: The Strategic Uses of Political Violence* (copyright © 1964 by Princeton University Press; Princeton Pa-

lessons the Communists are likely to have learned from their seizure of power in Eastern Europe 1944–48.

Soviet Military Occupation: A Necessary Precondition

Whatever may be said of the Communist seizures of power, one single feature of these seizures overshadows all the rest: they were preceded and made possible by Soviet military occupation of the area. In Eastern Europe it was not a question of whether the Communists could capture power. Rather the question was—or turned out to be—in what manner and at what time they would mount the positions of command.[1]

This was in part because the Western powers and more particularly Western public opinion did not appreciate the character of Soviet intentions toward the East Europeans. After all that had happened under Hitler the West was willing to recognize that the Soviet Union had a special security interest in the area and was therefore privileged to preponderant influence. There was also an element of horse-trading involved. Since the Western powers wished to have the final say in the Allied Control Commission for Italy and later Japan, they had to grant the Soviets final say in the Control Commissions for Hungary, Rumania, and Bulgaria. What the West did not understand was that the

---

perback, 1965), pp. 77–116 (with omission of pp. 108–10). Reprinted by permission of Princeton University Press.

[1] Of the many general works covering this period probably the most stimulating and insightful is that by François Fejtö, *Histoire des Democraties Populaires* (Paris 1952). Hugh Seton-Watson's *East European Revolution* (London 1959), by a leading British authority, emphasizes the sovietization of the area. A useful American work is Robert L. Wolff, *The Balkans in Our Time* (Cambridge, Mass. 1956), which unfortunately excludes developments in Greece. Ernst and Rudolf Neumann, eds., *Die Sowjetisierung Ost-Mittleuropas. Untersuchungen zu Ihrem Ablauf in den Einzelnen Ländern* (Frankfurt/M 1959) is a collective work by expellees, which suffers from failure to deal with the Nazi occupation of the area as a major factor in preparing the way for sovietization. Ygael Gluckstein's *Stalin's Satellites in Europe* (London 1952) is a Marxist presentation concerned primarily with demonstrating the instability of the Communist regimes. The bibliography presented in these footnotes was compiled by Katharine M. Burks, but the comments are mine. Thanks are also due to several of my colleagues in Radio Free Europe, Munich, who have read and criticized the manuscript, in particular to Jaromir Netik, Slobodan Stanković, and Kazimierz Zamorski. None of these gentlemen, however, assumes any responsibility for the interpretation presented.

USSR regarded the installation of Communist dictatorships as the absolute minimum guarantee of its security interests in the East European area. This understanding came only with the Prague coup of February 1948. Before the coup the Czechs had demonstrated a capacity for democratic self-government and they had shown a willingness to follow the precepts of Moscow in foreign policy in exchange for autonomy in domestic affairs. This is why the Prague coup created such a stir in the Western World and why it may be taken as the beginning of the cold war.[2]

It is also questionable whether the Western powers would have acted differently had there been general public understanding that Soviet security requirements entailed Communist dictatorships in Eastern Europe. During the period of military operations the British had repeatedly proposed sending Western forces into Eastern Europe. The Americans had firmly resisted all these proposals on the grounds that such diversion of forces would delay or endanger the planned landing in Normandy and might even result in a Soviet occupation of Western Europe. The Americans were in effect saying that Eastern Europe lay beyond the perimeters of Western power.[3] As it turned out, the areas of military occupation were identical with the zones of influence. The growing belief of the Russians that they were free to do in Eastern Europe largely what they pleased was in no way diminished by the speed, not to say haste, with which the bulk of the American armies were withdrawn from Western Europe after the conclusion of hostilities.

It was a cardinal principle of Soviet policy not to permit the emergence in Eastern Europe of any local centers of authority which could offset the presence of the Soviet military. This principle underlay Soviet behavior during the Warsaw rising, which took place in the late summer of 1944, after Soviet forces had pushed the Germans back to the outskirts of the former Polish capital.[4] Militarily, the rising was directed against the *Wehrmacht,* but politically it was aimed at the USSR. The Poles wished to present the oncoming Russians with a *fait accompli,* a Polish government—however rudimentary—located on Polish territory and owing nothing to Soviet assistance. It is significant that the Poles made no effort to coordinate their plans with Moscow, although such

[2] For a good discussion of the postwar settlement in Eastern Europe, see C. E. Black, "Soviet Policy in Eastern Europe," *Annals of the American Academy of Political and Social Science,* CCLXIII (1949), 152–64.

[3] A scholarly statement by a participant is Philip E. Mosely, "Hopes and Failures: American Policy toward East Central Europe, 1941–1947," in Stephen D. Kertesz, ed., *The Fate of East Central Europe: Hopes and Failures of American Foreign Policy* (Notre Dame 1956), 51–74.

[4] Probably the best brief account of the raising is that given by S. L. Sharp in his bitter but penetrating and knowledgeable *Poland: White Eagle on a Red Field* (Cambridge, Mass. 1953).

plans had been under serious consideration by the London exile government at least since Stalingrad. It is equally significant that the units of the Polish underground army which, on instructions from London, contacted the Soviet forces when they first crossed into Polish territory, were promptly disarmed and deported to the Soviet Union.

Had the Warsaw rising succeeded, the Soviets could probably not have brought in the Lublin government in their baggage-train, as they were shortly to do. This is why the Soviet Union, despite the world-wide scandal produced by its behavior, made no serious effort to come to the aid of the Polish insurgents. It is not true to say that the USSR rendered no assistance whatever; in evident embarrassment some supplies were dropped by parachute, roughly as much in quantitative terms as the Western Allies from their much more distant bases were able to bring in. At the same time the Soviets flatly refused a request that British aircraft be permitted to land on Soviet-controlled territory east of Warsaw; such landings would have sharply increased the amount of aid the British could have given. The Soviet leaders appear to have kept clearly in mind the precept that war is fought not so much to defeat the enemy as to realize certain political objectives.

Soviet policy toward the Slovak rising in the fall of 1944 was not essentially different, though owing to different circumstances it was by no means so embarrassing to the USSR. The Slovak rising represented a *mariage de convenance* between elements of the puppet army of the "independent" Slovak state and a diverse local leadership in which Communists played an important role. Had the rising shown real prospects of success, the rest of the puppet army might well have crossed over to it. In this event there would have emerged a hybrid regime with a left-oriented but independence-minded Slovak leadership resting upon a nationalist-oriented Slovak army. From the Soviet point of view such a regime would no doubt have been preferable to the nationalist-minded but anti-Communist government that a successful Warsaw rising would have produced. Nonetheless, Moscow was deeply suspicious and feared "whether even in this case it was not a mere attempt at saving Slovakia's territory for capitalism by means of a staged uprising."[5]

[5] Václav Kopecký *ČSR a KSČ* [The Czechoslovak Republic and the Communist Party of Czechoslovakia] (Prague 1960), 348. For the rising itself see Peter A. Toma, "Soviet Strategy in the Slovak Uprising of 1944," *Journal of Central European Affairs,* XIX (1959), 290–98; L. Hory, "Der slowakische Partisanenkampf 1944/45," *Osteuropa,* IX (1959), 779–85; R. Urban, "Der slowakische Partisanenkampf 1944–45 (eine Ergänzung)," *Osteuropa,* X (1960), 779–85; A. L. Nedorezov, "Vostaniye Slovatskogo naroda v 1944 g." [The Uprising of the Slovak people in 1944], *Novaya i Noveyshaya Istoriya,* no. 6, (1959), 3–17. For a general consideration of the Slovak question in its relation to Communism see J. Netik and J. Franko,

Moscow offered the insurgents little or nothing in the way of support as the *Wehrmacht* moved in to mop up.

The Hungarian resistance organization (*Magyar Nemzeti Függetlenségi Front*) was not sufficiently active or influential to entertain any thought of armed uprising. Its efforts to establish contact with the Soviet high command remained without result. An attempt by Horthy to go over at the last minute (October 15, 1944) failed, and although one of the Hungarian armies crossed over to the Soviet side, it was ultimately disarmed and taken prisoner.

The Rumanians had succeeded where the Hungarians failed. On August 23, 1944, some three weeks prior to Horthy's failure, they managed to take both the German and Soviet commands by surprise, change positions, and reenter the fighting on the Allied side. To judge from the attitude of the Rumanian Communist leaders then resident in Moscow, the Russians were unhappy and chagrined. The Rumanian Communist exiles argued that the "events" of August 23 made necessary an intermediate period of collaboration with the bourgeois elements, a development that these exiles frankly regarded as unfortunate. For their part, the Soviet military did not turn Northern Transylvania, which they had occupied during the course of the fighting, over to Rumanian administration until the installation (March 1945) in Bucharest of a coalition government satisfactory to Moscow. Meanwhile Moscow had apparently toyed with the idea of a separate Transylvanian state.[6]

In the case of Bulgaria, the Russians suddenly declared war (September 4, 1944) and occupied the country. Almost at once (September 9) the Communist-led Fatherland Front took over the government by *coup d'état*. The government overthrown by the Fatherland Front had been in office less than a week; it had been moderately agrarian in its political views and looked to the US and Britain for support. After the *coup* Bulgarian forces were permitted to fight alongside Partisan and Soviet troops in the liberation of Yugoslavia and Hungary.

Thus Soviet policy makers went to considerable lengths to prevent the emergence in Eastern Europe of any power centers not under Communist control. Beyond the control of the policy makers was the development of a Communist power center with political resources of its own, i.e., the Yugoslav Partisan movement with its Albanian and Slavo-Macedonian appendages. The plain and almost miraculous truth is that the Yugoslav and Albanian Partisans fought their way into power over the opposition of both the German and Italian occupying armies and also of conservative nationalist forces such as the Croatian *Ustaša*,

---

Communism and Slovakia: A Documentary Analysis of Communist Policies (Munich: Radio Free Europe 1960), in mimeograph.

[6] R. V. Burks, *The Dynamics of Communism in Eastern Europe* (Princeton 1961), 155–57 and especially n. 17.

the Serbian *Chetniks* and the Geg *Legaliteti.* Such outside help as the Partisans received came from the Western allies. The Soviets did not even send a military mission to Tito until July 1944, when the outcome of the fighting in Yugoslavia was already clear. They had turned down repeated Partisan appeals for assistance, for shoes, medical supplies, almost anything. The Soviet reluctance was in part the result of their own pressing needs; in part it resulted from a fear that Partisan radicalism—the Partisans insisted on wearing red stars, organizing "proletarian brigades" and setting up local soviets (Commitees of National Liberation)—would make Soviet cooperation with the Western allies difficult. At one point Moscow even offered to recognize the royal Yugoslav government in London. Given Stalin's suspicious nature, however, and his instinct for the political, it may also be that the Soviet dictator viewed with reserve the emergence in Eastern Europe of any power center with significant local support, whatever its ideological allegiance.[7] At any rate, Partisan-Soviet relations were not free of serious disturbance during the period of the fighting and, after the liberation of Yugoslavia, they tended to deteriorate.

Perhaps the clearest proof that Soviet occupation of Eastern Europe was the decisive element in the seizure of power is provided by the case of Greece. There was nothing to prevent the establishment of a people's democracy in Greece except the fact that in negotiations taking place in Moscow in October 1944 Greece had been allotted to the British sphere of influence, and the British insisted on bringing back to Athens the royal government in exile. When fighting broke out in Athens between the Communist-led guerrilla forces and the government troops (supported by British units), and when it became clear that the latter would soon be overwhelmed, the British rushed in the reinforcements necessary to turn the tide. Thus even where the Communists were strong enough locally to seize power under conditions of occupation and civil war, they could not accomplish the seizure in a country which lay within the sphere of influence of an unfriendly power.

We can imagine the sequence of developments had the British been able to carry out one of their favorite wartime projects and push an Allied army through the Ljubljana gap. Allied troops would soon have been engaged with the Partisans (Tito once told Stalin that he would

[7] We are not of course speaking of popular majorities but of irregular armies victorious in civil war which had mass following and had set up institutions of local government in the areas under their control. On the question of Soviet policy Milovan Djilas, *Conversations with Stalin* (New York 1962) varies between the view that the Soviets simply did not understand what was going on in Yugoslavia during the Partisan war (8–11) and the view that Stalin was instinctively opposed for reasons of state to the formation of revolutionary centers outside of Moscow (132, 183).

attack immediately any Allied troops which put foot on Yugoslav soil). Slovenia and perhaps parts of Croatia would have shortly developed pro-Western governments. Only Soviet intervention could have prevented the partition of Yugoslavia into Communist and royalist halves.[8] In short, the prerequisite of Communist rule in any country of Eastern Europe appears to have been that country's inclusion in the Soviet sphere of influence. This was true even in countries (Yugoslavia, Albania, Greece) where Communist guerrillas had defeated their opponents in civil war and commanded extensive popular support, just as it was true in countries (Poland, Rumania, East Germany) where the Communists were little more than a handful of revolutionaries without important local adherence. This is probably only another way of saying that the armies of small states, guerrilla or otherwise, cannot contend successfully with the modern armaments of great powers.[9]

Divergencies of View Among the Communists

The principal question, then, which confronted East European Communists in 1944 with regard to the seizure of power was not the whether, but the how and the when. On these issues East European Communist leaders appear to have been divided. So, apparently, was the Soviet leadership. This division did not embrace a disputed succession, though maneuvering for position in the event of Stalin's death was involved, nor was it affected by a conflict of interest between major Communist powers. It was basically an honest division of opinion on policy and was rooted in divergent estimates of the situation which con-

[8] In this connection it is worth quoting a leading Czechoslovak Communist on the possible division of Czechoslovakia. "We left for Bratislava on May 9, 1945 . . . Beneš proceeded toward Bratislava cherishing his pet notion that U.S. troops advancing in Western Bohemia might reach Prague. We approached Bratislava in a gloomy mood; we did not want to think of the possibility of the Americans coming to Prague. For should this happen it would mean that we ourselves would have to stay away from a Prague occupied by U.S. troops. It would have meant the Kosice government stopping in either Bratislava or Brno, as well as the possibility that Czechoslovakia might be divided into two parts—just as later on happened with the territories of Germany and Austria." Kopecký, 384.

[9] Feodor T. Konstantinov, ed., *O Narodnoy Demokratii v Stranakh Evropy: Sbornik Statey* [People's Democracy in the Countries of Eastern Europe: A Collection of Essays] (Moscow 1956) emphasizes the importance of the Soviet army in the establishment of the peoples' democracies.

fronted the Communist movement. The evidence is skimpy in its details. The broad outlines of the dispute as it developed in the early postwar years, however, seem well established and parallel closely the familiar divergencies between "revisionists" and "dogmatists."

On the one side were the radicals, who regarded their party opponents as overestimating the economic stability and military strength of the "capitalist" states, while underestimating the power and revolutionary *élan* of the "socialist" movement. The radicals advocated the early seizure of power in Eastern Europe and the open installation of proletarian dictatorships. They wished to revive the Comintern, go back on the arrangement which put Greece in the Western sphere, and thought it unnecessary to conciliate public opinion in the West.

On the other side were the moderates, who held to the view that "capitalism" had reached a new plateau of stability through reform, and would probably avoid a serious economic crisis for some time. In seizing power they wished to pick up as much local support as possible, and to conciliate Western opinion where feasible. The moderates thought in terms of coalition governments and "peoples' democracies." They opposed heavy reparations deliveries from the former enemy states of Eastern Europe. They were against stirring up guerrilla war in Greece and they first tried to put off the revival of the Comintern and then to reduce its size and importance (thus the Cominform).[10]

Obviously the argument between the two groupings varied with the circumstances of the country to be taken over. In Rumania, where popular support for the Communists was so exiguous as to exclude any thought of a free election, the argument revolved around the "events" of August 23. The Rumanian Muscovites, those who had spent at least the war years in the Soviet capital, wished to denigrate the importance of these "events," pointing out that they made necessary a period of collaboration with bourgeois elements and thus postponed the day of final reckoning. The Muscovites seemed to be sorry that Rumania had very largely escaped the devastation of actual battle, thus leaving the traditional social order and way of life intact and undisturbed. On the

[10] For the divisions in the Communist camp see especially Ernst Halperin, *The Triumphant Heretic* (London 1958). Halperin fought in the International Brigade in Spain, where he learned to know many of the key Yugoslav Communists, and reported from Belgrade for the *Neue Zürcher Zeitung* in the early 1950's. *Informatsionnoye Soveshchaniye Predstaviteley Nekotorykh Kompartii v Pol'she v Kontse Sentyabrya 1947 Goda* [Conference of representatives of some Communist parties held in Poland toward the end of September 1947] (Moscow 1948) reproduces the speeches given at the founding of the Cominform and reflects the policy change involved in its establishment. See also Franz Borkenau, *Der Europäische Kommunismus. Seine Geschichte von 1917 bis zur Gegenwart* (Bern 1952).

other hand, the "nativists," those who had spent the war years in Rumania, seemed glad that the country had come through the war with so little physical damage, praised the "events" of August 23 as decisive for the national history, and enormously exaggerated the role which the Communist party had played in them.

There was a similar divergence of views in the Czechoslovak party. One group, which seems to have been composed mainly of *apparatchiks,* wished to seize power upon the return of the government in exile to Prague (1945). Communists or fellow travellers held key positions in the administration and the army; the party was numerically much stronger than the Rumanian or Polish parties which seized power in 1944–45; and Communism as a doctrine was identified with such popular events as the liberation of the country from the Nazis, the expulsion of the German minority, and the nationalization of industry. An opposing group, which appears to have drawn its strength from among Communists working the bureaucracy and trade unions, advocated another course. They opposed the use of force for the time being and proposed a period of collaboration with the non-Communist parties during which the Communist Party of Czechoslovakia (CPCS) would gradually build up its popular following and acquire in free elections a majority in the national parliament. After this demonstration of the popular will Communists could make the necessary arrangements for permanent tenure of office. Meantime the world would have been edified by a powerful example of peaceful transition from bourgeois to socialist democracy.

No doubt the same or a similar issue was a source of discord in other parties. There is, for example, evidence to suggest that a group in the Greek party opposed the resort to force both in December 1944, and in September 1946. But we know little that is specific about this or other comparable quarrels. Our knowledge of the Czechoslovak and Rumanian cases is largely the result of revelations made by the parties themselves for reasons of their own, in the Czech case by Gottwald shortly after the seizure of power in February 1948, and in the Rumanian case by Gheorghiu-Dej and others in the aftermath of the XXII Congress of the Soviet party (October 1961). It is worth noting, moreover, that Tito, when he was at the height of popularity and influence with the Bloc in the fall of 1947, publicly criticized those satellite Communist leaders who were unable to distinguish between a bourgeois parliamentary government and revolutionary one. But what is most important is that there were significant divergences of view within at least some of the parties concerning the timing and the method of the seizure of power in a situation in which the ultimate issue was hardly in doubt.

Typology of Take-Over

Eastern Europe is above all a variegated area, ethnically, geographically, economically. Within the framework of the generalities outlined in the preceding paragraphs the particular circumstances faced by each party during and after the Second World War often varied widely and it is instructive to categorize the parties according to the type of process by which they came to power. There is, first of all, the case in which in the circumstances of enemy occupation a party built up guerrilla forces and waged both a hit-and-run war with the occupier and a civil war with rival local guerrilla organizations. The action against the occupier did little more than discommode him and had little effect upon the outcome of the war, but it did serve to identify the Communist party with the national interest, especially since the Communists were usually more active in fighting the foreigner than were their local competitors. Having made clear their commitment to national defense the Communists were able in the long run to overcome their guerrilla enemies, who were frequently led by increasing fear of ultimate Communist seizure of power to collaborate with the foreign enemy. This in turn led the Western Allies to give more aid to the Communist resistance forces. The world was confronted with the confusing spectacle of the democratic allies giving military support to Balkan Communists (which Communist Russia failed to do) while the pro-Western anti-Communists in the Balkans collaborated with the Nazi and Fascist invaders. When the fortunes of war forced the Axis to withdraw, control of the territory thus fell almost automatically into the hands of the Communist guerrillas. In these countries there were not even important Socialist forces to deal with; the Socialists had been relatively unimportant to begin with and they were easily absorbed by the front organization which formally gave political guidance to the guerrillas. This was the situation in Yugoslavia, Albania, and Greece.[11]

[11] Yugoslavia will be dealt with at some length. For the seizure of power in Albania the most important contribution is that of Stavro Skendi. See his "Albania Within the Slav Orbit; Advent to Power of the Communist Party," *Political Science Quarterly*, LXIII (1948), 257–74; and also Skendi, ed., *Albania* (New York 1956). See also the anonymous "History of the Albanian Communist Party," *News from Behind the Iron Curtain*, IV (1955), 3–10, and V, 22–30. Julian Amery, *Sons of the Eagle: A Study in Guerrilla War* (London 1948) is an unusually penetrating eye-witness account of the Albanian civil war by a British officer who was attached to the Albanian royalists. The most revealing book on the Greek guerrilla struggle is undoubtedly that of C. M. Woodhouse, *Apple of Discord: A Survey of Recent*

A second case is that in which local Communists enjoyed significant popular support, relatively speaking, where the party had an important history, but where it possessed nothing in the way of guerrilla troops because there had been no civil war and in fact little underground activity. The terrain was not very propitious for guerrilla activity—but in any case the local populations had tended to collaborate with the Axis, sometimes out of national self-interest, at other times in skillful accommodation to *force majeure.* Within the shadow of Soviet tanks the local Communists began to rebuild their popular following and to play the dominant role in a coalition of anti-Fascist parties which in all sincerity shared many objectives with the Communists, such as the nationalization of industry or the expulsion of German minorities. In these circumstances the party made a patient effort to attain as large a measure of popular consent as possible, even on occasion going to the extreme of holding free elections. The final take-over was thus delayed for some time. In this category we have Hungary, where the last act was the forced resignation of Prime Minister Ferenc Nagy in September 1947, and Czechoslovakia, where the final scene was the formation of a new Gottwald government in February 1948.[12]

An interesting variant of this second case is provided by Bulgaria. There the Communist party had had a long and dramatic history and had given proof of considerable popular support. There also the regime and people had collaborated with the Axis, despite strong Russophile sentiments, because the Axis permitted the Bulgarian army to take

---

Greek Politics in their International Setting (London 1948). Woodhouse was the head of the British military mission to the Greek guerrillas. W. H. McNeill, *The Greek Dilemma: War and Aftermath* (New York 1947) is a closely reasoned presentation based on documentary sources and interviews; L. S. Stavrianos, *Greece: American Dilemma and Opportunity* (Chicago 1952) is more sympathetic to the guerrillas.

[12] The case of Czechoslovakia will be dealt with in detail. Ferenc Nagy and Stephen K. Swift, *The Struggle Behind the Iron Curtain* (New York 1948) is a biographical account of the Communist seizure of power by the Hungarian premier and leader of the Smallholders. Stephen D. Kertesz, *Diplomacy in a Whirlpool: Hungary Between Nazi Germany and Soviet Russia* (Notre Dame 1953) views the same process within the framework of international relations; Kertesz "The Methods of Communist Conquest: Hungary 1944–47," *World Politics,* III (October 1950), 20–54, is also useful. For the regime view see Deszo Nemes, *Magyarorszag Felszabadulása. Magyarorszag Fejlodése a Felszabadulás utan* [*The Liberation of Hungary. The Post Liberation Development of Hungary*], rev. ed. (Budapest 1960). A semi-official Soviet view is presented by L. N. Nezhinsky, "Iz istorii ukrepleniya Narodno-Demokraticheskogo stroya v Vengrii (1947–48 gg.)" [History of the Consolidation of People's Democracy in Hungary (1947–48)], *Novaya i Noveyshaya Istoriya,* no. 1 (1960), 92–103.

possession of much of Macedonia, territory that Sofia claimed for its own. The Macedonian Communists refused to take orders from Tito, who commanded them to lead a rising, and instead took their orders from the Bulgarian party, which instructed them to take service with the Bulgarian forces "in order to keep in close touch with the masses." Only toward the end of the war, when Axis defeat was a matter of time alone, did the Macedonian Communists renew their allegiance to the CPY and join in the partisan fighting.

But the Russians did not permit the Bulgarian party to negotiate its way to power through a parliamentary maze. Suspicious of the negotiations which Sofia was entertaining with the Western Allies in Cairo, though these were faithfully reported by the Westerners to Moscow, the Soviets without warning declared war on Bulgaria on September 5, 1944, occupied the country within forty-eight hours, and installed a Communist-dominated government. It is true that the BCP came to power as part of a coalition of anti-Fascist parties, and that an election was later held in which the Communists only claimed to have received 55 percent of the popular vote. But scarcely a week elapsed between the Soviet occupation of the country and the Communist takeover. Undoubtedly considerations of Soviet national security had much to do with this hastening of events.[13]

In addition to the cases of guerrilla conquest and parliamentary infiltration there is what might be called the baggage-train government. This type literally occurred in Poland and East Germany, and happened to a substantial degree in Rumania. Each of these countries had a long history of conflict with the Russians over frontier questions and two were adjacent to the Soviet Union and therefore major security concerns. Each state, furthermore, had been occupied by Russian or Soviet armies many times. Each had only a miniscule, sectarian, and slightly ridiculous Communist party, which could not overcome a taint

[13] For developments in Bulgaria see the official view as presented in *The Trial of Nikola D. Petkov. Record of the Judicial Proceedings, August 5–15, 1947* (Sofia 1947) and the opposition viewpoint as given by Michael Padev, *Dimitrov Wastes No Bullets* (London 1948). A good picture of the operations of the Bulgarian partisans is to be found in *There is a Spirit in Europe: A Memoir of Frank Thompson* (London 1948). For the strength of the Bulgarian Party see Joseph Rothschild, *The Communist Party of Bulgaria: Origins and Development 1883–1936* (New York 1959). The regime has provided us with a collection of documents, *Bulgarskata Komunisticheska Partiya v Resolyutsii i resheniya na Kongresite, Konferentsiite i plenumite na TsK* [The Bulgarian Communist Party in the Resolutions and Decisions of the Congresses, Conferences and Plenums of the CC], III (1924–44) (Sofia 1954), IV (1944–55) (Sofia 1955). The Soviet view is presented in F. T. Konstantinov, *Bolgariya na Put' k Sotsializmu* [Bulgaria on the Road to Socialism] (Moscow 1953).

of treason. In Poland there was—despite unsuitable terrain—a vital, hard-hitting, and daring underground army, but it was overwhelmingly anti-Communist and anti-Russian, as well as anti-German. In Rumania there was little underground activity of any sort. The Rumanian government participated in the German march to the east in the hope of territorial gain, and the strongest and most active of the extremist elements was the fascist-minded Iron Guard.

Thus in both Rumania and Poland elections were held only after the Communists were safely ensconced in power. Actually Warsaw first held a plebiscite on such questions as whether the electorate approved of the new and gently advantageous western frontier along the Oder and Neisse rivers. Only then did Warsaw venture to rig an election. The new Polish Communist government, which came to be known as the Lublin committee, was first established on Soviet territory and subsequently advanced to Warsaw in the rear of the Soviet forces. The Warsaw rising, discussed earlier in this essay, can be viewed as a Polish attempt to forestall the arrival of the Lublin committee. The government in Bucharest was turned over to the Communists on the direct orders of Soviet Foreign Minister Vyshinsky in early March 1945. The chief of the new government was Petru Groza, a Transylvanian lawyer who had headed a Communist front as early as the 1930's. However, neither Groza nor his cabinet could have lasted throughout one day had it not been for the support of Soviet bayonets. The popular approval which either the Polish or the Rumanian party could have mustered in 1945 was minute, even in comparison with Communist popular strength in the other countries of Eastern Europe.[14]

[14] Virtually all accounts of the seizure of power in Poland are strongly partisan. Noteworthy are *The Rape of Poland* (New York 1948) by Stanislaw Mikolajczyk, the leader of the defeated Peasant party, and *I saw Poland Betrayed: An Ambassador Reports to the American People* (Indianapolis 1948) by Arthur Bliss Lane, the American ambassador in Warsaw from 1945–47. Much more objective is the only history of the Polish Communist party in English, M. K. Dziewanowski, *The Communist Party of Poland: An Outline of History* (Cambridge, Mass. 1959). For the regime view see W. Gora, *PPR w Walce o Utrwalenie Wlodzy Ludowej. Od PKWN do Rzadu Jednosci Narodowej* [The Polish Workers' Party in its Struggle for the Consolidation of the People's Power. From the Polish Committee of National Liberation to the Government of National Unity] (Warsaw 1958). Also W. Gora, J. Golebioroski, R. Halaba and N. Kolomejczyk, *Zarys Historii PPR: Lipiec 1944–Sierpien 1947* [Outline of the History of the Polish Workers' Party: July 1944–August 1947] (2nd. ed., Warsaw 1962). For a Soviet view see N. Fedotenkov, "K voprosu ob etapakh v. narodno-demokraticheskoy Revoliutsii v Pol'she" [The Question of Stages in the People's Democratic Revolution in Poland], *Voprosy Ekonomiki,* no. 1 (1958), 57–65. Rumanian developments are dealt with by Alexander Cretzianu, ed., *Captive Romania—A Decade of Soviet Rule* (New York 1956)

In many respects the East German satellite presented the clearest case of baggage-train government. The Polish and Rumanian regimes, at the least, could claim to represent historic nations each with a mythos of its own. East Germany was not a nation, but rather a rump with a population whose real interest lay in reunion with the larger West Germany. The Polish and Rumanian regimes could gain support from even anti-Communists on vital territorial issues. The government in Warsaw could and did plead that its continuing tenure was prerequisite to the retention of the Western territories, which not only constituted a fourth of the area of the reconstituted state, but also provided it with the mineral resources of the Silesian basin and, for the first time in centuries, an access to the Baltic Sea not threatened by Germans.[15] In Rumania, the imposition of the Groza government was followed at once by the return of Northern Transylvania to Rumania administration. In the winter of 1944–45 there had emerged in this area, annexed by Hungary on August 31, 1940, a fellow-travelling local government rooted in the Hungarian minority. Until the advent of Groza, this local administration appeared to have Soviet patronage and nourished hope of some degree of continuing independence. But East Germany, in addition to being separated from its western counterpart, had to proclaim its approval of the loss of East Prussia, Pomerania, and Silesia, provinces which had been indisputably German for hundreds of years. Free elections in West Berlin indicated that the strength of the once powerful German Communists had fallen below five percent of the electorate. As long as it was physically possible for East Germans to escape westward, they would do so in great numbers. The German Democratic Republic, as the Soviets called their artificial creation, was one of the few states in the world to be characterized (until 1961 at least) by a declining population.

The East German regime had thus less in the way of popular support or national *raison d'être* than either its Rumanian or its Polish counterpart. It was in its origin almost wholly a creature of Soviet fiat, represented by some 22 Russian divisions stationed on East German

---

and Ion Gheorghe, *Rumäniens Weg zum Satellitenstaat* (Heidelberg 1952). The former is a collaborative work by a group of Rumanian exiles, the latter a presentation by a Rumanian general who served during the war as military attaché in Berlin. For an official view see *30 de Ani de Lupta a Partidului* [30 Years of Party Struggle] (Bucharest 1951) and *Lectii in Ajutorul Celor Cara Studiaza Istoria PMR* [Lessons to Aid the Study of the History of the Rumanian Workers' Party] (Bucharest 1951).

[15] For the Oder-Neisse territories see the fundamental study by Elizabeth Wiskemann, *Germany's Eastern Neighbors: Problems Relating to the Oder-Neisse Line and the Czech Frontier Regions* (New York 1956). The book has been severely criticized by German scholars.

territory. The Soviet blockade of West Berlin in 1948–49 was in considerable part an effort to endow the Pankow government with greater viability by making the whole of Berlin available to the German Democratic Republic as its capital, and by simultaneously cutting off the escape hatch through which thousands of East Germans fled, thus offsetting and enfeebling the disciplinary measures taken by the regime. In one sense the periodic crises over Berlin have been the result of a Soviet effort to endow a regime installed by Moscow with some of the real attributes of sovereignty.[16]

There is a curious geographic conformity to our typology of Communist seizure of power. The guerrilla Communists, those who fought their way into power without Soviet assistance, were all located in the rugged karst highlands of the Dinaric Alpine chain, an area with a well-established tradition of insurgency, embodied in the legend of the haiduks and the klephts. This area—roughly comprising the states of Yugoslavia, Albania, and Greece—is backward, poorly endowed with natural resources, and of secondary strategic importance to the USSR. It is the most nearly comparable to the underdeveloped territories of Asia, Africa, and Latin America. The baggage-train governments, on the other hand, are located in two countries immediately adjacent to the Soviet Union, in Poland and Rumania, and in an artificial country geographically contiguous with the first of these and having unusual strategic interest from the Soviet point of view, i.e., in Eastern Germany. The parliamentary Communists—if we may thus refer to those who sought to achieve power with a maximum appearance of popular consent—are to be found in Czechoslovakia and Hungary, countries closely identified with the West that have relatively high living standards and well established parliamentary institutions. In each country there had been extensive collaboration, whether *de jure* or *de facto,* with the Axis. The territorial arrangements of 1945 gave both Hungary and

[16] Ernst Richert, *Macht Ohne Mandat. Der Staatsapparat in der sowjetischen Besatzungszone Deutschlands* (Cologne 1958) is a profound study of the theory and inner workings of a satellite totalitarian regime. J. P. Nettl, *The Eastern Zone and Soviet Policy in Germany 1945–50* (Oxford 1951) is a comprehensive analysis which also deals with the place of the zone in the eastern bloc. Carola Stern, *Porträt einer bolschewistischen Partei. Entwicklung Funktion and Situation der SED* (Cologne 1957) is a useful handbook. For a Soviet view see G. N. Goroshkova, "Narodnye komitety nakanune obrazovaniya Germanskoy Demokraticheskoy Respubliki (1948–49 gg)" [The National Committees on the Eve of the Formation of the German Democratic Republic (1948–49)], *Novaya i Noveyshaya Istoriya,* no. 5 (1959), 22–40. The official interpretation is to be found in "Grundriss der Geschichte der deutschen Arbeiterbewegung," *Einheit. Zeitschrift für Theorie und Praxis des Wissenschaftlichen Sozialismus,* special issue (August 1962).

Czechoslovakia a common frontier with the USSR for the first time in their history. In a way, Bulgaria fits into all three categories. It was mountainous enough, and had enough of an insurrectionary tradition to have produced a major Communist guerrilla army—had the political situation favored such a development. It had a strong enough Communist movement to have permitted the seizure of power by way of parliamentary maneuver, and it was strategically significant enough for the Soviets to have imposed a Communist government immediately upon its liberation from the Axis.

There are, however, various features of the Communist take-over in Eastern Europe which do not conform to this basic geographical pattern, but which are common to all states, or to groupings of states which are not identical with the division into baggage-train, guerrilla, and parliamentary seizures of power. One of the universal characteristics was the effort of the Communists to achieve a monopoly of popular and reformist causes, such as the breaking up of the great estates where these still existed, the nationalization of industry, and the denazification of the bureaucracy. Another was the tendency of the Communist parties to admit to their formal membership large masses of persons who were at best little more than sympathizers and at worst opportunists seeking safe haven from a Nazi past; indeed the bulk of party membership everywhere came to be made up of opportunists. A generalization which applies to the whole area except for the guerrilla states (Yugoslavia, Albania, Greece) was the development of splinter peasant parties. These were secretly controlled, or at least strongly influenced, by the Communists, and were supposed to compete with long-established peasant parties, or in any case to confuse and disorient the electorate. Two other generalizations apply to smaller areas. The forcible fusion of the Communist and Socialist parties was an important development only in those states in which Social Democracy had been a major force during the interwar period, i.e., in East Germany, Poland, Czechoslovakia, and Hungary. In the last two, which both experienced the parliamentary transition to Socialism, the possession or infiltration of key ministries by the Communists played an important role. The ministries concerned were those of interior, national defense, agriculture and education.[17]

[17] For a sympathetic view of Communist land reform see Doreen Warriner, *Revolution in Eastern Europe* (London 1950); the nationalization of industry is dealt with by S. Doernberg in "Iz istorii bor'by dlya natsionalizatsiyu krupnoy promyshlennosti v Vostochnoy Germanni [The History of the Struggle for the Nationalization of Heavy Industry in Eastern Germany], *Novaya i Noveyshaya Istoriya,* no. 3 (1960), 104–19. An account of the destruction of the Social Democratic parties in Poland, Czechoslovakia, and Hungary is given in Denis Healey, ed., *The Curtain Falls; the Story of the Socialists in Eastern Europe. Foreword by Aneurin Bevan* (London 1951). The mass

These various eddies and patterns, however, are only overlays on the fundamental types of power seizure, guerrilla warfare, outright imposition by the occupying authority, and parliamentary manipulations. A closer examination of two of these types, guerrilla seizure and parliamentary manipulation, will reveal the infrastructure of each and will make possible a certain amount of informed speculation as to what the Communists may have learned from their experience in Eastern Europe that would affect their approach to the seizure of power in other parts of the world.

The Case of the Yugoslav Partisans

The prime case of guerrilla warfare is represented by Yugoslavia. The terrain of Yugoslavia, particularly that of the provinces of Bosnia, Herzegovina, and Montenegro, is conducive to this kind of warfare. It is rugged enough to provide good cover and safe hideouts and militates against the use of tanks and other heavy military equipment. It is also sufficiently poor and forbidding and far off the beaten track to be unattractive to an occupying authority whose major military interest in Yugoslavia was in any case the maintenance of its lines of communication, which, naturally enough, ran through the plains and the valleys. An additional element was the fact that the mountain zones are food deficit areas that normally import edibles from the plains of Serbia and the Banat. The effect of the Axis occupation was to cut off these imports and ultimately to reduce the mountaineers to the desperate expedient of raiding other villages for food.

The tradition of this mountain area in particular, and of the Yugoslav peoples in general, favored insurrection. There were not only the colorful *haiduks* of high *Turkish* times, who had nicely mixed brigandage with patriotic acts of resistance, but there was also a whole series of heroic national acts stretching far back in time. The Montenegrins under their *vladika,* or prince-bishop, had by more or less constant hard fighting maintained a precarious independence throughout the five hundred years of Turkish rule in the Balkans. The Serbs of Serbia proper had undertaken the first successful rebellion against the Turks in 1804, while the Serbs of Bosnia had begun the insurrection of 1875 which led to the Russo-Turkish war and the Treaty of Berlin. The Bosnian Serbs had also assassinated the Austrian Archduke, Franz Ferdinand, in 1914 in the hope of bringing about a war of Serbian unification. The Croatians under their leader Jellačić had played a

---

entrance of opportunists into the East European parties is described by Burks, 49–53.

significant part in the revolutionary risings which swept through Austria in 1848, and they were recognized as providing some of the Habsburg emperors' best soldiers.

While terrain and tradition did not necessarily favor the Communists as such, taken together they did produce a state of affairs from which the Communists by training and doctrine were better able to draw profit than their opponents. When Axis reprisals for acts of resistance produced mass graves and burned-out villages, the tendency of the *Chetniks,* the nationalist-oriented Serbian resistance guerrilla force, was to draw back and limit military action. The *Chetnik* commander Mihailović was fearful that this kind of bloodletting would impair the nation's chances for political survival. The Communist reaction to Axis reprisals, however, was to undertake raids designed to provoke more of them. Most of the terrified survivors would then flee to the hills where they of necessity turned to the Communists for weapons and food.

A more important factor in the ultimate success of the Partisans, however, was the ethnic problem of Yugoslavia. The Axis occupation brought with it the disintegration of the Yugoslav state, a creation of only some twenty years standing. In the north, parts of the Voivodina were taken over by the Hungarians. Slovenia was divided between Germany and Italy. Croatia was set up as an "independent" state and given the ethnically variegated and much contested province of Bosnia-Herzegovina. To establish permanent control in this province, where the Croatians (Catholics) constituted only a minority, Zagreb coddled the Bosniaks, or Moslem population, and created a special force (*Ustaša*) which set about exterminating the Serbian (or Orthodox) element. This attempt at genocide turned out to be an important factor in the Communist seizure of power, since many of the survivors sought refuge and succor among the Partisans. Further to the south, Montenegro was restored to a shadowy existence, the Albanian-inhabited territory of Kossovo (together with a small slice of Macedonia) was given to Albania, while the bulk of Macedonia was turned over to the Bulgarians. The rump of Serbia proper resembled in size and shape the independent kingdom of 1912.

It was the dismemberment of the Yugoslav state that, as much as anything, accounts for the ultimate victory of the Communists. The *Ustaše* and the Croation *Domobran* (or militia) represented Croatian particularism. Both the armed forces of the Nedić puppet government in Belgrade and the *Chetnik* fighters of Mihailović, centered in the hills of central Serbia, stood for the restoration of a Serb-dominated Yugoslavia as the time of King Alexander (1921–34). It was precisely this Serbian domination that had alienated the Croats. The Communists, on the other hand, were in their composition and outlook a truly Yugoslav movement. They had cadres and organizations in every part of the former Yugoslav state; in this respect no other force, whether resistance or collaborationist, could match them.

In the underground movement of the interwar period, the Communists had met and mastered the very problem which in the end had destroyed royal Yugoslavia, the problem of Serbian hegemony. In the early 1920's the leadership of the CPY had been predominantly Serb, though the bulk of the party following was probably non-Serb. The two elements, Serb and non-Serb, quarrelled bitterly over whether the existing Yugoslav state should be preserved in its essentials after communism came to power, or broken up into its component ethnic parts. The Comintern threw its support to the non-Serbs, since Soviet policy favored the dissolution of Royal Yugoslavia because of its membership in the Little Entente, an alliance system in part directed against the USSR, and because of King Alexander's policy of granting refuge to White Russian exiles. In the long run, the non-Serbs got the upper hand in the party leadership, thus helping to preserve for the period of Partisan fighting the truly pan-Slav character of the party. The outcome of the ethnic struggle in national politics was, of course, the reverse. The Serbs managed to maintain their dominant position in the army, the bureaucracy, and the national life. This created such dissatisfaction among the non-Serbs as to prepare the way for the military collapse of Royal Yugoslavia in 1941 and the subsequent outbreak of civil war.

Thus in the 1920's the Comintern had pressed upon the East European parties the advocacy of the principle of national self-determination, including the right of secession. In the conditions of factional conflict in the Yugoslav underground the effect of this policy was gradually to destroy the hegemony of the Serbian comrades over the Yugoslav Communist party and to replace it with a leadership of non-Serbian Communists—Croatians, Slovenians, Montenegrins, and *prechani* (members of the Serbian minorities in Croatia, Bosnia, etc.). In the midst of battle the Communists could raise the banner of national unity because their Partisan troops included Croats as well as Serbs, Slovenians as well as Montenegrins. Indeed as the fighting went on, other elements joined the Partisans in significant numbers: Bosniaks, Macedonians, ultimately even Serbs from Serbia. As the Partisans liberated this or that area they set up institutions of local government, Committees of National Liberation (similar to the Soviets of the Russian revolution) that reflected the multi-national composition of the movement. The Communists also established a central government in the mountains, the Anti-Fascist Council of National Liberation of Yugoslavia (AVNOJ).

Perhaps the success of the Communists was also in part due to what might be called the religious character of their faith and doctrine. In the Balkans there had been for many centuries a tendency to identify religion and nationality. The *Ustaše* spared the lives of those Serbs willing to accept Catholic baptism. Serbs, Croats, and Bosniaks, for example, spoke virtually identical tongues; even the dialects of the language cut across the ethnic boundaries. It could be asserted without fear of great error that a Serb was an Orthodox Croat, a Croat a Catholic Serb, and a Bosniak a Moslem Serbo-Croat. For those who joined Tito's movement, communism, replacing traditional faiths, became in a sense the hallmark of Yugoslav nationality.

Like other emergent nationalisms, that of the Yugoslavs had a dynamic and expansionist character. Already in 1941 we find Partisan emissaries organizing a Communist party in Albania. In the ensuing years this party functioned *de facto* as a section of its Yugoslav patron. Preparations were also made for the merger of the Albanian state with a federal Yugoslavia as a sixth republic alongside the republics of Slovenia, Croatia, Bosnia, Montenegro, and Serbia. In the merger, the Albanian-inhabited autonomous region of Kossovo was to be joined with the "autonomous" Albanian republic.

The Partisans also had their eyes on Slavic Bulgaria. They revived the Comintern's scheme for a Balkan federation, argued that the new Yugoslavia was a proper nucleus for it, and arrogantly invited Bulgaria to accept the status of a Croatia or a Montenegro. The Bulgarian Communists were confused and embarrassed by this proposal, since they had been the great proponents of Balkan federation in the 1920's. A more important stumbling block to the merger, however, was the disposition of Macedonia, a province divided among Yugoslavia, Bulgaria, and Greece, with a preponderantly Slavic population in the parts controlled by the Slavic powers, and an over-whelmingly Greek population in the rest. The Bulgarians claimed all the Slavs of Macedonia as their own, whereas the Partisans considered them to be a separate Slavic people. After some negotiation, the Yugoslav and Bulgarian Communists agreed that Macedonia (including its Greek inhabited seacoast) should be reunited and made a separate member of the new federation. For a time, indeed, missionaries from Yugoslav Macedonia were permitted to spread the doctrine of Slavo-Macedonian nationalism in Bulgarian Macedonia. The Greek party was brought in on the arrangement in exchange for promise of military assistance in the seizure of power and there began (1946) a Greek civil war which was largely engineered by the Yugoslav Partisans in the interests of their version of Balkan federation. Since the Yugoslavs apparently also entered into negotiations with the Hungarian and Rumanian Communist regimes, it is clear that under their aegis a new center of Communist authority was emerging in Eastern Europe. It should also be remembered that the Partisans provoked more than one crisis by their efforts to seize the city of Trieste, to serve as the Yugoslav port on the Adriatic, just as Macedonian Salonika was to have served as the outlet on the Aegean.

Two further remarks must be made about the Yugoslav case. The first of these is that the Soviet leadership did not welcome the developments that we have just described. It was not only that the Soviets were unable to aid the hard-pressed Partisans in 1941–44; they also thought that Partisan policy ran counter to Soviet interests. By being openly revolutionary, and by settling the question of the future Yugoslav regime while the fighting was going on, the Partisans risked rousing the suspicion of Russia's Western allies and undermining their collaboration with Russia against the Germans. Instead of setting up local Soviets and organizing a government on the mountain, the Partisans should, in the Soviet view, have continued to collaborate with Mihailović and to have postponed the political issue until the fighting was over.

The Soviets, moreover, were not pleased with the Partisan scheme for organizing a Balkan confederation. They could not openly oppose the scheme, since it was a veritable part of Marxist canon, and there was factional conflict in Moscow which gave the Yugoslavs reason to hope for Kremlin support. But in actual practice the Soviets did what they could to slow down the realization of the project and in the end it was a major factor in producing an open breach between Belgrade and Moscow. Thus the revolutionary process in the Balkans was by no means under strict Soviet control, even though Moscow was the center and supreme arbiter of the doctrine in whose name the revolution proceeded. From Moscow's point of view the revolutionary movement was pretty much out of control. The schism of 1948 was only a doctrinal, and therefore public, recognition of this fact.

The second conclusion to be drawn from the Yugoslav case is that the key element in the Communist victory was the ability of the Partisans to identify themselves with a true Yugoslav nationalism, one which seemed to offer an alternative to the bloody ethnic war which had been the outcome of King Alexander's pan-Serb Yugoslavia. It is still true that the Communist party could probably not have a won a majority in a free election if one had been held in 1945, and that its solution of the nationalities problem was largely (if not entirely) restricted to the Communists and their supporters. But it is also true that the Communists would probably have been the largest single party, in ballots cast, in any free election, and perhaps the only party whose electorate did not consist overwhelmingly of the members of a given ethnic *souche*. The opposition to the Communists was and remained largely particularistic, envisioning solutions which involved the disintegration of the Yugoslav state. And when after 1948 it became evident that the Communists could, and had, defended Yugoslavia's national interests with skill and devotion, a kind of popular acceptance, or at the least a confident truce, set in.[18]

[18] The most revealing single work on the Partisan War is Stephen Clissold,

CZECHOSLOVAKIA AND "PEACEFUL TRANSITION"

Thus in Yugoslavia, guerrilla war combined with nationalism in a very complex ethnic situation to produce a Communist victory. In Czechoslovakia, by contrast, the Communist regime was not a product of guerrilla war. Compared to the Yugoslav case, resistance had been unimportant, and the Czechoslovak Communists did not dispose of anything resembling a guerrilla army. It should be recalled, however, that the postwar provisional government, in which the Communists gained a position of predominant influence, was created as a result of negotiations between Beneš, Gottwald, and Stalin in Moscow in March 1945. At that time, Subcarpathian Ruthenia had just been annexed by the Soviet Union and Soviet troops were rapidly advancing over much of the rest of the country.

It seems probable that the Czechoslovak Communists could have seized power in 1945, upon the liberation of the country from German occupation. Soviet units were stationed throughout the land. During their advance these forces had permitted the Communists to enter newly liberated areas ahead of representatives of the parties which made up the London exile government. In the liberated areas, the Communists organized local National Committees, or soviets. While all the recog-

---

Whirlwind, An Account of Marshal Tito's Rise to Power (London 1949). A member of the British mission to the Partisans, Clissold was evidently given access to Partisan documents. Vladimir Dedijer, *Tito Speaks: His Self-Portrait and Struggle With Stalin* (London 1953) is the official biography, and merits careful reading. For an insightful but somewhat journalistic overall interpretation, see the previously cited work by Halperin. Constantine Fotić, Yugoslav ambassador to Washington during the Second World War, strongly defends Mihailović in *The War We Lost: Yugoslavia's Tragedy and the Failure of the West* (New York 1948). Elizabeth Barker, *Macedonia, Its Place in Balkan Power Politics* (London 1950) is a nearly classic exposition. For a Soviet viewpoint, see V. K. Volkov, "Nekotorye voprosy osvoboditel'noy bor'by Yugoslavskikh narodov v gody Vtoroy Mirovoy Voiny v osveshchenii Yugoslavskoy istoricheskoy literatury" [Some Problems of the Liberation Struggle of the Yugoslav Peoples in the Second World War in the Light of Yugoslav Historical Writing], *Novaya i Noveyshaya Istoriya,* no. 5 (1960), 126–38. See also Burks, Chapter VI, for the available data on the ethnic composition of the Partisan army. For the Albanian party see *Cështje të ndërtimit të Partisë. Material e dokumenta.* [Questions Dealing with the Building of the Party. Materials and Documents] (Tirana 1948), Vols. I–VIII.

nized parties were represented, the Communists filled the key positions with their own followers and from the very beginning they had the upper hand in local government. Moreover, they had been given control of a number of key ministries—and important influence in others—with the formation of the first post-liberation government in negotiations conducted in the Soviet capital. The Communists had: the ministry of interior, and therefore control of the police; the ministry of information, which licensed newspapers and distributed newsprint; agriculture, which allowed them to preempt for themselves the popular cause of land reform and in particular to distribute the landed properties of the expelled Sudeten Germans to their own followers and sympathizers; social welfare, which permitted them to develop broad sympathy and support among the masses through increases in pension, medical insurance, and the like; and education. The prime minister, although a Social Democrat, was clearly pro-Communist, and the chief of the Army general staff was a fellow traveller. High ranking cadres were placed in foreign affairs and other key ministries.

In these circumstances no one can doubt the ability of the Czechoslovak party to have taken power in 1945. The question is rather why the party waited for three years. This was in part because the party could afford to wait. There was throughout the country a revolutionary mood, compounded of bitterness against the treason of the minorities, who had made possible the catastrophe of 1938–39, the disintegrative effect of seven years of Nazi despotism, and the influence and prestige of a friendly Slav power which, espousing a revolutionary doctrine, had liberated the country. The population, moreover, was socialist-minded. Virtually everyone believed in government ownership of banks and industry, in economic planning, and in a far-reaching social security program. Thus on many crucial matters of legislative policy it was very difficult for the opposition to put up much of a struggle without appearing reactionary. Furthermore, the Czechs at least did not think of the Communist party as a foreign element, alien to the national tradition. In the interwar period the party had operated legally and in the open, much as any other radical party, and had been the third or fourth largest in a field of eight major parties. And now, for a variety of reasons, the party's prestige and influence was at an all-time high. In 1945 it was evidently the single strongest party by a wide margin and it did not seem out of the question that in a free election it could carry a majority of the voters with it.

A more important factor in the evident restraint of the party in 1945 was Soviet foreign policy. In East-West relations there was an important carry-over of wartime collaboration and the extent of Soviet-American disagreement on such important issues as the treatment of Germany and the interpretations of the Yalta accord was not yet clear. Czechoslovak democracy was held in particularly high regard by Western public opinion and Moscow very probably saw no reason to exacerbate East-West relations (already strained) by an unnecessary *coup d'état*. The Soviets permitted a free election in Hungary, a former Axis partner, in 1945. Furthermore there was a huge bonus in prestige for the international Communist movement if for once a country could be conquered by parliamentary means, especially one as highly industrialized as Czechoslovakia. Such a victory would underline the Marxist doctrine of inevitable world revolution and give new impetus to the movement. In 1945 there was much to be gained and little to be lost by refraining from taking over in Czechoslovakia. True, as has been mentioned, there were differences of view on this issue in both the Soviet and Czechoslovak party leaderships; but the radicals did not get the upper hand until the international situation had deteriorated sharply.

It is exceptionally instructive to study the tactics which the Czechoslovak Communists worked out in these circumstances. It cannot be affirmed that everything they did in the three years 1945–48 was designed primarily to increase their popular following. Many of the measures which they took they would have taken in any case; some lines of action they continued after the opposition had been finally defeated. Much of what they did was also done by other East European parties, sometimes before, sometimes after, these parties had come to power. But it is also true that there was little the Czechoslovak Communists did from which they did not try to manufacture prestige and popularity for themselves. From the welter of these election-oriented actions, policies, and programs, two deserve particular emphasis, e.g., Communist manipulation of the party situation, and Communist exploitation of the minorities problem.

At the very beginning of the resumption of the parliamentary process, even before the liberation of the country, the Communists succeeded in outlawing certain parties as Fascist and reactionary. The most important of these were the Agrarians and the Slovak Populists. The Populists had stood for Slovak separatism and had been responsible for the government of the Nazi puppet state; they were clearly tarred with the Fascist brush. The Agrarians, on the other hand, were a peasant party with a following in both Slovakia and the Czech lands. Electorally speaking, they had been the largest party in interwar Czechoslovakia and, although relatively conservative, they could most certainly not be regarded as Fascist or even reactionary. Thus the party system presented to the voters included the parties of the center and the left, but not those of the right, and the powerful and stubborn peasant party was banned. This fact accounts in some part for the revolutionary atmosphere which prevailed.

The accepted parties, moreover, were not given freedom of operation, but were bound together in a National Front which put forward a a common program. Within that Front the four parties which could claim the title "Socialist"—the Czechoslovak Communists, the Slovak Communists, the Social Democrats, and the National Socialists—formed a special inner grouping, the Catholic Populists and the Slovak Democrats being degraded to a secondary role. The Communist cause was aided further by a split among the Social Democrats into a left wing which preferred to merge with the Communists, and a right which fought a hard battle to preserve the party's independence.

The National Front was easily dominated by the Communists. To begin with there was the size of the Communist party itself, which had more paid secretaries than all the other parties together. Furthermore the Communists leadership followed a policy of building up mass membership in order to impress the local electorate and the world with its popularity. By the time of the *coup d'état* the CPCS had some two million members, the bulk of them nominal; this membership was comparable in size to the vote cast for the Communist ticket in the free election of 1946. Approximately two of every five adults in Czechoslovakia was a member of the party.

Communist domination was also facilitated by the absence of anything like an institutional opposition. As we have seen certain parties and points of view had been eliminated from the official roster and the remaining parties were bound together in a common front with a common program. Deputies and factions which disagreed with this or that aspect of official policy could resign or retire from the field, but they could not join a public opposition or threaten the hold of the coalition in power, and thus could not affect policy. Since there was no such thing as an opposition press, the other side of any issue was rarely discussed. Voters could express, as they freely did in 1946, their preference among the official parties, but except by giving the Communists a majority they could not change the government or its policy.

As a democracy without institutionalized opposition, Czechoslovakia was a democracy without genuine debate, political alternatives, or real public life. The power struggle between the Communists and their opponents took place behind a façade of apparent agreement and cooperation. The masses of the population did not understand what was going on until after an irrevocable decision concerning their fate had already been reached. It was not until Jan Masaryk, foreign minister and son of the founder of the Czechoslovak state, committed suicide (or was murdered) that the voters understood what had actually transpired during the "parliamentary" maneuverings of February 1948.

The Communists of course did their best to persuade the voters to give them a majority. The party was instrumental in bringing about the lowering of the voting age to 18 years, on the correct assumption that this would increase the Communist share of the total vote. The Communists pushed successfully for land reform measures, although Czechoslovakia had had a thorough-going land reform in the 1920's, and although long-range party policy called for the restoration of the great estates in the form of collective farms. The Communists sponsored amplification of the existing social welfare legislation. Through their control of local government (the National Committees) they played a decisive role in the redistribution of the properties left behind by the evacuated Germans; in the 1946 election it was precisely in the border districts where the German population had been concentrated that the Communists rolled up their heaviest vote. In three such districts the Communists polled an absolute majority. It is characteristic of their tactics that in this Sudetan area they had made final title to the newly distributed properties dependent upon the outcome of the election.

Beyond the machinery and chicanery of their electioneering, however, the Communists sought to identify themselves with the interests of the Czech and Slovak nations by appealing to their primitive instincts for survival. They sponsored the expulsion of the Sudeten Germans, whose overwhelming support of the Henlein party and of Hitler had been a prerequisite of the dismemberment of 1938. It is true that the other Front parties officially took a position in favor of expulsion, but no one could mistake the fact that it was Soviet power and Soviet policy which were ultimately responsible for it, and that it was part of a broader movement of German withdrawal, expulsion, and resettlement that was occurring under Soviet aegis all over Eastern Europe. The Czechs (and those Slovaks who were also settled in the evacuated areas) were bound to an eastward orientation not only by the sharing of the booty, but by the fear that any revival of German power might bring with it the return of the three million expellees and a wreaking of vengeance. The expulsion of the Germans, moreover, greatly reduced the number of those who would vote for the non-Communist parties.

The Communists also attempted to expel the Hungarian minority in southern Slovakia. This minority, one-half million strong, had not only welcomed enthusiastically the reunion with Hungary in 1938; it also possessed some of the best farm land in Slovakia. But here the Czechoslovak party ran into the bitter opposition of the Hungarian Communists, who evidently carried the issue to Moscow on appeal. After some hesitation, Soviet military units stationed in northeastern Hungary turned back the large numbers of the minority which the Slovak authorities had set in motion across the border. The Communists also played upon the Slovak desire for autonomy or independence, which had found expression in the clerical Fascism of Father Tiso's independent Slovakia (1939–45). They awarded the Slovaks some separate institutions, a national council or parliament, and a board of trustees or government, which had jurisdiction in purely Slovak matters. When, however, in the general elections of 1945 some 70 percent of the Slovaks voted for other than the Communist party (as contrasted with 57 percent of the Czechs) the Communist leadership in Prague began to whittle down the concessions it had made to Bratislava. Had the effort to expel the Magyars succeeded, however, the Slovak attitude toward both Communism and the separate institutions might have undergone a different development.

The efforts of the Communists to gain a mass following in Czechoslovakia and maneuver themselves into power by parliamentary means were thus far-reaching and shrewdly calculated. Nonetheless, despite their shrewdness and planning, despite the fact that for many reasons they were working in an exceptionally favorable environment, the Communists failed to achieve their objective. They were unable to win a majority in a free election. They were forced to resort in the end to a *coup d'état*. This fact has been somewhat disguised from public view because the so-called "events of February" began with an anti-Communist parliamentary maneuver undertaken by the leaders of the other parties. This made it easier for the Communists to carry out a *coup* which, in a major reversal of policy, they had probably been intending for some time to execute in any case.

The decline in Communist electoral strength became evident in a number of ways. In student elections at the universities during 1947 the Communist percentage averaged out at no more than twelve. Union elections also revealed an unfavorable trend and the Social Democratic party, at a convention held in November, 1947, overthrew its fellow-travelling leadership. In January a confidential poll of the public, taken by the Communist-controlled ministry of information, revealed (before it was stopped) that in the country as a whole the party would attract only about 25–30 percent of the voters, as compared to the 38 percent of the general election of 1946. New elections were scheduled for May, 1948; to avoid a significant electoral defeat the Communists would have to strike in the spring.

The degeneration of East-West relations had meantime considerably reduced the Kremlin's concern for Western sensibilities and interests. Increasing international tension also strengthened the hand of the extremists in the world Communist movement; these were at last able (September 1947) to organize a truncated version of the Comintern, the Communist Information Bureau or Cominform. In December, the Greek rebels announced the establishment of a government in the mountains. In February 1948, there was the Prague *putsch*. In March, the Communists were frustrated in an attempt to seize power in Finland, as described in another chapter of this book. In April began the land blockade of Berlin. The spring of 1948 also saw the initiation or intensification of guerrilla uprisings in Burma, in Malaya, and in the Philippines. Clearly, world Communism had gone over to the offensive.

The *putsch* itself was a fairly standard operation. The stage was set by the resignation of 12 non-Communist ministers in protest against the appointment, by a Communist minister of interior, of district police chiefs in the national capital taken exclusively from the ranks of the Communist party. The opposition scheme was to force the resignation of the entire cabinet over the issue, make the Communists share the police positions with the other parties, and permit President Beneš to form a new cabinet in which the totalitarian party would have a lesser, though still prominent role.

Actually the anti-Communists had missed their great opportunity in July 1947, when Moscow had forced Prague to withdraw its acceptance of the US invitation to participate in the Marshall plan. Even the Communist ministers had favored participation. Action by the democratic leaders at this juncture and on this issue would have placed the Communists before the devastating choice of defying Moscow or standing alone against the best interests of the country. In November 1947, furthermore, the Communists were able to stage a dress rehearsal for their *coup*. By showing that some members of the Slovak Democratic party were conspiring against the republic, they provoked a crisis in the course of which the Democrats were deprived of their absolute majority in the Slovak board of trustees (cabinet), thus annulling the free election of 1946 insofar as Slovakia was concerned.

The Communists countered the resignation of the 12 non-Communist ministers by threatening the use of force. They had enough key positions in the army to make uncertain the transmittal to operational units of orders issued by the president's office. They had enough people in the state radio to make difficult and perhaps impossible a presidential appeal over the heads of the chiefs of staff. They had control of the police, who dispersed with bullets the only demonstration to be made against the *putsch*—the demonstration of the students of the University of Prague. The police also distributed arms to a Communist-organized "workers militia," which paraded ominously through the streets. Moreover, the Communists let it be understood that, in the event they were overthrown, the Soviet units stationed in eastern Germany and in Hungary would march. The threat became more palpable with the sudden and mysterious arrival in Prague of Soviet deputy foreign minister V. A. Zorin.

In addition, the Communists were able to paralyze or gain control of the other parties, their organizational headquarters, and their newspapers. Through their influence in certain ministries, notably interior, the Communists had gotten into the personal dossiers of many of the opposition political leaders. They had used this information to blackmail members of the other parties into secret collaboration. And they had sent personnel of their own to penetrate the other parties. During the crisis day of February the Communists called for the organization of action committees. Composed of Communists and fellow travellers, these committees sprang into existence and, under the shadow of the "workers militia," took over control of newspapers, banks, the headquarters of national front parties, the national committees, and other key institutions. Overnight the commanding personalities of these institutions were pushed aside and replaced by relatively unknown persons subject to Communist discipline.

Faced with this situation, President Beneš acceded to the demands of the Communists that they be permitted to form a new government without the participation of the "obstructionist" ministers. The President then *de facto* withdrew from public life. He has been severely criticized. But in all fairness certain imponderable elements in the situation which he confronted should be recalled.[19]

[19] Perhaps the most enlightening work on the seizure of power in Czechoslovakia is that of Otto Friedman, *The Breakup of Czech Democracy* (London 1950). Friedman is strongly oriented toward the psychological aspects of the Communist takeover. D. A. Schmidt, *Anatomy of a Satellite* (Boston 1952) is an analysis by a New York Times correspondent and is particularly useful for its amassing of evidence on the factional conflict within the party. I am grateful to Paul Zinner for the loan of a paper he presented at the Annual Meeting of the American Historical Association in December 1961 entitled "Communist Seizures of Power: Czechoslovakia." His "Marxism in Action: the Seizure of Power in Czechoslovakia," *Foreign Affairs*, XXVIII (July 1950), 644–58, remains essential until the appearance of his forthcoming full-length analysis. Reference should also be made to a series of articles by Gordon Skilling, notably "Revolution and Continuity in Czechoslovakia, 1945–46," *Journal of Central European Affairs*, XX (1961), 357–77, and "The Breakup of the Czechoslovak Coalition, 1947–48," *Canadian Journal of Economics and Political Science*, XX (1960), 396–413. For the expulsion of the Sudeten Germans see the work of Wiskemann already cited. An account by one of the democratic leaders is presented in Hubert Ripka, *Czechoslovakia Enslaved: the Story of the Communist Coup d'État* (New York 1950). See also Joseph Korbel, *Communist Subversion of Czechoslovakia 1938–1948. The Failure of Coexistence* (Princeton 1959) and Edward Taborsky, *Communism in Czechoslovakia, 1948–1960* (Princeton 1961) for scholarly treatments by eyewitnesses. The official version is to be found in Chapter IX of Pavel Reiman and others, eds., *Dějiny Komunistické Strany Československa* [History of the Communist Party of Czechoslovakia] (Prague 1961).

The alternative to surrender was probably civil war. The Communists and their supporters represented perhaps a third of the nation. They were armed, organized along totalitarian lines, and backed by Soviet Russia. In the event that Beneš successfully conspired with local Czechoslovak army commanders, he would have serious fighting on his hands; Soviet aid would almost certainly be forthcoming in whatever degree was necessary to achieve a Communist victory. Defeat was therefore inevitable unless aid could be procured from the West. After what had happened in 1938, could Western aid be counted upon?

It seems doubtful that Beneš gave serious consideration to the alternative of civil war. He had from the beginning staked the restoration of the Czechoslovak state on agreement with the Soviet Union. He did not wish his London government to be replaced with one organized in Moscow, which is what happened to the Poles. He and his advisors hoped against hope that Moscow would exchange loyal support of Soviet foreign policy, for which the predominant position of the Communists in the Czechoslovak government after 1945 served as guarantee, for a wide measure of domestic autonomy. To bolster their courage for this venture, Beneš and his associates deluded themselves with the belief that the Soviet government was somehow essentially democratic and compromise-minded. When it turned out that the Communists and Russia would accept nothing less than total power and total control, Beneš no doubt saw himself, his policy, and his country as finished.

Another ending to this chain of events is of course conceivable. But it must be kept in mind that vital Soviet interests were at stake. Successful defiance of Moscow's authority by the Czechs and Slovaks would probably have threatened Soviet control in neighboring Hungary and Poland, and perhaps in Eastern Europe generally.

In the event of civil war in Czechoslovakia and an urgent appeal from Beneš, Washington's reaction would have been difficult to predict. On the one hand, US policy was not yet deterred by a Soviet nuclear capability. On the other, conventional Soviet strength stationed in Europe was such as to presage early Soviet occupation of Western Europe in any general conflict. To point to American support of the royal Greek government in 1947–49, or to American military intervention in South Korea 1950–53, is not really germane, since both were areas that had been assigned to the Western sphere of influence. Would the United States have taken serious risk of general war in order to preserve Czechoslovak autonomy within the Communist empire? And, if it came to that, would the US have fought a general war in order to liberate Eastern Europe from Soviet control? Beneš evidently thought the answers to such questions would be in the negative. Who can with authority gainsay him?

. . . .

The Lessons for the Communists

Although the events in Eastern Europe described in the preceding pages represent major gains in territory and prestige for the international Communist movement, there are some general limitations on the applicability to other areas of whatever the Communists may have learned from them. The seizures of power in Eastern Europe were a direct result of the occupation of the area by Soviet armies and followed hard upon a major military upheaval which had been a traumatic experience for all the peoples involved, victors as well as vanquished. This upheaval had created a whole new political situation. Given the present nuclear stalemate between East and West it seems unlikely for the foreseeable future that there will be a general war in the course of which Soviet or Chinese forces will come in victory to occupy major new areas. Efforts to extend communism will probably be subject to a precept of limited risk, and in general the rules of the game will be different from those obtaining in Eastern Europe during 1944–48.

It is also the case that the populations of Eastern Europe through long association with the Russians had developed deeply ingrained attitudes toward them and their political wares, whether positive, as in the case of the Bulgarians, Yugoslavs, and Czechs, or negative, as with the Rumanians, Hungarians, and Poles. Such attitudes served as major conditioning factors in the tactics and strategy of Communist take-over, as is illustrated by the imposition of a baggage-train government on the Poles and the development of "parliamentary" Communism among the Czechs. Because of the peculiarities of Soviet geography, this kind of situation could repeat itself for Moscow only in the Moslem cultural area stretching between the two cities of Istanbul and Kabul. In this general area the Turks and the Iranians would be ill-disposed towards any doctrine or movement coming from Russia, while the Kurds and the Armenians would be more favorably inclined. For the Chinese, such traditional attitudes would be found in south-east Asia and the adjacent archipelagoes. These attitudes would have been particularly affected by the local role of the overseas Chinese. Elsewhere in the vast reaches of the underdeveloped world, however, such traditional attitudes would play only a minor role.

Whatever lessons the Communists may draw from their experience in Eastern Europe will of course be filtered through the screen of their doctrine, their dogmatic convictions, and the national interests of their principal powers. The European Communists have been inclined to lay great stress on their experience in Czechoslovakia. The CPCS now presents the "February events" as its specific contribution to the common storehouse of Marxist-Leninist theory, claiming that it has shown the way to the peaceful transition to Communism that will characterize the historical epoch now beginning, that of the preponderance of the Socialist camp. The Asians in turn lay great stress on the fundamental role of wars of liberation in colonial and semi-colonial areas; these wars have their closest analogue in the Partisan experience of the Yugoslav party. The Chinese will not, however, be inclined to learn much from the Yugoslavs. Aside from having preceded the Yugoslavs in the successful conduct of guerrilla operations, they regard Tito and his party as both deviants from and traitors to the world Communist movement. The conflict between Soviet and Chinese Communists; which is reminiscent of the Bloc-wide quarrel between extremists and moderates in 1944–48, will have a continuing influence on the tactics and strategy of Communists everywhere.

The official European Communist view of the Czechoslovak experience is that it represents a new form of the transition to the dictatorship of the proletariat. In this form, owing to the liberation of the country by outside but friendly forces, the proletariat shares control of traditional bourgeois institutions—parliament, the ministries—with the bourgeoisie. By applying pressure from above as well as from below, the proletariat secures a majority in the parliament, and legally as well as factually transforms that body into an instrument of revolution. Examples of pressure from above are the arrest of "treacherous" opponents by a Communist-controlled police force and the propagation of revolutionary slogans through the ministry of education. Examples of pressure from below are strikes, the organization of labor brigades, or other activity of "mass" organizations. Throughout the process the proletariat retains possession of firearms, and it is this which persuades the bourgeoisie to hold its hand until too late. Thus it becomes possible to undertake the construction of Socialism without having first to rebuild a country devastated by civil war, and this is the original and positive feature of the new transition form.[20]

[20] The most authoritative Communist version is that of Jan Kozak, *How Parliament Can Play a Revolutionary Part in the Transition to Socialism and the Role of the Popular Masses. Introduction by the Right Honorable Lord Morrison of Lambeth, C. H.* (London 1961). See also his "Znacheniye natsional'noy i demokraticheskoy revolyutsii v Chekhoslovakii dlya bor'by rabochego klassa za sotsializm (1945–1948 gg.)" [The significance of the national and democratic revolution in Czechoslovakia for the struggle of the working class for socialism (1945–1948)], *Voprosy istorii KPSS,* no. 4 (1962), 72–91. I am especially indebted to H. J. Hajek of Radio Free Europe

Aside from the difficulty that this operational model presumes a decisive preponderance of Communist state power in the area, whether through military occupation or otherwise, the official presentation neglects mentioning other factors peculiar to the situation in Czechoslovakia. These include: the feeling of the population that it had been abandoned by the Western powers at Munich; widespread hatred of the German oppressor and fear that he would return; and a long-standing tendency passively to accept foreign rule and domination as a part of the natural order. In sharp contrast with their Polish first cousins, the Czechs have not risen in rebellion against a foreign oppressor for more than three hundred years. Insofar as parliament is the linchpin of the new transition process, there is the further difficulty that in most underdeveloped areas parliament—where it exists—is in no wise the anchor institution of the government system, but rather a foreign grafting without roots of its own. The Czechoslovak ideologists themselves constantly speak of their "contribution" in terms of advanced industrial countries. Only in the very broad sense that occasional situations may arise so favorable to the Communists that the threat of force will suffice to put them in power is the Czechoslovak example a useful prototype.

The Yugoslav model has a wider application. There exist many parallels between conditions in the Balkan peninsula and in the other underdeveloped areas of the world. In the karst highlands of Yugoslavia, Albania, and Greece there is poverty, economic retardation, isolation and, partly as a consequence of these, a complex and difficult ethnic situation. We are reminded of the mountainous backwardness and ethnic variegation of Indo-China, or of the harsh veldt and the mixture of races which constitute the boiling pot of South Africa. Above all there is the decisive fact that in the nuclear age guerrilla war can be carried on for months and even years without major risk of escalation into general conflict.

One of the major lessons which the Yugoslav experience suggests is the usefulness and reliability of the peasant and mountaineer as guerrilla fighters in the cause of communism. Doctrinally, the peasant guerrilla force is a far cry from the embarricaded proletarians of the Communist manifesto. But Mao and the Chinese leaders had achieved wonders with a peasant-based movement even before the outbreak of World War II, and had modified the doctrine accordingly. After the break with the Cominform the Yugoslavs allowed themselves to be openly critical of their erstwhile Greek colleagues, whom they accused of grossly underestimating the importance of the peasant in the Greek civil war. The

---

for an *ad hoc* paper entitled "Peaceful Way to Socialism: the Czechoslovak Experience" (15 June 1962).

Yugoslavs asserted that the Greek comrades persisted in believing until too late that the final and decisive assault would be carried forward by the workers in the cities.[21] In Yugoslavia as well as in Greece the overwhelming body of peasants and mountaineers came to the Communist colors without any previous indoctrination in Marxism or even without any awareness that such a creed existed. In contrast, the workers in the cities, who had been propagandized for at least a generation, worked steadily for the relatively high wages paid by the invader and sent financial contributions to the mountain fighters surreptitiously.

A second lesson suggested by the Yugoslav case is that guerrilla revolutions develop pretty much according to their own local requirements. There was in Yugoslavia serious disruption of the traditional social order. This was in the first instance the long-standing result of the impact of influences stemming from much richer and more sophisticated national cultures. The presence of communism itself as an envious reaction was one evidence of this. There was in the second place a profound ethnic and religious conflict in the country, and nowhere more profound and exacerbated than in the poverty-stricken highlands. The conflict had made impossible the governance of the state except by dictatorship. We must add to these things an ancient tradition of insurrection in the face of great odds. As the catalyst came defeat in war and occupation by foreign armies, which cut off the mountain areas from their normal sources of food imports. The multi-faceted civil war that broke out subsequent to the occupation was a phenomenon *sui generis* from which the Communists emerged victorious in considerable part because they faced up to the local requirements of battle.

Thus it is difficult to control or even to influence a guerrilla war from distant centers such as Moscow or Peiping. The guerrillas need arms and supplies from the outside, but relative to the area controlled by them and the damage done, the quantities needed are small. The Yugoslav Partisans captured most of their equipment from the enemy; the ammunition and the medical supplies dropped to them were not of Soviet or other Communist origin. The organization of local government along Soviet lines was essential to the ultimate conquest of power, and the flaunting of Communist symbols and slogans necessary to the maintenance of morale. In the view of the Partisans, such organization and such flaunting could not be foregone simply because of a temporary requirement of Soviet foreign policy for good relations with the Western allies.

The lesson for Moscow and Peiping is one of larger tolerance for the local requirements of guerrilla revolution and a willingness to accept, at least temporarily, wide variations from traditional Marxist practice.

[21] S. Vukmanović-Tempo, *Il Partito Comunista e la Lotta de Liberazione Nazionale* (n.p. 1951).

And for the local revolutionaries the lesson is the converse. They can assume from the beginning that on many issues they know better than Moscow or Peiping; that the success of the rising does not depend on getting Moscow's or Peiping's opinion on every matter of importance; and that other sources of outside arms and supplies than the capitals of world communism exist. It is not to be excluded that the Soviet experience with Yugoslavia is one of the minor factors which accounts for the increasing Soviet reliance on more traditional methods of statecraft (long-term loans, dispatch of technical personnel, gifts of military equipment) in attempting to subvert the non-Communist governments of Asia, Africa, and Central and South America. In Moscow's view the development of secondary centers of Communist power, whether based on guerrilla armies or not, is not necessarily identical at this stage of history with the best interests of the movement. Much depends on whether serious risk of military escalation is involved and on how far the subordinate center is capable of following a foreign policy of its own. At the same time Peiping has manifested an interest in promoting guerrilla wars in very nearly any and all circumstances; evidently the advantages to Peiping of a world in violent upheaval outweigh the risks of the emergence of new and independent centers of Communist power.

The final and perhaps the most important lesson of the Yugoslav guerrilla experience concerns the key role of national feeling. This is something about which Marxism-Leninism has a great deal to say, but always in a negative vein. That is, the cadres must take such feeling into account in order that it not retard the forward movement of revolutionary forces; once the exploitation of man by man has ceased, national feeling and national aspirations will expend themselves harmlessly in folk dancing and the celebration of national holidays. The lesson of Yugoslavia, however, is that nationalism is not a temporary impediment to the revolution; it is more nearly its motor force. Frontier problems, ethnic quarrels, and language issues are central to the revolutionary process and not peripheral. The Partisans won out over their better equipped and better fed local enemies in large part because they stood for Yugoslav nationalism as opposed to Croat or Serb particularism. They were able to do this probably because they represented a new (if secular) religion, which pushed aside and replaced the characteristic Catholicism, Orthodoxy, and Islam of such discrete national groups as the Croats, the Serbs, and the Bosniaks. The Bulgarian Communists, although ethnically of the same *souche* as their Yugoslav comrades, remained apart from the Partisan struggle on account of the Macedonian issue; it was this same issue that blocked the merger of the two parties and the two states after the seizures of power. Finally, much of the *élan* and vigor of the Greek guerrillas of 1946–49 came from the small Slavo-Macedonian population of northern Greece, who thought of themselves as fighting for a united and independent Macedonia. These Slavophones, as the Greeks call them, constituted as much as two-thirds of the Greek guerrilla force.[22] This terrain of nationalism and national conflict is in the long run the most treacherous for the Communists but in the short run the most fruitful.

[22] For the role of the Slavophone see Burks, Chapter v.

II

The Political Structure of Communist Systems

THE primacy and monopoly of political power exercised by the Communist party is probably the most significant common feature of all the ruling Communist systems. By and large, each of the Communist political systems has observed the Leninist principles that the party must serve as the driving force in society and that its membership must be limited to those who are actively dedicated to building a Communist society, although the particular interpretation attached to these principles differs considerably among the various Communist parties in power. Party membership, nevertheless, remains indispensable for all who aspire to positions of political leadership.

The nature of party control and its continued pre-eminence within each Communist state has depended upon a number of key factors: whether the party's acquisition of power was the result of an indigenous movement, or was organized and imposed from abroad (see Section I): whether the political leadership chose to utilize the party as the major channel of control or relied heavily on other institutions in society as well (the military establishment, the secret police, the personal secretariat of the top leader, etc.); the degree of opposition that the party leadership perceived as threatening to its political control (the Church, mass discontent, externally supported subversion, internal party factionalism, etc.); and the degree to which the imperatives of modernization, such as the need for highly specialized expertise in policy-making, have compelled the party to modify its structure and activities, as well as to seek new sources of information and support. Despite individual variations, each Communist party passed through a period of extremely centralized political control following its acquisition of power, and has now entered a phase in which it must re-evaluate its role and its relationship to the other institutions within an industrializing or an already industrially mature society.

An accurate description of the party's overwhelming de facto position in society cannot be found in the constitutional documents of Communist states. The detailed formal provisions of Communist constitutions, outlining the structure and functions of the governmental organs (Council of Ministers, ministries, state committees, legislatures, etc.), obscure the reality of a highly bureaucratized, overcentralized and overstaffed state apparatus that has usually performed as an obedient transmission belt for the central party apparatus.

At most, the state organs have traditionally been responsible for policy execution rather than policy formulation, or have served primarily a symbolic function for the regime. Recent evidence suggests, however, that there is increasing concern on the part of Communist leaders and various strategically placed groups (judicial authorities, parliamentary deputies, legal specialists, prominent dissenters) that constitutional form ought to be provided with some content. A number of Communist regimes have carried out significant modifications of the state structure, frequently in order to demonstrate the changed nature of society as it moves from the consolidation of socialism toward the building of communism. Soviet ideologists, in particular, have long been concerned with how Marx's predictions concerning the "withering away" of the state apparatus in Communist societies will in fact be achieved. The Yugoslavs have tried to attack the bureaucratization of the socialist state through the reduction and decentralization of governmental functions to regional and local authorities, directly and popularly elected.

The high concentration of decision-making power at the summit of the political structure in Communist systems, most notably in the top party organs, has made the personal characteristics, attitudes, and behavior of individuals who occupy these high-ranking positions an important area for inquiry. In recent years, social scientists have embarked upon an extensive investigation of Communist political elites, which, with the exception of Yugoslavia, has meant the incumbents of central party bodies. The underlying assumption of this research is that the early socialization experiences and career patterns of an individual directly affect his chances for elite entry, and once elite membership is acquired, past experiences and associations will affect his political values and patterns of behavior. The hierarchical structure of party organizations in Communist systems, in which all major decisions are made at the Central Committee level or above and routinely imposed upon lower party organs and non-party structures, makes it most fruitful to examine the changing composition of the party elite. Careful investigations into the probable causes behind these changes and their impact on political development have been a highly useful, if difficult, area of study.

As the articles in this section reveal, research on Communist political elites has been aided by the availability of biographical data on the personal backgrounds of party leaders. Despite the frequently noted limitations of such data, elite researchers have been able to extrapolate a great deal of important and interesting information (Klein and Hager, Ludz). Survey-interview techniques in more accessible Communist societies such as Yugoslavia, and the content analysis of elite publications, have provided other means of pursuing these questions.

Inquiry into the internal structure and operation of party and state organs has proved an equally difficult task for the foreign researcher. Thus, most studies on these questions rely primarily on the analysis of published materials and necessarily employ more descriptive (Funnell, Fisk) or standard "Kremlinological" techniques (Kanet, Skilling).

The Role of the Communist Party

THE COMMUNIST PARTY OF THE SOVIET UNION

Yaroslav Bilinsky

NOVEMBER 16, 1964, the Central Committee of the CPSU, meeting a month after Khrushchev's ouster, endorsed the countermanding of Khrushchev's reform which had split the Party into an industrial and an agricultural wing.[1] This is not the place to argue what caused the coup d'état: the personal ambitions of his lieutenants, reverses in Soviet domestic and foreign policies, the anger of the Party's organization men over Khrushchev's attempts to shake them up, or a combination of all three. But the structure and function of the CPSU have been far from negligible factors in the 1964 conspiracy. The bulk of this chapter will attempt to show the organizational changes in the Party after Khrushchev. But since it is not always possible to disentangle such changes from politics, I will briefly comment on the rise and fall of several Party leaders of high and intermediate rank.

Khrushchev's overthrow had been stealthily prepared and was smoothly executed. Apart from the secret police there were involved both the Party Presidium (in April 1966 renamed the Politburo) and the Central Committee (the latter to be henceforth abbreviated CC).

[1] *Pravda,* 17 November, 1964, p. 1.

Firm evidence is lacking on how many CC members were present and how many voted against Khrushchev. It is significant, however, that no official claim was made that the CC had voted unanimously, as did the USSR Supreme Soviet the following day in relieving Khrushchev of the Premiership.[2] In view of all these loose ends it is difficult to compare the role of the CC in 1964 with that it played in the 1957 crisis. Almost immediately after the successful coup Brezhnev started undoing two of Khrushchev's reforms: the bifurcation of the Party and the establishment of a joint Committee on Party-State Control with its network of subordinate units. The first counterreform was accomplished quickly, but it was not until December 1965, almost fourteen months after the coup, that the Party-State Control Committee was dissolved.

At the CC meeting of October 14, 1964, Suslov reportedly opened his five-hour indictment of Khrushchev by accusing him of disrupting the efficient functioning of the Party organization in vain attempts to improve the economy. Much of the chaos, said Suslov, arose after November 1962.[3] What did the Party reforms of late 1962 really entail? What had they been designed to accomplish and why were they being undone so quickly after Khrushchev's ouster? Following the November 1962 CC plenum, which debated the administration of the national economy, the Party was reorganized in strict accordance with the "production" principle. In Moscow, three separate bureaus of the CC were set up for the supervision of the Soviet economy, each headed by a Secretary of the CC who was not a member of the Presidium but presumably worked closely under the senior Presidium members and the First Secretary (Khrushchev). They were the CC Bureau for (Heavy) Industry and Construction (under A. P. Rudakov), the Bureau for Chemistry and Light Industry (P. N. Demichev), and that for Agriculture (V. I. Polyakov). Similar bureaus for industry and for agriculture were set up at the level of the republic CC's and, exceptionally, in three territorial (*kray*) committees of the Kazakh SSR and the provincial committees (*obkoms*) of nine Autonomous Republics (the Bashkir, Buryat, Dagestan, Mari, Mordovian, Tatar, Udmurt, Chechen-Ingush, and Chuvash ASSR's). Apart from those three *kray*-

[2] Ibid., 16 October, 1964, p. 1. In his plausible account Page states that the CC quorum had been carefully selected to exclude many of Khrushchev's supporters. Nevertheless, one third voted against Khrushchev's "resignation." See Martin Page, *The Day Khrushchev Fell* (New York: Hawthorn, 1965), pp. 44, 64. Myron Rush, however, in his *Political Succession in the USSR* (New York: Columbia University Press, 1965), p. 151, doubts that the CC was convened at all. For a good analysis of Khrushchev's fall see Hunter Alexander's unpublished conference paper, "Khrushchev's Removal" (5th Annual Meeting, Southern Slavic Conference, Lexington, Ky., 1966).
[3] Page, op. cit., p. 55.

koms and nine special *obkoms,* formal coordination of the production branches did not extend below the republic level.

A majority of the *kraykoms* (5 out of 9) and of the *obkoms* (at first 70, by November 1964 as many as 80 of the approximately 134 *obkoms* in the country) were split into two independent committees: the industrial or agricultural *kraykoms* or *obkoms.*[4] In some territories or provinces in which one or the other mode of production predominated only one committee was set up: either an industrial or an agricultural *kraykom* (*obkom*). Under the industrial *kraykoms* or *obkoms* there would be the city committees (*gorkoms*), about 602 in number, the urban district committees (*gorodskie raykomy*), of which there were about 343, and numerous primary organizations whose members served either in industry itself or in enterprises servicing industry. In the countryside the hierarchy was somewhat more complicated. Under the agricultural *obkoms* (or *kraykoms*) there stood, as of January 1, 1963, 1,711 Party committees of *kolkhoz-sovkhoz* production administrations, including in that number some Party committees in the Far North, the taiga or mountainous areas. (By November 1964, their number increased to 1,670 committees of *kolkhoz-sovkhoz* production administrations and 153 committees in underpopulated areas). The *kolkhoz-sovkhoz* production administration Party committees themselves had been consolidated from among approximately 3,202 rural district committees before November 1962; the *kolkhoz-sovkhoz* production administrations had been set up after the March 1962 CC meeting, but without the corresponding Party committees, which were established simultaneously with the industrial-agricultural bifurcation after November 1962. At the lowest level were the agricultural primary organizations encompassing both members who were directly engaged in agriculture and those in related service organizations.

Moreover, to complicate matters even further, special provisions were made for small industrial enterprises located in basically rural areas. For purposes of Party organization they were grouped together under "zonal industrial Party committees." On January 1, 1963, there were 352 such zonal industrial committees, by November 1964 their number had increased to 440. A parallel reorganization was carried out in the Soviet structure, and, less importantly, in the Komsomol and the Trade Unions.

[4] See the description in E. I. Bugaev & B. M. Leybzon, *Besedy ob ustave KPSS* (Moscow, 1964: 2nd rev. ed.), pp. 102–5, and later figures in "KPSS v tsifrakh (1961–1964 gody)," *Partiynaya zhizn',* 1965, No. 10 (May), p. 17. First source henceforth abbreviated as *Besedy . . . ,* second as *Part. zh.* Four figures were taken from "The Party in Figures (1956–1961)," *Part. zh.,* 1962, No. 1 (January), pp. 44–54, translated in *Current Digest of the Soviet Press* (*C.D.S.P.*), Vol XIV, No. 3, p. 6. See also Table 1.

To help us visualize the extent of the reform let us compare the Party organization in the Gorky province (Russian SFSR) before and after the reform. The province has a total population of 3.7 million, of whom 2.0 million live in cities. It contains several thousand enterprises and almost 900 *kolkhozy* and *sovkhozy*. Before November 1962 the Gorky *obkom* had jurisdiction over 12 city committees, 6 urban and 48 rural district committees, and a total of 4,300 primary Party organizations. After the split the Gorky industrial *obkom* supervised 18 city committees, 6 urban district committees and the Party committee of the Volga shipping line. Altogether it had jurisdiction over 2,416 primary organizations with more than 126 thousand members. The Gorky agricultural *obkom* assumed control over 18 *kolkhoz-sovkhoz* production administration Party committees, the Party committees of the provincial agricultural organizations and enterprises (probably the agricultural machinery supply organization and similar), with a total of 1,614 primary organizations and 44,000 members.[5]

According to two Western students of the reform—one a specialist on agricultural, the other on industrial administration—its purpose was really not to transform the Party into an organ of direct economic administration; for the Party had always been deeply engaged in supervising the economy.[6] On the contrary, paradoxical as it may sound, the real objective appears to have been to allow the Party to extricate itself from a host of economic administrative minutiae, to help it consider problems of long range significance. This was to be achieved by a better division of labor. Prior to the reform the united *obkom* would include some industrial and some agricultural specialists on its staff, work would proceed according to campaigns ("Produce more industrial goods!" "Strengthen agriculture!"), and only part of the staff would really participate in discussions, while the Secretaries would be overworked.[7] Hough has also persuasively demonstrated that ideological work need not have suffered after November 1962: the propaganda sections attached to industrial *obkoms* could have tailored their appeal to the urbanites, the agricultural propaganda sections would have been more successful in dealing with peasants alone.[8]

In practice the reforms did not work out too well. Cleary noted already in the middle of 1964 that the line of responsibility between the

[5] *Besedy . . .*, pp. 102, 104–5.

[6] J. W. Cleary, "The Parts of the Party [concentrating on agriculture]," *Problems of Communism,* Vol. XIII, No. 4 (July–August 1964), pp. 55–56, 60; Jerry F. Hough, "A Harebrained Scheme in Retrospect," ibid., Vol. XIV, No. 4 (July–August 1965), p. 27.

[7] Cleary, loc. cit., p. 60; Hough, loc. cit., pp. 28–29; also *Besedy . . .*, pp. 102–03.

[8] Hough, loc. cit., p. 29.

chairman of the *kolkhoz-sovkhoz* production administration (the Government official) and the Secretary of the corresponding Party committee was left rather murky, with the result that some Party officials started legislating on exceedingly technical matters.[9] The zonal industrial production committees do not seem to have done much of anything possibly because judging by a later example they were orphans lost in a labyrinth of jurisdictions.[10] Coordination of industrial and agricultural activities on the regional level proved impossible.[11] Material that appeared in the Soviet press after the November 1964 CC meeting which decreed the reunification of the Party make clear both some of the advantages and the overwhelming disadvantages of the November 1962 split.

On the positive side it was admitted that "more specialists have appeared among the guiding Party cadres."[12] Also praised at the conference in December 1964, at which the reunification of the *obkoms* and *raykoms* was carried out, were various technical and economic councils attached to many *gorkoms* and *raykoms,* some of which had been set up prior to November 1962, but whose work was stimulated by the recent emphasis on efficient supervision of industrial and construction enterprises.[13] Among the liabilities were listed:

1. The tearing asunder of the *rayon* that had formerly been a single economic administrative unit. The functions of Party, Soviet, and economic administrative organs at that level were not clearly delimited, tempting Party organs into usurping the functions of economic administrators.
2. Lack of coordination among Party and administrative officials at the *kolkhoz-sovkhoz* production administration level, as had been pinpointed by Cleary several months before.
3. A growth in the staffs of the *oblast* and *kray* organs and a "serious weakening" of the staffs at the crucial *rayon* level.
4. Increasing difficulty in transferring responsible personnel (*kadrov*)

[9] Such as artificial insemination of cows (Cleary, loc. cit., p. 58) or telling the director of a hatchery's incubator not to use eggs that are over ten days old (G. Shitarev, "Partiya—rukovoditel' sovetskogo naroda," *Part. zh.,* 1965, No. 18, September, p. 32).

[10] Cleary, loc. cit., p. 59 and P. Rukavets, "Kamni na doroge," *Part zh.,* 1964, No. 22 (November), pp. 41–42.

[11] Hough, loc. cit., pp. 29–31, sees in this the main shortcoming of the reform.

[12] See editorial "Fidelity to Leninist Organizational Principles." *Pravda,* 18 November, 1964; or *C.D.S.P.* Vol. XVI, No. 45, p. 4.

[13] See V. Klychev & R. Tveritina, "Komissiya sodeystviya teknicheskomu progressu," *Part. zh.,* 1964, No. 22 (November), p. 26: and editorial, "Edinstvo, aktivnost', delovitost'," ibid., 1965, No. 2 (January), p. 9.

from industrial to rural committees (the obverse side of professional specialization).

Insofar as urban Party workers had been helpful in the countryside, as officially alleged, but doubted by the present writer, this last accusation may be a serious one. In any case, it seemed to have created among the rural Party apparatus the feeling that they were left to fend for themselves in a field of second priority, devoid of the glamour of true "socialist production." The status of the *kolkhoz-sovkhoz* production administration Party Secretaries was, moreover, made nearly equal to that of the administration chairmen, whereas previously the rural *raykom* had lorded over the district executive committee (*rayispolkom*) administrators, not to mention individual collective farm chairmen.[14]

The two men who apparently were put in charge of the Party's reunification were Nikolay V. Podgorny and Vitaly N. Titov. Podgorny, a Ukrainian by nationality and the graduate of the Ukrainian Party organization (Kharkov was his political "home town") had been drawn into the Presidium by Khrushchev as an alternate member in 1958, was made a full member in May 1960 and a CC Secretary in June 1963, simultaneously with Brezhnev's reelection to the Secretariat. This has led to speculation that Khrushchev used Podgorny as a "counter-heir" against Brezhnev.[15] After Khrushchev's overthrow Podgorny, for a time, became Brezhnev's deputy for Party organizational questions: for it was he that gave the report "On Merging Industrial and Rural Province and Territory Party Organizations and Soviet Bodies" at the November 16, 1964 CC plenum.[16] Titov, another Ukrainian, had been Podgorny's successor in the Kharkov Party organization, in 1961 was transferred to Moscow to work on Party personnel matters and in November 1962 was made chairman of the newly created CC Commission for Organizational-Party Questions and simultaneously elected Secretary of the CC. Titov and his Commission seem to have been used by Khrushchev to counterbalance the power of Krushchev's Deputy (Secretary for cadres) and chief rival Frol R. Kozlov.[17] With Kozlov

[14] Editorial, "V interesakh dela," ibid., 1964, No. 23 (December), pp. 5–6; Hough, loc. cit., p. 31.

[15] Rush, op. cit. (note 2), p. 137. Podgorny, however, seems to have been handicapped by not being a Russian.

[16] *Pravda,* 17 November, 1964, p. 1.

[17] See Rush, op. cit., pp. 171–72; Merle Fainsod, *How Russia Is Ruled* (Cambridge: Harvard University Press, 1963; 2nd rev. ed.), p. 221; Grey Hodnett, "Khrushchev and Party State Control," in Alexander Dallin & Alan F. Westin, eds., *Politics in the Soviet Union: 7 cases* (New York: Harcourt-Brace-World, 1966), pp. 147–48n. *Besedy* . . . on p. 148 describes the work of the Party Organs Department but does not distinguish it from that of the Commission for Organizational Questions.

gravely ill (he was released from both the Presidium and the CC Secretariat at the November 1964 plenum) and Brezhnev preoccupied with the duties of First Secretary, Podgorny and Titov set about restructuring the Party. By April 1, 1965, they had reunited 80 *obkoms* and 5 *kraykoms,* abolished two territorial (*kray*) committees in Kazakhstan (the West-Kazakhstan and South-Kazakhstan *kraykoms*) and all of the 440 zonal industrial production committees. As many as 738 city committees were set up, compared with 602 in 1961, but 208 of the new committees were given the job of co-ordinating both urban and rural Party organizations. 396 city district committees were established (an increase of 53 over the 343 existing in 1961). It is rather noteworthy that while the Party has abolished the 1,670 *kolkhoz-sovkhoz* production administration Party committees it has not restored the full complement of rural district committees existing prior to November 1962: Instead of some 3,202 rural *raykoms* in 1961 there were created only 2,434 rural *raykoms* in 1965.[18] (The changes in the organizational network from 1961 through mid-1967 have been briefly summarized in Table 1). The writer has not been able to analyze what happened to all the individual Secretaries of the *kraykoms, obkoms, gorkoms* and *raykoms:* Who was made First Secretary of the reunified committee and who became a Deputy Secretary or worse. The figures, however, indicate beyond any doubt that a major reshuffle of personnel took place. In view of the subsequent fate of Podgorny and Titov we may also want to bear in mind the warning in an important 1964 editorial that the reunification would lead to the release of a certain number (*nekotoroe chislo*) of *oblast* and *kray* personnel. The editorial urged that these officials be reemployed at the *rayon* and the lower (primary?) level. Their knowledge, experience, and, "if possible," their personal interests were to be taken into account, but Party discipline should on no account be relaxed.[19] I have seen no figures on the actual transfers downward in the Party hierarchy, but I would imagine that the demoted Party officials were none too happy with the new reorganization.

The Party State Control Committees under Khrushchev have been the subject of a thorough study by Grey Hodnett. From 1923 to 1934 the Party's Central Control Commission and the State's Workers and Peasants Inspectorate had been merged. Stalin undid this union in 1934: Khrushchev, possibly already at the 20th Party Congress in 1956, and quite explicitly on the eve of the 22nd Party Congress was thinking of reestablishing joint Party-State control committees.[20] Despite some

[18] See "KPSS v tsifrakh (1961–1964 gody)," loc. cit. (note 4), p. 17.
[19] "V interesakh dela," loc. cit., p. 6.
[20] Hodnett, loc. cit., pp. 115, 120, 131–32.

opposition from fellow-Party leaders, notably Frol R. Kozlov, the joint Committee on Party-State Control (CPSC) was set up at the November 1962 CC plenum under the direction of young and ambitious Aleksandr N. Shelepin: veteran Komsomol leader (under Stalin and Khrushchev), former head of the secret police (KGB) from 1958 to 1961, and since November 1961 CC Secretary. Upon taking over the chairmanship of the CPSC Shelepin was also made a USSR Deputy Prime Minister.[21] According to a summary of the Committee's statute in *Pravda* the CPSC was given rather ambitious tasks in fighting waste and red tape in the economy and administration, but the struggle with political deviants was not stressed.[22] A Soviet commentary on the Party Statutes emphasized that the Party State Control Committees were not only to ferret out dishonest bureaucrats but to uncover ways and means of achieving more efficient production: to find hidden reserves to help introduce new techniques.[23] The real purpose of the new creation appears to have been to commit the full authority of the Party to the control over the economy; it was a logical corollary of the Party's simultaneous bifurcation.

What were the limitations imposed on the work of the new Committee? The Party Control Committee that had jurisdiction over Party disciplinary matters was not abolished, only renamed the Party Commission, implying that the new organ would not be allowed to initiate the expulsion of Party members.[24] At the highest level, the CPSC was made subject to the Party CC's, and the *obkoms* on the one hand and to the CPSC at the All-Union or Republic levels on the other. The Control Committees below the *oblast* level, however, answered only to the *oblast* or Republic CPSC's, "though they required the formal 'approval' of plenums of local Party committees."[25] In practice, while the chairmen of the Republic and *oblast* CPSC's had to be approved by the Party Organs Department of the All-Union CC, their subordinates were usually handpicked by the regular Party officials at the corresponding levels, subject to the veto of the Republic CPCS. At the lowest level the numerous "groups and posts of assistance" to the local CPSC's had their chairmen appointed by the Secretaries of the Party primary organizations.[26] In short, while the committees were to include representatives from the trade unions, Komsomol, press, workers, collective farmers and

[21] On Shelepin's career see *Who's Who in the USSR,* 1965/66 (Montreal: Intercontinental Book & Publishing Co., 1966, (2nd ed)., pp. 753–54.

[22] See outline statute of CPSC in *Pravda,* 18 January, 1963, p. 2. Also Hodnett, loc. cit., p. 149.

[23] *Besedy* . . . , p. 44.

[24] Hodnett, loc. cit., p. 147.

[25] Ibid., p. 149.

[26] Ibid., p. 150.

Table 1
Intermediate and Local CPSU Organizations, 1961–67

	October 1, 1961	*November 16, 1964*			*April 1, 1965*	*July 1, 1967*
		Divided		*Remain joint or exclsv.*		
	United	*separate industr.*	*sep. agric.*	*ind. or agric.*	*United*	*United*
Territory (*Kray*)	143	5	5	4	7	6
Province (*oblast*)		80	80	(54)[a]	133	133
National district (*okrug*)	10	—	—	—	10	10
City Committees (*gorkomy*)	602	—	—	(602+)	738	747
City District Coms. (*gorraykomy*)	343	—	—	(343+)	396[d]	417
Rural District Coms. (*sel'skiye raykomy*)	3,202	440[b]	1,670[c]	—	2,434[d]	2,746

[a] Figures in parentheses rough estimates by author.
[b] So-called zonal industrial production administration Party committees.
[c] So-called *kolkhoz-sovkhoz* production administration Party committees. To which number should be added 153 Party committees in the Far North, the taiga and similar underpopulated areas.
[d] To which numbers should be added a total of 17 Party committees having the right of *raykoms.*

SOURCES: "The Party in Figures (1956–1961)," *Partiynaya zhizn,* 1962, No. 1 (January), pp. 44 ff., translated in *Current Digest of the Soviet Press,* Vol. XIV, No. 3, p. 6 for 1961 figures (I have deducted from 157 the 14 Republican CC's); "KPSS v tsifrakh (1961–1964 gody)," *partiynaya zhizn,* 1965, No. 10 (May) p. 17, counterchecked against E. I. Bugaev & B. M. Leybzon, *Besedy ob ustave KPSS* (Moscow, 1964; 2nd ed.) pp. 102–4; and "KPSS v tsifrakh," *Part. zhizn',* 1967, No. 19 (October), p. 19.

intelligentsia, the Party tried to maintain close control over the CPSC's at all levels. This was made the more urgent by the mass character of the CPSC's network: by February 1964, i.e., within a year of their actual establishment the CPSC's had a total membership of 4 million, in 1965, their number is said to have reached 5 million.[27] But their

[27] Ibid., p. 155, and Christian Duevel, "Ser'eznaya neudacha Shelepina v bor'be za vlast', in Radio Liberty, Munich, *Ezhednevny Informatsionny Byulleten* (Henceforth abbreviated *E.I.B.*), 13 December, 1965.

real power of enforcing compliance by economic administrators does not seem to have been very great. As late as January 1965 V. Zaluzhny complained in a party journal that when a CPSC uncovered economic waste and lax personnel policies in a sector of the Byelorussian railroad, the responsible deputy director heaped on them "coarse insults." It took an appeal by the local CPSC to the republic CPSC to have that deputy director sharply reprimanded.[28] Hodnett summarizes the evidence thus:

> The CPSC of the Central Committee, with its local organs and assistance groups, soon became involved in a broad variety of activities, including sponsoring various nation-wide campaigns against waste, reducing redundant administrative personnel in agriculture, resolving high-level disputes among industrial administrative agencies, and formulating detailed proposals on technical matters. The main targets of the CPSC were industrial managers, engineers, bookkeepers, planners, and high state administrators. Judging from published material, party *apparatchiki* did not seem, directly at least, to have been much affected.[29]

Yet the possibility could not be excluded that in 1963–64 CPSC's were slowly groping their way toward greater power. That possibility became acute when—apparently for services rendered in the overthrow of Khrushchev—at the November 16, 1964 plenum Shelepin was immediately elevated to full membership on the Presidium skipping the customary candidate stage. An ambitious man could use the CPSC network to build his "empire" within the Party. Hodnett noted tentatively that after November 1964 the "CPSC was indeed beginning to remove some high officials from office."[30] In the summer of 1965 Christian Duevel, head of Radio Liberty's Research Division, noticed a muted war being carried on between the CPSC network and regular Party committees in the pages of Soviet newspapers: as late as August 3, 1965, the CPSC's were being lavishly praised and regular Party organs called upon to "develop their initiative by all means." Within three weeks the wind had changed, the papers—mostly notably an editorial in *Pravda* on September 4, 1965—started exhorting the Party to exercise leadership over the groups and posts of assistance to the CPSC. This was termed an inseparable part of Party personnel policy. A broad hint was dropped that the assistance groups would function more successfully if their chairmen would be drawn from among the Deputy Secretaries of the regular Party organizations. Apparently in 1965 there had developed somewhat of a tug of war between the regular Party

[28] V. Zaluzhny, "Sovetskiy khozaystvennik," *Part. zh.*, 1965, No. 1 (January), p. 48.
[29] Hodnett, loc. cit., p. 152.
[30] Ibid., p. 152n.

hierarchy, headed by Brezhnev, and the CPSC chain of command under Shelepin over the staffing of the "assistance groups": the emphatic assertions that leadership over the CPSC's was an "inseparable" part of Party work, that in a "majority" of cases the chairmen of the "assistance groups" were Deputy Party Secretaries, that it was "perfectly understandable" that such groups would carry out their task better, would seem to indicate a lot of underlying tensions.[31]

The denouement came at the December 6, 1965 CC plenum. Speaking on behalf of the Presidium Brezhnev charged the CPSC's with unspecified "shortcomings." He did not say that a mass of freewheeling Party-State controllers might interfere with the extension of certain limited decision-making powers to industrial managers and with the newly centralized national economic administration. Instead he used the lame argument that time had come to draw more persons into the *people's* control movement. Had not Lenin established the goal "to draw *all* the working masses, both men and, *in particular, women,* into participation in the workers' and peasants' inspection?" (The old CPSC's were not exactly small organizations with their membership of 5 million!) Brezhnev's most revealing statement was that the "agencies of peoples' control did not control the work of the Party agencies."[32] It is probably in this field that disagreements had lately arisen. In any case, however feeble the excuse, the newly formed Agencies of People's Control were no longer to be headed by Presidium member and CC Secretary Shelepin: the chairmanship over the new Agency was given to a second-rate figure, one of Shelepin's deputies, Pavel Kovanov, who did not even succeed to the Deputy Prime Ministership which was vacated by Shelepin.[33] Thus Shelepin has been removed from the source of potential power and his empire appears to have been reduced in fact if not in law to another one of the numerous mass (*obshchestvennye*) organizations in the country. Half a year later the Deputy Chairman of the USSR Committee on People's Control asserted that the

[31] See M. Krakhmalev, "Avtoritet zovoevan delom," *Izvestiya,* 3 August, 1965, p. 1; and in contrast the editorial, "Great Party Cause," *Pravda,* 4 September, 1965, p. 1, or *C.D.S.P.,* Vol XVII, No. 36, pp. 15–16. Also Duevel, "Ser'eznaya neudacha Shelepina v bor'be za vlast'," *E.I.B.,* 13 December, 1965.

[32] *Pravda,* 7 December, 1965, p. 1.

[33] On Shelepin's dismissal from the Deputy Prime Ministership in order to allow him "to concentrate his activity at the CC of the Party" see *Izvestiya,* 10 December, 1965, p. 3. Pavel V. Kovanov, a teacher by training had been working in the Party apparatus since 1944. Second Secretary of the CP of Georgia from 1956–62, then one of Shelepin's deputies at the CPSC. See his official biography in *Deputaty Verkhovnogo Soveta SSSR: Sed'moy sozyv* (Moscow, 1966), p. 217.

controllers numbered as many as 6 million. From reading his article it is hard to avoid the impression that it is six million relatively innocuous busybodies too many.[34]

The reunification of the Party and the abolition of the CPSC's should not, under any circumstances, be interpreted as a diminution in the Party's well-established right to control economic administration: only the forms of control may have been slightly simplified.[35] Under Brezhnev as under Khrushchev, or Stalin, for that matter, the Party official is in a quandary to decide how much of his attention should be devoted to ideological and political work, how much to economic matters, and what form the latter activity should take.[36] "Petty tutelage" over economic administrators is impermissible and Party meetings should be distinguishable from factory or farm director's conferences,[37] but what does this mean in practice? An authoritative survey of Party conferences and congresses that took place shortly before the 23rd All-Union Party Congress in early 1966, quotes approvingly from the resolution of the September 1965 CC plenum:

> The Party Committees, without substituting for economic personnel, are obligated to concentrate their main attention on organizational work, on the selection, assignment and education of responsible personnel (*kadrov*), on the control over the execution of Party and State directives, on strengthening the Communist education of the toilers.[38]

This is about as meaningful as the injunction that Party officials should be good dedicated men. An honest, realistic picture of the interrelationships between the Party and economic administrators is provided in the following excerpt from a letter of a Party official.

> There arise many deficiencies in planning, in the operational administration of the economy, bottlenecks appear in the supply of

[34] See V. Zaluzhny, "Narodny kontrol'," *Part zh.*, 1966, No. 13 (July), pp. 14, 19.

[35] A recent Soviet commentary points out that the Party primary organizations have been given the formal right of control over the work of the administration since the 18th Party Congress in 1939. See V. Ososkov, "Kommunisty i proizvodstvo." *Part. zh.*, 1965, No. 19 (October), pp. 27–29.

[36] See the analysis by Howard R. Swearer, "Changing Roles of the CPSU under First Secretary Khrushchev," *World Politics*, Vol. XV (October 1962), pp. 20–43 *passim*.

[37] V. Degtyarev, "Rol' pervichnoy partorganizatsii v razvitii proizvodstva," *Part. zh.*, 1967, No. 3 (February), pp. 12, 15.

[38] Editorial, "Sovershenstvovat' formy i metody partiynoy raboty," *Kommunist*, Vol. 42, No. 4 (March 1966), p. 50.

> raw materials, and lo and behold, the [Party] department starts playing the role of a dispatcher: communicates with various authorities; decides questions of supply; "knocks together" the heads of factory directors; its instructors "keep hanging" [*"vysyat"*] on the telephone lines and, of course, keep writing a multiplicity of memoranda and reports. This is confirmed, in particular, by the work of the industrial department of the Kuznetsk *gorkom.*
>
> The question arises: How can one under these circumstances avoid the meddling (*vmeshatl'stva*) of Party officials with the decision-making function of the enterprise management? *We get a charmed circle: on the one hand, we enjoin* [them] *not to substitute* [for management], *on the other hand, we require them to quickly "find out what's what and bring some order into the joint"* [*srochno razobrat'sya, navesti poryadok*]. With such an approach the duplication of the work of economic administrators becomes inevitable.[39]

The author ostensibly criticizes only the work of specialized departments of local Party organizations, but actually his strictures apply to the Party as a whole.

The 23rd Party Congress, the first after Khrushchev's ouster, which according to the Party statutes should have met in the fall of 1965, was postponed until March 29, 1966 without any official explanation.[40] Apparently some loose political ends had to be tied up before the Congress could be safely convened. The emasculation of Shelepin's CPSC's has already been commented upon. It is also important to note that for eight months in 1965 the CC Secretariat Department of Party Organizational Work, the Party's personnel division, had to get along without a high-ranking head. Shortly *after* the March 1965 CC meeting, V. N. Titov was demoted from chairman of the All-Union CC Commission for Organizational-Party Questions to Second (i.e., personnel) Secretary of the Kazakhstan Party. He formally lost his CC Secretaryship at the next CC plenum in September 1965, but no successor was appointed in his stead: the plenum merely filled the post of the CC Secretary in charge of agriculture, that had been left vacant since the dismissal of Polyakov

[39] See V. Tolstov, "Shtatnye i vneshtatne," *Part zh.,* 1965, No. 22 (November), p. 41 (emphasis added). For other revealing materials on the relations between the Party and economic administrators see Degtyarov, loc. cit., pp. 8–16 *passim,* and, above all, the resolution of the CC CPSU "O rabote partiynogo komiteta sovkhoza 'Mikhaylovskiy, Paninskogo rayona, Voronezhskoy oblasti," *Part. zh.,* 1967, No 7 (April), pp. 3–6.

[40] The postponement was discussed at the September 1965 CC plenum, but nowhere did the Soviet press print Brezhnev's report on that question or the discussion. See *Pravda,* 28 September, 1965, p. 1, and *CDSP,* Vol. XVII, No. 38, p. 3.

in November 1964, by appointing to it F. D. Kulakov.[41] No reason for Titov's demotion was given. Titov may have made enemies during the reunification of the Party which was completed by April 1, 1965, or even earlier during the three years that he served as Khrushchev's personnel chief, formally under Kozlov. In view of Titov's background (he had been First Secretary of the Kharkov Province Committee from 1953–1961) it may not have been altogether accidental that in July 1965 the CC singled out the Kharkov Province organization for a scathing attack on the subject of Party admissions: allegedly the Kharkov *obkom* had been very lax in supervising Party admissions with the result that many unworthy young people were admitted to the Party.[42] It was only at the December 1965 CC plenum that Ivan V. Kapitonov was appointed Secretary for Party Organization Work, the post that had been left open since early April. Kapitonov is an old Russian Party apparatchik, who in March 1954 had achieved the important post of First Secretary of the Moscow *obkom* but fell into Khrushchev's disfavor and was demoted to the less important Ivanovo *obkom* Secretaryship in 1959. After Khrushchev's fall he was put in charge of Party personnel work in the Russian Republic and sometime between the September and December CC plenums he appears to have been given more important position of personnel chief for the Union Republics.[43] But the most important development in December was the retirement at the December 1965 Supreme Soviet session of Mikoyan from the Presidency of the Soviet Union (apparently due to genuine bad health) and the election in his stead of Podgorny, who in 1964 had been made Brezhnev's deputy Secretary for Party personnel questions.[44] As a full Presidium member he had outranked Titov in that capacity. There may have been muted policy disagreements between him and Brezhnev in the field of economics, Podgorny being regarded in the West as more liberal or moderate, pro-Liberman and light industry, closer to Kosygin than to Brezhnev.[45] Podgorny, too, being a graduate of the Kharkov

[41] *Pravda,* 6 April, 1965, p. 2., and September 30, 1965, p. 1.

[42] "O ser'eznykh nedostatkakh v rabote Khar'kovskoy oblastnoy partiynoy organizatsii po priemu v partiyu i vospitaniyu molodykh kommunistov: Postanovlenie TsK KPSS, 20 iyulya 1965 g.," *Part. zh.,* 1965, No. 15 (August) pp. 24–25; or *Spravochnik partiynogo rabotnika: vypusk shestoy* (Moscow 1966), pp. 383–86. A later editorial admitted that such shortcomings were not limited to the Kharkov *oblast.* See 'Soblyudat' ustavnye trebovaniya o chlenstve v KPSS," *Part. zh.,* 1966, No. 18 (September), p. 4.

[43] See his official biography in *Pravda,* 7 December, 1965, p. 1. Also *Le Monde,* 8 December, 1965, p. 6.

[44] *Izvestiya,* 10 December, 1965, p. 1.

[45] Clearest on this is Bernard Péron in his portrait in *Le Monde,* 11 December, 1965, p. 4. Also *New York Times,* 10 December, 1965, p. 1.

Party organization, the scandal in July over Party admissions may have had a sharp political point. Podgorny's departure opened up a very important problem: Who would become Brezhnev's ranking deputy for Party organizational affairs?

The long-awaited Party Congress finally met on March 29, 1966. I propose to comment only on those aspects of its sessions that are immediately relevant to Party organization, starting with changes in Party admission policies, the turnover of local (*raykom*) Secretaries, the problem of unpaid Party staffs, then proceeding to a brief analysis of the leading Party organs: the CC, the renamed Presidium and the CC Secretariat.

In the last section of the Central Committee report to the 23rd Congress Brezhnev dealt with Party organizational matters. He stressed first of all that local Party committees should be more careful in selecting candidates for admission and later suggested that the Party statutes be changed to require that new candidates be recommended by Party members of at least five years' standing (not, as previously, *three* years' status) and that decisions on expulsion from membership taken by the primary organization be made final on confirmation by the *raykom* and *gorkom,* subject to the right of appeal to higher organs. He also proposed that a statement be added to the preamble of the Party statutes that "the Party rids itself of persons violating the Program and the Statutes of the CPSU and compromising by their behavior the high calling of a Communist."[46] Only one other lowly speaker stressed this point: the First Secretary of the Turkmenian Party Ovezov.[47] Incidentally, it is most important to note that only very few members of the Party Presidium were given the floor. Besides Brezhnev there were Podgorny, speaking ex-officio as titular President of the USSR; Kosygin, the USSR Prime Minister; Shelest, the spokesman for the CP of Ukraine; alternates Rashidov and Mzhavanadze, speaking for Uzbekistan and Georgia respectively; and alternate Shcherbitsky addressing himself to the Ukrainian economy. Conspicuous by their silence were Shelepin, Suslov, Mikoyan, Kirilenko, Voronov, Polyansky, Mazurov, Shvernik. In 1961, under Khrushchev all full Presidium members with the exception of soon to be disgraced Voroshilov would be allowed to address the Congress, not to speak of full members holding joint appointments in the CC Secretariat such as Shelepin and Suslov in 1966.

Brezhnev's strictures against the admission of unworthy Party members amounted to a call for a "gentle purge." From Table 2 a drop in the total Party admissions in 1966 in comparison with the period of Khrushchev's predominance (1957–64) may be observed, even though

[46] *Pravda,* 30 March, 1966, p. 8.
[47] Ibid., 3 April, 1966, p. 2.

the Party did not change appreciably in its socio-economic and ethnic components (see Table 3).[48] A later article in *Partiynaya zhizn'* makes clear that as a result of the tightening of requirements at the 23rd Congress, new admissions to Party candidate status (in 1966 510,955 persons) were the lowest since 1958 (480,507 persons). The article further stresses that in 1966 12,000 applications for candidate status and as many as 36,000 applications for admissions to full membership were disapproved.[49] Moreover, a comparison of various figures shows that the number of persons separated from the Party in 1966 (62,868 who were expelled for disciplinary reasons and 17,244 who had been automatically dropped for losing contact with their primary Party organizations) substantially exceeded the number of Party members or candidates separated for the same reasons under Khrushchev: in 1963, 34,045 persons had been expelled and 14,422 had been automatically dropped for having lost contact. Moreover, in 1963 only 20,987 Party candidates were dropped upon being refused admission as full Party members, in 1966 there was 36,000 such cases. In summary, in 1963 under Khrushchev, a total of 69,454 Party members and candidates were mustered out for a variety of reasons, in 1966, under Brezhnev, about 116,112 were forced to leave and fewer new candidates were admitted.[50] This is not a big purge, but compared with Khrushchev's rule the turnover is rather high.

On the other hand, Brezhnev seems to have been anxious to obtain the favor of the professional Party apparatus, the local Secretaries and their deputies, whom Khrushchev meant to shake up by introducing the principle of "systematic renewal" in Section 25 of the 1961 Party Statutes. (Basically, at least one quarter of the members of the All-Union

[48] Two notable exceptions to the rule appear to be the increased number of Party members of less than 10 years' standing; a result of the heavy admissions in 1963 and 1964; and a relative decline in the number of Russian Party members, from 63.54 to 61.86 per cent of the total. Also noteworthy is the increase in the percentage of Ukrainians, from 14.67 to 15.63 in the years 1961–67. (See Table 3). Titov may have helped as Party personnel chief. Nevertheless, in 1959 Russians numbered 54.65, and Ukrainians 17.84 per cent of the country's population.

[49] Cf. "Priem v KPSS i nekotorye izmeneniya v sostave partii za 1966 god," *Part. zh.*, 1967, No. 7 (April), p. 7, with "The Party in Figures (1956–1961 loc. cit. (note 4), p. 3.

[50] "Priem v KPSS . . . ," loc. cit., p. 8; "KPSS v tsifrakh (1961–1964 gody)," loc. cit. (note 4), p. 10. Less explicit figures would indicate that in 1960 Khrushchev expelled or dropped from the Party only 40,333 members or candidates—see "The Party in Figures (1956–1961)," loc. cit., p. 4. See Section 16 of 1961 Party Statutes for dropping Party candidates who fail to get admitted as full members, in *Zapisnaya knizhka partiynogo aktivista, 1966* (Moscow, 1965), p. 60.

Table 2
Growth of Party Members
(Figures as of January 1 of corresponding year)

Year	*Number of Members & Candidates*	*Absolute Increase*	*Percentage Increase Per Interval*	*Percentage Increase Per Annum of Interval*
1946	5,510,862	——	——	——
1953	6,897,224	1,386,362	25.16	3.59
1957	7,494,573	597,349	8.66	2.17
1961	9,275,826	1,781,253	23.77	5.94
1962	9,891,068	615,242	6.63	6.63
1963	10,387,196	496,128	5.02	5.02
1964	11,022,369	635,173	6.11	6.11
1965	11,758,169	735,800	6.68	6.68
1966	12,357,308	599,139	5.10	5.10
1967	12,684,133	326,825	2.64	2.64

SOURCE: "KPSS v tsifrakh," *Partiynaya zhizn'*, 1967, No. 19 (October), p. 9.

CC and of the Presidium were to be renewed at each successive election, one third of the members of Republican CC's, of *kraykoms* and *obkoms*, and as much as one half of the members of the Party organs below).[51] In their desire to fulfill and overfulfill the planned quota, the Party organizations had gone rather far. In 1962 as many as 62 per cent of the Secretaries of primary Party organizations were changed, whereas in previous years the turnover had been about one third. As Brezhnev complained at the Party Congress, the turnover running close to 60 per cent in the last years, two thirds of the primary organizations' Secretaries were retired only to fulfill the rotation quota. Another source mentioned that at the Party elections which took place late in 1963 and early in 1964 as many as 77.4 per cent of members of urban *raykoms* and 75.5 per cent of the *gorkom* membership were rotated out (instead of the required 50 per cent): so were 69.2 per cent of *obkom* and 57 per cent of Republican CC members (their quota being 33 per cent).[52] Not surprisingly, the Party officials complained against this after Khrushchev's fall.[53] As a later editorial put it:

[51] *Zapisnaya knizhka* . . . , p. 62.
[52] *Pravda,* 30 March, 1966, p. 9; *Besedy* . . . , p. 124.
[53] G. Popov, First Secretary of the Leningrad *gorkom,* "Partiyny rabotnik," *Pravda,* 30 May, 1965, p. 2.

Table 3
Comparative Profile of CPSU Members (Selected Years)

	N	%	N	%
Length of Party Membership[a]	*January 1, 1962*		*January 1, 1967*	
10 years or less	—	39.0	—	48.3
11–20 years	—	56.2	—	20.8
21–30 years	—		—	25.9
30 years & over	—	4.8	—	5.0
Education[b]				
Completed higher	1,349,535	13.7	1,771,070	13.9
Incomplete higher	282,061	2.9	325,985	2.6
Completed secondary	2,693,457	27.2	3,993,119	31.5
Total	9,891,068	100.0	12,684,133	100.0
Employment in Branches of Economy[c]	*January 1, 1957*		*January 1, 1967*	
Industry	1,786,273	23.83	3,195,718	25.19
Construction	205,132	2.74	666,380	5.25
Transport	550,268	7.34	838,019	6.61
Agriculture	1,442,571	19.25	2,336,412	18.42
Total	7,494,573	100.00	12,684,133	100.00
Nationality[d]	*July 1, 1961*		*January 1, 1967*	
Russians	6,116,700	63.54	7,846,292	61.86
Ukrainians	1,412,200	14.67	1,983,090	15.63
Byelorussians	287,000	2.98	424,360	3.35
Uzbeks	142,700	1.48	219,381	1.73
Kazakhs	149,200	1.55	199,196	1.57
Georgians	170,400	1.77	209,196	1.65
Azerbaydzhanians	106,100	1.10	162,181	1.28
Lithuanians	42,800	0.44	71,316	0.56
Moldavians	26,700	0.28	46,562	0.37
Latvians	33,900	0.35	49,559	0.39
Kirghizians	27,300	0.28	39,053	0.31
Tadzhiks	32,700	0.34	46,593	0.37
Armenians	161,200	1.67	200,605	1.58
Turkmenians	27,300	0.28	35,781	0.28
Estonians	24,400	0.25	37,705	0.30
Others	866,100	9.00	1,113,263	8.78
Total	9,626,700	100.00	12,684,133	100.00

SOURCES: (a) "KPSS v tsifrakh (1961–1964 gody)," *Partiynaya zhizn'*, 1965, No. 10 (May), p. 13; "KPSS v tsifrakh," ibid., 1967, No. 19 (October), p. 15. (b) "KPSS v tsifrakh (1961–1964 gody)," loc. cit., p. 11; "KPSS v tsifrakh," loc. cit. (1967), p. 14. (c) "KPSS v tsifrakh," loc. cit. (1967), p. 17. Percentage added. (d) "The Party in Figures (1956–61)" *Partiynaya zhizn'*, 1962, No. 1 (January), pp. 44ff., translated in *Current Digest of the Soviet Press,* Vol. XIV, No. 3, p. 5. "KPSS v tsifrakh," loc. cit. (1967), p. 14. Percentage added.

> Such an arbitrary regulation narrowed down the number of mature and experienced workers who could be elected to Party committees, infringed on the rights of Party activists, showed a negative impact on the activity of the primary Party organizations.[54]

Brezhnev proposed to the Congress to abolish Section 25, which was duly accepted.

Another issue in which Party officials are strongly interested is to obtain a sufficient number of paid Party personnel to help them carry out their work. Khrushchev, on the contrary, had cut the rolls of paid Party staffs substituting for them unpaid voluntary activists. In 1963 such *vneshtatnye partiynye rabotniki* totaled more than 320 thousand. In that year the apparatus of the Moscow City committee was reduced in comparison with 1950, though the number of Party members in the city had increased by more than 70 per cent. 92 per cent of the 8,436 primary organizations' Secretaries in Moscow were not paid from the Party treasury. In the Proletarsky district in Moscow only six per cent of the Party staff were paid.[55] In Estonia from 1961–64 paid Party personnel were reduced by 20 per cent, in their stead in the capital Tallin alone as many as 50 diverse volunteer (*vneshtatnye*) commissions were set up, which employed as many as 1,100 unpaid Party members.[56] A particularly important volunteer commission was that which provisionally reviewed the credentials of applicants to Party admission.[57] I have not found any discussion of this sore matter at the 23rd Congress but there are at least two straws to indicate that the wind has quietly shifted into the opposite direction. One member of a voluntary commission on personnel matters was reprimanded for insisting that the commission's chairman, not the secretary of the primary organization, should continue to present a candidate's credentials to the *raykom* bureau, as had been done before.[58] More importantly, alternate Politburo member Kunaev, who is said to be a close protegé of Brezhnev's, wrote in late 1966, that the CC of the CP of Kazakhstan had reviewed and condemned "the mistakes and perversions" in the Party's work with

[54] Editorial, "Zakon zhizni partii," *Part. zh.*, 1966, No. 9 (May), p. 5.

[55] *Besedy* . . . pp. 170–71. This trend had started already in 1957. See Fainsod, op. cit. (note 17), p. 230.

[56] A. Vader, "Sovershenstvovat' obshchestvennye formy raboty," *Part. zh.*, 1964, No. 19 (October), p. 21.

[57] See Fainsod, op. cit., p. 228; I. Vasil'ev et alii, "Soblyudat' Leninskie printsipy," *Part. zh.*, 1964, No. 20 (October), pp. 34–38, esp. p. 35; and editorial, "O vneshtatnykh partkomissiyakh (Obzor pisem)" *Part. zh.*, 1965, No. 9 (May), pp. 39–43.

[58] See E. Bronshteyn's letter, and reply in *Part zh.*, 1966, No. 17 (September), p. 47.

volunteers and had recommended the Party committees to set up "only those voluntary sections, councils and commissions which actually help to increase the role of the "regular Party committees as organs of political leadership."[59]

Turning to the higher Party organs, Brezhnev's proposal to revive the practice of convening All-Union or All-Republican Party Conferences between the Congresses might constitute an effort to detract from the authority of the CC plenums and the quadrennial Congresses. But Congresses' power is more symbolic than real, and so far no All-Union Party Conferences have been called. Of symbolic importance is also the abolition of the CC Bureau for the RSFSR: it appears to have been set up in 1956, when Khrushchev courted the non-Russian nationalities, in order to indicate that the CP of the Soviet Union was not to be identified with the CP of Russia.[60] Brezhnev may have been right in pointing out that even with the RSFSR Bureau the more important questions of Russian Republic Party organizations were being discussed in the Presidium and Secretariat anyway.[61] Of greater importance have been the changes involving the CC, the Presidium and the Secretariat.

At the October 14, 1964 CC plenum Suslov allegedly accused Khrushchev of watering down the authority of the CC. The Committee was being convened in increasingly large sessions, with many non-members attending as experts personally invited by Khrushchev. The meetings eventually turned into spectacular shows, at which strangers would outnumber the CC members. Khrushchev thus deprived "the members of the highest organ of the Party of any real opportunity to discuss and criticize policy."[62] At the 23rd Congress Brezhnev hinted that the authority of the CC plenums ought to be increased.[63] From the official announcement of the September 1965 plenum it does appear that Brezhnev himself was not averse to inviting a reasonable number of

[59] See D. Kunaev, "Kollektivnost'—vysshiy printsip partiynogo rukovodstva," *Part. zh.*, 1966, No. 19 (October), p. 11, and the analysis by Christian Duevel, "Novoe istolkovanie 'kollektivnogo rukovodstva' (po retseptu Brezhneva?)," *E.I.B.*, 2 November, 1966.

[60] Officially the reason for setting up the RSFSR Party Bureau was "to provide more concrete and effective leadership of the 78 provinces, territories and autonomous republics of the Russian Republic." See Khrushchev in *Pravda,* 15 February, 1956, pp. 1ff., or Leo Gruliow, ed., *Current Soviet Policies II: The Documentary Record of the 20th Communist Party Congress . . .* (New York: Praeger, 1957), p. 58b.

[61] *Pravda,* 30 March, 1966, p. 9.

[62] Page, op. cit. (note 2), p. 56.

[63] *Pravda,* 30 March, 1966, p. 8.

non-members to a particularly important meeting,[64] and there is a lingering suspicion that he did not invite Khrushchev's supporters to the October 1964 meeting. On the other hand, the full membership of the CC was kept remarkably stable: a record number, four-fifths or 139 of the 175 1961 full members were kept on in 1966. Of those who were not reelected in 1966, 9 had died between the Congresses, one (Dauleunov) had been expelled by Khrushchev in 1963, and only 26 were forced out under Brezhnev (including Adzhubey, who was dropped November 16, 1964). To accommodate the 27 promotions from alternate status (including that of Rudakov in 1962), the five rehabilitated members (e.g., Voroshilov, Matskevich) and the 24 completely new admissions, a total of 56, Brezhnev has had the CC expanded from 175 to 195. Brezhnev seems to have gone almost out of his way to keep on the CC, the Party's and the country's functioning parliament, as many Party notables as possible.[65]

At the Party Congress Brezhnev also suggested that the Party Presidium be renamed the Politburo, because this is how it was called during Lenin's lifetime and because the latter name "more fully reflected the character of the activity of the highest political organ of our Party, which directs the Party's work between the CC plenums."[66] There was little harm in changing this particular designation. More significant is, as pointed out by Dr. Duevel, that three rather important speakers at the Congress emphasized collective leadership in the Politburo and Secretariat (N. A. Murav'eva, the chairman of the Auditing Commission, who spoke immediately following Brezhnev; N. G. Yeogorychev, Secre-

[64] The announcement read: "Invited to participate in the work of the plenary session of the CPSU Central Committee were the first secretaries of province Party committees, the chairmen of the Union-republic Councils of Ministers, the second secretaries of the Central Committees of the Union-republic Communist Parties, Ministers and chairmen of state committees of the USSR, officials of the apparatus of the CPSU Central Committee and the USSR Council of Minister, and the editors-in-chief of central newspapers." See *Pravda*, 28 September, 1965, p. 1. To take just one example, B. V. Popov, II Secy. of the CP of Lithuania was not a member of the 1961 CC. Khrushchev used to invite to CC plenums even deserving shockworkers, e.g. to the June 1959 plenum—see *Ezhegodnik Bolshoy Sovetskoy Entsyklopedii na 1960 god,* p. 11. The frequency of the meetings under Khrushchev and Brezhnev, on the other hand, is about the same: at least two meetings a year.

[65] For more details see Y. Bilinsky, *Changes in the Central Committee Communist Party of the Soviet Union, 1961–1966* in The Social Science Foundation and Graduate School of International Studies, University of Denver, *Monograph Series in World Affairs,* Vol. 4, No. 4 (1966–67), pp. 26 *et passim.*

[66] *Pravda,* 30 March, 1966, p. 9.

tary of the Moscow City Committee: and V. S. Tolstikov, Secretary of the Leningrad *obkom*),[67] while an exceedingly low-placed delegate, Mrs. Yu. D. Filinova, *raykom* Secretary from the Saratov *oblast,* used a formula so flattering to Brezhnev: "the Politburo headed by the Secretary General."[68] Her superior, Saratov *obkom* Secretary Shibaev, appears to have been punished for this indiscretion.[69] It is also worth noting that Podgorny, once Brezhnev's deputy, did not utter a single word on the proposed change in names.[70] The emphasis on collective rule probably was a subtle reminder to Brezhnev not to follow the footsteps of Khrushchev who in October 1964 had been accused of violating that principle in the Presidium.[71]

Even more important was the somewhat reserved and cool proposal by Yegorychev to rename Brezhnev's office the Secretaryship General, which had been set up by Lenin after the 1922 Party Congress.[72] None of the subsequent speakers who supported this proposal dared to breathe a word about the fact that the term had become closely associated with Stalin's career and that it was for that reason that Khrushchev assumed the title of First Secretary in 1953. Duevel has tried to interpret the change in Brezhnev's title as a "Greek gift": Lenin had indeed thought of the Secretary General as the executor of the Politburo's will, Stalin had overridden the Politburo, thus after assuming Stalin's title Brezhnev would have to be more careful.[73] This interpretation, however, was not borne out by Brezhnev's last words to the Congress.

In a remark, which was not printed in *Pravda,* Brezhnev emphasized that the plenary meeting of the CC, which took place shortly before the end of the Congress, "proceeded in an atmosphere of unity and solidarity."[74] Then, with a somewhat aggressive immodesty, he said:

> The plenum unanimously elected as Secretary General of the CC and member of the Politburo of the CC Comrade Brezhnev [here

[67] Ibid. 30 March, 1966, p. 10: 31 March, 1966, pp. 2–3. Duevel, "Novye Politbyuro i Sekretariat Tsentral'nogo Komiteta KPSS," *E.I.B.,* 14 April, 1966. The latter is an excellent analysis based upon close monitoring of Moscow Radio, and on *Pravda.*

[68] *Pravda,* 3 April, 1966, p. 5.

[69] He had been elected to the Congress's Presidium but not to the editorial commission charged with drafting the Congress's resolution on Brezhnev's report—see *Pravda,* 30 March, 1966, p. 1, and 5 April, 1966, p. 1.

[70] See his speech in *Pravda,* 1 April, 1966, p. 4.

[71] Page, op. cit., p. 56.

[72] *Pravda,* 31 March, 1966, p. 2.

[73] Duevel, "Reorganizatsiya otnosheniy mezhdu sekretariatom i presidumom TsK KPSS," *E.I.B.,* 6 April, 1966.

[74] Duevel, "Novye Politbyuro . . . ," loc. cit. (note 67), p. 1.

he paused to wait out the applause]. The Plenum also unanimously elected as members of the Politburo of the CC CPSU Comrades . . ."[75]

The Western radio monitors and the Western correspondents pricked up their ears when for the first time since 1954 Brezhnev announced the members of the Politburo and of the Secretariat in order of seniority rather than the accepted Russian alphabetical order. Full members of the Presidium were: Brezhnev, Kosygin, Podgorny, Suslov, Voronov, Kirilenko, Shelepin, Mazurov, Polyansky, Shelest, and Pelshe.[76] Mikoyan and Shvernik were dropped, possibly because of advanced age. This is clearly a ranking according to political importance, not according to the date of admission to the Politburo-Presidium. Zorza of *The Guardian* sees in the new Politburo an inner body of four (Brezhnev, Kosygin, Podgorny, and Suslov), which may be a plausible assumption. But it is more difficult to accept his hypothesis of several outer concentric circles, for the Russian alphabet then repeats itself three times (Voronov-Shelepin, Mazurov-Shelest, Pelshe).[77] Rather interesting in any case is the low position of Shelepin and Polyansky (the latter a full Presidium member since 1960, like Podgorny). Among the candidate members were: Demichev, Grishin, Mzhavanadze, Rashidov, Ustinov, Shcherbitsky, Kunaev, and Masherov, with a possible interpretation of the verbatim announcement to the effect that the election of the last two was not unanimous.[78] The ranking of the Secretaries was as follows: Brezhnev, Suslov, Shelepin, Kirilenko (new), Demichev, Ustinov, Andropov, Ponomarev, Kapitonov, Kulakov, Rudakov. Most noteworthy is the disappearance of Podgorny, who had been "promoted" to head the USSR Supreme Soviet, and the relatively high position of Shelepin's. It looks as if Suslov had been made Deputy Secretary General responsible for cadres, despite the fact that he is known to be ailing. This merely postpones the solution of the problem. The man to watch as possible successor to Suslov as Deputy Secretary General for Party Organization would be Kirilenko, who is a full Presidium member and has had experience in managing Party affairs in the Russian Republic. Most importantly, a few hours after the original broadcast of Brezhnev's speech Soviet news media (*TASS*, and then *Pravda*) excised Brezhnev's announcement of the elections from the text of his final speech to the Congress and restored the alphabetical order of Presidium members and Secretaries, the only ex-

[75] Ibid., p. 8.
[76] Ibid., p. 1. Confirmed in *Le Monde*. 9 April, 1966, p. 4; and by Victor Zorza, in *The Guardian*, 9 April, p. 9.
[77] Zorza, loc. cit.
[78] Duevel, "Novye Politbyuro . . . ," loc. cit., p. 5.

ception being Brezhnev, listed first a Secretary General.[79] It would appear that some influential leaders in the Soviet Union—though not Brezhnev himself—did take the principle of collective leadership seriously enough to try to quash—somewhat *ex-post-facto*—disputes over the political ranking of individual colleagues.*

Lack of space does not allow me to comment on such facts as occasional violations of voting procedures in local Party elections,[80] and the growing snobbism in the Party toward relatively uneducated manual and clerical workers.[81] Nor can I, for lack of material, interpret the unusually sweeping attack on the CC of the CP of Estonia by the All-Union CC in March 1967: Judging by the resolution the Estonian Party leaders have done hardly anything right in the field of personnel policy.[82] Nor can I analyze here the involved and somewhat murky fall of the "Komsomol group": in May 1967 Shelepin's successor and presumed collaborator V. Semichastny was dismissed from the chair-

[79] *Pravda,* 9 April, 1966, p. 2.

* When the article was going to press the official stenographic transcript of the Party Congress has come to my attention (*XXIII S'yezd Kommunisticheskoy Partii Sovetskogo Soyuza, 29 marta—8 aprelya 1966 goda: Stenograficheskiy otchët.* Moscow 1966, 2 volumes). Unlike *Pravda* it lists the Party leaders in order of seniority ibid., Vol. II, pp. 292–93). This authoritative later source, which is, however, more esoteric than *Pravda,* almost fully confirms Duevel's analysis based on radio monitoring tapes. The only discrepancy is that the stenographic report does not draw a distinction between Kunaev and Masherov on the one hand and the rest of the *alternate* Politburo members on the other: all eight are said to have been elected "truly unanimously" (*edinodushno, edinoglasno*), all of them meriting simple applause after the announcement of each name (*aplodismenty*). Duevel may have been overly suspicious, or the stenographic report may have been overly "edited." In any case, the "applause protocol" is not without interest to students of collective leadership. Among the *full* Politburo members, Brezhnev alone has been accorded "stormy applause not abating for a long time" (*burnye, dolgo ne smolkayushchie aplodismenty*). Significantly, he was *not* given a standing ovation. The inner circle of Kosygin, Podgorny and Suslov received "stormy continuing applause" (*burnye prodolzhitel'nye aplodismenty*). All the rest from Voronov on down (Voronov, Kirilenko, Shelepin, Mazurov, Polyansky, Shelest and Pelshe) had to make do with "applause" pure and simple.

[80] See, e.g. the despatch from Baku, Azerbaydzhan, in *Pravda,* 23 February, 1966, p. 2.

[81] An interesting example of this is A. Bobicheva's letter in *Part. zh.,* 1965, No. 22 (November), p. 64. The author, a Party member of 20 years' standing, was prevented from being elected deputy Secretary of a factory Party organization because she was merely a typist.

[82] "V Tsentral'nom Komitete KPSS: O rabote TsK Kompartii Estonii s rukovodyashchimi kadramy," *Part. zh.* 1967, No. 6 (March), pp. 8–12.

manship of the secret police,[83] late in June Yegorychev was dismissed from the Secretaryship of the important Moscow City Organization (his successor is alternate Politburo member Grishin, who had headed the Soviet Trade Unions),[84] and in the first half of July 1967 Shelepin was appointed to head the Soviet Trade Unions.[85] At the September 1967 CC plenum Shelepin was released from the (vital) CC Secretaryship to be able to fully devote himself to the (second-rate) Trade Union job.[86] Also released from the Secretariat (in June) was Andropov who succeeded to Semichastny's K.G.B. post. Andropov, however, was given a consolation post: a candidate membership of the Politburo.[87] It is the first time since Beria that a K.G.B. chief occupies a seat on the Politburo. In this reshuffle the Party organization was not directly affected, unlike in December 1965: the 1967 power-struggle was much more "economical," possibly had foreign policy overtones.[88] A much less controversial change has been the election of Mikhail S. Solomentsev to CC Secretary in charge of Heavy Industry at the December 1966 CC plenum: he replaced Rudakov, who had died in July of 1966.[89]

In summary, Brezhnev has tried to undo some of Khrushchev's attempts on the old and tried ways of the Party apparatus: the industrial and agricultural production branches, the network of Party State Control Committees, the principle of rotating out entrenched Party bureaucrats, of surrounding them with unpaid activists. Brezhnev's party is one of allegedly Leninist and possibly quasi-Stalinist restoration. He emphasizes the difficulty of admission and the easiness of expulsion. From the leaders' viewpoint, this may be exactly what the country needs as a counterweight to the limited economic reforms and the spreading ferment among its intellectuals. Brezhnev has been lucky in his politics: he has deftly dislodged first Podgorny and then Shelepin. But judging from the events at the 1966 Party Congress his position is not unchallengeable. The future will show how easily the crown of a Secretary General rests on his head.

[83] *Pravda,* 19 May, 1967, p. 6.
[84] Ibid., 28 June, 1967, p. 1.
[85] Ibid., 12 July, 1967, p. 1.
[86] Ibid., 27 September, 1967, p. 1.
[87] Ibid., 22 June, 1967, p. 1.
[88] See the commentary in the Western press: *The New York Times,* 29 June, 1967, p. 7, and 12 July, 1967, p. 20; *Le Monde,* 30 June. 1967, p. 3; Victor Zorza in *The Guardian,* July 12, 1967, p. 9. All these sources link Yegorychev's career to Shelepin's (Yegorychev, too, started his career in the Komsomol) and intimate that Yegorychev took a very bellicose stand at the June 1967 CC plenum which discussed the Six Days' Middle Eastern War.
[89] See *Pravda,* 14 December, 1966, p. 1, for announcement and short official biography.

THE METAMORPHOSIS OF THE CHINESE COMMUNIST PARTY

Victor C. Funnell

As a revolutionary party, armed with a revolutionary theory, a ruling Communist Party faces a task still harder than revolution in adjusting to its new administrative role, and in bringing its unique power to bear on a range of pressing and complex administrative problems. It first of all faces the dilemma that its initial success in winning power, and its subsequent preoccupation with holding power, may divert or dilute the original ideological concepts that gave it birth. Revolutionary virtues are now less endearing to the new Communist rulers, seeking consolidation and stability, and increasingly committed to the status quo. This transition from revolution to administration is generally a severe and chastening experience for young revolutionary regimes. Experience of office tends to lead away from the ideological response, and toward greater pragmatism in everyday decisions. In the process, the Party undergoes a subtle metamorphosis from left to right. It institutionalizes the revolution, and recruits vast new bureaucracies. Its goals change, and with them change the motives of the new people that the Party seeks to attract, and indeed has to attract, if it is to succeed. At the same time, it is forced to rely on large numbers of personnel who previously served its erstwhile enemies.

This new functional role of the Party frequently collides with its revolutionary instincts and experience. It is an unaccustomed role, and easily induces feelings of unease. Necessary decisions may impinge on the purity of the doctrines. A note of compromise is introduced. In foreign affairs, too, the Party's identity with the state leads to national policies that cloud the universal relevance of its message. The ideology that has become only partially relevant at home may then even

From *Studies in Comparative Communism*, IV, 2 (April 1971). Reprinted with permission of the author and the editor.

become an impediment to relations with other countries. Particularly is this so where those countries share the same basic ideology, and whose internal development has run a similar course. Polycentrism in the Communist world is, thus, simply the external reflection of the innumerable modifications to doctrine imposed on Communist parties in facing their own internal circumstances over the years. In each case, internally and externally, the process can be expected to continue, to deepen and widen, as changing conditions dictate, and to be hastened by every shifting alliance and maneuver in national and world affairs.

The case of China is strikingly relevant to this theme. The cultural revolution in China illustrates in an acute form all the tensions generated by this process of adjustment. These tensions have arisen notwithstanding all the experience and training of the Chinese Communist Party before 1949, which might have been expected to provide useful lessons and precedents in the exercise of power. To some extent this is true, and the practical experience of Mao and his associates in their guerrilla base at Yenan contrasts with the largely conspiratorial activities of Lenin and the Bolsheviks prior to 1917. This very fact, however, has proved something of a disadvantage, in hindering the inevitable adjustments that have to be made when the Party assumes supreme power. The formulation of revolutionary doctrines under Mao's leadership, the working out of organizational training and techniques, and the growth of a native self-confidence are all owed to the Party's earlier period of tutelage, and it is from that period that its operational principles are derived.

These principles, as expounded by Mao in his *On Coalition Government* in 1945, consist essentially of three things: the integration of theory and practice, the mass line, and the practice of self-criticism. It is these techniques, or "styles of work" as the Chinese call them, which are the hallmark of the Party, and which are supposed to govern all organization and execution of policy in subsequent years. They are considered as applicable today as when they were first formulated thirty years ago. The practical concern for the integration of Marxism-Leninism with the objective of revolution in Chinese society is the essence of Mao's thought, as revealed in his major works, and is held to elevate him to the position of a contemporary Lenin. The formula of "Marxism-Leninism-Mao Tse-tung thought," as enshrined in the new Party constitution, is clearly intended to establish Mao's claim to universality. This is not simply a national innovation, in other words, but an extension of basic doctrine, and the relevance of Chinese Communism stretches out beyond Asia, to Africa, Latin America, and the world.

The genesis of the mass line similarly reaches back to the period when the Party was struggling for power. Not the least of Mao's attributes is his skill as a political tactician, fully comprehending the need for a zigzag route, in an Asian setting, toward the Party's goals. What at times appears as a *lack* of principles is no more than the ability, which many another politician might envy, to profit from every external circumstance. To a Party raising its army and its revenues from a peasant base, the necessity for identifying its policies with popular causes, such as land reform, or the patriotic war against the Japanese, became a simple question of survival. The Party's links with the masses in the countryside, and the thoroughness of its appraisal of their feelings, became the essential guidelines for its scope of action. Here, too, as the originators of the techniques of "people's war," the Chinese would claim to find its application valid for other peoples in other lands.

The third style of work, involving criticism and self-criticism, has been a potent force in a disciplinary context in maintaining Party cohesion in the rigorous and extended conditions of national and civil war. Abuses apart, it is seen as an exemplary exercise in self-renewal and rededication to the cause. Following the guidelines established during its first coordinated use, in the great rectification movement in the Party in 1942, criticism and self-criticism have become a feature of Party life and organization.

Here, then, is the operating mode or ethos of the Communist Party of China, evolved in the course of its rise to power. The success of the Party in 1949 has not unnaturally tended to elevate its work styles into a rigid code, and to obscure the necessity for flexibility in a new and changing environment. The Party has become the prisoner of its own experience. Hence, many of its subsequent difficulties have been of its own making, as it has clung tenaciously to its well-tried techniques among the masses. These are techniques which are best suited to making revolution, to mass mobilization and taking and holding power, and which are less obviously relevant to the needs of stable administration and regulated production. The very centralization and uniformity demanded by the system have been less than adequate as a framework for the diversified requirements of a modern industrial and military establishment. These pose unprecedented social and political problems for the Party, the solution to which may, in the long run, tend to poison the wells of political inspiration and fervor.

Nevertheless, the Party in China has relied extensively on its proven political techniques in coping with the objective difficulties it has encountered in the administrative field since the new phase in its history ushered in 1949. It has kept effective power in the hands of Party committees in all sectors of the economy and society, and it has never ceased to believe that constant ideological education is the remedy for every tension and contradiction within the system. The greater the setbacks in production, or in foreign affairs—to take but two examples—the more the Party clings to its political message, enshrined in "the thought of Mao Tse-tung." When the two come together, as in the failure of the "great leap forward" and the communes, and the simultaneous worsening of relations with the Soviet Union and other socialist countries, the greater is the pressure within the Party to reclaim its revolutionary heritage and relive its earlier successes. It may also hope to recapture some of its earlier enthusiasm, and to infect both cadres and masses in this sense. To this may be attributed the apparent conviction of Mao and his colleagues that there are still revolutionary victories to be won at home, and revolutionary virtues to be instilled in young and old alike. The attempt to circumvent annoying and unfamiliar difficulties by returning to the simplicity of Yenan seems irresistible to the Chinese leaders.

The attempt to substitute a revolutionary black-and-white for the postrevolutionary gray, which has inspired many domestic campaigns, culminating in the cultural revolution in 1966, succeeds only in emphasizing the increasing irrelevance of the official ideology to the current situation. To the aging leaders of the Party, those for whom (and Mao especially) the doctrines of Yenan are graven on tablets of stone, the danger of a growing gulf between the Party and the masses may not always be apparent. For them, indeed, the mere fact of a discrepancy between ideals and practice may point to the necessity of increased indoctrination in the verities. At lower levels of the Party, however, where there is daily and first-hand knowledge of the fusion of doctrine and action, as in the whole technological-managerial sphere of operations on which the Party must rely so heavily for the modernization of the country, awareness of the self-inflicted difficulties of the Party imposed by doctrinal rigidity at the top must be acute. There is, thus, the possibility not only of a dangerous divergence between the Party and the masses, but a further strain within the Party itself, between the formulators of policy above and the practical executants below. For the latter, constant exhortations to read Mao's works on "the foolish old man who removed the mountains," or the memory of Dr. Bethune, can scarcely appear an adequate or relevant guide to daily routine.[1]

In the Soviet Union, it has not been found necessary constantly to adopt the prerevolutionary writings of Lenin as an exclusive guide to action in all years subsequent to 1917. Indeed, Lenin himself felt it expedient to make significant revisions. Successive leaders have similarly interpreted the doctrines in a way they found most expedient. In China

[1] Mao's "three most constantly read articles" in China are *Serve the People* (1944), *In Memory of Norman Bethune* (1939), and *The Foolish Old Man Who Removed the Mountains* (1945).

this is not so. There, there are no latter-day emendations of the doctrines that served the Party so well in its revolutionary days, and the Russian exercise in Leninist exegesis provokes only hostility and suspicion. For the Russians, on the other hand, the Chinese tendency in Sino-Soviet polemics to quote the pristine utterances of the Bolshevik leaders against them must appear both tedious and infantile. To the sophisticates in the Kremlin, Chinese fundamentalism seems the earnest prattling of a recent convert, or "like someone trying to assert at noon that the day is only dawning."[2]

In China, reliance on the word of Mao is all the more necessary, as the Russians have not failed to point out, due to the lack of any formally adopted Party program. Whether a program, if adopted, would necessarily prove more realistic, or any more binding on the leadership, is questionable. The experience of the Communist Party of the Soviet Union, with its twenty-year program adopted in 1961, leads one to think that it would not. Moreover, a program may in any case be of secondary importance to a party, whether Russian or Chinese, whose primary concern is the strength of its apparatus. In the absence of such guidelines in China, as the Russians now also like to point out, the cult of personality flourishes. There is an obvious connection between the lack of a Party program in the Soviet Union under Stalin, and a similar lack in China under Mao. It is the same symptom of the dictatorship of personality and a departure from Leninist norms as the irregular holding of Party congresses, or holding them not at all.[3]

This situation cannot fail to affect Party organization and the nature of the cadre operation. It accentuates all those stresses and strains, those "contradictions," to which Mao addressed himself in 1957. They include the tensions inherent in such Party concepts as democratic centralism, collective leadership and individual responsibility, and hierarchical and lateral authority. In the broader, social sphere they embrace the tug-of-war between Party control and administrative decentralization, the relationship of the intellectuals and the underlying "red and expert" controversy, the increasing disparity between the incomes of peasants and city workers, the conflict between minority nationalism

[2] Editorial, *Party Life,* broadcast on Moscow Radio, April 22, 1964, *Summary of World Broadcasts* (SWB), SU/1535.

[3] See, for example, Kuusinen's speech at the CPSU Central Committee plenum in February 1964, published in *Pravda,* May 19, 1964, and broadcast on Moscow Radio (*SWB,* SU/1558): "The Party's leaders have in fact freed themselves from all Party control. There have been no CCP Congresses for many years, and its representative organs play an increasingly decorative role." Only three Party congresses have been held in China in the past twenty-five years (in 1945, 1956, and 1969), and only nine altogether since the Party's foundation in 1921.

and Han "chauvinism," and between Party ideology and liberalizing tendencies.

These instances, which could be multiplied indefinitely, serve to illustrate the extent of the price the Party has to pay for its monopoly of power. That price is a chronic sense of insecurity. The failure to consult the Party inevitably excites the leadership's susceptibility to the suspicion of impurity in the Party's ranks and the slightest breath of internal opposition. Great as is the power of the Standing Committee of the Politburo, fear of subversion is greater. Constant political campaigns and "rectifications" are the concomitants of the sense of insecurity that pervades the Party structure, and which itself is a product of the almost total absence of that "democracy" which, according to the Party statutes, should counterbalance "centralism." Centralization is, in fact, the dominant characteristic of the Chinese Party, particularly in the wake of the cultural revolution. In the wider sphere as well, the failure to consult the masses in any meaningful sense leads to the same preoccupation with any thought or action that is not subject to the guidance of the Party, and the same search for security in devices of control and supervision, such as the division into small groups, of one sort or another, of the whole population. In this, the country accurately mirrors the Party.

In a constitutional context, the Party has only itself to blame. It took the Soviet Union twenty-two years before, in 1939, it felt able to relax the discriminatory conditions of Party membership sufficiently to include workers, peasants, and intelligentsia on equal terms. In China, on the other hand, after only seven years in power, the Party at its Eighth Congress in 1956 established common conditions for membership, regardless of social position. As a commentary on the comparative speed of advance toward a socialist society in the two countries, the Chinese action was considered premature by the Russians.[4] For the Chinese, however, it testified to a confidence in the internal Party structure, and the consolidation of Party control in the country, that was shortly to be disproved in the great rectification campaign in 1957 and the challenge to the leadership in 1959.

Distortion of the Party's Operational Principles

The effect of these twin absolutes of power and security is to distort the Party's own operational principles. The mass line evolved in response to the Party's need for close and continuing contact with the

[4] Editorial, *Party Life*, see note 2: "And this was in a country incomparably more petit bourgeois than Russia was."

population, at a time when it was in need of mass support to sustain it against its foes. The two-way flow of policies and ideas that the mass line supposedly incorporated subtly changed with the defeat of those foes in 1949. It then became a means of manipulating the popular response to the policies arbitrarily decreed by the Party's high command, and ensuring receptivity to the ideology officially enthroned in Peking. Since the Party was itself the highest representative of the "people," or of those people included in the "revolutionary classes," it could only follow that the Party's policies were the embodiment, the supreme expression, of the popular will. In this identification of the Party with the "people," already postulated by Stalin in the Soviet Union (who also identified himself with the Party), the mass line became simply a question of the propagation and implementation of Party policy. It was then less a question of mass support than of the enforcement of policies ostensibly approved by the masses. In the process, the upward transmission of information and opinion, an integral part of mass-line operation, has become a nationwide system of reporting, which enables the Party to sound out pockets of resistance and take appropriate action. Once again, the Party applies to the country at large its own code of behavior, whereby every Party member is required to report to his superior authority, not only on his own circumstances but also of those with whom he comes into contact. This is a system which the Russians, doubtless hypocritically, have asserted "creates worthless people, slanderers and careerists."[5] In this way, many an activist has brought himself to the attention of the Party organization, and launched himself on a career as a cadre or Party member.

The practice of criticism and self-criticism serves the same end. Whether it was ever anything other than a means of enforcing a spurious unity may be questioned. There can be little doubt that its disciplined use during *cheng-feng* at Yenan in 1942 forged a cohesive organization out of some very disparate human material, on the basis of a uniform ideology, which was essential to eventual Communist success. The point is, though, that there was then an element of voluntariness, insofar as those who were subjected to the process, or subjected themselves, may be presumed for the most part to have been convinced Communists, or at least adherents to the cause. Many of them had already made the trek to Yenan in preference to Chungking. After 1949, on the other hand, there was no longer any opportunity for the display of preferences. Criticism and self-criticism, as practiced on a national scale since then, can hardly be expected, even by Party leaders, to produce a monolithic unity of all ethnic and social groups across the length and breadth of the country. Ideological unity has been replaced

[5] Ibid.

by the minimum requirement of ideological conformity. The technique has the more practical purpose of ironing out the contradictions that arise in the body politic in the normal course of administration, and easing the introduction of new policies in accordance with the vicissitudes of the Party line. Conducted always at the Party's decree and under the Party's guidance, it is also a disciplinary instrument in directing criticism at selected targets, be they fallen leaders, such as Liu Shao-ch'i, or discredited policies. The cadre or citizen who wishes to avoid becoming a target himself will naturally take care to make his self-criticism sound convincing, and his criticism of the object of execration as wholehearted as possible.

The "united front" has undergone the same transmutation. At one time intended to unite all those who felt some affinity, whether their motives were revolutionary, patriotic, intellectual or simply personal, in establishing a national government and restoring some semblance of economic stability to the country, it has since become a device for harnessing the talents and supervising the political education of non-Party personnel of value to the regime, and particularly, of course, the intellectuals and technocrats. The history of the "united front" since 1949 is symbolized in the vicissitudes of the Chinese People's Political Consultative Conference (CPPCC), which was set up on the foundation of the regime as the institutional expression of Mao's *On New Democracy* (1940), and the highest representative assembly of the new state. Composed of delegates from every sector of national life, including the Party and the army, it drew up the *Common Program* and the *Organic Law of the Central People's Government* at its first session on September 29, 1949. With that, its usefulness seemed to have terminated, as the Party settled itself more securely into the seat of power. In 1954, when its role under the terms of the new Constitution was superseded by the National People's Congress, the CPPCC remained as a powerless appendix of the state, wherein were gathered members of the "democratic" (i.e., non-Communist) parties, and leading non-Party personages. Their only task in subsequent sessions, meeting concurrently with the National People's Congress, appears to have been to applaud, echo, and implement every decision of the Party and the state. Now, in the course of the cultural revolution, this body has vanished into limbo, together with the "united front" concept itself.

These palpable changes in style and content are, in fact, the Party's response to its changed circumstances since 1949. That is to say that, in practice, the Party's pretension to absolute power requires the extention of its political and administrative control, through methods of organization and operational techniques, over the whole of the population. In turn, this has led to a close structural involvement of the Party in all aspects of administration, and the creation of an ever-larger number of cadres to carry out the Party's unfolding program of socialization. In the Soviet Union, by 1936, the Party had become "the leading core of all organizations of the working people, both public and state."[6] The same is essentially true of the People's Republic of China where, in Mao's words, "The force at the core leading our cause forward is the Chinese Communist Party."[7] In many areas, this involvement has led to a duality of role in the Party and the state by the same individual, which is particularly marked at the higher levels. It is a method of organization that leads to an impressive concentration of power, enabling the Party to control the state machine in the person of the identical individuals in each sphere. Thus, it can be said that Mao and his half-dozen principal lieutenants in the Standing Committee of the Politburo represent the effective decision-making and coordinating group at the head of 750 million Chinese people.

The Power Structure

In this power structure the Chinese comrades have faithfully followed the Soviet model, and the pattern is one shared with other Communist regimes. The real test of the effectiveness of the Party-directed administration, however, comes at the intermediate and basic levels of command. Here the Chinese, as has happened in other Communist countries, have been faced with a constant search for the correct balance between centralization of authority and local initiative. This is a critical problem for all Communist regimes, and the solution is elusive. It also requires the perfection of devices of supervision at lower levels, which in turn increases the already formidable bureaucratic element. These problems arise as the ineluctable offshoot of a ruling Communist Party's involvement in administration. Having set itself up as the supreme arbiter of policy, the Party must then contrive the machinery to carry that policy out. In so doing, it is not surprising if, having smashed or emasculated the old bourgeois state machinery, it is obliged to replace it with itself. It is not surprising if, in the process, the Party becomes identified with the administration, whatever the theory may say about its "vanguard" role in society. Nor is it surprising that this provokes a host of unwelcome problems, in accentuating the bureaucratic tendencies of a Communist regime.

[6] Article 126, Constitution of the Union of Soviet Socialist Republics.

[7] Opening address at the first session of the First National People's Congress of the People's Republic of China, September 15, 1954, *Quotations from Chairman Mao Tse-tung,* Foreign Languages Press, Peking, 1966, p. 1.

Despite the experience of their seniors in the Communist Party of the Soviet Union, it cannot be said that the Chinese have had any greater success. They have fallen into the same trap. Neither has been able to steer a middle course in practice between detachment and excessive control, though both these faults are equally condemned. "Unfortunately," Khrushchev said at the Twentieth Congress of the CPSU in 1956, "many Party organizations draw an absurd distinction between Party political work and economic activity. . . . The CPSU is the ruling Party and everything that happens on our Soviet soil is of vital interest to the Party as a whole, and to each Communist. A Communist has no right to be a detached bystander. . . . This, of course, does not mean confusing the functions of Party bodies with those of economic agencies or the substitution of Party bodies for economic agencies."[8] Exactly the same dilemma faces the Chinese.

An attentive listener to Khrushchev was Liu Lan-t'ao, an alternate secretary in the Chinese Party's central secretariat, and a deputy secretary of its Control Commission. Three years later, in 1959, in an authoritative directive, he stated that some people "claimed that the Party could only render political-ideological leadership but not organisational leadership over non-Party organisations, lest it should interfere with the independence of these organisations. . . . Obviously, this kind of idea is absolutely wrong. In fact, there is no such thing as 'independence' from the leadership of the Communist Party. . . . Of course, this is not to say that the Party may monopolise all the daily work of government organs, civil groups, and other non-Party organisations, and mix up the difference in principle between the Party and these non-Party organisations."[9]

The close similarity of these comments cannot be thought to arise simply from notes taken by Liu Lan-t'ao three years before, and must therefore be attributed to a perennial dilemma of Communist parties in power. Nevertheless, there was no intention of relaxing the rigidity of Party control. The basic principle was comprehensively restated: "To assure the unified leadership of the Party it is necessary to place all revolutionary organisations—no matter whether they are government organs, army units, or civil groups, whether they are political and legal departments such as public security bureaux, courts and procuratorates, or departments in financial, economic, cultural, educational, scientific and public health fields—under the unified leadership of the Party Central Committee and local committees at various levels, in order to

[8] *Pravda,* February 15, 1956, quoted in M. Fainsod, *How Russia Is Ruled,* Cambridge, 1965, p. 239.

[9] "Chinese Communist Party Is Supreme Commander of Chinese People in Building Socialism," *Jen-min jih-pao,* September 28, 1959 (translated in Union Research Service, Hong Kong, Vol. 17, No. 5).

carry out the general line and general mission of the Party."[10] The hope, rather, seemed to be that the situation could be met by an adjustment in the working relationship of Party committees with non-Party organs, and in giving individual responsibility to qualified personnel within the context of collective leadership. This appeared to contain, like so many other aspects of Party administration in China, its own inherent contradiction.

If in the past the principle has been often flouted in practice in Party committees, where the secretary naturally tends to assume personal command, so in the state sphere, and particularly where it may involve the complicated relationship of technically qualified non-Party personnel working under the direction of ideologically trained but otherwise unqualified Party members, the tension has at times become acute. The system seems one almost guaranteed to produce the kind of friction it is designed to overcome. At the same time, of course, it is designed to ensure the maximum political control, if necessary at the expense of professional considerations. The advantage claimed for the system by Liu Lan-t'ao was that it ensured unified Party leadership over all aspects of administration, while simultaneously stimulating a sense of responsibility among non-Party personnel. That the latter may have become necessary owing to the inescapability of the former seems not to have occurred to him.

It was clear, however, that the Party's rejection of any compromise in this sphere had led, to a large degree, to the withering of state institutions and their replacement by the Party machine. This was demonstrated in various ways. In some areas, particularly at the level of local government, and in such organs as the *hsien* (county) people's councils, the state body had become an appendage of the local Party committee. At best, there was confusion between the jurisdiction of the two. In some central ministries the same situation prevailed. In the Ministry of Education for example, even directives of the State Council tended to be treated as less important and less urgent than those emanating directly from the Party. The problem of authority was acute. Some non-Party ministers had become mere figureheads in their own ministries. If there were exceptions, of ministers who had normal relations with the Party factions in their ministry, it was only as a result, as one minister admitted, of "a series of struggles."[11]

The root cause of all these problems of Party involvement in admin-

[10] Ibid. As a leading *apparatchik,* Liu has subsequently met his nemesis in the cultural revolution.

[11] Chang Nai-ch'i, Minister of Food, and Vice-President of the China Democratic National Construction Association. For these and other strictures on the Party's role in administration, see R. MacFarquhar, *The Hundred Flowers,* London, 1960, chapter 4.

istration was ably urged in 1957 by the leading journalist, Ch'u An-p'ing, editor of the *Kuang-ming jih-pao*. He drew the basic distinction between political direction and operational control. "I think a party leading a nation is not the same thing as a party owning a nation," he said, making the same point that Milovan Djilas was propounding at almost the same time in his theory of the Communist Party as a "new class." The Party had become the political expression of the collective ownership by a political bureaucracy of nationalized property. "Isn't it too much," Ch'u asked, "that within the scope of the nation there must be a Party man as leader in every unit, big or small, whether section or sub-section; or that nothing, big or small, can be done without a nod from a Party man? . . . I think this idea that the world belongs to the Party is at the root of all contradictions between the Party and non-Party people."[12] The Party's response, however, was swift. The flowers that bloomed in 1957 had became noxious weeds. In the following six weeks, Ch'u An-p'ing had resigned, had been criticized by his son, and made a public confession of error. The Party's monopoly of control in every sphere was not negotiable.

This goes to the heart of the crisis encountered in China in recent years, and the cultural revolution itself. Either a stable working environment is created, where the man with the knowhow can get on with the job, where responsibility is matched by authority, where there is scope for technical skills, initiative is suitably rewarded, opportunities correspond as far as possible with professional merit, and where administration and production are conducted on rational and impersonal —that is, on bureaucratic, Weberian lines; or, everything is subjected to Marxist analysis and ideological criteria, class struggle and revolutionary virtues are accentuated, political priorities predominate, even in a factory, and as a consequence Party members are the people with the authority, the people who count in any given situation.

This is to state the alternatives rather starkly. In fact, there is some compromise. The exact balance at any particular time may vary, depending on the state of the economy or the strength of the Party and its domestic campaigns. The stratification of income and status fostered by the elevation of professional criteria may need balancing by a reassertion of ideological motivation and an emphasis on the political virtues. Broadly speaking, the professional alternative was stressed during the years of the first five year plan (1953–57), under Russian influence, and again in 1961–62, in the aftermath of the "great leap forward" and the failure of the communes. The political drive that accompanied these latter campaigns in the years 1958–60 was increasingly in evidence after 1962, culminating in the frenzy of the cultural revolu-

[12] Ibid.

tion.[13] The guidelines of "class struggle, production struggle and scientific experiment," which are supposed to have governed domestic policies in recent years, and which reflect the chastening experience of the Party early in the last decade, would seem to be a nice paper compromise which is frequently difficult to achieve in practice. This continual search for a workable compromise can sometimes lead to the combination of ultimately incompatible elements, such as those expressed in "the principle of integrating politics in command and material incentive."[14]

THE CRUX OF THE CONTROVERSY: "RED" VS. "EXPERT"

This conflict between the "red" and the "expert" is the most disruptive possible for a Communist administration. Much as it may desire modernization and the adoption of scientific techniques in management and production, the Party is unable to tolerate the political and social concomitants of economic development. This is an area where it faces defeat, for economic development appears in many respects to be at odds with revolutionary fervor and momentum. One profits at the expense of the other.[15] This is the crux of the controversy in China. It also lies at the heart of much controversy between the Russians and Chinese. If the Soviet Union is now a "revisionist" power, this has much to do with reliance on the more remote economic levers of monetary incentives and the adoption of profitability as an index of industrial efficiency. It is, surely, more than a coincidence that the first duty of a Party member in the Soviet Union relates to productivity, techniques, and skills. If China, on the other hand, is still a "revolutionary" power, even though it may have taken a cultural revolution to achieve it, this has very much to do with the elevation of political values (enshrined in Mao's thought) throughout the country, the managerial role of Party committees in the factories, and a revulsion from the notion that the

[13] These periods have been called, respectively, "bureaucratic" and "campaign" phases. See M. Oksenberg, "The Institutionalisation of the Chinese Communist Revolution: The Ladder of Success on the Eve of the Cultural Revolution," *China Quarterly,* No. 36, Oct.–Dec. 1968, pp. 61–92.

[14] This was the formula adopted at the first National Political Work Conference for Industry and Communications, as reported by Peking Radio on April 3, 1964 (*SWB,* FE/1521).

[15] For a somewhat contrary view, see R. W. Lee, "The *Hsia-Fang* System: Marxism and Modernisation," *China Quarterly,* No. 28, Oct.–Dec. 1966, pp. 40–62.

possessor of technical qualifications is any more valuable, or entitled to any greater rewards, than a humble peasant. It is, surely, more than a coincidence that the first duty of a Party member in China is to study and apply the doctrines of Marx, Lenin and Mao.

This whole question has its great significance for the administrators who run the country, both inside and outside the Party, the Chinese cadres who are the executors of policy decided by the Politburo. For them, it must often be difficult to establish their priorities. The cadre concept and cadre training and techniques are something particularly owed to the pre-1949 epoch, when Mao had before him the Russian, and especially the Stalinist, example of Party-building and cadre deployment. If the ideal is something closer to a guerrilla leader than an office-bound administrator, then clearly the amount and value of work done is not to be measured by the number of papers shuffled into the out-basket. How should, say, officials of a Ministry of Machine-Building maintain revolutionary fervor in dealing with the technical requirements of their department? Some nice distinctions must be drawn, and some fine interpretations given to their instructions. With experience they can presumably learn to interpret all these in the way intended, sensitive to every nuance and change of emphasis. Success will depend on a correct sense of timing and anticipation. The official must know the mind of his superior in the hierarchy, though his obedience must not be so unquestioning as to lead to his undoing when the policy changes. He is, after all, expendable, and can conveniently be blamed when things go wrong. This is a system where the man with strong convictions, unless it be in the Party's infallibility, will not last long. It is a system which favors the clever rather than the good. Even so, he must be very clever to survive—a Mikoyan rather than a Voznesensky, or a Chou En-lai rather than a Liu Shao-Ch'i.

Nor is it a question of policy alone. Additional recruitment and the growth of a larger and larger cadre force bring their own problems of momentum. Sheer bureaucratic bulk may actually impede the efficient execution of Party policies, especially by the time the directives have reached the lower levels. The bureaucracy itself becomes a factor in the power structure, and it is in a very strategic position to influence the course of events. Concessions may have to be made to it, and consciously or not, policies may be tailored to its predilections and capacity. Generally speaking, it can look forward to constant expansion, and a consequent extension of its power, as a direct result of the Party's monopoly of power and decision-making. Despite attempts in China to prune this growth through administrative decentralization, and the *hsia-fang* (send-down) movements for state and Party officials, involving their demotion to lower levels and employment in manual labor, the numbers of cadres have continued to rise. The definition of a "cadre" in China is notoriously imprecise, and the official figures would seem to be somewhat narrowly defined, as cadres in "Party and government work." In 1949, there were claimed to be 720,000.[16] By 1956, the year of the Party Congress, there were over 5 million.[17] If the numerous activists, and cadres of mass organizations and rural production units, were included, the resultant figure would be a much more meaningful guide to the bureaucratization of the Communist Chinese regime since 1949. By 1963, there were 20 million cadres leading production work in the countryside alone.[18] Their total number today, in all categories, must run into tens of millions. This development lends further force to the Weberian dictum that, in socialism, "the dictatorship of the official and not that of the worker is on the march."[19]

The Party itself has greatly increased in size. The last official figure, 17 million, was given in a speech by Liu Shao-ch'i in 1961, on the occasion of the fortieth anniversary of the Chinese Communist Party.[20] By 1964, according to *Pravda,* membership had reached 18 million.[21] Subsequent reports of further recruitment in various provinces, and in the army, may well indicate an additional 2 million by 1966.[22] Thus, on the eve of the cultural revolution the Party membership in China had reached its highest figure of some 20 million. While recent events have undoubtedly caused some decimation in the ranks, it is still the case that the approximately 20 million members of the largest Communist Party in the world form the core and base of the Chinese bureaucracy. Of these, only 3.4 million, or 17 percent, belonged to the Party prior to 1949. Significantly, nearly 17 million, or 83 percent, joined the Party after it had come to power, and the majority of these joined after the start of the five-year plan in 1953.[23] Human nature being what it is, it is perhaps not over-cynical to see in this the material attractions of Party membership, nor quite irrelevant to infer the comparative appeals of revolution or career prospects. This, in fact, was precisely the point

[16] New China News Agency (NCNA), September 30, 1952.

[17] Derived from figures given in speech by Tsai Chang, first secretary of the Women's Work Committee of the Party, in *Eighth National Congress of the CCP,* Peking 1956, Vol. II (Speeches), p. 280.

[18] Editorial, *Jen-min jih-pao,* July 4, 1963. See also, my review in *China Quarterly,* No. 16, Oct.–Dec. 1963, pp. 157–59.

[19] *Der Sozialismus,* quoted in Gerth and Mills, *From Max Weber,* London, 1964, p. 50.

[20] NCNA, June 30, 1961.

[21] As broadcast on Moscow Radio, *SWB,* SU/1541.

[22] Provincial broadcasts from Anhwei, Heilungkiang, Hopei, Shansi, Shanghai, Sinkiang, Szechuan and Tibet, in *SWB,* FE/2207.

[23] Derived from the percentage figures given by Liu Shao-ch'i in 1961, when membership was seventeen million. He said 80 percent of these had joined since 1949, and 70 percent since 1953.

made by the Party's Secretary-General, Teng Hsiao-p'ing, in his report on the new Party constitution in 1956, when he said, "In the past, a person's decision to join our Party generally meant that he was prepared to struggle, at the risk of his personal freedom and even his very life, for the interests of the masses and for the supreme ideal of human society. Nowadays, however, it is more likely to find people who have joined the Party for the sake of prestige and position."[24] Membership of the Party in China, as elsewhere, bestows power and prestige on the recipients, as well as increases the conveniences of daily life and opens the avenues for promotion. The 20 million, in a population of 750 million, are an elite corps of which the over 3 million older members form a ruling stratum.

Within the Party's own bureaucracy the same trend has been marked. This is a pyramid whose apex grows with its base. The self-administration of the Party has become more complicated and more demanding. In 1956, when the total membership was 10.7 million, Teng Hsiao-p'ing pointed out that there were over 300,000 Party cadres above the rank of county Party committee members. The ratio of general Party membership to cadres at that level was 36 to 1. "Nevertheless," he added, "there is a universal feeling that there are not enough of them."[25] No official figure for this ratio has since been published, though it can only have been altered upwards by the increase in membership and in Party branches.

The Russians appear to have no comprehensive information either. Perhaps only the Albanians know. However, the Soviet journal *Party Life* referred to this question in 1964 in the following words: "It is well known that the less Party democracy there is, the more numerous the Party apparatus becomes. In no Communist Party is there such a vast apparatus as in the CCP."[26] The article cited three examples by way of illustration. In the Fushun coalfield, in 1960, there were evidently 3,500 Party members and over 100 full-time Party cadres. The ratio in this case was 35 to 1. At the Shanghai diesel works, there were 510 Communists and 25 full-time Party workers, or a ratio of 20 to 1. While at Anshan, 24,000 Party members had no fewer than 2,500 full-time Party and non-Party cadres to look after them. This rather different ratio was, roughly, 10 to 1. Admittedly, this is not much to go on. It would seem to be little better or worse than the Soviet Union, say, in 1922, when the ratio was 25 to 1.[27] We may also contrast Teng Hsiao-p'ing's figure of 300,000 leading cadres in the Party in 1956 with Stalin's enumeration of the equivalent ruling caste in the Soviet Union

[24] *Eighth National Congress,* Vol. I, p. 91.
[25] Ibid., p. 220.
[26] See note 2.
[27] M. Fainsod, op. cit., 180.

in 1937, as comprising up to 200,000 people.[28] In total numbers, of course, the Chinese Party apparatus is much bigger. If a modest ratio of twenty members to one full-time Party cadre is assumed, the CCP would have a million full-time cadres on its rolls. The essential situation, however, was well expressed in the *Party Life* article: "In recent years the Chinese press has publicized less and less about the questions of Party life, and only touched on methods of Party leadership. This is becoming virtually a closed question, and some sort of military secret."

There is then the problem of ordering and controlling this huge bureaucracy of cadres throughout the country. The great growth in the size and diversity of the cadre force since 1949 has drawn attention, first of all, to the question of demarcation. The recruitment of cadres with varying qualifications at different times on thc basis of shifting criteria, such as technical expertise, ideology, age, or provincial or racial origin, forced a reorganization of the Party's administrative arrangements by 1956. At the Eighth Party Congress that year, Teng Hsiao-p'ing announced, "In the Party's work of administering cadres an important improvement in the last few years has been the division of administration according to rank and department so as to coordinate it with the work of political and professional inspection and supervision."[29] This presumably referred to appropriate division of work within the Party's Organization Department, rather than separate responsibility by each department of the Secretariat for cadres in its own field. The Chinese here inherited the problem faced by the CPSU in 1930. The first five-year plan, the socialization of industry and commerce and the collectivization of agriculture created an unprecedented demand for cadres. The bottleneck caused by centralized administration delayed their placement, and hindered the Party's work of supervision and control. The CCP's answer, apparently, was to adopt the Soviet solution, introduced by Kaganovitch at the Sixteenth Congress of the CPSU in 1930, for the streamlining of the Organization Department into several functional subsections. This rearrangement by 1956 paralleled, and in fact preceded, the broad decentralization of state administration the following year. Whether the new structure was still found satisfactory in the commune movement in 1958, or whether subsequent experience led to a constant search for a workable balance between centralized control of cadres and decentralization of administration, similar to the experiments in the Soviet Union over the years, there is insufficient information to judge. The destruction of much of the Party's machinery, including the Secretariat, in the cultural revolution will certainly leave scope for innovation in reconstituting the Party's authority. This point

[28] Ibid., p. 132.
[29] *Eighth National Congress,* Vol. I, pp. 221–22.

was deliberately left vague in the new constitution adopted at the Ninth Party Congress in April 1969, and which, without any specific reference to a secretariat, simply stated that "a number of necessary organs, which are compact and efficient, shall be set up to attend to the day-to-day work of the Party, the government and army in a centralized way."[30]

If centralization, however, is to remain a key principle, then the same pattern of hierarchical authority and demarcation can be expected to reemerge. Bureaucracy brings in its train such relevant questions as pay and status, tenure and promotion, and requires some measure of rank and scale. This problem had already arisen in China in the course of the first five-year plan. As in the Soviet Union under Stalin, it was found that the promotion and transfer of cadres was best facilitated on the basis of job ranking and salary scale. Thus a whole-scale process of stratification was officially sanctified in 1955, with the introduction of a comprehensive scale of salaries covering every cadre in the country, including the Army, and with "every little rung on all the multiple steep ladders of authority marked out with bizarre precision."[31] This salary structure has been a feature of Communist rule in China. It is paralleled by the division of the industrial work force into graded wage differentials, between industries as between individuals, patterned on the Soviet model. The integration of salaries and status by 1955, therefore, implicitly conceded the importance of material incentives for cadre morale and performance. This attitude received definitive expression in the major wage reform of the following year when workers in strategic industries, intellectuals, and administrative staff received salary increases of 10–18 percent.[32] Party cadres, too, received their salaries from the State on the same basis.

This was an extremely important development in confirming and contributing to the metamorphosis of the Chinese Communist Party. It marked a tendency that, if unchecked and allowed to grow, might have led, and was leading, to "revisionism" in the Party's ideology and the bureaucratization of administration in China. The sudden decision to communize in 1958, to emphasize the "red," to restore payment in kind in preference to cash, to abolish piece rates, and to rely on mass participation instead of individual expertise, can be seen in this context

[30] Chapter 4, Article 9. This constitution is remarkable for its brevity, containing only twelve Articles altogether, compared with sixty in its predecessor, and seventy-one in the equivalent Soviet document.

[31] I. Deutscher, *The Prophet Outcast: Trotsky, 1929–40,* London, 1963, p. 299. See my article, "Social Stratification," *Problems of Communism,* Vol. XVII, March–April 1968, pp. 14–20.

[32] See speech by the Minister of Labor, Ma Wen-jui, to the National People's Congress in June 1956, *Current Background* (U. S. Consulate General, Hong Kong), No. 405.

as an attempt to halt the trend. The failure of these policies then gave way to a further growth of the stratification process in the years of comparative laissez-faire after 1961, and in the planned development of the economy in a new five-year plan due to begin in 1966. It is, surely, significant that on both occasions, in 1958 and again in 1966, the beginning of a five-year plan was overwhelmed by a Mao-inspired mass movement throughout the country.

The Conflict of Ideas Within the Party Leadership

These divergent policies point to the acute conflict of ideas that has assailed the Chinese leadership in recent years. The conflict came out into the Party arena at the Lushan plenum of the Central Committee of the Party in 1959. The failure of the "great leap" strategy encouraged its opponents, not only in the Central Committee but also at lower levels of leadership, who took heart from the results achieved by the more pragmatic policies that then ensued. Their opposition was aroused again, however, when it become increasingly clear after 1962 that what was intended—not least, by Mao himself—was a further return to political over administrative priorities. Delaying action and attempts to assume the leadership of the new political movement were insufficient, as it proved, to deter the Maoists from launching an all-out offensive in 1966 against this stubborn internal resistance. There was then no possibility of averting civil war within the Party. The wounds opened in 1959 had not only not healed, but they had festered. Presented as a conflict between Marxist and "revisionist" ideas, or the proletarian road versus the capitalist, the cultural revolution in fact developed along sternly Leninist organizational lines, with control of the apparatus as the prize.[33] Personnel have been appointed, and as suddenly removed. Rival organizations have been set up. There has seldom been a stranger injunction by the leader of a Communist Party than Mao's, to "bombard the headquarters."[34]

It is important to remember that even after his removal as head of

[33] "The main target of the revolution under the dictatorship of the proletariat is the bourgeois headquarters hidden within the apparatus of this dictatorship. It is against this Section . . . that we are making revolution." Editorial, *Hung-ch'i,* No. 13, 1967, in *Peking Review,* August 11, 1967, p. 7.

[34] Mao's *ta-tse-pao* (big-character poster) appeared with this inscription on August 5, 1966.

state in 1959, Mao remained leader of the Party, and it is in this capacity, however nominal, that he has attacked the Party in the cultural revolution. It is easy to dismiss this as a power struggle for unchallenged control of the machine, dressed up in ideological terms. On the other hand, if Mao's control was incomplete, this casts doubt on the reality of his leadership. In either case, to launch an attack on the Party bureaucracy without at the same time calling Mao's own leadership into question was a somewhat delicate and risky undertaking. With the help of considerable hindsight, and on the basis of Maoist charges against Liu Shao-ch'i, it is possible to postulate the long-term existence of dual loyalties and a dual concept of Party organization in China, that until 1958 at the least lived out an uneasy compromise.[35] The suggestion here is that while Liu is the real Bolshevik, the elitist, and organization man of the Party, Mao has always placed greater faith in mass action and the Party's links with the masses. None of this, however, invalidates the thesis that a struggle for power within the Party is the main content of the cultural revolution. More credibly, one may see Mao not as a Dubcek-style reformer attempting to create a more popular image for the Party and its policies, but as a die-hard centralist, bent on creating a new structure built around his personality and doctrines. Mao's actions closely resemble the Stalinist precedent in the Soviet Union, and in many respects appear designed less to build a strong Party in his own image than to weaken it as an obstacle to his own undiluted power.[36] Certainly, the existence of an enormous Chinese bureaucracy can be seen as a cumbersome and immobilizing influence on national life, less pliable and more resistant to personal manipulation, jealous of its prerogatives, and increasingly ill-adapted for a revolutionary role. Like Stalin, Mao first presided over the creation of this bureaucracy, and then fell upon it. In reaching outside the Party, to the Red Guards and the army, and his personal entourage, there is a striking parallel between the methods of Mao and Stalin.

In the circumstances, the whole operating code of the apparatus is vitiated. The basic postulate of democratic centralism is unity at the top which is enforceable at every lower level. There is no reason to suppose that Mao is any less attached to this principle than Liu Shao-ch'i. Failing this, the Party becomes subject to the same factional activity and the same ideological latitude as may characterize its bourgeois rivals

[35] For a discussion of this, see the contribution by J. W. Lewis to the article, "The Roles of the Monolithic Party Under the Totalitarian Leader," *China Quarterly,* No. 40. Oct.–Dec. 1969, pp. 50–57.

[36] Leonard Schapiro, ibid., pp. 46–49, and Conclusion, pp. 61–64. See also, his article, "Reflections on the Changing Role of the Party in the Totalitarian Polity," *Studies in Comparative Communism,* Vol. 2, No. 2, April 1969, pp. 1–13.

in democratic states. Whether democratic centralism is, in fact, not best suited to activity of a revolutionary and conspiratorial kind is a question that is not irrelevant to the administrative approach of a Communist Party in power. It raises the further question, as to whether a Communist Party that surrendered its Leninist principles of organization would necessarily cease to be Communist. To strike at its organization is to strike at the powerful heart of a Leninist party. It may then have to rely less on the strength of its apparatus and more on the persuasiveness of its ideas. So long as the dispute is unresolved, the warring elements represent alternative policies and a rudimentary approach to a two-party system. To Communist parties as at present constituted, however, this appears as the kiss of death. To submit themselves and their policies to any genuine form of electoral approval might imperil their position. So long as the Party, in the countries where it has come to power, continues to demand an absolute monopoly of decision-making and policy formulation, joined to unquestioning obedience from its members, so long will it continue to face disturbing and apparently insoluble problems in the region of production-planning, administrative decentralization and bureaucratic solidification. So far, it has merely reacted to these problems, without any attempt at a long-term solution in terms of its own internal Party structure. Thus, there is a built-in tension between the centralized apparatus and the increasingly pluralistic development of the economy and of society.

The Party is, therefore, likely to continue to be the object of active or passive resistance. While its monopoly of control, backed where necessary by military forces, makes it unlikely that this resistance could get out of hand, the possibility becomes a probability that whatever changes take place will do so, first and foremost, within the apparatus. The Party itself then becomes the forum of conflict, rather than any external battle-ground. This is precisely what has happened in China, in the cultural revolution. To the question why, if there are so many stresses and strains in the apparatus, does it not fall apart, the answer is that it has. The disarray in the Party leadership is the reflection of the tension and dissension that afflicts administration at much lower levels, and that is found in every sphere of national life.

In domestic terms, the Maoist injunction to "make revolution" ensures a continuance of turmoil. Class struggle is to continue under the dictatorship of the proletariat, and its focus is the individual. As so often in the past in China, classes are equated less with social background than with ideological standpoint. The class struggle, therefore, even reaches into the Party, notwithstanding the orthodox definition of the Party as the vanguard of the proletariat. Class enemies may be found within the instrument of proletarian dictatorship as well as without. The Maoist equation of "revisionism" with "capitalism," whereby even the former President of Communist China can be called a "capitalist-roader," is doubtless an oversimplification, yet not totally devoid of content. If the hallmarks of a Marxist-Leninist revolutionary are a fanatical sense of universal mission, and a resolute refusal to compromise with the class enemy wherever he may be found, these are surely more characteristic of Mao than of Kosygin. They are explicit in Mao's doctrines, and the acid test of a revolutionary in China, as opposed to a revisionist, has become his adherence to the thought of Mao Tse-tung. It might be added that the same test is applied by Maoists to members of foreign Communist parties as well. To postulate the end of class struggle, to claim that the Party has become the Party of the whole people, as has been done in the Soviet Union, is tantamount to going over to the enemy. In Maoist eyes it is the same symptom of surrender as a policy of "peaceful coexistence" with states with differing social systems. This identification of revisionism with capitalism and imperialism then makes intelligible the constant Chinese claims that the Soviet Union is "in collusion" with the United States, in Vietnam, over the nuclear test-ban treaty, at the United Nations, militarily, politically, and diplomatically.[37]

There is no hiding the fact, however, that the development of the economy and of society in China since 1949 closely follows the Soviet pattern. Indeed, it was precisely Mao's appraisal of this growing internal "revisionism" that led him to the cultural revolution. After twenty years, the country is already some way along the "revisionist" road. The changes in the character of the Party, and the growing bureaucratization of the apparatus, have already been referred to. Almost every charge made by the Maoist leadership against the revisionist Soviet Union can find a parallel in China. These include the use of economic incentives in industrial and agricultural production, wage grades and bonuses, the relaxation of restrictions on private plots and livestock, extending loans for promoting private production, the allocation of land and fixing production quotas on the basis of work teams, encouragement of the profit motive in free markets, class stratification, growing wage differentials between cadres, technicians and ordinary workers, and commercial agreements with firms in capitalist countries.[38] Further charges extend into the field of education and cultural policy, the oppressive use of State machinery, and Party membership and composition. The point is not that Russia is "revisionist" while China is

[37] It will be interesting, in this context, to see how the Chinese Communist media treat the current development of China's relations with the Nixon administration. Russia's hostility to this unexpected liaison is already plain.

[38] *How the Soviet Revisionists Carry Out All-Round Restoration of Capitalism in the U.S.S.R.*, Foreign Languages Press, Peking, 1968.

"revolutionary," but that both exhibit these characteristics of revisionism to a marked degree.

This must raise once more the question of Mao's contribution to this development. For the first ten years of the Chinese People's Republic, when China wholeheartedly adopted the Russian aid and technical advice, Mao was head of both the Party and the State. The fact that thereafter he realized the potential political and ideological dangers attendant on this development cannot obscure his primary responsibility. The charges now laid at the door of Liu Shao-ch'i, Teng Hsiao-p'ing, and other leaders are not, therefore, wholly convincing.

Since the radical break with Soviet policies was made in 1958, it is arguable that it was only then, and particularly after the 1957 Moscow conference, that Mao became aware of the extent of the doctrinal revisionism that succeeded Stalin's death in the Soviet Union. That is not to ignore the interplay of personal and nationalist influences that later turned a crack into a chasm, but it is to suggest that the initial impetus was ideological. In this case, Mao's apparent lack of qualms about the evident bureaucratization and nationalism that had already evolved in the Soviet Union under Stalin can only be explained in terms of China's comparative weakness, Stalin's personal prestige, and possibly, a predilection of Mao in favor of centralized control and personal authority as outweighing other unwelcome tendencies. Once these factors had changed, the latent and growing hostility of Mao to the pattern of evolution in the Soviet Union was given free rein. This analysis, therefore, lends further support to the characterization of Mao as a Chinese Stalin, presiding over a growth of bureaucracy, state power and social stratification, to the extent that he retains the means of their manipulation through the use of extra-Party and personal instrumentalities.

The metamorphosis of the Chinese Communist Party is, therefore, likely to continue under Mao as it has in the past, and in response to the same processes of economic and social complexity that have arisen in the Soviet Union. Mao's preoccupation with ideology and the political superstructure in the cultural revolution has not only deepened the divisions in national life, but has, curiously, left virtually unscathed those underlying features in the economy and society that are thought to give rise to revisionism. Already, the element of centralized control and personal authority has been severely weakened by the events of the past five years. Mao's death will remove the last break on the accelerated tempo of change that must inevitably ensue under his successors. A reconstituted Party under new leadership may then endorse the definitive emergence of Communist China from its revolutionary phase. The real victor of the cultural revolution is not Mao, but Liu Shao-ch'i, and those forces of bureaucratic and Party solidification that he has come to represent. Time, in China, is on the side of the "revisionists."

THE FALL OF NOVOTNÝ IN CZECHOSLOVAKIA

H. Gordon Skilling

THE deepening political crisis in Czechoslovakia in the sixties resulted from the failure of the Novotný regime to deal adequately with a series of acute problems and from the growing awareness of the fundamental flaws in the political system. This culminated in the fall and winter of 1967 when the crisis first permeated the topmost organs of the Communist party of Czechoslovakia. In meetings of the Central Committee and Presidium from September on, the division of opinion among the members became ever sharper and more serious. Largely unknown to the general public, or even to the mass of party members, a furious debate, unique in the history of these bodies, raged. The central issue was defined, in somewhat euphemistic terms, as "the cumulation of functions," in other words, the holding of more than one post by a single person. In fact, the discussions centered on the question as to whether Antonín Novotný should continue to be first secretary of the party as well as President of the Republic. Moreover, the entire work of the party under his leadership and the basic weaknesses of the political system as a whole came under vigorous attack. The members of the leading organs divided into distinctly separate camps, with some favoring, and others opposing, a basic change in the party's methods of action. A long, hard, defensive struggle, waged in vain by Novotný and his supporters, ended in early January with his ouster as first secretary and his replacement by Alexander Dubček.

The clash of the contending forces occurred at the sessions of the Central Committee (CC) at the end of October 1967, in late December, and in early January 1968, and in intervening meetings of the Presidium.[1] The threat to Novotný's position was, however, heralded at

From *Canadian Slavonic Papers,* XII, 3 (Fall 1970). Reprinted by permission.

[1] Nothing is known with certainty about the Presidium meetings. The

earlier meetings. Even in February, critical voices were raised within the ranks of the Central Committee, to the great dissatisfaction of Novotný. In particular, Maria Sedláková, editor-in-chief of the Bratislava *Pravda,* blamed the passivity of the masses squarely on "those who are responsible for the management of the fate of society." Others, including Černík, were critical of the party's work.[2] The crisis deepened in the summer, when the party was openly challenged during the Writers' Congress.[3] Soon thereafter Novotný resolved to take the offensive. In a speech on 1 September he declared: "Our democracy is a class democracy, and our freedom is a class one. Only the Communist

---

minutes of the CC meetings, covering some 1,500 pages, have not been published. Two months after the change of leadership, on 4 March 1968, the Presidium issued, for party use, a 19-page summary of the issues involved in the discussions but deliberately avoided identifying the position taken by individual CC members. This was published only in 1969, in a collection of decisions and documents relating to 1968, *Rok šedesátý osmý v usneseních a dokumentech UV KSC* (Prague, 1969) (henceforth cited as *R.š.o.*), pp. 7–25. A fuller report based on the minutes, and citing some speakers briefly, was published in a series of articles in *Život strany and Pravda* (Bratislava)—"How It Was in January," by V. Mencl and F. Ouředník. Excerpts are given in R. A. Remington (ed.) *Winter in Prague, Documents on Czechoslovak Communism in Crisis* (Cambridge, Mass., and London, England, 1969), pp. 18–39. See *Život strany,* no. 14 to 19, July, August, and September 1968. An even fuller analysis, by V. Mencl alone, was issued in printed form, but not for public circulation, by the party's Ideological Department, under the title "The Historic January Plenum," in a booklet, *50 let Ceskoslovenska 1918–1968* (Prague, October 1968), pp. 66–125. Another version, also based on the minutes but dealing primarily with December and January, was published abroad in the Journal *Svědectví* (Paris), IX, no. 34, 35, 36 (Winter 1969), 147–82 (henceforth cited as *Svědectví*). A briefer version of this, by Pavel Tigrid, the editor of *Svědectví,* is given in his article "Czechoslovakia: a Post-Mortem," *Survey,* No. 73 (Autumn 1969), pp. 133–64 (first part). The Mencl and *Svědectví* reports are selective and do not give an entirely clear picture of the course of the discussions. They differ in many respects but on the whole corroborate each other. The following is based mainly on these two sources, which are cited, however, only where it seems desirable. Although the Mencl chapter and the joint Mencl-Ouředník articles are in many cases the same, citations are made, where necessary, from the fuller, Mencl chapter. In most cases the same material is also to be found in the published articles.

[2] Mencl, op. cit., pp. 82–83.

[3] See Z. A. B. Zeman, *Prague Spring: A Report on Czechoslovakia 1968* (Harmondsworth, 1969), chap. 3; Pavel Tigrid, *Le printemps de Prague* (Paris, 1968), pp. 141–70.

party, and not this or that group that thinks of itself in this role, is called upon to follow and direct the political process, and where necessary, to correct inadequacies and errors . . ."[4] In retrospect, this important address can be regarded as a clear signal of the intended renewal of a hard-line policy which would include stringent measures against dissidents.[5]

This counterattack manifested itself openly at the CC plenum at the end of September, when punitive actions were taken against certain writers and *Literární noviny,* the organ of the Writers' Union. An aggressive tone pervaded almost all the speeches, particularly that of Jiří Hendrych, the party's ideological chief, who condemned the "oppositional" and even "anti-Communist" character of the Writers' Congress and of *Literární noviny* and asserted the necessity of "class freedom," not "abstract freedom."[6] On the surface it seemed that Novotný had carried the day, since the overwhelming majority of the Central Committee endorsed the severe measures and hence approved the "hard line." There were, however, voices raised in opposition, and in an event previously unheard of, several votes were reportedly cast against the proposed actions.[7] Although this was a small, almost token opposition, it was significant as the first instance of open resistance on the floor of the Central Committee, and an example for the future.

Meanwhile, discussions were taking place within the party, at all levels, in preparation for the CC session which was to be held in late October and which was to consider, *inter alia,* the official draft "Theses on the Position and the Leading Role of the Party in the Present Stage of Development of Our Socialist Society." Although this twenty-odd-page document was not made public, either then or later, it was presumably circulated within the party for discussion. Extensive materials poured into Prague headquarters from the party organizations, embodying many criticisms of the work of the party and proposals for re-

[4] *Rudé právo,* 2 September 1968. See also Mencl, op. cit., pp. 83–84.

[5] Mencl (pp. 85–86) describes the secret directives of the eighth department of the CC apparatus supervising state administration, especially the army, security, and the courts, for an offensive against anti-socialist elements in literary and scientific circles. See also J. Kokoška, "How It Was in the Army," *A-Revue,* no. 12, June 1968, pp. 28ff.

[6] See *Rudé právo,* 28, 29, 30 September 1968, for the published speeches.

[7] Vodsloň is reported to have been one of those who openly opposed the actions taken (Mencl, op. cit., p. 83). Others who opposed may have been Slavík and Kadlec, but no opposition speeches were published, and no negative votes recorded. In a moderate speech, Dubček criticized the failure to implement party decisions concerning the proper exploitation of Slovak economic resources. *Rudé právo,* 29 September 1967, transl. in R. A. Remington (ed.), op. cit., pp. 13–16.

form.[8] However, in a speech in mid-October to district and regional secretaries, Novotný made it quite clear that he was not ready to make any serious concessions to the growing desire for reform. He declared that "the party would exercise its leading role everywhere, and would use those measures which it recognized as suitable in each concrete case." He rejected what he termed non-Leninist conceptions of the party's role, according to which the party was to carry out "predominantly, or even exclusively, so-called conceptual (*koncepční*) work, the elaboration of objectives and program, and politico-ideological activity," whereas other organs, such as the government, had "the task of carrying out their own directing and so-called operational activity."[9]

When Hendrych presented a sketch of the discussion materials and presumably the draft Theses to the October plenum, he did so in a form that apparently differed from that originally approved by the Presidium. Although this introductory statement was also not published at the time, or later, its content and presumably that of the draft Theses, may be roughly deduced from an article published by Hendrych in a subsequent number of the party's organ *Život strany*.[10] The emphasis was laid on "the need to deepen the leading role of the party" in order to meet the needs arising out of the technical and scientific revolution and the new economic system, and to overcome the "passivity of some Communists." Recognizing that in domestic affairs the "class struggle" had ceased to be the main motive force, Hendrych proclaimed the requirement of "a regulating force which will combine varied interests in a single current of action by the whole of society." In international affairs, where a bitter class struggle of the two opposing systems persisted, the mission of the party was to develop "socialist class consciousness and international feeling." Although the need to replace outdated methods by new ones was stressed, almost no concrete indication was given, at least in this published version, as to what was to be changed, except for the greater use of "science," including the social sciences, in the management of society, a better implementation of party decisions, and an improvement in the party's inner life. In general, the report did not suggest that any significant change in prevailing political procedures was contemplated, but rather that party control would be strengthened. It was bound to awaken great dissatisfaction among those bent on achieving thorough reforms.

Bitter and sharp discussion, unknown in previous CC meetings, was

[8] See R. Bajalski, *Borba* (Belgrade), 9 January 1968. None of this was published, so that it is impossible to know how the Theses compared with this material from the lower party organs and how far the Theses went in advocating specific reform.

[9] Mencl, op. cit., pp. 86–87.

[10] No. 24, November 1967, pp. 1–4.

touched off by Alexander Dubček, First Secretary of the Slovak Communist Party, who openly criticized Novotný for the use of materials different from those approved by the Presidium, and who proceeded to deliver a comprehensive critique of the party's methods of operation. Although he referred approvingly to the Theses as raising "the historically significant questions," Dubček found fault with it for failing to deal adequately with many issues, and himself drew on materials submitted by certain regional party organizations, in particular those of South Moravia and East Slovakia. He proclaimed the need for the party to exercise a leading role, but stressed the urgency of a "fundamental turn," and "essential changes in the work of the party," in line with what he termed the qualitatively new stage of society's development. The party must "lead, not direct, society." "The government must govern. . . ." Treading on more delicate ground, he warned that the danger of conservatism was no less than that of "the liberal tendency" and advocated "a struggle of old and new," "progressive and conservative," a struggle which, he said, would involve "concrete people." It was essential, he concluded, "to clarify the relations of work in the central organs, to make some further demands on the work of the Central Committee, to work out a long-term party program, and to adopt a standpoint on the cumulation of functions in the highest organs of the party, government, National Assembly, and the national economy generally." Dubček also spoke at some length on the Slovak question, emphasizing both the indispensability for full national equality of Czechs and Slovaks and for unity of Czechoslovak "statehood" and recommending a new program in nationality relations. With this speech, which stressed the urgency for basic changes and openly raised the sensitive question of the duplication of jobs at the highest level, Dubček had thrown the gauntlet to Novotný.[11]

The subsequent debate revealed that Dubček was not alone in his discontent. Other speakers, notably Sedláková and F. Kriegel, described the serious situation in which the party found itself, and the need for drastic change.[12] When Martin Vaculík, a candidate member of the Presidium, criticized Dubček, imputing "personal" motives for his attitude, it became obvious for the first time that there was division within

[11] Mencl, op. cit., pp. 88–89. A full text was published in late 1968 in a collection of Dubček's speeches. *K otázkam obrodzovacieho procesu v KSČ* (Bratislava, Oct. 1968), pp. 3–16. It was later reported that the Theses themselves had referred to the "harmful" effect of the cumulation of functions without, however, relating this general idea specifically to the posts at the highest level. See *R.Š.o.*, p. 22.

[12] Mencl, op. cit., pp. 90–95. Other critics of the party's work were reportedly Slavík, Sobolčík, V. Kadlec, J. Špaček and O. Volenik.

the highest ranks in the Presidium. After the plenum had gone into closed session, with only full members and candidates present, Novotný delivered a passionate speech in which he censured Dubček's work as head of the Slovak party and accused him of expressing "narrow national interests." This drew a sharp response from Dubček's colleague, V. Bil'ak, who reminded Novotný of the damage caused in the fifties by the charge of nationalism against Slovaks, and urged a CC meeting in a few weeks, to include all members of the Slovak party's presidium. A similar proposal by Josef Borůvka not to close the session at this time and to continue after a two or three weeks' recess was not passed, nor was Kriegel's proposal for secret voting. In the end the Theses were passed, not unanimously as requested by Novotný, but with thirteen votes against.[13] Novotný promised that there would be further discussion of the work of the central organs and especially of the government.

The official report on the October plenum, which did not include even censored texts of speeches delivered, concealed the division of opinion at the apex of the party and asserted the doctrine of its leading role in somewhat traditional terms.[14] "The party is the leading political force, the ideological center, the cognitive and directive organism of socialist society. It unifies and directs all the essential aspects of social life and organizes the working people for the realization of socialist and Communist aims." The report continued, in words that echoed, although somewhat ambiguously, Novotný's formulation in mid-October: "In its activity it concentrates on the conscious programing and the conceptual direction of the general social process. From state and economic organs it demands full responsibility for the operative and perspective management of their respective spheres on the basis of the political line set forth." It was not possible, however, to separate "the conceptual and organizational" sides of the party's activity. "The party's action may not be limited merely to cognitive work. The party must in its activity penetrate all spheres of social life and, through the medium of Communists, influence the development of the whole of society."

Oncc again it appeared that Novotný had scored a victory and successfully defended his position. It was evident, however, at least to those "in the know," that the top leadership was split and that the issues of the controversy had not yet been finally settled. In the weeks that followed, Novotný's position significantly worsened. The Strahov student demonstration, and its brutal suppression by the police, which occurred on the very evening of the final plenum meeting, led to widespread public criticism of the police action and further discredited the "hard-line" policy.[15] Novotný's absence in Moscow for eight days immediately

[13] *Svědectví,* p. 149.
[14] *Rudé právo,* 1 November 1967.
[15] See Zeman, op. cit., pp. 75–83.

following the plenum, for the celebration of the 50th anniversary of the Soviet revolution, may have permitted those opposed to his continuance in office to organize. Although the evidence is scanty, it seems that, by this time, the Presidium was split in half over the issue of party reform, including Novotný's holding the two top positions of party and state. Dubček, J. Dolanský, O. Cerník, D. Kolder, and eventually Hendrych were reportedly urging a division of the two offices, and criticizing Novotný's work as first secretary.[16] This created an impasse in the preparations for the December plenum and resulted in a very vague compromise resolution which referred only to the implementation of the Theses in relation to the central organs, including the settlement of the problem of the cumulation of functions.[17]

A one-day visit to Prague by Leonid Brezhnev on 8 December remains shrouded in mystery. During Novotný's trip to Moscow he had, by his own admission, been unable to speak at length with the Soviet leader but had urged Brezhnev to visit Prague, presumably hoping that this would strengthen his own position. Later, again according to Novotný, a telephone call by Brezhnev led to an acceptance of this invitation. Nothing was known of this to the Central Committee members or even, seemingly, to the Presidium.[18] During his brief stay in Prague, the Soviet chief did not meet with the full Presidium, as was apparently planned, but talked separately with individual members. He is generally believed to have declined to interfere in the affair and to have left the Czechoslovak leaders to settle it themselves.[19] Since Novotný was not removed at that time, it may be presumed that Brezhnev took no steps to support his ouster and may have urged his continuance in office. He may have left Prague confident that Novotný would weather the storm. On the other hand, his apparent "neutrality" did not strengthen Novotný's hand and may have cleared the way for his eventual removal by his opponents. Certainly, Novotný was not able, later, to rely on Soviet support to avert his ouster.

16 There were various reports circulating in Prague of a presidium divided 8 to 2, or 6 to 4 and, eventually, with a shift of position by Hendrych, of a deadlock of 5 to 5. The five listed above as opposing Novotný are named by Mencl (p. 97). *Svědectví* gives the same names and lists the others, Chudík, Laštovička, Lenárt and Šimůnek as supporting Novotný (p. 151).

17 *R.š.o.*, op. cit., pp. 9–10.

18 For this and for Novotný's explanations see *Svědectí*, pp. 150, 152.

19 Mencl, op. cit., p. 99. Cf. Kolder's statement to this effect in *Svědectví*, p. 167. Hence the oft-quoted phrase, later attributed to Brezhnev *"Eto vashe dyelo!"* ("This is your affair"). The report in *Svědectví*, however, quoting Hendrych, assumes that Brezhnev threw his support to Novotný at this time (p. 150).

When the Central Committee gathered on December 19, one week later than previously scheduled, it was soon evident that great dissatisfaction existed both with the proposed resolution submitted by the Presidium (which was referred back in the end) and with the lack of information concerning the actual differences within the topmost organ and the visit by the Soviet leader. Novotný did little to dissolve the dissatisfaction. Speaking somewhat defensively, he apologized for his statements disparaging the Slovak leaders, sought rather weakly to explain the visit by Brezhnev, and dealt at length with the dangers of the international situation. On the question of the separation of the top offices, he spoke of alternative solutions to this problem and, it seems, suggested postponement of a decision for several months.[20] Critical speeches were made by F. Vodsloň, Z. Fierlinger, and Dr. F. Šorm, the head of the Academy of Sciences, but the real storm of debate was initiated by the economist, Dr. Ota Šik.

Referring to the growing "political discontent of the people" and the "declining activity and interest of party members," Šik made a devastating criticism of the entire party system as it had operated, including the suppression of criticism and the "immense cumulation of power in the hands of some comrades, especially comrade Novotný." Separation of the functions of President and first secretary must be carried through without delay. Concretely, he proposed the resignation of Novotný as first secretary and the selection of a successor by a secret vote of the plenum. This would follow the nomination of two candidates, together with several new presidium members, by a special commission, which would not include any members of the Presidium. He also advanced a series of measures for the democratization of the party so that the Central Committee would, in fact, become the supreme organ between congresses, and not merely "an assembly which always unanimously approves proposals submitted in one version by the Presidium." Central Committee secretaries would be responsible to commissions which, in turn, would be responsible to the Presidium and the Central Committee plenum. Secretaries would be limited to two terms of office and would be excluded from other state functions. All elections would be secret. Cadre policy would no longer be an instrument in the hands of one person but would be permeated with "the spirit of collective party leadership." The Presidium would be authorized to work out a political and economic action program which would assure the solution, as soon as possible, of the burning questions that had piled up.[21]

The dramatic statement touched off three days of sharp debate which

[20] *Svědectví*, pp. 151–53; Mencl, op. cit., pp. 98–99.

[21] Text is given in *Svědectví*, pp. 154–57; see also Mencl, op. cit., pp. 100–2.

were followed, after a Christmas break, by three more days of discussion, beginning on 3 January. The conflicting tendencies were more and more clearly defined.[22] The conservative group was largely satisfied with the *status quo,* blamed existing problems on "Western ideological diversion," and urged an even more emphatic implementation of the methods of directive administration. The progressive group regarded the situation as one of grave crisis and urged the need for a thoroughgoing democratization of the party and the development of socialist democracy. The central issue had, however, become the separation of the functions of secretary and President and, as it became clear that such a division was unavoidable, when, and in what form, it should be effected. The conservatives sought a postponement, hoping to secure time to defend Novotný's position. The divergence of opinion thus became somewhat confused as a number of issues, including Novotný's leadership, the division of functions, and the matter of postponement, were intertwined.

The initial reaction to Šik's speech was mixed. A number of persons, including J. Lenárt, M. Chudík and O. Šimůnck, opposed his proposals, arguing that many of them fell outside the competence of the Central Committee, and in varying degrees defended Novotný's tenure of office. Both Lenárt and Chudík warned of the international repercussions of a change in leadership, especially in neighboring socialist states, particularly in the German Democratic Republic (GDR). An impassioned speech in defense of Novotný was made by Vera Dočkalová who, although admitting that all was not in order, denied that there was a crisis in the party and declared that the leader had the confidence of the entire nation.[23] Others took a somewhat ambiguous position. J. Piller, for instance, was critical of Novotný but was doubtful of the wisdom of the immediate division of functions. Progressive spokesmen, such as V. Slavík, J. Válo, and a number of others, were in favor of a separation of functions. Dubček is not reported to have spoken. His colleague, Bil'ak, however, censured Novotný's policy toward Slovakia and the Slovak party and urged an immediate solution of the problem of the division of functions. Alois Indra, a cabinet minister, criticized the limitations placed on the actions of the government and of individual ministers.

Novotný, confronted with these hard realities, resorted to a new defensive maneuver, informing the Presidium, and later the plenum, that he was "placing the function of first secretary at the disposal of the plenary session of the Central Committee," and pledging that he would

[22] A good summary of the conflicting positions is given in the Presidium's later report, *R.š.o.,* pp. 13ff. See also interview with O. Šik, *Kulturní noviny,* 29 March 1968.

[23] Text in *Svědectví,* p. 158.

abide by any decision that was made.[24] This shrewd move, which was not a full resignation, would have left the question of separation open and would have involved a delay in its final resolution. Thereupon Dubček, on behalf of the Presidium, proposed that the final decision, including the choice of a successor, be deferred until 3 January, when the plenum would resume its deliberations. Once again a turbulent debate began, mainly centering on the question of postponement, with some favoring immediate action and others accepting the proposed delay; with some defending, and others criticizing, Novotný. It was during this third day of discussion that the Presidium members and secretaries were requested to speak and were thus compelled to commit themselves openly. Most of them favored a division of functions, but a few, including Šimůnek and Chudík, opposed this and warmly defended Novotný.[25] In the end, an overwhelming majority supported the proposal, made by Vilém Nový and accepted by the Presidium, to postpone the discussion until January 1968 and to leave the decision on separation to a consultative group which would include, in addition to all Presidium members, a representative from each regional party organization.[26] No reference was made to the political content of the plenum debate in the brief communiqué issued after the meeting. Only the Central Committee's decision on economic questions was published the following day.[27]

During the two-week period between the plenary sessions there were, no doubt, many efforts made on both sides to prepare the ground for the final struggle in January. It was at this time that steps were taken in military circles to try to influence the decisions of the Central Committee, or perhaps even to use armed force to prevent the ouster of Novotný. These activities were conducted, it would appear, primarily by Miroslov Mamula, head of the eighth department of the party secretariat

[24] Text, ibid., pp. 159–60.

[25] Those who reportedly spoke in favor of the separation included Kolder, Vaculík, L. Štrougal, V. Koucký, A. Kapek, Sabolčík, Černík, Dolanský, Dubček, and perhaps Hendrych and S. Sádovský. Smrkovský favored immediate separation of the two posts. Whether he spoke on this occasion or at the January sitting is not clear, as the two main sources differ on this point. The content of his address, about which there is little difference in the sources, suggests that it was delivered in January. See below.

[26] Mencl and Ouředník, op. cit., no. 19; *Svědectví*, p. 168. The latter reports that the consultative group was also to propose Novotný's successor, suggesting that the issue of separation had already been settled. Those appointed to the group were: J. Piller, F. Červenka, F. Samec, J. Černý, O. Paul, J. Borůvka, J. Špaček, O. Voleník, later replaced by M. Čapka, A. Perkovič, E. Rigo and M. Hladký. F. Barbírek was added later.

[27] *Rudé právo*, 22 and 23 December 1967.

responsible for state administration, and Gen. Jan Šejna, the secretary of the chief party committee in the Ministry of National Defense.[28] Mamula had, in effect, direct supervision of all the relevant ministries, in this case National Defense and its chief party organization, and was thus able to bypass, to a considerable extent, the Main Political Administration in that ministry, headed by Gen. Václav Prchlík. Already in September and October 1967, Mamula was seeking to implement in the armed services the hard line set forth in Novotný's first of September speech and in that delivered at the plenum at the end of that month. During and after the October plenum, he and General Šejna continued their pressures but were rebuffed by the Minister, General Lomský, and by Prchlík. Both Mamula and Šejna were reported as being convinced of the danger of a "counterrevolution" engineered by the West and carried through by the oppositional elements within the party. The party's leading role, and socialism, were endangered, they believed, and a situation comparable to Hungary in 1956 existed. Both Mamula and Šejna made clear their opposition to the division of Novotný's functions and to his removal from power.[29]

[28] For this, see the series of articles by J. Kokška "How It Was in the Army," published in the journal of the Chief Political Administration (CPA), *A-Revue*, no. 12–16, from June to August 1968. These articles were based on archival materials and interviews with many of the participants except, of course, Gen. Janko, who had in the meantime committed suicide, and Gen. Šejna, who had defected to the U.S.A. These later events tended to lend corroboration to the charge that these two were involved in some kind of dubious activities. Gen Šejna, however, in a later interview in *The New York Times,* firmly denied that he had attempted a military coup (*The New York Times,* 26, 28 August 1968). M. Mamula made a similar denial. See *Reportér,* III, no. 23 (5–12 June 1968), pp. 7–9. See also the article by Gen. E. Pepych, who at that time had been deputy chief of the CPA, *Obrana lidu,* 24 February 1968, and an interview with Gen. Djur, ibid., 6 April 1968, the latter cited at length by Pavel Tigrid, op. cit., pp. 189–90. Cf. brief comments on the episode in *Svědectví,* ibid., pp. 168–71.

[29] For their statements see *A-Revue,* no. 12, pp. 33, 35–36; no. 13, pp. 24–26; no. 14, p. 37; no. 15, p. 27; no. 16, p. 37. In the last-named source Gen. Šejna, for instance, declared that "certain opinions, in their essence, tend to call forth distrust in the leadership of our party and Comrade Novotný as the first secretary of the party. . . . There is no doubt that the dissemination of various opinions and moods, and calumnies, as well as the expression of distrust in the highest organs of the party, strike deeply at the very essence of the existence of the party as the leading force in our society, and tend to destroy its ideological and action unity, whether the bearers of such opinions or moods are aware of this or not."

In early December there was a call-up of troops for military exercises, concluding on 18 December, the day before the plenum began. These training exercises had been decided on earlier, but holding them at this time may have been designed to exert influence on the Central Committee discussions. During and after the plenum at the end of December, General Šejna continued his efforts to convince high-ranking military personnel such as, for instance, General Lomský and General Djur, a deputy minister, that there was a threat to socialism, thus awakening fears in their minds that the armed forces might be misused for political purposes. Lomský, Djur, and Prchlík rejected Šejna's arguments and overtures, and Prchlík informed the political chiefs at lower levels to be prepared to ward off the danger of a "misuse" of the army. General Lomský later quoted himself as having said to Novotný on the telephone: "I defend the principle that the army may not be misused in the present situation. By either side . . . ! We are not, after all, somewhere in Africa!"[30] General Janko, another Deputy Minister of National Defense, was apparently more receptive to Šejna's arguments.[31] Throughout the holiday season, General Janko was said to have had many meetings with Šejna and reportedly took steps to place military units in a state of readiness for possible action. He is said to have ordered some military leaders to Prague and to have arranged for a tank brigade to go to the capital at a certain time. Meanwhile, Mamula had reportedly drawn up a list of over one thousand persons to be arrested, and had warrants ready and signed for that eventuality.[32] Even if these reports are true, it is not entirely clear whether these moves were, in fact, preparations for military action in defense of Novotný's position, or whether they were designed to exert a psychological influence on the military leaders and on the CC members and thus to discourage any steps which would weaken Novotný's power.

When the plenum resumed in January, it was at once evident that there was still strong resistance to Novotný's removal. At the outset, the Prime Minister, Lenárt, spoke at length on proposed changes in the work of the government but urged care in consideration of the question of dividing the top functions. Novotný, in his opening remarks, admitted errors in his work, but in essence rejected the case of his critics. In principle, he expressed agreement with the idea of separating the two posts, but cleverly shifted the discussion to the question as to when and how this might take place, clearly seeking to delay action. The Presidium, too, had submitted an ambiguous resolution, which in effect left the matter to be settled at the next plenum, in accordance

[30] Ibid., no. 14, p. 38.
[31] Ibid., no. 14, pp. 36–40; no. 15, pp. 27–28, 33; no. 16, p. 40.
[32] *Svědectví*, p. 169.

with recommendations that would be made by the Presidium and the consultative group.[33] A number of speakers, including Sedláková, V. Minač, and Josef Smrkovský, reacted vigorously by proposing that the decision be made at once, at that very sitting. Others, including General Lomský, Lenárt, and the Foreign Minister, Václav David, warned that the international situation argued against the removal of Novotný. General Lomský was somewhat ambiguous, since he strongly defended Novotný and spoke of the threat from imperialism, but did not oppose or support the separation of posts.[34] Lenárt once again emphasized the danger that the removal of Novotný would pose for the GDR, and for Ulbricht's position. These arguments were sharply countered by other speakers, including the Slovak, Josef Válo, General Prchlík, and Josef Smrkovský.

Smrkovský delivered a major speech which was similar in many ways to the earlier one by Šik and which helped to turn the tide.[35] Proclaiming his own support for the closest relations with the USSR, he denied that any individual or group could arrogate the right to be the guarantor of this relationship and denied that it was necessary, as Chudík apparently had suggested, to consult the Soviet leaders. They would no doubt respond, he argued, that it was up to each individual party and its organs, which "know best the situation," to solve its internal problems. There was, in the party, no tradition of "separatism" toward the international Communist movement and no reason to "doubt the international position of this Central Committee or any part of it." Smrkovský also denied that any group could claim a monopoly of the interests of the working class, and opposed any tendency to place the workers against the intellectuals. He rejected the charge of nationalism against the Slovaks and stressed that Czech-Slovak relations were not entirely "in order." In this "historic moment" of the party's history, there was urgent need for "a democratization" of society and for basic changes in the party's manner of work. This should begin with the addition of new blood to the Presidium, and a division of the functions of secretary and President. In favor of the latter, he said, were the greater part of the Central Committee, including half the Presidium, the majority of the Slovak Presidium, and all the Central Committee secretaries. He urged that the latter question be settled at once, at this session, by secret ballot, with a choice between alternative candidates. It was not enough, he said, for Novotný to place his position at the disposal of the Central Committee; he ought to resign, as he should have done much earlier. "Novotný, as the highest functionary with the greatest concentration of

33 Partial text in Mencl and Ouředník, op. cit., no. 19.

34 Mencl, op. cit., pp. 110–11; *A-Revue,* No. 15, pp. 28–30. Later Lomský said that he had been in favor of the division of functions.

35 Text given in *Svědectví,* pp. 160–66. See fn. 25 above.

power, also bears the greatest share of responsibility for the existing situation." The new secretary should act as chairman of the Presidium, as "first among equals," thus guarding against concentrating too much power in the hands of an individual. More than this was needed, however, if the party was to regain the confidence of the people—a positive program that would unite all "who wished socialism without deformations," and "a rehabilitation of the ideas for which the majority of us have dedicated our lives."

Meanwhile, the center of deliberations was transferred to the joint meetings of the Presidium and the consultative group. On the fourth of January this body proposed that the issue of separation of functions be settled at this very plenum and that the Presidium make its proposals known on the following day. Discussions in the plenum on the fourth indicated continuing opposition in some circles, including General Rytíř, the Army's Chief of Staff, who described Novotný as a "firm representative" in the defense against imperialism and urged a delay in settling the question of division.[36] Nothing is known with assurance of the discussions in the consultative body on the actual succession to Novotný. Reportedly, Novotný rejected Smrkovský or Šik, and his own suggestions, including B. Laštovicka, Lenárt and Vaculík, were not acceptable to others.[37] Finally, agreement was reached on Alexander Dubček, who was approved by Novotný and was prevailed upon to accept. There was also concurrence on the addition of four new members to the Presidium.

This proposal was submitted to the plenum on the fifth of January by Novotný, who declared that he was relinquishing his post in the interest of party unity and saw in Dubček a "guarantee" of "the strengthening of that unity." In the discussion that followed, some opposition voices were heard, including O. Pavlovský and V. Šalgovič, but in the end the recommendations were approved unanimously. In his acceptance speech, Dubček revealed his initial reluctance to accept the post, and declared his intention to work as "first among equals." He pledged himself to carry out the "intentions" of the Novotný leadership, especially in strengthening both Czechoslovak statehood and the relationship with the Soviet and other Communist parties. He thanked Novotný for his past work, urged an objective evaluation of it, and expressed the hope of Novotný's continued assistance.[38]

There was an ironic epilogue associated with the efforts of General Šejna to prevent the ouster of Novotný. At meetings of the presidium of the main party committee in the Ministry of Defense on 3 and 4 Jan-

[36] Mencl, op. cit., pp. 112–13; *A-Revue*, No. 15, pp. 32–33. *Svědectví* places this speech on the third of September (p. 170).
[37] *Svědectví*, p. 171.
[38] Text, ibid., pp. 173–74.

uary, Šejna sought to persuade his colleagues of the dangers of the situation, and eventually convinced them of the need for a letter to the Central Committee setting forth the views of the party members in the Ministry. Early in the morning of the fifth, at about 8 A.M., more than an hour before the CC plenum was to open, an enlarged meeting of the party committee, including approximately one hundred and twenty persons, began its discussion of the draft of such a letter. Šejna spoke of the threat to the party as the leading force, and was opposed, among others, by General Djur and General Čepicky, deputy Chief of Staff, and was supported by General Janko. The content of the letter was modified, but in its final version strongly opposed the division of the functions of secretary and president as a threat to party unity and to the implementation of the thirteenth congress line and the October plenum decisions. It rejected also the slander of comrade Novotný, "whom we know as a consistent defender of the party's line, and of the alliance with the Soviet Union, and as a defender of the fulfillment of the international duty of our party." In the final vote, taken between 1 and 2 o'clock in the afternoon, the letter was overwhelmingly approved, only Djur opposing it. It was too late—the plenum had already taken *its* decision and Novotný had been removed.[39]

The final Central Committee communiqué, published on 6 January, was a compromise revealing little of the vigorous debate that had preceded the decision, and thus implicitly reducing the significance of the change in the first secretaryship.[40] The report contained not a single word of direct criticism of Novotný's many years of rule, and indeed expressed appreciation for his "devoted work" and praise of his "significant successes." Dubček was described as "in his own person maintaining the continuity of party leadership." The profound disunity within the ranks of the Central Committee during the sessions from October 1967 to January 1968 was veiled by references to the "broad discussion" that had occurred and the "complete unity of opinion" that had resulted. Although there was reference to the "existing inadequacies in the methods and style of work," including "inner party democracy," the only specific changes mentioned were the separation of the functions of the presidency and the first secretaryship, and a future "improvement of the activity" of the government and the Slovak National Council. Moreover, the measures taken were said to be designed to implement the conclusions of the thirteenth congress in 1966, and of the

[39] The episode is described in *A-Revue,* No. 16, pp. 34–43. The text of the letter is given there in part. See also Djur's interview, *Obuana lidu,* 6 April 1968.

[40] *Rudé právo,* 6 January 1968, and *R.š.o.,* pp. 5–6. A fuller version of the January resolution was published in *Tribune,* 15 October 1969.

Theses on the Position and Task of the Party approved at the October plenum, suggesting that a modification of methods, rather than a change of objectives, was envisaged.

Despite the ambiguities of the public record, there were potentialities of future change inherent in the situation. The significance of the removal of Novotný from the top party post, terminating fifteen years of almost unchallenged rule, could not be concealed or minimized. As in similar cases in all Communist countries, the repercussions of such a shift in leadership could hardly fail to be tremendous. The general public, and the mass of party members, knew little or nothing of the background of the decision. Yet, as we have seen, it was the product of three months of bitter debate in both the Central Committee and the Presidium, reflecting deep splits within the top leadership and profound dissatisfaction with the person of Novotný and with his methods of governing. This conflict at the top also mirrored powerful forces of social discontent and strong public pressures which had begun to be expressed during the final decade of his rule. Although the Central Committee was composed entirely of Novotný appointees, it had assumed a new and important role by becoming a forum of debate and an instrument for the transition to a new leadership. The removal of Novotný from the party secretaryship undermined the system of personal rule which he had built up over many years. The person of Dubček, although largely unknown and somewhat ambiguous in its significance, represented a new generation and, it seemed, suggested a new style of rule. The breaking up of the traditional "cumulation of functions" by the separation of the top state and party posts opened up the possibility of restoring some degree of independence to the government, the assembly, and the mass organizations, hitherto dominated and directly controlled by the party. Basic reforms in the party itself, including the subordination of the Presidium and secretariat to the Central Committee, and the emergence of the first secretary as "first among equals," were other possible consequences of the January decision. The process of "democratization," however uncertain, unintended, and ill-defined, had begun. The first signs of "spring" had come to Prague.

The State Apparatus

THE RISE AND FALL OF THE "ALL-PEOPLE'S STATE": RECENT CHANGES IN THE SOVIET THEORY OF THE STATE*

Roger E. Kanet

SINCE Khrushchev's removal from power, a number of the economic and political changes which he had fostered have been reversed. For example, almost immediately after his fall the division of the party into industrial and agricultural sections was replaced by a single, unified party structure. A few months later the economic districts into which the Soviet Union had been divided were disbanded and the All-Union ministries re-established. In the area of political theory, Khrushchev's successors have instituted major revisions in the concept of the state during the period of the building of communism. At the XXII Party Congress in 1961, the concept of the all-people's state was proclaimed as "one of the most important developments of contemporary Marxist-Leninist scientific thought."[1] According to the Party Program adopted at the Congress:

The working class is the only class in history that does not aim to

From *Soviet Studies* XV, 1, (July 1968). Reprinted by permission of the author and *Soviet Studies*.

* I wish to express my appreciation for comments by Robert C. Tucker on an earlier version of this paper and for suggestions made by Jaroslaw Piekalkiewicz.

[1] V. I. Pavlov, "Nekotorye voprosy teorii obshchenarodnogo sotsialistic-heskogo gosudarstva (v svyazi s materialami martovskogo plenuma KPSS)," *Sovetskoe gosudarstvo i pravo* (hereafter *SGiP*), 1962, no. 7, p. 3.

> perpetuate its power. Having brought about the complete and final victory of socialism—the first phase of communism—and the transition of society to the full-scale construction of communism, *the dictatorship of the proletariat has fulfilled its historic mission and has ceased to be indispensable in the USSR* from the point of view of the tasks of internal development. The state, which arose as a state of the dictatorship of the proletariat, has in the new, contemporary stage, become a state of the entire people, an organ expressing the interests and will of the people as a whole. . . . The Party holds that the dictatorship of the working class will cease to be necessary before the state withers away. The state as an organization of the entire people will survive until the complete victory of communism.[2]

Recent Soviet writing has significantly revised the theory of the all-people's state as expounded in the last years of Khrushchev's leadership of the party. Although the term "all-people's state" is still used occasionally, it is no longer viewed as an essentially different type of state from the dictatorship of the proletariat. According to the Theses of the Central Committee of the CPSU for the fiftieth anniversary of the October revolution, the all-people's state merely "continues the work of the dictatorship of the proletariat. . . ."[3] One Soviet theoretician has argued that, except for the disappearance of the repressive functions, "all the other aspects of the essence of the state of dictatorship of the proletariat remain."[4]

The purpose of this paper will be to examine the concept of the all-people's state and the recent changes which have occurred in its interpretation. In the course of this examination we shall attempt to clarify three questions concerning the theory: 1) the development and exposition of the doctrine; 2) its relationship to classical Marxism-Leninism; and 3) the reasons for the recent revisions in the theory.

[2] XXII Party Congress, *The New Soviet Society: Final Text of the Program of the Communist Party of the Soviet Union.* With annotations and an introduction by Herbert Ritvo (New York, 1962), pp. 165–68; emphasis added.

[3] "50 let Velikoi Oktyabr'skoi revolyutsii. Tezisy Tsentral'nogo Komiteta KPSS," *Pravda,* 25 June 1967. However, more recently *Pravda* has begun once again to speak of the all-people's state without any reservation. For example, in an editorial on the role of the soviets it is stated that they are important for the "further strengthening of our all-people's state" ("Kommunist v soviet," *Pravda,* 9 December 1967). See also the editorial entitled "Sovetskaya demokratiya," *Pravda,* 5 December 1967.

[4] V. M. Chkhikvadze, "Razvitie narodnoi sushchnosti sotsialisticheskogo gosudarstva," *SGiP,* 1966, no. 10, p. 8.

The Theory of the All-People's State

At the XXII Congress Khrushchev explained that, "Naturally, when socialism had triumphed *fully* and *finally* in our country and we entered the period of the *full-scale building of communism,* the circumstances necessitating the dictatorship of the proletariat disappeared; its internal tasks had been accomplished."[5] Prior to the publication of the Draft Program in July 1961 no mention had been made in any Soviet publication of the all-people's state. In fact, as late as 1960 Soviet writers were arguing that ". . . a superclass state power never existed. In fact, the state always acts in the interests of a class, is led by class motives. . . ."[6] This same view of the necessary class character of the state can be found in numerous other Soviet publications in 1959 and 1960. For example, in attempting to refute revisionist ideas which opposed the dictatorship of the proletariat, A. P. Butenko, who later wrote a number of articles in defense of the new concept of the all-people's state, maintained that

> . . . the state, above all, is a class phenomenon, as well by its origin as by the role which it plays in every given society. This circumstance is so essential that without it the state would cease to exist as such. Classness is the general, constant trait of every state; also the state of the dictatorship of the proletariat, which does not differ from any other state in this regard. . . . *Superclass states do not exist; the state cannot be other than the organ of the ruling class.* The essence and role of any state are determined entirely and fully by the interests of that class whose tool it is, or more exactly, of the economically ruling class.[7]

As is clear from these citations, the concept of an all-people's state did not develop before the publication of the Draft Program in 1961,

[5] N. S. Khrushchev, "O Programme Kommunisticheskoi partii Sovetskogo Soyuza," *Pravda* and *Izvestiya,* 19 October 1961; translated in Charlotte Sarkowski and Leo Gruliow (eds.), *Current Soviet Policies, IV: The Documentary Record of the 22nd Congress of the Communist Party of the Soviet Union* (New York, 1962), p. 102.

[6] G. K. Soseliya, *Revizionizm i marksistskoe uchenie o diktature proletariata. I: 90-e gody XIXv.—30-e gody XXv.* (M. 1960), p. 155.

[7] A. P. *Butenko et al., Protiv sovremennogo revizionizma v filosofii i sotsiologii* (M. 1960), p. 245. See also A. Denisov, who condemned contemporary revisionists for coming out "in the role of propagandists of the decadent and long-bankrupt theory of a superclass state," *Sushchnost' i formy gosudarstva* (M. 1960), p. 36.

although some of the characteristics attributed to it had been referred to earlier.

In the period immediately following the introduction of the new concept, a veritable flood of articles appeared in the Soviet press explaining the characteristics of the all-people's state and attempting to prove that the change in theory was not only in the spirit of Marxism-Leninism, but that the theory itself was also contained in the classical Marxist writings. Although the state continues to exist during the period of the construction of communism, it is a different stage in the development of the socialist state.[8] But, even though the state of all the people and the dictatorship of the proletariat are not different types of states, but only different stages in the development of socialist society, they do differ qualitatively, for the socioeconomic basis of power in the two forms varies. In the state of all the people there no longer exists an exploiter class which must be suppressed, and thus the entire population is represented by the state.[9] These qualitative differences between the two stages are indicated by the various characteristics, or tasks, of the two. For example, the all-people's state is the first state in history that is not the organ of rule of a particular class, but the organ of the expression of the will of all the people. Since there is no exploiting class to suppress, it is clear that this function of the state—including the state of the dictatorship of the proletariat—no longer exists in the Soviet Union:

> During the transition from socialism to communism, the socialist state will even further develop its key constructive activities. But now, as communism arises from socialism in which there are no exploiting classes, the workers' class does not need to dominate, as there is no one to dominate. There are no exploiters, no classes or class desires which hinder the development of socialism. In such a situation, the socialist state is no longer a state of proletarian dictatorship, for *the tasks of the latter have been accomplished.*[10]

[8] A. I. Lepeshkin, "Obshchenarodnoe gosudarstvo i ego osnovnye cherty," *SGiP,* 1961, no. 3, p. 22. Lepeshkin divides the history of socialist society into three stages: 1) the dictatorship of the proletariat, which is the period of change from capitalism to socialism; 2) the period of gradual transfer of the dictatorship of the proletariat to the all-people's state, during which all the conditions for the period of full-scale creation of communism are prepared; and 3) the period of the all-people's state, which develops after the full and final victory of socialism.

[9] Ibid., p. 27, and V. O. Tenenbaum, "Ob osobennostyakh obshchenarodnogo gosudarstva," *SGiP,* 1963, no. 2, p. 6.

[10] A. P. Butenko, "Sovetskoe obschchenarodnoe gosudarstvo," *Kommunist,* 1963, no. 13, p. 30, emphasis added.

The all-people's state is distinguished from the dictatorship of the proletariat, 1) by a broadening of the basis of socialist society to include all the population, 2) by changing functions of the state, which now include the creation of communism and the transfer of state administration to public organizations, and 3) by the extension of democratic methods of rule.[11] The most important characteristic of this new form of the state is the attraction of all the people into the administration of the affairs of society.[12]

Throughout all the articles which dealt with the state of all the people emphasis was placed on the fact that under this new form of the socialist state the coercive role would be much less important and the primary place would be taken over by those organs of the state which carry out economic and cultural functions. There would be increased stress on the role of recommendation and counseling, and those methods which use direct, compulsory orders would become less important.[13]

Although the Communist party was also viewed as a party of all the people and not merely the party of a single class, the proletariat was to continue to play the leading role in Soviet society during the period of the all-people's state. In fact, the role of the party as the leading force in the construction of communism was to be further developed and the Communist party strengthened in all spheres of activity.[14] Socialist democracy would be extended to the entire population and public organizations would play a more important part in the management of state affairs. The broadening of the democratic base of society was to take place by a greater participation of the population in state administration, further participation of public organizations in the direction of

[11] F. M. Burlatsky, "O nekotorykh voprosakh teorii obshchenarodnogo sotsialisticheskogo gosudarstva," *SGiP,* 1962, no. 10, pp. 5–6. See also Lepeshkin, op. cit., pp. 6–7, and M. T. Baimakhanov, "K voprosu o yuridicheskoi prirode protsessa perekhoda nekotorykh gosudarstvennysh funktsii k obshchestvennym organizasiyam," *SGiP,* 1962, no. 8, p. 26.

[12] Lepeshkin, op. cit., pp. 7–8. Burlatsky defines the all-people's state as "the organ of the power of all the people, with the aid of which society accomplishes the construction of communism, the direction of economic and social processes, protects the freedom and socialist equality of the citizens, socialist law and order, provides defense and maintains relations with other countries" (op. cit., p. 4).

[13] A. S. Fedoseev, "Rol' Sovetskogo sotsialisticheskogo obshchenarodnogo gosudarstva v stroitel'stve kommunizma," *SGiP,* 1962, no. 4, p. 31. According to Fedoseev, the primary tasks of the all-people's state include the following: 1) the creation of the material-technical base of communism; 2) the accomplishment of the control of work and demands in the economy; 3) the guarantee of the development of the welfare of the people; and 4) the preservation of the rights and freedoms of Soviet citizens (ibid., p. 30). See also Pavlov, op. cit., p. 10.

[14] Pavlov, op. cit., p. 10.

economic and cultural construction and, finally, by a further democratization of the organs of government.[15]

After completing this brief review of the theory of the all-people's state, we wish to examine the relationship of the doctrine to the classical Marxist-Leninist theory of the state. According to the Chinese Communists, the new theory is a revision of Marxism-Leninism and will lead to the overthrow of the dictatorship of the proletariat and its replacement by that of another class.[16] They argue that both "Marx and Lenin maintained that the *entire* period before the advent of the higher stage of Communist society is the period of transition from capitalism to communism, the period of the dictatorship of the proletariat." They base their criticism on statements from Marx and Lenin which they interpret to mean that no such thing as a non-class or superclass state can exist.[17] This argument is the same as that used by Soviet writers before the XXII Party Congress. According to the Chinese, the so-called state of all the people is nothing but an old device used by reactionary classes to cover up their dictatorship, and the classical Marxist writers exposed this idea long ago. In his *Critique of the Gotha Program,* Marx stated: "Between capitalist and Communist society lies the period of the revolutionary transformation of the one into the other. There corresponds to this also a political transition period in which the state can be nothing but the revolutionary dictatorship of the proletariat."[18] In *The State and Revolution* Lenin took the same position:

> The essence of Marx's doctrine of the state has been assimilated only by those who understand that the dictatorship of a *single* class is necessary not only for class society in general, not only for the proletariat which has overthrown the bourgeoisie, but also for the *entire historical period between capitalism and classless society, communism.*[19]

[15] Yu. M. Kozlov, "Novyi etap v razvitii sotsialisticheskoi demokratii," in D. I. Chesnokov (ed.), *Nekotorye aktual'nye voprosy marksistsko-leninskoi teorii* (M. 1963), pp. 211, 212–14; see also Pavlov, op. cit., p. 7.

[16] Chou Yang, "The Fighting Task Confronting Workers in Philosophy and the Social Sciences," Speech at the Fourth Enlarged Session of the Committee of the Department of Philosophy and Social Sciences of the Chinese Academy of Sciences held on 26 October 1963 (*Peking Review,* 3 January 1964, p. 20).

[17] See "Letter of the Central Committee of the Chinese Communist Party to the Central Committee of the Communist Party of the Soviet Union," *The New York Times,* 5 July 1963, p. 8

[18] Karl Marx and Frederick Engels, *Selected Works in Two Volumes,* 5th impression (M. 1962), vol. II, pp. 32–33.

[19] V. I. Lenin, *Selected Works* (London, 1935), vol. VII, p. 34; emphasis added.

The Soviet authors replied that Marx and Lenin, in referring to the dictatorship of the proletariat during the period of transition from capitalism to communism, meant only the first stage of communism, or socialism. Butenko accused the Chinese of isolating themselves "from life with a fence of quotations" and argued that it is quite clear that, in so far as the crushing of exploiters is concerned, the transition to communism means the transition to the first stage of communism—i.e. to socialism. "Thus, both Marx and Lenin agree, basically, that the dictatorship of the proletariat is necessary for the transition from capitalism to the first stage of communism—socialism—although both Marx and Lenin frequently called this transition to socialism the transition to communism."[20]

In this dispute, the Soviet writers were on very weak ground. Although it is true that Marx and Lenin did use the terms "communism" and "socialism" interchangeably, a brief glance at the texts which were quoted by the Chinese and which the Soviet side attempted to explain away shows that Marx and Lenin were not referring to the first stage of communism. In the statement by Lenin it is clear that "classless society" does not refer to the first stage of communism, but to the higher stage of full communism. Besides, later in *The State and Revolution* Lenin mentions specifically both stages of communism and makes quite clear the distinction between the two.[21] Another indication that the Soviet interpretation of classical Marxism is inaccurate is the statement of Engels in *Socialism: Utopian and Scientific:*

> When at last [the state] becomes the real representative of the whole of society, it renders itself unnecessary. As soon as there is no longer any social class to be held in subjection; as soon as class rule, and the individual struggle for existence based upon our present anarchy in production . . . are removed, nothing more remains to be repressed, and a special repressive force, a state, is no longer necessary. . . .[22]

The Chinese offered additional arguments for the retention of the dictatorship of the proletariat. First of all, there are classes and class struggles "in all socialist countries without exception." Secondly, remnants of the old exploiting class are still attempting to stage a comeback and new capitalist elements are constantly being generated. Finally, the dictatorship of the proletariat is needed to handle correctly the relations between the working class and the peasantry, the consolidation of their economic and political alliance and the creation of conditions which will

[20] Butenko, "Sovetskoe obshchenarodnoe gosudarstvo," pp. 23–24.
[21] Lenin, *Selected Works,* vol. VII, pp. 83ff.
[22] Marx-Engels, *Selected Works,* vol. II, pp. 150–51.

lead to the gradual elimination of the class differences between workers and peasants.[23] Butenko replied that Soviet thinking does not assert that there exists a classless society in the Soviet Union but rather that these classes are not antagonistic to one another. Besides, the exploiting classes in the Soviet Union were liquidated long ago, and the Chinese attempts to equate criminal elements in the Soviet Union with exploiting classes are as "remote from Marxism as witches' incantations from scientific research." The socialist ownership of the means of production makes exploitation impossible, for there remains no objective socio-economic basis for the development of exploitation. Finally, the result of the Chinese approach to the relations between the workers and the peasants is to suggest that the workers' class can only guide the peasantry and other working people by means of dictatorship, which is a gross distortion of Marxism-Leninism.[24]

Actually the arguments which the Soviet writers advanced to defend the new theory are not particularly convincing. It is extremely difficult, for example, to reconcile the view that the state is not necessarily an instrument of class rule—since a particular stage of social development can serve the people as a whole and not merely a single class—with those statements of Lenin which refer to the state as "the product and the manifestation of the irreconcilability of class antagonisms" and as "an instrument for the exploitation of the oppressed class."[25]

One of the questions which arise from an examination of the Soviet literature on the all-people's state concerns the reasons for the change in theory. It seems safe to assume that Khrushchev and his associates saw the need for reviving fervor among the members of the party and for replacing passive bureaucratism with initiative. The new theory was aimed at stimulating the younger generations of Soviet citizens to active participation in the building of communism, as their elders were stimulated by the desire of building socialism in the Soviet Union. In order to facilitate the building of Communist society the party needs the active support of the entire population and not merely that of party members. By increasing the participation, at least in theory, of the entire population in state affairs, Soviet leaders apparently hoped to obtain more enthusiastic support for their programs.

Another related purpose for the innovation in the theory of the socialist state was the emphasis in the Khrushchev era on rewards rather than on brute coercion as a means of control in the Soviet Union. The revision was also related to the process of de-Stalinization, and Stalin was accused of delaying the development of the all-people's state by demanding the strengthening of the dictatorship of the proletariat

[23] "Letter of the Central Committee of the CCP . . . ," p. 8.
[24] Butenko, "Sovetskoe obshchenarodnoe gosudarstvo," pp. 31–32.
[25] Lenin, *Selected Works,* vol. VII, pp. 8, 13.

when there no longer existed an exploiting class which needed to be suppressed.[26]

Recent Reinterpretations of the All-People's State

In the past few years, Soviet interpretations of the nature of the socialist state have shifted back to a more "orthodox" Marxist-Leninist view. In fact, the all-people's state introduced by Khrushchev is relatively seldom referred to by name. In a major theoretical article in *Pravda* early in 1967, Professor D. I. Chesnokov presented the new interpretation now prevalent in Soviet writing. He complained about those revisionists who "belittle the role of the socialist state" and who "demand that it be abolished, that it wither away almost the day after the victory of socialism." According to Chesnokov, there are those in the Soviet Union who have

> improperly contraposed the socialist, all-people's state to the state of the dictatorship of the proletariat and statehood to public self-government.
>
> Actually the Program of the CPSU does not speak about a radical change in the essence of the socialist state, but about stages in its development. Similarly, statehood and public self-government are not mutually exclusive. The birth of socialist statehood is also the birth of self-government by the people.[27]

An examination of the Party Program of 1961 indicates clearly that the concept of an all-people's state was contraposed to that of the dictatorship of the proletariat and that this was not the work of later interpretations of the Program. According to the Program, "the dictatorship of the proletariat has fulfilled its historic mission and has ceased to be indispensable in the U.S.S.R."[28] Khrushchev's interpretation of the Program which was approved by the XXII Congress, noted that "A state of the entire people represents a new stage in the development of the socialist state, a *most important milestone* in the evolution of socialist statehood into Communist public self-government."[29] This

[26] N. P. Farberov, "Obshchenarodnoe gosudarstvo—zakonomernyi rezul'tat razvitiya gosudarstva diktatury proletariata," *SGiP*, 1962, no. 7, pp. 16–18, and A. P. Kositsyn, "Ob osnovnyeh etapakh razvitiya sovetskogo sotsialisticheskogo gosudarstva," ibid., 1961, no. 3, p. 29.
[27] Chesnokov, "Sovetskoe gosudarstvo, ego vospitatel'naya rol'," *Pravda*, 27 February 1967.
[28] *The New Soviet Society*, p. 166.
[29] Khrushchev, op. cit., p. 101.

seems to indicate that the originators of the concept of the all-people's state did see it as something quite different from the dictatorship of the proletariat.

According to the new interpretation, the all-people's state is merely a new stage in the development of the socialist state which is "characterized by the fact that, with the disappearance from Soviet society of class antagonisms, the state ceases to be an instrument of class rule. Therefore, an important component has disappeared—the suppression of class resistance by the exploiters, without which it is not a dictatorship of the proletariat." However, "all the other aspects of the essence of the state of the dictatorship of the proletariat remain. . . ."[30] The Soviet theoreticians are now attempting to show that

> . . . it follows that the present Soviet state, which expresses the will and interests of all the people, is not an essentially new state, different from the socialist type of state. It is also a socialist state, in which, in conformity with the changes in the economic and class structure of society, the traits of general democracy inherent in it from its very beginning come to light more deeply and broadly. Quite properly the dictatorship of the proletariat is also called popular, in so far as it expressed the will and interests of all toilers from the very beginning—i.e. the majority of the people—and developed in the direction of ever greater expression of its all-people's essence.
>
> What is involved, therefore, are two stages of development of one and the same type of state, while the newer, higher stage retains and develops the traits which characterized the state of the dictatorship of the proletariat as a new, higher type of state. . . .[31]

However, when the doctrine of an all-people's state was introduced in 1961 it was pointed out most clearly that the dictatorship of the proletariat had been rule by one class, while its successor, the all-people's state, was "an organ expressing the interests and will of the people as a whole."[32] The only explanation for the reinterpretation is that it represents an attempt to explain away one of the most important revisions of Marxist-Leninist theory introduced during the regime of Khrushchev.

Besides arguing that the all-people's state is merely an extension of the dictatorship of the proletariat without any essential changes, one Soviet theoretician has complained that some writers have interpreted the Party Program

[30] Chkhikvadze, op. cit., p. 8.
[31] Ibid., pp. 8, 15.
[32] *The New Soviet Society* . . . , p. 167.

as if our state had already lost its class nature, as if the socialist state had ceased, or was ceasing, to be a class state, and was even losing the character of political power. But that, of course, is clearly running ahead and is very harmful both for theory and practice.

Although the Soviet state has become the expression of the will and interests of all the people and no longer appears as the dictatorship of a class, it does not cease to have an entirely class character, nor is it deprived of class content until the objective grounds for the existence of classes have disappeared. This does not exclude the possibility and necessity of speaking of the well-known evolution of the class nature of the Soviet state in accord with the development of the all-people's state.[33]

This view is quite different from the one expressed by Soviet writers only a few years ago when they emphasized that, although classes continue to exist in the Soviet Union, the all-people's state was to attract all the people into the administration of society.[34] Actually, the terms remain the same, but the emphasis has changed very drastically. Some Soviet theorists can imply that the dictatorship of the proletariat still remains in existence in the Soviet Union. Professor Chesnokov, for example, has stated: "Having *raised the Marxist-Leninist teaching about the dictatorship of the proletariat to a new level,* our Communist party has drawn important theoretical and political conclusions about the attributes and functions of the state under socialism and about the maintenance, under specific conditions, of the state in a Communist society."[35]

Probably the most important practical consequence of the new interpretation of the all-people's state concerns the role of public or social organizations in the Soviet Union during the period of transition to communism. According to the doctrine as developed in the early sixties, there was to be a gradual transfer of state functions to public organizations during the period of the construction of communism.[36] Theore-

[33] Chkhikvadze, op. cit., p. 12. See also V. M. Chkhikvadze and N. P. Farberov, "V. I. Lenin o sotsialisticheskom gosudarstve," *Kommunist,* 1967, no. 5, p. 23.

[34] Lepeshkin, op. cit., pp. 6–7.

[35] Chesnokov, "Sovetskoe gosudarstvo . . . ," p. 1; emphasis added. See also A. I. Ermolgev, *Nekotorye aktual'nye voprosy marksistsko-leniniskoi teorii* (M. 1966), p. 56.

[36] Baimakhanov, op. cit., p. 26. See the Party Program on the role of public organizations (*The New Soviet Society . . . ,* pp. 178–83). Even before the introduction of the idea of an all-people's state, Soviet writers spoke of the development of public organizations to take over the functions of the state. For example, in 1960 Professor Chesnokov himself came to the con-

ticians called for the strengthening of popular control over the activity of the state apparatus, the development of agricultural organizations to control production, the expanded participation of the populace in the supervision of the courts, and so forth.[37] In conjunction with the expansion of the role of public organizations, local soviets were to increase in importance during the period of the construction of full-scale communism.[38]

Some recent articles in the Soviet press, however, have downgraded the importance of the public organizations and have re-emphasized the functions of the state organs in the building of Communist society: "The soviets are the democratic basis of the Soviet state system and the only representative and sovereign organs of the people, for they embody their will and unity, their sovereign power."[39] Various authors point out the shortcomings of the public organizations which have been created in accordance with the recommendations of the Party Program:

> The organs of voluntary public bodies are rising so rapidly that definite difficulties have developed, not only in their leadership, but even in registering them in an organized fashion. . . . Unfortunately, the passion for "new" forms and the numerical growth of public organs has not yet ceased. At times various councils . . . are created, which are not called for by the demands of life.
>
> Conditions in the voluntary public bodies suffer from a number of inadequacies; in part, from confused working regarding the character, basic tasks, and rights and duties of the organs of a public voluntary nature.[40]

Other Soviet writers are more explicit in their complaints against the development of public organizations:

---

clusion that "At the present stage of Communist construction, it seems expedient to transfer to public organizations, above all the state functions of cultural and educational work. . . ." (Chesnokov, *Ot gosudarstvennosti k obshchestvennomu samoupravleniyu* (M. 1960), p. 37).

[37] See Pavlov, op. cit., pp. 7–8; E. A. Lukasheva, "O vospitanii pravosoznaniya i pravovo kul'tury v period razvernutogo stroitel'stva kommunizma," *SGiP,* 1962, no. 7, p. 45.

[38] See M. Piskotin, B. Lazarev and D. Gaiderkov, "Sovety, demokratiya, samoupravlenie," *Kommunist,* 1962, no. 4, pp. 13–24.

[39] M. G. Kirichenko, "Sovetskaya sotsialisticheskaya demokratiya: puti i formy ee razvitiya," *SGiP,* 1965, no. II, p. 131.

[40] A. M. Zhilin, "Povyshenie roli mestnykh sovetov i razvitie obshchestvennykh nachal v ikh rabote (Po materialam Gor'kovskoi oblasti)," *SGiP,* 1966, no. 5, p. 64.

> Unfortunately, the authors of various scientific works and several practical workers reduce the problem of the development of socialist democracy to a one-sided enthusiasm for its voluntary forms and, proceeding from this, they contrast public to state organizations. The notion has been growing that the problem of the maturing of Communist public self-government may be reduced to a mechanical replacement of state by public forms, to the speeding up of the transfer to public organizations of state functions in the area of distribution, services for the population, the safeguarding of social order, culture, etc. Actually the development of the socialist state into Communist public self-government is a process which affects the system of all state and public organizations. Of course, the transfer of some functions of the state organs to public organizations has an important meaning, but nevertheless, that does not make up the most important part of the process of the development of socialist statehood in present conditions. For example, under the socialist mode of production the strictest control of society and the state over the measure of work and of consumption is an objective necessity. Public organizations actively participate in this control, but with the preservation of the leading role of the state.
>
> The development of public forms of socialist democracy must occur in interaction with the state forms.[41]

In an article reviewing Soviet literature on the political organization of socialist society, V. V. Varchuk and V. I. Razin have argued that there are "two sets of apparatus, as it were. One is the state apparatus and is sufficiently developed and basically stable. . . . The other apparatus is the public one and is poorly organized, unstable, operates only on the basis of enthusiasm and serves as an object of the most varied investigation." In other words, the public organizations do not perform the functions for which they were established. In fact, Varchuk and Razin imply that, although the membership of these organizations is relatively large, they have not actually taken over the functions of the state apparatus. If this is the case, they say, "it means that the enlistment of the public is being carried out only for the sake of enlistment itself, for the sake of the records (*radi otchetnosti*). . . ."[42]

The new interpretation of the functions of the Soviet state has re-established the priority of the state apparatus in the fields of education,

41 V. Chkhikvadze and V. Kotok, "Sovetskaya sotsialisticheskaya demokratiya," Kommunist, 1966, no. 5, p. 57.

42 V. V. Varchuk and V. I. Razin, "Issledovaniya v oblasti politicheskoi organizatsii sotsiali-sticheskogo obshchestva", *Voprosy filosofii,* 1967, no. 4, p. 143.

the protection of law and order, and so forth. Professor Chesnokov, who only a few years ago argued that "it seems expedient to transfer to public organizations above all the state functions of cultural and education work," now speaks of the "further development of the educational function of the socialist state."[43] Although he once argued that "questions of the observance of law . . . to an ever greater extent become a matter for the public organizations," he now sees the protection of public order as an "important aspect of the activity of the Soviet state."[44]

The public organizations, which were established in order to reduce bureaucracy in the Soviet Union, have proved to be extremely inefficient and, obviously, much more difficult to control than the state apparatus. The attempt is now being made to bring these organizations under the control of the organs of the state and to expend more effort in drawing people into the state machinery itself, where they will not only acquire the feeling of participation, but will also be under closer supervision by the party.

The Future of the All-People's State

The changes which have occurred in the interpretation of the all-people's state actually rob it of much of its meaning as a major revision in Marxist-Leninist theory. As we have noted, the role of public organizations is being played down and the importance of the state apparatus emphasized. These changes fit in with the general trend which has developed in the Soviet Union since the removal of Khrushchev from power more than three years ago, and which has been reaffirmed in the Central Committee Resolutions on the fiftieth anniversary of the Soviet revolution. The socialist state will continue to fulfill the basic functions of the construction of communism, and the process of its gradually withering away has once again been put off into the distant future.

In the actual functioning of the Soviet government, the new interpretations of the socialist state will have very little effect. Even under the

[43] Chesnokov, *Ot gosudarstvennosti* . . . , p. 37, and *id.,* "Sovetskoe gosudarstvo . . . ," p. 2. The Theses of the Central Committee of June 1967 also speak of the continued growth of the "economic-organizational and cultural-education functions" of the socialist state during the period of Communist construction ("50 let velikoi Oktyabr'skoi Sotsialisticheskoi revolyutsii," p. 3.

[44] Chesnokov, *Ot gosudarstvennosti* . . . , p. 36, and *id.,* "Sovetskoe gosudarstvo . . . ," p. 3.

all-people's state as originally conceived, the Communist party retained full control of the state apparatus and of all the public organizations. In fact, the party was called upon to play an even more important role during the period of the all-people's state than it had in the past.[45] This aspect of the theory of an all-people's state has not changed, for it is the party which is to direct and lead, the party which will be the ultimate decision-maker. One of the obvious reasons for the recent revisions which have occurred in the theory of the socialist state is the desire of the party apparatus to facilitate its control over the population, while at the same time increasing its popular support. This, the party officials feel, can better be accomplished through the traditional state apparatus than through the new public organizations.

[45] Pavlov, op. cit., p. 8.

POLITICIZED BUREAUCRACY: COMMUNIST CHINA*

Ezra F. Vogel

In many Western states, there is an important distinction between the roles of the politician and the civil servant. The politician is a generalist concerned with the manipulation of power, with the balancing of interest groups, with the organizing and molding of opinion, and with major policy questions. Depending upon fluctuations in relative support, he is subject to rapid rise and fall in power. The political role does not necessarily constitute a career and sometimes is not even a full-time occupational specialty.

In contrast, the civil servant is expected to remain politically neutral. He does not ordinarily take an active part in political campaigning or make political utterances, and he is expected to be sufficiently insulated from political pressures that he can perform his duties under a variety of politicians of varying political views. He is in principle appointed and promoted on the basis of universalistic qualifications. His work is commonly delimited to certain specified tasks, and his line of work constitutes a career. He rises by orderly procedures, depending on vacancies in the organization and his relative seniority and qualifications.

In Communist China, as in many other Communist countries, no sharp line divides the politician from the civil servant. All political leaders are simultaneously bureaucrats, and bureaucrats are not expected to be politically neutral; even if they are not party members they are expected to be devoted to the Communist cause and to specific

From Fred W. Riggs, ed., *Frontiers of Development Administration* (Durham: Duke University Press, 1970). Reprinted by permission of the publisher.

* This chapter was originally prepared for presentation at the annual meeting of the American Political Science Association in New York City, September 1966.

policies as well. Even in Western countries the top-level bureaucrat may be simultaneously a politician and a bureaucrat, but in China this mixture of politics and civil service penetrates the official hierarchy from the top to the bottom.

The Basic Strain: Political Loyalty Versus Competence

The fusion of politics and bureaucracy in one organization gives rise to a basic tension: how can the political function of aggregating power interests be balanced with the bureaucratic functions of rational administration?

One of the clearest and most explicit expressions of this conflict is found in discussions about the recruitment and promotion of personnel. Soon after the Communist takeover, during the early attempts to rationalize cadre policy, the issue was phrased as to which criterion was more important, "virtue" (*te*) or "ability" (*sai*). Should a person be promoted because of his virtue, his proven loyalty to the regime, or his ability, his capacity for performance? Later, in various organizations, the question was raised in terms of power and authority. Who should have power, the "red" or the "expert"? In a country like the United States where political activity is separated from the civil service, there may still be a power struggle between the political parties and the bureaucracy but this is not reflected in recruitment and promotion because the organizations are largely separated. In Communist China, where the bureaucracy and politics are fused, each case of appointment and promotion involves the same tension between political loyalty and competence.

As a result, the Chinese bureaucracy has not been able to establish purely universalistic criteria for appointment and promotion. The appointment to a bureaucracy cannot be made on the basis of competence alone. In fact, because of the importance of political loyalty, the Chinese Communists have never utilized any kind of objective test for admission to the bureaucracy, nor have they even been able to establish any other purely universalistic criterion such as years of education.

As in other Communist countries, the problem of establishing universalistic criteria for competence is made immeasurably more difficult because the poorer peasants and workers, those defined as the most loyal, are, by most measures of competence that might be devised, the least competent. The problem in China is much worse than in most other Communist countries because of the very low rate of literacy at the time of takeover and the fact that virtually no one in the loyal classes, the workers and peasants, was fully literate.

Although it is difficult to draw a sharp line between the literate and illiterate because of the many semiliterates who could read perhaps several hundred characters, the percentage of the population which was illiterate at the time of takeover has been estimated as high as 85 percent to 90 percent. On almost any kind of universalistic test of competence, the bourgeois and landlord classes despite their low political reliability would perform very well. Hence, no universalistic measure has been used for admission to cadre ranks or promotion within cadre ranks. One would expect that this problem would become less acute as the general level of education rises and the literacy rate rises. However, today, twenty years after takeover, although a whole age cohort has gone through the school system under communism, the desire to avoid universalistic measures of appointment and advancement remains as intense as ever. Even in school systems where educational performance can hardly be neglected, there has been continued embarrassment about the results of achievement tests which discriminate against the "right classes," and recently the regime has announced a renewed determination to do away with admissions examinations.

At the same time, however, performance criteria cannot be neglected entirely. The Chinese Communists want results; they want to make China into a modern state, with modern technology and industry, and they want this quickly. They have recognized that this requires competent personnel and, especially during the first five-year plan, they made a serious effort to improve the quality of personnel. The regime had to develop some standards for selecting and promoting those who performed better, and this was particularly apparent in the industrial, commercial, agricultural, and financial spheres where output is subject to more-or-less precise quantitative measurement.

The problem has been how to introduce these considerations of competence without making the "wrong social classes," the bourgeois and landlord classes, appear more competent. Since for political reasons the concern for competence has to be diluted, competence cannot be evaluated by strictly universalistic criteria. The regime had to develop other methods for evaluating competence, and the method devised was to evaluate performance not by test but by committee. The committee could make allowances for political loyalty, and it was hoped that the fact that it was a group rather than an individual making the decisions would limit nepotism and the formation of cliques. Competence is ordinarily evaluated not in terms of generalized abilities or knowledge but in terms of ability to perform a specific job. This evaluation of work performance can be conducted by either or both of two groups: a "small group" (*hsiao tsu*) of work peers or the "leadership small group" (*ling tao hsiao tsu*) in charge of a given unit. This method of evaluating competence is by no means pure; it is a compromise between considerations of politics and competence, and it is a compromise in which relative weight can be adjusted continuously as each case is considered.

Similar tensions and compromises between bureaucratic and political standards are reflected in the handling of the question of specialization. To a considerable extent the nonspecialist (*tuo mien shou*), the many-sided person who fills in wherever needed, is held up to the officials as the ideal for all to emulate, but in the context of the work setting, the nonspecialist (*wan chin yu*) may be regarded as an incompetent amateur. In part, of course, the Chinese problem is exacerbated by the fact that there are only a small number of specialists who have taken a regular training program and that there are large numbers of practitioners of any given specialty who have not received standardized training. The common compromise which is held up for cadres to follow is the requirement that functionaries should be prepared to move from one job to another as assigned, but that they should develop competence in a specialty while working on the job.

The tension between competence and loyalty, between the specialist (*nei hang*) and nonspecialist (*wai hang*), has been a continuous and intense one. The fight is intensified because the only method the children of the bourgeois and landlord class have to legitimize their activities and points of view is by stressing performance standards. There is no underlying Chinese value which stresses the importance of academic freedom or any other kinds of freedom. The person who wishes to insulate himself from greater political pressures has only one legitimate basis of appeal, the importance of competent work for meeting the goals set by the regime. Even during the Hundred Flowers, when considerably more direct expression was permitted, one main line of criticism had to do with political interference with specialists who were trying to do their own work. Just as concern for specialized competence is used by those alienated from the system as a focus for resistance or at least relief from political pressures, so it is an object of attack by those who are concerned about the political successes of the regime. People are criticized, for example, for thinking only of their work and not the Thoughts of Chairman Mao, which has become a symbol for political commitment to the system as a whole.

The precise balance of power between the "red" and the "expert" has varied considerably. In times of greatest mobilization, as during the collectivization campaign in 1955–1956 or the Great Leap Forward, political considerations tended to assume priority, and the "red" gained in relative power. In times of comparative stability, as during the period of the first five-year plan and in the relatively free period following the Ninth Plenum in 1961, the "expert" gained in relative status. In the case of a direct conflict between the "red" and "expert," the "red," the political considerations, have taken priority, as expressed in the slogan "Politics Take Command" (*Cheng chih kua shuai*).

Career patterns in Communist China also reflect the mixture of political and rational-bureaucratic considerations. Aside from the unstable early period following takeover when vast numbers of positions were opened up and functionaries were frequently shifted from one job to another as demanded, career patterns have generally followed a fairly regular progression much as one might expect in an ordinary bureaucracy, with some striking exceptions that have occurred for political reasons. The exceptions are concentrated at the time of rectification campaigns when political considerations take on greater primacy. At the time of rectification campaigns, despite the variations in content and seriousness, the politically vulnerable are attacked and sacrificed. At the end of a rectification campaign, new openings are available as a result of the removal of the politically vulnerable, and the politically reliable, those who played a key role in the exposure and criticism of the politically unreliable, are promoted. In other words, under ordinary circumstances promotions within the apparatus are likely to be based on annual assessments when rational-bureaucratic considerations of competence are given greater weight, but at the time of rectification campaigns, promotions and demotions are more likely to be based on political considerations.

Although no formal distinctions are made between functionaries who are more concerned with political matters and functionaries more concerned with administrative matters, informally there does tend to be a difference. Broadly speaking, it is possible to distinguish two general career patterns. The one, the political career pattern, is based primarily on activism and loyalty to the party. The person seeking this career is more likely to be from the proletariat or peasant class and to have had fewer social relationships with the wrong classes and is thus less vulnerable politically. He is likely to have a relatively "low cultural level," (i.e., have less education) and to be assigned a job where greater trust and less competence is required. He is, for example, more likely to be in party organizational and public security work.

In contrast, another career pattern is based chiefly on competence, on general intellectual ability and specialized technical skills. This person is more likely to come from a bourgeois or landlord background or at least to have had more contacts with people from this background and to feel more at home in this kind of setting. He tends to have a high level of education and to be assigned jobs where political reliability is less of an issue and knowledge and skill are more important. He is, for example, more likely to be engaged in economic, educational and cultural, and united front activities. Thus, within the politicized bureaucracy there is an embryonic differentiation between the political and the rational-bureaucratic careers. However, as the Chinese Communists make clear with their motto of "red and expert," they hope to limit the amount of differentiation which takes place. Their aim is to have those who are reliable politically become experts at their work and to have those who are experts become politically reliable, i.e., to prevent a sharp differentiation of political from rational-bureaucratic.

The Politicization of Bureaucratic Functions

As a result of the lack of differentiation between political and administrative matter, many activities which we Westerners think of as bureaucratic are affected by this politicization.

First of all, a very high level of political commitment is expected of everyone in the bureaucracy. Everyone is expected to express this commitment frequently in his small group meetings; study sessions and propaganda meetings are called to reinforce this basic political commitment. Cadres are expected to be familiar with and committed to major Communist party policies and directives.

The demands for conformity in political thinking go far beyond what is ordinarily expected of functionaries in a rational-bureaucratic setting. Deviations are not permitted, and those whose mere comments might cast doubt on their loyalty are often prosecuted with great vehemence. These demands for conformity are analogous to, but more severe than, the demands for loyalty that are sometimes made on American civil servants by their political leaders.

The demands which can be placed on cadres go far beyond the performance of special tasks. Although they may be given specialized assignments they are expected to perform almost any work that might be assigned to them, regardless of how remote from their ordinary specialty, including assignments to farm work in the countryside. Their work may have fairly routine scheduling, but they will be expected to work far beyond the usual time under special pressures.

Disciplinary measures are applied to insure political reliability. Communist China's bureaucracy has not witnessed the violence of purges in Russia in the 1930's, but it has institutionalized what Donald Klein of Columbia University refers to as the "semipurge," and the cultural revolution amounted to a serious purge at all levels. Cadres who are not responsive to political leadership are sent away for study or physical labor for periods of time and then returned to work, although often at a somewhat lower position. This practice tends to maintain a high degree of responsiveness to political pressures from above even if it derives more from anxiety than from spontaneous enthusiasm.

The bursts of political activities and the pressures generated within the bureaucracy are disruptive of ordinary routine procedures. Nowhere is this more apparent than in the campaign, a time of intense political mobilization. Work is sometimes disrupted or even stopped, and ordinary decisions are held in abeyance while all energies are concentrated on the primary task expressed in the campaign. Although bureaucratic functions are disrupted in these times of political intervention, some attempt is made to limit the disruptions caused by the campaigns, and this has been particularly striking since the Great Leap Forward campaign because it so disrupted ordinary operating procedures that it caused the overall work a major setback. An attempt is made to control the timing of these political campaigns so that they interfere minimally with routine activities, and this is feasible since most of the political pressures emanate from above rather than rising spontaneously from below. For example, the annual rectification campaign in rural cooperatives is ordinarily held in the winter, immediately after the fall harvest and just before the spring planting. Rectification campaigns in schools are conducted in shifts so that someone is left on duty and work is disrupted only minimally.

Because the bureaucracy is not neutral, changes in political policy are more disruptive to bureaucratic organization than in Western countries, where the bureaucracy is more insulated from political considerations. All officials in the bureaucracy of any consequence are expected to express strong commitments not only to the overall party but to the main outlines of current policy. Thus, responsibility for errors in policy lie not only in the hands of a few decision-makers, but in the hands of large numbers of bureaucrats. As a result, any time an important policy change is made, bureaucrats must undertake a thorough confession of their own previous errors. When a new policy comes down, not only must everyone study the new policy, but all those most closely identified with the old policy must criticize themselves for their errors.

This is true even in such a simple matter as the adjustment of local production quotas. If provincial officials announce a given quota for agricultural or industrial production and if as a result of meetings with the ministerial officials concerned the quotas are later adjusted, the local officials must confess their errors in setting the previous quota. In rational-bureaucratic settings, the neutrality of the bureaucracy permits it to adjust to the changes in policy without internal disruptions, but in Communist China because all policy decisions require more commitment from the bureaucrats, it is not possible to adjust to changes of policy so gracefully. In some cases officials identified with a given policy must even be sent away for a period of study when a new policy is announced. This replacement is more like what one would expect of an outdated or unpopular politician in the West, rather than of a bureaucratic official, and the replacement of a Chinese bureaucrat also reflects the fact that he is playing a political role.

Needless to say, bureaucrats are anxious to be criticized only as often as necessary, and the frequent changes in policy have led bureaucrats in China to seek some degree of neutrality that would protect them from being criticized if policy should change. Over the years this has had the effect of making lower-level bureaucrats cautious in going beyond the directives from higher authorities when they endorse present policies. They say what it is necessary to say to support such policies, but they often phrase their statements so that it would be difficult to criticize them even if the policy should change. If, for example, the general approach coming from higher levels is to give more consideration to people's wants at a given time, a local official might say, "We should avoid being commandistic and study actual situations in order to unite with the masses," a statement which would be difficult to criticize even if a hard line comes down at a later time.

Many problems which are viewed in the West as problems of work morale, accident proneness, and waste are treated in Communist China as political problems. Indeed, any problem where personal motivation is relevant is regarded in China as a political problem. If a person is slow, late to work, involved in an accident, or wastes materials he is likely to undergo an examination of his "thought" to prove that he is basically committed to the regime. Even reorganizations of organizational structure are likely to involve examination of political thought, especially if some of the members are to be dismissed or transferred down to productive activities.

The Bureaucratization of Political Functions

But just as what we Westerners think of as bureaucratic organization takes on a political coloring, the political activities in China also take on a bureaucratic coloring. Political leaders are not freewheeling agents outside the bureaucracy but paid officials who are given the same benefits as other bureaucrats. They operate within the framework of bureaucratic organization and bureaucratic procedures.

In Communist China, the masses have relatively little political power, and the effective power base of the politician is inside the bureaucracies.

The issues that arise inevitably involve the respective bureaucratic organizations, and it is difficult to separate policy from interbureaucratic struggles over funds and power.

The nature of the Chinese Communist control system makes it very difficult to develop political parties or even closed cliques within the bureaucracy. The balance of power is clearly in the hands of the higher authorities, who can break up incipient cliques by sending in outsiders or by transferring insiders. Political groups might better be described not as cliques but as semicliques in which functionaries of like interest, educational level, place and language of origin, etc., tend to work together on given issues. But the person whose support one aims to recruit is not someone with generalized influence, or just any important person sympathetic with a cause, but rather a bureaucrat whose position permits him to influence the way a decision is made. One may try to mobilize those members likely to be sympathetic to support a given issue, but the politics of getting support on any issue is determined by the formal bureaucratic structure relevant to the point at issue.

One of the problems with the system as seen by the top leaders is that basic policies quickly become bogged down in bureaucratic operations. The higher authorities attempt to keep a fairly open political structure by widespread use of special cadre meetings, task forces, and campaigns. But over the years, even campaigns which are designed to promote the maximum amount of flexibility in energizing the system tend to be carried out in relatively set bureaucratic patterns.

Advantages and Disadvantages of Politicized Bureacracies

The main purpose of this chapter has been to describe and analyze the nature of a politicized bureaucracy rather than to evaluate its effectiveness. Evaluating the effectiveness of a system as complicated and large as the Chinese Communist organization requires a far more ambitious effort. However, several striking features deserve comment.

One of the impressive characteristics of Chinese Communist bureaucratic organizations, the largest the world has ever known, is the remarkable speed with which it can be mobilized for effective action. To be sure, the effectiveness derives partly from a very large propaganda network, but it is immeasurably aided by the high degree of politicization of the bureaucracy. Because functionaries do engage in continuous political study and because those in responsible positions are highly politicized, the bureaucracy can be mobilized in a way that officials in Western representative democracies cannot. During the Great Leap

Forward bureaucrats throughout the country not only worked overtime but even slept overnight in their offices for a period of months; such dedication is probably rare in the annals of bureaucracy even under wartime conditions.

Despite the concerns of the Chinese leadership, the chief problem arises not from resistance to mobilization but from the lack of resistance. Because the bureaucracy is not an autonomous organization concerned with civil administration, it cannot provide the stable balance wheel that bureaucracies in many countries provide. In China, there are no bureaucratic procedures or practices which are not subject to attack and modification in the event of mobilization. Forms and reports may be dispensed with, leading bureaucrats sent to work in factories and farms without replacement, and remaining bureaucrats may devote their energies to the current campaign without regard to the ongoing responsibilities of the bureaucracy. Indeed, this was precisely the problem with the Great Leap Forward. With the massive mobilization, routine administrative tasks were neglected. In the end this proved the undoing of the mobilization efforts. It was the failure of administrative organs to provide coordination and to scale down targets and practices to reasonable limits that caused the serious difficulties. Indeed, so serious were these difficulties that the regime has since been much more cautious in upsetting ordinary bureaucratic operations, but the general problem has not entirely disappeared.

The subjection of bureaucrats to political evaluation and criticism has also had a serious effect on morale, just as political pressures and risks in the United States during the McCarthy era exacted their toll on bureaucratic morale. The impact of the fear of criticism is to make bureaucrats more cautious and less innovative than they might otherwise be. Although lower-level bureaucrats in China are continuously told to adapt policies to the local situation, they are reluctant to take any moves without getting specific approval from their superiors. The bureaucrat in China is not even protected by bureaucratic rules and procedures and simply performing his job properly is not adequate protection. The result is to make him dependent, not on rules, but on the wishes of his superiors. He comes close to being an "obedient tool," but he is not likely to be a creative innovator in performing his assigned tasks. His goal is not to perform a specific job well but to please his superior.

I have not tried in this brief essay to give a general and rounded treatment of bureaucracy in Communist China but to highlight what I believe to be one of its most salient characteristics, the fusion of political and bureaucratic concerns, and to examine some of the results of this phenomenon. In this very central characteristic, the state bureaucracy functions much as it does in the Soviet Union despite the very different stages of economic development in the two countries. Most Western social scientists have argued that the development of independent rational-bureaucratic organization has been functional for economic modernization, but this is not the Chinese view. Even in the Soviet Union there is no evidence that the fusion of politics and bureaucracy is in imminent danger of being dissipated. This fusion is probably even less likely to be abandoned in Communist China.

THE CONSTITUTIONALISM MOVEMENT IN YUGOSLAVIA: A PRELIMINARY SURVEY*

Winston M. Fisk

ONE of the critically important trends in the government and politics of the East European Communist states in recent years has been the quite steady and rapid development in Yugoslavia of some striking forms of pluralization and institutionalization of power, and of some concomitant fairly well enforced legal restrictions on power. The development is often called by the Yugoslavs their movement toward "constitution-

From *Slavic Review,* XXX, 2 (June 1971), pp. 277–97. Reprinted by permission.

* This article is a report of the first results of a continuing study. It began when the writer held a Fulbright research professorship in Yugoslavia in 1965–66. Since then it has received generous support from the American Philosophical Society, Claremont Men's College, the Claremore Fund, and the Henry Salvatori Center; the writer records his thanks to these organizations. Several related aspects of the subject are somewhat speculatively explored in Winston M. Fisk, "A Communist *Rechtsstaat?*—The Case of Yugoslav Constitutionalism," *Government and Opposition,* 5, no. 1 (Winter 1970): 41. The writer owes a special debt of gratitude to Professor Jovan Djordjević of the University of Belgrade and to Professor Fred Warner Neal of the Claremont Graduate School. The study is based almost entirely on participant interviews and direct observation (both now readily possible) in Yugoslavia since September 1965. It is necessarily preliminary and partial, since so little work has been done directly on the subject by Western scholars. It explores the thesis that at least in the Yugoslav setting a Communist regime can generate a form of genuinely constitutional rule, and that the Yugoslav movement may well be a real and lasting affair, and an alternative in the future of Communist regimes. The conclusion so far is that the thesis is about halfway proven, and that some tenable hypotheses about *why* and *how* such rule gets generated are now emerging.

alism and legality."[1]** However, though Titoism has been much studied, this particular movement,[2] one of the most far-reaching and fundamental of all of the Titoist innovations, has received little explicit examination in Western scholarship,[3] even in such a colorful manifestation as the exercise by the new constitutional courts of the power of judicial review over major legislation approved by the party. This article deals with the nature and dynamics of the movement and with some implications it may have.

An influential Yugoslav political scientist and theoretician suggests the central position in the Communist world that the Yugoslavs assign to this movement: "Modern society tends to set up a more complex organization of power, more decentralized and more stable. . . . the institutionalization of political power is, at present, the main and even historical problem of the socialist state and society."[4] The view expressed in this and in the large body of similar Yugoslav statements leads to the quite dramatic assertion the Yugoslavs are now making (which, among other things, runs contrary both to orthodox Communist doctrine and to the usual practice of Communist regimes when fully in power) to the effect that Communist states are similar to other states in this vital respect and that Communist states, as they become modern, contain forces which tend to generate political orders that have, *mutatis mutandis,* some of the characteristics of classic Western constitutional-

** This article was written before the adoption of a new constitution by the Yugoslav Federal Assembly in February 1974. [Editors' Note]

[1] *Ustavnost i zakonitost;* see chapter 7 of the 1963 Yugoslav federal constitution.

[2] "Movement" is common in both official and scholarly Yugoslav usage and is probably the best term available, but it may suggest more strength and inevitability in the development than Westerners would be willing to recognize.

[3] Thus, though there has been some good journalism, there are few articles in the scholarly journals touching the matter in any depth. Representative of recent books is H. Gordon Skilling's valuable *The Governments of Communist East Europe* (New York, 1966), which gives the movement little treatment. George W. Hoffman and Fred Warner Neal, *Yugoslavia and the New Communism* (New York, 1962), though still basic, was published before the 1963 constitutions and numerous other important events affecting tbe movement. Mention must also be made of Phyllis Auty's admirable *Yugoslavia* (New York, 1965), but it is addressed to broader issues. Two recent books are Wayne S. Vucinich, ed., *Contemporary Yugoslavia* (Berkeley and Los Angeles, 1969), and M. George Zaninovich, *The Development of Socialist Yugoslavia* (Baltimore, 1968).

[4] Jovan Djordjević, "Political Power in Yugoslavia," *Government and Opposition,* 2, no. 2 (February 1967): 207.

ism.[5] This is a large assertion indeed, and its basis needs to be examined.

Ghiţa Ionescu, in an outstanding contemporary analysis of the political dynamics of Communist East Europe as a whole, offers the following as one of his conclusions:

> This analysis of the political societies of the European Communist states has concentrated on the study of their present realities. If one were to attempt to forecast their future one would do so by singling out the two features which have shown such a basic continuity in these realities that they might be considered as two irreversible trends. The first is that the pluralization and the reinstitutionalization which follows from it will continue to lead to the dissolution of the Apparat. The second . . . is that the European Communist states will in the future become more European than Communist.[6]

This interpretation raises with renewed force the often-discussed suggestion that these Communist regimes, after their messianic, terrorist, and revolutionary youth, may be slowly headed toward something like a sedate, law-abiding, and respectable middle age.

The Yugoslav movement toward pluralization undoubtedly will influence the general East European trend, whether or not Yugoslavia is *a* or *the* "model," or "pattern," or "leader." The Yugoslavs argue that it is none of these, partly from conviction that every country must find its own way to socialism from its own traditions, habits, and "objective circumstances," and partly from shrewd political analysis.[7] However, they are clearly saying not only that constitutionalism is a natural and inevitable movement for Yugoslavia but also that the other East European Communist regimes will sooner or later move decisively toward constitutionalism and legality.

To be sure, both Ionescu and the Yugoslavs may be overstating the matter, and certainly simple ideas of convergence must be treated with

[5] "Constitutionalism" is a slippery term, but it can be useful. See the clarifying recent discussions by Sartori, Morris-Jones, and Vile: Giovanni Sartori, "Constitutionalism: A Preliminary Discussion," *American Political Science Review,* 56 (1962): 853–64; W. H. Morris-Jones, Communications, *American Political Science Review,* 59 (1965): 439–40; M. J. C. Vile, *Constitutionalism and the Separation of Powers* (Oxford, 1967).

[6] Ghiţa Ionescu, *The Politics of the European Communist States* (London and New York, 1967), p. 271.

[7] Their most common explanations of their influence are (1) that they are respected because they were the first anti-Stalinists and the first to experiment with devices (e.g., the market) that everyone now agrees are promising and (2) that all the East European countries have some conditions and some problems in common.

great caution. Further, Ionescu would not want the trends he notes to be projected as something fixed and automatic. In addition, the Yugoslav situation may have significant unique features. And so on. The affair requires careful analysis before we can begin to explain it, let alone make predictions.

At least three major phenomena of contemporary Yugoslavia that are especially vital to the constitutionalism movement because of their pluralizing and institutionalizing effect have advanced considerably beyond their rather small beginnings (if these are in fact real beginnings) elsewhere in Eastern Europe.[8]

One of the three phenomena is that the Yugoslavs are now attempting, probably for the first time in any Communist regime, to govern *politically*. There is now a good deal of political activity in Yugoslavia in the classic Western sense, a sense well expressed by Bernard Crick: "Politics, then, can be simply defined as the activity by which differing interests within a given unit of rule [e.g., a nation] are conciliated by giving them a share in power in proportion to their importance to the welfare and survival of the whole community."[9] Furthermore—an important point—this political activity goes on to a decisive and increasing degree through the ordinary channels of government and politics (e.g., legislatures, interests groups, executive and administrative organs, public opinion, law, etc.) rather than through party or covert channels. And the Yugoslavs in their own thinking have moved away from the simplistic utopianism (and then absolutism) of traditional Marxism-Leninism and *apparat* rule. They are addressing themselves to the problems of the organization of political power among institutions, at least as much in the manner of Western politicians and political scientists as of orthodox Communists. They have built up a rather developed and potent set of governmental-political institutions which lie in the way of return to authoritarian "administrative" rule. These are prominent realities in contemporary Yugoslavia. There is, not quite but almost, an institutional settlement.

The second phenomenon is the new economic order. All the East European countries have moved away from a postwar economy that was almost totally centralized and Eastward-oriented. The Yugoslav shift—the last major steps taken in the "economic reforms" begun in 1965 and still continuing—is drastic and has been widely discussed.

[8] The movement is of course affected by the whole of Yugoslavia's historical experience and present circumstances—e.g., the nationalities problem, the historical fact of self-liberation, the personalities of Tito and his associates, the country's status as a nonsatellite, and so forth. The three phenomena seem of most immediate causative political relevance, but certainly long and complex chains of causation lie behind them as well.

[9] Bernard Crick, *In Defence of Politics*, rev. ed. (Baltimore, 1964), p. 21.

The elements most significant for constitutionalism may be summarized briefly: the federal budget declines in importance nearly every year; the Plan is indicative and predictive only, not detailed and compulsory; the workers' council system and enterprise autonomy are established; investment is now largely out of the hands of the federal government; the market dominates in most fields; and the economy is, as the Yugoslavs say, "entering into the international division of labor." The political power that grows out of economic power has in many respects been decisively pluralized.

The third phenomenon is experimentation. The Yugoslavs have been innovative; many significant methods and ideas in government and politics have been tried out. And many of the experiments are like genies, who once let out of the bottle of authoritarian and ideological rule are hard to force back in. Some of the experiments (e.g., functional representation in legislatures) are old ideas but have rarely been put to the test before. Some (e.g., a constitutional judicature with broad powers of judicial review) are classics borrowed from Western tradition and revised for Yugoslav use. Some (e.g., judicially enforced administrative law for the protection of the citizen against unlawful government action) are fairly standard in the West but are little known in Communist regimes, and have been expanded in Yugoslavia beyond what is customary in the West. Some (e.g., the development of economic law and litigation by specialized courts, much like the medieval law merchant) are startling revivals of the past in today's world. Some (e.g., developed drafting and information services, both technical and policy-oriented, for the legislatures) are methods long thought in the West to be good ideas but seldom adopted. Some (e.g., drastic decentralization and "de-étatization" of government) are more or less new. Some (e.g., workers' self-management in economic enterprises and in all other "working organizations," including to a degree even government) are new attempts to apply ideas that in various forms have existed for years in reformist thought. Some (e.g., the new and increasingly more limited role of the party) are revolutionary in Communist thought and practice. Out of such experimentation many elements of the constitutionalism movement have emerged.

It may be held that the political order in Yugoslavia today functions through four main clusters of processes, each with its associated bodies of doctrine and structure of institutions.

The first of these clusters is governmental pluralism. This somewhat unsatisfactory term is intended to include federalism and decentralization but to exclude the curious phenomenon of "de-étatization," which, though related to governmental pluralism, is at root part of the second cluster, social self-government, which in turn, though certainly pluralist, is a social and political matter that stands in a substantial way apart from government. The third cluster is what the Yugoslavs call "assembly government," or the "assembly system." This is the embodiment of Yugoslavia's special version of the old Marxist idea of unity of power. The fourth cluster has to do with the governmental and political side of the legal order. Its most spectacular aspect is the constitutional judiciary, in existence since 1964 and employing with increasing vigor the power of judicial review against both federal and republic action. As we shall see, however, there are many other vital governmental and political uses which the Yugoslavs make of law and the courts.

We shall discuss these four clusters separately, though they are interactive and interdependent. First, however, we must clear up a vital threshold question, that of the position of the party.

The Party and the Movement

Usually in an analysis of a Communist regime, primacy is given to the party and its *apparat*. For some years the Yugoslav party has insisted that in important respects such is not the case in Yugoslavia. That is probably true. With the progress of the constitutionalism movement, the party is no longer the major center of policy formation, decision-making, or policy effectuation, even informally.[10] The causes for this change need not detain us; the important fact is that it has taken place, freeing our four clusters to dominate the polity.

More and more the party is staying away from everyday governing and politicking. Thus it is fairly well established that nobody (except Tito, an exception less important than it might seem) may hold high office in both the party and the government. This is not a rule of rigid separation, but certainly deviates sharply from Soviet practice. And most of the party line deals only with broad issues and in broad terms, leaving some room to urge differing policy views without disloyalty to the party. The party, by established and repeated policy, at least formally eschews a role *as authority;* it asserts that it is no longer "an instrument of power" but an "ideological force" only. Observation and interviews in policy processes bear out this official picture, as do documents drawn from these processes. Matters are especially clear in the complexes of legislative processes which play an important part in the

[10] Reservations must be made for basic and long-range policy, for certain policy areas (e.g., foreign relations), and for some emergency situations (e.g., the Ranković affair), none of which are directly relevant here.

polity. Both general inquiry and specific legislative episodes suggest that, especially at the higher levels, policy is being made by the overt legislative processes rather than offstage in party caucuses.[11]

The party is fully committed in doctrine and in practice to the constitutionalism movement; it sees the pluralization and institutionalization of power as the future of the political order, and expects to find its place in such an order. Its motives are only in part libertarian. The party came to the conclusion years ago that only in the constitutionalism movement could be found the economic dynamism and political stability that Yugoslav socialism must have to survive. This view continues to be reinforced, although the movement is still not accepted by some conservative elements in the party (and interestingly enough is suspected by some semianarchistical young liberals as being "bureaucratic" and too formal).

Thus the Yugoslav constitutionalism movement is an extraordinary course for a Communist regime to have undertaken. If the party does complete, and maintain, this shift from instrument of power in an authoritarian system to merely an ideological and catalytic agent in a more or less constitutional system, something new will have been discovered about the potentialities of Communist rule. Some scholars have begun to discuss the future of the monolithic party, and whether such parties alone can run modern states.[12] Yugoslav events already are shedding considerable light, and will shed much more, on what may be an alternative.

Governmental Pluralism

For the Yugoslavs, governmental pluralism begins with federalism, both because of the doctrinal and practical centrality they give to it and because it rests upon some of the most fundamental facts of Yugoslav society—especially the existence of the several major nationalities, with their own territories and strongly felt separate histories and traditions. The prewar solution to the problems these conditions produced was suppression and Serbian hegemony. The solution during the period of Communist dictatorship (roughly 1945–51) was suppression, centralization, and an attempt to ignore the whole matter. The current solution, expected to be permanent and likely to be, is a constitutional one—a

[11] Several detailed legislative histories were done in the course of the present study.

[12] See, for example, the symposium, "The Dead End of the Monolithic Parties," *Government and Opposition,* 2, no. 2 (February 1967).

complex federalism of a special and perhaps unique character along with a decentralization perhaps equally complex and unusual.

At the threshold, however, one encounters doubt among commentators that Yugoslavia's constitutional federalism is of any real significance. The main reasons for this doubt are two. One is the doctrine that federalism is a transitional form, a way station on the road either to consolidation or dissolution.[13] The second is the doubt that any Communist regime will give up strict and discretionary control. The second point seems not to apply to the Yugoslav party. And the Yugoslavs are making a determined effort to avoid both of the developments that the doctrine of the transitory nature of federalism contemplates. Thus the republic capitals, when we look at specific events and policy issues, are clearly independent and major centers of power.[14] Indeed, it is significant that many able Yugoslav politicians, well qualified to judge which way the wind is blowing, have left Belgrade and are pursuing their careers in their home republics. The question of stability against dissolution remains, but so far no real tendency toward dissolution can be detected. Though separatist ideas exist, they stop short of real substance.

Yugoslav federalism is not the familiar classic type in which power is distributed between central and constituent governments in supposedly watertight compartments. Rather it is part of a large scheme of cooperative decentralization. For example, the communes (*opštine*), in theory and it seems increasingly in practice as the constitutionalism movement goes on, are not regarded as permanent creatures or even subdivisions of either the federation or the republics.[15] Rather they are seen as the building blocks, the natural and basic units of the whole system, dealing directly and on a plane of at least formal and juridical equality with republic and federation alike.[16] (Thus they draw their status and powers directly from the federal constitution.) Further, this official equality seems often to have some reality; for example, the political muscle that a vigorous commune can show at least in dealing

[13] See, for example, William H. Riker, *Federalism: Origin, Operation, Significance* (Boston, 1964).

[14] One major intention, and probable consequence, of the December 1968 amendments to the federal constitution was to make the republics more independent by strengthening their position in the federal legislature.

[15] The communes have been much examined by Yugoslav social scientists, but there is little on them in English. One study by an American scholar is Jack C. Fisher's *Yugoslavia: A Multi-National State* (San Francisco, 1968).

[16] Thus, under the federal constitution of 1963, the regime's central political as well as legal declaration, the commune is "the basic sociopolitical community" (article 96), "autonomously" passes regulations and determines its own revenues (article 99), and is the repository of all governmental powers not assigned by the constitution to the republics or the federation.

with many of the lesser federation and republic agencies is often substantial, and matters tend to be worked out by negotiation and cooperation rather than by command from the top.[17] And the movement seems to be toward the communes—for strong economic reasons (e.g., the communes now are the principal founders of new economic enterprises) as well as for reasons of governmental pluralism.

Relations between republics and the federation are increasingly collaborative and cooperative—and constitutionalized. Of particular interest are the recurrent heated disputes between them over "basic" and "supplementary" legislation. These problems arise out of the inevitable frictions of any federation, but specific form is given them by a Yugoslav innovation in the constitutional law of federalism.

Under articles 160 and 161 of the constitution of the federation the federal government can legislate on a wide range of subjects—so wide that at first glance little room seems left for the republics. But there is a catch. Only in two major areas—foreign policy and foreign trade, and the national security—is the federal legislative power exclusive; only there can it enact what are called "complete" or "comprehensive" laws (*potpuni zakoni*), which can exclude any republic legislation.[18] The federal government does have a rather undefined power to enact "general" laws (*opšti zakoni*), but these are hardly laws at all. (They have no binding force, obligate nobody, and create no enforceable rights; they are little more than hortative guides which the republics and communes are expected to take broadly into account in their own legislation.)

The disagreement comes over the "basic" laws (*osnovni zakoni*). These are real laws, lying between "complete" and "general" laws, and have binding force. They comprise most of the federation's constitutional jurisdiction. But they are intended to be framework enactments only—that is, declarations of general policy—and are almost inoperative until supplemented *and made effective* by subsequent republic legislation. Thus the federal jurisdiction is sharply limited.

The republics are becoming more and more keenly jealous of their prerogatives of supplementation and effectuation, and they wage vigorous political, bureaucratic, and juridical battles against basic laws which they think go too far and encroach unconstitutionally on republic policy-making territory or, on the other hand, do not go far enough and

[17] This is strengthened by the communes' very considerable constitutional jurisdiction in the administration of federal and republic laws. See, for example, articles 96 and 101. The republics may be strengthened somewhat by the December 1968 amendments to the federal constitution.

[18] See, however, section 2 of amendment 16 of the December 1968 amendments.

do not take the responsibility they should under the 1963 constitution's division of powers.

Increasing economic decentralization appears in all the standard indicators. Thus, significantly, investment policy is now largely out of the hands of the federation and into the hands of republics, communes, other sociopolitical communities, independent investment banks created in part by the communities but not ruled by them, and individual economic enterprises.

For reasons such as these Yugoslav governmental life is not simply federal but is pluralized in ways that include but go beyond classic federalism—a system in which decentralization, dependent upon and defined and structured by constitutional principle, has proceeded on a dozen fronts and seems likely to proceed further.

Social Self-Government

Central to this constitutionalism-based *governmental* pluralism, but even more fundamental, is the master concept of all Yugoslav political thought and practice and the *political* mainspring of Yugoslav constitutionalism. This is the radically pluralistic self-government in the sociopolitical communities (i.e., governmental units) and the working organizations (i.e., economic and other institutions). The basic idea has been appearing here and there in Marxist thought for years, connected with the dream of the coercive state withering into some kind of idyllic cooperative socialist commonwealth. The venturesome Yugoslavs, however, with their penchant for translating farfetched Marxist theory into action, put the idea into sweeping practice. The decisive Yugoslav contribution is that their cooperative utopia is to be grounded in a constitutional system rather than dependent upon some indeterminate end to conflict.

To the Yugoslavs, social self-government is a most important phenomenon in their polity. Indeed, some Yugoslav theorists find socialism itself a second-level matter, existing for the sake of social self-government and at bottom adopted to make it possible. The roots of social self-government are of course in Marx. But they are seen increasingly by the Yugoslavs as being in an early, "humanistic," anthropologically oriented Marx. It should be added, however, that the Yugoslav theoreticians contend that these humanistic and anthropological strains continue through Marx's later thought and are a vital part of his mature system overlooked by other Marxist scholars, especially those under Russian influence. The Yugoslavs in short, with Yugoslav self-confidence, see themselves as the true expounders of the whole of the doctine, and the Russians and their followers as putting forward a version that is both truncated and distorted.[19]

Social self-government began in 1950 with workers' councils in industry. It was some time before these groups really worked their way out from under party and government domination. Worker's self-management and enterprise autonomy, another aspect of social self-government, now appear established, perhaps especially the latter,[20] it is impossible to speak with precision because not enough empirical investigation has been done. Yugoslav social scientists find a high degree of development and strength in these areas,[21] especially in enterprise autonomy, as do the few Western scholars who have looked at the matter extensively. Evidence collected in the present study is limited but tends to bear this out. For example, the investment banks, so important to the economy and so natural a place for party and government influence to hang on, now function quite independently and are highly influential,[22] thus the National Bank of Yugoslavia is back to the classic central banking functions, note issuance, monetary policy, and foreign exchange management, along with only a small amount of advising on investment matters when asked.

From industry, social self-government has spread to most aspects of life, even to government agencies and the courts. The newspapers continually report instances in which it has been extended or strengthened. Social life is somewhat further along the road than political life, for most social groups now are self-governing. But political life does not lag far behind. One finds pluralism and cooperativism to an extent never before operative in a Communist political order. The Westerner, however, is not so likely to see parallels with Western pluralism in Yugoslav society as he is to see something more familiar to him than the traditional monolithic communism.

19 This Marxist humanism is usually associated with the advanced and supposedly rather heretical *Praxis* group, but it is actually more widespread than that and is to be found in virtually all circles of Yugoslav thought except the most conservative, which are becoming more and more isolated.

20 This is true despite the still somewhat ambiguous position of the enterprise director, who is in some measure a representative of the governmental units or agencies that founded or regulate the enterprise.

21 Major studies have been carried out by the Institute of Social Sciences of Belgrade and by several of the government institutes for public administration.

22 This has been fostered by the catastrophic failure of the political factories (uneconomic factories established by political influence and for political reasons) and by quiet foreign pressures in connection with international loans and grants.

Two tendencies in the thinking behind social self-government constantly appear and must be distinguished. One is toward decentralization, the more specifically federal and governmental aspects of which we have already mentioned; Yugoslav theory and practice extend it broadly into devolution outward and downward of a large number of governmental and political activities. The Yugoslavs tend to hold as a matter of faith, doctrine, and practical conviction the drastic view that many processes of governing are better in the hands of small units, that much of governing really is "the problems of our street," and that larger problems and processes and units are often basically epiphenomena.

The second tendency is toward "de-étatization," a less familiar and even more drastic matter. This is the Yugoslav policy, well developed and vigorously practiced, of transferring as many governmental functions as possible (and the Yugoslavs argue that the possible number is large—startlingly large to the Western observer) to nongovernmental and quasi-governmental organizations, often in the nature of cooperatives. For example, much of social insurance (a large field) has already gone this route. More is expected, and there are newspaper accounts almost daily of new instances of "de-étatization."

The classic Communist practice has been toward centralization and "étatization." The Yugoslavs are reversing it. What is emerging is neither Western nor Soviet.

No useful statistics are available, but the social self-government movement is clearly broad and deep, and seems to be gaining momentum. It is regarded as one of the society's principal weapons in what is for Yugoslav Marxism the greatest task and the greatest challenge: the conquest of man's alienation from his work, society, and government.[23] The Yugoslavs describe it, with some justification, as a radically new approach for communism to governing and the problem of freedom under government.

Yet social self-government is firmly established. Consider, for example, its political-constitutional position. The 1963 constitutions were major political commitments. They have deeply influenced ideology, public opinion, and government practice, and thus have measurably restricted the power of those who promulgated them. The Yugoslav power-holders, including the party, are now less free than before they committed themselves so unreservedly (as they continue to do) to the 1963 constitutions. After over thirteen years of discussion and experiment, social self-government was in 1963 implanted as deeply into the

[23] Some proposals are a little bizarre, yet are seriously intended and may well be tried. One, for example, is that sections of highway, when built, would be handed over to nongovernmental enterprises to operate and maintain, with revenues coming from tolls.

system by the constitutions and the politics of the constitution-making processes as anything could be, aside from socialism itself. Further, this position has been strengthened and defended not only politically and by government and the pressures of public opinion but also by the now potent and independent Yugoslav judiciaries, both regular and constitutional. Indeed, this is one of the principal duties of the constitutional judiciary (of which more will be said in a moment) and understandably so, for a complex and novel body of law, constitutional and otherwise, is required to keep all these complex arrangements in order.

The Assembly System

Social self-government is the great principle of the Yugoslav *political order*. What the Yugoslavs call "assembly government," or the "assembly system," is their great principle of *governmental organization*,[24] and presents other major aspects of their constitutionalism.

As with social self-government, the assembly system is rooted in Communist doctrine, here the Marxist idea of unity of power, though that particular term is regarded now as a Russian one and inappropriate for Yugoslavia. This idea is that governmental power is to be concentrated in the elected assemblies, with the political executive and the administrative system subordinate and directly responsible to them. Thus the executive is seen as more or less a committee of the assembly, and the assembly as itself supervising the administration.

The Yugoslavs assert that they are seeking democratic rule and political freedom through constitutionally regulated social self-government. The assembly and assembly government are regarded as the capstone of social self-government and one of the greatest means whereby that system is protected and effectuated, because the assembly is the place where all the self-governing entities are represented and interact. Structurally, therefore, the heart of the Yugoslav governmental system and of constitutionalism is the assembly. One may ask if the assembly is much of a political reality in the Yugoslav constitutional scheme, and how it actually functions in the system. The question of political reality has to come first, since only if it can be answered affirmatively do the assembly's functions have any significance.

What of the position of the assembly system within government itself, especially on the crucial issues of relations between the assembly and the political executive and the relative degree of real control the two

24 The principle appears throughout the 1963 constitutions; see, for example, articles 163 and 225 of the federal constitution.

exercise over the administration? The evidence collected for this study is limited largely to the federal government, so we speak mainly of it, although there is also evidence to indicate that trends in the republics are similar. Several lines of inquiry were explored. Six will be mentioned here briefly.

First, the pronouncements of power-holders and influential theoreticians were examined. These have considerable importance—if the public takes them largely at face value, and it usually does—in committing the regime and in arousing expectations that can be disappointed only at the price of a loss of legitimacy and public support so heavy that the regime would hardly want to pay it unless driven by dire necessity (such as serious internal disruption or external threat). The trend is clear, with no serious reservations or caveats in recent years.[25]

Second, a study was made of the general expression of opinion in newspapers and journals and by intellectuals, working officials, ordinary politicians, and so forth. Here the trend is equally decisive. In ordinary informed, responsible, and moderately influential circles the assembly system is regarded as both accepted and acceptable at its constitutional face value, and as the established future of Yugoslav governmental organization. The significance of this is twofold. First, it adds to the commitment of the regime to the system. Second, it indicates that the system is now entrenched in political ideas; the Yugoslavs would now find it difficult to imagine government in Yugoslavia organized and functioning in any other way.

The third line of investigation is perhaps more concrete: it has to do with the movement of political personages of the upper and middle levels out of the political executive (and even out of offices in the party) and into the assembly. A useful empirical and semiquantitative study could be done, but the evidence seems to indicate that the movement is strong and that politicians see a good future in the assembly.

The fourth area of interest lies in the changing relations between the agencies, the political executive, those associated with the Federal Executive Council (roughly the counterpart of the Western cabinet), and the assembly. The agencies—secretariats, administrations, councils, and so forth—are in many cases moving closer to the assembly and away from the executive. A good example is the federal Secretariat for Legislation and Organization, an agency especially concerned with interrelationships within the government. Interviews and other evidence over several years showed a distinct shift in the agency's perceptions of its role and in its actual functions.

[25] The trend was recently reconfirmed by the public debates on the December 1968 amendments to the federal constitution and at the ninth congress of the party in March 1969.

The fifth line of inquiry centers on the assembly committees and commissions. External evidence shows them to have a high level of power, which continues to rise. Internal evidence from interviews indicates that they think of themselves, and rightly, as the real centers of policy-making and as the supervisors of the administration and the executive. In some instances they have not yet been able fully to act as such, but they are mostly pretty well along the road.

Finally, there are case histories of specific episodes of policy-making. These tend to confirm, in the form of concrete examples, the foregoing.

To the Western political scientist this march toward assembly hegemony raises the question of general laws of growth—for example, may the Yugoslavs not be encountering some of the familiar problems of Western legislatures, including those of separation of powers? The Yugoslavs, both theorists and politicians, have been concerned for some time over separation; and two schools of thought, tugging in two ways in the constitutionalism movement, have emerged. Both accept an independent and powerful judiciary, which Yugoslavia now has.

One school is the more orthodox and traditional. It holds that social self-government and an independent judiciary plus (a Marxist touch) a classless society are enough to protect against all the dangers separation is said to protect against. Indeed to some extent this school continues to accept the usual Marxist argument that separation is merely a bourgeois device to help prevent the working class from reaching power. But this school is uncomfortable; it is as aware as anyone of the distortions and tyrannies that have sprung up in other Communist regimes.

The other school of thought has the advantage of the argument on this point. It contends that there are still conflicts and contradictions in Communist societies, including Yugoslavia, and that they produce oppression and distortions against which separation in the proper form and amount is helpful, as irresponsible executives and nominally supreme but actually feeble assemblies elsewhere in Communist East Europe have not been. This school sometimes goes a step further and argues that proper separation can be of permanent value both to *competent* government and to freedom, and for the protection of political rights (including the vital right of social self-government) against the much-hated "Stalinism" and "bureaucratism."

The issue now is being brought into sharp focus by the problem of responsibility. The 1963 constitutions provide that executive officials are to be "responsible" for the discharge of their offices. High on the current agenda is the enactment of statutes effectuating this. But the point is made that an executive official cannot justly be held responsible unless he has some independence—which entails some separation, as does the necessity of having an agency of government able effectively to bring him to account.

The upshot is that political scientists can look forward to a most illuminating working out in practice of one of the classic issues of the discipline, and to the first real attempt by a Communist regime to grapple in concrete terms with this issue.

The same is true of another important issue: what should be the internal organization of a legislature? The Yugoslavs recognize that their particular constitutionalism requires an effective legislature, and they have been working on the matter. The novel 1963 constitutional scheme for the federal assembly has been further developed by practice and by the April 1967 and December 1968 amendments, and the republics are following suit. The 1963 scheme provided at the federal level (the republics were similar, *mutatis mutandis*) one chamber of general jurisdiction, the Federal Chamber representing the communes and the republics, and four specialized chambers representing the working organizations in four major fields—the economy, education and culture, social welfare and health, and social self-government. There was a Chamber of Nationalities incorporated, more or less, in the Federal Chamber and representing the republics. The 1967 amendments strengthened the Chamber of Nationalities, and the 1968 amendments dropped the Federal Chamber in favor of a further strengthened Chamber of Nationalities, now the chamber of general jurisdiction. Throughout, legislation (with some exceptions) was and is adopted by the general chamber and the relevant specialized chamber—the two acting together as a bicameral body.

This scheme of combined general and functional representation has been in operation long enough to make some tentative conclusions possible. It produces a high level of expertise in committee work and floor debate, and has brought into legislative life in the specialized chambers some highly qualified people who would not be likely to take posts as general legislators, thus improving both the quality and the legitimacy of the assembly in general. And the device of having the general chamber, the chamber of the generalists, the professionals, the politicians, and the functionally specialized chamber, representing subject-matter expertise and the interests of the concerned groups, all work together seems to be operating well and productively.

As to the actual legislative process, the Yugoslavs, in their quest for legislatures competent to play the large role that the constitutionalism movement envisions for them, have made two striking innovations. One is procedural, dealing with the forms and stages in which proposals are considered. Traditional procedure, followed in most Western legislatures, is for a proposal to be drafted as a complete bill and then considered in that form throughout the legislative process. The Yugoslavs employ an ingenious departure. A proposal passes through several distinct forms of drafting, usually beginning as a collection of rather general and broadly phrased "theses" and moving only slowly and by stages into bill form. It goes through several equally distinct stages of discussion and debate, moving from policy to specifics, before enactment. One's impression is that this process helps to produce well-structured and fruitful discussion, often better than what emerges in some of the long-established and more experienced legislatures of the West. An understanding of the Yugoslav procedure helps in part to explain a matter which often raises Western suspicions—the near unanimity of the final votes. Differences and opposition have been compromised, argued down, or abandoned as hopeless in earlier stages, rather than simply repressed or excluded from debate, in the familiar authoritarian style—though traces of this may survive in some forms. Certainly the innovation increases the effectiveness of assembly influence over policy.

A second innovation with significance for policy control is the provision of two kinds of drafting and advisory services. One is the Secretariat for Legislation and Organization. Standing between the agencies (and to a lesser extent the political executive) and the assembly, this secretariat assures that all legislative proposals, at all stages, reach debate only after expert legal scrutiny and effective administrative-executive discussion, and with full documentation both from the agencies involved (and the political executive to whatever extent it is involved) and from the earlier stages of legislative consideration.

The second kind of service is the Legislative-Legal Commission. This is a small bureau of highly qualified legal experts attached directly to the assembly. Its function is not to do the routine drafting—though it does a little—but to review proposals in the light of existing legislation and policy. The commission is very influential, and very competent. The Yugoslav legislature is thus in several respects well armed for its dealings with both the political executive and the administration and for its constitutional role as the center of policy-making and supervision.[26]

[26] One must not be too sanguine; the assembly has a long way to go before it achieves the assured power and expert skill of a Commons or a Senate, and it may fall prey to Western legislative ills (e.g., obstructive committee empires, democratic face versus oligarchic core, and the rest). And of course it always will be profoundly different from them—built on and serving profoundly different social and political orders. But it *is* developing, and in interesting ways. For example, if and when some form of effective opposition develops in Yugoslavia (and there are a few small signs, emerging out of the constitutionalism movement), its center may well be in the legislature and its shape and functions influenced by that setting.

LAW AND CONSTITUTIONALISM

The most spectacular manifestation of the legal-judicial element in the Yugoslav political order, and in some respects the crown of the constitutionalism movement, is the work of the constitutional courts, the first and so far the only ones in any socialist state. They were established under the 1963 constitutions, one in each republic and one for the federation. The latter so far is much the most important. The constitutions provide extensive judicially enforceable standards both for the limits of the powers of government and for the relationships of the various parts of government to each other—that is to say, for two of the great traditional functions of constitutionalism, the *garantiste* function and the frame-of-government function.[27] The constitutional courts are given broad duties, and broad powers, to enforce these standards. (Thus they have the power of judicial review over virtually all acts of government, including all legislation in both areas, along with what appears to be ample political and procedural resources to make this power effective.) These powers the courts have exercised quite vigorously.

The jurisdiction of the federation court is extensive, and a mixture of the political and the judicial. In part it is a court in the traditional style, in part it is a high constitutional council, and in some part it is an unusually powerful and high-level complaints bureau. It is also a vital coordinating commission, charged with the task of general supervision of Yugoslavia's exuberantly complex governmental system. The court has exercised this jurisdiction actively, and it seems likely to continue to do so. Its own inclinations clearly lie in this direction, public criticism has advocated that it be even more forceful, and the evidence is that the party and other influential circles are fully committed to its support.

The court was created for two major purposes: (1) to serve as a great agency to mediate, coordinate, and keep in constitutional order the tumult of forces released by federalism, the assembly system, decentralization, social self-government, and "de-étatization," and (2) to be a judicial and political defender of constitutionalism and law against the "bureaucratic" use of power by officials and government.[28]

For various reasons the court began with rather minor matters, and felt its way both in its substantive powers and in its procedure.[29] In

[27] Sartori, "Constitutionalism," pp. 853–64.

[28] See Winston M. Fisk and Alvin Z. Rubinstein, "Yugoslavia's Constitutional Court," *East Europe*, July 1966, pp. 24–28, at p. 24.

[29] This and much of what follows is largely based on interviews with court members and others beginning in 1965.

recent years it has developed more confidence and has been moving energetically into substantial undertakings. For example, in June 1967 the court for the first time held as unconstitutional major portions of important federal laws, and this in the conceptually difficult and politically hot area of federation-republic relations.

Some changes in the statute of the court and its constitutional provisions are currently in progress. They are rather minor. But major expansion and strengthening of the court's functions and powers are to come soon. It is a going, prospering, and developing concern.

So far the court has been concerned primarily with the frame-of-government aspect of its constitutional jurisdiction—with federalism, social self-government, and the logic and interrelationships of the constitutional system generally. One large task involving all three has been to see that the complex masses of legislative materials produced by Yugoslav "normative activity" under governmental pluralism, the assembly system, and social self-government are ordered and rationalized in terms of the federal constitution—a detailed, carefully drafted, and demanding legal document as well as a broad political statement. Progress has been made. Yugoslav law is getting into pretty good constitutional order.

Important developments are apparently under way in another of the court's major jurisdictions, and one central to the *garantiste* aspect of constitutionalism, epitomized in its power to "safeguard . . . basic freedoms and rights established by the constitution" (article 241 of the federal constitution). The court has moved slowly here but is beginning to gather momentum as it gets its other tasks in hand and develops its procedural machinery for handling cases in this class—usually quite individual matters turning upon specific sets of facts.

In all its categories of cases the court is having increasing success in getting its decisions recognized as not only disposing of the particular matter but also as authoritative precedents for other courts and for government agencies and entities, some of which have been stubborn on occasion and jealous of their democratic prerogatives. The court has been firm and in the end largely successful.

The court has another great area of constitutional power and responsibility which, unlike its others, has no American parallel. At first glance it is likely to cause the American observer concern that it would divert too much of the court's energies into political functions as a constitutional advisory council and academic functions as a research center in constitutional law, or even seriously impair its independence and detachment as a court. This function is the court's power and duty to "keep itself informed" concerning events bearing on the effectuation of constitutionalism and legality and to "offer to the Federal Assembly its opinions and proposals to pass laws and take other measures to secure constitutionality and legality and to protect the . . . freedoms and rights of the citizens and organizations" (article 242).

So far, however, the court has coped well with its many roles. It began by establishing itself as a court, with strictly judicialized procedure, producing a flood of case decisions and adhering meticulously to judicial style generally. It has recently begun to allow itself more latitude, but without reducing its judicial air. And its recommendations to the assembly have had much impact, both on legislation and on public opinion.

The Yugoslavs have also developed other innovative legal-judicial institutions in their quest for effective "constitutionalism and legality" within a Communist state. One which is rather mundane and technical but whose importance must be counted high is the system of administrative law and litigation.

The Yugoslav constitutional judicature is in part the result of borrowings from the West, notably from America, and in part the creation of contemporary Yugoslav imaginativeness. The system of administrative law and litigation has older domestic roots. However, it is nearly as much an innovation in the Communist world as the constitutional judicature.[30] The problem of imposing on the administration legal controls that are effective and just without crippling the administrative process is a conundrum that besets all developed polities. Working partly imaginatively and partly with inherited materials, and under the impulse of the constitutionalism movement, the Titoists seem to have created a rather satisfactory solution.

Yugoslavia's tradition in both major branches of administrative law—the setting of legal standards for administrative behavior and their enforcement by judicial action—goes back to the Council of State of the Serbian kingdom of the 1860s and to the Austro-Hungarian heritage in the northwest. It was strong in the interwar period, when the judiciary and the Council of State were among the few really respected segments of that troubled monarchy. The tradition was decisively built upon by the Titoists. It survived even the postwar dictatorship, and then was brought into prominence when the movement toward legality, and later constitutionality, began about 1951.[31]

In 1952 the federal law on administrative disputes (amended and strengthened in 1965) was enacted. For the first time in any Communist

[30] The Russian procuracy, for example, is an internal administrative control and a tool of the state, not a system of judicial control of administrative action as the Yugoslav judicature is. See Glenn G. Morgan, *Soviet Administrative Legality* (Stanford, 1962).

[31] It is significant that one is often told in Yugoslavia that many of the present leading administrative law scholars and judges got their training in the interwar Council of State.

regime the courts were given substantial independent control over administrative actions. Until then the standard Communist doctrine had been that the courts and the administration were to be completely separate, with the administration controlled only by itself and by the organs of popular power, which commonly meant in practice no effective controls at all. The 1952 statute established judicial control of administrative procedure, building on what had existed. The 1957 law on general administrative procedure (also amended and strengthened in 1965) codified the rules for administrative procedure itself—the internal rules for justice within the administrative machine.

Much has been drawn, in Yugoslav tradition and in the two statutes, from French and Austrian sources and from the civil law generally. But much is specifically Yugoslav. Further, the Yugoslav system in many respects goes beyond existing models, and gives Yugoslavia a system of administrative law and judicial enforcement which compares well with most other systems in justness, effectiveness, and modernity.

The enforcement of the two statutes and the rest of the corpus of administrative law (which is large, because case law, received doctrine, and special statutes all play important roles) is in the hands of special departments of the republic and federation supreme courts, and makes up roughly a quarter of their work. Such empirical studies as exist (the Serbian Institute for Public Administration did an extensive one), and interviews with informed participants and scholars, suggest that enforcement works well and is now independent of undue political influence. Individuals and organizations litigate against all manner of governmental and quasi-governmental agencies and win a fair proportion of the cases. An examination of a number of case files and of a larger number of judicial decisions in several courts suggests that the cases are substantial, well argued, and well decided. Further, the evidence is that the administration is in general law-abiding—this is strongly borne out by interviews with judges—with cases being litigated in the main over legitimate differences of opinion.

Yugoslav administrative law also features another protective aspect. Every Yugoslav enterprise, or other entity using social property, is subject to the federal Social Accounting Service, which has broad powers of inspection and surveillance and is charged with assuring that social property is used in authorized fashion and for authorized purposes. This powerful agency is, however, also subject to a developed system of administrative law. Here again the performance of the law, the courts, and the agency itself seems creditable.

In summary, Yugoslavia seems in important and far-reaching respects to be becoming a *Rechtsstaat*. Of the alternatives open to a Communist political order situated as it is, it has made this unlikely choice. Subject to sharp limitations dictated by its ideology, history, and circumstances (it is a smallish and rather poor Communist country, with severe internal strains and also with all the deep problems of its location in Southeast Europe, trying to overcome centuries of underdevelopment and misrule and experimenting with a novel and shaky system), Yugoslavia has elected to commit its political future in major respects to a form of constitutionalism and rule of law.[32] Whatever one may think of constitutionalism as a basis for organizing government and politics, or of conceptualizing them—and schools of modern political science have doubts on both scores—the Yugoslavs have taken the plunge. Their adventures should be followed with interest. Unlike other Communist nations, Yugoslavia has adopted law and constitutionalism, as contrasted with ideology, administration, *apparat,* or party, as the primary means of social coordination, organization, and control, and as the means and language of its politics. And law and constitutionalism have become to a degree what Deutsch calls "the nerves of government."[33]

Yugoslav constitutionalism is a challenging and unusual movement in contemporary politics, especially in the Communist world. We conclude with a rather speculative comment about its causes.

A grand question is, When does political freedom emerge, and survive? Yugoslavia has a considerable degree of it, as things go in Communist East Europe, and seems to be maintaining it and acquiring more.[34] Hoffman and Neal (in *Yugoslavia and the New Communism*) established the accepted causal analysis of this aspect of Yugoslav affairs through 1962. But their analysis does not fully explain the constitutionalism movement.

Berman and Hazard and others have shown that, contrary to oversimplified ideas of the extent of Soviet totalitarianism, the Soviet Union

[32] This asserts that the 1963 constitutions are important and are, so to speak, genuine—not mere propaganda or misleading façades. However, these documents need to be read with some care. They are political and social pronouncements. As the Yugoslavs say, they are constitutions of a society as well as of a legal order. As such pronouncements, they appear to the casual observer to be suspiciously full of windy political rhetoric. But they are intended to be legal instruments as well, and when they are read in this light the political rhetoric falls into its proper place and one sees the sharply reasoned and precisely drafted legal framework. To this framework the Yugoslav regime has committed itself, beyond possibility of withdrawal except at a heavy price.

[33] Karl W. Deutsch, *The Nerves of Government* (New York, 1966).

[34] We will be more sure of this if the 1968 amendments to the penal code, giving Yugoslavia one of the most enlightened systems of criminal procedure in Europe, are fully applied in political cases.

does have an effective and important system of law.[35] But Yaney has shown that Russia has never had, and does not now have, a genuine *legal order,* "a commonly recognized *legal system* based on abstract governing principles," and that this has been one vital cause of the continuing Russian tradition of autocracy. He says, "Soviet and tsarist statesmen alike have generally regarded *themselves* as preservers of their people's 'freedom.' They have always assumed in practice that society by itself was not free, that individual subjects were unable to protect their own interests except by appealing to persons in power. . . . In such a milieu only the ruler and his favorites have stood for 'freedom.' "[36] And this is because of the lack of a legal order on which to build more liberal states, because such states have to be built on *generally accepted* legal relationships—which cannot be created out of thin air by government fiat. So Russia has always been governed autocratically.

Herein lies a decisive difference. The Titoists, partly consciously and partly unconsciously, make the opposite assumption, and see in their country a legal system on which to build. And for good reason. The comparative richness and strength of the Yugoslav legal order and its traditions are apparent both from direct experience and from the literature.[37] Not many contemporary Western political or social scientists recognize a legal order as a major independent variable, a great causative social and political dynamic in its own right. But all astute tyrants, Stalinist and otherwise, have shown that they recognized it as such when they make its corruption a first order of business as soon as they come to power.

[35] See, for example, the convenient summaries of their basic work in Harold J. Berman, *Justice in the U.S.S.R.*, rev. ed. (Cambridge, Mass., 1963), and John N. Hazard, Isaac Shapiro, and Peter B. Maggs, *The Soviet Legal System,* 2nd ed. (Dobbs Ferry, N.Y., 1969). See also Hazard, *Law and Social Change in the USSR* (London, 1953).

[36] George L. Yaney, "Law, Society and the Domestic Regime in Russia, in Historical Perspective," *American Political Science Review,* 59 (1965): 380 and 383, emphasis added.

[37] Some sense of this can be obtained even from the dryly precise bibliographical entries in Fran Gjupanovich and Alexander Adamovitch, *Legal Sources and Bibliography of Yugoslavia* (New York, 1964), and the latest of these entries are for 1961, when the current renaissance in the creation, and study, of Yugoslav law was just beginning.

The Political Decision Makers

THE IMPACT OF THE POLITICAL STRUCTURE ON THE RECRUITMENT OF THE POLITICAL ELITE IN THE USSR*

Gerd Meyer

* The development of a Party bureaucracy as a well entrenched political elite, alienated from the masses, has characterized the Soviet political system in the last five decades. The *de-facto*-dictatorship of the Party in the socialist countries presents one of the most serious problems to modern Marxist theory which tries to reconstruct a theory of democratic socialism. This article (originally prepared for the VIII World Congress of the International Political Science Association, Münich 1970) is part of a larger study being prepared on the problem of "Socialist Democracy and the Recruitment of the Political Elite in the USSR." Here we will present a descriptive, empirical analysis of the subject, within a loosely defined structural-functional framework. Its results shall be used later for a study that, from a Marxist point of view, will be much more critical and theoretical in its approach to the Soviet system. The lack of a fully elaborated theoretical basis should not lead to the misunderstanding as if this study implicitly intends either to defend any functionally corresponding, negative phenomena in non-socialist systems or to criticize a socialist system on the basis of a so-called "value-free" empiricism or an anti-Marxist concept of democracy.

I. Political Elite and Political Structure in the Soviet System: Conceptualizing Their General Relationship.

In the Soviet system, both the political structure and the recruitment of the political elite are basically determined by the particular relationship between polity, society, economy, culture, and ideology, and the complex role of communist political leadership within this context. It is only within this wider framework that we can understand and define the two concepts of "political structure" and "political elite" in the case of the USSR.

The Soviet political elite has the right and the capability to decide authoritatively, or at least to influence substantially, all policies affecting the society as a whole, and also to direct and control their implementation. It not only performs many functions very similar to those of most of their non-communist counterparts, but it also:

a) directs and supervises all important activities in an economic system where the state owns all means of production, and is responsible for the planning, the general administration, and often even the day-to-day management of the production process;

b) defines and guards detailed norms of legitimate social and political behavior, and ensures compliance with them, particularly by a carefully supervised socialization process;

c) mobilizes support, requires loyalty, and legitimizes the rule of the Communist Party on the basis of an official state ideology by an extensive political education and continuous propaganda.

The Soviet political elite thus politicizes all important social activities. Its top Party leadership group tries to achieve efficient integration of the various subsystems, bureaucracies, organizations, and groups by close, centralized, and comprehensive political-ideological control, by mediation, coordination, and arbitration in the relations between elite sub-units, or, if necessary, also by coercion. Moreover, the "combination of complementarity and rivalry among separate but interlocking bureaucracies has ensured, and probably will continue to ensure the top leadership in Moscow against possible undermining of the central power by other elite elements."[1]

From *Il Politico*, University of Pavia, XXXVI, 1 (1971). Reprinted by permission.

[1] F. Barghoorn, *Politics in the USSR*. Little, Brown, Boston, 1966, p. 199.

To achieve these goals, the Soviet leadership has set up, commands, and works within a specific political structure, i.e., a relatively persistent pattern of the formal and informal distribution of political power, resources, and authority.[2] The concept of political structure, as used here, not only defines the institutionalized or non-institutionalized power relations between the political elite, the sub-elite, and the non-elite, but also between the various sub-units of the political elite itself.

The political structure of the Soviet system is also one of the most important of a group of factors which determine the process of recruitment and the outlook of the political leadership. As these factors can hardly be isolated from each other, it is, therefore, extremely difficult to measure their impact exactly. As a rule, it will be only possible to state the mere fact of the influence of the political structure on the recruitment process and/or to determine more or less precisely its approximate strength as an independent factor.

The political structure of the Soviet Union is characterized by the authoritarian, but no longer totalitarian, rule of a relatively small group of political leaders, who are distinguished from the rest of society by a unique concentration of social, economic, and political power.

The Soviet political elite does not allow the autonomous development or public competition of political and social forces, which would present a substantial limitation or serious challenge for its own overall control. Political resources (i.e., social power, such as specialized skills and knowledge, professional experience, especially in largescale management, individual political talent, influence on the basis of income, status position, or organizational association, group support, etc.) and legal rights can be used for effective participation in the political decision-making process only within the formally provided, or informally tolerated, channels of interest articulation and aggregation, and in accordance with the Party's general line of policy. In the USSR, there are no independent political or social organizations whose leadership as a legitimate socialist "counter-elite" could present a political and/or personal alternative to the ruling political elite.

The influence of dissenting, "liberal" intellectuals, mainly writers and scientists, who gained considerable publicity in the West, is difficult to assess precisely. Yet, as a whole, this group has very probably only marginal influence on the authoritative policy-making process. But they may articulate the views of a far larger number of citizens, and thus represent and enhance an important, but suppressed potential for political change.

[2] The first part of: S. Bialer, *The Soviet Political Elite: Concept, Sample, Case Study* (unpublished Ph.D. Thesis. Columbia University, New York, N.Y. 1966) contains some points with regard to the concept of the "Soviet political elite" in general which I found helpful to develop my own conceptualization of this specialized subject.

So, as a rule, the almost monopolistic political power is only exerted within the formal structure of political authority. In the Soviet system, therefore, the political elite may be defined as the political-social aggregate of incumbents of high executive offices in the most important political decision-making units. As an additional, though not constitutive, criterion nearly all of them also hold membership in predominantly symbolic, representative institutions, such as the USSR Supreme Soviet and its Presidium, or the CPSU Party Congress and, most important, its Central Committee (CC). This in only a very rough definition of the political elite, based on institutionalized power positions. More precisely, we should distinguish between a potential political elite and a "core" political elite, a small group of professional politicians at the very top of the Soviet system. In terms of actual behavior, the members of the potential political elite only occasionally use, directly or indirectly, their potential or limited influence on the decision-making process when their interests are directly at stake or when then they get involved by others for consultation, support, or implementation of certain policies. The small nucleus of professional politicians, the "actual" political elite, continuously and extensively uses its far reaching power to influence all basic decisions of the Soviet leadership organs. This top elite consists of most of the members of the CPSU Presidium/Politburo, the CPSU CC Secretariat, and the Presidium of the USSR Council of Ministers.

Operationally, the political elite may best be defined as the members of those leading organs of the most important political decision-making units which, by a cross-organizational sample, are represented in the CPSU Central Committee, and its Central Auditing Commission. If taken together, the institutionalized assessment of leadership positions, as indicated here by the Soviet political elite itself, the available information, and the implicit consensus in non-Communist research publications make this definition appear to be the least arbitrary, though of course not a fully satisfactory one. According to this definition, the members of the Soviet political elite 1953–1970 are those office-holders listed in the Appendix.

Unfortunately, for obvious technical and organizational reasons, it was impossible to do the necessary largescale, empirical research by a computerized data analysis of this huge population of ca. 2,000 persons. Moreover, several students in this field have announced the preparation or publication of comprehensive studies.[3] Nevertheless, a considerable number of studies, prepared on other aspects of the Soviet political elite, provide ample data we can well use as empirical evidence

[3] S. Bialer, F. Fleron, C. Beck, G. Zaninovich, M. Gehlen, G. Skilling, and others.

in our analysis. The methodological problems connected with the use of empirical data in Soviet studies, e.g., accuracy, classification, typology construction, analysis of trends and correlations, theory building, etc., cannot be discussed within the limits of this paper.

The political structure of the Soviet system, as set up and changed according to the goals, interests and perceptions of its political elite generally influences the recruitment of its political leadership in the following ways:

a) it determines the formal and informal distribution of power and authority among the main bureaucracies and their leading organs, as well as within the top leadership, to decide on or to influence the selection of new members of the political elite (procedures, organization, methods, criteria, and general policies of elite recruitment);

b) it determines how much influence and which positions and opportunities for advancement to political leadership are provided by the various bureaucracies, institutional or informal channels, and career stations;

c) it determines which functions and roles have to be performed in different status positions, and consequently, which political and professional career backgrounds are required and favored by the system;

d) so, in general, it determines the frequency distribution of different career patterns in the political elite, its political-professional characteristics, its structure and composition.

As the political structure changed constantly during the various periods of post-Stalinist rule, its impact differed considerably over time. The development of the political structure in the USSR was characterized by the essentially unaltered, political predominance of the Party since 1957, and a continuously changing, informal distribution of power and authority among, and partly also within, the four most important bureaucracies (Party, state—including the economic administration—, military, and police) as well as among the leading party and state organs (CPSU CC, its Presidium/Politburo and Secretariat; Presidium of the USSR Council of Ministers). Even more in a constant flux, and often hardly recognizable, is the scarcely defined distribution of power within the top political leadership, between its groupings and individuals, who as members of the all-dominant CPSU CC Presidium/Politburo decide the fate of the Soviet system. Since 1956, we also find a growing internal differentiation of the functions, status positions, and the organizational structure of the top leadership organs. "It may be posited that the group basis of Soviet politics almost always combines cleavages between and associations of formally-organized and officially recognized elite collectivities with informal and hidden, but nevertheless persistent and effective formations of elite individuals."[4]

These brief remarks on the political structure of the USSR were, of course, not intended as an exhaustive analysis of the subject. We only wanted to emphasize some traits and elements of the Soviet political system which have particular importance for the recruitment of its political elite, and whose impact we are now going to study in greater detail.

II. Formal Organization and Political Control in the Recruitment Process: Top Leadership Politics and the Power of the Party.

The formal organization of the recruitment process as part of the political structure is characterized by pseudo-democratic election procedures, the legally guaranteed privilege of the Party to control directly or indirectly all appointments of politically important officials, and, finally, by a highly standardized, planned, centrally supervised, and carefully engineered selection of all leading cadres, except for the small group of top politicians. By these means, the Party tries to achieve a regulated, rational, calculable, flexible, and systemicly functional recruitment of its political elite, favorable both to the stability and creative development of the Soviet system.

Formally, most of those who hold an important political office are directly or indirectly elected by representative bodies of their organizations.[5] But, in reality, the Soviet politician essentially is an appointed, coopted, or self-selected politician. Elections ratify, legalize, and legitimize previously decided choices of candidates. The only exception to this rule occurred in 1957, when an appeal was made to the CPSU CC as the "supreme arbiter" in an open clash of two rival groups of top leaders. It decided against an already ailing majority of its Presidium and in favor of its First Secretary. As a result, the defeated were ousted at once or later, whereas the victor staffed the Presidium with his adherents. It is only since 1966 that the CPSU CC has the formal right to elect its General Secretary. A single leader or a

[4] S. Bialer, op. cit., pp. 136–37.

[5] For a detailed study of the election procedures, rules, and turnover rates see: M. Lesage, *Le renouvellement des dirigeants du Parti Communiste de l'Union Soviétique,* "Revue française de science politique," vol. 14, 1964, pp. 1134–1154.

"primus inter pares" like the present (1970) General Secretary could lose office only by death or if a majority of the CC Presidium/Politburo, who opposed his leadership and who has the support of the CPSU CC, were able to oust him, and to take over the supreme power by itself. Elections are the legal or constitutional form of status assignment, but do not decide the result of the recruitment process. Elections confirm, but do not bring about personnel changes.

The control of the recruitment of the political elite is one of the most important privileges of the Party leadership, and one of the most efficient instruments for wielding its supreme political power. The organizational structure and the working of the staffing mechanism, including the nomenclatura system, have been described elsewhere in greater detail.[6] For our purposes, we will only briefly outline some structural aspects. The much criticized, but probably still existing nomenclatura lists a certain number of important offices and positions together with their past, present, and possible, future incumbents. It stipulates, too, which particular official(s) has (have) the right to appoint, dismiss, or transfer an incumbent of a specific position.

The CPSU CC Presidium/Politburo is "the ultimate authority on selection, assignment, promotion, and training of personnel."[7] It decides on general recruitment policies and career development programs; it defines criteria for advancement and supervises the performance of high officials. It has reserved the right to staff about sixty key positions at the top exclusively on its own and to give the consent to all appointments of members of the political elite.[8] Formally, this body makes most of its decisions collectively. But except for a varying number of very important appointments, most of these tasks are performed by the General Secretary in close collaboration with a senior CC secretary and the head(s) of the CPSU CC party organs departments(s) and their staff members, who are responsible for the selection of the leading cadres.[9] All appointments on the upper echelons of all important

[6] Cf. e.g., Senate Committee on Government Operations. Subcommittee on National Policy Machinery of the US: *Staffing Procedures and Problems in the Soviet Union.* U. S. Government Printing Office, Washington, D.C. 1963; B. Lewytzkyj, *Die Nomenklatur. Ein wichtiges Instrument sowjetischer Kaderpolitik.* In: "Osteuropa," vol. 11, 1961, pp. 408–12; A. Lebed, *The Soviet Administrative Elite: Selection and Deployment Procedures.* In "Studies of the Soviet Union" (Münich), vol. 5, 1965, pp. 47–55. See also Bialer, op. cit., pp. 45–46.

[7] Senate Committee, *Staffing Procedures,* p. 9.

[8] Cf. S. Bialer, op. cit., p. 46.

[9] J. A. Armstrong, *The Soviet Bureaucratic Elite.* New York, 1959. His chapter 6 deals with the career backgrounds, group characteristics, political importance, and the vertical mobility of the medium-level staff agencies of the Ukrainian Party, and also of the CPSU in general.

bureaucracies are either handled directly by the Party Secretariat or must have its approval. Every bureaucracy, especially the state administration, has a more or less far-reaching autonomy in its staffing policies, depending on the power and the degree of independence it has achieved under its leadership. The hierarchical structure and the one-man leadership, in connection with other, more informal methods of elite recruitment, often allow the head of a bureaucracy a considerable freedom in the selection of his aides; but for the appointment of his direct subordinates he always needs the consent of his superiors, often by a collective decision, and also of the Party, i.e., usually the CPSU CC Central Administration.

Thus by its power to grant access to and promotion within the authority structure, a strong central Party executive, predominantly staffed with professional politicians and Party *apparatchiki,* tries to control, direct, and integrate all elements of the political elite.[10] Yet the recruitment of the Soviet political elite is not only determined by its formal organization and authority structure, but also by a number of directly intervening, informal factors, structures, and processes.

In the USSR, the recruitment of the top political leadership is characterized by the lack of generally accepted rules which would define a clear-cut, stable distribution, the legitimate exercise, and orderly transfer of power and authority in the supreme political organs. This leads to a never-ending struggle for more power and security among its members. The top political leaders hitherto gained their position either by filling the power vacuum created by the death or the ouster of a monocratic leader, or as victors and survivors in an "open" competition for supreme leadership; or they were coopted into this group by a ruling oligarchy or a more or less preeminent individual leader, or by a combination of two or more of these ways. The members of the CPSU CC Presidium/Politburo, in particular, are essentially self-appointed leaders, who "elected" themselves by virtue of arrogated power. Besides other factors, it is, above all, the control over the selection of leading personnel, the power to create, to change, and to abolish positions and organizational structures, and the ability to muster support by powerful personal followings which are decisive for a leader's advancement and tenure of office. An established, leading Soviet politician is only able to hold his office not so much by any "constitutionally" vested or "democratically" legitimized authority, but, above all, by demonstrating the success of his policies, and by maintaining sufficient personal support among his peers as well as by his subordinates. In general,

[10] For the career background of Central Party Apparatus Staff officials in the CC see F. Fleron, *Cooptation as a Mechanism of Adaptation to Change: The Soviet Political Leadership System.* "Polity," vol. II, n. 2, Winter 1969, p. 184, table 3.

there are no effective, formal provisions to limit the tenure of officials belonging to the Soviet political elite. The new Party statute, adopted in 1961 under Khrushchev, stipulated a regular turnover of one quarter of the CPSU CC and its Presidium (but not its Secretariat!) every four years, and at higher rates (33% and 50%) also in the committees and bureaux of lower levels. It also limited in general the tenure of membership in the principal organs of the Party to three sucessive terms, i.e., to twelve years. But it exempted the CPSU CC, all higher Party secretaries and, if a 75% quorum of the electors were achieved, also "Party personalities of recognized authority and outstanding qualities."[11] These rules clearly favored the upper echelons by granting them lower turnover rates, and thus stabilized oligarchical and bureaucratic tendencies among the well entrenched political elite. Moreover, because of the unwillingness of the top leadership and the already built-in loopholes, this system of automatic rotation was never really put into effect for the upper echelons of the Party. In reality, it only affected its intermediate and lower strata, and led to an undesiredly high turnover of experienced and qualified personnel. In 1966 as in 1962, the requirements for the CPSU CC were only formally met by finally demoting members who already were more or less on their way down. In the case of the CC, the prescribed quota were achieved either in a similar way or by enhancing its membership. Consequently, in 1966, the fixed quota were abolished by an amendment of the Party Statute, and only the general "principle of systematic renewal and continuity of leadership" was retained.[12] Among others, this development shows that the top political leadership, and probably most members of the political elite, do not want to give up voluntarily the advantages of a *de facto* unlimited tenure of office. It was impossible to introduce an effective rule that would have helped to provide the system with a dynamic, innovative leadership by a periodical renewal of established office-holders. No inescapable, "blind" mechanism was allowed to influence independently the degree of vertical mobility in the political structure. The top leadership still wants "to elect" itself, and decide on the cooptation of its peers. Party politicians stick to the privilege of authoritarian direction and tutelage of the recruitment process for their subordinates as a main basis of their power.

In the USSR, the constituency of a political actor who wants to enter the political elite is not the electorate, but, above all, the Party leadership. It is the skillful maneuvering within various bureaucracies, the poli-

[11] Cf. the Party Statute of 1961.

[12] Cf. the Party Statute as amended in 1966. For details of this development and of the inner Soviet discussion of this problem, see B. Lewytzkyj, *Generations in Conflict*. "Problems of Communism," vol. 16, Jan./Feb., 1967, pp. 37–38, also M. Lesage, *Le Renouvellement des Cadres,* op. cit., *passim.*

tics and tactics towards the ever present superiors and peers, the ability to impress and to influence the record-keeping cadres agencies of the Party, the demonstration of professional-political ability, personal loyalty, and ideological conformity that determine the advancement of a Soviet bureaucrat-politician. Having become a member of the political elite, especially as head of a bureaucracy or a Party functionary, he will try to enhance his share of authority, or gain maximum autonomy to recruit administrative aides and political supporters. As a result, this fierce competition for power more or less undermines the principle of collective leadership. Furthermore, it imperils the stability of the authority structure, the efficiency of central control, and the implementation of general policics in the recruitment process. The answer to the question "who selects?" and "who is selected why?" depends largely on the current state of a mostly hidden, continuous power struggle, not only at the top, but in all segments of the political elite. The dynamics of a leadership system, which since Stalin's death has combined elements of monocratic and oligarchical rule in a wide range of mixing proportions, make the recruitment process often appear as incalculable, irregular, and erratic. Very often, therefore it is difficult to analyze and to understand from outside the frequent, and mostly unforeseeable, shifts of leading personnel which we will now study in some more detail.

Our approach to look at the power struggle as a process by which individuals gain or lose offices does of course not claim to be a complete analysis of this complex phenomenon. In the case of the USSR, however, these are the most fruitful and reliable data we can use for an empirical study of the recruitment of its political elite. We also want to emphasize that not only individuals are involved in the power struggle, but also formal or informal groups, who together often act in the interest of institutions, nationalities, or various other, similarly large "constituencies."

There are several ways and techniques by which an individual bureaucrat-politician can use his more or less far-reaching influence on the recruitment of leading cadres to enhance his power and to work on his ascendancy to top leadership.

A very common one is to build up powerful, personal followings of political supporters. One major source of loyalty is the leader's ability to promote his adherents or otherwise to further their career, mostly in close connection to his own advancement. Thus patronage and lasting career associations strongly influence many politicians' way to the top. As a result, in all important bureaucracies, we find numerous informal clans and power cliques, more or less stable alliances of ambitious office-holders and status-seekers, associations for mutual support, reinsurance, and career-building. We find them on all echelons of the politically relevant organizations, along vertical and horizontal lines, often with their apex in Moscow. They are scattered all over the country, and their size ranges from a handful to a maximum of probably a hundred. Although the Party statute strictly bans any factions, these "unconstitutional" power groups still exist behind the façade of "monolithic unity," "democratic centralism," and "collective leadership" in the Party, and impair the objectivity of the elite recruitment. Careful studies have traced and analyzed the rise and fall of many of these groups whose members often heavily rely on the unpredictable political fate of their sponsor.[13]

There are different degrees of dependence between a leader and his supporters which, in many cases, is not easy to determine. There are "clients" who owe their career totally or mostly to patronage, e.g., L. P. Beria's[14] and N. S. Khrushchev's clienteles.[15] A second category may be called "allies" who owe their career only partly, but on some steps decisively to their superior partner.[16] Finally we can find more or less independent partners who have formed a coalition with a top leader, and thereby gained some advancement, but who do not owe their membership in the political elite predominantly to him.[17]

But having achieved themselves a top position, many of these sup-

[13] To name only some of the most important and comprehensive ones: R. Conquest, *Power and Policy in the USSR. The Struggle for Stalin's Succession 1945–1960.* New York, London, 1961; R. Pethybridge, *A Key to Soviet Politics: The Crisis of the Anti-Party Group,* Praeger, New York, 1962; M. Rush, *Political Succession in the USSR.* New York, 1965; H. Tatu, *Le Pouvoir en URSS.* Grasset, Paris, 1967. (*Power in the Kremlin,* London, 1968, New York, 1970.)

[14] Cf. B. I. Nicolaevsky, *Power and the Soviet Elite. The Letter of an Old Bolshevik and Other Essays.* London, 1965; R. Conquest, op. cit., Ch. 9. See also his elaborate, brilliant study of the "Leningrad Case 1949/50" (Ch. 5) and the "Zhdanov group" and the purges in Georgia 1951–53 preceding the fall of Beria (Ch. 7). Beria's most important clients were V. N. Merkulov, V. G. Dekanozov, S. A. Goglidze, P. I. Meshik, L. E. Vlodzimirsky, V. S. Abakumov, M. D. Bagirov.

[15] M. Tatu made the distinction between "clients," "allies" and "independents" in an analysis of Khrushchev's following in 1960 (op. cit., p. 24). Some of the more important of Khrushchev's clients are A. I. Kirichenko, Ye. A. Furtseva, L. I. Brezhnev, V. A. Churaev, I. A. Serov, L. R. Korniets, and many others. See also J. A. Armstrong, op. cit., ch. 10.

[16] E.g., A. B. Aristov, N. G. Ignatov, N. J. Belyayev, O. V. Kuusinen, (cf. M. Tatu, op. cit., p. 24); K. F. Katushev in his relation to Brezhnev F. R. Kozlov (till 1960), and many others in their relation to Khrushchev (cf. M. Tatu, op. cit., p. 539) and V. E. Semichastny to A. N. Shelepin (cfr. ibid., pp. 536–38).

[17] E.g., A. N. Kosygin, M. A. Suslov, and D. S. Polyansky in their relation to Khrushchev (cf. M. Tatu, op. cit., p. 24).

porters begin to take openly a more or less independent, often oppositional, or even hostile stand towards their former patron, and can well oust him as his peers. Moreover, Khrushchev's lieutenants began to form their own personal followings, e.g., F. R. Kozlov[18] and G. T. Voronov.[19]

Usually the head of such a following tries to base his power not only on his personal influence and the allegiance of his protégés. He often holds a central or regional key position, mostly with substantial influence in higher Party organs. He will try to staff key positions and institutions in the Soviet political structure, such as the Party bureaux and secretariats, the Party organs department and other cadre agencies, the command posts in the police and the armed forces, the directorates of the mass media, etc.—with his most reliable and able adherents. The promotions and removals after Khrushchev's fall show that these positions are the most sensitive, insecure, and crucial ones during changes in the political leadership.[20]

The hierarchical political structure and the system's built-in rivalry of bureaucracies also favor a patron's efforts to control the recruitment in an important institution, or in part of it, and to entrench himself and his associates in one or several organizational units. Many political leaders attempt to enhance their power by defending and expanding their institutional authority and political autonomy in order to achieve advancement for themselves and their supporters, or, at the top, to strengthen their position among peers (e.g., L. P. Beria: police apparatus, cross-organizational patronage[21]; G. M. Malenkov and the "anti-Party group": USSR government, central planning organs, industrial administration, foreign service till 1956[22]; N. S. Khrushchev: Party apparatus, especially CC Secretariat, CC Bureau for the RSFSR, territorial Party organizations; also coalition first with two, after 1957, with one military group, the "Zhukov" and "Stalingrad" group.[23]

As proved by Stalin, Khrushchev, and Brezhnev, the Party apparatus and especially the powerful and prominent office of CPSU CC First

[18] M. Tatu, op. cit., p. 137.
[19] Ibid., pp. 133–34.
[20] Cf. M. Tatu, op. cit., Ch. V, *passim;* Y. Bilinsky, *Changes in the Central Committee: The Communist Party of the Soviet Union 1961–1966.* (Monograph series in "World Affairs," Vol. 4, 1966–67.) University of Denver, Denver, Colorado, 1967, pp. 3–7.
[21] Cf. R. Conquest, op. cit., Ch. 9; B. Meissner, *Umschau* (reports), "Osteuropa," Vol. 8 (1953), pp. 278–89 and 458–65.
[22] Cf. Conquest, op. cit., Ch. 12.
[23] Cf. the detailed study of R. Kolkowicz, *The Soviet Military and the Communist Party,* Princeton University Press, Princeton, N.J., 1967, esp. Appendices I–IV.

Secretary are the most favorable springboard to gain superiority and even sovereign leadership in the Soviet system. But even after his victory in 1957, Khrushchev probably did not have unrestricted command of the recruitment process. There is some evidence that, since 1960, he sometimes had to negotiate for promotions of his allies and that he had to accept compromise appointments. He also was not able to replace as many *obkom* first secretaries as he wanted after 1961, and he probably caused growing resistance among the "old" secretaries against the "newcomers" and the reorganization that brought them to power.[24]

Sometimes these career groups originate from and are based on the leader's control of a regional Party organization, and/or previous cooperation with his supporters in one part of the country (e.g., Khrushchev: Ukraine, Moscow; Zhdanov, Kozlov: Leningrad; Podgorny: Kharkov, Ukraine; Brezhnev: Dnepropetrovsk, Kazakhstan). This kind of association can be connected with a preference for certain nationalities.

We also find many followings with cross-organizational and cross-occupational alignments (Beria: predominantly police officers, but also many supporters in other groups[25]; Khrushchev: with some exceptions, the complete spectrum of groups). A political leader may also try to get the support of various professional groups by providing them with influential or prestigious positions, as e.g., Khrushchev did for many young industrial managers and administrators.

Representative organs, especially the CPSU and Republic CCs, with their prestige and potential power, can be used by a patron to award supporters and to improve his own position. The technique of "packing" the CPSU CC, was widely used by Khrushchev during his ascendancy. After having exchanged about two fifths of the Republic and regional first secretaries between 1953 and February 1956, Khrushchev had the support of about three fifths of the CPSU CC at the XX Party Congress.[26] However, "the gain made by direct negotiation in the Presidium was about as great as that secured, or staked, through the Party Organs Department."[27] In 1959, about 60% were likely supporters among the CPSU CC full members.[28] In 1961, he removed

[24] Cf. M. Tatu, op. cit., pp. 69–101, 127–40 and 176–207, especially pp. 99–100, 106, 135.

[25] B. Meissner, op. cit., lists supporters or allies in the Party, state, military, Komsomol, trade unions, courts, and among the writers.

[26] See the careful study of T. H. Rigby, *Khrushchev and the Resuscitation of the Central Committee,* "Australian Outlook," Vol. 18 Sept. 1959, p. 174, and also his article *How strong is the Leader?* "Problems of Communism," vol. 11 (1962), p. 3.

[27] R. Conquest, op. cit., p. 285.

[28] Ibid.

half of the membership of the 1956 CC, increased the number of full members by one third, and so was able to bring in a large number of his adherents. But the rule that the CC Presidium oligarchs negotiate the composition of the CPSU CC was still valid. It was even more valid in 1966 when 80% of the 1961 CC members were reelected. Only seven of the 56 new members were clearly Brezhnev's allies of the "Dnepropetrovsk group." Seven other new members obviously were rewarded by full membership for their role in the coup against Khrushchev.[29]

In order to gain power a political leader often has to move against his rivals and adversaries by diminishing their personal and institutional support. In case of a clear-cut victory, the defeated and their supporters are removed sooner or later.[30] M. Tatu speaks of a "pre-Congressional purge" in 1961 when "hundreds of officials," 20 full members, and over a third of all *obkom* secretaries were replaced.[31] Quite often we hear of regional "purges" where the central leadership moves against often well-entrenched clusters of Party or state officials on lower echelons. Or it happens that only a single *oblast* or republican first secretary is demoted, sometimes in the presence of a CPSU CC secretary. These interventions from above are often designed as an indirect attack on a peer rival.[32] Or a leader may be able to place one of his associates as

[29] Cf. Y. Bilinsky, op. cit., p. 5.

[30] See the following examples: Beria group: immediate, sweeping purge of most of his helpers, only some "trials" in later years: Malenkov's following: in 1955, demotion in his closest associates (e.g., N. N. Shatalin, G. F. Aleksandrov, P. K. Ponomarenko, A. F. Zasyadko, A. I. Kozlov), and many of his allies among the local Party secretaries (cf. R. Conquest, op. cit., pp. 256–60); "Anti-Party group": six out of eight prominent members immediately removed from CC Presidium, but some only later and gradually demoted; Khrushchev's following: only closest associates immediately demoted, others in 1965 and 1966; e.g., A. Adzhubei, L. Ilyichev, Z. T. Serdyuk, P. A. Satyukov, V. H. Polyakov, Z. Senin, M. A. Polekhin, M. A. Charlamov, some of them heads of important newspapers, journals, mass media (cf. Y. Bilinsky, op. cit., pp. 4–5); also two thirds of all industrial *obkom* first secretaries appointed by him in 1962–64 (see detailed statistics in G. Hodnett's article: *The Obkom First Secretaries,* Slavic Review, vol. 24, Dec. 1965, pp. 636–52).

[31] M. Tatu, op. cit., pp. 127–28.

[32] For example, I. V. Spiridonov's removal in 1962: Khrushchev vs. Kozlov (cf. C. A. Linden, *Khrushchev and the Soviet Leadership, 1957–1964.* Johns Hopkins Press, Baltimore, Md., 2nd print, 1967, pp. 139–42). Demotion of the Party secretaries in Kazahstan 1962–63; Kozlov vs. Brezhnev (cf. M. Tatu, op. cit., pp. 514–15). Demotion of V. A. Shurygin 1963: Khrushchev vs. Voronov (cf. M. Tatu, op. cit., pp. 374–75). Removal of V. I. Titov, N. A. Sobol 1965: Brezhnev vs. Podgorny (cf. M. Tatu, op. cit., pp. 499–502).

a kind of control agent into the institutional domain of a rival or adversary.[33] Khrushchev often carefully "checked and balanced" the power and authority of his lieutenants and rivals.[34] In order to solve the succession problem, he first informally designated an "heir presumptive" as "second Secretary"; but in 1963 he apparently chose to build up an "heir" as well as a "counter-heir" who balanced each other for about a year.[35]

Another very important device to enhance his own authority and capability to promote supporters is either to infringe upon a rival's institutional power basis or to create new organizational units by splitting up or recombining existent structures of authority.[36]

[33] Malenkov, in moves against Khrushchev, placed N. N. Shatalin into the Party Secretariat (March 1953) and P. K. Ponomarenko as First Secretary of the Kazakhstan CC (February 1954). The latter, in return, was "checked" by L. Brezhnev, a protégé of Khrushchev, who also managed to appoint N. S. Patolichev as Deputy Foreign Minister in a move against V. Molotov (July 1955). Molotov even had to give up his office of Foreign Minister, and had to share responsibility in this field with D. T. Shepilov, a follower of Khrushchev (June 1956). In 1960, many of Khrushchev's allies, probably as a compromise, were sent from the Party into the governmental administration, whereas the Deputy Chairman of the USSR Council of Ministers, F. R. Kozlov, entered the Party Secretariat (cf. M. Tatu, op. cit., pp. 69–100). Since 1965, L. Brezhnev has sent many high-ranking Party *apparatchiki* into the state administration (e.g., the appointments of M. A. Sholokhov in 1968, and some others in 1965, cf. M. Tatu, op. cit., pp. 464–65; he also insured the Party's control of the mass media (ibid., pp. 465–66).

[34] For example, F. Kozlov vs. A. B. Aristov, later I. V. Titov in cadres direction (cf. M. Tatu, op. cit., pp. 86, 135). M. Suslov vs. L. Ilyichev in ideological questions (cf. ibid., pp. 200–3, 208–10) G. T. Voronov vs. V. M. Churaev, later M. T. Yefremov in the CPSU CC Bureau for the RSFSR (cf. ibid., pp. 134, 291–93).

[35] The arrangements were the following: June 1957–January 1960: A. J. Kirichenko; February–June 1960: Probably L. Brezhnev; July 1960–June 1963: F. R. Kozlov; June 1963–October 1964: L. Brezhnev and N. Podgorny.

[36] Only a few of the more striking examples shall be mentioned: 1) the reorganization of *Gosplan* in 1955, impinging the Malenkov group's realm; 2) the steadily growing numbers of CC secretaries and alternate or full CPSU CC Presidium members during Khrushchev's rise 1953–60; his creation of the CPSU CC Bureau for the RSFSR in 1956, which he always staffed with his supporters whenever he was able to; 3) the moves and countermoves of the "Khrushchev group" and the "anti-Party group" as manifested in the fight for the reorganization of the economic administration in 1956–57: first strengthening, then crushing nearly all of the central power, thus dissolving the power basis of many of Khrushchev's adversaries; 4)

The extent to which an individual political leader will be able to aggrandize and use his power and authority to influence the recruitment of the political elite depends strongly on the state of the constantly changing political structure. It is highly important to what degree the top leadership is monocratic or oligarchical. The nature, the number, and the success of the different ways of gaining superiority and advancement, as described above, will differ during various stages of the power struggle. Although there is more or less rivalry among the lieutenants of a predominant single leader the actual, manifest, and full-scale competition for power, open to all potential contenders, is essentially a post-vacancy selection process.

Two periods of oligarchial rule (1953–57, since 1964) showed some similar characteristics:

- relatively small purges of the closest associates of the former "monocrat";
- no high turnover of leading personnel essential for the functioning of the system;
- a more or less stable, but still rather precarious power balance among the main oligarchs;
- more or less successful moves of one oligarch or work to oust a rival and to promote supporters;
- a widening of participation in the power struggle, because institutional and other groups become potential allies and followings for a leader; and
- a more or less intensive revival of institutional rivalries, and even clashes.[37]

After the coup in 1964, we could observe a remarkable phenomenon almost unknown in Soviet politics: the rehabilitation in the form of a political "comeback" or reinstallment of many high officials who had fallen into disgrace under Khrushchev.[38] Their new positions, how-

---

Since 1960, progressive recentralization with increasing power for the central economic administrators; many of them were either independents or opponents of Khrushchev. The division of the Party in 1962–63 gave Khrushchev the opportunity to promote many young industrial administrators to *obkom* or *gorkom* first secretaries in industrial areas. Detailed empirical material is presented by J. A. Armstrong, *Party Bifurcation and Elite Interests,* "Soviet Studies," vol. 17, April 1966, pp. 417–30; G. Hodnett, *The Obkom First Secretaries* (see note, 30, 4); 5) The undoing of nearly all of Khrushchev's reorganizations in 1965 strengthened the Party apparatus, but also considerably the central economic administration, and provided the opportunity to appoint numerous new ministers.

[37] Cf. R. Conquest, op. cit., Part III; M. Tatu, op. cit., Part V.

[38] After Stalin's death, we only find e.g. S. D. Ignatiev, T. Sodelava, M. Baramiia, and A. Rapava reentering the political elite. Tatu mentions a

ever, were usually not as high-ranking as those they held before, and it would definitely go too far to speak of a "counter-elite" of the demoted as Z. Brzezinski did. In both cases, we saw the gradual rise of a "primus inter pares" among the oligarchy, in the case of Khrushchev even of a supreme leader. Brezhnev has been far less able to pack the Party apparatus with his allies. The post-Khrushchev oligarchy is also far more stable, and has not yet (1970) experienced any large shake-ups, except for rather limited ones in a particular territorial or functional unit. Since 1966, there have been very few significant reorganizations which would have clearly favored one of the oligarchs. During the last five years, collective decision-making, negotiations, consultations, and compromise probably prevailed in the recruitment of leading cadres, with the General Secretary slowly, but steadily improving his position within the Party apparatus, and also in the general leadership of the Soviet system. But we should be aware that there is no "iron law" that an oligarchy will inevitably lead to a one-man rule. In the USSR, all leadership structures between oligarchical and monocratic rule, as a result of the self-selection process at the top, are possible.

III. Political Structure and Career Patterns.

In the first chapter, we made some remarks on what functions the political leadership has to perform in the Soviet system, and how the correspondingly set up political structure influences in general the political-professional career patterns of its political elite. As information is lacking on the precise nature of the work done by the incumbents of most leadership positions, we will not deal with the impact of the specific division of labor and the network of roles as constituted by the characteristics of offices in changing organizational arrangements. We

---

considerable number of officials who experienced this fate, belonging to a broad range of institutional and professional alignments, e.g., N. K. Baybakov (p. 462), D. A. Kunaev and other former Kazakhstan Party functionaries (pp. 514–15); V. V. Matskevich, F. D. Kulakov, and other leading agricultural personnel (p. 496), N. A. Mukhitdinov, N. N. Organov (p. 539), P. Lapin (p. 539), K. E. Voroshilov, N. Y. Zakharov and other military officers (Linden, p. 264), M. Y. Shcherbitsky (p. 513), A. F. Zasyadko, and V. N. Novikov (p. 118). Cf. Z. Brzezinski, *The Soviet Political System: Transformation or Degeneration?* "Problems of Communism," vol. XV, Jan.-Feb., 1965, pp. 1–15.

can infer from our previous remarks that the Soviet political elite will not (and does not) consist of politicians with career backgrounds as parliamentarians, leaders of publicly acting, well organized interest groups, and, with some exceptions, of members of the so-called professions (lawyers, doctors, writers, artists, scientists, journalist, etc.). We rather find political leaders with a career in one or two of the main Soviet bureaucracies, the top leaders predominantly in the Party apparatus. In contrast to non-Communist societies, most of them are "bureaucrat-politicians," not "electoral politicians"; far more of them have experiences in economic administration and management. In contrast to most non-Communist societies, we also find some "ideologists" with considerable political influence. With very few exceptions, the unique position of the Party in the Soviet system makes it impossible to be recruited into the Soviet political elite without being a member, if not an activist, in the CPSU. The system requires and favors the recruitment of a political leadership that combines general executive skills with some specialized knowledge and experience, particularly in the technical and economic field. The growing scope and complexity of Communist leadership and the second-rank importance of the economy call for the generalist, the "multiple executive," the "free-floating apparatchik" (S. Bialer), who is able to integrate, lead, control, and manage the whole of polity, economy, and society; but, to a certain degree, he also has to be a specialist who is able to apply these attributes to particular fields of work. We would expect, therefore, that the career background of a growing number of members of this managerial political elite would show an increasing inter-occupational and inter-organizational mobility.

There is no comprehensive empirical study of the career background of our elite population; but we do have some very detailed studies of samples which deal with the various aspects of mobility (vertical, horizontal and geographical, inter-occupational, interorganizational) and which try to analyze and typologize the emerging career patterns. We will only be able, and not always in a very systematic way, to use these limited data to answer our question.

G. Fischer constructed four career types in his study of 306 high-ranking Party executives who held office between 1958 and 1962[39]:

• 1. *Dual Executive*—"a party executive (with or without technical training) who as a rule did extensive (four years or more) work of two

[39] George Fischer, *The Soviet System and Modern Society,* Atherton Press, New York, N.Y. 1968. His sample of Party executives contains (cf. p. 25). 1) USSR secretaries and heads of major departments in the CPSU CC Central Administration. 2) Republic first, second, and capitals (including Moscow and Leningrad) first secretaries. 3) *oblast/kraj* first secretaries (including autonomous republics and *oblasts*).

kinds within the economy, technical work and party work, prior to getting a top party post."

- 2. *Technician*—"a party executive (with or without technical training) who did extensive technical work, but not extensive party work, within the economy."

- 3. *Hybrid Executive*—"a party executive who received technical training but had no extensive work in the economy."

- 4. *Official*—"a party executive whose career includes neither technical training nor extensive work in the economy.[40]

Sixteen percent of this sample were Dual Executives; 29%, Technicians; 11%, Hybrid Executives; and 44%, Officials.[41] His calculations show that "10% of the Soviet politicians in the sample were Dual Executives in 1958 as against 17% in 1962. That shift suggests something of a trend"[42]; accordingly the percentage of officials went down.[43] "Two main occupational shifts take place during the careers of most top executives. The first shift is from an initial white-collar skill to a second one. The second shift takes place when an executive gets a top party post."[44] Before getting a top Party post, two thirds of the Dual Executives, but only 46% of the Officials went through the intervening step of "sub-leadership" posts (i.e., party second secretaries in *oblast* or Republic capitals, Republic or *oblast* government council chairmen). "In general, the past careers of Dual Executives appear to be the most varied, their rate of change between occupations the highest and their upward move the most orderly."[45]

Of G. Fischer's sample 21% of the Dual Executives were full CC members in 1956, but 52% in 1961; for the other groups the statistics are the following[46]:

Technicians—1956: 32%; 1965:46%
Hybrid Executives—1956:44%; 1965:68%
Officials—1956:28%; 1965:43%

"From 1956 to 1961, there is a much greater rise in percentage of Dual Executives to the CC than of Officials,[47] men with at least a small amount of technical economic skill fare much better in their standing at the top than do men who lack experience altogether."[48]

[40] Ibid., p. 39.
[41] Ibid., p. 39.
[42] Ibid., p. 52.
[43] Ibid., p. 56.
[44] Ibid., p. 49.
[45] Ibid., p. 51.
[46] Ibid., p. 127, table 6. 4.
[47] Ibid., p. 129.
[48] Ibid., p. 128.

M. Gehlen, in a study of career types among party *apparatchiki* in the CPSU CC 1952–66, confirms that "there has been a steady increase in the number and percentage of persons coopted into the higher echelons of the apparat who have functional specializations in the economic sector of Soviet society." Particularly "production oriented specialists in the industrial sector," and, to a lesser extent "agricultural specialists" have risen in number.[49] Between 5–10% spent their previous career in the "government bureaucracy" or as pedagogs-propagandists, whereas there is a sharp decrease of "pure" Party functionaries. The number of years spent as specialists by *apparatchiki* increased sharply.[50] In 1966, two thirds of them had more than six years' experience as specialist; one fourth each spent 25–50% or 50–75% of their career as specialist, but still more than a third, 25% or less.[51] Specialists begin their Party work "primarily in the district, city, or provincial organizations of the CPSU," because those units are most immediately responsible for supervising the technical as well as the general aspects of industrial and agricultural productivity.[52] The increase of specialist experience among Party *apparatchiki* was strongly correlated with a rise in the percentage of those who hold the post of *obkom* first secretary at the time of their initial election to the CPSU CC (1961–1966: ca. 75%).[53] "The change that is manifest is one of moderate emphasis on some specialist training and experience with a continued emphasis on extended service in the apparat." We can observe "a slow but steady encroachment of the technocrat-specialist *apparatchiki* on the provinces of the political-ideological functionary."[54] This is also indicated by the increasing number of CC members with higher and technical education.[55]

F. Fleron, in a similar study of the CPSU CC full members 1952–61, distinguished between "two types of officials: 1) those who entered the political elite at very early stages in their careers and who thus had

[49] M. Gehlen, *The Soviet apparatchiki:* In: R. B. Farrell (ed.), *Political Leadership in Eastern Europe and the Soviet Union.* Aldine Publishing Co., Chicago 1970, p. 147. His sample of Party executives comprises all Party *apparatchiki* who held full membership in the CC since 1952 and "who were either central Party secretaries, members of the apparat of republic Party organizations, or provincial Party secretaries." (cf. p. 140)
[50] These trends, but based on partly different data and calculations, are also indicated by the study of Y. Bilinsky, op. cit., table 9.
[51] M. Gehlen, op. cit., pp. 147–49.
[52] Ibid., p. 150.
[53] Ibid., p. 153.
[54] Ibid., p. 154.
[55] Cf. M. P. Gehlen, M. McBride, *The Soviet Central Committee: An Elite Analysis,* "American Political Science Review," vol. LXII, Dec. 1968, p. 1233.

little opportunity to form close ties with a professional-vocational group and 2) those who entered the political elite in mid or late career and who had probably established very close professional-vocational ties outside the political elite. The former are called recruited officials, the latter coopted." The former spent less, the latter more than seven years in a professional or technical vocations. Fleron found "a marked increase in the proportion of individuals who had been coopted into the CC and the Presidium/Politburo." Correspondingly, he notices "decreases in professional politicians in the Soviet political elite."[56]

Three carefully documented studies on the *obkom* first secretaries by J. A. Armstrong, J. F. Hough, and G. Hodnett, show that in the last four years of Khrushchev's leadership, there was a limited change in the career backgrounds of this group.[57] Its large majority which held office before and after the Party reform in 1962 only had the "political" experience of party work for ten years or more, but no exposure to "economic administrative" work in *sovnarkhozes,* leading Soviet organs, or big plants.[58] Thus most of the *obkom* first secretaries in agricultural *oblasts* did not have a technical-economic training, but were Party *apparatchiki,* many of them also graduates of the Higher Party School.[59] The industrial *oblasts* were led predominantly by younger functionaries who combined experience in Party work and technical-economic skills.[60] The "Party-technocrat" was clearly preferred to the "pure specialist" or "the manager at the production front." Thus the career backgrounds between the "old" and the "new" secretaries were different—but by far not as much as was often thought.

The Party still is the most important channel of advancement to political leadership.[61] G. Fischer noticed that more than two thirds of the top Party officials in his sample, spent at least a year in Party or para-Party organization work.[62] M. Gehlen found a "declining role in Komsomol activity as a requisite for recruitment into the CPSU ap-

[56] F. Fleron, *Career Types in the Soviet Political Leadership.* In R. B. Farrell (ed.): *Political Leadership in Eastern Europe and the Soviet Union.* Aldine, Chicago 1970, p. 123, 135.

[57] Cf. J. A. Armstrong, *Party Bifurcation and Elite Interests* (see note 36, 4a); G. Hodnett, *The Obkom First Secretaries* (see note 30, 4); J. F. Hough, *The Soviet Elite I: Groups and Individuals,* "Problems of Communism," vol. 16 (Jan./Feb., 1967), pp. 28–35. *The Soviet Elite II: In Whose Hands the Future?* "Problems of Communism," vol. 16 (March/April 1967), pp. 18–25.

[58] Cf. G. Hodnett, op. cit., pp. 647–48.

[59] Cf. J. A. Armstrong, op. cit., p. 420.

[60] Cf. G. Hodnett, p. 468.

[61] See also M. Gehlen/M. McBride, op. cit., p. 1234.

[62] G. Fischer, op. cit., p. 107.

parat."[63] But this trend may have been reversed after the 1966 Party statute amendments.

A very rough analysis of the career backgrounds of the full (FM) and candidate (CM) members of the present Politburo (PB 1970: N=19) and the CPSU CC Secretariat (CCS 1970: N=11) shows that nearly all of them (28) spent, on the average, slightly more than ten years in the central Party administration (PB: FM=13, CM=ca. 7, CCS=11 years). 27 of the entire population of 30 spent even longer periods in the Republic or *oblast/kray* Party apparatus (PB: FM=17.5, CM=14.5, CCS=12.6 years). Two men (PB-FM N. Kosygin=27, PB-CM/CCS D.F. Ustinov=24 years) spent extremely long periods in the central government; one man, PB-CM D. A. Kunacv, spent 17 years on regional government level (mostly RSFSR). Excepting these extreme cases, six PB-FM spent, as a mean, eight years in the central government, but only three PB-CM and four CCS about did so for three years. Three PB-FM and PB-CM each spent about three years, two CCS about four years in regional governmental bureaucracies. About half of the Politburo has worked, as a mean, for more than two years in the technical-economic field; but eight out of ten secretaries had more than three years experience in this field, one even seventeen. Two members of the Politburo worked for extremely long periods in the Komsomol (13 and 20 years); yet the other five as well as four secretaries spent three to four years in this organization. Half of the Politburo, but only three secretaries had some exposure to political work in the armed forces, but usually for less than two years. A considerable portion of both organs did some academic-scientific-pedagogic as well as farm or factory work, usually for less than two years. Only a few members each had been involved in ideological or propaganda work.

We only emphasize the fact that the members of both organs are still predominantly professional Party politicians. In the Politburo the overall experience with government work seemed to be longer than in the Secretariat, whereas the latter concentrated a slightly stronger technical-economic background.

Above all, we learn that mostly generalists, not specialists are running the Soviet society. Yet, as we have seen already, specialized knowledge and skills, i.e., non-Party professional training and work becomes increasingly important. This is well reflected in the growing number of top politicians who have not only been Party *apparatchiki*.[64] Thus about a third of all members of both organs spent extremely long periods, i.e., more than ten years, in non-Party bureaucracies or fields of work. Though not nearly as representative as the CPSU CC, both bodies

[63] M. Gehlen, op. cit., p. 143.
[64] For comprehensive statistics see F. Fleron, op. cit., pp. 123–135.

comprise and constantly broaden a considerable range of specialized career backgrounds, particularly in the economic field.

Yet, the strategic elite of the USSR combines technocratic with political-ideological leadership. The pattern of circulation, vertical and horizontal, of the Soviet political elite is characterized by the usually high rate of interchange between high positions in the government (including the economic) bureaucracy and the corresponding posts in the Party apparatus, except for some specialized career services. J. A. Armstrong gave empirical evidence of frequent transfers of *oblast* and Republic Party secretaries between state, Party, and police agencies in the Ukraine 1939–1956 before they got their post.[65] Particularly with regard to present or future "multiple executives," S. Bialer, in his study of the Soviet political elite, speaks of a "vertical fusion of personnel of those two organizations."[66] This applies especially to the top positions at each organizational level.

But there is some evidence, too, that, under Khrushchev, the transfers *from* the governmental, especially the economic administration, *into* the Party apparatus were more frequent than vice versa.[67] Furthermore, those who once secured a higher Party position tend to advance and to stay within the Party apparatus.[68] But this trend, if it existed at all, has probably been reversed to a certain extent by Brezhnev's and the oligarchy's policy of staffing high positions in the state bureaucracy and the mass media with Party *apparatchiki*. During the Khrushchev era, the rate of all types of circulation went up considerably. This trend continued also after his ouster. But the abolition of the automatic rotation system and the praise of the experienced, longstanding Party functionary and his specific professional skills probably led to an increased stability in career assignments, to lower turnover rates, and to further professionalization, at least in the Party apparatus and its intermediate level.[69]

The rate of interchange not only differs over time, but also with regard to different organizations. Especially economic administrators in agriculture, in the defense industries, and in the planning organs show a sustained non-generalist occupational association in spite of all existing

[65] John A. Armstrong, *The Soviet Bureaucratic Elite*. New York, 1959, ch. 4, esp. pp. 54–57. See also his analysis of the career patterns of *oblast* and Republic first secretaries, 1939–56, pp. 47–49.

[66] S. Bialer, *The Soviet Political Elite: Concept, Sample, Case Study*. Unpublished Ph.D. thesis. Columbia University, New York, 1966, p. 108.

[67] See the three detailed analyses of the career lines of *obkom* first secretaries in the three studies 1960–65 mentioned in note 57.

[68] Cf. S. Bialer, op. cit., pp. 109–14. See also M. Gehlen, op. cit., pp. 151–53.

[69] Cf. Carl A. Linden, op. cit. (note 32, 1), pp. 254–59.

inter-organizational mobility.[70] This is even more true for the intermediate and upper level officials in the field of propaganda and agitation, ideology, political education and indoctrination.[71] Since their early career, most of them have been professional Party *apparatchiki,* but their specialization prevents them from becoming the generalist type of leader. Moreover, the number of top positions available for them, and, hence, their proportion among top leaders is relatively small.[72] The top positions in this field seem to be increasingly open to non-professionals in the post-Khrushchev era.[73] Nearly closed career services are the foreign service (also the foreign trade administration), the police, and the army. But there are some significant exceptions.

Since I. A. Serov was removed in 1958, the heads of the police administration(s) always have been politicians, often followers or at least political partners of the First Secretary. In the army, it is the head and many senior officials of the Main Political Administration who normally have a career background as Party functionaries. Since 1957, the foreign service has had a professional diplomat as its head. But, since 1953, many Soviet ambassadors in Communist countries, and also some in non-aligned states, have been or are former high Party officials. For them, these posts usually represented degradation, for many only one station to final disgrace.[74] Some of them replaced career diplomats; a few had a comeback or pomotion to higher positions in the USSR later on.

The career pattern of many ambassadors in the East bloc shows a phenomenon which has become more and more familiar in the Soviet system: the stepwise and the partial demotion. We know of numerous cases where former high-ranking Party leaders were demoted to inferior, but politically still important posts. We have already mentioned ambassadorships; relatively frequent are also the posts of *obkom* first secretary, second-ranking central ministries, and representative positions in the Soviets. Thus, most incumbents of these positions are on their way up, or just stagnant, but some are also on their way down. The

[70] Cf. S. Bialer, op. cit., pp. 109–12. See also the data on the career lines of the agricultural group among the *obkom* first secretaries 1960–65 in the three related studies of note 57.

[71] Cf. J. A. Armstrong, *The Soviet Bureaucratic Elite,* pp. 96–101.

[72] G. Fischer, *Soviet System and Modern Society,* pp. 111, 114.

[73] M. Tatu, *Power in the Kremlin,* op. cit., ch. 5 and postscript and the personnel changes in early 1970.

[74] To name only a few examples: P. Abrasimov, Yu. Andropov, A. B. Aristov, A. Basov, I. A. Benediktov, G. A. Denisov, N. A. Mikhailov, V. M. Molotov, N. N. Organov, P. K. Ponomarenko, G. M. Popov, M. G. Pervukhin, A. M. Puzanov, I. F. Tevosyan, S. W. Shervonenko.

offices the latter ones are allowed to hold clearly reflect the power structure of the Soviet system.

Demotions and promotions, two aspects of the vertical mobility of the political elite depend, among others, in their scope on two other elements of the political structure. The power struggle among individuals and institutions generates a limited competition of various bureaucracies, organizational sub-units, professional groups and personal followings for the most influential and the most prestigious positions in the system. By "purges" and reorganizations the number, the character, and the set-up of positions available for promotion is increased or diminished. One particular characteristic of the Soviet leadership system, the "interlocking directorate" or the combination of top offices in the Party and government hierarchy by a single incumbent, tends to limit the upward mobility within the political elite.[75]

Another structural element, however, the institution of candidate membership in the CPSU and Republic CCs and Presidia/Politburos tends to enlarge the number of available prestige positions, and, to a limited degree, presents an institutionalized, regular process of advancement.

Twenty-eight or ca. 15% of all alternate members of the 1961 CC were among those 56 persons who were promoted to full CC membership in 1966. Of the 31 candidate members of the CPSU Presidium/Politburo 1953–1970, 13 or ca. 44% were elected full members of the Politburo later on. On the average, they spent about two and a half years as candidates and had a slightly longer tenure than Presidium members who did not go through this intervening step.

After 1960, however, candidate membership became less and less a stepping-stone to full membership but more a status symbol in a relatively closed body.

But except for these fragmentary or other, often scattered, data, especially on the *obkom* first secretaries or equivalent echelons, and on turnover rates for offices and organs, we have no sufficient empirical data to construct a theory of the vertical mobility of the Soviet political elite which would indicate trends and correlations.[76]

[75] See e.g., the charts 2 and 8 showing overlapping memberships in top political organs of the USSR in F. Barghoorn, *Politics in the USSR*, Little Brown, and Co., Boston, 1966.

[76] Very helpful to get a rough idea on the vertical mobility of the lower strata of Party officials in our elite sample are J. A. Armstrong, *The Soviet Bureaucratic Elite*, New York 1959, *passim*, and the three studies mentioned in note 57. See also Y. Bilinsky, op. cit., tables 10–13 for the CPSU CC.

For technical reasons two chapters dealing with the representation of institutional groups in leading CPSU and Soviet organs and with centralism, federalism and the representation of nationalities could not be reprinted in this article. They will be presented in the context of the larger study.

Appendix

(The Soviet Political Elite)

1. PARTY.

a) Union level: full and candidate members of the CPSU CC, its Central Auditing Commission, and its Politburo/Presidium; CC secretaries, heads of CC commission, bureaux, departments and sections and their deputies.

b) Republic level: all members of the (political) bureaux and secretariats and heads of departments of the Republic CCs.

c) First and second secretaries of *oblasts/krajs,* autonomous republics and *oblasts,* and metropolitan or capital cities.

2. GENERAL AND ECONOMIC STATE ADMINISTRATION.

a) The Chairman and the Deputy Chairmen of the Presidium of the USSR Supreme Soviet and the Chairmen of its two chambers.

b) Council of Ministers: all members of the USSR Council of Ministers, the deputy Ministers of the more important ministries, leading officials of ministries, state committees, and central agencies; the All-Union and Republic economic planning agencies; the chairmen and most important ministers of the Republic councils of ministers; chairmen of the executive commission of the *oblast* (or similar as in 1c) soviets.

(For 1957–64, the corresponding positions in the *sovnarkhozes* and planning organs of various levels have to be included.)

3. MILITARY.

Minister and deputy ministers of defense; commanders-in-chief and deputies of the most important units of the armed forces and of military districts (including the forces in the GDR, CSSR and the Warsaw Pact Forces); heads of the political administrations of these units and areas and their deputies; a limited number of generals in the central staff.

4. FOREIGN SERVICE.

Minister of Foreign Affairs and deputy ministers; heads of departments and their deputies; heads of sections; the ambassadors to all Communist, the more important non-communist countries, and to the UN.

5. POLICE, PROKURATURA, JUSTICE.

a) Police: according to the changing administrative structure, heads of departments and their deputies of the USSR and the Republic ministries and/or state committees responsible for the police administration; heads of *oblast* (or similar as in 1c) police apparatus.

b) Prokuratura: USSR Prosecutor-general and his deputies, Republic prosecutors-general.

c) Justice: Members of the USSR Supreme Court, chairmen of the Republic Supreme Courts.

6. KOMSOMOL.

Members of the bureau and the secretariat of the USSR Komsomol CC; first and second secretaries of the Republic Komsomol CCs.

7. TRADE UNIONS.

All members of the Presidium and the Secretariat of the All-Union and Central Council of the Trade Unions; the chairmen of the most important, individual trade unions on Union level; the chairman and his deputies of the Rep. Pres. of the Rep. Central Councils of the Trade Unions.

8. OTHER MASS ORGANIZATIONS.

Chairmen and their deputies of various other mass organizations on the Union level.

9. CULTURAL ORGANIZATION, PRESS.

a) Cultural organizations; top officials of the writers', composers', etc. union.

b) Press: editors-in-chief and their deputies of TASS, the important central and some Republic Party, state, and military newspapers of, important political, economic, professional, scientific, literary, and general journals.

10. SCIENTIFIC ORGANIZATIONS, INSTITUTES OF HIGHER EDUCATION.

Directors and top officials of the more important scientific centers, the Institute of Marxism-Leninism, the Academy of Sciences, and similar institutions, the Higher Party School, and important universities, etc.

THE NINTH CENTRAL COMMITTEE*

Donald W. Klein and *Lois B. Hager*

In the half-century history of the Chinese Communist Party (CCP), only nine congresses have been held.** Since six of these were convened during the first seven years, only three congresses have been held since the Sixth Congress in 1928. If the Seventh Congress in 1945 can be characterized as the consolidation of Mao's rule over the CCP, and the Eighth Congress in 1956 as the consolidation of the CCP's mastery over the China mainland, then the Ninth Congress, held in 1969, is the story of the victors and victims of the Cultural Revolution.[1]

In analysing the Central Committee (CC) it is necessary first to explain our general conception of its functions. It is difficult to regard the CC as a policy-making body; indeed, its large size virtually precludes this possibility. Moreover, the CC holds relatively few plenary sessions—the Seventh CC (1945–56) held only seven plenums and the Eighth CC (1956–69) only 12.[2] In fact, CC membership has been in recent years a badge of recognition or a reward for things done. With rare exceptions, membership has signified that a man holds other positions

From *The China Quarterly*, London, No. 45 (1971). Reprinted by permission of the author and the editor.

* Roy Hofheinz and Michel Oksenberg read earlier versions of this article and made many helpful suggestions. We also want to thank Sheriden Dillon and Susan Horsey for invaluable research assistance. May 1970 is the terminal date for the information in this article.

** The Tenth CCP Congress was held in August 1973, but no substantive analysis of the newly elected Central Party organs has been published to date. [Editors' Note.]

[1] The official communiqué summing up the Congress described it as a "congress of unity and a congress of victory."

[2] The Party Constitution adopted in 1956 provided that the CC should meet at least twice a year, but no such provision is contained in the new version.

within the CCP itself or within one of the other hierarchies (such as the People's Liberation Army (PLA) or the State Council). Furthermore, rather than a decision-making body, the CC has probably served more as a useful avenue for top policy-makers to transmit ideas to the various strata of the society and for the same policy-makers to receive opinions from "below"—both from institutions such as the PLA and from geographic units such as provinces.

In order to comprehend the continuities and discontinuities reflected in the new CC, we need to characterize the CCs elected in 1945 and 1956. The 1945 CC, which had 77 full and alternate members, consisted principally of the Long Marchers plus an infusion of northerners[3] who had distinguished themselves during the Sino-Japanese War. Viewed in another fashion, it could be divided into one group represented by the Party and army high commands in Yenan and a second group of top military officers who held the key commands in the field. Apparently as a reflexion of Mao's "style" in dealing with his political opponents, a few places were reserved on the Seventh CC for fallen leaders (*e.g.*, Wang Ming). A decade later the Eighth Congress elected a CC of 97 full and 73 alternate members (and another 25 alternates were added in 1958 at the second session of the Eighth Congress). There was remarkable continuity between this and the previous CC: most of the surviving Seventh CC full members were re-elected, and most of the alternates were promoted to full membership. In addition, 130-odd persons reached CC status as full or alternate members for the first time in 1956–58; these men were "new" to the CC, but with few exceptions they had all been prominent in the Party for two or three decades.[4] The 1945 CC emerged from the wartime situation but the 1956–58 group reflected the necessities of managing a huge and populous nation, and was thus top-heavy with Party and government administrators. The trend begun in 1945 of having significant representation from the north grew markedly in the 1956–58 elections. Once again, a few places were reserved for men who were, in Mao's eyes, dissident elements (*e.g.*, Wang Ming and Li Li-san). It is not wisdom-

[3] By "northerners," which is our own term, we refer mainly to the men who established the important Communist base in Shensi prior to the Long March. Shensi served as the haven for Mao and his Long Marchers when they arrived there in 1935–36. Most of the northerners were native to Shensi or one of the nearby provinces. For a description of the Shensi base, see Mark Selden's articles on the subject in *The China Quarterly*, Nos. 28–29 (October-December 1966, January-March 1967).

[4] See Donald W. Klein, "The 'Next Generation' of Chinese Communist Leaders," *The China Quarterly*, No. 12 (October-December 1962), pp. 57–74.

through-hindsight to remark further that the Eighth CC was largely predictable. This is simply because it was so reflective of the key organs of authority (*e.g.*, most of the provincial Party first secretaries, the ministers of the key ministries, and the chiefs of the most important military organs). Continuity and stability were the watchwords of the Eighth CC, but virtually no allowance was made for the hypothetical "brilliant young administrator" who emerged only after the Communists assumed power. In retrospect, as one of us has already speculated,[5] this failure to give voice—if only symbolically—to emerging talent was perhaps the major shortcoming of the CCP leadership which was still ruling the nation on the eve of the Cultural Revolution in 1966.

The Ninth CCP Congress, held in April 1969 and attended by 1,512 delegates, elected 279 full and alternate members to the Ninth CC. Many observers have already commented on the large number of Eighth CC (1956–69) members who were not re-elected to the Ninth CC. This is certainly true, but to get a more sharply etched view of the continuities and discontinuities we must look back to the Seventh CC (1945). Setting aside those who died between 1945 and 1969, as well as those purged *before* the Cultural Revolution,[6] two related points stand out. First, two-thirds of the full members surviving from the 1945 CC were re-elected in 1969, but only one-third of the alternates.[7] In other words, the most senior echelon of the Party in 1945, that is, those most closely associated with Mao, survived far better than the next echelon. The point would not be worth labouring except that so much attention has been given to the fact that some of Mao's closest associates for many years—most notably Liu Shao-ch'i and Teng Hsiao-p'ing—were among the leading victims of the Cultural Revolution. The second point that emerges is related to the first, namely, all but two (K'ang Sheng and Ch'en Po-ta) of the 27 survivors to 1969 from the 1945 full and alternate members were in one of the central-south China Soviet areas (principally the Kiangsi Soviet) *or* made the Long March.[8] There were of course several Long March victims during the Cultural

[5] Donald W. Klein, "A Question of Leadership," *Current Scene* (Hong Kong), Vol. V, No. 7 (30 April 1967).

[6] Of the 44 full members elected in 1945, nine were dead and six had in effect already been purged (although one of the six may have been ill rather than purged).

[7] These figures work out to 20 who survived and nine who were purged during the Cultural Revolution.

[8] We draw the distinction between the men in the central-south bases and the Long Marchers to highlight those in the former group who remained behind in the south when the Long March troops left Kiangsi in 1934. Notables in this group include Ch'en I and Teng Tzu-hui.

Revolution, but the most striking fact is that *all* nine of the surviving Seventh CC members and alternates who did *not* make the Long March and whose origins were in the north were purged during the Cultural Revolution. P'eng Chen and Po I-po are among the best known members of this category. In brief, a comparison of the Seventh (1945) and Ninth (1969) CCs reveals that Mao's much heralded inner core remains largely intact, whereas the "northern" element (most heavily concentrated among the 1945 alternates) has been systematically eliminated.

The successive "generations" of leaders elected to the CC in 1956–58 were as badly hit as the Seventh CC alternates. Except for the 1945 full members, Table I demonstrates a remarkable consistency among "losers" during the Cultural Revolution, and indicates that the date a man assumed a seat on the CC had little or no bearing on the reasons for being purged. Perhaps there is some justification for the Cultural Revolution accusations that Liu Shao-ch'i, Teng Hsiao-p'ing and P'eng Chen "took control" of the Party apparatus. All three were for many years enmeshed in organizational aspects of Party work, and perhaps were in a position to dominate the selection processes for CC membership. (The figures on the table are adjusted by removing those already purged before the Cultural Revolution, such as Kao Kang, as well as those who died prior to the Ninth Congress.)

Table I

"Generations" of CC Members Not Elected to the Ninth CC, 1969

		No.	%
Group I	(the "hard core" of Long Marchers elected full members in 1945)	9	31
Group II	(alternates, several of them "northerners," elected in 1945)	15	68
Group III	(full members elected in 1956 who had not previously been full or alternate CC members)	24	75
Group IV	(alternates elected in 1956)	40	73
Group V	(alternates elected in 1958)	16	76

HOW "NEW" IS THE NEW CENTRAL COMMITTEE—INITIAL ASSOCIATION WITH THE COMMUNIST MOVEMENT

The abundance of unfamiliar names is one of the more striking things about the Ninth CC, even for those who follow closely the activities of the Chinese elite. Of the 170 full members on the new CC,

122 (or 72 per cent) had never been CC members or alternates. (In 1956 there were 33 new members—or 34 per cent.) Only five of the 109 Ninth CC alternates had held full or alternate membership previously, and these were probably special cases.[9] Looking at the continuity or discontinuity between the Eighth and Ninth CCs, there were 120 Eighth CC full or alternate members still living in 1969 who were *not* re-elected to the Ninth CC,[10] and only 53 who were.

Thus, at first sight, it is tempting to assume that the surviving Maoist inner-elite by-passed several "generations"[11] of leaders and opted for the introduction of men nurtured in the post-1949 era.[12] To test this assumption, it is useful to introduce some basic biographic details. Perhaps the best test is to pose the question: when did the Ninth CC members enter the Communist movement? Although there are problems of data (information exists on about three-quarters of the full members and about half the alternates), it is evident that the majority of members

[9] The five are Wang En-mao, Teng Hua, Fang I, T'ang Liang and T'an Ch'i-lung. (It was clearly no coincidence that these five were the *only* ones elected to the Ninth CC who were *not* on the Ninth Congress presidium.) The election of these men, plus a few more elected to full membership, may have resulted from compromises, implicit or explicit, worked out during the troubled years of the Cultural Revolution. In particular, it appears that the election of Wang En-mao, the dominant personality in Sinkiang for many years, resulted from a compromise. He had been promoted to full membership in 1958, but was pointedly demoted to alternate status on the Ninth CC.

[10] There is abundant documentation to show that the overwhelming majority of the 120 men were purged. But there are some exceptions. For example, Li T'ao, Wang Wei-chou (now dead), Lo Kuei-po and Hsieh Chueh-tsai were favourably mentioned in the press subsequent to the Ninth Congress.

[11] For a view of "generations" as defined by CC membership, see Klein, "The 'Next Generation' . . . ," *The China Quarterly,* No. 12, and for another which concentrates on the PLA, see William Whitson, "The Field Army in Chinese Communist Military Politics," *The China Quaterly,* No. 37 (January-March 1969), pp. 1–30. In 1960 Edgar Snow was told by a "man very high" in the Party that after Chiang Kai-shek's 1927 coup against the CCP there were only 10,000 Communists left, and "today there are about 800 of us—survivors of all the years" since 1927. "By and large," the official continued, "the country is being run and for some years will be run by those 800." See Edgar Snow, *The Other Side of the River* (London: Victor Gollancz, Ltd., 1963), p. 331.

[12] In this regard, the final communiqué of the Ninth Congress seems to stress the newness of CC membership by pointed references to "new proletarian fighters who have come forth in the . . . Cultural Revolution," "outstanding Party members working at production posts in factories and rural areas," and PLA "combat heroes."

have been associated with the Party for two decades or more. If the 63 peasants and workers who make up 23 per cent. of the Ninth CC are omitted from the calculations, on the theory that they were elected to meet the requirements of mass representation, the figures are considerably higher. In Table II, the figures are given first (regardless of whether or not there is information on initial association with the Communist movement), and then these are "adjusted" by removing the peasants and workers.[13]

Table II
First Identification with Communist Movement

	By end of Long March %	*By end of Sino-Japanese War* %	*By* 1949 %
CC full members (170)	55	66	69
Full members, excluding workers-peasants (135)	70	81	84
CC alternate members (109)	21	31	48
Alternates, excluding workers-peasants (81)	29	42	65

Table II requires further elaboration. First, if and when information becomes available for an unknown category of 44 persons (apart from the 63 peasants and workers), it seems likely that many of them will date their association with the CCP to the pre-1949 period. Secondly, the percentages for long-term association with the Party are substantially higher for the largest and one of the most important groups—the 110-odd men whose primary responsibilities are in the military establishment. Next, the table does not reveal the fact that some of the post-1949 recruits into the Party were very elderly; the best example being the scientist Li Szu-kuang, who was admitted to the CCP when nearly

[13] We used an admittedly loose definition for "first identification with the Communist movement." The figures are probably conservative in that the earliest information about a man often suggests he was already a Party member for several years. This assumption may serve to balance out the further supposition that many of the "unknowns," in our information joined the Communists, at a much later date. In any case, Table II is meant to be suggestive, and nothing more.

70. There appears to be no cluster of men of relative youth who hold significant posts. Yao Wen-yuan, about 40, seems to be the exception proving this rule. In sum, there is very little "new blood."

AGE

The previous paragraphs raise another question and, in part, suggest an answer: what is the average age of the Ninth CC member? The data for full members is fairly good (69 per cent.), but marginal for the alternates (20 per cent.). For full members, the average age in 1969 was 59; for the alternates, it was 53. Both figures (especially for the alternates) would doubtless be somewhat lower if we had better information. Nonetheless, it is fairly evident that there is no substantial difference in this regard between the Eighth and Ninth CCs: in both instances the average member was elected to the CC sometime in his fifties.[14]

NATIVE PROVINCE

The statistical base for place of birth roughly parallels that for age. Available information on native provinces, if correlated to initial experience in the Communist movement, testifies to the durability of the old-time revolutionaries who formed the backbone of the pre-Long March Soviet bases in Hunan (Mao's native province), Hupeh (Lin Piao's province), Kiangsi and Szechwan.

Prior to the Cultural Revolution a knowledge of the native provinces of CC members was useful to historians of the Communist movement, and it is only a slight exaggeration to state that the peripatetic history of the CCP could be plotted on a map by examining such data.[15] Inferential evidence suggests that the dominance of Chinese Communist leaders from the central-south provinces continues to characterize the

[14] See Klein, "The 'Next Generation' . . . ," *The China Quarterly,* No. 12, and Chao Kuo-chün, "Leadership in the Chinese Communist Party," *The Annals of the American Academy of Political Science,* January 1959, pp. 40–50.

[15] Roy Hofheinz, Jr., "The Ecology of Chinese Communist Success: Rural Influence Patterns, 1923–45," in A. Doak Barnett (ed.), *Chinese Communist Politics in Action* (Seattle: University of Washington Press, 1969), p. 20.

Table III
Native Province

(Full members: 102 known; 68 unknown)
(Alternate members: 32 known; 77 unknown)

Hunan	—	21
Kiangsi	—	19
Hupeh	—	18
Szechwan	—	13
Honan	—	9
Fukien	—	9
Kwangtung	—	6

(All other provinces have five or fewer, and six have none.)

Ninth CC. The inference is drawn from data on many of the younger military men (for whom specific native province data are lacking); the locale of their early associations with the CCP suggests that many of them are native to one of the central-south provinces. Moreover, the early careers of many others suggest wartime service in one of the north-north-west provinces where the Communists had border regions, or in those areas in east-central China where the Communist New Fourth Army operated. If this extrapolation of data proves correct, then the native province concentration of about three-quarters of the Ninth CC members will roughly parallel the Seventh and Eighth CCs.

Once again, special comments are required in connexion with the worker-peasant category. We assume that the overwhelming majority of the workers and peasants are native to the place where they work at present.[16] The remarkable evenness of worker-peasant representation on the Ninth CC from *all* parts of China—based on present work locale—makes it quite clear that a decision to this effect was made at the Ninth Congress. If data on worker-peasant native provinces become available, it would give the impression that all provinces are equally represented simply because the worker-peasant category represents such a large percentage of the total CC. In short, there is a broad continuity

[16] From 1949 to the Cultural Revolution, work locale and native province bore only a marginal relationship for most important Communist leaders. But in the case of the worker-peasant group, there seems to be a very strong correlation; this has already been demonstrated in some biographical sketches published in China since the Ninth Congress about the workers and peasants now on the CC.

with the past in terms of native provinces, but this might be sharply qualified by the worker-peasant category and how one interprets the importance of this category in the political processes in China.

We have already suggested that historians of the Communist movement have an interest in provincial origins, but this has also fascinated those who view the CCP in terms of cliques. One of the most familiar themes is that because Mao hails from Hunan he has favoured his Hunanese colleagues. In more recent years similar claims have been made for Hupeh, Lin Piao's native province. To provide a partial test of these theories we have computed the number of Hunanese, etc., on the Eighth CC who were purged (*i.e.,* those not elected to the Ninth Congress excluding the 22 Eighth CC members who died before the Congress). Table IV lists only eight provinces, but these eight represent the native provinces of 75 per cent. of the Eighth CC members.

Table IV
Purge Rate of Eighth CC Members by Native Province

Province	*Total Members*	*Purged* (no.)	*Purged* (%)	*% above or below average rate of purge*
Hunan	42	31	74	+ 5
Shensi	15	14	93	+24
Szechwan	14	8	57	−12
Hupeh	14	6	43	−26
Hopeh	14	11	79	+10
Kiangsi	12	7	58	−11
Kiangsu	9	7	78	+ 9
Kwangtung	9	6	67	− 2
All other provinces and unknown	44	30	68	− 1
Totals	173	120	69	

If nothing else, these figures demonstrate that Hunanese does not carry a passport for survival so long as Mao lives and, while the survival rate is higher for men from Lin Piao's province of Hupeh, the figure is still not very impressive. Most striking are the figures for Shensi and Hopeh, which reinforce our contention that, for whatever reason, the northerners were the greatest losers.

EDUCATION

Paucity of data precludes thorough treatment of the educational background of the Ninth CC members. In general, it appears that relatively few men received much higher education *before* joining the Party, and that, in contrast to the Seventh and Eighth CCs, a greater percentage of them are directly beholden to the Party for whatever education they may have received in civilian or military schools. It is almost certain that far fewer of the present CC members were educated abroad in contrast to the impressive number on the Seventh and Eighth CCs. This is not surprising; the majority of Seventh and Eighth CC members educated in schools abroad went before 1927. From that year until 1949 most of the emerging talent was involved in the two decades of military struggle with the Nationalists and Japanese. An interesting fact emerges regarding the Soviet-trained members of the Chinese elite. At least 37 members of the Eighth CC who had received some training in Moscow were still alive in 1969 but no less than 24 of them were not elected to the Ninth CC. (We should note, however, that this is almost identical with the 69 per cent. general purge rate, thereby indicating that Soviet training neither helped nor hurt a man's chances for re-election.) Also for the first time, the CC now has two men who undertook post-graduate research in an American university. Ch'ien Hsueh-sen holds a doctorate from the California Institute of Technology, and by the time he returned to China in 1955 he was regarded as one of the world's greatest rocket experts. The other man, Chu Kuang-ya, received his doctorate from the University of Michigan in 1950 and then returned to China to teach nuclear physics at North-east People's University and then Peking University.

FOREIGN TRAVEL

There is also a clear divergence between the Eighth and Ninth CCs with respect to foreign travel. Prior to the Cultural Revolution, two-thirds of the Eighth CC members had traveled abroad; or rather more if those who fought in the Korean War were added.[17] In contrast, only just over a quarter of the members of the Ninth CC members have been abroad and about half of these were also in the Eighth CC. (The figure

[17] For statistics on the foreign travels of Eighth CC members, see Donald W. Klein, "Peking's Leaders: A Study in Isolation," *The China Quarterly*, No. 7 (July-September 1961), pp. 35–43. Unlike some categories examined in this paper, information on foreign travel is generally very good.

would be about two-fifths of the Ninth CC if Korean War participants are added.) As we shall mention again in another context, foreign experience is a marginal characterization for most of the Ninth CC members, particularly those who have not previously held CC membership.

WOMEN

The women of China received a boost, if only a symbolic one, from the elections to the Ninth CC. On the previous CC there were only eight women (4 per cent), but all eight had impressive revolutionary credentials, and in no case could their election be attributed solely to the fame or importance of their husbands. On the new CC the 23 women members represent a doubling of the percentage (8 per cent, while 10 per cent. of all CCP members are women), but well over half are peasants or workers. Five of the women are married to some of China's most important figures—Mao, Lin Piao, Chou En-lai, K'ang Sheng and Li Fu-ch'un. The wives of Chou and Li are the only women who were also members of the Eighth CC (the six others were dropped); both have been revolutionists since the May 4th Movement, and Ts'ai Ch'ang (Li Fu-ch'un's wife) is the sister of one of Mao Tse-tung's closest friends (Ts'ai Ho-sen) from the years before the establishment of the CCP. The Party credentials of Yeh Ch'ün and Ts'ao Yi-ou (the wives of Lin Piao and K'ang Sheng) are dubious, to say the least. Much the same can be said about Chiang Ch'ing, despite the concerted efforts of contemporary scribes to depict her career as one of great importance stretching back for many years.

NATIONAL MINORITIES

There is no striking difference between representation on the Eighth and Ninth CCs in terms of national minorities. There were nine national minority figures on the Eighth CC, and now there are at least 13.

WORKERS, PEASANTS AND THE CC

We have already asserted the view that CC membership almost always signified the holding of some other specific position of political importance within one or more of the various hierarchies. In other words, the CC consisted of representatives from the most crucial interest groups who, because of their long experience and generally superior education, were able to articulate these interests at the highest political levels. Now the unprecedented introduction of workers and peasants gives rise to new questions about the nature of the CC as an institution.

At least 63 workers and/or peasants are on the new CC, and there are good reasons to assume that the 10 members about whom little or nothing is known are mainly from these two groups. The worker-peasant group is about evenly divided, in percentage terms, between full (20 per cent.) and alternate (26 per cent.) status. Only a handful work in Peking, and the balance is rather evenly spread among the provinces. In fact, only Ningsia appears to be without a worker or peasant on the CC. Most of the peasants are brigade-level CCP secretaries or senior commune officials, and the majority are vice-chairmen or standing committee members of the Revolutionary Committee in their respective provinces. Several of them received national recognition before 1969 as deputies to the National People's Congress. Although data are very scanty, the peasants seem to be relatively young (some in their early thirties). The characteristics of the peasants are generally applicable, *mutatis mutandis,* to the workers.

It is tempting to dismiss the workers and peasants as little more than a symbolic group, but to do so might mean a failure to grasp an important message which Mao was trying to communicate. It is noteworthy that the communiqué regarding the opening of the Ninth Congress strongly suggested that peasants and workers would get seats on the CC.[18] Mao's sense of identification with peasants and workers (especially the former) is well known, and he may be attempting to give institutional expression to the idea that "only a peasant (or worker) can express the peasants' (or workers') interests." We might also pay heed to the changes regarding qualifications for Party membership. The 1956 Party Constitution asserted that membership was "open to any Chinese citizen who works and does not exploit the labour of others" while the 1969 revision reads: "Any Chinese worker, poor peasant, lower-middle peasant, revolutionary armyman or any other revolutionary element . . ."

[18] "As compared with any of the previous congresses of our Party, there have never been such great numbers of delegates of Party members from among industrial workers in factories, mines and other enterprises and from among the poor and lower-middle peasants in people's communes, . . ." *Peking Review,* No. 14 (4 April 1969), p. 8. Midway through the congress a plenary session was held which adopted Lin Piao's political report. On that occasion Ch'en Yung-kuei, a peasant, and Wei Feng-ying, a worker, were among the very few to give speeches aside from such old stalwarts as Mao, Chou En-lai, Ch'en Po-ta and K'ang Sheng.

CHART I
CCP Central Committee:—1928-69

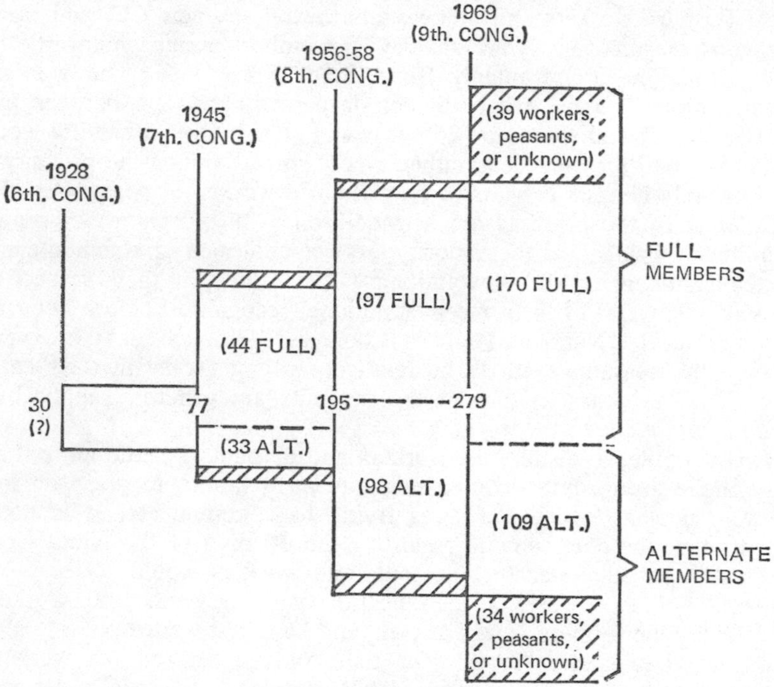

In the current tense political atmosphere in China, it is unlikely that a seasoned Party veteran would brusquely disregard the opinions of a worker or peasant. But in the longer run, we assume that the political skills of more experienced leaders will have the effect of neutralizing the voice of the workers and peasants. For the present, of course, this remains a moot point. In Chart I we have attempted to illustrate graphically a conception of the new CC in relationship to the past. The shaded areas between 1945 and 1969, representing only a very small percentage, indicate membership held by those essentially divorced from the daily political processes, *i.e.*, a combination of Mao's old political opponents and a few very elderly comrades with revolutionary credentials reaching back to the turn of the century. The Ninth CC is completely devoid of Mao's old political opponents and death has claimed virtually all the elderly revolutionaries. Thus, the

CHART II
Seventh, Eighth and Ninth Central Committee Members
Working in Peking

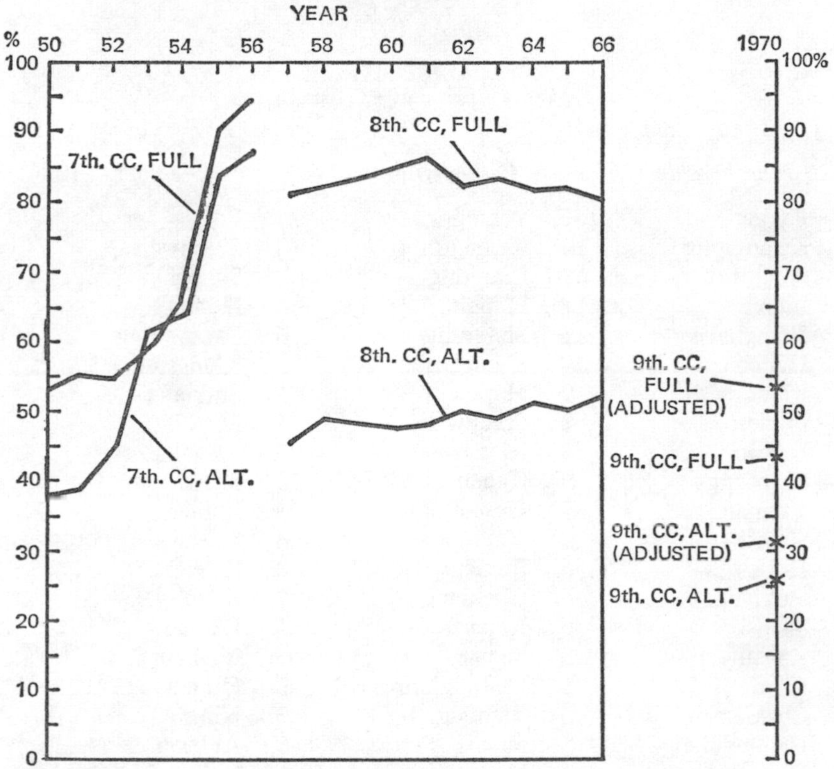

post-1969 shaded areas represent the workers and peasants (plus a few unknowns). The Ninth CC is about 30 per cent, larger than the Eighth CC in absolute figures, but if our supposition, that the workers and peasants will play only a marginal political role, is correct, then the difference in size is only fractional.

WORK LOCALE

Another conspicuous characteristic of the new CC is the decentralization of the work locale of both full and alternate members. Prior to the Cultural Revolution, 66 per cent. of the entire CC worked in Peking and only 34 per cent. in the provinces. The figures now read 36 per cent. in Peking and 64 per cent. in the provinces, or 45–55 per cent. if these figures are adjusted by removing the worker-peasant category. This in turn suggests that the inner-elite made the specific decision that the majority of the CC members should work outside the capital.[19]

Table V
Work Locale of CC Members

Total CC Membership (279)		*Full Members* (170)		*Alternate Members* (109)	
Peking	100	Peking	73	Peking	27
Kwangtung	14	Kwangtung	10	Szechwan	6
Szechwan	11	Liaoning	8	Shanghai	5
Liaoning	11	Hupeh	6	Honan	4
Shanghai	11	Shantung	6	Kwangtung	4
Hupeh	10	Shanghai	6	Kiangsu	4
Kiangsu	9	Hopeh	5	Sinkiang	4
Fukien	8	Szechwan	5	Hupeh	4
Honan	8	Kiangsu	5	Tsinghai	4
Shantung	7	Kansu	4	Shansi	4
Yunnan	7	Honan	4	Fukien	4
Shansi	7	Yunnan	4	Shensi	3
Hopeh	6	Fukien	4	Kweichow	3
Sinkiang	6	Chekiang	3	Kirin	3
Shensi	6	Inner Mong.	3	Liaoning	3
Kansu	5	Shansi	3	Yunnan	3
Kirin	5	Heilungkiang	3	Hunan	2
Chekiang	5	Tientsin	3	Ningsia	2
Heilungkiang	5	Shensi	3	Anhwei	2
Hunan	4	Hunan	2	Heilungkiang	2
Tientsin	4	Kiangsi	2	Kwangsi	2
Tsinghai	4	Kirin	2	Tibet	2
Inner Mong.	4	Sinkiang	2	Chekiang	2
Anhwci	3	Anhwei	1	Shantung	1
Kiangsi	3	Kwangsi	1	Hopeh	1
Kwangsi	3	Tibet	1	Tientsin	1
Kweichow	3	Tsinghai	0	Kansu	1
Tibet	3	Kweichow	0	Kiangsi	1
Ningsia	2	Ningsia	0	Inner Mong.	1
Unknown	5	Unknown	1	Unknown	4

[19] In a 1958 speech, Mao Tse-tung observed that "comrades working in local areas will eventually come to the center. Those working in the center

These adjusted figures—45 per cent. in Peking and 55 per cent. in the provinces—are almost precisely the same for CC members in the take-over years when the consolidation of political control was an issue of the highest priority. Given the considerable turmoil of the Cultural Revolution, the coincidence may be more than accidental. Chart II demonstrates the previous high degree of centralization, together with the decentralization of the Ninth CC.

Further refining these work-locale figures, we find that a greater number (73 persons, or 43 per cent.) of the full members work in Peking than do the alternates (27, or 25 per cent.). Moreover, there is a full member in all but three provinces, and at least two full *or* alternate members in *every* province. Not surprisingly, there is a broad (but by no means perfect) correlation between the distribution of CC members and the population of provinces (see Table V).

In terms of an occupational breakdown, virtually all of the 15–20 top policy-makers (Mao, Lin Piao, Chou En-lai *et al.*) are in Peking. About a third of the 110-odd people whose primary responsibilities are in the military field are in Peking while the rest are scattered fairly evenly throughout the provinces. Similarly, of a rather loosely defined group of 60–70 administrative generalists, whose main tasks are within the Government and Party hierarchies, about a third are in Peking and the rest are scattered throughout the provinces. Both the latter groups have more full than alternate members in Peking (38 per cent. v. 29 per cent. in the case of the military men, and 50 per cent. v. 26 per cent. for the administrative generalists).

INSTITUTIONS AND SYSTEMS

The State Council

Having attempted a rough profile of CC members, we turn to an examination of the institutions and systems[20] in China in relation to the new membership. Are there sets of facts, or even crudely drawn

---

will eventually die or be overthrown. Khrushchev came from a local area. The local class struggle is sharper, more similar to a natural struggle, and closer to the masses. These are the favorable conditions possessed by the local comrades as compared with comrades at the center. The state of Ch'in was first a kingdom and then an empire." "Selections from Chairman Mao," *Translations on Communist China*, No. 90, *Joint Publications Research Service* (Washington), No. 49826 (12 February 1970), p. 46.

[20] For details on systems in China, see A. Doak Barnett, *Cadres, Bureaucracy, and Political Power in Communist China* (New York: Columbia University Press, 1967), esp. pp. 6–9 and 456–57.

trends, which mark distinct changes in the Chinese political system, or have we witnessed changes of form but not substance? Aggregate elite analysis can never supply definitive answers to such questions; at best it can only suggest partial answers and raise issues which political scientists, historians, sociologists, etc. can grapple with in their own fashion. Some of the most important questions concern the national administrative hierarchy. In post-1949 China, administration has centered in the State Council (the cabinet), a key institution whose activities cut across several of the most important systems, particularly in the field of economics.

If one assumes that fewer State Council ministers and vice-ministers[21] on the CC indicates a diminution of authority and the opportunity to articulate interests, then the State Council emerges as a less important organ. On the Eighth CC, no less than a quarter of the members were drawn from the ministers and vice-ministers. Moreover, this group of men probably possessed a unique familiarity with one another because virtually all of them were stationed in Peking. In contrast, large percentages of the men in the other crucial hierarchies, such as the Party apparatus and the military establishment, were by definition scattered throughout the provinces (*e.g.,* provincial Party secretaries and military district political commissars and commanders). On the Ninth CC, only 10 per cent. of the members are ministers or vice-ministers, although the percentage would be slightly higher if the worker-peasant category were deleted. Equally revealing is the fact that at the time of the Eighth Congress (1956–58), two-thirds of the nearly 50 ministries had at least one full or alternate member on the CC, whereas only one-third of the ministries are represented on the new CC. (Those which currently have the most representatives are the State Planning Commission (six), the Ministry of National Defence (five) and the Ministry of Public Security (three)[22]). If these figures have any real meaning, they might suggest a lower priority in various economic fields, or at least a reduction in the economic responsibilities which the State Council exercised for so many years.

The Military Establishment

The well-known rise in importance of the PLA during the Cultural Revolution is, of course, heavily reflected in the composition of the Ninth CC. A good deal of secrecy surrounds the work of the Party's

[21] As used here, ministers and vice-ministers are equated with State Council commission chairmen and vice-chairmen, *e.g.,* the chairman of the State Planning Commission.

[22] The figures for "representation" in these ministries are almost certainly inflated. Lin Piao, for example, is calculated in these totals by virtue of his position as Defence Minister.

Military Affairs Committee (MAC), but at present it includes among its leading members at least 17 CC members, including, of course, Mao's designated heir, Lin Piao. The PLA's General Staff, the Rear Services (logistics) Department, as well as the various service arms (*e.g.*, the Navy and Air Force), are also well represented. On the eve of the Cultural Revolution these units had about 10 CC-level persons in leading posts; the figure is now three to four times that number. In all, there are 40–50 CC members and alternates in Peking whose major functions are in the military sphere, in addition to several more top policy men who devote much of their attention to military affairs.

One of the most striking facts about the military figures is that the majority (70–80 per cent.) are working in the provinces. There is about an even break between the political commissars and commanders, and some men, of course, hold both kinds of posts. Not surprisingly, more full than alternate members occupy the key positions in the 13 military regions, which stand above the military districts in the hierarchy. Except for Tibet, all regions have at least two full members holding the top posts,[23] and most have about five full or alternate members. In total, at least 63 full or alternate members have assignments in the military regions. There is less of a concentration of CC representation in the 22 military districts; in contrast to the 63 men in the regions, there are 32 in the districts (12 full members and 20 alternates). There also appears to be a pattern in the districts that more of the CC members and alternates hold political commissar posts than command assignments.

In view of the abundance of military personalities on the Ninth CC, and particularly because so much attention has been given to the alleged "militarization" of the Chinese leadership, it is worth noting that military figures from the Eighth CC survived no better than their civilian colleagues in terms of re-election to the Ninth CC. In this regard, long-term association with the PLA was no more a passport to success than being a native of Hunan.

Revolutionary Committees

So much has been written about the provincial-level Revolutionary Committees that little more need be added here. No less than 77 (or 45 per cent.) of the 170 full members and 43 (or 39 per cent.) of the alternates are chairmen, vice-chairmen, standing committee members, or members of these committees. These figures and percentages would be increased to a marked extent if we added the 40-odd

[23] By top posts we mean commander, political commissar, deputy commanders, and deputy political commissars, as well as the generally described "responsible persons."

generically defined "responsible persons" who probably hold one of the four posts mentioned above. Except for Tsinghai, where there is a vacancy, all provinces have a CC member or alternate as the Revolutionary Committee chairman. And, as one might expect, the overwhelming majority of chairmen are full CC members. Every provincial-level committee has at least one CC member or alternate, with the greatest concentration in Shanghai, Szechwan (10 each), Kwangtung (nine), Honan, Peking (seven each), Sinkiang, Yunnan (six each).

The predominance of military personnel in the revolutionary committees is particularly evident. With a few marginal exceptions, most chairmen qualify as military figures. This point is reinforced by the fact that six of the chairmen are concurrently commanders of military regions and another six are the political commissars. Moreover, two more are commanders of military districts and still another six are the district political commissars. The interlocking directorate is equally apparent in terms of many of the lesser revolutionary committee position holders (*e.g.,* vice-chairmen, standing committee members). This provincial-level interlocking directorate is, of course, nothing new to the Chinese People's Republic. Prior to the Cultural Revolution it was dominated by the Party apparatus, but now it is dominated by PLA figures.

Senior revolutionary committee officials currently shoulder many responsibilities formerly undertaken by the ranking officials in the old Party provincial committees and government administrations. It is appropriate, therefore, to inquire into the fate of former first secretaries and governors, most of whom still serve in the provinces. On the whole, the governors fared far better than the secretaries. Nine of their numbers, or one-third, were re-elected or elected to the CC. On the negative side, three former CC members who had been governors were dropped. Seven of the first secretaries, or one-fourth, were re-elected to the CC, but an impressive 14 (50 per cent.) who had been CC members were purged.

Other Institutions and Systems

Finally, we would like to examine briefly some other fields of specialization by examining senior officials in various organizations in terms of the Eighth and Ninth CCs. Here again we can only be suggestive, and there would doubtless be important qualifications if these organizations and institutions were scrutinized in detail. (In all cases, persons who died before the Ninth Congress were omitted from our calculations.)

Communist Youth League. Eight men who had been leading League officials at some time between 1949 and 1964 held seats on the

Eighth CC—none survived to the Ninth CC. Among the eight were such important men as Hsiao Hua, Liao Ch'eng-chih and Hu Yao-pang.

All-China Youth Federation. Twelve men who held important federation posts at some time between 1949 and the Cultural Revolution were concurrently Eighth CC members. Only two survived to the Ninth CC, but both of them—Su Yü and Hsieh Fu-chih—are obviously more closely linked to the PLA than to youth work. Two other former federation officials, the familiar Yao Wen-yuan and the nuclear physicist Chu Kuang-ya, were elected for the first time to the CC.

All-China Federation of Trade Unions. Twelve Federation officials from the 1949–66 period were on the Eighth CC. Eight were not elected to the Ninth CC, including two of the most important in the everyday federation activities, Liu Ning-i and Li Chieh-po. None of the four elected to the Ninth CC (*e.g.,* Ch'en Yun) has been active in the labor federation since the 1950s. Only one man, Chang Kuo-hua, who still serves with the federation but who was not on the Eighth CC, was elected to the Ninth CC.

Foreign affairs specialists. Foreign affairs specialists, as defined by past association with the Ministry of Foreign Affairs, have never been well represented on the CC. They fared no better on the Ninth CC. None of the six men who had been former ambassadors and who were members of the Eighth CC was re-elected to the Ninth CC, nor was former vice-minister of Foreign Affairs, Chang Han-fu. On the positive side, Chou En-lai and Ch'en I were re-elected, and two current ambassadors, Huang Chen and Keng Piao, were elected for the first time. In a broad sense the failure to place many foreign affairs specialists on the CC can be correlated to the fact that experience abroad is not a striking characteristic of the Ninth CC.

Scientists and science administrators. Twenty-one men, who were members of the Eighth CC, held posts before the Cultural Revolution on the State Council's Scientific and Technological Commission (or its predecessor organizations, the Scientific Planning Commission and the National Technological Commission), or in one of the departments of the Academy of Sciences. Thirteen of the 21 were not re-elected to the Ninth CC. On the other hand, six men associated with these organizations, but not previously on the CC, were elected to the Ninth CC. Among them were the well-known scientists Ch'ien Hsueh-sen and Li Szu-kuang.

Political Science and Law Association. Five former officials of this organization served on the Eighth CC, but only one, the elderly Tung Pi-wu, was re-elected to the Ninth CC.

Party Central Control Commission. Fourteen full or alternate members of the Party's Control Commission, the body set up in 1955 in direct response to Kao Kang's alleged "anti-Party" plot, held seats on the Eighth CC. Ten of them failed to be re-elected to the Ninth CC. The senior Control Commission official, Secretary Tung Pi-wu, was re-elected, but three of the five deputy secretaries were among the 10 dropped. Two alternate members of the Commission who had not previously served on the CC were elected to the Ninth CC. Of special interest is the fact that no provision was made for the Control Commission in the new Party Constitution.

CONCLUSION

After the *Sturm und Drang* of the Cultural Revolution, few observers of China would have been surprised to find an almost complete new cast of characters at front stage. But, to continue the metaphor, we seem to have witnessed the emergence of understudies who have been waiting in the wings for many years. There is little to indicate that the hypothetical "brilliant young administrator and activist" who reached maturity in the past decade has now emerged to hold crucial posts. On the contrary, as we have demonstrated, the Ninth CC members are fairly elderly and have served the Communist movement for many years.

But there are, to be sure, some striking innovations in the Ninth CC. We have stressed the worker-peasant element as a new dimension to the study of the CC, although the significance of this change remains to be determined—not just within the CC, but throughout the various nationwide administrative hierarchies. To the extent that the new CC is representative of broader trends, it also appears that a number of interests are no longer well represented at the highest political levels.

Another striking departure from the past is the increased role of the military establishment. This raises a number of possibilities. Among the more important questions are those of allegiance and priorities. If the military men continue to perform many civilian tasks, will their prime allegiance be to the PLA? And how will they react to the allocation of scarce materials and skilled manpower for civil functions? There is a substantial body of literature on the important role of the military in the modernization process, but prior to the Cultural Revolution the Chinese did not seem to follow this pattern. The new composition of the CC may be an institutional expression of new approaches on questions of development. Perhaps, for example, there is some crucial relationship not readily apparent in the large percentage of military men and the high degree of decentralization that characterizes the Ninth CC.

We have also suggested that some previously laid "tests" of the political process are now open to serious question—such as the primacy of Hunanese. In like fashion, it appears that formal education, which was previously quite impressive among CC members, is now less of a factor for aspiring Party members. If true, this may be still another expression of Mao's well-known aversion to the worst trappings of formal education (for which he is erroneously charged with being anti-intellectual).

The dramatic innovative trends suggested by the composition of the Ninth CC are intellectually stimulating for all students of China. And there are those who would doubtless argue that the changing trends are paralleled by "transformed" Chinese leaders as a result of the Cultural Revolution. This may be true, but it has yet to be demonstrated over the long run. In any case, the discontinuities with the past should not blind us to the fact that various continuities persist. We may be in the midst of Act II, Scene III, but the play continues.

THE SED LEADERSHIP IN TRANSITION

Peter C. Ludz

THIS article proposes to analyze the top leadership of East Germany's ruling Socialist Unity Party (SED) in terms of the rival political groups it encompasses, the career patterns of the spokesmen of these groups, and their contending views on the domestic and foreign policy options open to East Germany. Focusing on the personal characteristics of the men who will one day succeed the 77-year-old Walter Ulbricht and who already participate extensively in shaping East Germany's course seems justified because, as we shall try to show, the personalia of the individuals composing the major elite groupings reflect, in a very direct fashion, the major social processes at work in the GDR. The careers, convictions and life styles of different groups of party and state functionaries are intimately tied to specific ongoing social developments; hence their biographic data—the rise and decline of specific types of *apparatchiki* and experts—can also be read as indicators for East Germany's political and economic development and, above all, for the resolution of East Germany's basic problem, to which all others are subsumed: the dilemma of how to combine modernization with stability. Before turning to the discussion of the East German leadership, it might therefore be useful to sketch here the nature of this problem and its special application to East Germany.

At bottom, the problem—one that exists in all polities—is to find the proper balance between the frequently contradictory requirements of modernizing a political and social system while keeping intact the char-

Peter C. Ludz, "The SED Leadership in Transition," *Problems of Communism* (Washington, D.C.), May–June 1970. *Problems of Communism* is a bimonthly publication of the United States Information Agency.

acter and identity of its core institutions and its essential leadership group—what is known in political science terminology as system modernization and system maintenance. These two processes, far from being mutually exclusive, are complementary; no political entity of any complexity could perpetuate itself for long without making at least a minimum provision for both. But, in any given case, there is bound to be tension between the requirements of modernization and those of stability; and, almost inevitably, there are bound to be differences within the leadership group (and in the society at large) concerning the correct mix of the two elements. Those who identify with the status quo will tend, out of conviction as well as from a well-defined sense of their own interests, to accentuate the need for system maintenance and downplay the need for modernization; modernizers can be expected to take the converse approach.

Though the processes of system modernization and system maintenance (or system preservation, as it has sometimes been called) constitute what in Hegelian terminology might be called a "dialectic unity," they obviously are never in perfect equipoise in any system at any specific time. One tendency may predominate for long periods of time, or there may be considerable fluctuations from one tendency to the other. In the specific case of East Germany, these forces did not really come into full play for the first fifteen years of SED rule because the GDR had not attained a sufficiently high level of industrialization to qualify as a fully articulated modern system, being instead a "system-in-construction" whose social processes were not advanced enough to conform to the patterns of system maintenance and modernization. However, when these patterns finally did emerge during the early 1960's, it became clear in retrospect that they had been decisively conditioned by the political and economic developments of the 1950's.

In this earlier period the political structure installed in East Germany by the Soviets after World War II was securely based on the *de facto* monopoly of the SED over the political life of the state, while the economic organization—copied from the Stalinist model of Soviet development—operated, like its prototype, on the principles of complete centralization of the economy and tight party control. Both sub-systems served their purpose: the political structure ensured popular compliance, while the economy showed consistently high growth rates. And while there was some opposition among both theoreticians and managerial types to economic overcentralization on account of hidden inefficiencies, demands for change were overridden and did not become major political issues.

The situation changed radically in the early 1960's. The dislocation caused in agriculture by a new program of forced collectivization in

1960 and, more importantly, the traumatic impact of an abrupt drop in industrial growth rates in 1961–62 generated doubts as to the continued stability of the existing economic model. Moreover, the Liberman debates which took place in the Soviet Union in 1962, providing open recognition that some of the main features of the Stalinist system were no longer appropriate to an industrialized economy, strengthened the hand of those in the East German leadership who, in the past, had unsuccessfully advocated changes in the economic system. In 1963, Ulbricht made the decision to update at least the economic sector of East Germany, while attempting to preserve the old order in the political sector.

Change vs. Stability

It was at this point in time, when the SED leadership (and some perceptive Western observers) recognized that East Germany had attained the status of an advanced industrial society, that the cycle of system modernization and system maintenance was initiated. In this case, circumstances clearly called for modernization; it was implemented in the economic reform of 1963 and took three approaches: the diffusion of decision-making authority from the central economic agencies to associations of nationalized enterprises (the VVBs or *Vereinigungen Volkseigener Betriebe*) and the enterprises proper; the rationalization of work processes in the central and regional economic bureaucracies; and the improvement of training methods geared toward fostering initiative and independence in managerial personnel. In short, the kind of process was undertaken which political scientists have called the extension of sub-system autonomy. While the reform was not entirely restricted to the economy (indeed, as implied above, it was vigorously applied to the organization of research and training), the major implementing agencies were in the field of economics: the State Planning Commission and the associations of nationalized enterprises, as well as various central and regional agencies of the party and government—all of which were thoroughly reorganized in the spring of 1963. The result was nothing short of astounding: administrative and industrial executives at all levels acquired, within a very short time, a managerial sophistication which led to an economic dynamism unparalleled in Eastern Europe.

However, by 1965 the process of modernization gave way temporarily to a counterbalancing trend emphasizing system maintenance at the expense of system modernization. Whether this reaction was in response to pressure from the post-Khrushchevian Soviet leaders, who were embarking on a similar policy in the USSR, or whether the conservatives in the East German leadership felt threatened by the sweep and rapidity of economic modernization, the years 1965–67 saw a return to the predominance of system-maintenance processes designed to safeguard the power and authority of the ruling group. A development in 1964 both antedated and presaged this trend—the transformation of the so-called "production committees" in enterprise plants. Initially established in a few enterprises in 1963 for the purpose of providing a convenient administrative roof for various party and mass organizations in the enterprises, the production committees were converted in 1964 into instruments whose primary function was supervising the enterprise managers.[1] Starting in early 1965, control over all segments of party, government, economy and society was noticeably reinforced. An important example was the creation, in December 1966, of so-called Social Councils (*Gesellschaftliche Räte*) attached to the VVBs, whose task it was to advise and supervise the VVB management boards, which previously had been given a rather free hand in running the associations.[2]

Since 1968, the trend in East Germany has been back toward modernization, for somewhat paradoxical reasons. Partly because of the collapse of the Czech economy in the aftermath of the Soviet invasion, and also because of the increasing difficulties experienced by the Soviets in their own economy, East Germany has been called upon to respond to expanded East European and Soviet demands for commodities and technical know-how. Fulfilling this task has required an expansion of East German economic capabilities, which in turn has given new impetus to the demand for modernization.

This trend may not go unchecked. The unexpectedly cordial reception accorded by the population of the East German city of Erfurt to West German Chancellor Willy Brandt during his visit there is just one event demonstrating that the state's political situation has not yet been stabilized. Therefore, despite East Germany's economic progress, its relatively high standard of living and a growing sense of social cohesion, the current leadership may decide at some time that the problems of system maintenance must take precedence over the problems of system modernization, and may revert to stabilizing measures.

[1] See, for example, Peter C. Ludz, *Parteielite im Wandel,* Köln und Opladen, Westdeutscher Verlag, 1698, p. 136ff. It should be noted that the Soviet Union had pioneered this type of organization by establishing production committees in several Leningrad enterprises early in 1963.

[2] *Cf.* Paul Liehmann *et. al., Leiter und Kollektiv in der sozialistischen Wirtschaft,* Dietz Verlag, Berlin, 1967, p. 101ff.

The Experts

In turning to analyze the effect of these broad social tendencies on the SED leadership, it must be kept in mind that the identification of specific leadership groups with definite trends must be qualified. On the one hand, certain groups and individuals have a definite stake in either modernization or preservation by dint of their past history, their philosophy, their organizational association, and their career patterns and interests. On the other hand, the identification cannot be pushed to the point where an individual or a group is totally identified with modernization at the expense of stability, or *vice versa.* At least, this is not the case in East Germany where the modernizers are thoroughly integrated into the political system and where the stabilizers do want to see an extension of East German capabilities and are willing to accept a certain amount of modernization. All groups in the East German leadership advocate a mix of stability *cum* modernization. However, the mixes are sufficiently varied to permit categorization of the Politburo of the SED into clearly different wings.

At one end of the spectrum is the group of leaders who promote modernization and change, consisting of the younger and professionally educated members of the Politburo. If one takes the age 45 and the possession of an advanced education as the minimum criteria for inclusion in this group, one of the fifteen full members and five of the six candidate members of the Politburo qualify on both counts. All members of this group were recruited into top positions in the party because of their contributions to East Germany's economic, technical and scientific performance; and their future success in the party depends clearly on the continued dynamism of the economic system. Hence their commitment to modernization is both intellectual in nature and prompted by self-interest.

At present, the single most important individual in this group is Günter Mittag, a full member of the Politburo and Central Committee Secretary for the Economy (born 1927). Five others hold candidate membership in the Politburo. They are Werner Jarowinsky, Central Committee Secretary for Trade and Procurement (born 1927); Georg Ewald, an agricultural expert, who also sits on the Presidium of the Council of Ministers (born 1926); Walter Halbritter, Director of the Office of Prices attached to the Council of Ministers (born 1927); Günther Kleiber, State Secretary for Data Processing on the Council of Ministers (born 1931); and Margarete Müller, a member of the Presidium and Secretariat of the Free German Trade Union Federation (born

1931). Mittag, Jarowinsky, Ewald, and Margarete Müller have belonged to the Politburo since 1963; Halbritter and Kleiber were elected to candidate membership in the spring of 1967. All of these people are experts in their specialized fields. All but Ewald hold either Ph.D. degrees from major universities or diplomas for advanced study at higher technical institutes. Thus their careers demonstrate that economic or technological competence has now become a means to achieve political power in the Communist stystem.

In an earlier work, the writer has described this group as the core of an "institutionalized counterelite."[3] The term "counterelite" is useful in two senses: it identifies the new breed of party cadres whose education, expertise, and career experience clearly differentiate them from the functionaries of the "Old Guard"; and it also reflects the fact that these younger experts and "technocrats" are regarded with a certain amount of suspicion by the *apparatchiki*. At the same time, this counterelite is "institutionalized" in that it has taken firm root in the apparatuses of the party, the state, and the economy. The members of the counterelite consider themselves convinced Marxists functioning within the political framework of the GDR. But their views on Marxism are quite different from the ideological concepts entertained by many older functionaries. They can best be characterized as pragmatically-oriented neo-conservatives, to differentiate them from the dogmatically oriented old-style conservatives in the leadership.

All of the above-named spokesmen of this group advocate a continuing process of economic and technological modernization in East Germany. They support economic reforms not as a matter of principle but as a matter of practicality—so long as the reforms are aimed at strengthening the industrial and agricultural infrastructure of the GDR and thereby increasing its political leverage *vis-à-vis* other countries. By the same token, when they criticize Politburo decisions, they are not criticizing the basic system or its ideological underpinnings but are rather opposing the imposition of economically inefficient measures by political decision-makers. It may be assumed that they favor improved relations between East and West Germany—again, mainly for economic reasons; they are less interested in the ideological subversion of West Germany or in ideological questions in general.

Within the group, Mittag unquestionably enjoys the most power and prestige, though lately Jarowinsky's star has also been on the rise. In December 1969, Jarowinsky was chosen to present the report of the Politburo to the 12th Plenum of the Central Committee (a key assignment since the report included a comprehensive review of recent economic and scientific progress, covering such subjects as automation and

[3] Peter C. Ludz, op. cit., p. 43ff.

rationalization of industry, developments in the construction and transportation fields, the state of agriculture, foreign trade, etc.).[4] To all outward appearances, however, there have never been any serious rivalries within the group—probably because their special areas of concentration have led to a natural division of labor. Thus Mittag has focused on special efforts to rationalize industry and transportation; Jarowinsky has concentrated on measures to raise the standard of living; while Ewald has been responsible since 1955–56 for improvements in agriculture.

Some Western observers believe that the Soviets maintain a guarded and even mistrustful attitude toward the younger reformers in the SED Politburo. Such opinions are difficult to prove or disprove. Mittag has visited the Soviet Union a great many times, together with Ulbricht and party stalwarts Erich Honecker and Willi Stoph. In the writer's view, there is nothing—at least on the surface—to indicate that Mittag does not enjoy good relations with the Soviet leaders.

The Dogmatists

Opposed to the group of modernizers is that wing of the Politburo which places the need for stability above the requirements of modernization. Generally older and less well educated than those belonging to the first group, functionaries by experience and true believers by conviction, members of this group tend to stress the supremacy of politics and ideology at the expense of economics and technology (which, in any event, they do not fully understand). They cannot, of course, express opposition to the modernization of East German society—in fact, they probably approve of certain political effects of the GDR's present rapid development, above all its growing influence with the USSR. But they clearly fear that an overly rapid pace of liberalization in the economy might spread to the political structure of East Germany and thereby constitute a very real threat to the power of the party and the preservation of the current system. Hence, they tend to be cautious about modernization even when the situation is well in hand, and to press for a reversal of the trend in times of crisis.

The views, affiliations, interests and policy objectives of this group are epitomized by the case of Erich Honecker, its leading spokesman.

[4] Werner Jarowinsky, *Bericht des Politbüro an die 12. Tagung des Zentralkomitees der Sozialistischen Einheitspartei Deutschlands, 12/13 December 1969* (Report of the Politburo to the 12th session of the Central Committee on the Socialist Unity Party, Germany, December 12–13, 1969), Dietz Verlag, Berlin, 1969.

In contrast to Mittag, Jarowinsky, *et al.*, who achieved high rank in the party because of their economic and technological expertise, Honecker reached his top-drawer position thanks to his political knowhow. The son of a veteran Communist, Honecker—who was born in 1912 and has been a party member since 1929—is considered by many to be Ulbricht's most likely successor. In recent years he has frequently been deputized by Ulbricht to act as the official representative of the East German party and state. More important, he holds key positions in the party and has managed over the years to build up a personal power base. Since 1958, he has been both a member of the Politburo and the Central Committee Secretary for military affairs and internal security, exercising crucial authority over the People's Army and other security organs of the GDR. As an old-style politician who has spent 40 years in the Communist Party, he has enjoyed the confidence of the older party *apparatchiki.* He has also maintained good relations with the leadership of the East German Communist youth movement (FDJ), which he himself founded and headed up in the first postwar decade (1946–55). In the traditional pattern of the professional party functionary, he has also put in two years of political training in the Soviet Union (1955–56). In general, Honecker fits the stereotype of the colorless, disciplined and cautious party bureaucrat who has little understanding of the "new economics" and who has never displayed much initiative in the area of policy-making. Ironically, it is in part these qualities —in combination with an unswerving devotion to Ulbricht—that have enabled Honecker to become number-two man in the party apparatus.

One possible indication of a recent weakening in Honecker's position perhaps ought to be mentioned. It is clear from his public statements that he has been strongly opposed to the idea of a rapprochement between East Germany and West Germany. For instance, in a speech delivered February 16, 1970, to the students of the SED Higher School "Karl Marx," he declared:

> There is no indication that the objectives of West German imperialism—which has at its disposal a strong and aggressive force that must not be underestimated . . . the army—have been changed under the regime of the Social Democrats. . . . What distinguishes the Social Democratic variant [of West German imperialism] is simply that it employs more flexible methods than those used by certain CDU/CSU politicians.[5]

While there is no way to verify the report, it has been rumored that Honecker raised strong objections to the initiation of discussions between West German Premier Willy Brandt and SED leader Willi Stoph

[5] *Neues Deutschland* (East Berlin), Feb. 22, 1970, p. 4.

(more on whom shortly). If this is true, Honecker's view certainly did not prevail—and his defeat on so crucial an issue may well be a significant political omen.

Some of the other "hard-line" conservatives in the party's top council ought to be mentioned. One is Paul Fröhlich, a member of the Politburo since 1958, and First Secretary of the SED Bezirk (regional) Party Committee in Leipzig since 1952 (born 1913). Another is Paul Verner, a Politburo member since 1963 and First Secretary of the immensely important SED Bezirk Party Committee in Berlin since 1959 (born 1911). Verner, who fought in the Spanish Civil War and later emigrated to the West during World War II, has become known primarily as an expert on Western affairs; he was also a cofounder with Honecker of the Communist youth movement. Still another member of the group is Alfred Neumann, who has been on the Politburo since 1958 and is now serving concurrently as First Deputy Chairman of the Council of Ministers (born 1909). Neumann's performance as an administrator has been unimpressive. He served as chairman of the short-lived People's Economic Council from its founding in 1961 until its dissolution in 1965. He then spent three years as a rather ineffectual Minister for Material Economy. In both roles he displayed a lack of understanding of the complexities of modern economics and little more talent for administrative organization.

The professional ideologues in this group of hardliners are Albert Norden (born 1904) and Herman Axen (born 1916). Norden has been a member of the Politburo since 1958 and has served as the Central Committee Secretary in charge of propaganda *vis-à-vis* West Germany and West Berlin since 1955. While he is a highly intelligent man, his intense dogmatism has always impelled him toward a strident and primitive approach in agitprop activities (one of his frequent themes is that the West German government represents little more than the old Nazi system in a new guise[6]). Norden has an obvious rival in Herman Axen, even though both belong to the conservative wing and though Axen is only a candidate member of the Politburo. Axen, who was editor-in-chief of the party organ *Neues Deutschland* for the decade 1956–66, has served more recently as the Central Committee Secretary in charge of foreign propaganda. (A third up-and-coming rival to both of these men is Werner Lamberz, who is not on the Politburo but who has served since 1967 as the Central Committee Secretary in charge of domestic propaganda.)

Considered as a group, the old conservatives obviously do not enjoy as much political power as they did in the 1950's and early 1960's. Since

[6] *Cf.* Norden's speech, ibid., March 8, 1970, p. 3.

they have relatively little knowledge or understanding of scientific, technological, and economic problems, their influence in a whole range of vital activity has been small. To all appearances, their most important external objective is to weaken the political and ideological fabric of the West German Federal Republic, and it is possible in many instances to show how members of this group have promoted contacts with and extended support to Communists, anarchists, and fellow travelers in West Germany; by the same token, the group takes a negative attitude toward any kind of dialogue with the democratic parties in the Federal Republic. Insofar as relations with Moscow are concerned, most members of the group seem to be limited to contacts with their Soviet counterparts—for example, personnel in the Soviet agitprop apparat. (Honecker is an exception, since he is a frequent visitor to the USSR and has many political contacts there.) Finally, on the domestic front, the group rejects any and every concept or measure that might promote modernization of the party apparatus, presumably because they fear that changes might alter power relations within the party to their further disadvantage.

The "Middlemen"

The remainder of the Politburo is comprised largely of advocates of a middle course between the two wings described above. This mediating posture seems to be dictated less by the search for an optimal balance between the requirements of modernization and stabilization than by the pragmatic recognition that maximum political leverage can be obtained from a flexible "centrist" position catering to—and drawing support from—the other two contending groups. The star proponent of this approach is party chief Walter Ulbricht, whose image as an ideological hardliner is often overdrawn in the Western press; Willi Stoph is in the chief supporting role, with Horst Sindermann and Kurt Hager as other important members of the "Center."

The group's characteristic approach to politics is exemplified by Walter Ulbricht's conduct in the leadership of the SED: on the one hand, he has been tough and unyielding with respect to the pursuit and protection of his personal political power; on the other hand, he has been flexible, adaptive, and open to compromise in policy determinations, generally seeking to achieve a balance or "integration" of various opposing forces in the party leadership. The first of these postures was most evident in the decade between 1950 and 1960, when Ulbricht was involved in the deadly game of eliminating his rivals for power (notably, Zaisser, Herrnstadt, Schirdewan and Wollweber).[7] The second of Ulbricht's postures was epitomized by his quick reaction to Khrushchev's announcement in November 1962 of a major reform in the party, state apparatus, and economic structure of the Soviet Union. Before any of the other bloc regimes acted, Ulbricht managed to formulate and announce a program of economic reform for the GDR, and implementation was already under way by the summer of 1963. Meantime, having recognized that a successful economic policy required new blood—or new brains—in the party leadership, he threw his support behind the aforementioned experts (Mittag, Jarowinsky, *et al.*), who were pressing for more authority, ensuring their election to the Politburo at the Sixth Party Congress of the SED in January 1963.

Just as Mittag and Jarowinsky represent the younger generation, Willi Stoph (born 1914) is the most important spokesman of the middle generation of pragmatic, flexible and organizationally gifted functionaries who have moved to the fore since 1963. In any speculation about the future leadership of the SED, Stoph must loom large; for while Honecker occupies the number-two spot in the party apparatus, Stoph has built up a comparable power base in the state apparatus.

To understand Stoph's current standing in the East German hierarchy, it may be useful to review the highlights of his long and varied career experience. Going back to the early postwar era, in 1945, Stoph—who had spent part of the war years undergoing intensive training in the Soviet Union—was assigned at the age of 31 to the newly-created central economic administration in the then Soviet zone of occupation in Germany, where his most notable achievement was the organization of the construction-materials industry. In 1948, he moved on to the Central Committee apparatus as head of its influential department for economic affairs. In 1951, he transferred into the new state administration of the GDR, devoting himself for the next four years to a series of high-level assignments directed toward the reconstruction of the East German economy. Meantime, in 1953, he was elected to the party Politburo. From 1955 to 1969, Stoph turned to quite different fields of endeavor, organizing first the People's Police and later the National People's Army. During this period, he served as Minister of Defense of the GDR and also as *ex officio* deputy to the Commanding General of the Warsaw Pact forces.

Stoph's combination of economic expertise and extraordinary organizational ability was, of course, precisely what was needed in the "new economic era" of the 1960's; so it is hardly surprising that he quickly came to occupy key positions of power in the regime. Since 1963, he has served as First Deputy Chairman (under Ulbricht) of the

[7] *Cf.* Carola Stern, *Ulbricht: A Political Biography,* New York, Praeger, 1966.

Council of State, the supreme policy-making organ or "inner cabinet" of the governmental apparatus; in addition, he has served since 1964 as Chairman of the Council of Ministers—that is, as chief coordinator of all the organs in the state administration. Under his leadership, the Council of Ministers has come to assume an even larger role in the direction of economic affairs, further enhancing Stoph's area of political leverage and influence.

While Stoph's fabled talents have been basically responsible for his ascent to power, his success must be explained in a larger context. In the first place, his pragmatic approach to problems represents a new style of leadership that has been essential as the SED moved away from its past dictatorial control over society to its present more flexible and more authoritative (as opposed to authoritarian) method of rule. In the second place, Stoph's rise is directly related to the evolution of East Germany from a semi-state demolished by war to the second strongest industrial power in the Soviet bloc; in consequence, the GDR has become indispensable to the Soviet Union for economic reasons as well as for political reasons. Stoph's role in East Germany's recovery and subsequent economic development has without question won him friends and supporters in his contacts with the Soviet elite, including party and government leaders, economic and technological experts, and military men.

Stoph's public posture shows that he is disinclined to engage in ideological rhetoric and suggests that he is disinterested in political intrigues and power rivalries within the Politburo. His political statements differ clearly from those made by dogmatists like Honecker and Norden, and insofar as style and manner of delivery are concerned, he is often more conciliatory than Ulbricht. This was quite apparent, for example, in his speech to the People's Chamber in March 1970,[8] reporting on the discussions held in Erfurt with West German Chancellor Willy Brandt. The tone of the report was measured and nonpolemical, although in substance it presented the collective view of the Politburo, which is firm in its stance on the conditions that must precede a genuine reconciliation with West Germany (these demands include West German support for international recognition of the GDR; agreement to a policy of noninterference in foreign policy; conclusion of a treaty renouncing the use of force; agreement to the application of the GDR for membership in the UN; renunciation of atomic weapons; and settlement of claimed West German debts to the GDR).

While it is rumored that Stoph has built up loyal and well-integrated staffs wherever he has been in charge, he is not the spokesman for an

[8] *Neues Deutschland,* March 22, 1970, p. 3.

entire group of functionaries in the sense that Honecker is. The very flexibility that has made the centrist line successful is a clue to the loosely-knit character of the coalition that supports it. Thus it would be misleading to single out Stoph as the one and only representative (next to Ulbricht) of the middle position between the two wings of the Politburo. Certainly another party leader who ought to be mentioned here is Horst Sindermann (born 1915). Before 1963, Sindermann had made something of a name for himself as an agitprop specialist—specifically, as chief of the department of press and radio at the national level of the party apparatus. Like many other party leaders who are currently counted as influential, Sindermann got his real boost at the Sixth Party Conference of the SED in 1963. At the same time that he was elected to candidate membership in the Politburo, he was also appointed to the position of First Secretary of the regional party organization for Halle. This region has reportedly posed particular problems of administration, since it has a mixed economy embracing both large industry and agriculture. To all appearances, Sindermann has performed well in the job. In addition, his knowledge of the central party apparatus, his organizational talent and his experience in propaganda activities mark him as one of the most promising of all the 15 regional party first secretaries in terms of political potential. In sharp contrast to most of this group, Sindermann's political statements place him unambiguously and squarely among the flexible "centrists" in the party leadership. The three other regional secretaries who belong to the Politburo—Paul Verner (for East Berlin), Erich Mückenberger (for Frankfurt an der Oder) and Paul Fröhlich (for Leipzig)—must be counted as belonging to the wing led by Honecker. Most of the 11 remaining Bezirk secretaries, who sit on the Central Committee but not the Politburo, have also given evidence of being oriented toward the dogmatic wing of the party.

A final figure who ought to be mentioned among the important political functionaries of the "center" is Kurt Hager (born 1912). Since 1954 Hager has served without interruption as the Central Committee Secretary in charge of ideological matters. Since 1963, he has also been chairman of the ideological commission of the Politburo (and a full member of that body). While Hager is an ideologue by nature and by profession, the support he has given to various reform policies places him in the middle group of party leaders around Ulbricht. In particular, he has been open to the modernization of education—and, in fact, has proven very adept at tying the political need for a continued level of ideological indoctrination to the practical need for a better and more efficient educational system in the GDR. According to informed sources, he is personally responsible for the reform of the Higher Party School "Karl Marx" and the Institute for Social Science attached to the

SED Central Committee[9]—institutions that have gained greatly in stature during the past few years and can no longer be viewed as mere educational factories turning out propagandists versed in Marxism-Leninism. Thus, whatever the polemical overtones of Hager's public statements, he must be recognized as a modernizer in the field of ideology and, as such, an influential member of the Ulbricht team.

In concluding the discussion of this group, certain similarities should be noted between its approach and objectives and those of the group around Mittag. A rationalistic, pragmatic style of problem-solving is a common characteristic of both Stoph and Mittag. Efficiency in operating the economy is a major goal of Stoph, as it is of the young pragmatists in the Politburo. And, it seems safe to say, the expansion of East Germany's economic and trade relations with the West, and with West Germany in particular, seems desirable to leaders of both groups. Such trade, by making available to East Germany sophisticated machinery and advanced know-how, will quicken the speed of her modernization, expand her economic capabilities, and thus give her more political leverage in Eastern Europe.

The Balance of Power

Like all political systems, that of Communist East Germany has developed a mechanism to adjust the conflicting requirements generated by the processes of system maintenance and system modernization. The key role in achieving the necessary balance is played by the system's political leadership, which serves as a steering mechanism equilibrating the system in response to various pressures from within and without.

In the case of East Germany, that role has been fulfilled by the Politburo of the SED with some adroitness, but with less than complete success. Shifting several times from a policy accentuating system maintenance to one emphasizing system modernization and then back again in response to various contradictory pressures such as the internal need for greater economic productivity and administrative decentralization (1961–62), the Soviet example of recentralization (1965) and Soviet and East European requirements for greater output and efficiency (1968), the East German leadership has managed to generate dynamic growth in a liberalized economy, while maintaining a somewhat precarious stability in the political system.

[9] See, for example, Ernst Richert, *Die DDR Elite,* Rowohlt Verlag, Reinbek bei Hamburg, 1968, p. 71.

Perhaps the most important clue to understanding the leadership's performance is to be found in the composition of the group. All members of the ruling elite are thoroughly committed Communists; hence they possess considerable coherence and unity. At the same time, the leadership is sufficiently differentiated so that various groupings (they do not really qualify as full-fledged factions) can be discerned; and this difference is based precisely on the priority which they variously accord to the need for modernization and stabilization. The younger group of technological experts put the main emphasis on innovation and change, particularly in the field of economics, while the dogmatists care most about safeguarding the dominant position of the SED. In between stands the pivotal group of pragmatists whose continuous aim it is to establish a middle position that is acceptable to the entire SED Politburo, both on domestic issues and on the question of relations with the Federal Republic of Germany.

If this balance-of-power arrangement at the top has determined East German policy in the past and does so in the present, can it be expected to survive the eventual demise of its single strongest figure, Walter Ulbricht, who is 77 years of age? Clearly, no one leader in the Politburo combines in his person Ulbricht's power, his prestige at home and abroad, and his long experience. Nor is any one group sufficiently strong enough to assume total power. It seems most likely that representatives of all three groups will share the succession, at least initially. Probably they will be Honecker for the dogmatic wing, Stoph as the advocate of the middle, and Mittag as the representative of the pragmatists. Alternatively, various two-man teams can be projected; the most plausible is the combination of Stoph and Honecker.

While the exact composition of the leadership must remain a matter of speculation, one thing seems quite certain: on balance, both external and internal pressures presently favor the forward march of the East German economy; in this situation, the experts and the pragmatists tend to have the upper hand, and their influence is bound to remain strong for the foreseeable future.

WALTER ULBRICHT resigned suddenly, and apparently not voluntarily, as First Secretary of the SED Central Committee and as Chairman of the National Defense Council in May 1971; he was succeeded by Erich Honecker. Therefore, Mr. Ludz's tentative assessment of the post-Ulbricht leadership is in order. The following pages are from part of a longer article, "Continuity and Change Since Ulbricht," *Problems of Communism,* XXI, 2 (March–April 1972), and are reprinted by permission.

[Editors' Note]

Developments on the Home Front

When we turn to consideration of the East German domestic scene, perhaps the single most striking fact to be mentioned is the smoothness with which the switch in the top leadership was accomplished and the lack of repercussions—at least in public—in the months that have since passed. Thus, only a few weeks after Ulbricht's resignation as party secretary, the Eighth Party Congress conducted its business with very few signs of confusion or reaction over the changes taking place. (Even the firmest of Ulbricht's former supporters did not seem to raise an eyebrow over the fact that Honecker barely mentioned the former leader in his address to the Congress—which Ulbricht, incidentally, did not attend.)

Ironic as it may sound, this surface serenity may well be explained by the essential instability of the East German political system—or, more accurately, by the recognition of that instability on the part of the party leadership that dominates the system. That there have long been tensions and rivalries within the SED is well known; in fact, in an article in this journal less than two years ago, the present author analyzed in some detail the tendency of the SED leadership to divide into three basic groupings of reform "technocrats," hard-line "dogmatists," and pragmatic political "centrists."[1] These rivalries certainly did not suddenly dissipate with Ulbricht's fall; but there may well have been tacit (or explicit) agreement among all elements of the SED leadership that they must pull together for the time being or else take the risk of triggering reactions that could imperil the party itself.

The SED's long preoccupation with the problem of its own political legitimacy and security is underscored by the background of its new top leader. Erich Honecker can best be described as a professional "political specialist." He established an early reputation for organizational ability in the years 1946 to 1955, when he was responsible for directing and building up the Free German Youth (FDJ), East Germany's Communist youth corps. Subsequently, in the central SED apparatus, he became the expert on all questions having to do with party organization, control and security. As CC Secretary for Security Affairs, he was the one man most responsible for the insulation of the SED from internal and external "contaminating" influences.[2] As Ulbricht's suc-

[1] Peter C. Ludz, "The SED Leadership in Transition," *Problems of Communism*, May–June 1970, pp. 23–31.

[2] For details of Honecker's background, see Peter C. Ludz, "The German Democratic Republic from the Sixties to the Seventies," Harvard "Occasional Papers" Series, Cambridge, Mass., Harvard University Press, 1970, pp. 48ff.

cessor, he now has the responsibility for the similar ideological and political insulation of the whole GDR.

In the past, Honecker's political concerns have inclined him toward alliance with the hard-line elements in the party, though he is also a pragmatic politician. For many years his position as Ulbricht's heir-designate was unquestioned; yet with the progress of economic reform, there was increasing speculation that he might have to share power in a collective leadership with the centrists (notably Politburo member Willi Stoph, who is also the GDR's Prime Minister) and the technocrats (possibly Guenter Mittag) in any successor regime. The fact that he has instead emerged as top man—with decisive control over the machinery of governance, at least for the time being—seems to indicate that the prevailing pressures within the party, and no doubt from Moscow as well, favored priority emphasis on the internal security and order of the East German state.

The internal trends of regime policy over the past several months tend to support this interpretation. On the one hand, there has been an effort to reinforce the ideological claims and to strengthen the political controls of the SED over East German society. The intensification of the policy of "demarcation" with respect to the FRG has already been mentioned—a policy which Honecker must hope will fortify his own position as well as that of the GDR by systematically instilling fear of the West German "enemy." Another development in the ideological area was the adoption of a directive giving increased weight to the political attitude, as opposed to the performance record, of applicants for admission to GDR universities, colleges and technical schools.[3] In the area of economic performance, the new regime has been able to step up control through the "growing responsibility" of the Workers-and-Farmers Inspectorate (ABI), which organizationally is under the direction of both the SED Central Committee and the Council of Ministers, and which has been assigned key responsibility for checking on the implementation of party resolutions affecting the East German economy and society.[4]

At the same time, the regime has tried to increase domestic political stability by taking steps to improve the morale of the East German people. The most important feature of the Honecker course in this respect is a planned rise in the living standard of the population. At the Eighth

[3] "Directive on Application Procedure, Selection, and Admission to On-Campus Study at Universities and Colleges—Admission Regulations," dated July 1, 1971, published in *Gesetzblatt der DDR* (East Berlin), Part II, 1971, p. 486.

[4] On the role of ABI, see Heinz Matthes, "Reliable Popular Control—Principle of Socialist State and Economic Management," *Einheit,* No. 6, 1971, pp. 715f.

Congress the SED adopted special resolutions to this effect, patterning them after similar resolutions that had been adopted at the 24th Congress of the CPSU. Willi Stoph reiterated the regime's intentions in his speech on the new Five-Year Plan, emphasizing that its "primary task" was to raise the "material and cultural living standard" of the East German population. The Plan itself set forth the prospect of a considerably greater volume of consumer goods and services over the next five years. Housing construction is also supposed to be increased and improved: for example, the plan calls for the erection of 500,000 new apartment units by 1975—representing an annual rate of increase that is considerably higher than that planned for either industrial output or investments.[5]

Probably this stress on meeting the people's needs was triggered in large part by the widening gap between the living standards of the GDR and those of the FRG.[6] While the economy of the GDR has made significant strides forward under the reform program, East Germans have still had to endure the role of poor relations vis-à-vis the West Germans, who have literally galloped along the road to prosperity. While the SED leadership could not fool itself about closing the gap in living standards in the immediate future, it apparently felt it had to offer the people some reassurance that conditions would improve and that they would soon have more of the amenities of life.

Interestingly, the East German leadership expects to achieve these improvements by restructuring priorities and inputs even while reducing the rates of expansion in overall industrial output and investments. Thus, industrial production, which increased at an average annual rate of 6.5 percent in the last five-year plan period, is to be increased only 3.9 to 6.4 percent over the next five years; similarly, investments, which increased annually by 9.7 percent in 1966–70, are planned at a lesser growth rate of 5.1 to 5.4 percent for 1971–75.[7]

Internal Politics

There remains the pivotal—and politically the most interesting—question of whether Erich Honecker has enough influence and/or clout to retain his present dominating role in the leadership.

[5] SED directive on the Five-Year Plan, loc. cit.

[6] For comparative statistics on living standards, see *Deutschland 1971: Bericht und Materialen zur lage der Nation* (Germany 1971: Report and Materials on the Situation of the Nation), Cologne-Opladen, Westdeutscher Verlag, 1971, especially Chap. V.

[7] SED directive on the Five-Year Plan, loc. cit.

Certainly there can be no doubt that Honecker has a significant power base which he built up during his years of control over the party security apparatus. An initial sign of the extent (as well as the limits) of his influence was provided by the personnel changes which were announced at the Eighth Congress.[8] His hand was evident in certain appointments to the Politburo, more pronouncedly in shifts on the Central Committee, and finally in the appointments of some first secretaries to the SED Bezirk Committees (the party overseers in the 17 basic administrative divisions of the GDR). Honecker showed a definite preference in these appointments for younger party functionaries (generally in their forties) whose careers have reflected a combination of political pragmatism, ideological activism and organizational capabilities, as opposed to the equally pragmatic but non-ideologically oriented technocrats whom Ulbricht tended to lean on in the last years of his leadership.[9] In a number of cases Honecker promoted personal associates from his years with the FDJ and the SED Secretariat.

Insofar as the Politburo is concerned, relatively few changes were made in the overall membership, giving the impression of continuity with the past. The composition was slightly altered to comprise 16 members and seven candidates, a rise of one in each category. To the surprise of some observers, none of the Old Guard party faithful (including, *e.g.,* Friedrich Ebert and Herbert Warnke[10]) were retired. In this respect, the East Germans again imitated the Soviets, who similarly kept their older functionaries on the new CPSU Politburo elected at the 24th Party Congress. From the point of view of Honecker's interests, two men promoted from candidates to full members of the Politburo—Werner Lamberz and Werner Krolikowski—could be considered his supporters and were probably selected at his bidding. Lamberz, born in 1929, epitomizes the relatively new and relatively young type of party ideologist who has eschewed the hard-line dogmatism of the past in favor of more flexible "scientific" and "strategic" approaches to Marxism-Leninism. Significantly enough, his interest has concentrated on the ideological aspects of the so-called "Western matter"—in other words, on the ideological-propagandistic conflict with the Federal Republic. His intellectual dexterity, as demonstrated in his published analyses,[11] would seem to make him an ideal collaborator for Honecker

[8] Party personnel actions taken at the Eighth SED Congress were published in *Neues Deutschland,* June 20, 1971.

[9] See Ludz, "The SED Leadership in Transition," loc. cit.

[10] Ebert also remains on the Presidium of the People's Chamber; Warnke continues as chairman of the National Board of the 7,000,000-member Free German Trade Union Association (FDGB), East Germany's largest mass organization, which he has headed since 1948.

[11] See, *e.g.,* his articles, "New Demands on the Ideological Work of the

in the latter's doubletrack course vis-à-vis the FRG. It also seems possible that Lamberz might develop into a serious rival for the now 66-year-old Albert Norden, a hard-line Politburo member who has long had dominant control over SED agitation and propaganda. The second newcomer to the Politburo, Werner Krolikowski, is another member of the 40-plus age group (he was born in 1928) who has risen in the party apparatus; he has been First Secretary of the Dresden SED Bezirk Committee since 1961, and he is considered a Honecker confidant. Two new candidate members of the Politburo are also regarded as Honecker appointments. Erich Mielke (born in 1907), has been Minister of State Security since 1957, and his elevation within the party no doubt reflects the regime's current emphasis on internal security. Harry Tisch (born in 1927), has been First Secretary of the Rostock SED Bezirk Committee since 1961; his allegiance to Honecker became evident at the Eighth Congress when he delivered a speech that indirectly but unmistakably criticized Ulbricht.

The trend toward promotion of "Honecker-type" functionaries was revealed in sharper focus in the composition of the new SED Central Committee approved by the Eighth Congress (whose 189 members and candidates again represent a slight enlargement over the previous CC[12]). Of the 11 former candidates raised to full membership on the CC, as well as eight new men appointed directly to membership, almost all came from the central SED apparatus or the Bezirk party administrations—and almost none from party members manning the economic agencies or directly participating in the economy. A similar tendency could be observed in the case of the 28 new candidates to the CC, although the stress was not so pronounced. Conversely, among the 15 members who lost their seats on the Central Committee, there was a striking preponderance of party members directly involved in economic and agricultural management. While it is beyond the scope of the present paper to provide a complete breakdown of age levels and backgrounds here, it is certainly valid to claim that the 40-year-plus group of professional party workers has been given special weight in the new Central Committee.

Party," in *Der Parteiarbeiter,* East Berlin, Dietz Verlag, 1969; "The Leninist Principles of the Scientific Management of Socialist Construction and Their Application in the GDR," in *Der Leninismus und der Revolutionare Prozess: Internationale theoretische Konferenz . . . vom 19. bis 21. November 1969 in Prag* (Leninism and the Revolutionary Process: International Theoretical Conference . . . November 19–21, 1969, in Prague), East Berlin, Dietz Verlag, 1970, pp. 67ff.; and "A Quarter-Century of Victorious History," in *Neuer Weg* (East Berlin), No. 3, 1971, p. 99ff.

12 The CC was increased from 131 to 135 members and from 50 to 54 candidates; see *Neues Deutschland,* June 20, 1971.

Finally, Honecker had an obvious voice in the appointment of at least three new first secretaries of the Bezirk party committees, all in important areas of East Germany (most other appointees were incumbents). In all three cases, the appointees had been top-level officials of the FDJ and had worked with Honecker during the decade that he built up the youth organization, in the process providing the "cadre reserve" of the SED. In East Berlin the chosen man was Konrad Naumann; in Frankfurt/Oder, Hans Joachim Hertwig; and in Halle, Werner Felfe (all born in 1928). It might be noted that a colleague of these men, Horst Schumann—Honecker's successor as chief of the FDJ for many years—had already been appointed first secretary of the Leipzig Bezirk Committee in 1970, upon the death of the incumbent, Paul Froehlich.

Honecker's ability to place a number of his supporters in key positions was certainly an indication of his considerable strength within the party. To all appearances, his influence among party functionaries is not due simply to the power of his position but reflects their genuine respect for the special talents he has demonstrated in dealing with intra-party organizational and cadre problems. According to report, he has built up good relations with leading officials at all levels of the SED apparatus, and he has made a point of being personally accessible to minor and local party officials.[13] Besides his following in the SED and the FDJ, he is said to have good contacts in the Nationale Volksarmee (National People's Army). In terms of personal leadership style, he is reported to lean toward directness and informality and to have a hearty dislike for bureaucratic pretense and red tape. So far he has shown none of Ulbricht's disposition to be authoritarian and dictatorial; in fact, he has gone out of his way to pay lip service to the principle of "collective leadership," even though he obviously has the final power of decision in all matters so long as he remains both First Secretary and Chairman of the National Defense Council (the second most important position in the GDR power structure).

Despite these many factors in Honecker's favor, the fact remains that he by no means possesses the degree of authority and prestige, either within the SED or in East German society at large, which Ulbricht enjoyed for many years. While his role in the party has given him an inside track in establishing a personal following, the narrowness of his specialization in matters of party organization, control and security could work to his disadvantage over time. The debit side of the coin is that he has played no part whatever—so far as is known—in overall economic and social planning or more particularly in the crucial re-

[13] See Harald Ludwig, "The SED before the Eighth Party Congress," *Deutschland Archiv*, No. 6, 1971, p. 596.

organization and modernization of the East German economic and educational systems since 1963. Nor has he distinguished himself in any significant way in the field of ideology. Thus he is in the position of having to rely for help in a number of areas on men who have been real, or who are now potential, rivals.

It thus seems entirely possible that a succession crisis might still develop in the GDR. As mentioned earlier, the very smoothness with which Ulbricht was eased out of the top spot suggests the probability that in the minds of at least some of the leaders, Honecker's assumption of power was an interim necessity subject to possible challenge when time and circumstances should permit. For years Honecker's chief rival in and out of the Politburo has been Prime Minister Willi Stoph, whose professional specialty is economic organization—a field in which Honecker cannot personally compete. A second, younger rival is the aforementioned Guenter Mittag, who in Ulbricht's last years was the leading light of the faction of technocrats who guided the course of economic reform. If a power struggle should develop within the Politburo at some future date, it could conceivably see an alignment of Stoph and Mittag—and possibly also Alfred Neumann as a source of conservative support—against Honecker.

The harder question is to determine who would stand by Honecker in the face of such a challenge. Besides Lamberz and Krolikowski, one probable supporter is Horst Sindermann, a tough-minded but capable ex-chief of the Halle Bezirk party organization, who has been on the Politburo since 1963 and who, in the wake of Ulbricht's ouster, was elevated—seemingly at Honecker's behest—to the post of Deputy Chairman of the Council of Ministers, making him a potential successor to Stoph. A clear sign that Sindermann has joined the "inner circle" of the Politburo leadership was the fact that he—together with Honecker, Stoph and Hager (but not Mittag)—made up the top SED delegation that visited Moscow in mid-May 1971, obviously to coordinate future Soviet-East German strategy. Sindermann was noted for his total loyalty to Ulbricht; whether he will show the same fealty to Honecker remains to be seen.

Another Politburo member owing his promotion to the new party chief is Paul Verner, appointed Honecker's successor as CC secretary in charge of security, organizational and cadre questions. Verner, whose experience with matters of internal security and order derives from many years as chief of the Berlin SED Committee, could probably be counted in Honecker's corner in the case of a struggle, but there is no way to be sure.

Summary

Latest developments at the time of writing seem to indicate that Honecker is in no immediate danger of such a political challenge and in fact has managed to strengthen his hand in the state apparatus as well as in the party.[14] Still, he is a political man attuned to all political possibilities, so no doubt his main order of business for the present and the foreseeable future will be to rally further support for himself within the SED and in the GDR at large, as well as among the Communist leaders in other Soviet bloc countries.

The importance of the latter fund of support probably means that he will hew rather closely to the lines of policy established when he took over from Ulbricht and will refrain—at least for the time being—from stepping forward with any dramatic innovations of his own, especially in the field of foreign policy. To repeat, then, the GDR can be expected to continue along a course of closer ties to the Comecon countries and firm support for Moscow's line on such international issues as the Sino-Soviet confrontation and the conflicts in the Middle East, Southeast Asia and other areas of the globe. In its policy toward the Federal Republic, the Honecker regime will continue to put great stress on the ideological differentiation of East and West Germany, even while moving in certain limited areas along the paths of possible cooperation with the FRG.

Concomitantly, the new regime will continue to pursue all possible tactics to upgrade the international status of the GDR. In this area it has rather good prospects for some success in the near future. There has been widespread sentiment favoring the admission of the GDR to membership in a number of organizations affiliated with the United Nations, including the Economic Commission for Europe (ECE), the UN Economic and Social Commission (UNESCO), and the World Health Organization (WHO). Moreover, a number of states, including Sweden, India and Japan, have indicated an interest in expanding their

[14] At the end of November 1971, Honecker, Paul Verner, and several presumable allies were appointed to the Council of State (Staatsrat), which is the third most important ruling body in the GDR (after the SED Politburo and the National Defense Council, both headed by Honecker). While Ulbricht remained chairman of the Council, his intimate associate Otto Gotsche—long head of the Staatsrat Secretariat—was removed. Guenter Mittag also lost his seat on the Council, though he remains on the Politburo. For the composition of the new Council see *Neues Deutschland,* Nov. 27, 1971.

official relations with the GDR. Finally, if a European Security Conference should ever be convened, as a number of states in both East and West would like, it is widely expected that the two German states would participate on a basis of equality.

At home, Honecker has a long way to go to match the image which Ulbricht managed to project of himself as the "father of his country." For the long run, it remains an open question whether Honecker will be able to assert and stabilize his authority in the face of potentially formidable—if presently latent—competition. All that can be said at the moment is that he has established a very good lead.

III

The Political Process in Communist Systems

THE increasing availability and reliability of information about Communist societies in recent years have prompted a large number of social scientists to inquire into the process of policy-making in these systems, particularly the role played by various loosely organized and institutional groupings. The existence and identification of such group influence in the policy-making process, as well as the appearance of more vaguely articulated demands by the general citizenry, are recent phenomena in the study of Communist systems. Many Western observers view this change in the political process as the inevitable consequence of socioeconomic developments that were initially launched by the Communists themselves. As a society modernizes and becomes more functionally differentiated and specialized, there is growing pressure for greater pluralism in political life, which is extremely difficult, if not impossible, to contain. The emergence of interest groups, although less numerous and effective than in non-Communist systems, has both affected and been affected by the changing role of the party in recent years. Group demands have been influential in the decision by various Communist parties to relinquish portions of their earlier control, while the reduction of party power has also fostered the growth and activity of groups in the political arena. How the individual Communist parties will react or adapt to the likely increase and political implications of such group pressure is a central question affecting the political development of these systems.

As Communist societies become more technologically developed, political leaders realize that they must begin to rely on technical expertise to supply and interpret the data necessary for effective decision-making. Indeed, in several of the more economically advanced states, the party has found it necessary to rely on technically trained non-party or nominal-party personnel for assistance in formulating policy, whereas in earlier years, only loyal party members were called upon to perform such tasks. This situation has led some observers to speculate on the possible superfluity of the party in a fully modernized society. In fact, some parties have already found it difficult to recruit highly trained specialists, particularly those experts in the physical sciences whose talents are crucial to political leadership.

Every society seeks to inculcate its values into the next generation, and Communist states have been particularly assiduous in this task. Soviet ideologists and educators, for instance, have sought for half a century to create the "new Soviet man," whose values and beliefs would differ markedly from those of prerevolutionary Russia, or from Western capitalist societies. The Soviet citizen of the 1970s has been socialized into preferring a socialist rather than capitalist economic system, but has yet to develop the other-oriented personality of the Marxist-Leninist ideal. How effective political socialization in Communist states has been depends in part on the persuasiveness of the regime, the citizens' apathy, hostility, or loyalty toward the political system, and the relative influence of various agencies of socialization (family, educational system, church, peer group).

Despite the persistent difficulty in collecting data, it is now possible to begin to study political socialization and political participation in an analytical rather than a merely descriptive fashion, as the articles in this section demonstrate. Hollander analyzes data collected and published by Soviet sociologists on the film-viewing preferences of Soviet citizens; she questions the effectiveness of one aspect of the socialization process. Vogel analyzes the impact on personal friendships of rectification campaigns sponsored by the Chinese Communist Party, with their demands for criticism of all "deviant behavior" of friends and colleagues. Each of the articles concerned with the role of interest groups either assumes or establishes that groups do exist and that they are able to influence the policy-making process. Oksenberg states the case most unequivocally for China, although he emphasizes that groups necessarily must utilize different techniques than those used in more democratic systems. Although the essays by Israel and Golan are largely descriptive, each raises important questions about the extent to which the regime can control or direct youth movements, whose members presumably have been socialized into support, if not belief, of the state's ideals and goals. At what point does the regime lose control and indeed become compelled to heed popular demands? Oliver examines the nature and fate of consumer demands, which are not championed by any organized group and remain, in Communist states as elsewhere, most easily ignored by the political leadership.

Political Socialization

From
SOVIET POLITICAL INDOCTRINATION: FILM

Gayle D. Hollander

SOVIET leaders, repeating Lenin, have frequently referred to film as "the most powerful means of educating the masses."[1] In the early days of Soviet power the cinema was, along with the newspaper and personal oral agitation, one of the three major instruments of political education. It did not require a literate audience, and it had the added advantage of visual presentation. Perhaps most important, the moving picture was a relatively new phenomenon, and as such, it acted as messenger of the modern world; this was a distinct asset to a regime which sought to present itself as an agent of progress. Like the newspaper, the Soviet film has had to yield its prominent place, sharing the political-socialization function with newer, faster media. It has become more and more specialized as a means of entertainment, although, along with other artistic forms in the Soviet Union, it is subordinated to politics. Its protagonists, like those in literature, are meant to serve as models and antimodels for Soviet citizens. Ironically, this formula-oriented regi-

[1] *Lenin, Stalin, i Partiya o Kino* (Lenin, Stalin, and the Party on the Cinema) (Moscow: State Publishing House for Art, 1938), pp. 7–8.

mentation has undermined its effectiveness both as an art form and as an agent of political socialization.

Since the decision to expose oneself to cinema involves more than the mere flicking of a switch or turning of a page, the film must have greater initial appeal than the television program or newspaper article. It is the focus of an evening's activity, requiring a change in the daily routine. Once the audience has gathered, however, the film has a monopoly on its attention, safe from the interruption of visitors and telephone calls. The message is therefore sure to be heard.

Expansion of Production Facilities

The last years of Stalin's regime were characterized by stagnation and low productivity in most of the arts. In 1952 only a few feature films were produced. These years of regimentation were frustrating, and there were increasing demands for new scenarios and motion pictures. After Stalin's death, discussion of the problems of the film industry was much more open and many changes were proposed. The new Ministry of Culture almost immediately released a production plan for twenty-five feature films and called a conference of young writers to discuss the problems of the motion picture industry. Part of the problem was that during Stalin's rule only trusted writers had been commissioned to write scripts, and a campaign was launched to draw new talented writers into scenario writing. There was a concerted drive to produce more feature films: by 1954, there were thirty-eight full-length films; by 1957, the number had jumped to ninety, and the number has continued to grow. By 1963 the number was one hundred thirty-three and in 1967, one hundred seventy-five.[2] There are presently more than forty film studios in the Soviet Union. In March, 1963, the State Cinematography Committee of the National Council of Ministers was formed so that the Soviet film network was given administrative status similar to that of the press and the broadcast media.

The increase in output was paralleled by a growing concern over the content of these new films which were to reach the public in much greater numbers. This period saw a revitalization of the "new Soviet man" concept. Interpretations of Socialist Realism, the formula for Soviet artistic production, began to broaden. In 1957 it was decided to

[2] Tsentralnoye Statisticheskoye Upravleniye pri Sovyetye Ministrov SSSR, *Strana Sovyetov za 50 Lyet* (Moscow: "Statistika" Publishing House, 1967), p. 288.

open a comedy workshop at Mosfilm Studio in order to bring together and stimulate people to work on this long-neglected and politically troublesome genre.

The political problems which have beset other art forms in this period have been troublesome in the production of feature films as well. Artists now knew that they could begin to produce less orthodox works, but they did not know how far they could go in certain directions. Many were to get into ideological trouble because of this uncertainty; but ultimately the zig-zag course of liberalization had a positive effect in stimulating the production of less orthodox and more interesting fare. There was increasing emphasis on contemporary significance and variety in films. Whereas the typical Soviet film hero of Stalin's day was more or less the prototypical "positive hero," in films of the late 1950's and early 1960's he began to be a complex human being, influenced by circumstances and doubts beyond mere ideological considerations. He was thus more credible and appealing to the film's viewers.

Changes in the Accessibility of Films

Along with the drive to increase production and improve content there was developed a drive to extend the film-projection network. The number of projectors grew from 52,300 in 1953 (40,500 of them in rural areas) to 153,000 in 1967 (130,000 of them in rural areas). Since the average film house in the Soviet Union seats about one hundred forty[3] this means that there are about 21.4 million cinema seats, the majority of which are in rural areas. The number of moviegoers increased over two and a half times during this period, and total attendance reached 4.5 billion in 1967. This is an average of two hundred ten visits per seat.

Individual Soviets have been increasing their rates of attendance as films grow more accessible and more attractive. The following table shows the pattern of rising attention to movies:[4]

[3] Yu. Kalistratov, "Nekotoriye Problemy Kinofikatsii Po Itogam Perepisi Kino Ustanovok" (Some Problems of Cinema Development According to Results of the Film Projector Census), *Vestnik Statistiki,* 4 (1967), p. 25.

[4] From *Narodnoye Khoziaistvo v SSSR v 1965 Godu,* p. 731 for 1950, 1958, and 1965, and M. Poluboyarinov, "Razvitiye Kinofikatsii v SSSR—Kratkiy Obzor" (The Development of Cinemafication in the USSR—A Short Survey), *Vestnik Statistiki,* 4 (1967), p. 24.

Average annual visits to movies per inhabitant:	1950	1958	1960	1965	1968
Total	6	16	17	19	20
Urban	11	22	21	20	21
Rural	3	12	12	16	18

The greatest increase occurred during the early post-Stalin years, when the drive to produce more and better films was at its height. Since then, attendance has risen more gradually, with little change in the last few years. At present the Soviet Union has one of the world's highest rates of movie attendance.[5]

The gradual decrease in urban attendance may reflect the introduction of television, because as the novelty began to wane (during the mid-1960's) movie attendance in cities seemed slowly to rise again. Rural moviegoing grew markedly from 1950 to 1967. Although rural people have a better chance to see a movie once it is being shown (because of the higher ratio of seats per population), they tend to see fewer films. Not only are fewer films shown, partly because rural movie projectors are nonstationary and there are great transportation problems, but rural people have a harder time getting to the place where films are shown. During bad weather the mobile projection unit may not reach an isolated village for months, and inhabitants have no way of coming to the club except by tractor.

The average number of visits to movies per person varies from republic to republic. The Russian Republic has the highest rate of film attendance, with twenty-one visits annually per person, and the Georgian and Armenian Republics vie for lowest place with eleven visits per person. If we separate urban average annual attendance from rural, a slightly different picture emerges. Lithuania and Latvia, each with an average annual per-person attendance rate of twenty-three, are highest; the Armenian Republic is lowest, with a rate of thirteen visits per year. In rural attendance the Russian Republic is highest with twenty annual

[5] *The United Nations Statistical Yearbook 1966* (Paris, 1968), Table 7.2, gives the following figures for average annual film attendance per inhabitant in 1965 for various countries: Ghana, two visits to movies per year per inhabitant; Liberia, 1.4 visits; United Arab Republic, two visits; United States, twelve visits; Burma, nine visits; Israel, twenty visits; Japan, four visits; Albania, four visits; Bulgaria, fifteen visits; Czechoslovakia, nine visits; Federal Republic of Germany, five visits; German Democratic Republic, seven visits; Hungary, ten visits; France, five visits; Portugal, three visits; Yugoslavia, six visits; Soviet Union, nineteen visits; Rumania, ten visits; Switzerland, eight visits; United Kingdom, six visits; and New Zealand, ten visits.

visits per inhabitant, and Georgia is lowest, with only five.[6] Again, the Baltic republics have a longer history of mass media usage than most of the Soviet republics. Why the Caucasus should be lower than the Central Asian republics, for example, is not clear.

Kotov reports that of one hundred members of the Brigade of Communist Labor he studied, 60 per cent regularly saw films, and that the time each person spent on this averaged out to half an hour per day.[7] Baikova reports that about 84 per cent of the people interviewed in her study saw films "regularly," with almost no differences between men and women.[8] Grushin reports that about 73 per cent of his sample saw films regularly "at least several times a month," again with no great variation between the sexes.[9] Beliaev also reports fairly close time expenditures on filmgoing for men and women; men spent an average of 18.9 minutes per day and women 16.7 minutes.[10] This means that women went to the movies about once a week on the average, and men slightly more frequently. Perhaps sex differences in time spent on movies are smaller than for other mass media because film attendance involves going out of the house, and is regarded as a social event; couples attend films together whereas joint participation is not so common for reading, listening to radio, or watching television.

On overall frequency of film attendance, Grushin reports that a very small percentage of his sample said they went daily, almost half said they went to the movies several times a week, and almost 30 per cent said they went several times a month;[11] this indicates that the sample is atypical, since it shows a much higher rate of annual film attendance than reported in the official figures above.[12]

Age seems to have a predictable influence: young adults are the

[6] *Narodnoye . . .* , loc. cit.

[7] L. Kotov, "Byudzhet Vremini," *Molodoi Kommunist,* 7 (1960), p. 34.

[8] 83.7 per cent of men and 83.9 per cent of women. V. G. Baikova *et al., Svobodnoye Vremya i Vsestoronnoye Razvitiye Lichnosti* (Moscow: Mysl' Publishing House, 1965), p. 136.

[9] 74.4 per cent of men and 72.3 per cent of women. B. Grushin, *Svobodnoye Vremya—Actualniye Problemy* (Moscow: Mysl' Publishing House, 1967), Table 11, p. 81.

[10] E. V. Beliaev *et al.,* "Workers' Time-Budget Research: A Method of Concrete Sociological Investigation," *Vestnik Leningradskovo Universiteta,* Seriia Economiki, Filosofii i Prava No. 4, 1961; translated in *Soviet Sociology,* I, 1 (Summer, 1962). Table 5, p. 50.

[11] Daily, 0.2 per cent; several times a week, 44.6 per cent; several times a month, 28.5 per cent. Grushin, op. cit., Table 9, p. 76.

[12] Since official figures always try to show a maximum of exposure, we conclude that it is the nature of the Grushin sample which is responsible for the excessively high rate of attendance.

most avid filmgoers, Grushin[13] reports a peak in the late twenties, with a sharp decline in the thirties, and after sixty, a slight increase. Beliaev reports a fairly consistent rate of attendance (averaging about twenty minutes per day) until over forty, when time spent on movies drops to an average of thirteen minutes per day.[14] This pattern is different from most other countries, where peak attendance comes earlier, before the arrival of children.[15]

The evidence on the effects of occupation offers us no clear pattern. Grushin reports that in his sample slightly more intellectuals reported going to movies regularly than did workers.[16] It would seem then that people in occupations requiring more training and education had a higher rate of film attendance. Beliaev, on the other hand, says that in his sample, workers spent more time on the average going to movies than did engineering and technical personnel.[17] Grushin reports that people with a secondary education are more likely to go to films than either those with an elementary education or those with a higher education.[18] The data suggest that perhaps there is a "critical optimum" of training and skill, at which level film attendance is highest, but we cannot draw any clear hypothesis from the evidence available.

Party members were reported by Beliaev to spend less time on movies than either Komsomols or non-Party people. They averaged a little

[13]

16–24 years	84.1 per cent	30–39 years	61.9 per cent
25–29 years	92.5 per cent	40–59 years	52.7 per cent
60 and over	56.3 per cent		

Grushin, op. cit., Table 11, p. 81.

[14] 18–30 years, 20.2 min/day; 31–40 years, 20.4 min/day; 41 years plus, 13 min/day. Beliaev, op. cit., Table 7, p. 5.

[15] The Soviet deviation from the general pattern may be explained in one of two ways. The average childbearing age may be somewhat later in the Soviet Union than in other countries because of housing shortages delaying marriages, etc. I could not find comparative statistics on average childbearing ages, so I am unable to substantiate this impression. More probably, the housing shortage has another effect which can also account for the phenomenon of late peak movie attendance. This is the fact that several generations are forced to live together; this means that grandparents are readily available for babysitting, allowing young parents more freedom to go out to movies than they would have otherwise.

[16] 80.2 per cent of technical intelligentsia; 81.3 per cent of other intellectuals; 75 per cent of workers. Grushin, op. cit., Table 11, p. 81.

[17] 20.8 minutes and 13.2 minutes. Beliaev, op. cit., Table 2, p. 49.

[18] 66.4 per cent of those with an elementary education; 79.2 per cent of those with a secondary education; and 72.4 per cent of those with a higher education. Grushin, op. cit., Table 11, p. 81.

less than one film a week while Komsomol members reported about one film a week and non-Party people a little more than one film a week.[19]

As we have indicated, rural film attendance is problematic for the majority of people. In most rural settlements films can be seen from time to time, though a few villages, even some in European Russia, are inaccessible for the mobile projection unit, and even for mail delivery. The villages studied by Soviet ethnographers seem to be exceptional in this regard. Kopanka, for example, has one film projection hall in the House of Culture and another in the village club. In the House of Culture, films reportedly are shown five times a week.[20] In Korablino, films are shown only in the club, and this seems to be true for most of the villages in Kalinin *Oblast*. Each stationary film unit there serves an area with a radius of three to five kilometers. As of 1963, there were 1,400 units serving 13,000 population settlements, or one projection unit per nine villages.[21] In Bezhetskiy *Raion* in 1960 there were only six stationary film projectors and twenty-two mobile ones, serving sixty-four population points; this is a somewhat better ratio than the average for the entire *oblast*. In Ves'yegonskiy *Raion* there were thirteen stationary and ten mobile units together serving forty-six population centers; again, this is much better than the average ratio.[22] Clearly, there is a rather uneven pattern of availability of movies to the rural population: some villages are well above average in exposure, and others well below.

In their average film annual attendance rates, the rural villages studied are also atypically high. In the Shovgen community near Maikop, the villagers reportedly have an annual film attendance per inhabitant of thirty in 1960;[23] the all-Union average was seventeen for that year, and rural attendance was sixteen per person. In Kopanka, a survey was taken on film attendance on the basis of nationality:[24]

[19] Party: 14.8 min/day; Komsomol: 18.4 min/day; non-Party: 21.6 min/day. Beliaev, op. cit., Table 8, p. 52.

[20] B. N. Yermuratskiy, G. V. Osipov, and V. N. Shubkin, eds., *Kopanka—25 Lyet Spustya* (Moscow, 1965), p. 89.

[21] V. I. Selivanov *et al., Korablino—Syelo Russkoye* (Moscow: Sovietskaya Rossiya Publishing House, 1961), p. 96.

[22] L. A. Anokhina and M. N. Shmeleva, *Kultura i Byt' Kolkhoznikov Kalininskoi Oblasti* (Moscow: Akademiya Nauk SSSR, Instituta Etnografii im. Miklukho-Maklaya, "Nauka" Publishing House, 1964), p. 320.

[23] M. G. Autlev *et al., Kultura i Byt' Kolkhoznovo Krest'yanstva Adygeiskoi Autonomnoi Oblasti* (Moscow-Leningrad: Akademiya Nauk SSSR, Instituta Etnografii im. Miklukho-Maklaya, "Nauka" Publishing House, 1964), p. 166.

[24] Yermuratskiy, op. cit., p. 100

Nationality	Number of Families	Once a Week	Twice a Week	Thrice a Week	Once a Month	More Rarely
Moldavians	1072	323	159	122	141	327
Russians	463	145	66	62	58	132
Ukrainians	57	11	16	11	9	10
Total	1592	479	241	195	208	469

This indicates that films must be changed fairly often; if there are six showings a week, and more than nine hundred families attend once a week or more, the program is either sufficiently varied, or these people are exceedingly tolerant of repetitious entertainment!

Exposure patterns for age are in keeping with our earlier findings. The Kalinin *Oblast* study indicates that there young people are the most avid filmgoers.[25] Most of them do not miss a single picture, and people know what is coming far in advance; word spreads quickly if films are good. Old people rarely go to the movies. In Korablino,[26] the five most popular films in one year in the early 1960's were seen by an average of one hundred seventy-eight people each, though we have no idea of how typical these audience sizes are for films shown there.

Film lectures are used quite frequently in the country as a means of trying to educate rural people in new agricultural techniques and propagandize the achievements of the Soviet countryside. There are indications that Soviet collective farmers are tired and disgusted with this fare, especially the image of rural life portrayed on the screen. They seem to feel it has little to do with them personally. The writer Yefim Dorosh, who specializes in writing on rural life, has expressed his feelings on Soviet documentaries about the countryside:

> Almost every time I see a documentary film about the countryside I feel uncomfortable and annoyed by turns. I am ashamed to listen to ordinary people who, owing to the circumstances of their everyday life, and accustomed to behaving naturally and simply, utter in wooden and stilted voices, words they do not commonly use in their everyday life, moreover, although they are speaking to one another, they seem to be addressing themselves to me, sitting in the theater. I am annoyed by the artificial tone in which the narrator talks about the land and the grain, the irrelevance and stupidity of his agrotechnical maxims and the tactlessness, to say no more, of his grandiloquent reflections on the history of the collective farm countryside.
>
> Another reason for my reaction, I think, is the inordinate zeal with which some makers of documentary films shoot tractors,

[25] Anokhina and Shmeleva, op. cit., p. 320.
[26] Selivanov, op. cit., p. 150.

combines, and electric milling machines, with the result that these are machines and pieces of equipment, although they have long since come into common use in the countryside and surprise no one, look like advertising displays.[27]

A former collective farm leader has expressed a similar impatience and disgust with the "culture of the peasants" approach of some films:

> You must bear in mind that all these broadcasts, films, and plays devised especially for the countryside, with their eternal bucolic jingles and folk dancing, are now being received by the farmers with ironical grins. They have no respect for second-rate culture. It is too bad that some people still do not understand that. We are interested in cybernetics and in space and in ballet. I am not idealizing anything. You have to be blind not to see how the country people have developed.[28]

At present the gap between urban and rural life styles is a very charged subject for most people, whether they are emphasizing or minimizing it. The press discussion of Yashins' story "Vologda Wedding," in which he describes the backwardness of village life is a good case. In *Izvestiya,* Yashin was bitterly criticized:

> No, Yashin is wrong in describing our village life! Such villages as Sushinovo, where "there is no electricity, no radio, no library, no club, and where the mobile cinema has not been seen for the last two years" are now rare. But this author makes a single case look typical.[29]

Yashin's fellow villagers came to his defense in a letter to *Literaturnaya Gazeta:*

> Yashin's notes mentioned that in the village of Skochkovo there had been no movie for more than a year. That is so. And in Yashin's home village, Bludnovo, where he grew up, in 1962 only two movies were shown in the year. The first movie was shown in April—and the last in December. Here we are still living in the second month of 1963 already but they still don't show movies to the collective farmers, we are still unable to see movies . . .[30]

27 Yefim Dorosh, "Authenticity of View—Notes on Documentary Films," *Pravda,* March 24, 1966, p. 3; *CDSP,* XIX, 12.

28 "This is How We Live, This is Our Stand—Interview with a Collective Farm Leader," *Komsomolskaya Pravda,* February 2, 1966, pp. 1–2; *CDSP,* XVIII, 5, (1966), p. 11.

29 "Two Rejoinders," *Izvestiya,* January 31, 1963, p. 4; *CDSP,* XV, 5, p. 31.

30 A. Yashin, "A Village Meeting Writes," *Literaturnaya Gazeta,* 44 (November 1, 1967), 4; *CDSP,* XIX, 46, p. 11.

Audience Studies

We do not know how many people see the average film, but the Soviet press has published figures on the number of people who saw a few of the most popular films in recent years. These are all Soviet films, products of the mid-1960's, which reflect a much more interesting style and content than films made in the 1950's and early 1960's. They include the following:[31]

	Audience
The Living and the Dead Part 1	41.5 million
Part 2	40.3
Believe Me, People	40.3
State Criminal	39.5
Native Blood	34.9
The Chairman Part 1	33.0
Part 2	32.3
Comrade of the Cheka	32.1
Fortress Actress	31.8

(These figures probably include only those who saw the films in theaters and not those who also saw them on television.) The magazine *Sovietskiy Ekran* (Soviet Screen) began in 1965–66 to conduct an annual audience survey to learn what readers of the journal thought of Soviet and foreign films, how many of them saw these films, and something about the audience. The first questionnaire form appeared in issue No. 24, 1965. The results of the questionnaire survey and the magazine's discussion of these results provided some of the most revealing information yet published about Soviet filmgoers and their reactions to what they see. Ten thousand people filled out and returned the questionnaires. The films named best were, in order of choice:[32]

1. *The Chairman,* chosen best by 53 per cent of the respondents (Mosfilm Studio)
2. *Divorce Italian Style* (French-Italian)
3. *Father of a Soldier* (Georgian Film Studio)
4. *There Once Was an Old Man and an Old Woman* (Mosfilm)
5. *Believe Me, People* (Gorkiy Film Studio for Children and Youth)

[31] M. Poluboyarinov, "People's Universities of Culture," *CDSP,* XV, 9, p. 23.
[32] See *Sovietskiy Ekran,* 10 (226), (May, 1966).

6. *The Garnet Bracelet* (Mosfilm)
7. *I Am Twenty Years Old* (Gorkiy Film Studio for Children and Youth)
8. *Judgement at Nuremburg* (USA)
9. *Ashes and Diamonds* (Poland)
10. *Operation "X" and Other Adventures of Shurik* (Mosfilm)

The film which took first place among Soviet films for the year 1965 is a two-part study of a collective-farm chairman and his village from the late 1940's until after Stalin's death in 1953. It is a frank and outspoken film, touching on the attitudes and conditions in the Soviet countryside which have been openly discussed only during the last few years. The film is especially significant because its frankness about Soviet agriculture and the collective farm system is said to have displeased Khrushchev, and it was suppressed for some time. When it was finally released during the first months following his ouster, people came from miles away to see it. This author, standing in line in a Moscow theater for tickets, overheard many many people who, being turned away, made comments like "But I came all the way from village X to see this film. You must have a ticket for me, Comrade!" At this point the film had not been distributed outside the larger cities, and people were apparently concerned that it might be withdrawn in the uncertain atmosphere of the succession period. The magazine RT commented on the choice of this film as the most popular; its conclusions are:

> More than half the filmgoers (53 per cent) named *The Chairman* as the best—a rare instance of unanimity in our contest.
>
> Let us recall that of all the films of 1965 *The Chairman* evoked the greatest controversy in our press. Some thought that for the first time the grim truth was being told about the countryside after the war; others thought that the film laid it on too thick, and still others that it offered too easy a solution to the conflict it portrayed. Some liked Part 1 and thought the ending false, others wanted the whole film to be consistent with the spirit of the ending.
>
> . . . .
>
> That *The Chairman* won first place clearly shows that it is truth that the viewer values in a film above all else, and not far-fetched pathos. The viewer yearns for truth.[33]

[33] "Films, Viewers, TV," RT, No. 24 (October 24–30, 1966), 2; *CDSP*, XVIII, 43, p. 8.

This article also commented on the fact that many good films are listed alongside very bad films as "most popular." The United Arab Republic picture *The Dark Glasses,* for example, was listed among the worst by most of the 10,000 moviegoers who responded, while about three hundred of them thought it was the best. *Wild Strawberries,* which the magazine calls one of the "masterpieces of the world cinema," was mentioned as best fewer times than *Dark Glasses*. The magazine concludes:

> The results of the content disclosed two attitudes towards films, the active, creative attitude and the passive, sponge-like one. Sometimes these two trends stand out against each other clearly, but more often than not they are curiously intertwined.
>
> Judging by the answers to the questionnaire, the passive attitude toward film perception seems to be the most widespread today; and this is not surprising. It has long been known that the subject matter of art creates the public capable of responding to it. A flood of dull pictures has swept over the viewer, corrupting his taste and undermining his faith in the seriousness of anything the screen can convey. . . . The spectator has been bred on a mass of ersatz and comes to regard truly serious works uncritically, passively.[34]

These remarks seem to indicate a growing awareness that the dull, monotonous quality of Soviet artistic production has had a stultifying, rather than politically inspiring, effect on its audience. It is a tacit admission that the Soviet artistic formula of Socialist Realism needs to be revised if the contemporary Soviet audience is to be stimulated by artistic production.

Gradually a demand for more sophisticated treatment of subjects is developing, and this taste is whetted by exposure to foreign films. *Sovietskiy Ekran* continued its "contest" the following year, publishing a questionnaire in issue No. 24, 1966. By March 1, 1967, 52,000 completed questionnaires (five times the number of the previous year) had been returned, indicating a tremendous desire on the part of the Soviet moviegoer to express his views. Thirty-six thousand women and 16,000 men chose the top three films:[35]

Film:	*Saw It*	*Thought It Best*
(1) *No One Wanted to Die*	75 per cent of all	35 per cent men
(Lithuanian Film Studio)		30 per cent women
(2) *War and Peace*	78 per cent men	34 per cent men
(Mosfilm)	91 per cent women	23.6 per cent women
(3) *Ordinary Fascism*	80 per cent men	17.7 per cent men
	70 per cent women	17.7 per cent women

34 Ibid., p. 9.
35 See No. 10, 1967, p. 1, by Yuriy Kosyryev.

It is interesting to note that two of these films (1 and 3) have to do with contemporary military-patriotic themes, and another, a classic, has to do with similar themes from Russian history. Russian film producers make a large number of such films each year, and they are extremely popular. These films keep alive the wartime memories of Soviet citizens, serving to recruit support for Soviet foreign policy by continually reiterating the themes of patriotism and peace. Such themes are also prominent in other Soviet artistic works, such as novels, short stories, and poems.

According to the Sverdlovsk study on the effects of television on movie attendance (see Chapter 4), people see more films in movie theaters than they do on television. This is interesting, since in the Soviet Union there is a lag of only a few months before new films are shown on television. It indicates that Soviet people are eager to see each new film, and are far from saturated with them. Eighty-five per cent of the people in the Sverdlovsk sample said they watched films on the movie screen rather than on television. The screen-to-television ratio changes as people grow older: while those under thirty-five go to movies most often, those sixty and over see more movies on television. People reported that they prefer to see longer, two-part films, such as *The Chairman* and *State Criminal,* at home because they take up such long blocks of time. One would suppose that this preference extends to a more recent Soviet film, *War and Peace,* which is usually shown on four evenings in sequence.

A recent article by the eminent Soviet film-maker Sergei Gerasimov stated the basic dilemma of Soviet films:

> As a rule, the chief complaint of critics and moviegoers about many motion pictures about our times is so-called grayness, a stamp of low quality. . . .

After lamenting the scarcity of films about current daily life and "Soviet man's peaceful labor," he went on:

> The Soviet cinema's direct focusing on the major questions of the development of modern history remains fixed and constant for us, inasmuch as our ideological and political goals—which are the underlying goals of the Communist Party's theory and practice—also remain constant and unchanging.[36]

The problem of evoking enthusiasm and interest from a well-educated audience starved for diversity with time-honored themes bound by the limits of political control is a real one, and it increases with time. It is not one which the present Soviet leadership, more conservative

[36] Sergei Gerasimov, "Force of Revolutionary Film Art," *Pravda,* December 29, 1970, p. 3; *CDSP,* XXII, 52, p. 36.

and concerned with ideological purity than Khrushchev, seems prepared to deal with head-on.

SUMMARY

Soviet films in the years since Stalin died have become more numerous and interesting, at times even controversial. The models of behavior presented in them have gradually become more complex, almost credible as human beings. This cannot but have had a positive effect on the cinema's efficacy as an instrument of political socialization, since some identification is necessary for any transfer of values and behavioral norms.

The Soviet film has become much more accessible to the population, especially in the countryside. Although rural attendance rates have increased faster than urban rates, the average annual attendance figure for country people is still below that of their urban counterparts. This is due to the difference in lifestyle of the two segments of the population: long distances and poor transportation, especially during certain seasons of the year, make attendance very difficult for rural people. While television seems to have had the temporary effect of slightly decreasing the rate of urban attendance, this is now leveling off. Television has not yet made a similar impact in rural areas.

Sex differences in film attendance are not so great in the Soviet Union as for exposure to other media. Young people are the greatest movie fans, especially those in their late twenties; after this, attendance declines until approximately retirement age. Party people spend less time on the cinema than do Young Communist League members, but non-Party people spend the most time of all. This again would indicate that the more political members of the Soviet population tend to be somewhat more utilitarian in their motivations to exposure to mass media than the rest of the population. Films usually convey little political information for immediate use.

The Soviet population is eager to see new films. Word of a new film's quality and entertainment value spreads quickly, and few wait until the film is shown on television before they see it. Audience research on the film audience is still in a fairly primitive state: we know less about motivations to exposure and reactions to films than we do about audience behavior for radio, television, or newspaper.

FROM FRIENDSHIP TO COMRADESHIP: THE CHANGE IN PERSONAL RELATIONS IN COMMUNIST CHINA

Ezra F. Vogel

In the first fifteen years of Communist rule on the Chinese mainland, personal relationships have undergone an important transformation, a transformation which testifies to the success of the régime in penetrating and influencing the private lives of its citizens. From the view of the individual, the change in personal relationships arises principally from the uncertainty as to whether private conversation will remain private or whether it will in some way be brought to the attention of the authorities. When one no longer confides in a friend for fear that he might pass on the information, either intentionally or unintentionally, an element of trust is lost. When a person no longer invites a friend to his home for fear the friend might see something that he would later be called upon to describe, the nature of the relationship is altered. When a person begins to watch carefully and think about what he might be revealing to his friend and wonders under what circumstances this information might be brought to the attention of the authorities, friendship as a relation of confidence and personal commitment is weakened.

To say that friendship as an ultimate value has been weakened is not to say that friendliness has gone. Indeed, a new morality which stresses friendliness and helpfulness between all citizens has become widely accepted. The new morality does not distinguish between people on the basis of personal preferences. Like the Protestant ethic in which all are equal under God, comradeship is a universalistic morality in which all citizens are in important respects equal under the state, and gradations on the basis of status or degree of closeness cannot legitimately interfere with this equality. This article is concerned with exploring the decline of friendliness and the rise of comradeship.

From *The China Quarterly*, London, No. 21 (January-March 1965). Reprinted by permission of the author and the editor.

The Risks of Friendship

The success of the régime in preventing friendships from interfering with what it defines as national goals and purposes has been achieved in large part because of people's fears. The fear arises because people are continually supplying information which causes friends to suffer. The opportunities for supplying information are legion and cannot be avoided entirely. Information may be supplied in private interviews, in small group discussions, or in large assemblies. It may be supplied formally or casually, wittingly or unwittingly.

Refusal to supply information about a friend is rare because it would cause the authorities to take a more serious view of the problem. When an individual refuses to testify against a friend, the case is no longer regarded by the régime as that of an idiosyncratic individual, but as a group of two and possibly more conspiring to resist the régime, and the risks become greater. For most citizens the question is not whether to supply information, but how and how much to supply to minimise the consequences for one's self and one's friend.

Although friendships have been broken as a result of information supplied, the profound effect on friendship in Communist China is not so much a direct result of cases of broken friendship as the indirect result, the growth of the feeling that it is not worth the risk to confide to a friend information which could potentially be damaging. In fact, supplying information about a friend does not necessarily lead to a break in friendship since both recognise the pressures to co-operate. Indeed, even under pressure, most people make serious attempts to minimise the rupture in personal relationships. If the opportunity is available, a friend will first consult the accused to find what information has already been supplied and then, in slightly different terms, supply the same information without giving forth any new "materials." Even if the opportunity for consultation is not available, the friend may try to guess what information might be known already to minimise the possibility of contradictory stories or new material which might increase the suspicions. Or he might supply testimony which, though critical of the accused, subtly presents the friend's good side or suggests mitigating factors. For example, this could take the following form: "Since he has done such goods things as ————, I was shocked at his being so base as to ————." If he suspects he will be called upon to denounce a friend in a small meeting, he may first ask the friend for suggestions about what to say. At a minimum he would apologise to his friend afterwards. But even if friendships do not break with criticisms they are often strained. There is a fine line between supplying the bare minimum of information and a little more than the minimum, and many friendships have turned on this fine line.

Although betrayal of friends is possible at any time, the greatest opportunities arise during rectification campaigns. At the time of these campaigns, lines between the loyal and the deviants are drawn more sharply, and the loyal must prove their loyalty by criticising their deviant friends. More meetings are held for expression of opinions about neighbours and fellow workers, and more histories of friends, and especially suspect friends, must be written. More wall posters must be hung to denounce those who have committed errors, and large assemblies called to publicise the more serious cases. Friendships are under the most serious strain during these campaigns, and the prevailing mood is that it is unwise to trust anyone.

Of course, campaigns are opportunities for those who bear old grudges to express them by finding evidence that one's object of hate made precisely the kind of mistakes that the campaign is designed to correct. Indeed, people with old grudges continuously watch their rivals and save up instances of potentially culpable behaviour for just such campaigns. One obviously tries to avoid letting such a rival obtain any information which he might later use for criticism.

In addition to the danger of rivals, two kinds of persons are considered especially likely to betray a friend: the activist-opportunist and the suspect. An activist who is anxious to join the Young Communist League or the League member anxious to join the Communist Party in order to advance his own career has to prove that he is very loyal to the régime. One of the best ways to prove it is by showing that friendships do not stand in the way of his loyalty to the régime, that when necessary he will report on a friend. Of course, there is considerable variation among activists as to how energetically they report on friends, but there are always some who even seek opportunities for reporting. Many eager young people feel that their chances of rising within the régime are improved if they can furnish exciting bits of information which cast doubts upon some of their fellows. Most superiors whose job it is to receive such information apparently prefer to feel safer and have more reports (even if some are not later substantiated) rather than run the risk of not getting information which is important. Hence, they are anxious to give sufficient encouragements and rewards so that activists will continue to bring in their "little reports."

The suspect is dangerous partly because he is in a somewhat desperate situation, and he is anxious to do something that might eliminate or at least minimise his difficulties. Reporting on friends is one obvious way to extricate one's self, and the continued pressures for supplying information are hard to resist. The suspect may first be called upon to supply very unimportant and seemingly irrelevant details, and this is then used as a wedge for acquiring more information.

The suspect is dangerous not only because he is more motivated to accuse others, but because he is called upon to give much more detailed information about all aspects of his life. The mere fact of being an acquaintance of a suspect is sufficient to implicate the other person. Indeed, the régime relies very heavily on such objective factors as who had contact with whom, who is related to whom, who lives near or works with whom. Even if not guilty by association, a person is at least a suspect by association.

Direct betrayal is certainly not the only danger of friendship, and perhaps not even the most important. The risks of friendship arise in large part from the masses of information which are continually gathered in autobiographies, school essays, small group discussions, and even in casual conversation. The many channels of gathering information make it possible that the most innocent sounding statement might eventually be used or distorted by the régime to discredit a friend. Several times during their school years, students are expected to write autobiographies which begin from the age of eight. All cadres, all people of importance, and all people who are under serious suspicions must also write autobiographies. Some people are called on to write annual reports about their activities. Checks are sometimes made to see that a person mentioned by another will in his own report mention the other. Furthermore, the discussions in small groups in the school, neighbourhood, or place of work may be used as information, and this information reflects not only on the person giving the information but on all other persons whom he mentions.

In school, children are called upon incidentally to tell about things at home. Although the primary purpose of these school discussions may not be to gather information about doubtful families, a teacher would be expected to pass on any reports that do create serious doubts about certain families.

Not only contacts, but even incidental details may create risks if reported. For example, any information about dress or house furnishings or eating habits, no matter how innocuous it may seem to the reporter, might be taken to mean that a person is not truly a member of the peasant or proletariat class.

The risks of friendship are thus almost omnipresent. They vary from serious accusations which might send one to labour reform or death down to the petty annoyances of neighbourhood jealousies being discussed in small group meetings which at most would lead to verbal criticism. The impact of these risks is not limited to friendships broken as a result of betrayal. The total impact is much more profound. It includes the reluctance to let any other person know something which might have adverse effects if known by the authorities. The possibilities of the other person casually mentioning or recalling it in a group meeting before thinking of the significance or of deliberately supplying critical information are so great that it is thought safer not to expose a friend to such information. But it is the very withholding of information from friends which changes the nature of friendship.

The Routinisation of Risks

In the period since 1949 not only has the régime had to develop and modify its techniques for governing, but also the people have had to learn how to live under Communist rule. In the early period, after a period of rumours and worries of the wildest sort, the people seemed to settle down to learning seriously what was expected of them. Not only did they have to study ideology, find out what they were expected to perform at work, and how they were to be organised, but they had to learn to live with the risks of friendship.

The risks of friendship became most apparent in the early campaigns; rural land reform, thought reform of the intellectuals, and 3-anti and 5-anti against cadres and businessmen. These campaigns involved self-criticism, criticism of others and struggle against those accused of thoughts and behaviour not in keeping with the purposes of the régime. Most people were apparently completely unprepared psychologically for being denounced by their friends, and the impact on those criticised in these early campaigns was sometimes devastating. People in Shanghai, for example, compared the 3-anti and the 5-anti campaigns to the 1929 Wall Street crash, and the feeling at the time was that one must be careful in walking along the street to watch for the bodies falling from tall buildings.

The risks have probably not become any less severe. The campaigns of 1955, 1957 and 1959 also involved large numbers of people, and the struggle sessions were also very intense. Although probably in no campaign were as many people killed as in the land reform and counter-revolutionary campaign, labour reform and labour re-education have continued on a sizeable scale. In addition to these major campaigns, group discussion, self-criticism and criticism continue between campaigns. While the risks of friendship have probably not lessened to any considerable extent, people have become more accustomed to it and have grown to treat it as a routine which does not upset their own personal equilibrium. They have become less concerned about whether a friend can be trusted and more willing to take for granted the need to be cautious. They have become less anxious about conversations with friends and more willing simply to exclude certain things from the discussion to avoid the tensions and strains in their personal relationship.

By virtue of having seen how the régime operates for a number of years, people have become much more skilful in distinguishing between what is risky and what is not. They know how to watch for clues that campaigns are in the offing, and they detect hints about kinds of behaviour likely to be criticised. They have become more sophisticated in supplying evidence. They know how to state their arguments in ways that sound sincere without presenting new information which would be damaging to themselves or their friends. They are less earnest in trying to state what they really believe and more willing to say what they think they are expected to say. Indeed, so clear have the procedures and practices become that people criticised by the régime often are considered not unfortunate but foolish, foolish for having taken stands which would almost inevitably lead to trouble. But there is still a measure of uncertainty, of surprises, and many people, because of their background or their class position, or their situation within a neighbourhood or work group, cannot escape risks no matter how well they understand them. And although people are more resigned to criticism, the experience of being criticised, denounced and isolated can still be very devastating.

Reducing the Risks

Although people are generally cautious in their conversations and their associations, they cannot avoid saying everything which involves risks, and the desire for intimacy leads people to take some small risks with people with whom they feel relatively safe. Great care is taken, therefore, in distinguishing the various degrees of risk in seeing various people and in talking about certain topics.

Obviously people avoid others who have more suspicious backgrounds. Children of landlords not only have difficulty finding partners when they reach the marriageable age, but they have difficulty in finding friends at all. People who have been criticised in a campaign and gone through a period of labour reform or re-education may, if they prove themselves, be allowed to return to their former work and salary, and some are even allowed to return to positions as high as they had before. But even if they return, it is hard for them to have close relationships with anyone except other people who have been similarly criticised. They are avoided not so much because they are generally despised for their errors. They are avoided because of the risks involved in associating with them.

People also avoid activist-informers, but here the danger is not of being seen with such a person but of saying something that might be used as "material" with unfortunate results. One must, of course, be polite to the activist-informer and avoid saying or doing anything that might antagonise him. But one also tightens up in his presence. When the Youth Leaguer comes around, people are respectful but aloof, and idle chatter usually ceases until he goes away, and people hurry to return to their work or to some place else. Sometimes it is not readily apparent which member of a group it is who is serving as informer. But over a period of time, judging by the criticisms that the superiors make and the opportunities for various colleagues to have acquired the knowledge on which the criticisms are based, one can generally determine who is serving as informer. Although people cannot physically avoid contact with activists in their own group, they can be much more on their guard.

People also avoid contacts with strangers, since one can never be sure what their standing with the régime might be. Even a relative in another city who was formerly in good standing with the régime might have fallen into disfavour without one's knowing about it. If he is now in difficulty, exchanging letters with him will cause a lot of "trouble" and many people feel that the risks involved aren't worth it; it is not the content of the letter but the mere fact of sending the letter which causes the trouble.

Similarly it is rare even for fellow professionals living in different communities to have much contact. Within a single urban area, one can keep well-informed on the current political standing of one's colleagues and thus have contact with the acceptable ones without running too much risk. With fellow professionals in other communities there is always a much greater risk, and hence people are reluctant to associate with fellow professionals from different communities.

People are similarly cautious in associating with people who have newly arrived from the outside, and even greater risks are involved in having too much contact with foreigners. Even members of the Party who are authorised to have such contacts with outsiders may be cautious since even they would be suspect if they had too much contact, just as before 1949 some cadres who had originally been sent to work as undercover agents in Kuomintang organisations were later suspect since they might have taken over some of the Kuomintang's attitudes during their association with it.

Adults are also cautious with children, not because of fear of being associated with certain children and not (except in very rare cases) because they are afraid that children will be called upon to betray them. It is because children often lack precautions in talking to others. Whereas most adults can be counted on to be cautious in giving out information which could conceivably reflect on their family or friends, children are often lacking in discretion, and they might unwittingly blurt out revealing information.

Rarely is anyone so foolish as to complain to a friend about the régime. Even if one were to complain about the food or clothing, this might be taken as a reflection of one's bourgeoisie background or—if not from a bourgeoisie background—of bourgeoisie influences in one's background or at least bourgeoisie tendencies in thought or behaviour. It is rare to invite others to one's home, especially if one has some articles of furniture or food that might be considered as bourgeois.

This does not mean that one cannot express opinions to one's friends, but one must always be careful to say things which if quoted will not be interpreted badly. One cannot say, "Oh, the food is bad this year," but one could if pressed defend a statement like, "It is a great pleasure to serve our great country, and what does it amount to if one has a few little inconveniences like having a little less rice." While the ability to express opinions in ways which do not reflect doubts about one's love for the régime is an art which is now highly cultivated, the expressions of subtle criticisms have not fully replaced the expression of frank criticism. Even two people with long-term loyalties and mutual fondness ordinarily do not express verbally their doubts, their troubles, their tribulations. It is not worth the risk, and there is commonly an implicit comrade's agreement that they will not say anything that would create in the other a conflict about whether or not he should reveal something. Indeed, there are modes of mutual understanding and fondness which do not require confiding one's innermost thoughts; and many people prefer not to strain the relationship by saying something that the other might be under pressure to reveal. It is not simply prudence and self-protection, but considerateness to the other and to their relationship.

The Limits of Influence and Help

Not only has friendship as a relationship of confidence greatly declined, but another kind of friendship has declined for very different reasons. This is the kind of relationship where one gave economic assistance or used his influence in an organisation to help a friend.

The reasons for this change are not hard to find. The régime has carried on a concerted attack on nepotism and the use of personal influence. In addition to enforcing severe sanctions against violators, the régime has placed the critical decisions about placement in schools or jobs in the hands of committees rather than single individuals. Very commonly outsiders do not even know who it is who makes the decisions. Entrance to schools or firms is decided by entrance examinations in combination with other criteria by a committee who do not even say why people are rejected or admitted. Because these decisions are made by committees and not by individuals, because the personnel on these committees is subject to frequent changes, and because their decisions are subject to review by other parts of the régime, it is very unlikely that one individual can be a personal benefactor. Of course, one person may recommend another and this may have some effect on the final decision, but the decision would be made by a larger committee and the person applying for the job would have to have the necessary qualifications as judged by other criteria. Even Communist Party members are subject to the same discipline of committee decisions and hence lack the power to offer help to people on the basis of particular considerations. It is true that Party members must be loyal and not just competent, but the loyalty is to the Party, not the Party secretary.

Not only do individuals ordinarily not have the influence to provide others with opportunities for schooling or employment, but few individuals any longer have the resources of private wealth to offer sizeable economic assistance to others. The régime has not had to rely on a concerted attack on "feudalistic" relations between people from the same locality, from the same school, or the same clan to weaken these friendship bonds between the benefactor and the recipient. They have been weakened by the inability of individuals to command the resources by which they can effectively serve as benefactors.

THE NEW ETHIC: COMRADESHIP

In place of friendship as a relationship of mutual trust and privacy or as a "feudalistic" relationship between benefactor and recipient, the concept of comradeship has become gradually diffused throughout the population. Originally the term comrade was used among the members of the loyal band of Communists to signify a faithful and trusted follower in the context of a wider society in which many people were not comrades. It implied a fundamental equality, and even today in Party meetings, Party members are regarded as fundamentally equal, even though in their work units they would have superior-subordinate relationships to carry out their activities.

With the takeover of the mainland and the enunciation of the New Democracy in 1949, the term "comrade" was gradually extended in practice to include the population at large. At first it was used for officials, and then perhaps gingerly and almost playfully (as with any group learning new terms) it was gradually used by people in talking to each other until it became fairly widespread. It was not used, however, among close friends. It was used to describe the relationship of one person to another in their role as fellow citizens. As one's activities and responsibilities as a citizen of the state came to play an important part in one's life, so did the relationship between citizens become a critical mode of interpersonal relations. It became the dominant basis for all interpersonal relations and was supported by propaganda and by the very small group discussions that played such a key role in the weakening of friendship.

The essence of the term comrade lies not only in the loyalty to Communism (counter-revolutionaries, landlords and other "enemies of the people" would not be addressed as comrades) but in the universal nature of comradeship. In a very fundamental sense, every citizen is a fellow comrade, and there is no longer such a sharp line even between friends and comrades. Part of the ethic underlying the concept of comrade is that there is an important way in which everyone in the society is related to every other person. Hence it is perfectly natural for people to address others whom they never met before. The other side of the concept is that one should not have special relationships with certain people which would interfere with the obligations to anyone else. A special relationship between two people is not considered sacred and not even praiseworthy; this would not be a comradely relationship and it would be considered suspect and illegitimate.

An important element in "comradeship" is the accent on "helping" other people. "Helping" is at times a euphemism for getting another person to fall in line and do what is expected of him, whether by logical arguments, forceful persuasion, or repeated reminders. This kind of "helping" is something that one should do for a comrade, for anyone else in the society. But "helping" also means spending time to be of assistance to a person in need. A student who is having trouble with his lessons should be helped by someone who can give the assistance. An old person on the street should be given assistance by someone located conveniently nearby. A newcomer to a group should be helped by someone already on hand to become acquainted with the new place, to find all the facilities that he will need.

There is a positive value placed on being of assistance to others, on spending time and energy to make things easier for them. Indeed, some refugees from mainland China find it difficult to adjust in Hong Kong to the fact that no longer are people really looking after them and caring for them.

Although activists are likely to be the best informers, they are also likely to be the best comrades. Activists are expected to and do in fact spend considerable time assisting their colleagues and neighbours. They assist new arrivals, they make suggestions for how to do things, they try to arrange help for the needy. Comrades are concerned for their fellow citizens, and this concern includes both seeing that they stay in line and that they be given assistance when they need it within the limits of the possibilities of the time and place.

Comradeship is also strongly egalitarian in its underlying ethic. Because of their work position, some people have considerably more authority and power than others. But as fellow citizens, as comrades, they are in many fundamental respects regarded as equals. A person who is a Party member or who has more education or a higher status in his personal relations with others is supposed to behave as an equal. Of course, this does not entirely work out in practice, but the underlying ethic is clear, and a case where it was not practised would be considered an abuse.

Variations on a Theme

The pattern of caution and reserve in personal relationships paradoxically is probably the greatest among Party members, whom the régime considers very reliable, and the intellectuals, whom the régime considers very unreliable. What is common to these two groups is that they are subjected to more study meetings, self-criticism, and criticism. The Party members are subjected to intense control because of their power and responsibility. Because of their power, the régime demands of them a much higher level of loyalty and discipline than it demands of ordinary citizens, and it exercises constant vigilance lest impure elements or impure thoughts affect the ranks of the Party. The intellectuals are subjected to intense control because of their unreliability, their lack of discipline, and because the régime recognises their potential for influence, especially influence on the minds of youth.

Party members who are least in danger of being rightists, *i.e.,* those with the purest backgrounds and thoughts, may have a feeling of security and camaraderie unknown anywhere else in the society. The Party, being the one organisation where frequent meetings and organisational strength are not suspect, gives its members a group spirit in place of more intimate friendship.

Factory workers and peasants are less subject to pressures, not only because they have a "good" class background but because the demands of keeping up production place some limits on the frequency and length of meetings. Since educational institutions can tolerate more political meetings without clearly and visibly affecting the results, they are more prone to such intrusions.

Peasants are subject to less intrusion than are factory workers partly because the rural organisation, even under the commune, is not as tight and highly controlled and structured as factory organisation. Partly peasants are less controlled because the distance from political power centres is farther and because the proportion of Party members, Youth Leaguers, etc., is less. Peasants may be just as reticent to express criticism to authorities, but the concern about private conversation being brought to the attention of authorities is certainly not as great as in other groups, and the extent to which opinions could deviate before being reported is undoubtedly much greater. This is not to say that peasants have not been affected by the same pressures; the régime's exploitation of local community cleavages, the sending in of outsiders into rural areas, and the informing activities of Youth Leaguers and local Party members have affected friendship patterns even in remote rural areas.

Closer Comrades

Although comrades are theoretically equal and close companions, in practice some are more close than others. While they would be reluctant to admit it, people who grew up under certain economic conditions and have been assigned a certain family status do tend to feel more comfortable with comrades who have been assigned the same status. When a comrade goes to the city or is assigned with other comrades to go to a rural area, he is likely to associate with comrades from his same area who can speak the same dialect and share the same local tastes in food and opera and join in discussion of local news or mutual friends. A comrade may feel tense in talking to a comrade who has power over him and become somewhat stiff and formal when talking to a comrade under him, but will relax with a comrade of about his own level. Though more intimate with comrades in his own small group, a person may feel freer with an acquaintance in another group because there is less danger that their conversation will have to be reported and discussed in a meeting. Young people of the same sex do not sense the slight embarrassment and reserve that can characterise relations between men and women. A better-educated person may feel somewhat cautious with a less-educated comrade because he cannot display his inward feeling of superiority, and the less educated may try to suppress the embarrassment he feels in trying to behave like an equal when he in fact feels inferior. Comrades of the same educational level do not have this problem.

So prominent are political considerations that subtle shadings in political attitudes often separate closer comrades from other comrades. Often these political shadings are not discussed openly, but they are sensed and understood. A comrade who was criticised in a campaign several years ago feels closer to another comrade who was criticised in the same campaign. An activist is more likely to feel comfortable with another activist; a League member can talk more easily to another League member. And, even within the Communist Party, a mildly enthusiastic Party member is more likely to feel closer to another who is mildly enthusiastic, a former rightist is likely to feel closer to another former rightist.

There are many ways to express this closeness. Comrades can talk together, go to movies, or go on walks together. While they are not in the position to do big things for each other like offer major financial assistance or find jobs, there are many little favours they can do for each other. They can share their tight rations, they can help each other with their washing or sewing. They can share their books or their clothes. They can assist each other with their lessons or their work. A comrade who has some special political information might in the context of some casual conversation simply say that it is not wise to do such and such, thereby indirectly warning of some impending political campaign. They would ordinarily avoid any kind of political discussion that might conceivably be embarrassing if later discussed with authorities, but they can make subtle criticisms in ways that would later be defensible. Within the confines of not discussing items which might be politically embarrassing later, there can be considerable loyalty between comrades, and the easy-going affability, kindness and considerateness which characterise friendship in other parts of the world are also found among comrades in Communist China.

Within certain confines, the régime has gradually grown to accept the existence of closer comradeship. The programme of having everyone discuss almost everything about himself and his friends which characterised China in the early period after takeover, has generally given way to a sharpening of the line between what the régime needs to know and what it doesn't need to know. As long as these relationships do not seem threatening to the régime and are kept within bounds, comrades are given freedom to be closer to some comrades than others. While comrades may associate fairly freely on an individual basis, they rarely assemble in a large group except under official auspices. Large groups are inevitably anathema since their potential for damage caused by unified opposition is much greater. Hence, any sizeable group must have its activities very carefully authorised, and its activities must be reported in great detail by very reliable comrades. Because their friendships are potentially more dangerous, men are watched more carefully than women, and old women are perhaps given more leeway in their friendships than any other group in the population.

The practice of not interfering with non-threatening relationships inevitably involves a distinction between the politically reliable and the politically unreliable. Comrades with very clean records of continued activism and support for the régime are given considerable leeway in forming close relationships. But the régime is much more suspicious of budding friendships when one of the pair has some "problems in his background." More frequent observations and reports are required of associates of suspects. Even without any special reason, suspects may be called upon to report on their activities and engage in criticisms of themselves and their comrades. Special meetings may be called, and if these friendships appear too close, they may suffer all the more and even be assigned to different (and often lower) positions in places where they could not possibly have contact with each other. Hence, those who have suspicious backgrounds must be much more cautious in forming relationships and more reserved even in seeing the same person too many times lest it lead to further suspicions. They are in fact, as the régime wishes them to be, relatively isolated.

While some comrades are in fact closer to other comrades, there is a limit as to how close they can become. The limit is dictated partly by fear, but it is supported by the ethic of comradeship which demands that friendships do not interfere with one's role as a citizen, that an individual's commitment with another individual not interfere with his commitment to the collectivity.

As a moral ethic, comradeship is very similar to the moral ethic governing work relationships in the West. One is expected to be friendly but not to form such deep friendships that they interfere with doing the work. In work relationships one can be considerate, kind and relaxed without developing a special private relationship and commitment to the other person. One can discuss some limited personal matters, but it is inappropriate to talk too much about one's personal tastes. If two people are continually together, whispering, going everywhere together, it is regarded as lack of consideration for the rest of the group.

What is unique about Communist China is not the presence of a universalistic ethic governing personal relations, but the absence of a private ethic to supplement the public ethic and support the commitment of the individual to his friend. In most Western countries, close personal relationships may exist outside of a work context giving personal support to the individual for the tensions which exist in his more formal work requirements. In Communist China, the universalistic ethic penetrates much more deeply into personal lives so that it is difficult to gain personal support from the tensions generated in the more formal relationships. This is not as severe a problem as one might imagine. For the citizen who is bitterly attacked by comrades, the combination of criticism and avoidance by friends can be devastating. But most Chinese people do not seem to require as high a level of personal support as people in many other societies. Their needs for dependent gratification are not so great, and the support of friends and especially of family members, even if expressed only by attitude rather than by potentially dangerous conversation, appears to be sufficient. But the individual is also tightly integrated into his small group, whether it be at work or in the neighbourhood, and to the extent that he cannot stand completely independent of social pressures and requires some support he is dependent on his small group which is closely integrated with the régime, and this support is conditional on his showing the proper political attitudes, a situation which gives the régime considerable leverage in getting the individual's co-operation. The general small group support for being a good comrade is not the same as the relatively unconditional support which a friend offers his friend, but it has become an important psychological substitute. A person relies on his comrades not only for expediency but to satisfy his desires for personal companionship.

The growth of the new universalistic ethic has been important to the régime not only because it reduces the threats to political control. It is important because a modernising society undergoing rapid social change and reorganisation requires a basis of personal relations which makes it possible for people of different social backgrounds, from different geographical areas, with different personal tastes to have relationships with each other. This can only be supplied by a universalistic ethic. But the all-pervasiveness of the universalistic ethic, its penetration into private lives can only be understood in terms of the régime's desires for the power to be able to influence people even in small matters of their daily lives. Because people rise into membership in the Young Communist League and the Communist Party partly because they have proved their willingness to place the goals of the Party above the goals of friendship, it has assured that the leaders, even more than the average people, will be comrades first and friends second.

THE SOCIAL EDUCATION OF CHILDREN IN BULGARIAN ELEMENTARY SCHOOLS

Peter John Georgeoff

The Role of the Elementary School Curriculum in Social Education

The elementary school curriculum is one of the strongest forces contributing to the social education of Bulgarian schoolchildren for their society. Essentially, it is divided into three parts: traditional schoolwork and class activities, including aesthetic studies and physical education; training in labor; and extracurricular activities. Both training in labor and extracurricular activities, in their present forms, are Communist innovations in the Bulgarian school curriculum—their equivalent is not to be found in the pre-Communist school program of Bulgaria.

The subjects forming the traditional part of the curriculum do not differ greatly from those that were included in the school programs before 1945, with the exception of the course on the elements of Communism. This course has apparently replaced Zakon Bozhi (The Law of God), a required course under the old regime which dealt with the basics of the Orthodox Christian religion. Otherwise, the courses forming the elementary school curriculum of the two periods are similar, at least in name.

Training in labor is the outgrowth of Communist ideology and seeks to combinc academic study with labor as an integral part of the school program (see Table 1). In practice, however, training in labor in grades 1–4 is little more than craft activities and the development of skills and habits in caring for personal and school property. The children are taught to use scissors and to paste; some instruction is given in making useful items for the home. In the middle and upper

From Georgeoff, Peter John. *The Social Education of Bulgarian Youth,* Chapter III, edited. University of Minnesota Press, Minneapolis.

grades (5–8), the students are given an opportunity to use equipment—such as saws and hammers for the boys and sewing machines and stoves for the girls. The kind and quantity of equipment available for such work differs from school to school. Generally, the demonstration schools are much better equipped than any of the other schools; for instance, the number of schools with power tools or modern kitchen equipment is still limited.

Table 1. Program of Education in Labor, Grades 1–4

Kind of Work	Hours Allotted per Year for Grade 1	2	3	4	Total
Work with raw materials	12	18	20		50
Work with paper and cardboard	24	16	16	12	68
Work with cloth	16	18	16	14	64
Model-building and field trips				24	24
Work on collective farms	10	10	10	12	42
Socially useful labor			31	31	62
Total	62	62	93	93	310

SOURCE: Ministry of Education & Bulgarian Academy of Sciences, Pedagogical Institute, *Uchebni programi za obshtoobrazovatelnite trudovo-politekhnicheski uchilishta, I–XI klas* (*The Course of Study for the General Polytechnical Schools, Grades 1–11*) (Sofia: the author, 1964), p. 95.

In actual practice, then, other means must be provided to train the students in labor. Sometimes the pupils are expected to police the schoolyard and hallways, to care for the school garden, or to plant and maintain the walks that lead to the school with shrubs and flowers. At other times, the children are sent to work in neighborhood establishments during periods when additional labor is needed. There they are supposed to perform simple work operations at their level of ability. In still other cases, work is contracted from industry for the children to perform in the school workshops.

Most of the schools also have a plot of land called the *trudovoopitno pole* (roughly translated, an experimental plot in labor—there is no exact equivalent). Here the students raise fruits and vegetables during the spring and summer months and conduct agricultural experiments. Again, in actual practice, there are relatively few such experimental and deliberately designed educational projects. The students frequently receive their training in agriculture by performing some simple operation on a collective or state farm: gathering fruit, harvesting vegetables, sorting or packing produce for shipment. If arrangements can be made for them to do so, all students are expected to participate in both industrial and agricultural production. Such an arrangement is not always possible owing to distance, difficulties of transportation, and housing problems.[1]

The third part of the elementary school curriculum falls under the general heading of extracurricular activities, although actually, *extracurricular* is a misnomer, since many of these activities are a required part of the school program. Only some activities taking place on the Day of Rest can be considered voluntary, and even then many school-organized activities are held that all children are expected to attend. The same is true for programs conducted at times other than during class hours. With the expansion of the *poli-internati* (all-day school), and the *internati* (full-time boarding school), more and more of the children's waking hours are under the supervision of the school authorities.

[1] There is some question about the actual reason compelling the Party and government to develop the program of labor training: Is it a method to obtain additional, inexpensive labor? Is it really intended as a training device? Or, is it a technique to help the students develop desirable attitudes toward labor? It seemed to the writer that it is probably all three. Certainly, the students are performing "socially useful work." If the operations require a low level of skill, with little or no training needed, then the increased production through the use of student labor may warrant the problems involved. In many cases, it seemed to the writer that this objective was all that was achieved. In other cases, it probably does serve as a training program, for the trouble of bringing the students to a certain level of performance is hardly worth the increased production, if any, that will be achieved. At times, it must also have as an objective the development of more positive attitudes toward manual labor.

The development of such attitudes—though part of Communist ideological dogma—has important implications for Bulgaria, a country still dominated by Oriental prejudices against manual labor in contrast to intellectual activity. Despite Communist pressures to the contrary, even today there is a tendency in Bulgaria for an intellectual—that is, a person with university training—to despise manual work of any kind, although it may be a necessary part of his chosen profession. Consequently, engineers and agronomists are sometimes inclined to leave many aspects of their work to the semiskilled technicians and the experienced unskilled laborers, rather than to roll up their sleeves and get to work themselves. It may therefore be that through compulsory training in labor in the schools, the Party hopes to develop a different set of attitudes about labor among members of the coming generation.

The extracurricular activities may be of many kinds. Some of them are carried on in various club and hobby groups—thus, a school may have a history club, a geography club, a club to study the commune, a hiking club, or a chess club. With the Party's increasing emphasis upon science and technology as a means of developing the country economically, many of the clubs that have recently been formed are in the areas of mathematics, physics, chemistry, general science, or biology. There are also folklore, folk-dancing, and singing groups.

The extracurricular work of all these clubs is a part of the Pioneer program within each school. The Pioneer leader of the school, who is specially trained and possesses not only teacher's credentials but also those for Pioneer work, assumes the responsibility for coordinating the work of the clubs. He, or more frequently she, receives a higher salary than do teachers of comparable rank and almost invariably is a member of the Communist Party.[2]

The extracurricular work of the clubs is coordinated with the Pioneer movement as a whole through the Pioneer homes in every city or town of any importance (approximately eighty in 1967) or through the Pioneer Palace in Sofia. Work of the clubs in science and technology is generally guided by the Stantsiya na mladite technitsi (Station of the Young Technicians) in Sofia through a special activity training program conducted by correspondence. There is another Station in Pernik, an important mining and industrial town.

In part, the children themselves are used to coordinate Pioneer homes, technical stations, and schools. The outstanding Pioneers of each school, as well as those children who have exhibited unusual talents and abilities in some area, are selected to attend the Pioneer homes and stations to receive additional training after school or on the Day of Rest. After such training, lasting usually about two years, they are designated "assistants" in their special areas and serve as monitors and helpers to the adult leaders in their respective schools.

Although training in labor and the extracurricular activities are ostensibly activity programs for children, they are permeated with ideological education. History groups study the Marxist-Leninist interpretation of history; geography clubs emphasize Marxist economics; the hiking clubs occupy much of their time on trips visiting historical landmarks of revolutionary or partisan engagements or the graves of fallen partisan and Communist heroes; and the folklore groups interweave an intense spirit of national pride with the study of their native cultures. Training in labor emphasizes not only technical proficiency at the children's level, but also the importance of the collective approach in meeting goals and

[2] Based on interviews and discussions with Pioneer leaders and with educators involved in the training of Pioneer leaders.

norms. It stresses what are thought to be the advantages of the collective or state farm in increasing agricultural production.

The academic part of the curriculum is also designed to prepare the children for the life they are expected to lead as adults, but since this will be considered in detail in later chapters, it is not dealt with at this point.

General Teaching Methods and Social Education

The teaching methods employed to effect the social education of students through the academic program do not differ appreciably from those used in other phases of classroom instruction.[3] The methods are neither unique nor necessarily inspired by Communist ideology, but typically follow the traditional European teaching patterns. This is not to say that these techniques do not lend themselves to the goals of Communist education—on the contrary, they are suited to do so, and it is for this reason that they continue to be used in the schoolrooms of Communist Bulgaria.

The use of the lecture technique is an excellent case in point. Despite some questions that have been raised recently in Bulgaria about its effectiveness, it still is probably the most widely used of all teaching methods.[4] In most cases, the teacher simply expounds upon the day's subject matter, and the students carefully take notes upon which they are later graded. Although the technique is more widely used in the middle than in the primary grades, it is nevertheless employed at all levels to some extent.[5] A superior lecture is considered to be one which is well organized, logically structured, and effectively delivered.[6] The children apparently are not encouraged to ask questions during the course of a lecture.[7] The lecture is the chief means of transmitting ideological ma-

[3] Much of the material in this section is based upon the book by Georgi T. Gizdov, *Pedagogika* (*Pedagogy*) (Sofia: Meditsina i Fizkultura, 1963), hereafter cited as *Pedagogy*.

[4] This statement is based upon the writer's own observations of classroom teaching practices in Bulgaria, his review of teaching methods, books, and his interviews with Bulgarian educators.

[5] The writer observed children in Grades 1, 2, and 3 being taught to copy material from dictation.

[6] This statement is based upon interviews with school directors and supervisors from the Ministry of Education, December 1964, in Sofia.

[7] In the course of his visits to various kinds and sizes of schools throughout Bulgaria, the writer never once observed a child interrupting a teacher during the course of a lecture.

terial to the students in the classroom. The presentation to the class is made in a concise, formal manner and is supposed to be assimilated by the children.

The discussion method is a second technique that is popular with teachers instructing at all levels of the elementary school.[8] *Discussion* in Bulgarian educational language means something quite different from the definition normally given to the word by American educators: By *discussion,* the Bulgarians mean a procedure in which the teacher poses questions to which the children reply by quoting or paraphrasing material they have learned from previous lectures or from reading the text. It does not mean a classroom situation in which children consider various alternatives to a problem or one in which critical thinking is being fostered. Communication is *between* the teacher and the students; seldom, if ever, is it *among* the children. If, by chance, some pupil wants to comment upon some fellow student's reply, he directs his statements to the teacher, not to the student provoking the response, and does so only after he has been recognized by the teacher. Verbal give-and-take among pupils in the classroom almost never occurs.

This formal approach—again, characteristic of traditional European classrooms—lends itself perfectly to Communist educational theory and practice. As used today in Bulgarian elementary school classrooms, there is incorporated within it many elements from Pavlovian psychology. The responses, depending as they do upon the texts or the lecture notes, are highly standardized, so that several children responding to the same question would give almost identical replies.

This discussion technique is used not only with factual material, whose range of correct responses is limited, but also with material that contains ideological and attitudinal elements. This approach allows for no appreciable deviation from the norm, certain predetermined responses. What might be regarded by a Westerner as an interpretation or a viewpoint is thus presented to the children as an absolute to be studied, memorized, and assimilated.

A class discussion on an ideological problem might proceed:

TEACHER: Why do all Bulgarian children love Georgi Dimitrov?[9]

[8] Gizdov, *Pedagogy,* p. 120.

[9] Georgi Dimitrov was leader of the Bulgarian Communist Party after World War I. In 1923 he was involved in an abortive revolution and had to flee the country, going first to Yugoslavia and then to Germany. When Hitler rose to power, Dimitrov was implicated in the burning of the German Reichstag. However, the accusation was never proved, and after a lengthy trial he was acquitted.

Dimitrov then went to the Soviet Union where he was made an honorary Soviet Citizen by Stalin and appointed Secretary General of the Comitern. After the Communists seized control of Bulgaria with the help of the Soviet

PUPIL: We love Georgi Dimitrov because he is one of the greatest sons of the Bulgarian people.[10]

TEACHER: That is correct! Why do we say that he was "one of the greatest sons of the Bulgarian people?"

PUPIL: We say that he was one of the greatest sons of the Bulgarian people because he loved his nation and her people and always worked for their welfare.

TEACHER: Can you give us an example?

PUPIL: He led the Bulgarian people on the road to socialism.

The remainder of the class period is conducted in a similar manner.

The third important instructional method, upon which much of the discussion method hinges, is the reading and study of the textbook assigned for the course. In the process, the acquisition of factual material is stressed as well as the memorization of the fundamental concepts presented by the book. Supplementary materials are sometimes assigned for students to read, and here, too, pupils are encouraged to acquire factual data and basic concepts by, essentially, a process of assimilation, rather than one of problem solving.

However, it is recognized that reading, as an educational process, has other purposes. Gizdov's widely used pedagogical text states the following: "During the instruction period, the student may read with these purposes in mind: (1) to memorize the content; (2) for understanding; (3) to deepen his knowledge—to acquire information that will supplement the text; (4) to evaluate critically the viewpoint of the author or to analyze the peculiarities of the material (its style or grammatical structure); and (5) to feel emotions."[11]

A few words need to be said about Gizdov's last two points. Where ideology is not a factor, students sometimes are encouraged to examine an author's viewpoint critically. Whether such analysis is encouraged or not depends a great deal upon the teacher's teaching methods, knowledge of the subject matter, and rapport with the class. But since so much of the material studied by students—especially that which lends itself most readily to analysis, such as literature or history—has an ideological character, the opportunities for students to examine an author's view-

---

Army in 1944, he returned to the country to become First Secretary of the Bulgarian Communist Party and Premier of Bulgaria. He died in a Moscow sanitarium in 1948 under suspicious circumstances. Today, he is memorialized in Bulgaria as is Lenin in the Soviet Union, and is considered to be the Father of socialist Bulgaria. His remains have been embalmed and placed on display in a tomb in Sofia's main square.

[10] Answers to teachers' questions in Bulgarian schools must always be given in complete sentences.

[11] Gizdov, *Pedagogy,* pp. 122–25.

point critically are greatly limited; where ideological elements enter, of course, no such examination is made. For those authors whose work differs from the current Communist line, the students are given access —if at all—only to selected excerpts from his writings, for the purpose of pointing out the shortcomings of his view and the superiority of the Party's position. Bulgarian writers of methods textbooks state the matter clearly: "Bourgeois . . . interpretations are to be presented only to the extent necessary for them [the children] to understand their intellectual shortcomings and their use as "scholarly" [quotations in the original] justification for the series of economic and political acts that have as their purpose the enslavement, oppression, and exploitation of the various peoples of the world."[12]

Lastly, the idea of reading a story to feel emotion contains important implications in the area of social education. Many of the stories available to the children are written with the distinct purpose of developing their attitudes about people and events.[13] Thus, stories about partisans and youth heroes are written in a highly sympathetic manner, with their sufferings graphically portrayed, so that the readers may be impressed with their determination and Communist ideals. Presumably the readers may feel impelled to follow in their paths. Stories about American minorities are written in the same style to obtain the sympathy of the children. On the other hand, Nazis, other fascists, colonizers, and imperialists are often lumped together as vicious, unscrupulous, and often stupid creatures to be outwitted by the workers.[14]

Other general classroom teaching methods that are described in books on pedagogy, but that appear to be seldom used in the process of social education, include laboratory work[15] and demonstrations.[16] Such teaching methods as group work, panel discussions, projects, or problem solving appear to be rarely used. Although some teachers (especially the older ones) and the professors of pedagogy are familiar with these tech-

[12] Pechevski, *The Methodology of Teaching Geography*, p. 165.

[13] Recent Western behavioral studies cast serious doubts upon the efficacy of these procedures in achieving the set objectives. The writer, however, is not seeking to evaluate the effectiveness of the techniques, but simply to describe and analyze them as they are used in Bulgaria.

[14] See the story by Veselina Genovska, "P"rvomaiski znamena" ("Banners of the First of May"), from Ivan Todorova, N. Bobeva, R. Gundova, & L. Shivacheva, *Chitanka za IV klas na obshtoobrazovatelnite trudovopolitekhnicheski uchilishta* (*A Reader for Grade 4 of the General Polytechnical Schools*) (Sofia: Narodna Prosveta, 1963), pp. 131–34, hereafter cited as *A Reader for Grade 4*.

[15] Gizdov, *Pedagogy*, pp. 125–27.

[16] Ibid., pp. 127–29.

niques, current policies do not favor their use in classroom teaching. Such procedures are, however, employed in the extracurricular programs of the Pioneer movement, which is permitting an increasingly greater amount of participation by the children in the development of their activity schedules. In the intermediate and upper grades, students are sometimes asked to give reports on various topics, but the procedure is considered to have serious limitations.[17]

Little attention appears to be given to individual instruction in teaching, regardless of the subject matter or the grade level. Of course, students having difficulties with a lesson may be helped by the teacher during the class period. Students can also receive help at the *zanimalna,* the study hall they may attend after their regular shift at school is out (most Bulgarian schools still operate in two or three shifts).[18] At the *zanimalna,* the students prepare their assignments for the next day and receive help, should they experience difficulties, either from the teacher of the course or from the *v"zpitatel* (in some of his duties as head of a *zanimalna,* the *v"zpitatel* actually assumes the role of a combined trainer and guardian). After they have completed their assignments, the children may participate in additional field trips, labor projects, or sports at the *zanimalna,* but these activities appear to bear little relation to their work in class. One reason for this is probably the fact that many *zanimalna* have children from several grades attending them.

In any event, although these provisions exist to give help to children experiencing difficulties with their schoolwork, almost no consideration is given to individual differences. Assignments in all subject areas are given to the classes as a whole. No attempt is made to tailor the work to the level of ability of the different children or to their particular interests. There is no grouping by ability levels within a grade.

Attempts are made to keep multi-grade rooms in each school to a minimum. Because school construction has not kept pace with enrollment, and most schools must operate in two shifts, it has been possible, generally, to limit the number of multi-grade rooms in a school. If, for one shift, there are not enough children in a certain grade to fill a schoolroom comfortably, the two shifts are combined. Nevertheless, multi-grade rooms do exist in many schools. The procedures employed in classes of this type, as far as could be determined by observation and inquiry, do not seem to vary from those used in rooms containing a single grade; the students in each grade simply had shorter lecture and discussion periods and a longer study period. No attempts were made

[17] Ibid., pp. 132–35.

[18] For a further discussion of this topic, see John Georgeoff, "Elementary Education in Bulgaria," *School and Society,* XCIV (February 5, 1966), 71–74.

to combine the classes with respect to any elements of the school program, and it appeared to this writer that such an arrangement would be contrary to the regulations of the Ministry of Education. This distinct separation of grades was true irrespective of subject matter or grade level.

There are no classroom activities in any curricular area, including the social studies. Because of the disrepute in which the project method as a classroom teaching technique is held, pupil research activities—except for occasional oral reports—are nonexistent. Schoolroom craft and construction projects relating to material covered in courses are never seen. Classroom dramatic activities are extremely limited—no puppet shows, skits, operettas, or shadow screen plays are part of the work in class. There is only one exception: children are encouraged to memorize poetry and to give declamations with great gusto, considerable flourish, some skill, and almost no self-consciousness. Patriotic and Communist themes very often are the subject of these poems.

Three other methods should be considered at this point: rivalry, cooperation, and criticism. Although these methods, in a sense, are not *teaching* methods since they are not a means of presenting content or information, they are employed intensively and continually during the process of instruction. Their use in Bulgarian schools is directly related to Communist ideology, and they form one of the bulwarks of Communist educational theory and practice.

Rivalry as a method of instruction is especially prominent in the early primary grades, although it is used to a considerable degree at all levels. In actual classroom practice, there appears to be little difference between *rivalry* in Bulgaria and *competition* in the United States. However, Bulgarian school officials insist that *rivalry* does not mean the same as *competition.* They maintain that *rivalry* is socialist in nature because its ultimate goal is the good of the community as a whole,[19] consequently, it is conducted on a friendly basis to see which child can study the most, perform some skill the best, or, as in the case of the Pioneer movement, do the largest number of good deeds, collect the greatest amount of scrap paper or metal, or gather the greatest quantity of wild, medicinal herbs. *Competition,* on the other hand, is regarded as individualistic, antisocial, selfish, and opposed to the public welfare, a remnant of degenerate bourgeois ideology. Socialist rivalry, therefore, is construed to be constructive and a characteristic that must be encouraged, whereas competition is to be avoided. Regardless of whether this is a distinction without a difference or not, the fact remains that socialist rivalry is widely employed to motivate individual pupils in a grade, rows in a class, classrooms in a school, troops in a Pioneer com-

[19] Interview with kindergarten teachers, December 13, 1964.

pany, and in every other situation where the technique can be used satisfactorily.

The use of rivalry as motivation is not restricted to children, but is extended to workers in order to stimulate greater production in factories, in the mines, and on the farms. The use of rivalry as part of the educational process thus prepares the children for adult life in communist society, where the goal will be to meet and exceed production quotas.

Recognition is given to the best pupils in a variety of ways. It may be simply in the form of praise before his peers. Most often, however, the award is extrinsic and takes a more tangible form: a badge with the hammer and sickle upon it; a Communist Party flag upon his desk; the designation of model pupil with the privilege of sitting near the teacher facing the class; the gift of a book, an article of clothing, or some other memento; or a trip to some place of interest. In a similar fashion, adults are recognized for achieving beyond their quotas: they are recognized as *udarniks* (heroes of labor), model workers, or outstanding workers; their pictures are placed at commonly frequented public squares; they are given monetary awards and other honors—such as medals, tickets to theatrical performances, sport spectaculars, and other special events, and, in exceptional cases, all-expense-paid trips to some of the other East European countries or to the Soviet Union.

Cooperation is also widely used as a method of instruction. The more capable students are encouraged to help weaker ones. Well-behaved students are expected to urge those who misbehave in class to change their ways. Members of a Pioneer troop are counselled to work together so that the troop as a whole can meet its quota in gathering scrap materials.

Thus, the extremes of rivalry and cooperation exist side by side as instructional techniques. Units and subgroups—such as rows in the room, classes, and Pioneer troops—are pitted against one another, and the individuals within each are urged to help all to meet and exceed the norm or quota. At the same time, the person within the particular unit or subgroup that contributes the most toward the common goal is singled out for honor. In many cases, outstanding individual achievement is recognized only within the winning group—therefore, in order for individual attainment to be honored, the group itself must first succeed. This procedure is sometimes referred to as cooperative rivalry, and through it Bulgarian pedagogues hope to achieve a delicate balance between friendly socialist rivalry and cooperation.

Such cooperation to achieve an end has its parallel in the adult world. Most of the workers in factories and other industrial establishments, on the farms, and in businesses such as department stores, shops, and hotels are divided into brigades of communist labor. These brigades are supposed to work together to meet a collective goal, such as a common work norm or a promised quota. Although within the brigade, each worker must attempt to exceed his own goal, he must also work for the interest of the group as a whole. Thus, should any worker of the brigade become ill or for some other reason be unable to do his share, the others are expected to work harder in order that the common objective can be met. Should the brigade fail in its purpose, all its members fail, no matter what each may have achieved himself. Members of a brigade of communist labor frequently are paid on the basis of whether or not the group as a whole meets its norm, not upon individual attainment alone. Consequently, the peer pressure to produce is sometimes enormous. In addition, members of the brigade are to spend a certain amount of their free time together after work—the time may be spent taking a course, studying some aspect of Communist ideology, taking a foreign language, attending the theater or opera, or reading and discussing books. Hence, through an emphasis upon cooperation and the collective approach in school, Bulgarian teachers are attempting to prepare their students for still another aspect of adult Communist society.

Finally, criticism is often used as a method of instruction. The criticism is usually made by a group as a whole, such as a class, and directed against an individual, although an individual may subject himself to self-criticism in front of his peers and his teachers. When a child has committed what his classmates or teacher considers an antisocial error, the group collectively discusses the matter and points out the error to the transgressor, who is expected to admit it, criticize himself for having committed it, promise to mend his ways, and ask his classmates to help him in his resolve. If, however, he persists in maintaining his innocence, or if he insists that whatever he has done is not an error, peer pressure will be exerted: Class members may attempt to ridicule him. They may send a student delegation to talk to his parents. They may ostracize him in their play and in their social encounters with him. They may demand that he remove his Pioneer neckerchief. Usually, only one or two of these devices are sufficient to persuade the offender to conform.

If this procedure fails to obtain the desired results—which is most unusual—the child's parents will be called to task by the school authorities and the parents' committee of the school. The Party secretary[20] at the parents' place of employment may be informed, and there they will be subjected to similar criticism themselves from the workers' committee. If everything fails, and the child is a discipline problem in school, he may then be sent to a reform school.

A discipline problem in the classroom is not necessary, however, for a criticism session to be held. Periodically, these sessions are held in each

[20] Among the duties of a Party secretary at a place of employment are certain disciplinary ones. Consequently, he can put considerable pressure on the child's parents at the place of work to persuade them to cooperate.

class, Pioneer troop, and cell of the Dimitrov Communist Youth League. During these sessions, the children routinely subject themselves to self-criticism, discussing before their colleagues what they have done well and where they have failed. Their fellow students comment upon what has been said, filling in details if anything has been omitted, and consider what further action, if any, need be taken.

This process has its parallel in adult life. Adults, too, must subject themselves to self-criticism and to the criticism of their peers. Industrial workers, collective farmers, teachers, college professors, musicians, artists—all must submit to the process. Social organizations have this practice, and even Party members must undergo public self-examinations—and that not only at their place of employment and in their social life, but also in their political organization. Moreover, each street or apartment house has its own general secretary and committee composed of certain "socially conscious" people who supervise conditions on their street or in their apartment building. Any resident who the committee considers derelict in some duty is subject to the process of criticism.

Criticism, as it is employed in the schools, thus prepares the children for the adult world, since they are becoming familiar with a process that will confront them throughout life.

Of the out-of-class general teaching methods, the most frequent is the field trip, called in Bulgaria the educational excursion.[21] Field trips are a requisite part of the curriculum, and entire classes of children with their teachers are frequently seen on the streets of any large town. A Bulgarian methodological textbook for the teachers' institutes gives the following categories of field trips: (1) to study nature; (2) to industrial establishments; (3) to places of historical importance; (4) to places of cultural importance (exhibits and museums); (5) for the study of the geography of the country; (6) to study the life of the people—social-centered field trips.[22]

All six kinds of field trips have implications for the social education of Bulgarian children. Nature study and field trips to study the geography of the country emphasize the "wonders and beauty of the fatherland." In field trips to industrial establishments, the economic growth of the country under Communism is stressed. Educational excursions to places of historical importance generally are visits to sites of partisan or revolutionary activity. Visits to points of cultural importance may be made to the Museum of the Revolution, the Museum of Ethnography, an art gallery, an exhibit of Bulgarian industrial products, or some similar place.

The importance of museums with exhibits on revolutionary topics are

[21] Gizdov, *Pedagogy*, pp. 129–32.
[22] Ibid.

obvious, but even visits to other institutions have importance for the children's social education. The Museum of Ethnography contains many exhibits of primitive Bulgarian life and of life today—that is, life before versus life after Communism. The Museum of Ethnography, in Sofia, which appears to include also practically everything available in the country relating to the field of anthropology, contains almost nothing on the Roman or Turkish period, per se. However, in general, these two periods are not ignored. Archaeological work is going on in the country, and a number of good finds have been reported, several of which date back to Thracian times. The Roman and pre-Roman period simply is not stressed—in all probability because it is so far removed from the present.

Exhibits and monuments of the Turkish period often have connected to them a certain revolutionary, nationalist flavor: buildings and sites where revolutionary leaders, such as Levski, lived; the dungeons where they were imprisoned; the stone blocks from which they were hung; and entire village-museums, such as Koprivtsitsa, where the center of an uprising against the Turks took place. Since the Russians were instrumental in liberating Bulgaria from the Turks, exhibits about this period help to reinforce the Party line, which aims to present Russia historically as a friend of the Bulgarian people.

In the art galleries, works on display are mostly realistic: tractor drivers, workers, soldiers, revolutionaries, and partisan tunnels. During the course of field trips to museums with their classes, teachers select certain of these art works and discuss them in detail with the childen, often placing more emphasis on content than on aesthetic merits. A trip to study the life of the people may mean a visit to a collective or state farm, a tour of some new workers' apartment buildings, a meeting with some industrial or agricultural group at their "home," or something similar. Thus, the field trip, as a teaching method in social education, is widely and intensively used. Regardless of the place visited, teachers almost invariably have opportunities to emphasize aspects of Bulgarian history or life that, it is believed, will develop a set of positive attitudes toward the nation, Communist society, and the Soviet Union.

Thus, the teaching methods used by Bulgarian teachers are selected to meet the educational objectives that the society has set for itself. Students are educated to become participating members of socialist society—vocationally, socially, and politically. All aspects of education are directed to the realization of these ends.

Interest Groups

INTEREST GROUPS IN SOVIET POLITICS: THE CASE OF THE MILITARY*

Roman Kolkowicz

I. INTRODUCTION

THE concept of political interest groups in a political system presupposes two conditions: (a) distinct sets of interests and values shared by groups or institutional memberships, and (b) the existence of "conflict" in the system, i.e., a modicum of tolerance for the public and private articulation of policy-relevant interests and values which are not necessarily those of the ruling elite. In pluralistic systems we have come to accept the idea and reality of interest groups as central to the political and social processes. They are presumed to be a vital factor in the political process and social transaction in which the political leaders manipulate or accommodate various interest group demands. In a totalitarian or authoritarian political system, however, where a single party claims hegemony in respect to political and social authority, the concept of interest groups needs some clarification, since the single party denies the

From *Comparative Politics,* II:3 (April 1970), pp. 445–61 and 470–72. Reprinted by permission.

* This article is based on a more extensive essay in *Interest Groups in Soviet Politics,* H. G. Skilling and F. Griffiths, eds. (Princeton, 1970).

very existence of such particularistic entities and views the possibility of their emergence as anathema.

In dealing with political process, social norms, and social "pathologies," Communist writers in the Soviet Union rarely talk about interest groups as we know the concept in the West, i.e., as a set of aggregate "constituencies" whose objectives are intra-systemic and not antisystemic, and whose interests, largely derived from their functional, regional, professional, economic, or social group orientations, are to influence policy makers in their particular favor. Communist theoreticians tend to view articulated group interests as a sign of antisystemic alienation from society and state, and, therefore, as a remnant of bourgeois society. They feel that such dissent, unless it can be directed and usefully channeled, must be eradicated. Institutional or particularist group loyalties and objectives which significantly depart from those of the Communist party are viewed as being "pathological." The only "interest groups" Soviet theoreticians and leaders recognize are the economically and historically conditioned social classes: the proletariat, the peasantry, and the intelligentsia. These three groups are assumed to have varying interests and values derivative of their class consciousness. Even these class differences, however, are eventually to be eradicated and subsumed within the classless communist society.

Clearly, we are dealing here with a political doctrine and with social values which diverge in a very basic way from those of many Western pluralistic societies. Let us briefly compare them:

Pluralistic Political Systems	*Soviet Authoritarian System*
Social "conflict" tolerated	Social "harmony" imperative
Diversity encouraged	Uniformity and unity stressed
Dissent intrasystemic	Dissent seen as antisystemic
Multiple sociopolitical loyalties	Primary loyalty: party
Decentralization of socio-political authority	Centralized hegemonic authority: party

It is apparent that the Soviet political and social ideals, which stress uniformity, harmony, and unity as basic desirable objectives would be antithetic to the formation and growth of particularist interest groups. And, indeed, Soviet leaders and theoreticians have in the past viewed Soviet society as an amorphous entity which the party could manipulate by means of various deliberate devices in order to maintain its malleability and commitment to the party's goals and to prevent it from crystallizing into groups and institutions whose spokesmen could challenge the party's hegemony. This party view of society was embodied in various Stalinist policies and declarations; it was described as having "demonstrated the 'mechanism' of the dictatorship of the proletariat; the transmission belts, the 'levers,' the directing force, the sum total of which constitutes the system of the dictatorship of the proletariat."[1]

Indeed, Western accounts of life and politics in the Soviet Union during the past four to five decades have spelled out the picture of a rule of terror over an undifferentiated populace and of a small group of men whose Byzantine intrigues and struggles for power absolutely determined the fate of the state, its institutions, and the individual citizens. Such accounts reduced all political activity to a single stage at the apex of the party hierarchy.

In defense of this simplistic presentation of a complex society, we must remember how relatively little reliable information on the Soviet Union was available to the West for many years, so that researchers were forced to make the most of official communications and the occasional statements of party leaders and had to try to derive both meaning and facts from the often laborious scrutiny of this output for any inconsistencies and irregularities. This task was the more difficult because of the distorted, idealized view of the Soviet scene—an idyllic picture of a classless, tranquil, and wisely guided society—that was propagated by the party-controlled media. Soviet society was presumed to be permanently "frozen" in an ideologically and politically determined mold and firmly ruled by party, the changes in the top leadership notwithstanding.

As we came to know, underneath the inhibiting burden of Stalinist dictatorship the Soviet Union was in reality being transformed into a complex industrial society, divided into a number of functional groupings, developing a vast bureaucracy. It came to include several institutions with strong loyalties and parochial interests, each constantly striving for a greater measure of autonomy. After Stalin's death, an accelerated process of loosening of political controls over society took place and the divergent institutional claims, which theretofore had been suppressed, became publicly articulated and advocated with various degrees of vigor. This perceived trend toward moderation in Soviet political and social life, the growing body of information on the Soviet Union, and the pressures for emancipation among Soviet satellites caused many Western students of Communist affairs to abandon the static view of the Soviet Union and to base their emphasis on expectations of change. Much recent research is focused on social and political change, and is devoted to analyses of Soviet phenomena starting with the premise that Soviet society is in the process of transition. This pres-

[1] A. Vyshinskii, in a 1948 Soviet publication, cited in Roman Kolkowicz, *The Soviet Military and Communist Party* (Princeton, 1967), p. 16.

ent analysis of the military's role as an interest group belongs to the latter category.

Among the various studies of Soviet interest groups, the military establishment seems to be the most promising and, at the same time, the most difficult. By virtue of its "apartness" from society, its formalized structure of authority and status, clearly discernible value system, and frequent disagreements and occasional conflicts with the political leadership, the military would seem to be best suited to the analytic scrutiny. Yet the analyst who attempts to investigate the role and place of the military by using Soviet sources encounters enormous difficulties, chief of which is recognizing and defining the military's separate institutional identity: its interests, objectives, and values. The reason for this apparent paradox stems from the fact that the Communist Party denies the military such a distinct identity. Through all available media it seeks constantly to reinforce an image of the military as a fully integrated part of the totalitarian system. And a large network of political controls within the military organization is designed to keep the latter fully responsive to party guidance, initiative, indoctrination, and other forms of manipulation. This effort has not fully succeeded, however, in suppressing the many strains and disagreements that exist between the two institutions.

Recent attempts to reappraise the role of the military and of other interest groups in the Soviet Union have been aided by a vast increase in the information on the Soviet Union, by an observable advance in the military's efforts to obtain institutional autonomy, and by the noticeable departure among Western academic disciplines from monistic and totalitarian monolithic concepts of Soviet political life. In short, it is possible to begin a reevaluation and reappraisal of the nature of the Soviet political and social processes by means of applying, in moderation, certain analytical criteria and hypotheses used in the study of Western political systems.

It would be useful to begin by positing several basic assumptions on the nature of Soviet political and social life: (a) that the political leaders and the basic political values and the ideology are inherently antimilitary, i.e., there is a profound distrust of the professional military men who possess the weapons and technology of war, the "experts in violence"[2]; (b) that the political norms of the Soviet system reject any

[2] Carl Friedrich and Zbigniew Brzezinski have found that totalitarian parties exert constant "efforts to prevent the armed forces from developing a distinct identity of their own" and that, as a result, the military lives "in an atmosphere of an armed camp surrounded by enemies." They maintain that "the Soviet handling of the army . . . comes closest to the model image of the complete integration of the military into the totalitarian move-

particularist interests, be they of institutional, functional, ethnic, or other nature, if such interests are articulated outside the norms and practices of the party; (c) that this rigid insistence on party hegemony and suppression of expression of group interests has been undergoing a progressive transformation brought about by several forces of change. These latter include modernization of the economy and the management of the state, erosion of ideological imperatives and the emergence of a new form of pragmatism, which considers certain forms of institutional or functional autonomy as necessary for the efficient management of the state,[3] the vast growth of Soviet political and military commitments around the globe which, within the delicate relationship of nuclear deterrence, necessitate substantial inputs into policy processed by experts of various sorts.

It becomes apparent, therefore, that the emergence of articulated group interests is a concomitant of a society which is becoming internally complex and politically committed, at home and abroad, to a grand political design dependent in turn on an efficient technological, economic, and managerial substructure. It might be inferred that the "pluralization process" in the Soviet Union is both of the "grass roots" variety and is partly engineered from above. In other words, the pressures of professional and institutional freedoms and group interests are selectively and carefully tolerated, and at times encouraged, insofar as such developments do not threaten the basic norms of that political system and as they serve to improve the problems of managing a multifaceted society. Such tolerance of interest group articulations may also serve the purpose at times of releasing political pressure from below at a low political cost.

II. CHARACTERISTICS OF THE MILITARY AS AN INTEREST GROUP

The Soviet military establishment satisfies many of the analytical criteria used by Western sociologists and political scientists in their definitions of an interest group: the military's value system is elitist and

---

ment." See their *Totalitarian Dictatorship and Autocracy* (New York, 1956), p. 281.

[3] In 1959 Prime Minister Nikita Khrushchev stressed the party's desire for "the inclusion of the widest strata of the population in the management of all affairs of the country"; he argued that such "an implementation by public organizations of several functions which at the moment belong to the state will broaden the political functions of the socialist state." Speech at the Twenty-first Congress of the Communist Party of the Soviet Union, 27 January 1959.

"inward"-oriented, tending to reenforce an institutional self-awareness and positive self-image; the military's "apartness" from the larger society fosters a sense of exclusiveness and engenders a strong reliance on the military community on the part of the community as a whole; the military's modes of dealing with the environment are similar to those of well-defined interest groups in other societies.

As an interest group the military tends to be highly self-centered, competing with other groups for status, resources, and influence.[4] The military's usual ways of influencing policy and social planning are mainly of the indirect and "reactive" kind. Although it possesses substantial *potential* and *inherent* political power, it rarely chooses to challenge the party head-on, even when its basic interests are denied. Instead, the military tends to resort to a form of "passive resistance," acting as a modifier or spoiler of policy by means of institutional inertia, bureaucratic obstructionism, appeals to sympathetic party factions, appeals to "political generals," and denial of its own expertise, which leads to erosion of efficiency, discipline, and morale. When looked at from a longer historical perspective than the two recent decades, this method of the military for dealing with undesirable party policies seems to have been successful for a variety of reasons. These include: the complexity of the military establishment and of warfare in the nuclear age; the rising political and military commitments of the Soviet state which result in a greater dependence on the military professionals; and the realization among military people, under a collective leadership regime, that a direct challenge to party supremacy tends to unify the party leadership against them, while a selective, patient exploitation of opportune political circumstances serves their ends much better.

The military's influences on the larger society are both positive and negative, or more properly, conservative and liberalizing. Essentially a conservative community of guild-like professionals, military officers largely view radical social, cultural, economic, and ideological positions maintained by other groups as undesirable and alien to their own moral code. In this respect their views are similar to those of the more conservative party members. The military establishment is also characterized by an acute sense of nationalism, fostering patriotic attitudes among its members and seeking to engender such values in the populace as a whole. Moreover, in seeking to further its basic institutional interests, the military interferes with and opposes various modernizing and liberalizing trends in the country. The officer corps generally prefers a social planning policy which subordinates consumer interests to those of defense needs, urging large allocations to heavy industry. It

[4] . . . Evidence in support of the military's competitiveness includes a number of RAND studies on Soviet military and economic affairs.

prefers an international arena which is less than tranquil and relaxed and depicts attempts to establish more relaxed relations with capitalist countries as dangerous to the state's interests.[5]

On the other hand, some of the military's institutional interests have a modernizing and liberalizing influence. The military rejects police-state controls; it presses for a greater autonomy of managerial, professional, scientific, and functional groups; it prefers a wider dispersal of state authority; and some of the younger and more highly-skilled elements in the officer corps stress a new form of functional and social pragmatism which rejects ideological intrusion and determinism.[6]

The military is not a very monolithic, homogenous institution. At times the officer corps shows deep splits brought about by inter-service rivalries, by varied attitudes toward military policies, and by a form of generation gap. When threatened by a challenge to its basic professional and institutional prerogatives and values, the military usually closes its ranks, however. Although the military shares some of the characteristics of other "interest groups" in the Soviet Union, it also profoundly differs from them because of its ambiguous position in the communist state: it is both the mainstay of the regime and its principal potential rival for power. The history of the military's relations with the party has, therefore, been rather unstable. Party leaders who have had little difficulty in dealing with many other groups and institutions that have challenged or threatened their hegemony are faced with the problem of how to control, and, when necessary, to coerce, the military without reducing its vigor, efficiency, and morale. Various attempts of the party to keep the military loyal and politically responsive without destroying its effectiveness have had mixed success.[7]

The disparity between the military's vital function in the state, on the one hand, and its unclear internal role and political influence, on the other, has led to ambiguous Western assessments of the military's place, status, and influence on Soviet policies. The main reasons for this uncertainty must be sought in the unique political context of the Soviet Union. The attitudes of the various communist ideologues toward professional armies have always been equivocal.[8] Both Marx

[5] For a recent analysis of the problem see Kolkowicz, *The Red Hawks on the Rationality of Nuclear War,* RAND Corporation, RM-4899 (March 1966) and *The Dilemma of Superpower: Soviet Policy and Strategy in Transition,* Institute for Defense Analyses, Research Paper P-383 (October 1967).

[6] For analysis see Kolkowicz, "The Impact of Modern Technology on the Soviet Officer Corps," in Jacques Van Doorn, ed., *Armed Forces and Society* (The Hague, 1968), pp. 148–68.

[7] See Kolkowicz, *The Soviet Military,* pp. 340–42 and *passim.*

[8] See Kolkowicz, "Una herejía santificada: Idea y realidad del ejército rojo," in *Estudios Internacionales,* II (April-June 1968), 64–84.

and Engels originally saw the revolution as a massive uprising of the lower classes led by a communist vanguard. Lenin remained vague about the military's role in a future communist society. With the establishment of the Soviet state, however, and in recognition of its growing need for a professional army, the party evolved a modus operandi with respect to the military. After the ouster of Trotsky in 1925, the new premier, Josef Stalin, established the Red Army's organizational structure, its relationship with the party, and its social and political roles. The Red Army became an adjunct to the party's ruling elite; the emerging officer corps was denied the full authority necessary to practice its military profession properly; officers' careers were kept in a state of perpetual uncertainty; and, finally, the closure-prone military community was forcibly exposed to the party's scrutiny through a complex system of control and indoctrination.[9]

Despite the controls and the incessant indoctrination imposed by Stalin, the new military establishment did not develop exactly along the lines desired by the party. The officer corps began to exhibit some of the characteristics of professional military officers in other political systems, stressing the need for greater professional autonomy. A typical military ethos developed, marked by elitism and detachment from society, expressed in the form of heroic symbols and a code of honor. At the same time, the functions and authority of the political officers were resisted and viewed as destructive. These tendencies toward institutional autonomy and professional independence were clearly incompatible with the party's objective of a politicized and controlled military organization.

The party's anxictics regarding the military are understandable. Since the state makes no formal provisions for the transfer of power, party leaders have come to view organized groups and institutions as potential rivals and challengers. Because of its organization, weapons, and philosophy, they see the military as the greatest single threat to their hegemony. It controls vast means of physical coercion; it is an integrated mechanism that can, in theory, respond to very few commands; and it is a closed group with an elitist, antiegalitarian value system.

As long as the terror machine was in operation, the military had few opportunities to develop spokesmen who could articulate its objectives and grievances. After Stalin's death, however, party leaders were divided by the struggle over his succession, the stabilized control mechanisms were weakened, and the military's views and interests emerged in the open. The brief tenure of Marshal Zhukov in the Ministry of Defense (1955–57) permanently strengthened the morale and

[9] Ibid.

stature of military professionals. Although his ouster in 1957 brought a temporary setback, the military has continued to gain in professional assertiveness and institutional maturity since that time. This improvement in the military's position has been aided by several developments: (a) The officer corps is becoming transformed from a group of relatively expendable commanders with minimal skills into a body of younger, more sophisticated and self-assured technocrats, who are becoming increasingly indispensable, individually and collectively, to the defense and political interests of the party; (b) The Soviet Union's extensive political-military commitments as a superpower would be severely compromised by a major open crisis between the two institutions, a situation which forces the party to be more circumspect in its treatment of the military; (c) The party's new pragmatism and heightened appreciation of most professional groups—managers, scientists, and the military among them—has further strengthened the latter's position in the state.[10]

In other words, conditions for the development of an inner cohesion and institutional self-awareness were inauspicious during the oppressive Stalin era. But the years since have witnessed a progressive ideological disillusionment, a new stress on functional and professional excellence, the reduction of the terror machine, and acceptance of the principle of collective leadership. These developments have greatly favored the military's role as an articulate interest group.

What emerges, therefore, from a study of the Soviet military is a realization that its institutional characteristics are those of all large professional establishments, regardless of their political-social environment: a high degree of professionalization and demands for professional autonomy; a professional ethos, including a strict code of honor and disciplines; and an organizational structure in which the levels of authority are easily discernible and very stable.

III. INTERESTS, VALUES, OBJECTIVES

A vital aspect of an interest group is the fact that it has certain interests and that it seeks to influence decision makers in order to maximize such interests. Let us, therefore, examine the essential interests of the military and determine in what ways it exerts influence on the political leadership and on society in general in order to advance its own basic interests.

The military's basic interests may be broadly divided into two categories: "ideological" and functional. In addition to such broad, all-

[10] See Kolkowicz, *Impact of Technology*.

military institutional interests, one can discern several subgroup interests which are usually related to certain policy and inter-service problems.

The "ideological" interests of the military refer to the traditional values, self-images, and beliefs of the military profession. The military's idealized self-image finds expression in numerous public statements by officers. A representative example of such views may be found in the statement of General Makeev, the influential editor-in-chief of *Red Star,* the main military organ:

> The concept of military honor has existed since time immemorial; it is as old as armies . . . bravery, selfless dedication, and military skill were revered. . . . There is a saying: the soldier is at war even in peacetime. But the soldier serves his prescribed time and departs into the reserves. The officer, however . . . is at war for a lifetime. How many inconveniences, how many trials! But the officer withstands all, overcomes all. He holds high his honor, the honor of the officer and citizen.[11]

Makeev rejects those views which impugn the social utility of the officer; he asserts that the officer's contribution to society is "no less necessary to the fatherland than that of a kolkhoznik (a collective farmer), agronomist, engineer, teacher, or doctor." He is opposed, too, to the lack of concern and antipathy of those in society who pursue their normal lives, "and while they sleep thousands of officers carry on their difficult duties."

The officers' idealized image of their profession, their duties, and their selfless service to their country (which are found in many other military establishments)[12] is resisted and rejected by the party functionaries. Such party views reject the "ideology of militarism" and the "idealistic philosophy" of the military which strive to "show the beauty and wisdom [of military life]."[13] They view such an idealized image of the military as contributing to elitist tendencies, to a sense of apartness from society and its problems—both unacceptable to the leveling pressures of the party.

The party's concern with the need for a constant politicization of the officer corps is well-known. The main objectives of this politicizing and indoctrination process have been spelled out in numerous guidelines to the political control organs in the military:

[11] General Makeev, quoted in *Izvestia,* 12 February 1963.

[12] See Morris Janowitz, *The Professional Soldier* (Glencoe, 1960); numerous others are cited in Kolkowicz, *The Soviet Military,* pp. 24–26, *passim.*

[13] V. I. Skopin, *Militarizm: istoricheskie ocherki* [Militarism: historical essays] (Moscow, 1957), p. 35.

> The political organs strive to . . . guard daily the uninterrupted influence of the party on all activities and affairs of the Armed Forces. . . . They must always approach problems in such a manner that the interests of the party and government, the interests of communism, are given priority. . . . The party demands that all aspects of military life be systematically penetrated. . . . The political organs must extend their influence into all facets of the activities of the forces . . . they must react to even the smallest deviations from Marxism-Leninism, to any opposition to the policies and directions of the party.[14]

The political control organs are instructed "to explain thoroughly the advantages of Soviet society and (the) state system over the capitalistic system . . . to inculcate in the military . . . an indestructible faith in the ultimate victory of communism." In order to be constantly informed about the internal affairs of the military, the political organs are urged to give "serious attention to the recording of discussions" during party meetings when the peculiar ritual of *kritika/samo-kritika* (criticism/self-criticism) is performed. "Here it is necessary to note the gist of every comment, and to put down precisely the basic views expressed by the communist as well as his suggestions." The reason for this constant scrutiny is explained: "A well-established informational system enables the political organs always to be on top of things and to react at the right time to deficiencies in the activities of the officer personnel. . . . Party information must correctly define the state of political morale among personnel."

The great importance the party apparat places on the politicizing effort of the officer corps is reflected in numerous ways. The political control organs play the key role in that task and their functions may therefore be summarized as follows: (a) to observe activities in the units and to pass on information to higher levels of the apparatus; (b) to politicize the officers through intensive indoctrination and political education; (c) to regulate the advancement of officers so that only politically desirable elements are promoted; (d) to supervise and control military as well as political activities in the units; and (e) to promote desired action or conduct through intimidation, threats of dismissal, public humiliation, or outright coercion.

In addition to these measures, the party also seeks to keep the military from institutional "closure" by involving it with social and party groups on the "outside": "Close contacts with party organiza-

[14] This citation is from a basic handbook "intended for Party-political workers" to assist them "in the organization of Party-political work among the personnel of the Soviet Army and Navy": *Partiino-politicheskaia rabota* [Party-political activities] (Moscow, 1960), pp. 47–70.

tions, and collectives of workers in factories, sovkhozes (state farms) and kolkhozes help soldiers and officers to better understand national interests and to prevent *'the emergence of castes'* in the military" (emphasis added).[15]

A conflict of "ideologies" is apparently inevitable because one of the party's basic objectives is to neutralize, equalize, and "depersonalize" all institutions and groups while claiming exclusive features only for itself. On the other hand, some professional and institutional groupings tend to develop distinct "personalities" and characteristics of their own.

The *functional interests* are embodied in the military's traditional and constant search for a larger freedom from the confining embrace and intrusions of the party apparatus. This basic interest is usually articulated less in terms of a particular group or institutional interest or of opposition to the party's right to exercise its supreme prerogatives, and more in terms of the best and most proper uses of its expertise. The military, therefore, resist "civilian" intrusion and domination within their professional areas because, they argue, such interference tends to undermine the efficiency, readiness, and responsiveness of the military organizations.[16]

The military's functional interests include: (a) authority to formulate strategic policies; (b) authority to influence allocation and planning policies of the government; (c) authority to exercise full command of the forces at its disposal; and (d) authority to manage its own internal affairs with minimal interference from the party apparat. Let us now examine these functional interests.

First comes the *maintenance of a high level of investments in heavy industry, since this sector of the economy is fundamental to the defense industry's needs*. This is probably the "military interest" with which Western readers are best acquainted. And, indeed, it represents a fundamental objective of the military establishment. The policy debates and disagreements on the proper proportion of investment in this sector of industry are as old as the Soviet state.[17] Recent military claims and the party's counter-claims on the proper proportions of investment were made by the Chief of the General Staff Marshal Zakharov and by Party Secretary Leonid Brezhnev. Thus, the latter declared: "The national economy must develop harmoniously, it must

[15] Colonel Rtishchev, *V pomoshch ofitseram izuchaiushchim Marksistko-Leninskuiu teoriu* [Handbook for officers studying Marxist-Leninist theory] (Moscow, 1959), p. 125.

[16] See Kolkowicz, *Dilemma of Superpower,* pp. 30–46.

[17] For historical survey, see John Erickson, *The Soviet High Command 1918–41* (New York, 1962); Dimitri Fedotoff-White, *The Growth of the Red Army* (Princeton, 1944); and Kolkowicz, *The Soviet Military.*

serve the interests of achieving . . . the constant rise in the people's living standards. The development of heavy industry must be subordinated to the requirements of constant technical reequipment of the whole economy. . . ."[18] The Marshal responded to this several months later in an argument for larger allocations to the heavy and defense industries: ". . . the Soviet people have in the past not for a moment failed to carry out V. I. Lenin's legacy: always to be on the alert, cherishing the defense capabilities of our country and our Red Army as the apple of our eye."[19] He then employed a historical analogy to make his case for "a powerful heavy industry—the foundation of foundations of the whole socialist economy and the firm defense capabilities of our country."

Second, the *maintenance of high levels of military budgets and expenditures is necessary to an efficient and effective military establishment.* As in the case of heavy industry, spokesmen for the military usually seek to impress political leaders with the urgency of the military's needs for large budgets and high levels of allocations. As a recent example of this tug-of-war between the military's views and those of party spokesmen, a policy struggle which took place on the eve of the Twenty-third Party Congress, where important and long ranging policy decisions are ratified, is typical. The military spokesmen emphasized the "economic base of the defense capabilities" which determines the "essence of a policy and the actual essence of war,"[20] stressing that "the nature of a war and its success depends more than anything else on the domestic conditions of the country."[21] They pointed out that "in a possible missile-nuclear war, economics will determine its course and outcome first of all and mostly by what it [the economy] is able to give for defense purposes before the war begins, in peacetime."[22] Consequently, they argued, "he who does not learn to defeat his enemy in peacetime is doomed to defeat in war."[23]

The party's response to these pressures by the military was to accommodate such demands while publicly asserting that the consumer interests would receive mounting attention and resource allocations.[24] Consequently, while sizable military research and development programs were continued and even expanded, and while the production of offensive and defensive strategic weapons as well as of conventional

[18] *Pravda,* 7 November 1964.
[19] *Krasnaia zvezda,* 23 February 1965.
[20] Colonel P. Trifonenko, ibid., 26 November 1965.
[21] Colonels Rybnikov and Babakov, ibid., 7 December 1965.
[22] Colonel Trifonenko, *Kommunist vooruzhennykh sil* (Communist of the armed forces), No. 1 (January 1966).
[23] Colonel Grudinin, ibid., No. 2 (February 1966).
[24] See Kolkowicz, *Dilemma of Superpower,* pp. 30–46.

weapons and military technology was increased, the military could publicly support the party's official line on consumer interests. Marshal Zakharov therefore reported to the Armed Forces on the results of the Twenty-third Party Congress by stressing that the next "Five-Year Plan" was to "achieve a significant rise in the living standards of the people and a more complete satisfaction of the material and cultural demands of all people . . . which will make it possible to direct increasingly greater resources toward the development of branches of industry which produce consumer goods."[25]

The third functional interest is *maintenance of high levels of internal political tension by depicting various international actors and situations as dangerous, unpredictable, or aggressive, in order to provide a sound rationale for large defense allocations and a high political status for the military.* It may be asserted that military professionals in all political systems tend to depict the international environment as more threatening to the security of their societies than any other for both objective and "subjective" reasons. In the Soviet Union the military had sought in 1954 to impress the political leadership with the fact that "the easing of international tension should not be overestimated; while the political leader who resisted military demands asserted the opposite."[26] Military spokesmen saw in 1965 "the current international situation as characterized by a sharpening of tensions and increased danger of war,"[27] while the political leader, who sought to curtail military expenditures, had suggested that "of late a certain relaxation of tensions has become apparent in international affairs."[28]

The military's public assertions on the dangers arising from the international environment are usually related to the party's attempts to reduce allocations, authority, or status to the military. Such warnings therefore serve the military as a correct and patriotic instrument for pressuring those party factions which would put the interests of the consumer or the "stomach" above the basic interests of survival of the nation or of the communist system.[29] A most recent example of such military rhetoric was connected with the deliberations prior to the Twenty-third Party Congress, when the Five-Year Plan was being debated. The military's arguments stressed (a) that "the policy and

[25] In *Tekhnika i vooruzhenie* (Technology and arms), No. 4, 1966.

[26] Marshal Timoshenko, November 1954, cited in Kolkowicz, *The Soviet Military,* p. 385.

[27] In *Kommunist,* No. 7, May 1965.

[28] Khrushchev, 1964, cited in Kolkowicz, *The Soviet Military,* p. 383.

[29] After Khrushchev's ouster his opponents criticized most of his policies. Among the many comments was the following: "It would be incorrect to see as the central purpose of Communism mainly the satisfaction of the 'needs of the stomach.' " Ibid., p. 384.

actions of the imperialists are intensifying the danger of a new world war" and this "is an undisputable truth,"[30] and (b) that nuclear war still serves as a rational instrument of politics, so that any "a priori rejection of the possibility of victory is harmful because it leads to moral disarmament . . . fatalism and passivity."[31] These two views, which were widely articulated by various military spokesmen, sought to counter antimilitary arguments.

Fourth, and last, is the *retention of authority to manage the internal affairs of the military establishment and to formulate strategic policies.* Political controls over the military in the Soviet Union have been discussed in numerous Western studies. The thrust of such studies has been to examine the various ways in which the party apparat politicizes and manages the officer corps. While the Soviet indoctrination and thought-control processes receive generous attention in the West, much less attention is given to the more recent problems in controlling the military, namely, the proper delineation of the military's authority to formulate strategic policy. During the Stalinist era the dictator usurped full authority to formulate strategic doctrine and policy, and the military played a limited role in the process. Only after Khrushchev came to dominate the party did the military begin to assume a minor-partnership role in these vital processes. Since his ouster the military have demanded a much larger role in the development of strategic doctrine and strategic planning.

The military's arguments are (a) that nuclear war is so complex that, in the words of Marshal Zakharov, military dilettantism in party leaders can be very detrimental, especially if these leaders lack "even a rudimentary knowledge of military strategy,"[32] and (b) that most major Western powers have entrusted their military leadership with full strategic planning authority, while Soviet military leadership plays a minor role in these processes.[33] The party's attitude, as recently expressed, is (a) that "attempts to prove that in modern war the political leadership has possibly lost its role have been decisively refuted by logic,"[34] (b) that "Marxists-Leninists do not assign the roles of generals absolute importance" since "the influence of even brilliant generals was at best limited to adapting the method of warfare to new weapons,"[35] and (c) that "because of their destructive properties,

[30] Colonel I. Sidelnikov, *Krasnaia zvezda,* 28 January 1966.

[31] Colonel Rybkin, "On the Essence of a Nuclear-Missile War," in *Kommunist vooruzhennykh sil,* No. 17 (September 1965), and reiterated in various writings in the winter of 1966.

[32] *Krasnaia zvezda,* 4 February 1965.

[33] Marshal of the Soviet Union Sokolovskii, in *Kommunist vooruzhennykh sil,* No. 7 (April 1966).

[34] V. Zemskov, *Krasnaia zvezda,* 5 January 1967.

[35] Ibid.

modern weapons are such that the political leadership cannot let them escape its control."[36] And, finally, the military was informed that, because of various complex tasks facing modern states, "it is absolutely obvious that the solution of these tasks falls completely within the competence of political leaders."[37]

The military's rather bold demands for a larger share in policy making are motivated by real concerns, stemming from Khrushchev's "hare-brained" policies, lest the political leaders will commit the armed forces to situations and policies without adequate preparation and capabilities. Another motivation for such military pressures is the High Command's desire to possess greater control over the vital planning activities involving the defense of the country.

CONCLUSION

Findings by this author suggest that the Soviet military is imbued with many characteristics usually associated with an "interest group." It has a distinct identity and self-reenforcing values; its members share similar educational backgrounds and professional goals and interests; it lives in an unfriendly social environment which sharpens its sense of corporate identity and creates a distinct modus operandi for dealing with challenges from the environment.[38] Moreover, unlike other groups in society, the military seeks and usually achieves distance and separateness from the larger society and its problems. The military may therefore be defined in part as a unique group in the Soviet Union, its uniqueness deriving from the fact that it is essentially a guild-like organization, seeking closure from the outside, living by its own rigid rules and mores, and constantly guarding its privileges and prerogatives. In broad terms, the military may be described as a conservative organization whose members generally prefer the status quo, i.e., firm governmental rule over an orderly and correct society in which it maintains its own strong identity.

Another aspect of the military's unique role in the Soviet state derives from the perpetual tension in its relationship with the party leadership. The military possesses the greatest reservoir of "organized violence" and this represents an inherent challenge to the absolute powers of the party elite. Moreover, the military represents the key

[36] Ibid.

[37] Ibid.

[38] For a more extensive examination of the military's modus operandi in dealing with its environment, see Kolkowicz, "The Military" in H. G. Skilling, ed., *Interest Groups in Soviet Politics* (Princeton, 1970).

instrument in the party's pursuit of political and military objectives at home and abroad. Thus, the party must accord to the military the necessary resources and professional freedom while, at the same time, exercising constant control, lest this military machine turn against the regime. This circumstance creates tensions between these two powerful groups and their relationship necessitates careful adjustment of mutual interests for the maintenance of internal stability. The historical record, however, suggests that as long as the military's basic interests are not denied, the generals and marshals find it easy to live with any kind of political leadership in the state.

While the military presents a monolithic facade externally, it is far from being a homogenous, tranquil community within. The military community is a complex amalgam of many varied interests, objectives, and parochial attitudes. Whenever its basic interests are threatened, however, members tend to unify and offer a concerted response to their challenges. In the absence of such threats, the military community has shown itself to be a veritable battleground of divergent ideas, interests, and objectives which reflect the impact of several new and profound developments that are affecting the larger society as well. These developments include: the phenomenon of collective leadership and the reduced internal role of the terror apparatus; the influx of new and complex technology into the military and, as a corollary, the growing influence of the military technocrats; the superpower role of the Soviet Union and the growth of the external commitments of the state; and, finally, the mounting complexity of nuclear warfare and the strategies and techniques for the conduct of such wars. Each one of these developments has had a liberating effect on the officer corps, endowing the military experts with a greater authority and role, reducing the power of the control organs, and making the officers more indispensable to the welfare and survival of the state.

If the military's influence and autonomy are enhanced by the mounting importance of its functions and expertise, and because of a certain dispersal of authority at the pinnacle of the party, does the military also seek to formalize this newly gained role in the governmental and political councils? In other words, what is the accessibility of the military leaders to the top ruling bodies of the state? While the military is represented in the Central Committee and in various lesser political bodies in the state, it is very doubtful that it exercises any significant political weight and influence there. Membership in the Central Committee is achieved largely through co-optation, at the pleasure of the party leaders, rather than by pressure from outside. Thus, the military has failed to obtain any real and formal political influence in the decision-making bodies of the party and government. In the past, the military tended to obtain important political influence during periods of profound internal crises in the party, when warring factions courted the military's support. Whenever such an internal party crisis healed, however, the military found itself without real influence or power, and actually suffered retaliation from the victorious political faction.[39] It may therefore be suggested that the military's political acumen is minimal; that it either finds itself satisfied with nonpolitical concessions from the party and seeks no political role; or that it lacks imaginative and bold leaders who could translate inherent and potential political power into reality.

What influence might the military have on the developing Soviet society? Potentially, the military could serve as a major vehicle for social and political change, since it has a monopoly of means of violence which could upset the internal political balance. The military, however, is unlikely to undertake such a role. Unlike the intelligentsia, the managerial-scientific-technocratic groups, the youthful dissenters, the ethnic groups, and other disaffected groupings with particular interests in various kinds of change, the military does not seek change nor does it evoke any trust or camaraderie from the other groupings. If anything, the military is looked upon by the others as a consumer of badly needed resources, as a blind instrument of various regimes, as a residue of social and political orthodoxy and blind adherence to party *diktats*. The military is seen as the institution which has most to gain from a deteriorating international environment, and as one which resists the relaxation of international tensions and disarmament efforts.

The military has a limited national "constituency," therefore, except for certain circles in the party and in the managerial-technocratic circles connected to defense industries. Only as the protector of the country from external threats does the military gain support and respect from society. Alas, such heroic and historical roles are rather quickly forgotten in the long interwar years, when society's interests turn toward social, cultural, economic, and private pursuits. In sum, the military differs profoundly from those interest groups in Soviet society whose particular interests and visions are also the larger objectives of hopes of people seeking urgent changes in the social, political, and philosophical realities of an authoritarian system.

[39] See ibid. for statistical evidence in support of this view.

OCCUPATIONAL GROUPS IN CHINESE SOCIETY AND THE CULTURAL REVOLUTION

*Michel Oksenberg**

THIS paper analyzes the interests and power of seven occupational groups in China: the peasants, industrial workers, industrial managers, intellectuals, students, Party and government bureaucrats, and military personnel. The evidence comes from two sources: 1) the activities of the members of these groups during the Cultural Revolution; and 2) revelations in the wall posters and Red Guard newspapers about their behavior from 1962 to 1966. The paper concludes that the configuration of power and influence among these groups will be an important determinant of Chinese politics in the years ahead.

ANALYTICAL APPROACH

A few years ago, when the totalitarian model of politics in Communist countries was in its heyday, little attention was paid to the ability of various groups in society to influence public policy. The totalitarian model led analysts to concentrate upon the dictator, his whims, the political intrigue among those around him, and the control mechanisms

Reprinted from *The Cultural Revolution: 1967 in Review* (Michigan Papers in Chinese Studies, No. 2) with permission of the Center for Chinese Studies, University of Michigan.

* I thank the participants of the "Year-in-Review" seminar for their helpful reactions to a shortened oral presentation of this paper. In addition, I profited from but have not done justice to the comments of several people who read an earlier draft of this paper: Thomas Bernstein, Mark Mancall, Edward Friedman, Robert Packenham, and Lyman VanSlyke. A grant from the East Asian Institute of Columbia University facilitated the typing of the manuscript.

which forced the populace to obey his commands. Barrington Moore and Isaac Deutscher stood out among the analysts of Soviet politics in the early 1950's for their willingness to look beyond Moscow to the power and influence of major groups in society.[1] Now, the totalitarian model has lost its earlier attraction, having proven unable to account for social change. Meanwhile, the approach employed by Moore and Deutscher has begun to win a wider audience, in part because in the early 1950's they suggested the possibilities of significant evolution in the USSR. Recently, Barrington Moore's study of the social origins of democracy and dictatorship again has displayed the analytical power of a study of the interrelationships among key groups in society.[2]

The Cultural Revolution provided a remarkable opportunity to view the structure of Chinese society in the 1960's. Prior to 1965, that view was obscured by the carefully nurtured image of a monolithic society led by a unified, cohesive elite. In 1966–67, the image was destroyed, revealing that the rulers were deeply divided and locked in bitter struggle. As the rulers lost their ability to provide unified, coherent guidelines to the nation, the various segments of society became more able to pursue their own interests. As a result, the Cultural Revolution made it possible to analyze the concerns of the major groups in society and their relative abilities to achieve their interests.

Before the substantive portions of the paper are presented, its analytical framework should be made clear. The analysis has four major conceptual underpinnings. The first concept involves the nature of groups and the ways they are able to articulate their interests. In common parlance, "group" has one of two meanings. One meaning is an "association," a collection of individuals who are formally organized for a purpose. When "interest groups" are discussed in the United States, people have the "association" in mind—a collection of individuals pursuing their common interests in concert. Another definition, more suited to the Chinese case, considers a group to be an aggregate of individuals with similar attributes, roles, or interests. Whether the members of the aggregate become aware of their similarity and form an association depends upon the context. But it is possible for the members of the aggregate, acting separately, to behave in the same way because of the similarity of their positions. In these terms, then, peasants can react to government policy as a group, that is, as an aggregate of individuals making similar decisions.

[1] Barrington Moore, *Terror and Progress USSR: Some Sources of Change and Stability in the Soviet Dictatorship,* Harvard University Press, 1954, and Isaac Deutscher, *Russia: What Next,* Oxford University Press, 1953.

[2] Barrington Moore, *Social Origins of Dictatorship and Democracy,* Beacon Press, 1966.

A second concept embodied in the analysis is that unorganized groups or aggregates can affect the policy formulation process. In democratic countries, aggregates have little trouble forming associations and gaining access to the key centers of decision making. In non-democratic countries, aggregates continue to pursue their interests, but since they are unable to organize, they must adopt different techniques. Manipulation of information, passive resistance, non-compliance, and cultivation of friends in high places of government are some of the indirect methods which enable groups to influence policy. The important research question, as far as China is concerned, is to determine how and to what extent each aggregate registers its demands.

A third aspect of the analysis is that some groups in society have a greater ability than others to influence policy. A number of factors determine what groups have the greatest power, but key among them are the degree of their organization, the relationship of these groups to the means of production, the values and attitudes of the particular culture, the international situation, and the interrelationship among various groups. The process of industrialization involves the removal, often violently, of some groups from the locus of power, and their replacement by new groups.

Finally, the fourth underpinning of group analysis is the notion that, to a considerable extent, politics involves the attempts by powerless groups to obtain power, while groups with power struggle to retain it. Moreover, the politics of a country to a large extent reflects the conflicts within the groups that have power. In societies where the military has power, for example, national politics comes to involve interservice rivalries, conflicts between senior and junior officers, and disputes between central headquarters and regional commands. If one can chart the distribution of power among various groups in a society, then one can predict what some of the important public policies and political issues will be.

The application of these concepts to the events in China in 1966–67 must not be misinterpreted as an attempt to explain the Cultural Revolution. Rather, this paper analyzes the Cultural Revolution for what it tells about one aspect of the structure of Chinese society. The seven broad occupational groups into which the Chinese Communists divide their society—peasants, intellectuals, industrial managers, industrial workers, students, Party and government bureaucrats, and the military—are examined briefly and crudely, with the following questions in mind: What were some of the salient characteristics of these groups? What did the members of these aggregates perceive to be in their interest? Did the aggregates have any common group interests, and if so, what were they? How did they pursue their interests? What power did they have to enforce their demands?

These questions are not easily answered. Without the opportunity to do field research, it is difficult to ascertain what people perceive to be in their interests. The activities of the members of different occupational groups during 1966–67 and statements in the wall posters and Red Guard newspapers about their attitudes and behavior provide some clues. In addition, occupational groups appear to have some similar characteristics, no matter what country is under investigation; the literature on the roles and behavior of members of these groups in the developing countries then provides inferences about some of their likely interests in China. Further, some information is available on the perceived interests of different occupational groups in pre-Communist China. By seeking convergence among the different sources of information, the analyst can roughly identify occupational group interests at the present time. It is harder to estimate the ability of these aggregates to articulate their interests and affect public policy, but surely the relevant data here include actual instances of members of these groups influencing important political decisions or public policy clearly reflecting the interests of the group.

An analysis of the activities of occupational groups during the Cultural Revolution admittedly provides only a limited perspective upon the extraordinarily complex events of 1966–67. But no single vantage will suffice in interpreting history of such sweeping proportions. Some of the valuable perspectives employed in other essays on the Cultural Revolution and purposefully eschewed here include analysis in terms of elites,[3] bureaucratic phenomena,[4] problems of industrialization,[5] and the Chinese political culture.[6] By approaching the Cultural Revolution from the perspective of occupational group interests, one of the oldest methods of political analysis, one hopefully will acquire additional in-

[3] For an analysis stressing this approach, see Philip Bridgham, "Mao's Cultural Revolution," *China Quarterly,* No. 29, January-March 1967, pp. 1–35.

[4] Analyses stressing this approach include: Franz Schurmann, "The Attack of the Cultural Revolution on Ideology and Organization," in Tang Tsou and P'ing-ti Ho, ed., *China's Heritage and the Communist Political System,* University of Chicago Press, 1968, and Chalmers Johnson, "China: The Cultural Revolution in Structural Perspective," *Asian Survey,* Vol. VIII, No. 1, January 1968, pp. 1–15.

[5] Analyses stressing this approach include: John W. Lewis, "The Leaders and the Commissar: The Chinese Political System in the Last Days of the Revolution," in Tang Tsou and P'ing-ti Ho, ed., *China's Heritage, op. cit.;* and Richard Baum, "Ideology Redivivus," *Problems of Communism,* May-June 1967, pp. 1–11.

[6] An analysis stressing this approach is Richard Solomon, "Communication Patterns and the Chinese Revolution," a paper delivered to the annual meeting of the American Political Science Association, September 1967.

sights into the structure of Chinese society and its relationship to the Chinese political system.

PEASANTS

Peasant Interests. An important desire of most peasants probably is to be free to cultivate, reap, market, and consume their crops; they wish to have less extracted from them, and more goods available for purchase at lower prices. Peasants particularly demand political quietude during the planting and harvesting seasons. They also want their government to protect them from disorder and the ravages of nature. In addition, to the extent that their aspirations have risen, China's peasants also want better educational opportunities for their children, more welfare, greater security, and a standard of living comparable to urban dwellers.

Articulation of Peasant Interests. Peasants have no associations to voice their demands. Nonetheless, the Cultural Revolution provided ample evidence that the peasants had brokers embodying and representing their interests. Recalling the disaster of the Great Leap, when peasant desires had been disregarded, many among the Peking leadership strove to anticipate peasant reaction to proposed policies. Moreover, upon occasion, outbreaks of violence in the countryside forced the officials to pay attention to peasant grievances.

The brokers came primarily from three sources: the officials in agricultural agencies, regional officials whose power stemmed in part from the performance of agriculture in their areas, and military officers. A number of leading agricultural officials, in particular Teng Tzu-hui, T'an Chen-lin, and Liao Lu-yen, were accused in the *ta-tze-pao* of seeking to expand private plots and free markets, to restrict the power of the communes, and to assign brigade plots to individual households, thereby restoring production responsibility to the family.

Teng, T'an, and Liao, in effect, were voicing the interests of their peasant constituents. The reason for their action seems clear. The performance of the agencies which they led was judged largely by agricultural production. They depended upon the peasants to fulfill the targets for which the agencies were held responsible. It was in their interest, therefore, to argue for measures and to secure targets congruent with peasant interests.

Similarly, regional officials occasionally represented the interests of the peasants in their area. The purge of Li Ching-ch'uan of Szechuan has proven fascinating in this regard. If the charges against him are accurate, Li was keenly aware of the peculiarities of the Szechuan agricultural system, and sought to win exemptions from the uniform, nationwide regulations Peking sought to impose. He took exception, for example, to marketing regulations which Mao had endorsed. He pointed out that (because of the terrain and scattered population) rural markets in Szechuan were different from the rest of the country.[7]

The military also had a vested interest in peasant morale. To the People's Liberation Army fell the unpleasant task of suppressing peasant unrest. Moreover, soldiers were recruited in the countryside, and troop morale was adversely affected by disenchantment at home.[8] The PLA conducted periodic surveys of troop morale, and monitored letters from home. When the surveys and monitoring revealed disenchantment at home, the military command apparently voiced its concern. As a result of these channels of communication, some military officers became particularly sensitive to the problems of the peasants and upon occasion acted as their representative. This is precisely what P'eng Teh-huai was doing at Lushan in 1959 when he expressed the discontent of the peasants with the commune system.[9]

In addition to representation by brokers, peasants acted on their own behalf. Such actions included failure to comply with directives—for example, hiding production and concentrating on private plots—and sporadic violence. The *Work Bulletin* described peasant violence in Honan province in 1960, while during the first half of 1967 there were persistent reports of small peasant uprisings and of an illegal influx of peasants into many Chinese cities.[10]

These means of voicing their interests, when combined with surveys measuring rural discontent and the visits by higher level officials to the countryside, added up to a general awareness in Peking of the desires and problems of the peasants.

Sources of Peasant Strength and Weaknesses. The power of the peasants to enforce their demands, however, was limited by the fact that they had no organization which could be considered their own. One wall poster indicated that some peasants were acutely aware of this problem:

[7] Radio Kweiyang, June 28, 1967.

[8] J. Chester Cheng, ed., *The Politics of the Chinese Red Army,* Hoover Institution, 1966. See pp. 12–19 for example.

[9] See *Peking Review,* No. 35, August 25, 1967, pp. 6–7 and No. 36, September 1, 1967, p. 14; Tokyo *Mainichi,* August 22, 1967.

[10] See *China News Analysis,* Nos. 645 and 647. For a dramatic account of one such uprising, see Joint Publications Research Service (henceforth JPRS) 44, 052, January 17, 1968, pp. 16–23.

> Workers have their unions, soldiers have theirs, and Party workers have a body to represent their interests. Why don't we have unions? . . . .
>
> The peasants have no voice. They have only 'formal' democracy. At the Second Conference of our Poor and Lower Middle Peasants Association, no decisions were made by us. All we had was a few days of free board and lodging.[11]

As anthropologists stress, peasants must overcome innumerable difficulties to become an organized, articulate, enduring political force.[12] Concerned with sheer survival and possessing only limited horizons, most peasants enter the political process rarely or not at all. They must depend upon sympathetic brokers to transmit their concerns to those who control the resources they want; barring that, their only recourse is non-compliance or violence.

This is particularly true in China, where the peasants are now bonded to the land. Owning only a small percentage of the land they till, unable to move without a hard-to-obtain permit, forced to deposit savings in state-regulated credit cooperatives which restrict withdrawals, peasants are largely at the mercy of lower level Party and government bureaucrats.

But it is easy to underestimate the power of the peasant aggregate. China's rulers must be at least somewhat responsive to the demands of the peasants because of their numbers (roughly 80% of the population) and their economic importance. Roughly 35% to 45% of China's net domestic product, for example, comes from the agricultural sector, and the bulk of China's exports are agricultural and agriculturally derived products.[13]

The Cultural Revolution demonstrated that political power still was rooted to a considerable degree in control over the peasants and agricultural surpluses. The purges of Li Ching-ch'uan, the powerful Szechuan official, and T'ao Chu, the former Kwangtung official, show how these men were somewhat responsive to peasant demands in order to encourage the peasants to develop the potential of their areas. On the

[11] *China Topics,* YB 415, February 23, 1967, part III.

[12] See especially Eric Wolf, *Peasants,* Prentice Hall, 1966, p. 91; and Mehmet Bequirj, *Peasantry in Revoution,* Cornell, 1966, pp. 14–15.

[13] For summary discussions of the role of agriculture in the Chinese economy, see especially: Alexander Eckstein, *Communist China's Economic Growth and Foreign Trade,* McGraw-Hill, 1966, p. 47; Marion Larson, "China's Agriculture under Communism," in Joint Economic Committee of the United States Congress, *Economic Profile of Mainland China,* Government Printing Office, 1968, Vol. I, esp. p. 205; and Feng-hua Mah, "Public Investment in Communist China," *Journal of Asian Studies,* Vol. XXI, No. 1, November 1961, p. 46.

other hand, officials in grain-deficit areas, more dependent upon allocations from central government storehouses, were less able to resist Peking directives. Heilungkiang, Shantung, Shansi, Kweichow, Tsinghai, Peking, and Shanghai—all grain-deficit areas—were among the first to respond to Peking's call in early 1967 to establish Revolutionary Committees. (There undoubtedly were other reasons for their response.) Here are indications of the persistence in China of the intimate relationship between power and agriculture. The peasant has not yet lost his crucial role as a source of bureaucratic power.

Peasants During the Cultural Revolution. The course of the Cultural Revolution indicates that by 1967 even the radicals were somewhat sensitive to peasant needs. The two strongest efforts to subdue the Cultural Revolution came precisely at those moments when the peasants probably most desired order. Although earlier efforts had been made, the Red Guards were finally told to cease their marches and return home in early February 1967 on the eve of the spring planting. The PLA received more vigorous orders than usual to assist the peasants in spring planting. These February directives, coming on the heels of widespread signs of peasant unrest, were issued only 45 days after the December 15th directive extending the Cultural Revolution to the countryside.[14] This apparently calmer situation prevailed until early summer, when the turmoil increased. As the fall harvest neared, however, the Peking authorities again recognized the constraints imposed by China's essentially rural character; in late August and early September, they took stringent measures to control the Cultural Revolution.[15]

The peasant desire to be left alone was recognized in other ways. There is remarkably little evidence that the agitational activity which marked the Cultural Revolution in the urban areas spread to the countryside.[16] To judge from the provincial radio broadcasts, the main undertaking of the Cultural Revolution in the countryside was the propagation of Mao's thought, primarily through the organization of Mao-study groups. In spite of all the condemnations, there were very few reports of actual seizure of the private plots or restriction of free markets. The announcements of a good harvest in 1967 further reflected the fact that the Cultural Revolution essentially had by-passed the rural areas. In short, the evidence strongly suggests that the interests of the peasants elicit a response from China's rulers.

[14] *China Topics,* No. 415, February 23, 1967.

[15] Crucial here was Chiang Ch'ing's speech of September 5, 1967. An excellent summary of this period is in Chalmers Johnson, "China: The Cultural Revolution in Structural Perspective," op. cit., pp. 10–15.

[16] John R. Wenmohs, "Agriculture in Mainland China—1967," *Current Scene,* Vol. V, No. 21, December 15, 1967.

Industrial Managers and Industrial Workers

Since the divergent interests of industrial managers and workers are what strike most Americans, it is wise to recall their common interests in China. Both usually have a vested interest in uninterrupted production, in protecting factory equipment from damage, and in maintaining industrial prosperity and growth. In China, both have a vested interest in the evolving factory management system, in view of the welfare and housing benefits it bestows upon them. Moreover, the deep economic depression following the Great Leap very possibly had underscored to many the commonality of manager and worker interests in resisting attempts by other groups to intrude upon their domain. In spite of common interests, however, industrial manager and worker have rarely joined together to influence the course of Chinese politics.

Against this background, the events from December 1966 to February 1967 assume historical significance. They suggest that China's industrial sector has begun to come of political age. With a few exceptions, the industrial managers and workers, apparently acting in concert, resisted the efforts by parts of the bureaucracy and organized students to intrude upon areas they deemed to be their prerogatives. Within one month of the decision to extend the Cultural Revolution to the factories, the order was quietly but significantly tempered. If China's rulers had been unified in their support of the spread of the Cultural Revolution to the factories, the ability of the industrial managers and workers to temper its course would have been questionable. But the move was initiated only by a radical segment within the Party and government bureaucracy, who required student support. More noteworthy, the considerable opposition within the bureaucracy indicated that since the Great Leap, the industrial managers and workers had acquired strong allies among the top officials.

The exact story of industrial cities in late 1966 and early 1967 has yet to be told, but enough is known to warrant a brief description.[17] In the stormy period following the August 1966 Eleventh Plenum, the

[17] As a start, however, see: Evelyn Anderson, "Shanghai Upheaval," *Problems of Communism,* January-February, 1968, pp. 12–22; "Sources of Labor Discontent in China: The Worker Peasant System," *Current Scene,* Vol. VI, No. 5, March 15, 1968; Andrew Watson, "Cultural Revolution in Sian," *Far Eastern Economic Review,* April 20, 1967, April 27, 1967, and May 4, 1967; and Neale Hunter, "The Cultural Revolution in Shanghai," *Far Eastern Economic Review,* June 1, 1967, June 22, 1967, and July 6, 1967.

Red Guards were repeatedly told that they were not to enter factories without prior approval of the factory employees, nor to interfere with production. One of the strongest warnings came in a November 10, 1966, *People's Daily* editorial, which said,

> Revolutionary students should firmly believe that the worker and peasant masses are capable of making revolution and solving their problems by themselves. No one should do their work for them. Special attention must also be paid to preventing interference with production activities . . . from the outside.[18]

But by December 9, the earlier policy was reversed and a more radical policy was adopted; the Red Guards were encouraged to enter the factories. In early December, in contrast to the November 10th editorial, a Red Guard newspaper could state,

> Chairman Mao has taught us, 'The young intellectuals and young students of China must definitely go among the worker and peasant masses . . .' The cultural revolutionary movement must expand from the young people and students to the workers and peasants.[19]

The formal decision allowing the students to enter the factories, promulgated on December 9, was made public in the important *People's Daily* editorial of December 26th.[20]

Five days later, the annual *People's Daily* New Year editorial indicated that there was considerable opposition to the measure. The editorial stated, "Any argument against carrying out a large-scale cultural revolution in factories and mines and in rural areas is not correct."[21] According to the rules of Pekingology, this sentence indicates that a strong debate was being waged. Moreover, by mid-January it was clear that the industrial managers and workers were undermining the December 9th directive. Rather than allowing the Red Guards to enter the factories, which might have led to damage of equipment, the factory managers encouraged their employees to leave the factories and travel to Peking to voice their grievances. Factory managers paid bonuses to their workers, promoted many of them, and gave them travel fare. Protesting Red Guard activities, it appears, factory workers went on strike, probably living off the bonuses paid them by their factory managers.

[18] "More on the Question of Grasping the Revolution Firmly and Stimulating Production," *Jen-min Jih-pao* (People's Daily, henceforth, *JMJP*), November 22, 1966, in *Survey of the Chinese Mainland Press* (henceforth *SCMP*), No. 3825, pp. 1–4.
[19] JPRS 40, 274, p. 34.
[20] For another analysis, see *China News Analysis,* No. 644.
[21] *Peking Review,* No. 1, January 1, 1967, p. 12.

The joint activities of managers and workers, assisted by some Party and government bureaucrats, were described in an "Open Letter" which stated:

> In recent days . . . , a handful of freaks and monsters have cheated the misled . . . worker masses, to put forward many wage, welfare, and other economic demands to the leadership and administrative departments . . . These administrative departments and leaders, acceding to these demands and not caring whether it is in accord with state policy or not, sign their names to hand out generously a lot of state funds.[22]

Those who encouraged the workers to put forth their economic demands were accused of setting the "revolutionary workers movement onto the devious road of trade unionism."

The situation in Shanghai became particularly critical. The railroad network was partially paralyzed due to a high rate of employee absenteeism, with serious disruptions from December 27 to January 9. Public utility services in Shanghai were disrupted; shipping in the Shanghai harbor was adversely affected. Similar reports came from throughout the country. By mid-January, Radio Peking and the New China News Agency (NCNA) had reported instances of worker's strikes and sabotage in such major cities as Tientsin, Shenyang, Chengtu, Chungking, Sian, Canton, and Hangchow.

Within a month of the December 9th directive, the radical attack upon the industrial sector had produced near-chaos. The first response of the leaders of the radical Party and government bureaucrats and their Red Guard student supporters was to win allies among the workers and to encourage conflict between managers and workers. Special appeals were made to the temporary factory employees (factories have two types of employees on their pay roll—permanent employees, who are paid according to the set wage scale, receive fringe benefits, and have a regular rank; and temporary employees, who are employed on special contract, receive lower wages, and can be dismissed easily during a recession). To gain the favor of the temporary employees, the radicals blamed Liu Shao-ch'i for originating the temporary employee system. They implied that one of the purposes of the Cultural Revolution was to abolish the distinction between permanent and temporary labor. At the same time, the radicals attempted to isolate the factory managers from their worker allies. The managers were attacked as anti-Maoists; the workers were excused for being duped. A series of student-worker meetings was arranged to build good will.

The tacit alliance, particularly between managers and permanent

[22] Radio Foochow, January 9, 1967.

employees, held firm and the government had to take stringent measures to restore industrial production. On January 15, Chou En-lai cautioned the Red Guards against hasty action. He implied that the action in Shanghai was too rash, adding that "we must. . . . see to it that business organizations truly carry out business operations."[23] Two days later, the CCP Central Committee and State Council jointly issued regulations to strengthen urban public security work.[24] On January 28th, an article by Mao Tse-tung entitled "On Correcting Mistaken Ideas in the Party," stressing the virtues of discipline and order, was reprinted, while on the next day, the State Council prohibited industrial workers from visiting their rural ancestral homes during the Chinese New Year. The efforts to keep the workers in the city, to keep the chaos in the cities from spreading to the countryside, and to restore urban order were receiving primary attention. To win back the permanent employees, on February 17 the Central Committee and the State Council decided to retain the distinction between permanent and temporary workers.

The stringent measures did not produce immediate results. They were intended to restore the confidence of the industrial worker, but they did little to assuage the fears of the factory managers, former capitalists, trade union leaders, and economic planners. The industrial sector apparently did not begin to return to normal until these groups also were mollified. To restore industrial calm, the vehement charges of "economism" levelled against the industrial managers began to be dampened in February. The press concentrated its attack upon "anarchists," meaning the Red Guards who persisted in their attacks on managers. The slogan so prominent in December and early January, "To Rebel is Justified," gave way to expressions of concern for the sanctity of property.

In view of the tacit manager-worker alliance, and the initial attempts both to split this alliance and divide the workers, the CCP Central Committee letter of March 18 has very special importance. Addressed jointly to the industrial workers and their leaders, the document officially recognized their common interests. Extremely mild in tone, the letter represents an almost total abandonment of the policy outlined in the December 26, 1966 *People's Daily* editorial extending the Cultural Revolution to the factories. The support given to the factory managers in the March 18 directive is worth quoting:

> As masters of the country, all workers *and staff* in factories and mines must, in the course of the Cultural Revolution, heighten

[23] *SCMP*, No. 3913, p. 2.
[24] For texts, see *China Topics*, No. 418, March 8, 1967.

> their great sense of responsibility and protect State property effectively . . .
>
> The Party Central Committee believes that in all factories and mines, the majority of cadres are good or relatively good. (emphasis mine)[25]

The mere issuance of these instructions did not restore industrial peace. The PLA also was instructed to enter factories to maintain discipline.[26] Workers who had joined the radicals were difficult to control, and factional strife among workers was a frequent phenomenon. Reports of worker absenteeism persisted. The effort to put factory production on a firm footing remained an elusive goal for the rest of the year.

Although these developments were important, the main significance of the events in China's cities from December, 1966 to February, 1967 should not be lost. In the heat of the Cultural Revolution, the industrial managers and workers, acting together, were able to alter drastically the intended course of the Cultural Revolution. The working class and their managers have moved closer to the center of power in Chinese politics.

INTELLECTUALS

In the broadest terms, intellectuals have three tasks. First, they pass the values and accumulated knowledge from one generation to another. Second, they increase the sum total of knowledge and create new works of art. Third, intellectuals criticize the society in which they live and point out alternative ways of ordering their society. Intellectuals can be distinguished according to the relative emphasis they place upon these roles. Thus, the teacher primarily transmits the knowledge of his generation to his students. The nuclear physicist is responsible for providing new information. The political satirist criticizes his society.

Depending upon the values of the society and the demands of the most powerful groups in the political arena, the particular roles performed by intellectuals command somewhat different rewards.[27] The

[25] *SCMP*, No. 3904, p. 9.

[26] For more detailed chronology see *China Quarterly*, No. 30, pp. 209, 232–33.

[27] For a general discussion, see Edward Shils, "The Intellectuals in the Political Development of the New States," in John Kautsky, ed., *Political Change in Underdeveloped Countries*, John Wiley, 1962, pp. 195–235.

Cultural Revolution demonstrated the political value of each of these roles in China.

Social Critic. The social critic was totally vulnerable to political control, as the attacks upon Wu Han and the Three Family Village with which he was associated revealed. To recall briefly, the historian Wu Han wrote on the virtues of the Ming minister Hai Jui.[28] Hai Jui had criticized a Ming emperor's alleged neglect of the peasants, and was removed from office as a result. Mao Tse-tung and those around him charged that Wu Han was using the story of Hai Jui as an allegory to attack Mao and defend P'eng Ten-huai, the dismissed Minister of Defense who had also protested against his leader's peasant policy. Mao, in short, was able to remove Wu Han and others after demonstrating that they were playing the role of social critic. This is not surprising for a society in which the distinction between criticism and disloyalty has often been blurred.

Transmitters of Values and Knowledge. The Cultural Revolution also showed that the transmitters of values and knowledge serve at the pleasure of the dominant political groups. As Mao's earlier optimism about the fate of the communist revolution gave way to a more pessimistic appraisal, he became more concerned with the educational process. While optimistic, he could afford to be lenient toward the past, for he believed China would not remain its captive. Later, the accumulated knowledge of the past and those who propagated it became threatening.

Several factors help to explain the political weakness of the propagandists, teachers, artists, and other transmitters of culture and knowledge. First, they had no economic allies, for few people's livelihoods depended upon them. Second, they were divided internally. Some younger "transmitters," such as the ideologues who came to the fore in late 1966—Wang Li, Yao Wen-yuan, Ch'i Pen-yu, and Kuan Feng—apparently were ready to assist in the removal of their superiors. Third, many "transmitters" had strong enemies among their students. Initially, the weight of tradition and knowledge and its concommitant responsibilities rests heavy upon students, and they tend to resent those who place it upon them. Students therefore were ready allies of the political groups who attacked the propagandists and teachers.

[28] For the editorials attacking Wu Han and the Three Family Village, see *The Great Socialist Cultural Revolution in China,* Peking: Foreign Language Press, 1966–67, 1–3. A collection of the satires attacking Mao, which appeared in the Peking Press in the early 1960's was reprinted in Taiwan: *Teng T'o shih-wen hsuan-ch'i,* Taipei: Freedom Press, 1966.

Researchers. At the very moment the critics were condemned and the teachers were attacked, the press pointedly praised other intellectuals for developing nuclear weaponry, synthesizing insulin, and improving medical techniques.[29] The increasing importance of China's scientific community enables this segment of the intellectuals to exert its claims. A reasonable assumption is that many scientists are willing to recognize the supremacy of any political leader, so long as they are able to pursue their intellectual interests. This seems to be the tacit bargain struck during the Cultural Revolution. In the 1966–67 reports of their work, scientists always paid homage to the inspiration they derived from Chairman Mao. In exchange, Mao appears to have made fewer demands upon the time of scientists during this campaign than he did during the Great Leap Forward. For example, the twelfth point of the Sixteen Point Central Committee Directive on the Cultural Revolution specifically exempted the scientists, stating:

> As regards scientists, technicians, and ordinary members of working staffs, as long as they are patriotic, work energetically, are not against the Party and socialism, and maintain no illicit relations with any foreign country, we should in the present movement continue to apply the policy of "unity, criticism, unity." Special care should be taken of those scientists and scientific and technical personnel who have made contributions.[30]

Among China's intellectuals, the scientists fared best in 1966–67. Unlike peasants, industrial managers, or workers, who were able to defend their interests only after an initial attack against them, the scientists saw their interests taken into account *prior* to the Cultural Revolution. Since their role in China's industrialization effort is valued by other groups in society, they appear to have representation at the center of power.

MILITARY

To appreciate the power and influence of the military in Chinese society, one must understand the position of the PLA during the Cultural Revolution. While most analysts agree that the PLA played a crucial role in 1966–67, they differ in their evaluations.

[29] *Peking Review,* No. 1, January 1, 1967, p. 15.
[30] *Peking Review,* No. 33, August 12, 1966, p. 10.

The PLA Rise to Power. Some analysts stated that the military had taken over. Impressive evidence exists to support this contention. PLA units were dispatched to factories and schools, where the troop commanders assumed important leadership functions. The PLA, already deeply immersed in such tasks as running the railroads and organizing propaganda prior to the Cultural Revolution, increased its responsibilities in these vital areas. When one looked at the top official in each of the provinces, one found that although a few of the new and surviving officials had careers within the CCP, most were former military officers. Some of them, such as Li Yuan in Hunan or Li Ts'ai-han in Kweichow, had risen from obscurity; their names were not listed in the standard biographic guides to China's leaders. In Peking, the national holidays were presided over by military men. Newspaper editorials throughout 1967 stressed the crucial role performed by the PLA in society. In 1967, Mao's closest comrade-in-arms and his likely successor was said to be the Minister of Defense and head of the Military Affairs Committee, Lin Piao. The nationally debated issues reflected the concerns of the military apparatus: the amount of time the army should spend in physical training versus the amount of time spent on the study of Mao's works, the role of the PLA troops stationed in factories and schools, the relations between the military and other sectors of society, the obligations of the regional garrison commanders to obey the center, and even the role of the navy in domestic peace keeping functions. When the leaders of the country are drawn from the military, when the issues debated in the press are of particular relevance to the military, and when the military stationed its troops in non-military units throughout the country, the evidence strongly suggests that a military takeover occurred.

Moreover, there were signs that the rise of the PLA was the result of a conscious rivalry with the CCP. The PLA had intimate organizational links with the Red Guards, who led the attacks upon the CCP apparatus. One of the key Red Guard units, for example, came from the Peking Aviation Institute, a school with close PLA connections. Some Red Guard newspapers also spoke of an organizational rivalry between the Party and the PLA. For instance, the Ministry of Railways and the PLA shared jurisdiction over the railways. The Minister of Railways, Lu Cheng-ts'ao, was accused of wanting to control the armed railroad personnel, who were under PLA command. Lu allegedly maintained:

> The Public Security Ministry controls its own public security forces. Why shouldn't the Railway Ministry control railway forces?[31]

[31] JPRS 41, 249, June 2, 1967, pp. 46–67.

Lu was accused of "wanting to usurp the power and authority of the PLA."

Invective in a similar vein had been directed earlier against Teng T'o, the dismissed editor of *Peking Daily:*

> We must warn Teng T'o and his ilk that the right to 'contend' is not allowed in the PLA, and the fighters of the people will wipe out those who dare to stick their nose into the army under the pretext of contention.[32]

These quotes hinting at a possible PLA-CCP rivalry lend weight to an interpretation of the Cultural Revolution that stresses a PLA takeover from the Party.

On the other hand, several factors made it misleading simply to state that the military seized power in China. First, the military apparatus in China lacked clear cut organizational identity and was thoroughly interwoven with the CCP. The commanders of the PLA who acquired power in 1967 probably were also CCP members. The rise to power of PLA commanders can be seen as a shift in the balance of power within the Party, with CCP members serving in the military sector taking power from those in charge of such internal Party work as organization and propaganda.

Second, not all elements in the military enhanced their position in 1966–67. In fact, many leaders of the PLA were purged. The most noteworthy cases included the dismissals of Chief-of-Staff Lo Jui-ch'ing, the head of the Political Department, Hsiao Hua, and Marshal Ho Lung, but the purge extended to garrison commanders, department heads, political commissars, and others.[33] If one is to speak in organizational terms, one cannot speak of a PLA takeover; one must speak of the seizure of power by specific units within the PLA. But here, no discernible pattern emerges, although there are some tantalizing hints. For instance, in recent years three newly appointed regional commanders came from the Shenyang garrison command,[34] Kiangsi province was occupied during the Cultural Revolution by troops dispatched from the Tsinan garrison command,[35] and the Wuhan rebellion was quelled, in part, through the dispatch from Shanghai of a naval force attached to the East China fleet.[36] A hypothesis that merits testing is that several army, navy, and air commands (such as Shenyang and Tsinan), perhaps owing allegiance to Lin Piao, acted together, that forces from these units occupied various areas, and that the newly risen military per-

[32] Radio Peking, May 24, 1966.
[33] In *China News Summary,* Nos. 188–94.
[34] Ibid.
[35] Radio Nanchang, September 6, 1967 and October 9, 1967.
[36] Radio Wuhan, October 22, 1967.

sonnel were drawn primarily from these units. But until firm evidence is uncovered, such hypotheses must be held in abeyance. Thus, the unqualified assertion that the PLA had risen to power glosses over the difficult yet crucial problem of a complex process within the PLA which led to the promotion of some and the purge of other military figures.

A third reason that the image of a "military takeover" needs qualification was its incompleteness. Many government and Party officials, even at higher levels, survived. Hunan provides a convenient example. Li Yuan and PLA unit 6900, which had been garrisoned in Hengyang, began to dominate news items from Ch'angsha. But Li appears to be the leader of a group that includes Hua Kuo-feng and Chang Po-sen, both of whom have long records of leadership in Party and government affairs in Hunan. Hua was First Secretary of Hsiang-t'an Special District in Hunan in the early 1950's, served as head of the provincial government's Culture and Education Office and the Party's United Front Department in the late 1950's, and was an active Party secretary and Vice Governor in the early 1960's. Chang's tenure in Hunan also dates back to the early 1950's, when he was head of the Provincial Party Finance and Trade Department. The Hunan pattern was observable elsewhere. Leaders of the PLA won positions of power, but their rise was not accompanied by the total removal of leading government and Party bureaucrats.

A fourth consideration against labelling the enhanced power of the military as a "takeover" was the noticeable reluctance of some military leaders to assume their new roles in domestic affairs. Military commanders in China were concerned with the capacity of their forces to fight against foreign powers. As the PLA became increasingly involved with domestic functions in the 1960's, of necessity it sacrificed some of its capacity to wage war. Lo Jui-ch'ing apparently was one of the officials opposed to the policy. Moreover, since the PLA automatically created enemies when it tried to restore order between conflicting groups and individuals, local commanders were reluctant to become involved. If the PLA intervened on the side of one Red Guard organization, the other side became disenchanted. If the PLA tried to work out compromises, then the organizations accused the PLA of not settling the dispute on the basis of principles. During the early part of 1967, many PLA commanders apparently tried to shield their units from the turmoil, but the spreading chaos could be dampened only through military intervention. To a certain extent, it was less that the PLA eagerly seized power than that it reluctantly filled an organizational vacuum.

Sources of PLA Power. Even with these qualifications, it remains true that the PLA significantly increased its power and influence. Part of the explanation for this rests in Mao's confidence in Lin Piao and the PLA, a confidence inspired by the political program carried out in the army from 1959 to 1965. Because the PLA stood apart from civilian society, ideological indoctrination probably could be carried out more effectively in the PLA than in other institutions in society. The effectiveness of the program in the PLA led Mao, who perhaps failed to discern the inherent differences between military and non-military organizations, to display impatience with the comparatively inefficient indoctrination efforts undertaken by the Party propagandists in civilian society, and to replace them with PLA personnel.

Another factor involved in the rise of the military was a personnel policy which enabled it to retain its vigor and extend its influence. Whereas other organizations in Chinese society frequently lacked institutionalized retirement processes, had aged leaders, and suffered from clogged channels of upward mobility, the PLA was able to transfer its older and less competent members to non-military organizations. Not only did the transfer of veterans to positions in government, Party, and industry enable the PLA to solve its own internal problems of mobility and retirement, but it also meant that the PLA saturated the non-military organizations with men whose loyalties may in part have belonged to the military.

A further reason for the rise of the PLA was the increased importance of the foreign and domestic functions it performs. In foreign affairs, the leaders of China believed themselves to be encircled by hostile powers. They give primacy to the acquisition of a nuclear capability. In the tense situation of the mid-1960's in East Asia, with problems of national defense a prime concern, it was perhaps natural that military men came to play a more vital role in national politics.

Domestically, although firm documentation is lacking, it appears that the rulers increasingly had to rely on coercive means to control the population. As their ability to elicit a mass response through idealistic appeals diminished and their initial wide-spread support waned, the leaders administered a more harsh criminal law. With the population growth and the possibly growing gap between urban and rural living standards, the rulers had to exercise increasingly stringent control over population movements. In 1966–67, the situation became acute, and force of arms became a major way of restoring law and order. Those who wielded the instruments of coercion, people associated with the PLA and the public security forces, rose to power as the demand for their skills increased.

Yet another source of military power was its control of rail, air, and major river transport, giving its members and their allies a mobility which people in other organizations lacked. During the rapidly evolving political situation in 1966–67, access to air transport proved especially important. Chou En-lai, for example, was able at several crucial junctures to fly to trouble spots to negotiate or mediate disputes. In other instances, key groups were flown to Peking. One day after the May 6th incident in Chengtu, for instance, several of those involved were already in Peking to discuss the Szechuan situation with Chou, Ch'en Po-ta, K'ang Sheng, and Chiang Ch'ing. Further, to communicate their message to the peasants, perhaps indicating an inability to use a recalcitrant propaganda apparatus, the leadership airdropped leaflets to peasants in Kwangsi and Hupeh province in the spring.[37]

An additional reason for the enhanced power of military personnel may have been their relative self-sufficiency. In contrast to members of other hierarchies, their organization produced a considerable portion of the goods they consumed. Moreover, the PLA had an important role in directing the machine-building industries, the mining and extractive industries, and the agricultural reclamation projects in China's border provinces. When production and delivery schedules fell behind, as happened in early 1967, the army may have been in a better position to sustain itself. (This observation, however, is a logical inference rather than an adequately documented conclusion.)

In sum, the principal reasons for the rise of the PLA were similar to those for the increased importance of the military in many of the economically developing countries.[38] It won the confidence of the national leader. It stood somewhat isolated from society, thereby retaining a vigor and *élan* which the CCP inevitably lost when it became so involved in societal affairs that its parts came to represent particular interests. The post-service affiliations of former military personnel enabled the PLA to extend its influence to other organizations. Its control of resources enabled it to have an independent base of power. Because the PLA and the public security forces were the coercive agents of the ruler, these organizations came to the fore as the maintenance of the state increasingly rested upon coercion. Moreover, since the reasons for their rise are likely to persist, military personnel seem destined to be at the center of Chinese politics for the foreseeable future.

Conclusion

The power and influence of the major occupational groupings in Chinese society, as revealed in the Cultural Revolution, can now be

[37] Radio Wuhan, March 8, 1967; Radio Nanning, February 28, 1967.

[38] See, for example, Lucian Pye, "Armies in the Process of Political Development," in his *Aspects of Political Development,* Little, Brown, 1966, pp. 172–87.

briefly summarized. The peasants influenced policy indirectly; their interests were voiced by sympathetic government and Party bureaucrats and the military leaders. The top policy formulators tried to anticipate peasant reactions primarily because of their economic importance.

In one of the significant aspects of the Cultural Revolution, the industrial managers and the industrial workers displayed their power to act swiftly and to affect policies ruinous to their interests. Members of these occupational groups appear to be acquiring increased power as China industrializes.

Intellectuals, increasingly differentiated in the roles they perform, differed in their ability to alter policy affecting them. Social critics were totally vulnerable to control, and teachers were shown basically to serve at the pleasure of the ruler. Scientific and technical personnel, however, saw their interests taken into account, particularly if they were engaged in research that gained them firm supporters among the military.

The students demonstrated that, when allied with elements of the bureaucracy and the military, they could become a powerful force, but that without allies, they were unable to remain a politically dominant group. Nonetheless, a study of youth suggests that their problems demand urgent attention, and for this reason their demands probably will elicit a continued response from those at the center of power.

Though many government and Party bureaucrats were purged, they displayed their ability to survive as an occupational group at the center of power. Their functions proved vital; moreover, they had learned some of the tactics necessary to defend their interests.

Finally, members of the military apparatus moved to the very center of power during the Cultural Revolution. An analysis of the sources of their power and influence indicates that their importance will persist.

This summary, however, has several limitations which should be made explicit. The occupational groups analyzed are broadly defined; in reality, each category includes many kinds of positions. For example, instead of analyzing Party and government bureaucrats as one group, a more rigorous analysis would examine the interests and power of the bureaucrats in the various functional systems into which the Party and government were divided; finance and trade, agriculture, forestry, and water conservancy, industry and communications, culture and education, law enforcement, and so on. A more rigorous analysis of industrial workers would distinguish among skilled and unskilled workers in large, medium, and small factories. Their attitudes and ability to affect public policy were probably different.

In addition, this paper's exclusive focus upon occupational groups neglects other important ways of subdividing the population, such as into geographical, attitudinal, ethnic, or class groups. Indeed, one would gain considerable insight into Chinese politics by asking the question:

What does the Cultural Revolution tell us about the relative power and influence of people in different geographic areas in China? Moreover, there is considerable evidence that conflict within the occupational groups was often based upon class and status groups. Among students, apparently, conflict sometimes broke out between children of cadres and children from less favored backgrounds. (The important United Action Red Guards, for instance, reportedly drew its strength from the children of cadres.) The conflict between the permanent and temporary workers was a struggle between two classes. Conflict between bureaucrats often involved disputes between high-ranking and low-ranking cadres. The pro-Maoist leaders apparently tended to draw strong support from the lower classes and status groups, a facet of the Cultural Revolution that does not become clear if one focuses solely upon occupational groups.

Moreover, the Cultural Revolution provides a narrow and unusual time span from which to view the interests and power of occupational groups. They were able to act upon their interests, in part, because of the diminished capacity of the elite to provide effective leadership. (One reason for their reduced capacity, however, was the increased ability of occupational groups to defend their interests. The two phenomena were inter-related.) If the rulers recapture their former strength, or if they resort to different techniques in order to elicit a response (for example, an increased use of material incentives), then the interests and abilities of various groups to affect policy will change.

Finally, another limitation of the exclusive focus upon group interests and power is its neglect of other important subjects, such as the role of ideas. A satisfactory explanation for the persistence of radical thought in China, so crucial for an understanding of the Cultural Revolution, must go beyond an analysis of student radicalism and the interests of occupational groups, for the radicals were found among all of them.[39] Ultimately, for a thorough understanding of Chinese politics one must integrate group analysis with an analysis of the leaders and the culture and ideas that move them.

In spite of these limitations, however, occupational group analysis enables one to approach China from a fresh vantage point. Transitory factors affecting Chinese politics, such as the power of a particular individual, factional rivalries, or a war on China's border, are blotted out in order to highlight more permanent developments. A clearer picture emerges of the occupational groups that will exercise the greatest demands upon the top leaders, no matter who those leaders might be.

[39] For sensitive studies of some of the sources of radicalism, see Maurice Meisner, *Li Ta-chao and the Origins of Chinese Marxism,* Harvard University Press, 1967, and Olga Lang, *Pa Chin and His Writings,* Harvard University Press, 1967.

This study suggests that in the years ahead, China's leaders will confront several occupational groups that will effectively articulate their interests: the military personnel, the government and Party bureaucrats, and increasingly, the industrial managers and workers. Moreover, the leaders will have to pay urgent attention to the problems of students, and respond to the demands of scientists and technicians. They will face considerable constraints in formulating their policies toward the peasants. It is highly likely that Chinese politics is moving into an era marked by intense bargaining between a weakened central leadership, its authority seriously eroded during the Cultural Revolution, and powerful occupational groups. The leaders will not be in an enviable position, as they attempt to reconcile and mediate the conflicting demands made by these groups.

BUREAUCRACY AND INTEREST GROUPS IN COMMUNIST SOCIETIES: THE CASE OF CZECHOSLOVAKIA*

Andrzej Korbonski

THE dramatic changes which took place in the Communist world after the death of Stalin in 1953 emphasized the need to move away from the narrow confines of area studies dominated, on the one hand, by the totalitarian syndrome developed by Friedrich and Brzezinski, and, on the other, by demonology practiced by the whole host of Kremlinologists, Sovietologists, and various other assorted experts on Communism—Soviet, Chinese and East European.

In the course of the last fifteen years it began to dawn upon some of the most perceptive authorities in the field that the traditional approach to Communist studies, characterized by the overconcentration on legal-institutional research and current events, has been yielding diminishing returns. The rapidly growing differentiation of Communist political systems put a question mark on the validity and usefulness of the totalitarian model based on the assumption of the monolithic character of Communist nation-states. Indeed, it may be argued that the model itself was developed at the moment when it no longer applied to the study of Communist societies, and that, however useful from the heuristic point of view, it bore little relation to reality. There is little wonder, then, that, beginning in the early 1960s, we have been witnessing the appearance of books, articles and papers challenging the utility of the traditional methodology and trying to come up with some alternative approaches. The movement in that direction was spearheaded by some

From *Studies in Comparative Communism,* IV, 1 (January 1971). Reprinted with permission of the author and the editor.

* Research for this article was conducted in Czechoslovakia during the academic year 1966–67 under the auspices of the Inter-University Committee on Travel Grants whose assistance is hereby gratefully acknowledged. The preliminary version of the article was presented at the meeting of the Western Political Science Association in Honolulu in April 1969.

of the best-known authorities in the field and that in itself helped to initiate a discussion concerning the future of Communist studies.

United in their dislike of the traditional approach each of them, however, went his separate way in trying to develop an alternative model. John Kautsky, interested mostly in political development and modernization, emphasized the sterility of the distinction between Communist and nationalist models of development.[1] Alfred Meyer, long unhappy with some if not all of the variables of the Friedrich-Brzezinski syndrome, suggested an alternative in the form of the bureaucratic model.[2] Robert Tucker, if I read him correctly, leaned somewhat toward Kautsky in trying to synthesize the traditionally distinct models of nondemocratic systems under the heading of "revolutionary mass movement regimes."[3] Finally, Gordon Skilling, influenced no doubt by developments in Eastern Europe, advocated the use of the group-theory approach to the study of Communist systems.[4]

It should not surprise us that in view of the thought-provoking and challenging nature of these contributions they should have met with considerable reaction, both positive and negative. Thus Richard Lowenthal, while accepting a number of Kautsky's insights concerning modernization, criticized him for equating Communism with nationalism in underdeveloped countries and for the near-abandonment of ideology as a significant variable in the Communist model of development.[5] Meyer's preference for the bureaucratic model of developed Communist polities, which, by the way, also emphasized the demise of ideology, was challenged by Brzezinski and, more recently, by Paul Hollander.[6]

[1] John H. Kautsky, "An Essay in the Politics of Development," in the collection edited by himself, *Political Change in Underdeveloped Countries* (New York, 1961); also his "Communism and the Comparative Study of Development," *Slavic Review,* Vol. XXVI, No. 1, March 1967, and the collection of essays, *Communism and the Politics of Development* (New York, 1968).

[2] Alfred G. Meyer, "USSR, Incorporated," *Slavic Review,* Vol. XX, No. 3, October 1961, and "The Comparative Study of Communist Political Systems," ibid., Vol. XXVI, No. 1, March 1967.

[3] Robert C. Tucker, "Towards a Comparative Politics of Movement-Regimes," *The American Political Science Review,* Vol. LV, No. 2, June 1961.

[4] H. Gordon Skilling, "Interest Groups and Communist Politics," *World Politics,* Vol. XVIII, No. 3, April 1966.

[5] Richard Lowenthal, "Communism and Nationalism," *Problems of Communism,* Vol. XI, No. 6, November-December 1962.

[6] Zbigniew Brzezinski, "Reply," *Slavic Review,* Vol. XX, No. 3, October 1961: Paul Hollander, "Observations on Bureaucracy, Totalitarianism, and the Comparative Study of Communism," ibid, Vol. XXVI, No. 2, June 1967.

Skilling's suggestion that the group-theory approach might be exploited profitably in analyzing Communist systems was brilliantly criticized by Andrew Janos, who felt that incipient pluralism in some Communist states was largely meaningless as a researchable category and that the application of the group approach, which, after all, was developed for the study of genuinely pluralistic societies, had little or no validity in this particular case.[7]

The discussion summarized above represented a very important step forward in the direction of instilling new life into the field of Communist studies which have long been suffering from stagnation, ossification, and parochialism. Of course, the wholesale criticism of the traditional methodology contained the proverbial danger of throwing out the child together with the bath. Still, the time has obviously come to take a look at some of the aspects of Communist politics which have been largely ignored or neglected until recently.

There is little doubt that many Communist political systems have been changing in a more or less dramatic fashion. Without going into the causes of these changes it is also clear that among the outcomes of these changes probably the most revealing were the gradual decline of the role of ideology and the emergence of a certain degree of pluralism. The former process has been reflected most visibly in the thoroughgoing bureaucratization of Communist systems, and the latter in the growing role and importance of interest or pressure groups. It ought to be stressed that neither the bureaucracy nor the interest groups represent the "ideal types" that one learns about from textbooks in Comparative Government. Still, they seem to exhibit, at least in my opinion, a number of characteristics common to groups and bureaucracies across the full spectrum of political systems. For that reason alone Skilling's suggestion to take a look at the group-theory approach appears to be well taken and the same applies to Meyer's bureaucratic model which offers an interesting object of study and research.

In order to move in the direction of analyzing bureaucratic and group behavior one should keep in mind the various caveats mentioned by the critics of the new approach. Regardless of the dramatic changes in some of them, the Communist societies are still largely idiosyncratic. Even though some of them reached a fairly impressive level of economic development, it does not follow that they were about to abandon some

[7] Andrew Janos, "Group Politics in Communist Society: A Second Look at the Pluralistic Model," (Paper presented at a meeting of the Project on Comparative Study of Communist Societies, University of California, Berkeley, March 1968).

of their peculiar features making them subject to Lipset's dictum concerning preconditions for a democracy. "Convergence theory" appears to have been successfully buried by Huntington and Brzezinski and the worst that could happen would be to resurrect it in the name of modernizing and integrating Communist studies with the rest of the discipline.

This article is an attempt to suggest some of the possible fields of research. It is restricted to only one country—Czechoslovakia—and it deals with the relationship between interest groups and bureaucracy, using the Czechoslovak economic reforms of 1964–67 as a case study. Its main purpose is, first, to come up with some factual information; secondly, to test in a highly preliminary fashion some of the hypotheses concerning bureaucratic and group behavior; and thirdly, to suggest possibilities for further research in that particular area.

Until very recently the existing literature dealing with East European political systems contained little or no discussion of bureaucracy and group representation. Most of the studies utilized the traditional country-by-country approach, emphasizing historical and institutional aspects of each state. To a large extent the form of the analysis was based on the standard model for viewing the Soviet society on the presumption that bureaucracy and the broadly defined groups—Party, the military, the secret police, and management—behaved in roughly the same fashion throughout the Communist camp. Only in the most recent period two authors, Gordon Skilling and Ghita Ionescu, made a valiant effort to depart from the traditional scheme by including in their repective studies an interesting discussion of groups and bureaucracies.[8] Otherwise, with the exception of Carl Beck's article in La Palombara's volume on bureaucracy and political development and a number of papers presented at various meetings, the cupboard was largely bare.[9]

The discussion that follows is based on interviews and research conducted in Czechoslovakia during the academic year 1966–67, ending some six months prior to the Prague "spring" of 1968. The main topic of my research concerned the preparations for, and implementation of, Czechoslovak economic reforms beginning in early 1964, which reached their peak in 1966–67.

[8] H. Gordon Skilling, *The Governments of Communist East Europe* (New York, 1966); and Ghita Ionescu, *The Politics of the European Communist States* (New York, 1967).

[9] Carl Beck, "Bureaucracy and Political Development in Eastern Europe," in Joseph LaPalombara, ed., *Bureaucracy and Political Development* (Princeton, 1963).

Supremacy of Ideology

Surprising as it may seem today, there is little doubt that by the time of Stalin's death Czechoslovakia had gone much farther than any other East European country in adopting and absorbing the Soviet political and economic model. Indeed, it may be argued that Czechoslovakia, perhaps even more so than the Soviet Union, provided a perfect illustration of the Friedrich-Brzezinski syndrome. Probably no other country in the Soviet bloc managed to elevate the official ideology to a position of absolute supremacy. Ideological considerations played a major role in just about every aspect of public and private life, penetrating into every corner of human activity. Among other things, they were responsible for the complete elimination of the private sector in the economy, something that even the Soviet Union hesitated to do, not to mention such otherwise orthodox stalwarts as Bulgaria and East Germany. It was ideology which was constantly invoked to justify a somewhat crude class struggle conducted along classic lines against the bourgeoisie and the intelligentsia, reaching extremes unheard of elsewhere in the bloc. The near-destruction of the Catholic church and of other religious bodies could also be traced to the doctrine. Finally, the educational system, especially in the field of social sciences, went much further than in the neighboring countries in imposing the ideological stamp on all phases of the learning process.

The second variable in the totalitarian syndrome, the Communist Party, also more than fulfilled the requirements of the model. Even though the Party accounted for a somewhat larger percentage of the total population than that suggested by Friedrich and Brzezinski, in every other respect it represented the ideal type. A series of purge trials, more frequent and wider in scope than in other East European countries, eliminated all vestiges of potential opposition within the Party, making it an obedient instrument in the hands of First Secretary Novotny and his clique. Party membership was a *sine qua non* of any advancement up the political, economic and social ladder. The degree of bureaucratization and centralization reached a very high level indeed and the Party bureaucrats dominated thoroughly the conventional government apparatus.

The National Front, the standard arrangement in all East European systems, included also two satellite parties—the Social Democrats and the People's Party—which acted as the transmission belts. The trade unions performed the traditional task of mobilizing the working class for the fulfillment of plans. Finally, the urban and rural youth were enrolled in the Czechoslovak Youth Association, which in addition to a massive indoctrination campaign kept supplying the already almost all-embracing Party with new members.

The reign of terror also reached impressive heights especially when compared with the rest of the bloc. Judging by the articles which appeared in the Czechoslovak press in the period between March and August 1968 and which dealt with the hitherto highly secret aspects of the Stalinist and early post-Stalinist era, the power of the secret police was probably greater than in the rest of the Communist camp with the possible exception of the Soviet Union. Moreover, it lasted considerably longer. Whereas the execution of Beria in 1953 and Khrushchev's condemnation of the rule of terror in his address to the Twentieth Congress of the CPSU in 1956 resulted in immediate repercussions throughout the bloc, Czechoslovakia proved to be the significant exception until the early 1960s when, finally, political prisoners began to be released and rehabilitated. The characteristic feature of the reign of terror was its highly ideological character which, combined with the typical arbitrary nature of secret-police operating procedures, resulted in terroristic campaigns directed against selected social groups. Family background and social origin became the criteria of political reliability.

Control over mass media and over the armed forces was also nearly complete. Before the mid 1960s Czechoslovak censorship was probably stricter than that in other Communist countries. One look at the quality of Czechoslovak books, newspapers, periodicals, films and plays was enough to convince one of the highly rigid and orthodox nature of Party controls. Again, as in the case of the secret police, these controls managed largely to survive the thaw which accompanied de-Stalinization after 1956. The same was true for the armed forces, which had been thoroughly purged, Sovietized and dominated by a Moscow-trained officer corps.

The final variable of the totalitarian model—the control over the economy—was perhaps more fully implemented than the remaining ones. In its zeal for ideological purity the Czechoslovak Party was highly successful in imposing the Stalinist model on the economy. Private enterprise was wiped out completely, especially in the non-agricultural sectors, and replaced by a centralized system of planning and controls. Collectivization of agriculture proceeded at a rapid pace and it was accomplished considerably ahead of the rest of the bloc with the exception of Bulgaria. The central planning apparatus was all-embracing, imitating to an iota the Soviet system.

Thus to an outside observer Czechoslovakia in the late 1950s represented an almost perfect illustration of the totalitarian model. The strength and pervasive nature of the system were best reflected in its ability to survive unscathed the 1956 crisis which shook the foundation of the monolithic bloc. It also helps to explain the fact that democratization of the Czechoslovak system came considerably later than elsewhere and that once it began it reached revolutionary proportions.

This is not the place to analyze in detail the gradual demise of the totalitarian rule in Czechoslovakia. There is little doubt that one of the major contributory factors was the state of the economy which by the mid 1960s necessitated the introduction of reforms aimed at a major transformation of the economic system. The reforms could not be contained within the framework of purely economic prescriptions and adjustments and, in the classical Marxist sense, spilled over into the political arena. This process of spillover is one of the most fascinating topics of research, fully deserving a major study of its own. The purpose of this paper is much more modest and it concerns only the way in which economic reforms in Czechoslovakia emerged as the result of the interaction between interest groups and bureaucracy.

To put the problem in its proper perspective it is necessary to provide a background for the reforms. The peculiarity of the Czechoslovak situation lay in the fact that in contrast to most of the other East European countries, the Czechoslovak economy was relatively well developed on the eve of the Communist takeover. Consequently, when the Stalinist economic model, intended for an underdeveloped country, was applied with a vengeance to a mature economic system, the results were predictable, and by the mid 1950s it became obvious even to the most die-hard believers in the universal applicability of Soviet model that something had to be done in order to put the economy back on its feet.

The outcome was a series of economic reforms introduced in 1958. Their purpose was threefold: organizational changes in industry; reduction in the number of obligatory success indicators; and improvement in the system of incentives. The interesting feature of the reforms was the fact that they were imposed from above without much prior discussion, and that they represented a mixture of centralizing and decentralizing measures. The organizational changes in industry consisted of a reduction in the number of independent state enterprises which were to be merged into a considerably smaller number of larger units. As such this particular measure represented an increase in the degree of monopolization and administrative concentration. It clearly expanded the power of bureaucracy especially at the higher, ministerial level. The second measure, which reduced the number of binding indicators, offset to some extent the former by giving greater authority to individual managers insofar as the planning of output was concerned. The same applied to the decentralization of investment decisions. The final reform, that of the incentives system, also strengthened the authority of the managers by granting them some say in financial matters.

COMMAND ECONOMY AND THE 1958 REFORMS

It may be said of the 1958 reform that by and large the power of the center, i.e., of the bureaucracy, remained largely unimpaired. To be sure, the bureaucrats lost some of their authority especially with regard to the fixing of the output targets and financial indicators but they retained and possibly even expanded their general control over industry, which became even more concentrated and centralized than before. The "command economy" continued to exist and, if anything, it got stronger as time went by and the economic situation began to deteriorate.

In 1963 and 1964 Czechoslovakia experienced an almost classic economic depression. The overambitious plan targets, extremely poor coordination between the center and the enterprise managers, poor harvest, severe drought and the stoppage of the very profitable China trade combined to bring the economy to the brink of a very serious crisis. It was clear that the 1958 reforms not only did not provide the required stimulus but, on the contrary, contributed to the difficulties. The reforms were clearly dysfunctional and it was only a matter of time before the old centralized system was reimposed.

It is probably true to say that the years 1963–64 represented a watershed in recent Czechoslovak history. The economic crisis and its gravity were apparently totally unexpected and shook the confidence of the highest Party organs. Even before the crisis it became clear that the relative position of the country within the bloc, characterized by relatively high living standards, also showed signs of decline and other countries such as East Germany, Hungary, and Poland began to catch up with their prosperous neighbor. Finally, the depression came fresh on the heels of the second de-Stalinization campaign decreed by Khrushchev at the Twenty-second Congress of the CPSU in October 1961. All of this combined to put the conservative Party leadership on the defensive for the first time since Novotny took over the reins from Gottwald in 1953.

The result was a rather striking change in the seemingly unassailable character of the totalitarian model. The Party leadership was forced by implication to admit serious errors in its economic policy. The power of the secret police, the crucial variable of the system, was greatly reduced. Political prisoners, many of them kept in jail since the late 1940s, were released and rehabilitated. Most of them were readmitted into the Party, creating a potentially dangerous nucleus of future opposition. The absolute Party control over the mass media also showed signs of weakening and in at least one case the press campaign contributed to the dismissal of one of the most highly discredited paragons of the Stalinist era. The economic failures also hurt the central bureaucracy, responsible for faulty economic planning. Furthermore, perhaps most significantly, the new atmosphere was reflected in the emergence of strong pluralistic tendencies in Czechoslovak society spearheaded by the intelligentsia, no longer the main target of the rule of terror.

On the eve of the discussions of the impending economic reforms in early 1964, the situation among the main protagonists in the debate was as follows. The bureaucracy—especially that connected with the Planning Commission, the economic ministries and government committees, and the Central Committee apparatus dealing with economic matters—was still powerful despite the setback caused by the 1963–64 crisis. As such it came close to the standard model of Communist bureaucracy so ably presented by Meyer and others. Inherently conservative and opposed to change, it frowned upon any experiments. It firmly believed that it possessed a monopoly of all wisdom and treated all other groups in society with contempt, refusing, at least initially, to take them seriously as partners in the discussions. Initially highly permeated with virulent ideology, by the mid 1960s its philosophy could be summed up in the relatively simple principle of "don't rock the boat." Politically it was firmly committed to the maintenance of the status quo accompanied by an occasional opening up of safety valves to let off the discontent of certain groups. By and large it proved to be quite adaptable to changing circumstances, delaying de-Stalinization as long as possible and then implementing it without the serious upheavals so characteristic of similar changes in the other bloc members.

Undoubtedly, part of the bureaucratic behavior could be attributed to the political culture of Czechoslovakia or rather to traditions that went back to the old Austro-Hungarian empire. Respect for the established hierarchical authority influenced Communist bureaucracy no less than that of Masaryk and Benes. The same was more or less true for the observance of purely bureaucratic procedures so dear to the hearts of the *kaiserliche-und-königliche* civil servants. In contrast to the less developed countries of the area where the tremendous increase in the bureaucratic apparatus had to be filled by recruiting groups and individuals who only recently had become socialized as part of an organized, urban milieu, the Czechoslovak bureaucracy as a profession enjoyed an honorable past and tradition going back several generations. Together with the system of values typical of a Central European middle-class society, the bureaucratic values managed to survive twenty years of Communist rule with relatively little damage, despite a large expansion of bureaucratic apparatus after 1948. In 1964 the Czechoslovak bureaucrats were ready to face perhaps the most crucial battle of the post-World War II period.

While the bureaucracy succeeded in outlasting Stalinism, the same was hardly true of the numerous groups characteristic of prewar Czechoslovakia. Following the usual pattern, the Communist rulers proceeded first to destroy the autonomous groups and then to replace them with a whole spectrum of transmission belts. By the early 1960s the process of *gleichschaltung* was largely accomplished and even a careful student of Czechoslovak society would be hard put to predict the revival of pluralism which was to take place soon thereafter.

The Groups in the Debate

For the purpose of the present discussion it is necessary to distinguish a number of groups which participated in the dialogue with the bureaucracy. By far the crucial role was played by the economists, especially those associated with a variety of research institutes attached to the Academy of Sciences, the Planning Commission and various ministries, as well as some universities and other academic institutions. This group, consisting probably of no more than 200–300 persons between the ages of twenty-five and forty-five, spearheaded the battle for reforms. Having obtained its university training in the post-1948 period, belonging almost to a man to the Party, it was rightly considered as a top elite within the system. It possessed a first-hand knowledge of the operating characteristics of the economy from both the theoretical and practical points of view. Many of its members were at some point in their careers employed in the actual running of the enterprises; some served as middle-ranking *apparatchiki* in the Central Committee apparatus; others began their careers in the Planning Commission and the economic ministries, while the rest chose to remain at the universities and other schools. By the mid 1960s nearly all of them were concentrated in a few, strategically located institutions devoted to economic research and teaching.

The majority of the trained economists were employed in industry and other sectors, in the government and Party apparatus, and in some institutions of higher learning, often outside the main urban centers of Prague and Bratislava. By and large they harbored a certain inferiority complex vis-à-vis their colleagues in the research institutes but generally shared their values and interests. On the other hand, a number of the older members of the profession centered around some schools and universities considered themselves as guardians of the orthodoxy and looked askance at the reforming zeal of the young Turks.

The next important group in the debate was the managers of the socialist enterprises. Like the professional economists, the managers were not a homogeneous group. Perhaps the most numerous subgroup consisted of individuals who managed to combine some economic training with faithful Party service and impeccable social origin. They were usually put in charge of the more important enterprises to fill vacancies caused by the ouster of the bona fide managers appointed in the pre-1948 period. Another subgroup was made up of typical Party hacks without economic background who reached the exalted status of managers by virtue of an honorable and long Party service which had to be rewarded somehow. Probably the least numerous was the subgroup composed of genuine, Western-type managers who succeeded in one way or another in overcoming bureaucratic resistance in getting the post.

The next strategically located group was the professional journalists. Some of them had economic training, others specialized in writing the editorials, still others edited some of the country's most popular literary and general-information weeklies. Because of their position they were able to open their media to the views of either or both sides to the debate. The most important journals had a nationwide circulation and thus the discussion could reach every corner of the republic.

By far the most numerous was the trade-union movement, which represented one of the most powerful pressure groups claiming to speak on behalf of the working class. In terms of potential political power it came close behind the top echelons of the Party and bureaucracy. Genuinely progressive in the early postwar period, by the mid 1960s it had become thoroughly bureaucratized and conservative. The preoccupation of the leadership with the maintenance of its status in the political infighting at the expense of defending workers' interests was responsible for the widening gap between the leaders and the rank and file which reached its extreme in early 1968.

The above represents a somewhat simplified picture of the existing groups. In addition to a number of subgroups within the few major groups one could still further subdivide them along national lines, with the Czech and Slovak components occasionally articulating separate interests of their own. A similar distinction could also be made with respect to the bureaucracy.

Before moving to a more detailed discussion of the interaction between bureaucracy and groups, one major question ought to be answered at this stage. It concerns the appropriateness of the use of the terms "group" and "group behavior." In his perceptive critique of the usefulness of the pluralistic model for the study of Communist societies, Andrew Janos considered the group model from a variety of viewpoints. In his opinion, in order to perform politically relevant functions, groups had to fulfill three major conditions. They were supposed to have a degree of integration, they had to be autonomous, and they had to be "representative" in the sense that the group membership responded to its leaders in a pragmatic rather than charismatic fashion.[10] The autonomy of groups also implied a degree of intergroup competition guaranteed by law or custom. On the basis of these criteria Janos concluded that no associations existing in any of the East European Communist countries including Yugoslavia fulfill the conditions enumerated above.[11]

From a highly rigorous point of view Janos is undoubtedly right. Yet a strict adherence to rigidly defined categories might prevent us from gaining useful insight into the working of a nondemocratic system such as Czechoslovakia. It is true that the existence of groups in that country was not guaranteed by law or custom. At the same time, however, in the mid 1960s the actors in the dialogue concerning economic reforms could hardly be described as pure transmission belts. While they continued to operate at the pleasure of the Party, which had presumably the power to limit and possibly terminate their activities, their behavior hardly resembled that of the obedient instruments that the Party used in the past to mobilize the population. On the contrary, as time progressed, the behavior of individual groups acquired an independent character which, even more importantly, was perceived as such by the membership. Even though the Party did not officially admit the legitimacy of group activity, it made little or no effort to suppress them. Each year it proved more and more difficult for it to do so and the group autonomy was growing.

The same was true with respect to the degree of integration which varied from group to group, usually with the sheer size of it. Some of the smaller groups—the research economists, the journalists, some managerial subgroups—exhibited a very high degree of cohesiveness and appreciation of their role as articulators of interests. They were united not only by their determination to press forward their demands but also by a number of other ties such as common university training, membership in professional organizations, participation in a number of formal advisory councils, conferences and seminars. Often a large number of individual members belonged to the same Party organization or a bloc committee. This interlocking membership provided also a network of communications. Meeting frequently on various occasions, members of individual groups were able to agree on their demands, on the strategy and tactics to be applied, and on targets to be attacked. In this respect they did not differ greatly from their Western counterparts.

The groups also appeared to be "representative" in the sense that the relationship between the official or informal leaders and the rest of the group was based on reciprocity and voluntary agreement. The leaders

[10] Janos, op. cit., pp. 5–6.
[11] Ibid., pp. 8ff.

emerged from the rank and file usually by virtue of their ability to obtain access to sources of decision-making, or because of their special skills to articulate group demands.

All of the above characteristics seem to imply that the Czechoslovak situation fell somewhere between the classic group model normally associated with Western democracies and the quasi-pluralistic model encountered at different times in such countries as Yugoslavia, Poland, and Hungary. Whether this means that the Czechoslovak groups ought to be considered as interest or pressure groups in the usual sense, or whether they should be treated as transitional aberrations, is a matter of personal preference. In my judgment they deserve to be considered as bona fide interest groups, however precarious their existence might actually be. This belief is strengthened by the fact that the group demands for economic reforms went far beyond the narrow demands one usually associates with corporatist bodies. It is quite clear that by advocating reforms of the economic system the proponents of the changes were fully aware of the important political repercussions of their action.

In the paper mentioned earlier, Janos, while admitting that groups in Yugoslavia came close to the Western model, considered them as falling short of the ideal since they were prevented by law from promoting political objectives.[12] While this is true in the formal sense and still further reinforced by the ideology which specifically denies the existence of antagonistic contradictions, i.e., particularistic interests and conflicts, the reality was far more complex. The borderline between economic and political inputs and outputs is at best a fuzzy one regardless of the political system in which they take place. One might perhaps separate the two in an underdeveloped society but hardly in a modern, industrial one. Thus the distinction made above strikes one as somewhat artificial although probably correct in a very narrow interpretation of the concept of interest group.

The suspicion that this narrow interpretation might cause us to lose sight of some interesting aspects of Communist politics is strengthened by an analysis of the group strategy and tactics during the debate on Czechoslovak economic reforms. The full story of the discussion can be reconstructed only in part but the degree of accuracy appears to be quite high, enabling us to trace the behavior of the different participants.

The process of reform-making appears to have been initiated in a rather innocuous fashion by a "discussion article" written in the fall of 1963 by four young economists, members of a working group created earlier in the year by the Party for the purpose of preparing the blueprint of the reforms. The article, which advocated a major transformation of the economic system, was sent to *Politicka Ekonomie,* an

[12] Ibid., pp. 12–14.

economic monthly published by the Economic Institute of the Czechoslovak Academy of Sciences. The editorial board considered the article to be of such importance that before deciding what to do with it it organized a conference attended by several hundred economists from across the nation to discuss the implications of the proposal. It may be presumed that the editors sought and received permission from the Party leadership for the staging of the meeting. As a result of the overwhelming support expressed at the conference, summaries of the article were duly published in early 1964, in *Politicka Ekonomie* and *Planovane Hospodarstvi,* the organ of the State Planning Commission.

Until then the discussion of the new economic model appeared to be purely academic and was confined to a fairly small circle of economists. The publication of the article implied, however, that the impact of the proposal reached beyond the narrow confines of the profession. The fact that censorship was not applied in this particular case meant that the green light must have come from the highest echelons of the Party. It was also at this time that the active leadership of the proponents of the reforms was taken over by Professor Ota Sik, the Director of the Economic Institute and a member of the Party's Central Committee.

Contrary to the usual interpretation known in the West, Sik's role in the reform movement was above all that of a salesman rather than author. A relative newcomer to the economic field, Sik embraced the proposed reforms wholeheartedly and became one of their foremost advocates. His membership in the Central Committee as well as his contacts in the Party bureaucracy put him in an especially advantageous position to sell the reforms to the Party leadership.

His efforts seemed to have met with success when in the late spring of 1964 the government agreed to set up a number of working groups which were given the task of preparing the detailed plan of reforms. The membership of the groups and numerous smaller subcommittees consisted of Party and government bureaucrats, planning officials, research and university economists, managers, and representatives of the trade unions. The commissions were organized along functional lines, each dealing with a particular aspect of the economy: planning and market; prices; investment; foreign trade; and others. According to available information, the committees met a number of times during the spring and summer of 1964 but showed little actual progress. The main reason appeared to be the attitude of the top Party leadership which experienced several changes of mind after having initially approved the reforms in early spring. The hot and cold wind blowing down from the Prague castle was hardly conducive to creating an atmosphere favorable for the reforms, and by the end of the summer even the most optimistic among the reformers became convinced that the reforms were dead, at least for the time being.

Quite unexpectedly the leadership did a turnabout and in October 1964 ordered the final draft of the proposed reforms to be ready for discussion at the forthcoming Central Committee plenum in January 1965.[13] Following three months of feverish preparations the draft was presented to the plenum, which duly approved it. The dissatisfaction with some of the provisions as well as with the slow progress in the implementation of some of the measures was largely responsible for a second draft, which was discussed and approved by the Central Committee in April 1966. It was this draft which became the blueprint of the first comprehensive reforms in the Soviet bloc.

Space does not permit a full discussion of the reforms and only a very brief summary can be presented here. The main thrust of the proposed reforms went in the direction of reducing the power of the center in controlling the economy in minute details. Individual managers were to receive greater authority in planning and disposing of their production, in setting prices and wages, and in investment decisions. The proposal also called for a wholesale overhaul of the fiscal and financial system by introducing new taxes and levies and reducing the role of the central budget. The most important aspect of the reforms was their comprehensive character, reflecting the lessons learned from the abortive 1958 reform. All in all the traditional "command economy" was to be replaced by a new system—a synthesis of market and plan.

The Resistance of the Bureaucrats

The reforms clearly represented a serious diminution of the power of the bureaucracy and it is not surprising that the latter resisted them to the hilt. The opposition came mostly from the middle-ranking bureaucrats in the Planning Commission, in the economic ministries, and in the various government committees dealing with prices, wages and other economic matters. Undoubtedly part of the resistance was due to the simple fear of losing their jobs and part to the dislike of seeing one's authority diminished. An interesting aspect of the opposition was the fact that most of the arguments used by the officials were couched in highly rational and pragmatic terms instead of the usual ideological ones.

Thus it was stated, for example, that there was really nothing seriously wrong with the existing system that some improvement in ad-

[13] According to stories circulating in Prague at that time, Novotny's change of mind was due to the fact that Khrushchev, during his last visit to Czechoslovakia prior to his ouster in October 1964, read the draft of the reforms and expressed considerable interest in them.

ministration could not take care of. In other words, there was no need for a massive overhaul of the economy but simply for some streamlining of procedures and tightening of controls. Furthermore, it was argued that the difficult economic situation made it impossible to engage in major reforms which would only aggravate the crisis still further. While some of the bureaucrats admitted the necessity of partial reforms, most of them claimed that the time was not appropriate and that only when the economy would get back on its feet would it be possible to put through some adjustments in the existing system. Another type of argument tended to emphasize the extremely low quality of management. According to that viewpoint the individual managers would be unable to cope with the new system. They could not be trusted with carrying out the provisions of the reforms since they had neither the qualifications nor the experience in managing the enterprises on their own without the guidance of the center.

One of the most interesting and politically significant arguments was directed at the working class, which was bound to be affected by the reforms. It was said that the major consequences of the new model would be a sharp increase in retail prices of foodstuffs and consumer goods; that a number of enterprises would be closed down, creating unemployment; that the traditional wage structure would be replaced by a highly differentiated system which would hurt the majority of the workers. The danger of inflation was constantly being invoked as the biggest obstacle to the reforms which in the eyes of the opposition had to be postponed until the economy regained equilibrium. The proponents of the reforms were pictured as hopeless romantics, and as abstract theoreticians without any practical experience and with little appreciation of economic realities.

Now and then another element, resembling some of the more sinister ideological arguments of the Stalinist past, was introduced into the discussion. Thus the advocates of the reform were overtly or covertly accused of being antiproletarian, of opposing socialist construction and favoring the return of capitalism to Czechoslovakia. The old class antagonisms were occasionally exploited in order to mobilize the working class against the reforms. In addition, the opposition attempted to convince the supporters of the new model that the Party could not afford to approve the reforms for political reasons since an approval would mean an admission of failure and thus it would play into the hands of the enemies of socialism. Since most of the supporters of the reforms belonged to the Party, Party loyalty and discipline were occasionally invoked in order to force the reformers to tone down their demands.

The arguments used by the bureaucracy were addressed primarily to the Party leaders and to their superiors in the government. In addition, the bureaucrats serving on the various committees entrusted with the preparations of the reforms tried to persuade the other participants, mainly the managers and the delegates of the trade unions, to accept their position. Having little or no access to the mass media, the opposition had also to rely heavily on spreading rumors and conducting a whispering propaganda in an attempt to discredit the reforms.

While the overwhelming proportion of the bureaucracy was opposed to the new economic model, there were some officials who appeared to be in favor of the reforms. Many of them occupied high posts in the administration to which they were called following the economic crisis of 1963–64. They were often recruited directly from universities and research institutes in order to ensure expert leadership of their respective ministries and agencies. They had a good deal in common with the advocates of the reforms and shared many of their interests.

Among the proponents of the reforms the major role was played by the above-mentioned research economists. They also used rational arguments emphasizing the utter bankruptcy of the old system, and utilized a variety of means to articulate their demands. To begin with, by virtue of their expertise, they played an important role in the numerous working committees formed to prepare the final draft of the reforms. It was there that they clashed frequently with the bureaucrats and also tried to persuade the other, hitherto uncommitted groups, to accept their ideas. Many of the economists were also employed as consultants in the various ministries and government committees which gave them the opportunity to present their views to the top-ranking government officials. While only one or two of the most vocal supporters of the reforms belonged to the Central Committee, they used their membership in order to sell the reforms to that important body. Many of the reformers were employed at some point in their careers in the Central Committee apparatus and this provided them with contacts in the Party bureaucracy. Some of them were used by the Party as special lecturers which permitted them to travel around the country and to popularize their proposals. One of the most interesting and probably least appreciated linkages between the reformers and the bureaucrats was the phenomenon of the "old school tie." Since there were only very few universities and other institutions of higher learning offering economics as a field of study, nearly all economists in the country knew each other and retained some form of contact even though their careers took different paths.

As indicated earlier, the key role in the discussions was played by the managers and the representatives of the working class. Both the proponents and the opponents of the reforms competed for their support. The advocates of the new model tried to impress the uncommitted groups with the gravity of the situation in a variety of ways. Apart from frequent contacts during the meetings of the preparatory commissions, the economists managed to organize a series of conferences and seminars to which they invited delegates from factories and enterprises. The reformers utilized every opportunity to make field trips to factories outside Prague and to meet with management and labor in order to articulate their views. They also sent out printed materials throughout the country to make their proposals known to as many interested groups and individuals as possible.

The economists employed at universities and other academic institutions also did their best to support the reforms. In this particular case there existed a rather interesting generational split. The younger members of the profession were wholeheartedly behind the reforms whereas the older generation, brought up on a heavy dose of the traditional doctrine, was unwilling by and large to change its ways and to adopt a more progressive attitude. Thus one could witness a kind of tug-of-war going on in the academic profession, with the younger members gradually winning the battle. The importance of this victory lay mainly in the fact that both sides competed for the attention of a captive audience composed of students who at some point had to make a choice as to what side to support. Since the students formed the backbone of the Czechoslovak Youth Association—a rather important interest group in itself—their support or opposition was of considerable significance.

The younger members had perhaps one major advantage over the conservatives. For one reason or another they seemed to have a fairly easy access to the mass media, especially newspapers and periodicals of both general and professional character. Thus they were able to present their views to a mass audience as well as to the other members of the profession. In this they were strongly helped by the journalists, the majority of whom accepted the reforms as necessary and inevitable. As a result, both the professional journals as well as the highly popular political and literary weeklies contained a large number of articles, editorials and interviews overwhelmingly favoring the new system.

Among the uncommitted groups the key role was played by the managers. The group appeared to be split three ways. The supporters of the reforms were offset by those who opposed the changes. The yardstick which seemed to determine the position taken by individual managers was their respective training and background. Many of the managers were appointed to their posts as a reward for faithful Party service. They had often no other qualifications, which, however, under the Stalinist system did not represent a major obstacle in their career. Within the framework of detailed central planning the role of the manager consisted mostly of seeing to it that hundreds of obligatory targets received from the center were achieved by his enterprise. He did not have to worry about selling his output nor about the quality of his products.

Even the sacred indicator of plan fulfillment did not look as threatening as it was commonly imagined. Usually if the enterprise did not fulfill the plan, it received a lower target the next year for the simple reason that the bureaucrats responsible for the given sector disliked being called on the carpet and preferred to avoid it by imposing a lower plan which could then be more easily reached. The manager's relations with the workers were also rather uncomplicated. Both were interested in getting highest possible bonuses and lowest possible targets.

For these managers the proposed reforms were anathema. They were worried as much about the impending loss of their jobs as about the magnitude of the tasks that awaited them. They were simply unable to cope with the variety of problems brought about by the reforms and their opposition could easily be understood. They also preferred the existing situation characterized by the persistence of the "seller's market," which guaranteed a steady demand for their products. As long as the enterprise order books were filled for the next ten years, there was little to worry about, regardless of the system. But one of the aims of the reforms was to reduce the pressure in the economy and to create a "buyer's market." Thus, in addition to the extra tasks imposed on the managers by the systemic reforms, there also loomed the new danger of reduced demand for their output and the unwelcome prospect of looking for buyers—a sharp contrast with the days when the buyers had to be turned away empty-handed.

The advocates of the reforms were in the minority. Some of them learned their profession prior to the imposition of the Stalinist model, others were trained in the most recent period. They were united in their dislike of the waste caused by the existing system and were strongly in favor of the reforms which would grant them the long-awaited opportunity to utilize their talents and experience.

By far the largest group was represented by managers who fell halfway between the two extremes. In many instances they also had little formal training and a good deal of Party service but, in contrast to some of their colleagues mentioned above, they had enough common sense to realize the havoc created by the old system. During the discussions preceding the reforms they managed to sit on the fence but in the final analysis they seemed to lean in favor of the reforms.

The final group which participated in the discussions and preparations for the reforms were the workers represented by the trade unions. Here the situation was quite complex. There is little doubt that the old system was not as unfavorable for the working class as may be imagined. While the income per head might have been fairly low, the income per family was not inconsiderable in view of the existing overemployment in the country. The prices of consumer goods were often heavily subsidized as were rents and the prices of social services. The trade unions provided an extensive network of recreational and cultural activities at a very low cost. The workers enjoyed a perfect security of employment as demand for labor continued to be very high.

In the short run the envisaged reforms would most likely result in a certain reduction in the living standard of the entire population. The reformers themselves anticipated some increase in retail prices partly as a result of a comprehensive price reform and partly as a consequence of the reduction or abolition of subsidies. There was also a strong possibility that a number of inefficient plants might be closed down, introducing an element of unemployment. The same was true for the attempted modernization of the industrial plant, which was likely to cause some technological unemployment as well. One of the major aims of the reforms was to get away from the extremely rigid wage structure by replacing it with much greater wage differentials based on skill, qualifications and productivity. Here again some categories of workers were bound to be hurt. In view of the changed role of the management, the honeymoon between the workers and the managers was also likely to come to an end.

All this contributed to the fact that the unions were hardly enthusiastic about the reforms.[14] Nevertheless, there is little evidence that the leadership did in fact oppose them strenuously. A possible explanation might have been that by the mid 1960s the leadership was thoroughly bureaucratized and fully dominated by the Party bureaucrats. Thus the leaders took their cue from the Party rather than from the rank and file, which was becoming more and more alienated. Possibly on Party orders, the delegates of the unions who participated in the consultations preceding the approval of the reforms remained largely noncommittal.

As was mentioned above, the first version of the reforms was approved in January 1965 and the amended draft in April 1966. In both instances the final outcome was the result of a compromise between both major protagonists. Neither side succeeded in getting all that it demanded. This was due not only to the inability of the top Party leadership to make up its mind but also to the speed with which some of the reforms were approved. Had there been more time it is quite possible that the reformers might have gained additional ground. As it happened, they preferred to take what was offered to them without risking a major defeat if they persisted in maintaining their initial position.

While the details of the reforms might be described as a compromise, the fact that the new model was approved at all represented a striking

[14] For a perceptive discussion of labor's attitude toward the reforms, see Vaclav Holesovsky, "Labor and the Economic Reforms in Czechoslovakia" (University of Massachusetts Labor Relations and Research Center, April 1968), pp. 2–6.

victory for those groups in Czechoslovak society which demanded change. It soon became clear that the economic reforms were only the first step in the process of near-revolutionary change which followed on their heels.

For the purpose of this paper, the most interesting phenomenon which emerged from the discussions of the reforms was the activity of the various groups in forcing the acceptance or rejection of the proposed changes in the economic system. A series of working hypotheses resulting from the foregoing presentation might perhaps be postulated as follows:

1) The totalitarian model of Communist societies appears to be no longer valid as an instrument of analysis. The bureaucratic model, which assumed a near-monopoly of power in the hands of bureaucracy, also seems to be somewhat too simple a device to be used indiscriminately. By process of elimination it would appear that the group model offers the most interesting insight into the workings of Communist systems.

2) Judging by the case study summarized above, the group behavior in Czechoslovakia resembled closely the behavior of groups in Western societies despite the presence of a Party which for ideological reasons was firmly opposed to the existence of autonomous groups.

3) It would also seem that some of the assumptions concerning the monolithic and ultra-conservative character of Communist bureaucracy might also be subject to revision. In the Czechoslovak case at least, the bureaucracy appeared to be almost as differentiated as some of the groups it faced in the discussions concerning the economic reforms.

Political Participation

CITIZEN DEMANDS AND THE SOVIET POLITICAL SYSTEM*

James H. Oliver

POLITICAL scientists interested in non-Communist systems have paid considerable attention to demands (expressions of opinion that an authoritative allocation with regard to particular subject matters should or should not be made by those responsible for doing so)[1] coming from the intra-societal (domestic) environments of these political systems. The importance of intra-societal demands, including citizen demands, for non-Communist systems is well established. Researchers interested in the Soviet political system have paid relatively little attention to intra-societal demands, especially demands coming from those whom David Easton would call citizen gatekeepers, i.e., citizens who convert their wants into demands by articulating them.[2]

From *The American Political Science Review,* LXII, 2 (June 1969). Reprinted by permission of the author and The American Political Science Association.

*I would like to thank Prof. John A. Armstrong for his valuable comments on an earlier version of this paper. I would also like to express my gratitude to the Inter-University Committee on Travel Grants for their support of my research in the Soviet Union.

[1] I will use the term "demand" only in this restricted sense. For a full discussion of the concept see David Easton, *A Systems Analysis of Political Life* (New York: John Wiley & Sons, Inc., 1965), Part II.

[2] For a discussion of citizen gatekeepers see Easton, op. cit., pp. 93–94.

The reasons for the neglect of research in this area are obvious enough. Quite apart from the problem of gathering useful data, there exists the question of whether demands from the intra-societal environment, and in particular citizen demands, are really important for a "totalitarian" system. Nothing like the politically autonomous interest groups of the Western democracies exist in the Soviet Union. Whatever demands come from the intra-societal environment are therefore largely grassroots demands from the populace, and there is reason to doubt that Soviet authorities feel compelled to heed such demands when formulating policy. Lenin's assertion that the Party is the vanguard of the proletariat was clearly a rejection of the idea that the masses should direct the Party. His successors have continued to assert that the Party leads the masses, and not the masses the Party. Stalin argued:

> The Party cannot be a real party if it limits itself to registering what the masses of the working class feel and think. . . . The Party must stand at the head of the working class; it must see farther than the working class; it must lead the proletariat, and not follow in the tail of the spontaneous movement.[3]

The 1961 Party Program clearly reasserted the doctrine of the primacy of the Party as the guiding force in society.

> The period of full-scale communist construction is characterized by a *further enhancement of the role and importance of the Communist Party* as the leading and guiding force of Soviet society.[4]

The directing element of the Party is much narrower than its total membership. Although Western scholars' estimates vary from under 1,000 to several thousand, they agree that the number of persons who really count in the formulation of policy in the Soviet Union is small.[5]

[3] J. V. Stalin, "Foundations of Leninism," *Problems of Leninism* (New York: International Publishers 1928), p. 73, as quoted in Merle Fainsod, *How Russia Is Ruled* (Cambridge: Harvard University Press, 1963), p. 137.

[4] Program of the Communist Party of the Soviet Union, reproduced from a supplement of *New Times* (No. 48), 29 November, 1961, in Leonard Schapiro (ed.), *The U.S.S.R. and the Future* (New York: Frederick A. Praeger, 1963), p. 310. Emphasis in the original.

[5] Compare Merle Fainsod, op. cit., p. 205; Derek J. R. Scott, *Russian Political Institutions* (New York: Frederick A. Praeger, 1961), p. 54; and Wolfgang Leonhard, *The Kremlin Since Stalin,* trans. Elizabeth Wiskemann and Marion Jackson (New York: Frederick A. Praeger, 1962), pp. 11–15. See also John A. Armstrong, *The Soviet Bureaucratic Elite* (New York: Frederick A. Praeger, 1959), Chapters I and II.

Furthermore, Soviet leaders have promoted not merely programs that were clearly contrary to the wishes of important segments of the general populace—collectivization—but also programs contrary to the wishes of segments of the elite—Khrushchev's bifurcation of the Party.

I. Some Hypotheses Concerning Demands of Soviet Citizens

The existence of an apparently limited political community, the lack of independent associational interest groups, the leadership's apparent contempt for mass opinion, the marked centralization of decision-making all suggest that demands from what Easton calls the intra-societal environment are far less important in the Soviet system than in the Western democracies, and even in many of the non-democratic but non-Communist states.

Certainly much of the work of Soviet-area specialists supports Easton's contention that although "there is still room for articulation of political demands" within totalitarian systems despite "the severe restrictions upon popular participation,"[6] the number and variety of gatekeepers—those who convert wants into demands by articulating them—is so restricted that input overload is not "likely to occur or even threaten."[7] He contrasts "modern totalitarian or dictatorial systems" with democracies, which, "within the limits imposed by other aspects of the political culture," encourage every citizen to participate in the system by tending his own gate, that is, by converting his own wants into demands by directing statements concerning the allocation of values to authorities.[8]

The hypotheses that in the Soviet Union (1) citizens are not encouraged to tend their own gates; (2) the number of gatekeepers is so restricted that input overload is unlikely to occur or even threaten; (3) demands from the intra-societal environment, and in particular citizen demands, are of little importance, seem tenable. I will try to show that these hypotheses, if not false, are true only in a very limited sense. In the course of my argument I also will attempt to clarify the way in which these demands are processed, and indicate some of the problems that arise in conjunction with their processing.

[6] Easton, op. cit., p. 110.
[7] Ibid., p. 93.
[8] Ibid., pp. 93–95.

II. Soviet Citizen Gatekeepers and Their Demands

Evidence that Soviet citizens tend their own gates and that higher officials require local officials to pay attention to the resulting citizen demands has existed ever since Merle Fainsod published his study of the Smolensk Province Party Archives in 1958.[9] In his chapter on the right of petition he noted that this right existed prior to World War II and that the citizens of Smolensk Province vigorously exercised it.[10] Fainsod also noted that citizen petitions had at least two functional consequences. First, the petitions (demands in Easton's terminology) served to expose and, therefore, inhibit misconduct at the lower administrative levels. Second, they tended to diffuse popular discontent and direct it from the center to local officials.[11]

The inaccessibility of Party archives, other than the captured Smolensk Archives, makes a replication of Fainsod's study impossible. Nevertheless, data available for Moscow and Leningrad clearly show that Soviet urban citizens in the 1950's and 1960's continued to make their demands known to local authorities, just as their rural counterparts had done during the pre-war period in Smolensk Province. By the 1960's thousands of citizen demands were pouring into the city raion (borough)[12] agencies and organs, either directly from the citizens or

[9] These archives were captured first by the German army during World War II and subsequently by U.S. forces. They are the only party archives open to non-Communist scholars.

[10] Merle Fainsod, *Smolensk Under Soviet Rule* (New York: Vintage Books, 1963), Chapter XX.

[11] Ibid., p. 408.

[12] Moscow and Leningrad are divided into a number of raions (city boroughs). Each raion has its "popularly" elected legislative assembly (soviet); executive committee (borough council), which is "elected" by the sovet; and numerous governmental administrative agencies. According to the legal theory of dual subordination, the raion soviet is subordinate to its electors and the "popularly" elected city soviet. The raion city executive committee is subordinate to its soviet and the city executive committee, and the raion administrative agencies are subordinate to their executive committee and the corresponding city administrative agency. Similar dual subordination exists for city organs and agencies, the next higher level for Moscow and Leningrad being the RSFSR.

In each raion there is a raion party organization consisting of the large raion party committee (raikom), which is "elected" by the larger raion party conference; the bureau of the raikom, which is "elected" by the raikom; and the party administrative agencies. The raion party organizations

via higher officials who simply sent any demands within the jurisdiction of a raion to that raion in the individual raw form in which the citizen had submitted it.

Whatever the route of the demands, the number was astounding. In the first four months of 1962 some 11,803 citizen demands poured into the offices of the Kirov raion of Moscow.[13] In the first half of 1963 officials of a single raion in Leningrad received over 15,000 letters and visits from the populace involving demands of various sorts.[14]

The demands themselves cover nearly the entire range of activities under the jurisdiction of the city governmental apparatus. The citizens complain about the quality of new construction; request additional housing space; and complain about the slowness of housing repairs and their quality. They make demands concerning the quality, assortment and availability of goods in stores and shops and the location of retail outlets and restaurants. They complain about the quality of service in retail outlets, restaurants, and consumer service facilities. They complain about taxi service; they make demands concerning mass transportation facilities. They express their concern about health facilities, about poor street lighting, about unkept parks, about cultural facilities, and about the condition of streets and sidewalks. They complain about the behavior of officials, and they complain about the activities of their neighbors. The regime that has undertaken, with great pride and deliberate purpose, more activities than any in modern history is confronted with demands covering a wider range of subjects than any regime in history.

The vast majority of citizen demands, whatever their topic, have certain common characteristics. They are specific demands from indi-

---

are subordinate to the city party organization, which also have a conference, city party committee (gorkom), bureau, and administrative agencies.

At each level the governmental organs and agencies are subordinate to their appropriate party organs and agencies. Candidates to governmental offices are selected, or at least approved, by the appropriate party organizations and by higher state organs and agencies. Party officials must be approved by higher party organizations.

[13] Decision of the Moscow Executive Committee of 29 June 1962 in *Biulleten' ispolnitel'nogo komiteta Moskovskogo gorodskogo Soveta deputatov trudiashchikhsia* (*Bulletin of the Executive Committee of the Moscow City Soviet of Working People's Deputies*), No. 15 (August 1962), p. 9. Hereafter this publication will be referred to as *M.B.*

[14] Decision of the Leningrad Executive Committee of 7 August 1963 in *Biulleten' ispolnitel'nogo komiteta Leningradskogo gorodskogo Soveta deputatov trudiaschikhsia* (*Bulletin of the Executive Committee of the Leningrad City Soviet of Working People's Deputies*), No. 18 (September 1963), p. 1. Hereafter this publication will be referred to as *L.B.*

vidual citizens involving limited and usually individual or neighborhood needs and wants. They are, in other words, raw demands. Because large autonomous interest groups, which exist in other modern societies are not permitted in the Soviet Union, these raw demands must be processed within the political system without the benefit of any prior efforts to sort, combine and consolidate them into general proposals for political action, but more about this later.

Most of the demands examined in this study are also apparently spontaneous and processed within the governmental apparatus. This obviously is not true of all demands. Fainsod's Smolensk study revealed that during the 1920's and 1930's some processing of citizen demands also went on within the party apparatus. No doubt it still does, although the inaccessibility of party records makes impossible a detailed discussion of party processing for any later period.

I can, however, state that the Party does play a considerable role in the processing of demands included within the electoral mandates, which are lists of demands that are binding, at least formally, on the local governmental officials to whom they are addressed. Furthermore, these demands often are not spontaneous.

To be included within an electoral mandate, a demand must be presented in a particular manner and meet certain criteria. It must be presented in a meeting called either to nominate deputies to the soviets or to present candidates for deputy seats to the electorate; it must be discussed by those present at the meeting with respect to its expediency and practicality; it must be adopted by a majority vote; it should involve matters of common concern to the electors; and it should be substantial enough to require inclusion in the plan for fulfillment.[15]

At the proper meeting a citizen may offer a demand for inclusion in the mandate, but frequently demands offered have been discussed first in the organs of public and voluntary associations.[16] These organs, of course, are dominated by party members. Furthermore, subjecting the proposed demands to public discussion may eliminate some of them. Discussions at public meetings are often rather open, vigorous and frank; but whether any resolution opposed by the party group present at such meetings stands any chance of being adopted is doubtful. The influence of the Party on the mandate has been clearly indicated by two Soviet jurists who state that the Central Committee considers the

[15] G. V. Barabashev and K. F. Sheremet, *Sovetskoe Stroitel'stvo* (Moscow: Iuridicheskaia literatura, 1965), pp. 374–75. See also I. A. Azovkin, R. A. Saforov and Iu A. Tikhomirov, "Deiatel'nost' deputatov mestnykh Sovetov v izribatel'nom okruge i na prozvodstve,' *Mestnye Sovety na sovremennom etape* (Moscow: Nauka, 1965), pp. 285–87.

[16] Barabashev and Sheremet, op. cit., pp. 375–76.

mandate an important means by which the Party sets tasks for the organs of state authority.[17]

III. Failures in Handling Citizen Demands

The thousands of raw demands pouring into the system create serious problems for local officials, especially the raion officials. They are in close contact with the populace and receive the major portion of citizen demands. The failure of hard-pressed raion officials to respond to many of the demands encourages citizens to route them through higher authorities in the hope that demands so routed have a better chance of attracting the attention of lower officials. Even so, a response is by no means certain. Between 1958 and 1960, 40 per cent of the demands received by officials of the Sokol'nicheskyi raion in Moscow had been sent via higher authorities, many of them, according to the city executive committee, for the second time. Of these, 50 per cent had not been disposed of within the required 20-day period.[18]

The failure of officials to fulfill citizen demands extends even to those legally binding demands included in the electoral mandate. Although their own record is not flawless, city officials often criticize raion officials for failures in this area. Many things go wrong. Sometimes officials simply ignore certain items in mandate, failing even to discuss them. Sometimes officials sacrifice items in a mandate in order to fulfill more important items in the plan. The plan has its priorities; and whatever standing mandate items may have in law, many of them do not enjoy much priority in the plan. Sometimes local executive committees fail to set a specific date for the fulfillment of some mandate demands, thereby making control over fulfillment difficult. Other times the executive committees find themselves without the resources needed to fulfill a mandate.[19]

Although the decrees of the raion soviets and city executive committees clearly show that local officials, especially raion officials, have trouble coping with the flow of citizen demands, little or no effort is made to stem the flow. On the contrary, evidence indicates that higher officials may view large numbers of demands flowing into the raions with

[17] Ibid., p. 374.

[18] Decision of the Moscow Executive Committee of 5 February 1960 in *M.B.*, No. 6 (March 1960), p. 10.

[19] For a discussion of some of the difficulties that arise concerning the fulfillment of the electoral mandate see E. Sovershaeva (Senior instructor of the Leningrad Organization-Instructor Department) "O rabote po vypolneniiu nakazov izbiratelei," in *L.B.*, No. 12 (June 1963), pp. 13–15.

enthusiasm. In 1962 the Moscow city executive stated it considered a large number of citizen demands on raion officials as desirable insofar as the demands indicated increased citizen activism. In the same decree the executive committee also stated it viewed large numbers of such demands as evidence of the raion officials' neglect of citizen needs.[20] Apparently, the city officials view a high volume of demands as a negative indicator for the performance of raion officials and a positive indicator for the existence of citizen support. This makes some sense. Certainly, an unusually high level of demands in one raion might indicate poor performance by raion officials, but at the same time indicate that citizens have confidence in the system's ability to satisfy their needs and wants.

Within the past decade the difficulties of the raion officials may have been aggravated by the demand of higher authorities that the raion officials adopt practices likely to increase both their work load and the flow of citizen demands. For example, city officials urged raion executive committees to hold "circuit" meetings at places where citizens work or live in order to facilitate citizen participation in the discussion of raion problems. They also urged raion officials to send out advance publicity on sessions of the raion soviets in order to give the citizens an opportunity to send in complaints and suggestions concerning questions on the agenda. The raion officials were supposed to consider these for inclusion in the draft resolutions submitted for adoption by the raion soviet. Authorities also ordered raion executive committee officers and raion agency heads to make periodic reports at public meetings and to use the meetings as opportunities to gather additional citizen demands.

The city officials and higher authorities claimed these practices brought officials into closer contact with the masses and improved their understanding of the masses' needs. The reluctance of some raion officials to adopt such practices suggests that they were not unaware that adoption would increase their work loads at a time when they were already having problems handling citizen demands.

IV. The Persistence of the Threat of Input Overload

The city and raion officials have only a limited ability to reduce the threat of input overload by correcting the conditions that give rise to the deluge of citizen demands. If the demands concern such limited prob-

[20] Decision of the Moscow Executive Committee of 29 June 1962 in *M.B.*, No. 15 (August 1962), p. 9.

lems as a specific street in poor repair, a dirty park, poor street lighting in a certain neighborhood, etc., the local officials can often effectively reduce the input load by correcting the conditions that give rise to the demands. Such corrective action ordinarily involves only the proper allocation and distribution of available resources, and this is within the capabilities of local officials.

When demands arise from conditions created by centrally determined investment and allocation priorities or certain basic characteristics of the economy, local officials can do little. For example, city officials can do something about demands concerning the poor quality of food in restaurants insofar as its quality depends on preparation and handling. They can satisfy the demands of citizens in a particular neighborhood for a restaurant in that neighborhood by using some of the limited resources available for such purposes to build a restaurant in that part of the city. However, they can do nothing to reduce effectively the flow of demands resulting from the general lack of restaurants or other service facilities because this lack results from investment decisions falling outside their jurisdiction.

In such cases city officials can fight for their share of a small pie; they can lend what support they can to whatever reforms are being discussed at higher levels; they can reassure the citizen that they are aware of the problems and are trying to do something to ameliorate the general conditions; and in individual cases they can provide some material relief. But the officials cannot change the basic conditions; consequently, they can do little that might reduce the input of demands resulting from those conditions.

As a result, many of the demands voiced by citizens in 1968 were the same as the demands voiced years earlier. This is occasionally revealed in local decisions. Thus, in 1963 the Leningrad soviet noted improvement in the work of service enterprises between 1958 and 1963, and pointed with considerable pride to expanded facilities. In the same decision the soviet noted that complaints from citizens had also increased. The reason is to be found in the growth figures reported in the decision. The per capita volume of services had increased by only 1.3 per cent over the reported period.[21]

[21] Decision of the Leningrad City Soviet of 24 June 1963 in *L.B.*, No. 14 (July 1963), pp. 1–2. As a result of an increase of 4.3 times in dry cleaning capacity between 1959 and 1961, the people of Leningrad could have their dry cleaning orders filled within twenty days in 1961. This was a considerable improvement over the sixty day period of 1959. However, according to the decision of the city soviet, demands in this area were still not being met. See the decision of the Leningrad City Soviet of 11 December 1961 in *L.B.*, No. 1 (January 1962), p. 4.

V. Disapproved Responses

Confronted with a difficult situation, the local officials resort to various disapproved tactics in an effort to conceal their failures in handling the deluge of citizen demands or to reduce it. Some simply falsify their reports by untruthfully claiming to handle properly a substantial proportion of received demands. Some try to reduce the flow by curtailing reception hours for citizens wanting to make oral demands. Other officials bury the demands by sending complaints for verification to those very persons against whom the citizens lodged them. Still others simply ignore citizen demands. These tactics provide some temporary relief, but at the risk of censure from higher authorities.

The citizens' perception of the inability of local officials to meet many citizen demands causes citizens to turn to disapproved devices for the satisfaction of their wants and needs. This fosters the rise of various small "businessmen," whose activities are both illegal and ideologically objectionable. Whereas demands addressed to authorities provide the regime with information on popular attitudes and official performance and with an opportunity to build support, the disapproved devices provide neither. They do, however, provide satisfaction for the citizen.

The disapproved devices may also serve some of the needs of local officials. No way exists to discover the motives behind the local officials' toleration of disapproved devices, but that they tolerate them is beyond doubt. The toleration may be indicative of actual corruption or simply a desire not to harass unnecessarily local citizens. Local officials also may tolerate formally disapproved devices because they see them as reducing their input load by providing an alternative way of satisfying citizen needs and wants.

Disapproved devices take various forms, some of which are serious from the regime's standpoint. There is the hardly concealed black market in currency and clothing illegally but rather openly purchased from foreign tourists. There is even a black market operation in public housing. A "businessman" may turn a profit by registering, quite properly, for new housing on the grounds that his current housing space is inadequate. When he receives new housing, he then exchanges it with another citizen for less desirable housing plus an additional material consideration. Again lacking adequate housing space, he places his name back on the list for new housing. Other devices are less ambitious, but no less illegal. Both private automobile owners and drivers of state owned trucks provide taxi service. Other citizens illegally make and sell consumer items or offer services for a fee.

The local official tolerating any of these activities runs a risk of being reported. Rather than use these devices, some citizens report to higher authorities both the person engaging in an illegal activity and the local officials tolerating it. Some of the reports may result from personal animosities; but the regime's considerable efforts to build socialist consciousness must have some effect, and some of the reports are surely motivated by a genuine sense of civic duty. Nevertheless, local officials sometimes ignore citizen complaints concerning illegal activities until investigations by higher authorities force them to act.[22]

Although the use of disapproved devices by citizens and the collusion of local officials pose serious problems for those seeking to impose the official norms, these problems should not be permitted to obscure the possible, if unintentional, beneficial consequences for the regime. If the regime successfully suppressed these practices, which so clearly violate officially prescribed norms, and if, as a result, citizens and local officials could no longer resort to them to satisfy their felt needs and wants, the level of popular dissatisfaction with the political leadership, its policies and the institutional structure it has established might sharply increase.

Propaganda and coercion may contribute to mass conformity to officially prescribed norms. However, the regime's willingness to tolerate (within limits) citizen gatekeepers and its inability to close off all officially disapproved means by which citizens can obtain satisfaction of needs and wants the regime is unable or unwilling to satisfy, may, by making life more tolerable, be no less important for the maintenance of popular acceptance or acquiescence in the system. Ironically, the use of disapproved devices by citizens, may, by reducing dissatisfaction, make less likely any challenge of what the ruling oligarchy regards as a legitimate right: namely, the right to impose on the people policies that the oligarchy allegedly believes to be in the best interest of the people, even when the people disagree.

VI. Approved Responses

There are approved means for reducing the demand input load. City officials may properly refer many of the demands they receive to raion officials for final action; but the raion officials are not so fortunate. They can refer some to public or voluntary associations such as the trade unions, the parents' committees attached to schools, apartment house committees, shoppers' councils, etc. These organizations may also directly absorb a certain number of demands. The trade unions devote

[22] See decision of the Moscow Executive Committee of 18 December 1962 in *M.B.*, No. 2 (January 1963), pp. 19–21.

some attention to working conditions and safety standards at places of employment. Parents' committees provide some material aid to children of needy families.

However, the ability of these organizations to handle or absorb demands is not very great. In fact, the small local voluntary associations—the parents' committees, apartment house committees, shoppers' councils, etc.—are likely to add to the flow of demands on raion officials. These groups are valuable primarily because they involve citizens in civic work, which helps build civic pride and support, and because they provide free labor for small civic projects such as clean-up and shrubbery planting campaigns. To a considerable degree, the effectiveness of the volunteer organizations depends on the amount of organizational aid the local officials are willing to give them. Therefore, the organizations are as likely to increase the work load of local officials as they are to reduce it. Some volunteer groups have become moribund for the lack of such aid, which suggests that some local officials may find the groups require more time and work than they are worth.

Although higher officials look with disfavor on the enlargement of paid raion staffs and forbid, without perfect success,[23] any unauthorized increases, they have encouraged local agencies to organize volunteer staffs. In 1961 the chairman of the executive committee of Moscow's Leningrad raion reported positively on the use of volunteers. His report also indicated the severe shortage of paid staff members at the raion level.

He reported that in 1948 the raion Cultural Department's staff consisted of the head of the department and one inspector for libraries. At the time it had under its jurisdiction one movie theater, two clubs and two libraries. By 1961 it had under its jurisdiction fifteen libraries, twelve clubs, two houses, of culture, sixty-five red corners, ten movie theaters, four music schools and six book stores. Its staff still consisted of the head of the department and one inspector for libraries. According to the chairman the work of the department improved greatly with the help of a twenty-nine member voluntary group composed of pensioners, housewives and workers from the various raion cultural institutions.[24] The executive committee chairman reported similar benefits from the use of volunteers in other departments. In the raion Department for the Allocation of Housing Space, an area of some sensitivity, he reported that the number of citizen demands answered in a period longer than twenty days declined from 750 in 1958, when there were no volunteers,

[23] Decision of Moscow Executive Committee of 7 January 1964 in *M.B.*, No. 2 (January 1964), pp. 13–14.

[24] A. Ia. Goncharov, "O praktike vovlecheniia obshchestvennosti v rabotu Leningradskogo raionnogo Soveta g. Moskvy," *Ot sotsialisticheskoi gosudarstvennosti k kommunisticheskomu samoupravleniiu*, pp. 298–99.

to around a dozen in 1960. The volume of demands pouring into this one department was enormous, numbering some 14,000 in 1959.[25]

Even though this was probably an exceptional success story, it does suggest the magnitude of the problem that confronts the raion officials. Volunteers would seem to promise some relief, and participation may provide the additional bonus of increased support. How much relief volunteers provide is a question that cannot be answered, but the following points should be noted in addition to the above report.

First, a number of raions were slow to adopt the practice of using volunteers, despite criticism from above concerning the quality of their work in handling citizen demands, and despite prodding from above to seek a remedy through the use of volunteers. This refusal to use volunteers simply may indicate organizational inertia. It also may indicate that the creation of effective volunteer staffs required a considerable amount of work by already busy paid staff members, and that all such experiments were not as successful as the one in the Leningrad raion. Furthermore, the Leningrad city executive committee warned that the use of volunteer staffs to check on the fulfillment of decisions did not relieve raion officials of responsibility for the quality of work in their raions,[26] thereby suggesting that the quality of volunteer work was not always high and that raion officials tried to hide behind volunteers in an effort to evade responsibility for shortcomings. Finally, I was told that by 1965 there was some problem in maintaining public enthusiasm for volunteer work, some of which was not voluntary in the strictest sense of the word. Pseudo-volunteer participation is unlikely either to provide efficient help or build support.

In addition to the use of volunteers, city officials have urged the raion officials to reduce the red tape and paper shuffling that so often accompanies the handling of citizen demands. The available data indicate that many raion officials quite needlessly add to their own burdens. In February of 1963 the Moscow city executive committee noted that despite a 1960 decision ordering raion officials to cease demanding numerous unnecessary forms, certificates, and notarized documents from citizens before undertaking such routine administrative matters as changes in residence, school registration and the issuance of passports, the practice continued, especially in Kuybyshev, Sverdlov and Timiriazev raions. The demand for notarized documents was so great that in a 21-month period one notary office in one of the raions notarized over 625,000 documents. The housing exploitation office of the Sverdlov raion had demanded and received in a single year over 75,000 certificates of various sorts from the citizenry. In the same raion

[25] Ibid., p. 295.

[26] See unsigned article, "O rabote obshchestvennykh otdelov po kontroliu ispolneniia reshenii," in *L.B.*, No. 10 (May 1962), p. 13.

a citizen wishing to acquire better housing had to present not only various forms, certificates and documents, including a personal financial report, but also fill out a seven-page questionnaire containing nearly 200 questions.[27] In view of the small size of the raion staffs such figures are astounding. The executive committee decision gives no indication of why the raion officials persisted in the use of procedures that increased their own work load despite contrary orders from higher authorities. Such procedures apparently had been standard at an earlier date. Perhaps some raion officials believed a large amount of documentation provided them with a ready defense against charges from above that they were giving housing or other material goods or services to unqualified applicants.

VII. The Use of Deputies

Higher officials have encouraged raion officials to work with the deputies "popularly elected" to the soviets and to weld them into an effective work force. This also may increase the work load of raion officials. The effective use of deputies requires considerable organizational work and other aid from the raion executive committees and their administrative agencies.[28] Furthermore, one of the major jobs of the local deputy is to transmit his constituents' demands to the local officials. Therefore, an effective deputy can add significantly to the total input of citizen demands.

On the other hand, the deputy can also relieve the local officials of some of their burdens by undertaking the initial investigation of demands, and the verification of the fulfillment of official decisions concerning them. Deputies also can organize the citizenry to work for the satisfaction of their own demands on a self-help basis. This activity is very helpful to local officials when they find themselves in the awkward position of not having the resources to meet citizen demands, especially the legally binding ones included in the electoral mandate. For example, deputies in one raion, faced with the prospect of having to tell their

[27] Decision of the Moscow Executive Committee of 21 February 1963 in *M.B.*, No. 4 (February 1963), pp. 23–24. See also decision of Leningrad Executive Committee of 25 March 1960 in *L.B.*, No. 9 (May 1960), pp. 3–6.

[28] See decision of the Leningrad Executive Committee of 4 June 1956 in *Sbornik reshenii i rasporiazhenii ispolnitelnogo komiteta Leningradskogo gorodskogo Soveta* (Leningrad, 1958), pp. 5–10. See also decision of Moscow Executive Committee of 12 October in *M.B.*, No. 20 (October 1965), pp. 1–5.

constituents that the raion had no resources to build a shop that had been included in the mandate, organized the citizens, issued appeals to enterprises for material aid, and led the citizens in the construction of the shop.[29]

The deputy does not confine his activities to the electoral mandate. He is expected to hold office hours in public places for the collection of demands from his constituents. He must periodically report to them on his work and hear their demands at public meetings. He also receives numerous letters from constituents. The citizen demands may involve matters of concern to the entire district, such as those pertaining to the quality of food in local restaurants, the need for new shops, or the lack of adequate cultural and recreational facilities. Other demands may be highly personal and relate to such matters as the enrollment of children in special schools, or disputes with neighbors, or even trouble within the family. No problem is supposed to be too personal or too small to take to the deputy.[30] He is supposed to take the same interest in the personal affairs of his constituents as the old ward politician did in American cities. The reason is probably the same in both cases. Personal attention builds popularity and support for the administration. Once the deputy receives a demand, he should investigate it, present it to local authorities if it has merit, and make certain that the citizen gets some sort of response from the officials, even if only a verbal one.

VIII. Desirable and Undesirable Citizen Demands

The demands discussed up to this point have been ones that the authorities, at least the higher authorities, regard as desirable and think should be given some measure of gratification, either material or psychic. The authorities undoubtedly regard many of them as legitimate and routine claims for goods or services—housing, housing repairs, pensions, etc.—to which the claimants are officially entitled. Authorities may find other demands desirable because they provide feedback on regime policies, reveal popular attitudes, or provide information on the performance of lower level functionaries. The authorities may value some merely as acceptable means for people to vent their frustrations.

Certainly, local officials who try to suppress or conceal demands of this sort run the risk of censure from above. The higher authorities' ob-

[29] A. Zhuravlev (Chairman of the Petroslaviansk Settlement Executive Committee), "Metodom narodnoi stroiki" in *L.B.*, No. 16 (August 1963), pp. 21–22.
[30] *Vechernii Leningrad,* 26 November 1964, p. 1.

vious desire that desirable demands receive some type of satisfaction is understandable. By satisfying the demands the authorities build support and cultivate in the minds of the citizens the belief that their demands are efficacious. This sense of efficacy itself may lead to greater support, and it almost certainly encourages citizens to submit additional desirable demands. This provides additional opportunities to build support and assures the continued flow of needed information to the authorities. The very fact that the citizens use official channels, rather than the disapproved but available means, to satisfy their needs and wants is itself an indication of support.

Undoubtedly, the authorities do not regard as desirable all citizen demands flowing into the system. The sources used in this study contain no information on whatever directives may exist concerning the handling of undesirable citizen demands. Consequently, any discussion of undesirable demands must be speculative.

Soviet citizens are more or less aware of the extent to which the regime is willing to act at a given time to meet certain kinds of demands. Whatever shortcomings the Soviet mass media may have as general news sources, they quite carefully provide information concerning official policy lines on the various subjects for which established policy lines exist. Research on Western political systems has shown that political participation is related to a sense of efficacy. No way exists to verify this hypothesis in the Soviet Union; but it seems reasonable to assume that there, too, active participation such as stating demands will vary according to the citizen's perception of the efficacy of his actions.

The authorities may try to discourage some demands by simply ignoring them, but the Soviet press provides clear evidence that the authorities also actively try to discourage certain demands. A mild form of negative response is the article reporting that certain nameless individuals hold an unacceptable view. Other articles will single out particular individuals. Sometimes the press will publish a letter (selected from among the thousands the Soviet press receives daily) containing a disapproved demand and follow it with crucial commentary. Mass media content of this sort must inhibit persons considering making similar demands.

In his study of the Smolensk Archives, Fainsod noted that citizen petitions expressing deep hostility to the regime were simply referred to the police for action. As a result, by the mid-thirties, such petitions nearly disappeared from the archives.[31] The sources used in this study do not enable me to determine whether such petitions existed in the 1950's and 1960's, but I can state that the Soviet citizen knows that the careless expression of certain opinions may arouse police interest. This is not to say that the citizen never expresses such opinions; but he does

[31] Fainsod, *Smolensk Under Soviet Rule*, pp. 378–79.

so cautiously, being selective about to whom and where he expresses them.

The norms governing acceptable demand expression, although not nearly as restrictive and inhibiting as some in the West seem to think, effectively restrict the citizen's expression of demands. His awareness of these limitations has the effect of reducing the number of demand inputs flowing into the system and, even more important, of restricting their content. The regime is thus protected from the possible consequences of a divisive public debate on basic policy questions.

IX. The Limited Impact of Citizen Demands on Official Discussion

The impact of citizen demands, or more precisely the impact of the data that results from the aggregation of citizen demands by local officials, on the deliberations of local decision-makers is difficult to determine because of the lack of access to the minutes of the most important local decision-making bodies: the city executive committee and the bureau of the city party committee. Nevertheless, a few observations, based on the local press reports of meetings of the full city party committees of Moscow and Leningrad from 1953 to 1967, are possible.

These reports have certain shortcomings. They are not verbatim accounts, but extended summaries. No way exists to determine the effects of censorship on the reports. Nevertheless, the reports are extensive summaries, attributing specific remarks to specific speakers. The speakers themselves constitute a fair cross section of that part of the local elite with an interest in the matter under discussion. Finally, the press reports provide the only accessible source of information on the deliberations of the local elite.[32]

The city party committees discussed various topics, among which were the state of housing construction, consumer goods production, and the state of retailing and various consumer and communal services. These were areas of governmental activity that gave rise to numerous citizen demands. During the course of these meetings, speakers sometimes stated that citizen needs, wants, complaints, or requests in some area were not being met. However, the speakers usually attributed the failure to meet citizen demands to the poor performance of some particular agency, institution, enterprise, or branch of the economy and

[32] For examples of such discussions see: *Vecherniaia Moskva,* May 30, 1956, p. 2; December 9, 1960, p. 1; and *Leningradskaia Pravda,* February 28, 1961, p. 1; April 25, 1961, p. 1.

never to centrally established policies and priorities. In other words, speakers occasionally used aggregated data on citizen demands to raise more general demands, but the more general demands themselves were limited. Speakers used the citizen demands as an indicator of how well some agency, institution, or branch of the economy satisfied the needs or demands of the populace within the limits set by centrally established policies and priorities.

Even this limited use of citizen demands has not been common. The members of the local elite are subject to various pressures; but of these pressures, the pressure of public opinion is not among the strongest. As a result the local elite is not very responsive to it. The Party leads the masses, not the masses the Party. The aggregated data on citizen demands are treated like any other aggregated data on performance. The information provides an opportunity to act and is taken into account, but it provides no compulsion to act. Indeed, aggregated data on unmarketable stocks of consumer goods may seem more compelling than aggregated data on consumer complaints about goods purchased. The speakers from the various agencies, institutes, and organizations have their own particular demands to promote. They are spokesmen not for the citizenry, but for some segment of the governmental, party, or economic apparatuses; and they usually use aggregated data on citizen demands only when the data supports their own particular perceived interests.

To assert that the party and governmental officials have no regard for public opinion or the welfare of the citizenry would be incorrect; but even the highest ranking city officials—the secretaries of the city party committee—have only a limited ability to cope with the more general problems implicit in the aggregated citizen demands. They can provide some satisfaction for the demands by calling on the government agencies fulfilling the housing construction program to build better housing. They can call on enterprises to produce more and better consumer goods. They can support the requests of the city construction agency, the city trade agency, or the city consumer services agency for more resources. The city party officials' demands directed to the center are, no doubt, often influential because of their political standing in the system. However, even they can call only for the most efficient use of available resources to attain centrally determined goals; goals that might or might not be consistent with the satisfaction of citizen demands.

X. The Importance of Demand Processing

The lack of any autonomous groups in the intra-societal environment capable of aggregating and processing the specific raw citizen demands into a program for political action that can serve as an alternative to the one advanced by the ruling oligarchy weakens the impact of citizen demands on official deliberations and policy making. In the Soviet Union the raw citizen demands are processed entirely within the political system. This imposes a burden on officials, but it also assures the leadership a greater amount of decision-making autonomy by sharply reducing the pressures of public opinion. At the same time it assures the leaders opportunities for building support and a flow of needed information.

This deserves further elaboration.[33] One may argue that in any society the political system's institutional structure, the composition of the political leadership and public policies generate frustration, anxiety and dissatisfaction among the people. The people respond in various ways, among which is the articulation of demands by individual citizens. In many societies this is followed by a collective redefinition of demands by various organizations involved in the political process. Many of these organizations are independent of the regime and some stand outside the political system, although linked to it. Thus political parties, both those participating in the government and those in opposition, pressure groups, and other organizations take raw citizen demands along with other materials and aggregate and process them into alternative programs and policies. This leads to activities, protests and movements seeking to implement new policies, to capture and even to modify or overthrow the existing institutional structure for political decision-making. The result is civil debate and conflict. Citizen demands do not merely offer rulers useful information and opportunities to build support, but generate additional strain within the society and pressure for changes in public policy, leadership composition and institutional structure.

In the Soviet Union the process is short-circuited at a critical point. Strains are generated; frustration, anxiety and dissatisfaction within the general populace exist; and citizens do articulate demands. However, these demands feed directly into the political system to be processed by members of the governmental and party apparatuses serving the ruling oligarchy. The lower level officials process and make use of citizen demands in ways that are useful to themselves, but they cannot, according to the norm they observe in self-interest and which they probably regard as legitimate, process the citizen demands into more general proposals that challenge the existing institutional structure, the policies and priorities of the leaders—unless given a signal that discussion of such matters is desired by the leaders—or the composition of leadership. In fact, established norms prohibit even the leading members of the polit-

[33] The following discussion is based on an adaption of a "Simplified Systematic View of the 'Collective Behavior' Approach to a Theory of Institutionalism" presented by Walter Buckley, *Sociology and Modern Systems Theory* (Englewood Cliffs, N.J.: Prentice Hall, 1967), p. 138.

buro from freely appealing to the public or groups for support on controversial matters.[34] Consequently the potential of citizen demands for generating additional strains and pressures for change is sharply reduced. On the other hand, the toleration and encouragement of citizen gatekeepers provide the officials and ruling oligarchs with opportunities to build support and a flow of information useful in adapting the system's structure and policies in ways the *leadership* believes appropriate, plus a means of reducing the erosion of support that may result from policies adopted and pursued with little regard for public opinion.

XI. Conclusion

Soviet citizens clearly tend their own gates and the quantity of citizen demands is sufficient to pose a serious threat of input overload at the lower administrative levels. The attempt to distinguish the Soviet political system from those of Western democracies on the basis of the absence of numerous citizen gatekeepers in the former and their existence in the latter is erroneous. Distinctions must be based on the kinds of demands that may be raised by these gatekeepers; the absence in the Soviet Union of institutions independent of the regime that can aggregate these demands; and the impossibility in the Soviet Union of using demands to create an alternative program to that advanced by the ruling oligarchy.

Citizen gatekeepers may be either an inevitable consequence of democracy or a necessary condition for it; but they are not a sufficient condition. In the absence of other democratic institutions, they may serve the interests of a dictatorship as well as they have ever served the interests of a democratic regime. They provide both with needed information and opportunities to build support.

This support may be built very cheaply. Not all demands need be given actual material satisfaction. The mere acceptance of a demand by local officials, some expression or indication of interest and concern (even if this amounts to nothing more than helpless thrashing about), can create support. The citizen is able to vent his grievances and make his wishes known. He may derive some release of hostility merely from seeing the discomfort of local officials as they struggle to meet his demands and suffer the criticism of higher authorities. Even this useless

[34] For a discussion of this point in the context of high level disputes over agricultural policy see Sidney I. Ploss, *Conflict and Decision Making in Soviet Russia. A Case Study of Agricultural Policy, 1953–1963* (Princeton, N.J.: Princeton University Press, 1965), p. 84.

effort may make the regime seem more human and interested in the welfare of the ordinary citizen. The more limited, the more private the demand and the more personal its handling by local officials, perhaps the greater the support generated for the regime, even though the regime persists in the policies that created the conditions that gave rise to the demand.

THE RED GUARDS IN HISTORICAL PERSPECTIVE: CONTINUITY AND CHANGE IN THE CHINESE YOUTH MOVEMENT*

John Israel

ALTHOUGH organised by students and young intellectuals, the Chinese Communist Party (CCP) has had a love-hate relationship with these groups. Throughout most of a quarter century of rural insurgency, the CCP was hard put to manipulate political activities among individualistic young urban intellectuals. In the mid-twenties, the Communist Youth League (YCL) resisted the Stalinist directives of Party leaders. During the war against Japan, thought reform was deemed essential to insure the loyalty even of those who had undertaken the arduous trek to the Border Regions. Furthermore, the CCP laboured under a doctrinal handicap: although students were invaluable for organising intellectuals, workers and peasants, it was embarrassing for the party of the proletariat to have to rely upon this educated élite. During the united front periods of the mid-20s and after 1937, students were defined as "petit bourgeois," which made them acceptable allies. After the CCP's break with Chiang Kai-shek in 1927, a more radical party line blamed these petit bourgeois for such Stalinist follies as the Canton Commune. Throughout the "united front from below" of the early 30s, students were divided into "progressive" proletarian and "reactionary" bourgeois elements, the former to be utilised, the latter to be excluded. The ideological conundrum remains even today.

Since taking power, the CCP, like the Kuomintang (KMT), has wavered between encouraging youth to study for national reconstruction and using them as political tools. Unlike the KMT, which feared

From *The China Quarterly*, London, No. 30 (1967). Reprinted by permission of the author and the editor.

* I would like to thank the Committee on Contemporary China of the Social Science Research Council, whose grant made possible this research, and the East Asian Research Center at Harvard University, which provided facilities for my work.

that youthful enthusiasm could open the door to Communist control, the CCP welcomed student activism which it had learned to manipulate before coming to power. Hence the CCP, despite its ambivalence, has consistently refused to exclude students from politics. Well before the proclamation of the People's Republic on October 1, 1949, nationwide student and youth organisations were brought under Party control. During the early 50s, these groups, like other mass organisations, became effective media for transmitting directives to vast numbers of people and promoting nationwide movements.

The principal youth organisation has been the Communist Youth League (called the New Democratic Youth League from 1949 to 1956). Its members—primarily men and women between 15 and 25—number perhaps 35 million (there have been no official figures since 1960). Membership in the Young Pioneers, an organisation of 100 million, is now compulsory for all schoolchildren of nine to 15. The CCP controls the League, whose cadres in turn control the Young Pioneers. Qualified Pioneers are absorbed into the League, qualified League members into the Party.

After 1949, the YCL faced two major problems in its relationship with the students. The first was a feeling of isolation, especially in the universities. During the 50s, when YCL cadres were a minority in institutions of higher learning, students recognised them as powerful but dangerous characters who were prepared to betray confidences and to report innocent slips of the tongue.[1] Hence an invisible barrier developed between self-proclaimed leaders and student masses. To study hard and minimise political involvement became a prevailing goal. The League employed various stratagems to reaffirm its pre-eminence. Group meetings, mutual surveillance, self-criticism and mobilisation for innumerable campaigns made it impossible to ignore politics. Rewards for "positive" thought and behaviour encouraged activists and have compelled even the serious scholar to make a pretence of co-operating with the League.

The second problem, opportunism, was encouraged by the very methods used to combat the first. To a generation of students educated entirely under communism, the path to success was clearly through the League and the Party. In 1964 the League's First Secretary, Hu Yao-pang, had to admit that "evil and degraded elements . . . have sneaked into the YCL."[2] More alarming was the probability that among the

[1] Now that YCL members are a majority in the universities, students are distrustful of the unscrupulous opportunists willing to exploit friends as stepping stones into YCL or the Party. Morris Wills (a student at Peita, 1956–62), unpublished manuscript on Peita. Cited by permission of the author.

[2] *Jen-min Jih-pao* (*People's Daily*), July 7, 1964, transl. in *Current Back-*

"evil and degraded" were sons and daughters of Party officials, youths who had taken advantage of their favoured position to avoid hardship and gain comfort.[3] The maintenance of quality has been further threatened by YCL's phenomenal growth, from half a million members in October 1949 to 12 million in 1954, 23 million in 1957, and perhaps 35 million today.[4] The transformation of a youthful élite into an unwieldy appendage of an entrenched establishment has eroded morale.

In the student upsurge of 1957 many YCL members joined the rebel ranks.[5] Appparently the lure of academic values had corrupted some of the presumed faithful, especially among the "bourgeois" whom the YCL had recruited in its search for educated cadres. To remedy the situation special efforts were made to enlist sons and daughters of the proletariat. However, the fact that they were often uneducated and incompetent simply increased the chaos of the Great Leap catastrophe.[6] By 1965 the League was in serious trouble. Said Anthony Sherman Chang and Wen Shih:

> The standards of the YCL are clearly low, its membership lagging; it contains not enough young people, and youngsters are not drawn to it, while on the other hand, it contains too many older persons who cling to their status or offices in this organisation. The "inheritors" of communism are not coming forward; while a dying generation tends to cling tenaciously to the positions of power, influence and prominence, though it is really incapable of producing any fresh approaches or new prospects.[7]

In the course of its recruitment drive of late 1965 the League welcomed qualified youths from non-proletarian backgrounds. This hectic and rather indiscriminate expansion has been variously interpreted as an attempt to placate progeny of upper-class parents or as an effort to

---

ground (*CB*) (Hong Kong: U. S. Consulate-General), No. 738 (July 30, 1964), p. 18.

[3] *China News Analysis* (*CNA*), No. 521 (June 19, 1964), p. 6.

[4] Figures through 1957 are from Klaus H. Pringsheim, "The Functions of the Chinese Communist Youth Leagues (1920–1949)," *The China Quarterly*, No. 12 (October–December 1962), pp. 90–91.

[5] *CNA*, No. 292 (September 11, 1959), p. 2; Roderick MacFarquhar, *The Hundred Flowers Campaign and the Chinese Intellectuals* (New York: Praeger, 1960), pp. 171–73.

[6] Tan Hsin-wen, "Chinese Communist Youth League Affairs and Youth Movements," *Communist China 1961* (Hong Kong: Union Research Institute, 1962), I, p. 64.

[7] Anthony Sherman Chang and Wen Shih, "The Political Role of Youth," in E. Stuart Kirby, ed., *Youth in China* (Hong Kong: Dragonfly Books, 1965), p. 138.

expand the YCL to offset the growing strength of the military.[8] The power struggle within the highest echelons of the Party and the demand for a generation of revolutionary successors doubtless were important causal factors. No matter the intention, the influx of eight million new members in a single year inevitably undermined whatever remained of the League's élitist élan.

The crisis in the youth movement was complicated by the CCP's endeavour to eliminate the distinction between the intellectual aristocracy and the illiterate masses. This was to be achieved by converting students into proletarians and proletarians into students. School admission standards were lowered and scholarships provided for working class children. At the same time, students were put to work in factories and on farms, the assumption being that proletarian life would produce proletarian thought. These efforts met with indifferent success. Many students equated manual labour with corvee service and discovered the virtues of the masses more evident in the abstract than in the concrete. Sons of the working class welcomed educational opportunities but they were coolly received by middle class schoolmates.

Hence the campuses became a battleground for the cold war between "red" and "expert," a conflict that continued after graduation between red cadres and expert managers, scientists and technicians. This war escalated after the failure of the Great Leap. Between 1961 and 1964 Party moderates managed to redress the balance in favour of expertise, but beginning in 1962 ideologues counter-attacked with a socialist education movement, forerunner of the cultural revolution. When radicals moved to sacrifice education in favour of indoctrination, the Youth League emerged as a relatively conservative force. In 1964 and 1965 it backed reforms that stressed leisure for students. Significantly the People's Liberation Army (PLA) opposed these measures in favour of a politically-conceived, village-oriented curriculum.[9] A Japanese correspondent who visited YCL Central Headquarters in October 1965 noted the reluctance of the organisation's leaders to discuss Maoist ideology except in the most perfunctory way.[10]

The muddled course of events in the early 60s widened the "gap between ideology and organisation," a pervasive problem in Chinese society.[11] The school system had grown enormously, but the slow pace

[8] See respectively Michel Oksenberg, "Communist China: A Quiet Crisis in Revolution," *Asian Survey,* VI, 1 (January 1966), p. 4; and *CNA,* No. 633 (October 21, 1966), p. 6.

[9] *CNA,* 617 (June 24, 1966), p. 3, and 633 (October 21, 1966), pp. 5–6.

[10] *Tokyo Shimbun,* December 21, 1966, transl. in *Daily Summary of Japanese Press* (hereafter *DSJP*), December 28, p. 20.

[11] Franz Schurmann, *Ideology and Organization in Communist China* (Berkeley: University of California Press, 1966), p. 493.

of economic recovery severely limited job opportunities for graduates. Attempts to place education upon an academic plane alarmed unqualified students while efforts to move in the other direction threatened the academically inclined. Meanwhile, even the new generation of proletarian students absorbed "feudalistic" attitudes of the old literati, disdainful of the uneducated and revolted by life in the countryside.[12]

The Creation of the Red Guards

The gap between ideology and organisation suggests the universal problem of ideals and realities that affects youth everywhere. Unlike most adults, young people generally believe that publicly promulgated values should find expression in reality. In China the proletarian youth who enters a higher middle school or university is especially sensitive to the official values of his society. As a beneficiary of the revolution, he has more reason than other people to take seriously Communist promises of a glorious future for the working class. He assumes the educational system will prepare him for leadership in that future. But, though granted preferential treatment, he discovers that the system is really designed not for him, but for the better-prepared children of the bourgeoisie, whom experience and indoctrination have taught him to distrust. For him, school means academic and social humiliation at the hands of the middle class.

The massive Youth League cannot rescue its millions of student members from this dilemma, especially since the unprecedented infusion of new recruits in 1965. By November of that year, the *China Youth News* found it necessary to exhort the handful of power-holding YCL politicians to allow greater leadership opportunities for their fellow students.[13] Members of "revolutionary" social classes continued to enjoy many advantages, but they were learning that proper class affiliation and political activism were no guarantees of success. With YCL students constituting a majority in the universities (and perhaps even in the higher middle schools), it was clear that many members would face a dreary future in the countryside after graduation. There was, however, a way to resolve, or at least postpone, this dilemma, a way which must have become increasingly attractive to Mao Tse-tung as he searched for revolutionary successors and allies in the power struggle: release these youths from the fetters of school and League bureau-

[12] Interview with Morris Wills, Cambridge, Mass., January 1966.

[13] *Chung-kuo Ch'ing-nien Pao* (*China Youth News*), November 18, 1965, transl. in *Survey of the China Mainland Press* (*SCMP*), (Hong Kong: U. S. Consulate-General), No. 3591 (December 6), pp. 11–13.

cracies, give them direct personal inspiration, arm them with the simplest possible ideology, and turn them loose against the "class enemy." This was the prescription for the Red Guards.

The allure of membership in the Red Guard élite was based upon many factors, which depended upon the individual: the desire to participate in the construction of a communist utopia, a prospect of gaining advantages in the relentless competition for education and employment, the enjoyment of comradeship, shared perils and a sense of group power and, by late summer, the opportunity for travel and adventure. Here was an outlet both for the opportunism spawned by a bureaucratic establishment and the idealism fostered through revolutionary indoctrination. In 1957 Premier Chou En-lai had predicted a youthful rebellion a decade hence, "if we don't change our bureaucratic ways."[14] Nine years later Mao assailed the bureaucracy with just such a rebellion.

At first there was no clear demarcation between the incipient Red Guards and the regular Party apparatus. But as officials at every level of the ruling structure came under attack, Maoist leaders circumvented the entrenched CCP-YCL machinery and called upon the nation's youth to act spontaneously. To the idealist seeking a "pure" cause the appeal was obvious. And to the young political climber the lesson was clear. The established order could guarantee neither advancement nor security; loyalty could be established only through an incorruptible mass organisation directly obedient to Mao. In this crusade, lower-class students would have licence, even responsibility, to attack the institutions and symbols of the corrupt society—the educational system which had confined them, the bourgeoisie which had despised them, and the officials who had made a mockery of their ideals and aspirations. Thus would the internal contradictions of the system be turned against each other in a crusade for a new order.

Were it not for the CCP's internal crisis, it is unlikely that the social problems of youth and bureaucracy would have been sufficient cause for the unleashing of the Red Guards. Liu Shao-ch'i's 50 days' bid for power in June and July demonstrated to Mao that extraordinary means would be necessary to extricate Liu and his Party machine from the seats of authority. However, even this power struggle was inseparable from the question of the younger generation. The problem of generations had grown acute as it became clear that many Party leaders accepted the post-Great Leap "normalcy" as more than a passing phase. A majority of China's population had been born since 1945. If youth nurtured by the state and conditioned by a bureaucratic environment failed to experience the equivalent of the Long March, the rural revolu-

[14] *People's Daily,* April 26, 1957.

tion and the war against Chiang, China's future leaders would be revolutionary in name only. Hence the entrenched conservatism of CCP organisation men not only thwarted Mao's aspiration for the present, but threatened to destroy his vision for the future. Without a generation of revolutionary successors all the dreams and sacrifices of the past would be for naught.

The quest for a method of passing on the revolutionary tradition had been in progress for several years before the birth of the Red Guards. The "recall bitterness" campaign sought to transmit it orally; exhortations to learn from Lei Feng, Wang Chieh and the PLA attempted the same thing through emulation. All were inadequate. Inured since nursery school to a bombardment of words, the younger generation could not be revolutionised through propaganda alone. The champion breaststroker of the Yangtze drew the obvious conclusion: "We learn to swim while swimming." Only a revolutionary struggle could produce revolutionary souls.

Months of preparation had been necessary before hundreds of thousands of youths all over China could spring into action. The earliest efforts, still under YCL leadership, may have been the juvenile and children's leagues, paramilitary organisations created in May 1965.[15] According to Asahi correspondent Matsuno Tanio, a nucleus of seven "revolutionary" Peking University (Peita) students received Mao's secret order to attack their president, Lu P'ing, in September 1965.[16] However not until early spring of 1966 are there clear indications of an embryonic Red Guard movement. The Red Flag Militant Team at Peita's middle school traced its origins to March, and a Canton refugee reported Red Guard-style harassment of teachers as early as March (Tsinghua Middle School Red Guards, who claimed national priority, were organised about May 21).[17] By mid-June at least one Canton middle school had a "cultural revolution students' congress."[18]

During the university purges in June, Party factions mobilised student support for and against the presidents of Peking, Nanking and other universities. The radicals who attacked these administrators as

[15] *CNA,* No. 633 (October 21, 1966), p. 5; Radio Chengchow, May 25, 1965; Radio Sian, May 31; Radio Nanchang, May 30; Radio Canton, May 30.

[16] Matsuno Tanio in *Asahi Journal,* October 2, 1966, transl. in *Summary of Selected Japanese Magazines* (hereafter *SSJM*), November 7, p. 20.

[17] Stanley Karnow, "Why They Fled: Refugee Interviews," *Current Scene,* IV, 18 (October 7, 1966), pp. 6–7; *Mainichi,* evening September 26, 1966, transl. in *DSJP,* September 28, p. 9; *Sankei,* evening September 29, 1966, transl. in *DSJP,* September 30, p. 31.

[18] *Yang-ch'eng Wan-pao,* June 24, 1966, cited in *SCMP,* No. 3470 (July 1), p. 16.

perpetrators of bourgeois education were among the original Red Guards who appeared two months later; defenders of the chancellors probably found their way into "rightist" Red Guard groups. The Maoist purge of school administrators appealed to proletarian youths who had ample cause for dissatisfaction with the status quo in education. Both Lu P'ing and Kuang Ya-ming, the president of Nanking University, were charged with discriminating against those of worker and peasant origin. At Peita, claimed the *People's Daily,* there were 31 such students among the 52 who dropped out of the 209-man class entering the physics department in 1960. Ten of the 31 were expelled from Peita, including seven of the eight industrial and agricultural cadres enrolled in the department.[19] This evidence suggests that the enforcement of academic standards had exacted a toll among those unqualified for a university education in a rigorous scientific discipline, especially those who had gained admission on political grounds.

The most dramatic encouragement for the student radicals was the June 18 postponement of the 1966–67 university enrolment and discarding of the current entrance examination system. The *People's Daily*'s statement that this was intended to aid the cultural revolution, encourage left-wing students, and strike a blow at the right was not an idle boast.[20] The proposal came from groups of seniors in two higher middle schools, the very individuals who would soon face the prospect of a career in the countryside if they failed to win college admission. Only a year earlier, the YCL organ, *China Youth,* had advised anxious middle school graduates to take the entrance examination and leave the decision to the state.[21] A great many college hopefuls inevitably had been disappointed by the results. Furthermore, the 1966 graduates included a much higher proportion of YCL members due to the massive 1965 recruitment which had concentrated upon the under-20 group. It was doubtful that all of these could be accommodated in college. No wonder that a group of graduating YCL seniors claimed to see no difference between the present examination system and that of China's "feudal" past.[22]

There was more than a little blatant opportunism in the suggestion of a number of middle school seniors in Peking that college entrants should be selected "from among those who stood firm and were active

[19] *People's Daily,* August 15, 1966, transl. in *SCMP,* No. 3767 (August 24, 1966) pp. 14–15.

[20] *People's Daily,* June 18, 1966, transl. in *Hsinhua News Agency Release,* June 19.

[21] *Chung-kuo Ch'ing-nien* (*China Youth*), No. 8 (April 16, 1965), transl. in *Selections from China Mainland Magazines* (*SCMM*), (Hong Kong: U. S. Consulate-General), No. 472 (June 1), pp. 1–2, and 476 (June 18), pp. 4–5.

[22] *Hsinhua News Agency Release,* June 20, 1966.

in the current great cultural revolution."[23] In effect they were asking that only persons like themselves, who were manifestly devoted to the proletariat, should be spared the ordeal of physical labour. What the young zealots had in mind for their bourgeois classmates was later spelled out by Red Guards at Peking's Hungyen Middle School:

> If the children of the propertied classes go to the farm villages, they will no longer wish to go to universities. That is because if they live with the farmers, they will learn a great deal of admirable ideology. This is very important. It is fully sufficient if they graduate from senior high schools.[24]

With the toughest academic competitors permanently exiled to the countryside and political qualifications substituted for examination grades, even the dullest student could compete. Through dedicated activity in the cultural revolution, he could hope to shape his own destiny more effectively than he could have through foreboding and impersonal examinations.

The June 18 announcement did not fulfill all the expectations of middle school seniors, but it did promise that college and middle school entrance would be based upon "a combination of recommendation and selection."[25] What is more, it called upon middle school authorities to see that graduating seniors be "accommodated" (kept in school) in those institutions where the cultural revolution was still under way, otherwise that they be sent to labour in farms and factories. What better incentive for seniors in higher middle schools to take the lead in the cultural revolution? Others followed, confident that political activities would be more important than ever in determining their academic futures.[26]

[23] *Hsinhua News Agency Release,* June 19, 1966.

[24] Statement made to a visiting group of Japanese, October 7, 1966, reported in *Asahi,* October 9, transl. in *DSJP,* October 8–11, p. 6.

[25] *People's Daily,* editorial, June 18, 1966, transl. in *Hsinhua News Agency Release,* June 19.

[26] The fact that middle school students were chosen for this role also reflected a widely-held belief that university students were unreliable. As one high official expressed it, "The state educates youths at primary schools and middle schools, spending much money on them, and when they proceed to universities, they are completely corrupted. . . ." See *Sankei,* evening, November 9, 1966, transl. in *DSJP,* November 15, p. 9. The Japanese correspondent who filed the report from Peking did not reveal the official's name; it seems improbable that it was Ronald Reagan. *The Free China Weekly,* February 3, 1967, p. 4, reports that Chou Pai-yun, a former Red Guard now on Formosa, estimates the percentage of students who support Mao as "100 in primary schools, 60 in junior high schools, 30

From early June through late July, Liu Shao-ch'i and his followers in the CCP Central Committee ignored Mao's desire for a profound revolution and attempted instead to launch a modest rectification campaign through the regular Party apparatus by dispatching work teams to government bureaus, schools, factories and communes. The terms frequently locked horns with cultural revolution committees of young Maoists organised under a variety of names, including "Red Guards." These zealots regarded the teams as tools of the establishment sent to seize leadership and stifle the revolution from below. Indeed, some teams did threaten the youthful radicals. In one Peking middle school of 1,700 pupils, the nascent Red Guards had increased from 14 on June 2 to 300 early in July only to shrink to 140 under pressure from the team.[27] The Maoists counter-attacked when they could. At Peking University, for example, an anti-Lu P'ing rally was turned against the head of the work team, and a group of faculty and student moderates, who filled the vacuum left by the president's removal, was successfully challenged by a radical Red Flag Militant Team from the associated middle school supported by Chiang Ch'ing (Mrs. Mao Tse-tung).[28]

This was not the only intervention by a prestigious figure in a school altercation. Between June and August, Tsinghua University and its middle school received visits from members of a work team including Yeh Lin (vice chairman of the State Economic Commission), Wang Kuang-mei (Mrs. Liu Shao-ch'i), Deputy Premier Po I-po, and Wang Jen-chung, subsequently vice-chairman of the cultural revolution group. (All of these were criticised by Red Guards in following months.)[29] Ch'en Po-ta and Mrs. Liu were said to have taken up residence on the campus.[30] It is likely that members of the work team joined forces with members of the student political aristocracy, including Mrs. Liu's daughter, against the insurgent Maoist radicals; the latter, in turn, interrogated the officials and barred their way to the campus.[31] The bitterness of the radicals was brutally expressed in a pamphlet of July 20 by a middle school Red Guard:

---

in senior high schools and none in college." Though exaggerated, this does reflect the scepticism of college students.

[27] Fukishima Udai in the *Asahi Journal,* October 16, 1966, transl. in *SSJM,* October 31, pp. 74–75.

[28] Ibid., p. 76; *Mainichi,* evening, September 26, 1966, transl. in *DSJP,* September 28, p. 9; "Foreign Expert," "Eyewitness of a Cultural Revolution," *The China Quarterly,* No. 28 (October–December 1966), p. 3.

[29] *Nihon Keizai,* January 5, 1967, transl. in *DSJP,* January 6, p. 21.

[30] "Foreign Expert," op. cit., p. 3.

[31] Ibid.

> For 17 years our school has been ruled by the bourgeois class. We shall not tolerate this any longer! . . . Old and young gentlemen, we tell you frankly, you all stink and you are nothing [but] rotten trash. . . . Formerly you were in a privileged position, sat on our heads and let your excrement fall on us to show that you were superior. Today you are under dictatorship and you suffer. . . . You thought you could make use of the temporary existing bourgeois education to climb higher up the ladder to become white experts, get into the university, join up with the "professors, experts." Your heart was set on a small car, a little modern house, a white coat, a laboratory . . . on enjoying comfort, affluence, a good reputation, a good salary. . . . Really wicked eggs! We tell you: if you do not wish to change, if you remain reactionary, we will not spare you! . . . your class hatred will stick to the points of our bayonets. Your guts will be dug out. . . .[32]

Chou En-lai visited the embattled Tsinghua campus on August 4 and August 22.[33] The urgency of these visits by China's leading diplomat was explained four months later in a wall newspaper which reported three students killed in bloody incidents on August 19 and 24.[34]

By the end of July, Mao deemed the situation so desperate that only extraordinary measures would suffice. Though it is conjectural whether the August showdown was precipitated by the power struggle alone or by a substantive issue such as Vietnam, it must have been obvious to Mao and Lin that Liu's work teams had to be stopped from extending their power and sapping the sources of revolutionary potential among the young. Final steps towards the unveiling of the Red Guards came in quick succession: on July 29, Mao, Chou and other Party leaders gave their blessings to a meeting of militant student groups from various Peking schools. There the name "Red Guards" probably was adopted officially. Red Guards reportedly participated as observers, and more likely as a Maoist pressure group, at the August session of the Central Committee plenary.[35] On August 16 students from all over China were convened and addressed by Ch'en Po-ta.[36]

[32] *CNA*, No. 636 (January 11, 1966), pp. 2–4.

[33] *Mainichi*, September 10, 1966, transl. in *DSJP*, September 10–12, p. 36; *Mainichi*, September 18, transl. in *DSJP*, September 20, p. 7; *Sankei*, evening, September 29, transl. in *DSJP*, September 30, p. 31; *Mainichi*, October 30, transl. in *DSJP*, November 1, p. 6.

[34] *Nihon Keizai*, January 5, 1966, transl. in *DSJP*, January 6, p. 21.

[35] *Sankei*, August 28, 1966, transl. in *DSJP*, September 1, p. 18; *Tokyo Shimbun*, September 12, transl. in *DSJP*, September 10–12, p. 44; Matsuno Tanio in *Sekai*, November 1966, transl. in *SSJM*, October 31, p. 37; *Mainichi*, evening, December 28, transl. in *DSJP*, January 13, p. 24.

[36] Wang Chang-ling, "Peiping's 'Great Cultural Revolution' and the 'Red Guards,'" *Issues and Studies*, III, 2 (November 1966), p. 20.

The official debut of the Guards at the Peking rally of August 18 was described in a news release as follows:

> "Red Guards," composed of the most active, the bravest and the firmest of the revolutionary students, packed the reviewing stands on both flanks of the Tienanmen gate and were scattered all about the square. Many of them were clad in khaki, with belts around the waist and red arm bands. These revolutionary students said that they were "Red Guards" for the defence of the Party Central Committee, Chairman Mao and Mao Tse-tung's thought.
>
> A number of the "Red Guards" went up onto the rostrum to pay their most profound and sincere respects to Chairman Mao and to present their arm bands to Chairman Mao, Comrade Lin Piao and other leaders. Tumultuous cheers broke out from the packed square as Chairman Mao, wearing the red arm band, waved his greeting to the paraders.
>
> "Red Guards" down below shouted joyfully: "Look, Chairman Mao is wearing our red arm band. He approves of our 'Red Guards.'" They cheered: "Long live Chairman Mao! Long life, long life to Chairman Mao!"[37]

The Red Guards began as a relatively select "organisation established by middle school pupils from the families of workers, former poor and lower-middle peasants, revolutionary cadres and revolutionary armymen." In the capital the Guards received direct encouragement from the cultural revolution group. The most detailed account available of the situation in the provinces comes from Wang Ch'ao-t'ien, a Red Guard leader from the First Middle School of Manchouli (a town on the Chinese Eastern Railroad near the Soviet border), who defected to Formosa.[38] The organisational impetus at Wang's school came from emissaries of Red Guard headquarters in Peking. The chain of command theoretically reached from the cultural revolution group and Red Guards were headed by the principal, who was also Party secretary, and the school's Party branch was responsible for choosing members from candidates who combined proper class background with "progressive" thought and "positive" behaviour. Of 700 students, 200 applied and 150 were accepted. Leaders included sons of high-ranking cadres. Hence, until early September there was probably little to distinguish the composition and power structure of provincial Red Guards from that of the Party and Youth League.

[37] *Hsinhua News Agency Release*, August 19, 1966.

[38] Wang Ch'ao-t'ien, *Wo shih i-ko hung-wei-ping* (*I am a Red Guard*), (Taipei: Chung-kuo Ta-lu Wen-t'i Yen-chiu So, January 1967), pp. 9, 49, and interviewed in *U.S. News and World Report*, LXII, 5 (January 30, 1967), p. 57.

The Red Guards in Action

In the half year after August 18, 1966, groups of Red Guards:

1. Appeared in eight Peking rallies where they responded ecstatically to the presence of Mao.
2. Covered China with the face and words of the Leader.
3. Turned China's schools into political battlegrounds for struggling against "reactionary" classmates and teachers.
4. Travelled the length and breadth of their country.
5. Physically clashed with government, Party and school authorities, workers, soldiers and other students.
6. Arrested high-ranking figures, crowned them with dunce caps, paraded them through the streets, hauled them before public rallies and forced them to confess their "crimes."
7. Assailed citizens and compelled them to change hairdos, dress and shoes, and to listen to sermons on the aphorisms of Mao.
8. Ransacked shops, intimidated owners, changed names on signboards and scrutinised wares.
9. "Smashed priceless private and public collections of art, burned old books, tore down historical monuments and structures, broke up Christian, Buddhist, Moslem and Taoist religious symbols and entered private homes to destroy family altars and furniture."[39]
10. Renamed streets, restaurants and other public places, *e.g.*, Wang Fu-ching Street became Resist Revisionism Road, Kuang-hua Road—Aid Vietnam Road, Eternal Peace Company—Eternal Red Company, *Ta-kung pao* (*L'lmpartial*)—*Ch'ien-chin pao* (*The Progressive*), Democracy Road—East is Red Way.
11. Harassed foreign visitors, diplomats, correspondents and nuns.
12. Performed an undetermined number of good deeds to assist workers, peasants, the aged, the infirm, etc.

Mobility was the Red Guards' trademark. Millions of youngsters swept across the map of China. Wang Ch'ao-t'ien said that 6,000 army vehicles had been allocated for Red Guard use in Peking alone, and that Red Guard travel in August and September had exhausted 20 per cent of the nation's annual transportation budget.[40] By mid-October freight cars were being used for passengers, trains were running three hours late, and the main Peking station had been reserved for the exclusive use of the Red Guards.[41] The official rationale for this expensive

[39] Tillman Durdin, in *The New York Times,* March 5, 1967.
[40] Wang Ch'ao-t'ien, op. cit., p. 17.
[41] *Asahi,* evening, November 28, transl. in *DSJP,* December 6, 1966, p. 28.

and expansive activity was embodied in the slogan, "Exchange revolutionary experiences," but the likely reasons were more accurately defined by Wang Ch'ao-t'ien: (1) After the crusade against the "four olds" had passed, idle students would have been easy marks for anti-Maoist agitators. To keep them occupied it was necessary to appeal to their curiosity and sense of adventure. (2) In taking advantage of a rare opportunity to visit Peking and see Mao, youth would reaffirm and strengthen their support for the Leader. (3) The mass rallies at the T'ienanmen were useful to intimidate opponents of Mao and of his chosen successor, Lin Piao. (4) The Red Guards would best be able to combat the "faction in power" in distant places, far from the coercive influence of their own local authorities.[42]

The only approximation to a quantitative analysis of Red Guard accomplishments is a report, presumably by Public Security Minister Hsieh Fu-chih, which credits them with the following "war results" as of October 3, 1966:

> 1. Attack Against the Enemy: (1) The arrests including land owners, rich farmers, counter-revolutionary elements, evil elements, and rightist elements, totalled 16,623 persons. (2) Members arrested in the act of counter-revolutionary moves totalled 1,788 cases. (3) Political cases other than the above totalled 3,368.
>
> 2. Confiscated Arms and Ammunition: 85 guns, 22 machine-guns, 13,700 rifles, 13,800 old model rifles, 1,368,000 bullets, 26,700 shells, 210,000 *chin* of ammunition, 389,000 detonation caps, 230,000 bayonets, 6,000 *chin* of poison and 13,600 copies of Chiang Kai-shek's portrait and Kuomintang flags.
>
> 3. Confiscated Properties: 1,198,000 *liang* of gold, 306,000 *liang* of silver, 9,789,000 pieces of silver coins, 3,558,000 *yuan* worth of U.S. dollars, 3,739,000 *yuan* worth of pounds and other currencies and 482,000 million *yuan* worth of cash and securities.[43]

But the soul of the movement cannot be dissected and enumerated. Photographs, films and reports of eye-witnesses indicate a fanaticism that sometimes reached terrifying proportions. Visitors who observed

[42] Wang Ch'ao-t'ien, op. cit., pp. 17–18.

[43] *Asahi,* January 9, 1967, transl. in *DSJP,* January 10, p. 6. Versions in other Japanese newspapers differ in some details. *Yomiuri,* January 8, and *Tokyo Shimbun,* January 9, transl. in *DSJP,* January 10, pp. 6 and 10, say "13,700 rifles and pistols, 13,800 spears," but fail to mention Chiang's portraits and Kuomintang flags. The *Yomiuri* adds that "land owners, rich farmers, reactionary elements, capitalists, etc., and their families—approximately 400,000 persons"—were expelled.

and interviewed these youngsters noted their doctrinal dogmatism and detected in their eyes the gleam of religious fanatics. Gradually, as a mass infusion of opportunists diluted the main stream of the movement and the peregrinations and rallies became more routinised, the majority of Red Guards began to resemble school-aged tour groups. The crusade had become a pilgrimage. Considering the vast numbers of youngsters involved and the high pitch of verbal acrimony, the overall level of physical violence was remarkably low.

The behaviour of the Red Guards does not lend itself to neat periodisation. First, a "time lag" separated events in Peking from those in the rest of China.[44] Secondly, most of their activities had appeared, at least in rudimentary form, by the beginning of September. One does detect, however, a widening division between the dedicated activists committed to political and ideological goals and the unsophisticated student masses, including local leaders like Wang Ch'ao-t'ien who had little idea what the movement was all about.[45] This phenomenon has been common to all modern China's student movements in which thousands of demonstrators have been reduced, within a matter of weeks, to a few hundred politicians. However, the process has now radically altered and, in a purely quantitative sense, reversed. Whereas previous generations had been drawn back to the classroom by the promise of academic reward and the threat of political punishment, between August 1966 and March 1967 there was no classroom to return to and only the apathetic and the heretic were threatened with punishment. Thus the mass of students continued to go through the forms of a political movement while sight-seeing and the true political activists were reduced to a handful of college-level groups allied with adult politicians. What had begun as a middle school mass movement had become the preserve of a few college students centred in Peking. The millions of young participants, especially rural boys and girls who had crowded into the cities, helped to preserve the chaotic atmosphere, but became an increasing political liability to the Maoists.

Still mindful of the danger of forcing complex events into a rigid series of "stages," we can note other changes of emphasis. During the first fortnight after August 18 the main thrust of the movement was against the "four olds"—old ideas, old culture, old manners and old customs—"feudalistic" anachronisms from China's distant past and "bourgeois" hangovers from her semi-colonial modernisation. The keynote was sounded in a Peking middle school poster: "DECLARATION OF WAR ON THE OLD WORLD." There followed an unleashing

[44] "Foreign Expert," op. cit., p. 4.

[45] Wang Ch'ao-t'ien, op. cit., p. 10; *U.S. News and World Report,* LXII, 5 (January 30, 1967), p. 57.

of attacks on bourgeois haberdashery and grooming, old names, fine foods, luxury stores and symbols of traditional religion and culture. Because these dramatic activities involved high school students, the Red Guards were labelled "adolescents," "teenagers" or "juvenile delinquents." Peking's college students may have been slow to appear because they were scattered about the country executing the important but less dramatic tasks as envoys of the cultural revolution.[46] In any case it was the initial core of Red Guard middle school students, relatively proletarian, uneducated and alienated from China's traditions, who were most disposed to launch an uncompromising assault against the old culture.

Besides gaining the Red Guards nationwide and worldwide notoriety, these activities wrought fundamental changes in their organisation. Attacks on popular customs and deep-rooted traditions isolated them from former sympathisers; many Red Guard groups in factories, public enterprises and women's organisations were dissolved.[47] Furthermore, during the iconoclastic crusade Party and Youth League authority evaporated, groups of students began to organise their own "rebel corps" and schools became anarchic. Wang Ch'ao-t'ien, who witnessed these developments in Manchouli, gives the following explanation:

1. The work teams had been withdrawn at the beginning of September, thereby freeing the students to make their own interpretations of the generalities found in the editorials of *Red Flag* and the *People's Daily*.

2. After the principal had been labelled a "revisionist" and "anti-Maoist element," the Party-League leadership was purged. Teachers who came under attack departed, leaving the school in the hands of the Red Guards.

3. Strong leadership has emerged in "Rebel Corps," possibly through the earlier efforts of Peking's Red Guard emissaries, but these leaders were more a provocative influence than a controlling force.

4. Mao had said that the cultural revolution would have to be a spontaneous creation of the masses. Under the circumstances, his words were taken at face value.

5. Threatened by Red Guard terror, the local Party Committee had fallen silent and lost its authority.

6. The Youth League had ceased all activities.

7. It was evident to the Red Guards that the local Party apparatus no longer enjoyed the confidence of Mao Tse-tung.

8. The national and regional apparatus of the Red Guards provided

[46] Matsuno Tanio in *Sekai,* November 1966, transl. in *SSJM,* October 31, p. 36.

[47] Wang Ch'ao-t'ien, op. cit., pp. 11–12.

only loose liaison and the cultural revolution group was unable to make its commands effective at the local level.[48]

Now the Red Guards had a sense of power. Courted by high officials and invited to travel to Peking, they were irresistibly drawn deeper into the vortex of the cultural revolution. As they gathered momentum, they gathered mass. No longer could the Red Guards be restricted to middle school pupils of "revolutionary" classes. Millions of university students and primary school youngsters clamoured for admission, and rigid class distinctions were discarded to accommodate a maximum number of volunteers in a powerful mass organisation. Maoist spokesmen now criticised students who clung to the "reactionary 'theory of family lineage.'"[49] By early October, 20 per cent of the membership of the Red Guard Military School was drawn from "non-revolutionary" classes and about 10 per cent. of the teachers and staff had also been admitted.[50] Scattered statistics indicate that by mid-autumn one-sixth to one-third of various student bodies were Red Guards.[51] While the movement broadened, Ch'en Po-ta tried to augment the authority of the cultural revolution group by calling upon children of high-ranking cadres to transfer leadership to sons of workers, peasants, soldiers and ordinary cadres.[52] Divested of leaders who were constrained by family interests, the Red Guards could be used against the "faction in power."

. . . .

Manipulation, Factionalism and Opposition

The inconsistency and ineffectuality of official restraints raise important questions about the Red Guards' command structure and their relations with individuals and factions in the CCP. Though affirming their direct responsibility to Mao, the Guards had more intimate contact with Ch'en Po-ta and Chiang Ch'ing, who supported them from their formative period, with Chou En-lai, whose diplomatic talents they frequently taxed, and perhaps with Lin Piao who, like Mao, remained behind the

[48] Ibid., pp. 14–15; *U.S. News and World Report,* LXII, 5 (January 30, 1967), p. 57.

[49] *People's Daily-Red Flag* editorial, January 1, 1967, transl. in *Peking Review,* X, 1 (January 1, 1967), p. 10.

[50] *Nihon Keizai,* October 12, 1966, transl. in *DSJP,* October 12, p. 22.

[51] *DSJP,* September 29, 1966, p. 3, October 12, p. 22; *SSJM,* October 31, p. 74; November 21, p. 26; November 14, p. 33; Wang Ch'ao-t'ien, pp. 3, 9.

[52] Wang Ch'ao-t'ien, op. cit., p. 50.

scenes. While Mao protected his invulnerability with a mantle of silence, his subordinates were left, divided, exposed and insecure to deal with his self-appointed guardians. Their position was unenviable, for Mao's youthful protectors—including those who were unwittingly being used by his opponents—acted in his name and considered criticism of themselves tantamount to criticism of the Leader.

The Red Guards were less restrained and more confused than any youth group in China since 1957. As Wang Ch'ao-t'ien (himself an organiser of Manchouli's East Flag Red Guard Rebel Corps) noted, "The Red Guards were created autonomously, lacked a unified organisation and had no discipline."[53] Only a few were directly responsive to the wishes of Mao's cultural revolution group. Clumsy and contradictory manoeuvres by rival backstage operators gave the movement a quality of channelled spontaneity and ineffective manipulation. Paradoxically an observer has found the Guards "naïve" and "ignorant" but "pure and unsoiled," "utilised by adults" yet "inebriated with a strange sense of victory."[54] The point is that not all Red Guards were utilised by the same adults and utilisation did not necessarily imply effective control. Probably most of them were only dimly aware of their relationship to warring factions. As Wang Ch'ao-t'ien recalled:

> When I was on the mainland I never heard it said that the Red Guards had factions. . . . I suppose that quite a few CCP big shots used Red Guards, each having Red Guards which he secretly organised and directed. This is something that would be known only by a small number of cadres who were directly used to operate the Red Guards. Most of the Red Guards, I have heard people say, are moths rushing towards a flame. They don't know why they are flying around blindly and aimlessly, but finally they fall into the flame and die.[55]

In Peking, from which the most detailed reports of factional warfare have come, the lines of division that rent the radical ranks were apparent as early as June 1966: YCL leaders loyal to the old Party apparatus versus those who jumped on the anti-P'eng Chen bandwagon; Red ideologues versus expert eggheads; middle school zealots versus university sceptics; dedicated activists versus part-time politicians. As the cultural revolution expanded, the situation became still more complex. Daily issues of strategy and tactics and the selection of new targets, with the resulting polarisation of forces, placed new strains on the Maoist alliance.

[53] Wang Ch'ao-t'ien, op. cit., p. 49.

[54] *Sankei,* evening, September 29, 1966, transl. in *DSJP,* September 30, pp. 33–34.

[55] Wang Ch'ao-t'ien, op. cit., p. 49.

These enormously complicated developments were hyperbolised at Tsinghua University:

> At first the university had the organisation of "Tsinghua University Red Guards" alone. After [members of the work team came] from June to July [1966], this organisation changed in quality into a "Red Guard group in support of them." In repulsion . . . the Chingkangshan Red Guards of Tsinghua University, the 88th Headquarters of Mao Tse-tung's Thought Red Guards, and the Provisional Headquarters of Mao Tse-tung's Thought Red Guards were born one after another. On December 19 . . . they were merged into the "Tsinghua University Chingkangshan Red Guards Corps.[56]

In many schools rival groups came to blows. By mid-September a Red Guard police force had been organised to expose spurious organisations in the capital and to keep legitimate ones under control. By October 26 it was known that the college-level movement was divided among three "headquarters": (1) the Municipal University-College Red Guards Headquarters, controlled by comparatively moderate "theorist factions" at Peita and Tsinghua; (2) the Municipal University-College Red Guard Head Office, in charge of the "investigation units" of the Red Guard police force; and (3) the Municipal University-College Red Guards Revolutionary Rebel General Headquarters, composed of radicals who had split off from the First Headquarters.[57] The Third Headquarters drew its support from the Aviation Academy (reflecting Lin Piao's influence), institutes for the performing arts (reflecting Chiang Ch'ing's) and specialised higher technical schools.[58]

Through bitter and protracted internecine warfare, the Third Headquarters emerged triumphant. It subdued the First in October, gained authority by staging the anti-P'eng rally of December 12 and attracted the support of Chou En-lai.[59] Public security authorities arrested its foes and drove survivors in the Second Headquarters to accept its left-wing hegemony.[60] Though vitriolic exchanges in the Red Guard press

[56] *Nihon Keizai,* evening, January 7, 1967, transl. in *DSJP,* January 11, p. 10.

[57] *Mainichi,* September 10, 1966, transl. in *DSJP,* September 10–12, p. 38; *Mainichi,* September 18, 1966, transl. in *DSJP,* September 20, p. 7; *Mainichi,* evening, November 23, 1966, transl. in *DSJP,* November 26–28, p. 9; *Sankei,* October 17, 1966, transl. in *DSJP,* October 27, p. 7.

[58] *DSJP,* December 23, 1966, p. 18; December 28, p. 2; December 29, p. 2; December 31, 1966–January 5, 1967, pp. 6–7; January 6, p. 32; January 11, p. 29; January 12, p. 5.

[59] *DSJP,* October 13, 1966, p. 16; October 27, p. 27; November 26–28, p. 9; December 17–19, p. 14; December 28, p. 9.

[60] See *Tung-fang Hung* (*The East is Red,* organ of the reorganised Second

reflected unresolved rivalries, by February the Third Headquarters was recognised as the Red Guards' "main command."[61]

As dauntless defenders of the Truth, Red Guards encountered opposition from many quarters. Sophisticated residents of Peking could do little but swallow their resentment of the hordes of rustic invaders, but elsewhere local Red Guards helped defend regional traditions, heroes and pride against the assaults of crusading comrades from the capital. Clashes with workers and peasants, mobilised in self-defence by influential enemies of the Red Guards, embarrassed the self-styled champions of proletarianism. Visions of a student-worker alliance faded when eligible workers were instructed to join militia rather than form Red Guard units, and a number of factory Red Guards were disbanded.[62] In view of the complicated and treacherous political situation in the factories and communes, students were understandably diffident about obeying the New Year's command to carry the revolution to the masses. Their reluctance was well advised. In Nanking, where they conspicuously obeyed, the result was bloodshed.[63]

One group which generally supported the Red Guards was the army. From the outset the Guards called themselves a "reserve force" for the PLA. Chairman of the National Defence Council Mao Tse-tung was marshal of the Red Guards, First Vice-Chairman Lin Piao vice-marshal, Third Vice-Chairman Ho Lung chief of staff. The army usually maintained order through passive means though, in the southwest, PLA units were called out on several occasions to subdue groups of Guards.[64] The Peking Aviation Academy, the only higher-level school in the capital under direct military control, was the foundation stone for the Third Headquarters. The PLA checked credentials and provided food,

---

Headquarters), No. 18, January 31, 1967; also *Mainichi,* December 28, 1966; *Asahi,* December 28, transl. in *DSJP,* December 28, pp. 9, 24; *Sankei,* December 31, transl. in *DSJP,* December 31, 1966–January 1, 1967, p. 23; *Sankei,* January 7, transl. in *DSJP,* January 11, p. 4.

61 *The New York Times,* February 9, 1967; *Tung-fang Hung,* No. 18, January 31 (see note 60); *Tung-fang Hung* (another publication of the same title, edited by the Tung-fang Hung Commune of the Peking Mining School), No. 5, January 28, 1967; *Chan Pao* (*The War Paper,* publ. by the Arrangements Bureau to Struggle against the Counter-Revolutionary Revisionist Clique of P'eng, Lu, Lo, and Yang), No. 3, January 19, 1967; and *Tsao-fan* (*Rebellion,* publ. by the Shanghai Publishing System's Revolutionary Rebel Headquarters), special issue No. 2, January 15, 1967.

62 *Kyodo,* November 4, 1966, transl. in *DSJP,* November 5–7, pp. 22–23; *Sankei,* November 23, transl. in *DSJP,* November 26–28, p. 18.

63 *Mainichi,* January 9, 1967, transl. in *DSJP,* January 10, p. 2.

64 *Tokyo Shimbun,* September 10, 1966, transl. in *DSJP,* September 10–12, p. 42; *The New York Times,* February 17, 1967.

lodging, medical care and transportation for millions of Guards. Reception stations in cities and villages were manned by PLA officers and troops. Wang Ch'ao-t'ien reported that one soldier "served" every carload of Red Guards en route from Peking to Canton, and Anna Louise Strong noted that in the capital "PLA representatives, in the proportion of one to 20 or 30 youths, lodged, ate and travelled around with the visitors and taught them to march in columns for reviews."[65] Thus the PLA brought its influence to bear through its nationwide logistic and liaison apparatus and doubtless exercised more direct control over specific groups. Its ostentatious assistance to itinerant youngsters and its disinclination to interfere with their controversial activities must have made an impression on the public, thereby according the Red Guards a coercive power that they otherwise would have lacked. At least one Guard went so far as to threaten, in print, that the youngsters' enemies would have to reckon with the army that stood behind them.[66]

What is less clear is the extent to which the army was used as an overall command structure. There were hints that army advisors would be attached to Red Guard units, possibly in the spring of 1967, but at the time of this writing it seems doubtful that this will eventualise. Indeed, in January a wall paper indicated that protests of Guards at Peita, Tsinghua and the Aviation Academy had forced the postponement of plans to place students under military authority. (The PLA had intended to send soldiers to carry out military training programmes in the colleges pending the resumption of classes in September 1967.)[67] This may mean that PLA attempts to cement an army-student alliance have, like Kuomintang attempts in the 30s and 40s, elicited a less favourable response from university than from middle school students.

The group whose relationship with the Red Guards remains most obscure is the Youth League. The Guards' only indisputable effect on the League was to eclipse it. Since YCL was the creature of the CCP, attacks on Party bureaus automatically placed the Red Guards at loggerheads with League membership. As an extension of the Party apparatus, the League must have appeared entrenched, bureaucratic and conservative. Guards labelled its expansion of 1965 a step towards revisionism.[68] For two weeks in October and November Red Guards at Shanghai's Futan University struggled with the League branch, which allegedly

[65] Wang Ch'ao-t'ien, op. cit., p. 23; Anna Louise Strong, *Letter from China,* No. 46, January 19, 1967, p. 2.

[66] *Wen-hui pao,* January 17, 1967, cited in *CNA,* No. 653 (March 31, 1967), p. 2. See also Wang Ch'ao-t'ien, p. 52; *Tokyo Shimbun,* December 20, 1966, transl. in *DSJP,* December 23, p. 18.

[67] *Sankei,* January 17, 1967, transl. in *DSJP,* January 17.

[68] *Tokyo Keizai,* October 15, 1966, transl. in *SSJM,* November 21, p. 27.

had compiled a black list of its enemies.[69] But anti-YCL activity centred in Peking, where wall posters accused Hu Yao-pang of scheming to create an "all-encompassing (*ch'üan-min*) Party," an "all-encompassing League," an "all-encompassing nation," and some Guards demanded the League's abolition.[70] In June, Peking's YCL committee was reorganised; in August *China Youth* and *China Youth News* were suspended. Hu Yao-pang and three other members of YCL's Central Committee were among the targets for a rally against the "bourgeois reactionary line" scheduled for December 31.[71] (There were no reports that the rally actually occurred.) In January a draft of new public security regulations appeared including provisions for punishing "leaders of the reactionary Communist Party youth organisations," who were lumped together with land owners, KMT agents and other subversives.[72]

However, the League apparatus may weather the storm. The crisis in the Federation of Trade Unions and the establishment of worker groups on the Red Guard model around the turn of the year inevitably affected YCL branches in the factories, but only in the schools was there clear evidence that YCL units were disrupted or disbanded. At the Red Guard Military School, students told Japanese visitors that they had been compelled to organise outside the framework of existing youth groups because these were "dominated by the minority power group, and it was not possible to have our views reflected." Though they had forced the school's YCL branch to dissolve, they looked forward to reconstructing it into a "bridge between the Party and the masses."[73] On March 14, 1967, Li Fu-ch'un revealed that the CCP Central Committee had yet to decide the future of the League; he left open the possibility that YCL, and perhaps even the Red Guards, would be reorganised.[74]

Vast numbers of the Red Guard rank and file must have been League members. Their class backgrounds and activist temperaments made them prime YCL material. In some instances, even the leadership coincided. If we accept Tillman Durdin's estimate that the peak number of Red Guards was far in excess of the usually cited figure of 22 million,

69 *Wen-hui pao,* January 24, 1967, cited in *CNA,* No. 653 (March 31, 1967), p. 2.

70 Wang Ch'ao-t'ien, op. cit., pp. 14, 29.

71 *Yomiuri,* December 31, 1966, transl. in *DSJP,* December 31, 1966–January 5, 1967, p. 16.

72 *Asahi,* January 13, 1967, transl. in *DSJP,* January 13, p. 32. The quotation is from *Asahi's* wording, not necessarily that of the original regulations.

73 *Sankei,* September 29, 1966, transl. in *DSJP,* September 30, p. 32; *Mainichi,* October 12, transl. in *DSJP,* October 13, p. 8. See also *Tokyo Shimbun,* evening, September 14, transl. in *DSJP,* September 17–19, p. 7.

74 Radio Sofia, March 21, 1967.

the organisation may well have included a solid majority of the League's members.[75] However, the average age of the Red Guards doubtless was lower than that in the League and, more important, in the Red Guards teenagers and youths in their early 20s were able to feel a sense of power which had been denied to junior (and most senior) members of the League. The Red Guards offered the League's impatient youngsters a unique opportunity for leadership and action and perhaps fostered the hope that some day they might remake the League in their own image.

The Red Guards in Retreat

By February 1967 the Red Guards had clearly outlived their usefulness. The political élite among them (those in Peking, Shanghai and other cities who had consummated alliances with Party and government factions) had failed to coalesce and was preoccupied with internal bickering. The vision of a grand union of students, workers and peasants, as well as the notion of the Red Guards as a reserve for the PLA, had failed to materialise. Many of the politically active units had proved unable to discriminate among targets and had disrupted vital operations of security, transportation and production. They had roused the ire of Chou En-lai by unrestrained attacks on the power élite and had especially antagonised Chou's ally, Security Minister Hsieh Fu-chih. On February 15 Hsieh dared to demand the abolition of the Third Headquarters and Red Guard liaison offices in the capital.[76] The Red Guard rank and file, on the other hand—especially those in lower and middle schools—had long since ceased to be politically significant. The task was to remove these teenagers from the cities to which they had flocked and persuade them to return to their schools and jobs in the smaller towns, the countryside and the border regions.

One step toward ending the Red Guard movement was to amalgamate warring factions under official auspices. Thus, on February 22, Peking's three college Red Guard headquarters were united in a 10,000-man congress, at which the principal speaker was Chou En-lai. The meeting's declaration (made public on March 2) expressed the hope that "revolutionaries of all circles" would soon "achieve a still greater alliance."[77] The delegates repudiated "mountaintopism, popularism, factionism, schism *and, above all, anarchism.*"[78] The message was

[75] *The New York Times,* March 5, 1967.
[76] *Yomiuri,* February 21, 1967, in *DSJP,* February 21, p. 29.
[77] Radio Peking, March 2, 1967.
[78] Ibid.; emphasis is my own.

further expounded in a March 1 Red Guard editorial in the *People's Daily,* which called for a reassertion of the "iron discipline of the proletariat."[79] The congress continued to function through its standing committee, which announced on March 9 that wall newspapers would henceforth be forbidden to reveal secret or unannounced Party documents.[80] By that time, according to a Japanese correspondent, the number of wall posters had already "decreased remarkably."[81] On March 26 a congress of Peking middle school Red Guards was held. Their final declaration, like that of the university students, advocated carrying the cultural revolution back to the schools, denounced anarchic tendencies, demanded discipline and vested power in a standing committee.[82]

The principal stratagem for defusing the Red Guards was to send them back to school. From the second week of February there were indications in the official press that the Guards were no longer needed outside of school. These pronouncements stressed the themes that power had already been seized, that the true revolutionaries were now in a majority, and that their main responsibilities were to defend positions already captured, close ranks with all possible individuals and groups, cease indiscriminate attacks on officials and organisations and pay more attention to remoulding their own souls. Exhortations to be thrifty, to encourage production and to prepare for spring planting were combined with specific pleas that Red Guards return to their points of origin. By February 4 student readers of wall newspapers were aware that primary schools would soon reopen and by the 12th they knew that secondary schools would follow suit. The official reopening date was to be March 1.[83] During the second half of the month this information was disseminated through the official press and radio. Shanghai and Peking primary schools reportedly opened on March 6, but the latter encountered serious problems in resuming operations.[84] On March 11 a summary of the "CCP Central Committee's Rules on the Great Proletarian Cultural Revolution in Colleges and Universities (draft)" appeared in Peking wall newspapers. It called for university and college students to return to their own campuses before March 20.[85]

The injunctions to return to classrooms were invariably accompanied by assurances that the cultural revolution had now reached a new and

[79] *People's Daily,* March 2, 1967.
[80] *Asahi,* March 10, 1967.
[81] Radio Tokyo, March 6, 1967.
[82] Radio Peking, March 26, 1967.
[83] *Yomiuri,* February 9, 1967; *Kyodo,* February 13.
[84] New China News Agency broadcast, March 6, 1967; *People's Daily* editorial, March 7.
[85] *Mainichi,* March 12, 1967.

higher stage, but the Red Guards would continue to play an important role in the schools, and that far-reaching educational reforms would follow. However, it was obvious that this was not an advance or even a tactical retreat; it was a major withdrawal.[86] After the reopening of schools, it is questionable whether the student movement will be able to regain momentum. More dubious is whether any of Peking's leaders will risk a recurrence of the chaos that followed the eruption of the Red Guards in the summer of 1966. Now they must compel millions of youths to leave the cities for reintegration into a rural environment. Moreover, even if the Guards are disbanded, members will recall the heady sense of power that they enjoyed in the latter half of 1966. The Red Guards leave Peking a legacy of new difficulties to compound the still unresolved predicament of the younger generation.

Some Tentative Observations

The actual or imminent decline of a group which has been given reason to hope for wealth, power or status often creates explosive situations. The proletarianisation of Germany's bourgeoisie in the early 30s provided fuel for the Nazis; the proletarianisation of China's in the late 40s aided the Communists. In the United States the radical right phenomenon has been interpreted as a reaction by groups which have lost their political, social and religious pre-eminence.[87] The dynamism of the Red Guards may be partially explained in similar terms.

During and after the Great Leap Forward, hundreds of thousands of ill-prepared proletarians were thrust into the middle and upper echelons of the educational system. They were led to believe that their favourable class backgrounds and "positive" political behaviour, once crowned with an education, would place them at the apex of the social order. But, Franz Schurmann has observed, education fosters expertise, and

[86] The strategy was similar to that adopted by the CCP at various junctures in the pre-1949 revolution when "objective conditions" made it impossible to continue nationwide student movements. For example, in December 1931, after the failure to turn an anti-Japanese movement into a revolution against Nanking, the CCP ordered its cadres to carry the revolution into the schools. The result was a four-year period of watching and waiting until conditions favoured a revival of nationwide activity.

[87] See Seymour Martin Lipset, "Beyond the Backlash," *Encounter*, XXIII, 5 (November 1964), pp. 11–24.

education in modern China has produced an urban bourgeoisie committed to "competition, individualism, and technical proficiency."[88] Even among present-day mainland educators there remains a strong residue of these Western attitudes. By the 60s, as it became evident that "redness" alone could not transform China, a renewed respect for expertise permeated the school system. The inevitable victims of this development were proletarian students—naïve, ambitious, over-indoctrinated under-educated youths who had been admitted during the high-tide of redness. Furthermore, job opportunities, even for graduates with favourable class backgrounds, remained poor. China's middle and higher educational systems had expanded faster than the economy's ability to absorb graduates. Hence every student realised that graduation most likely meant assignment to a remote village, possibly as a manual labourer. Few students, regardless of class background, anticipated this fate without anxiety and resentment. This bleak prospect and the fact that education had failed to fulfil expectations neutralised whatever reluctance students may have had to abandon education for agitation.

Morris Wills traces the student crisis to the Great Leap Forward. Before then, he writes,

> Most of the students believed in the campaigns launched by the Party. They felt that the cause of communism was good and they considered themselves a part of it. But with the failure of the Great Leap and the succeeding blunders the prestige of the Party ebbed and with it the confidence of the students. It became ever harder to associate oneself, one's destiny, with the cause of the Party. The cause of the Party and the cause of communism seemed to diverge.[89]

This was not entirely unprecedented, since even during the Hundred Flowers period student critics readily drew the distinction between the Communist Party and the communist vision. But post-Great-Leap disaffection is more prevalent and more serious, for it has occurred among post-revolutionary students of proletarian origin, not among bourgeois holdovers from the pre-1949 era. The crux of the problem is that students, taught that communism means a better life for the people, had observed Party cadres cynically preoccupied with personal and bureaucratic aggrandisement. Mao took this into account when, for the first time since the early 30s, he called upon his devotees to distinguish between the Party organisation and himself. By providing an acceptable outlet for youthful frustrations, the cult of Mao answered a vital psychological need. Such outlets were rare in a society where individual opportunities for emotional release had been denied and Party and League

[88] Schurmann, op. cit., pp. 51–52.
[89] Wills, manuscript.

bureaucracies no longer provided satisfactory substitutes. The Red Guards opened a new channel. Through absolute devotion to Mao and violent attacks on his enemies, they were encouraged to give vent to repressed resentments.

The Red Guards would crush the internal inconsistencies of Chinese Communism under the weight of a monolithic ideology. In place of two élites, based respectively upon ideology and education[90] they would create a single one drawing its power and prestige from an ideologically-oriented education. They would remove the barrier between the educated few and the untutored many by making students of workers and workers of students. Their new national constitution, based upon the dictatorship of the proletariat rather than the democratic united front, would grant legal precedence to the Thought of Mao and would ban all contrary publications, meetings, and associations. It would eliminate private ownership of the means of production, including vestiges of individual land holding; curtail political rights (such as they may be) of the propertied classes, right-wing intellectuals, "democratic parties and factions," and believers in God; and virtually outlaw religion.[91] China's future polity would be wholly popular and unabashedly totalitarian.

The creation of the Red Guards was a desperate gamble to spare China a grey, managerial bureaucratic fate; a final effort to prove that charisma, ideology and youthful zeal could triumph over political prudence and economic incentives; a crude, terrible, yet highminded attempt to rescue the permanent revolution from an agonising death. By the spring of 1967 the cultural revolution had lost momentum. The utopian vision had receded beyond the horizon. Not since the 1920s had students held real power in the CCP, and the present leadership, divided as it was, was not prepared to surrender control to a movement of teenagers.

At the Peking "unity conference" of February 22, 1967 Red Guards may have unwittingly composed their own epitaph when they declared, "Let us be revolutionary fighters to the end, and not just a flash across the stage of history."[92] Whether their historical significance will be limited to one of these stark alternatives remains to be seen.

[90] Schurmann, op. cit., pp. 8, 51.

[91] *Kyodo* release, in *Tokyo Shimbun,* October 27, 1966, transl. in *DSJP,* October 27, pp. 15–16.

[92] Radio Peking, March 2, 1967.

YOUTH AND POLITICS IN CZECHOSLOVAKIA

Galia Golan

It would be inaccurate to see the "revival" in Czechoslovakia in terms of a conflict of generations, or to attribute to this the radical changes of those startling eight months, for the issues were not specifically generational; more important, the forces in the struggle for power and leadership were not the young versus the old. Such a characterization was vigorously denied by Ota Sik in an interview immediately after the crucial central committee meeting which brought the liberals to power.[1] He pointed out that many of those who pushed hardest for change were among the oldest members of the party, including people like Frantisek Vodslon and Frantisek Kriegel. Indeed it was actually some of the youngest men in the Czechoslovak party such as Lenart, once regarded as promising "new blood," who stood by Novotny in many of the presidium and central committee battles. This is not to say that there was no generational problem in Czechoslovakia, or that it played no role in the movement for democratization. The problem was complex and constantly changing both in importance and function, and for this reason may be more easily understood within the context of three different periods: the pre-1968 liberalization; the period of the "revival," i.e., January to August 1968; and the invasion and post-invasion period.

Following the twelfth congress of the Czechoslovak Communist Party in December 1962, destalinization was at last undertaken in Czechoslovakia. This period, from early 1963 until 1967, might be called the pre-revival revival, during which certain elements within the party—principally liberal intellectuals, economists, and Slovaks—struggled to

From *The Journal of Contemporary History,* V, 1 (1970). Reprinted by permission.

[1] Prague radio interview, 21 and 26 February 1968, reported in *Bratislava Pravda,* 29 February 1968.

introduce thoroughgoing reforms, and when almost every area and aspect of Czechoslovak society came under scrutiny. One of these was the gap between the generations and the youth problem, though it must be added that only gradually did the youth emerge as anything of a force or issue with which the party had to contend.

Czechoslovak youth in the early 1960s was a disillusioned and generally speaking apathetic group, ashamed of its elders because of the Munich capitulation, and repelled by the regimentation, authoritarianism, and deceptions of the communist regime. It was precisely this apathy, or more accurately, this political indifference, which was of concern to the regime, as the liberals again and again pointed to the party's failure to win over the youth.[2] One survey concluded that among the students interrogated only some 11.4 per cent considered themselves politically active, while 47 per cent considered themselves politically neutral, 6.6 per cent passive, and 3.5 per cent "did not know."[3] Another study showed that only 11.3 per cent of the students who were members of the party joined out of "inner conviction"; 27.6 per cent joined for material advantage, 4.4 per cent under the influence of their environment, and 44.2 per cent for "other reasons," among which material motives and environment were predominant.[4] Still another study revealed that Czechoslovak youths were pacifists, uninterested in the army, and so desirous of peace that they "underestimate the motives of the enemy." Of the group polled, 20 per cent believed that the United States arms because of its desire for peace, and over 30 per cent said the United States arms for reasons other than war. Moreover, an astonishingly high percentage of nineteen year old boys were unaware of the existence of the Warsaw Pact (no doubt this figure has now declined).[5] In addition to these phenomena, juvenile delinquency was becoming a problem and young people were increasingly seeking pastimes, in groups or individually, outside the framework of the associations established and designed by the regime to organize their leisure time in the interests of the party. According to Vladimir Koucky, then a member of the Presidium, the institutions of higher learning had be-

[2] One article highlighted the dilemma of a teacher forced to present a new line every day, and the damage done to the young because "we tore down the old morality and left a vacuum." V. Kvardova, in *Kulturny Zivot,* 16 February 1963. Another article complained of the distortions fed the young and emphasized that they would not tolerate "the big lie." V. Zykmunt, in *Plamen,* 1963, 134. The failure to replace religious principles by anything constructive in the course of atheistic education was pointed out by V. Gardovsky in *Veda a Zivot,* February 1966, 65–70.

[3] M. Schneider, in *Zivot Strany,* March 1966, 13.

[4] Unsigned article in *Student,* 19 January 1966.

[5] *Smena,* 28 December 1965.

come hotbeds of "petty-bourgeois weeds and anti-Marxist attacks . . . new formations of technocratism, managerialism, mysticism, pro-Djilas pamphlets, the apotheoses of bourgeois democracy, and philosophical irrationalism."[6] Presumably to combat this, the party decided early in 1965 to establish party university committees, even though (or perhaps because) only 5 per cent of students were party members. The party admitted, however, that the problem was not limited to young intellectuals; Koucky pointed out that a poll of a provincial agricultural secondary school had revealed unsatisfactory attitudes towards work, lack of drive, and insufficient social responsibility.

While the party sought to solve these problems in a number of ways, including educational reform,[7] it placed the greatest blame for the situation on the Czechoslovak Youth Union (CSM), the organization designed to stimulate and direct youth and to shape its political activity. The CSM had been conceived as a unified youth organization designed not only to educate its own members, but also to exert an influence on the youth outside its ranks. In this it clearly had failed, as it became increasingly apparent over the years that instead of an organization for and of the youth, the CSM was a regime agency over the youth. Because of the fluid nature of its membership and the small number of communist members, it had by 1958 become the only mass organization under *direct* party control, instead of the usual indirect control exercised through communist members in an organization's leadership. In 1966 it covered 1,055,000 young people from the ages of 15 to 26, that is, about 50 per cent of those eligible for membership. Most of these were pupils and students, a reflection perhaps of the fact that CSM membership was one factor in admission to higher studies or other educational benefits.[8] Only 25 per cent of factory youth were CSM members and the percentage was even smaller among agricultural youth.[9] In the three years from 1963 to 1966 CSM membership had

[6] *Rude Pravo,* 24 October 1964: report by party ideological commission chairman Vladimir Koucky to the central committee. A conference on the growing problem of juvenile delinquency was held as early as 1963: Prague radio, 2 December 1963. In that year juvenile delinquency rose by 12 per cent: Bratislava radio, 8 March 1964.

[7] In 1964 and 1965 reforms were introduced in the primary and secondary school system, and the higher educational system respectively. Among other things they provided for greater differentiation within the educational system, more attention to the humanities, less time in production, entrance examinations for the academic secondary schools, an end to the cadre system for admission to the university, election of Rector and Deans, and student representation in the university scientific councils (senate).

[8] Prague radio, 27 May 1966; cf. *Rude Pravo,* 23 July 1965; *Mlada Fronta,* 25 April 1963.

[9] *Prace,* 24 April 1966.

dwindled by almost 400,000, from 1,418,783 to 1,055,000.[10] Membership had in fact become a largely formal matter, allegiances only superficial. Many a youth left the CSM as soon as he felt that membership was no longer necessary to his career. It was in part to correct this state of affairs that the party instigated a "Party Talks to Youth Campaign" in 1965 and called upon the CSM to reorganize and reform itself.[11]

The party's reaction was in fact a response to more than the situation in the CSM; it was an effort to stifle pressures which were beginning to gain dangerous momentum, from the party's point of view. The youth had been the first, perhaps the only, group outside the party to grasp early on the importance and possibilities of the campaign for reform launched within the party. Young workers as well as students had tentatively joined these forces by turning the traditional May Day outdoor poetry readings into political demonstrations.[12] In response to the liberalization in the cultural world, there appeared a new "generational" literature, numerous *avant-garde* satirical theatrical groups among the young, jazz and poetry-reading clubs, and a new, highly controversial journal for young writers called *Tvar*.[13] Moreover, in conjunction with

[10] *Mlada Fronta,* 24 April 1963; Prague radio, 27 May 1966.

[11] CTK, 13 January 1966.

[12] The most striking of these were the May Day demonstrations of 1965 and 1966. In 1965 the regime permitted the students to hold their traditional Majales Festival for the first time since 1956, when "revisionist" and "anti-party" slogans in the student parade had led the regime to prohibit the event. The posters in 1965 in Prague and Bratislava carried such slogans as: "Whoever cannot read or write can always quote," "Criticize only the dead," "As you grow older who will have to alter what you learned as a youth." In Prague the students brought the day to a climax by electing visiting beat poet Allen Ginsberg Majales King. One week later Ginsberg was expelled from the country for propagating "bourgeois attitudes" and corrupting the youth, since he was both a drug addict and a homosexual. Cf. *Rude Pravo,* 17 May 1965, speech by Novotny; *East Europe,* July 1965, 40; *Mlada Fronta,* 2, 22 May 1965; Prague radio, 14 May 1965. In May 1966 students and young workers held a demonstration in Prague carrying such slogans as "We want freedom, we want democracy," "A good communist is a dead one," and for the police "Gestapo! Gestapo!" Twelve youths were arrested and received five to ten months sentences by a Prague court on 24 May 1966. J. Ruml, in *Literarni Listy,* 21 March 1968.

[13] Some of this literature is discussed in J. F. Brown, *The New Eastern Europe* (London, 1966). The "generational literature" of such writers as Jan Benes, Milan Uhde, Ivan Klima, Jaroslava Blazkova, Ales Haman, and Milan Hamada came under severe party criticism, as did the satirical theatres. Cf. S. Vlasin in *Nova Mysl,* November 1964. The journal *Tvar* became the centre of a controversy within the Czechoslovak Writers Union and between the union and the regime in late 1965. It was finally shut

the intellectuals' pressure for changes in such organizations as the trade unions, and the creation of genuine interest groups with an effective role in society, the youth, particularly the students, began to press for changes in their own organization, the CSM. After months of discussion and warnings from the party,[14] the most radical of the proposals for CSM reform was presented at the national conference of university students in Prague, 18–19 December 1965, by Prague Technological Institute student Jiri Mueller. His plan outlined changes in both the function and the organization of the CSM.[15] He suggested that the union be broken down into a loose federation of autonomous professional groups, i.e., a students association, a young workers association, and an association of young farmers, each to be subdivided by age. These structural changes were designed for one purpose and one purpose only: to make the CSM a legitimate, independent representative of the youth by serving as a platform for its ideas and supporting them vis-à-vis the decision-making powers of the country. Mueller claimed that the CSM, as it stood, was a political organization (i.e., serving the party's interests and preparing the youth for the party) "without any possibility of acting as such." To act as such, Mueller argued, it must truly express the views of its members even to the extent of opposing the party if necessary. Concretely, he demanded an effective role for the CSM in the National Front, representation in all state bodies and in the National Assembly. In essence he was advocating the formation of a genuine political party.

The conference was favourably impressed by this proposal and set up an eleven-man committee under Lubos Holacek to look into its feasibility.[16] This marked the beginning of a controversy which was destined to make the youth issue one of the elements in the liberals' campaign against Novotny. The party's immediate reaction was to condemn Mueller's ideas as wrong or confused, arguing that there was no need for an opposition when there already existed ample opportunity for frank discussion within the party and CSM and between them.[17] Nonetheless certain liberals and moderates in the party recognized the importance of taking the students seriously. The then moderate Martin Vaculik, a rising star in the party hierarchy but still the liberal leader he had been in his earlier posts in Brno, pointed out that "a youth organization cannot merely imitate the organizations of the adults; it

down and its editor-in-chief expelled from the party. Cf. *Literarni Noviny,* 4 December 1965; V. Uhler, in *Zivot Strany,* April 1966, 17.

[14] Cf. for example Koucky's speech to the party central committee, *Rude Pravo,* 24 October 1964.

[15] *Student,* 26 January 1966.

[16] *Mlada Fronta,* 27 January 1966.

[17] *Rude Pravo,* 22 December 1965.

must find contents and forms of work which correspond to the needs, interests, and thinking of the young."[18] A later article in the party daily admitted that the young did not feel themselves part of a system they had merely inherited rather than created themselves: it was just this absence of "an active political relationship" to the system which had led to their apathy, opposition, and criticism. Implicitly criticizing direct tutelage by the party, the article concluded with the suggestion that a way be found to make the CSM "an authoritative and attractive component of our political system."[19]

Interestingly enough, it may not have been that Novotny feared that a serious generational gap had been or would be caused if the CSM were reorganized; rather it appeared that he was concerned with precisely the opposite, i.e. that the youth would join forces—were already doing so—with their elders among the liberals, who were at that time demanding such things as an opposition (within or outside the party), "integrated criticism," and so forth.[20] For this reason, apparently, Novotny acted to bring the movement to a halt. Addressing a young workers delegation in the spring of 1966, he strongly denounced Mueller's proposal. The conservative majority of the CSM leaders heeded this warning and also condemned the proposal as "one-sided and politically wrong."[21] The question was left for the CSM national congress in 1967, but before that meeting the party took stronger action. In December 1966, one year after the Mueller proposal, Jiri Mueller and Lubos Holacek were expelled from the CSM and from the university and drafted into the army.[22] After this move it was only to be expected that the June 1967 CSM congress did not concern itself with liberalization. These actions, together with other repressive measures introduced by Novotny in 1966 and 1967, irreparably alienated the students and set

[18] M. Vaculik, in *Nova Mysl,* 11 January 1966.

[19] *Rude Pravo,* 8 April 1966.

[20] Space does not permit an excursion into this subject. The reference is to a discussion conducted on these topics by intellectuals such as Zdenek Mlynar, Julius Strinka, Andrej Kopcok, Miroslav Kusy, Michal Suchy, and Michal Lakatos. Some of these ideas are discussed in an article by M. Schwartz in *Problems of Communism,* January–February 1967.

[21] Prague radio, 18 April 1966; *Rude Pravo,* 20 May 1966. It was typical of Novotny to deliver this warning to a delegation of workers rather than to the students themselves, for he had long played upon worker distrust of intellectuals in the hope of setting them one against the other, and thereby defeating the intellectuals' proposals while preventing the emergence of a potentially dangerous worker-intellectual alliance.

[22] Cf. *Reporter,* 6 March 1968, "The Case of Jiri Mueller."

the stage for a showdown.[23] The Slovak party, at least, seemed to grasp the potential danger of the situation, for its daily organ published an article by Academician and party theorist Miroslav Kusy and journalist Juraj Suchy which once again urged that attention be paid to youth as a distinct group. Without referring directly to the CSM, the reform of which now appeared unlikely, the two liberals argued that the youth must have some political outlet and some way to produce their own "generational programme." A programme devised by the older generation should not be forced on them; they should be allowed to propose their own solutions to their problems, to determine their own way of life in socialism, as well as the goals which they, as a generation, wished to achieve. "The youth which has no generational programme of its own," Kusy and Suchy argued, "cannot have positive aims and thus, as a generation, it must disintegrate; one part takes over the generational programme of the 'fathers' and becomes a conformist appendage, offering at most passive resistance, while the other part keeps to itself . . . slowly sinking into a position of criticism for criticism's sake, protesting against everything that exists." They concluded, as others had before them, that youth must be made equal political partners rather than mere political objects in society.[24]

This warning apparently went unheeded, coming as it did in August 1967 just when the regime was fully preoccupied with the faltering economy (and with complaining economists), as well as with recalcitrant intellectuals and demanding Slovaks.[25] The regime may well have thought the issue closed by the neutralization of Mueller and Holacek and the conservative trend of the June CSM congress. This was, however, a miscalculation, for just as the party central committee was meeting in what turned out to be the first of the three plenary sessions which brought the liberals to power,[26] the showdown came. A purely

[23] After weathering the crises of 1963 and 1964, Novotny gradually regained control and began to obstruct or even revoke many of the concessions he had been forced to grant under pressure from the liberals. The moves against the youth must be seen in this context.

[24] *Bratislava Pravda,* 2 August 1967.

[25] The economists were discouraged by Novotny's interference in and obstruction of the economic reforms; the intellectuals' rebellion at their June congress is well known; the Slovaks found their voice again when Novotny belittled their national aspirations by referring to nationalism as "reactionary." Novotny also moved against the young writers by the trial and imprisonment of Jan Benes, former editor of *Tvar,* in the summer of 1967.

[26] These are the meetings held at the end of October 1967 to discuss the role of the party, in December to discuss the splitting of the top government and party positions, and early January to elect a new first secretary. The move to get rid of Novotny crystallized at the October plenum.

non-political demonstration became the occasion for student demands differing little from those of the party liberals. It is not unusual for demonstrations, particularly student demonstrations, as we have seen them in the 1960s, prompted by purely material motives, even by minor grievances, to change their character, broadening out to include grievances against the political or socio-economic nature of society itself. Czechoslovak students and young workers had on previous occasions turned peaceful gatherings into anti-regime platforms, but in the early winter of 1967 the atmosphere was such—and the regime's reaction was a reflection of this atmosphere—that the student outburst was to be of great significance.

On the night of 31 October residents of the Prague Technological Institute's Strahov hostel took to the streets in protest against conditions in the hostel. Their peaceful candlelight march was dispersed by the police who even entered the hostel and indiscriminately beat up anyone found there.[27] This police brutality enraged the students (of many faculties and in other cities), who responded in the following days with meetings, demands, and threats of repeated demonstrations. Party conservatives realized the political nature of the student outburst and blamed it on western anti-communist propaganda, especially that of Radio Free Europe, and on the banned Writers Union weekly *Literarni Noviny*.[28] In response to the students' demands, an investigation was begun and the police were found guilty of "unduly harsh measures." The Interior Ministry was ordered to look into the affair, but the matter was left more or less in the air pending resolution of the crisis which had already reached an acute stage in the party's central committee.

The youth became something of an issue, and a relatively important one, as a result of the 1967 demonstration. The Strahov affair (as it came to be called) impressed upon the regime the need to look upon the youth as a stratum of society to which it would have to answer. Alexander Dubcek acknowledged that "among all the questions facing us today, that of the youth holds a special position."[29] Indeed the youth

[27] *Smena,* 19 November 1967. The candles were deliberate; one of the complaints was against electricity failures. Indeed the students went into the streets because that very evening, during one of their many sessions with youth officials (from *Mlada Fronta*) about the situation, the electricity failed again. *Rude Pravo,* 14 November 1967; *Prace,* 2, 3 November 1967.

[28] F. Kolar, in *Kulturni Tvorba,* 16 November 1967. Kolar also said that the police were just young workers trying to do their job. For this, students accused him of trying to drive a wedge between them and the workers; they even threatened to bring him to court. *Frankfurter Allgemeine Zeitung,* 22 November 1967.

[29] *Rude Pravo,* 23 February 1968.

themselves took advantage of the impact of the Strahov affair to form themselves into something of a vanguard of the "revival." They organized a great many rallies and meetings to which they invited leading political, cultural, and economic figures to answer their outspoken questions.[30] They did not restrict themselves to their own concerns, but put forward a list of comprehensive demands including freedom of the press, freedom of association, freedom of travel, re-establishment of a constitutional court, separation of powers within the government, investigation into the death of Jan Masaryk, solidarity with Polish students, and even changes in foreign policy (relations with Israel, equal status vis-à-vis the USSR, and so forth).[31] Nor was this activity limited to students; the students themselves sought to counter the conservatives' efforts to drive a wedge between workers and intelligentsia, sending letters to factory workers explaining their demands and arranging joint meetings and discussions.[32] The rallies themselves were by no means exclusively student affairs, any more than earlier May Day demonstrations had been composed exclusively of students, or, as *Prace,* the trade union daily pointed out (10 March 1968), any more than *Literarni Noviny* had lacked a large number of readers among the working youth. To aid the students in their efforts to cement their ties with young workers, *Prace* condemned the attempt to paint the Strahov affair as a class battle (young intellectuals against young workers, i.e., the police) and pointed out that most of the students were children of workers or party officials.

At this time there was some discussion of the generational aspect of the youth issue. On the most simplistic, perhaps vulgar, level, one indignant party member castigated the young for condemning past party actions: "It is true that we then proceeded harshly [in collectivizing agriculture]. You, the young, can now easily speak of the law and its sanctions. But at the time the towns had nothing to eat. If we had not been hard you would not be sitting here at all, or you would be crippled with rickets."[33]

While such an attitude (not an isolated phenomenon), sought to reduce the issues pressed by the youth to this type of over-simplification of a difference between generations, others feared that the attacks on the past might result in a wholesale rejection by the young of every-

[30] One of the largest and perhaps most interesting of these was held in Prague on 20 March. Some 6000 young people crammed the hall to question Smrkovsky, Sik, Goldstücker, and others. Prague radio, 20 March 1968; *Rude Pravo,* 22 March 1968.

[31] Ibid. See also *Reporter,* 3 April 1968, "Manifesto of Prague Youth"; Unsigned, *Student,* 29 May 1968.

[32] *Mlada Fronta,* 13 March 1968.

[33] *Bratislava Pravda,* 8 March 1968.

thing and everyone connected with the older generation. It was for this reason that the party made efforts to demonstrate that political age or youth, such as that demonstrated at the crucial party sessions, had nothing to do with chronological age.[34] Dubcek for his part urged party members not to fear such accusations but to prove their "political youth" by adopting the healthy scepticism and initiative of the young. That a problem nonetheless existed was pointed out by many who were disturbed by the distrust and disillusionment of the youth vis-à-vis the older generation. As one journalist put it: "they do not believe us, they do not believe that these changes are permanent"; or as another put it: "they saw at each step that practice was different from what was preached. And at the time of the exposure of the so-called personality cult the youth ceased to believe even the teachers."[35] The liberal writer Jan Prochazka sarcastically explained: "The young people's instinct made them understand that we usually do not believe what we say. And then we were surprised to realize that they have been losing their respect for us!" More specifically he added: "For the more intelligent boys and girls, it was hard to understand that in the history of other nations it was possible and permitted to pay homage even to tsars and tyrants, while in our own country there was no place in history for the man who was the founder of our democracy, who was neither a usurper nor the murderer of his own children, but an educated, democratic, and highly moral man, and this does not refer to T. G. Masaryk alone." Prochazka considered it foolish to think that young people believed all the lies they had been told or accepted the dogma uniformly presented them in schools: "It is an artificial pyramid. One day the wind will blow it down and the young people educated all these years in love of the USSR will one night go out into the streets and rejoice at an ice hockey victory in a manner which makes it clear even to the most uninformed that this does not concern ice-hockey alone."[36] Goldstücker echoed these sentiments when he told an Italian communist journal that "in general the young people are disillusioned by the evolution of Czechoslovakia."[37]

As these comments indicate, there was indeed a conflict between generations: the young distrusted the old, especially the party members, and found few people they could believe in since so many of even the liberals had Stalinist or opportunist pasts. There was little they could admire among their elders, for their aversion to the communists' mistakes, distortions, and terror had an earlier counterpart in the shameful sell-out at Munich, blamed on the leaders of the First Republic. But

[34] Cf. *Rude Pravo,* 29 January 1968.
[35] J. Ruml, in *Reporter*, 24 April 1968; *Prace,* 10 March 1968.
[36] J. Prochazka, in *Ucitelske Noviny,* 7 March 1968.
[37] *Rinascita,* 19 April 1968.

probably the greatest gap existed between the generations of communists, for among the non-communists at least the parents could and did maintain contact with their children by educating them (despite the influences outside the home) in the principles of the First Republic. A gap existed even here too, however, for the end of the First Republic and of the postwar Benes regime, plus the nature of the society which emerged after 1948, undermined any respect for authority and dispelled any interest in ideologies among the youth. There were no pat answers, no messianic solutions, and their ambivalence towards their elders, bordering on cynicism, was aptly expressed when Lubos Holacek said at a mass rally that student support for the progressives should not be taken as something assured. If, he explained, the "political monopoly of the Communist Party" failed to secure the activity of the masses, the students would have to seek another system.[38]

Though the gap indeed existed, the youth were well aware that their position could be improved only in the context of a general political change, and their demands were not limited to strictly youth needs; indeed, they were warned by one of their mentors, the philosopher Ivan Svitak, not to "solve only the narrow generational problems of youth." They should realize "that the decisive problems are the common human ones. You cannot solve them by advancing the demands of the young; you must grapple urgently with problems of all people."[39] In fact there was little or no conflict between the demands of the youth and those of the liberals. Even such ideas as federalization of the republic, urged by the older generation of Slovak communist nationalists, were sincerely shared by the Slovak youth whose nationalism appeared to be as strong as that of their elders.[40] Yet many students were to point out that while the words might be the same, and the slogans shared, there was a wide gulf between the generations as to the meaning of the words they used, such as democracy, rights, and so forth. This was one reason why they so sharply questioned their elders, demanding at every step actions rather than words.[41] Nonetheless, it may

[38] Prague radio, 20 March 1968.

[39] Ivan Svitak, in *Student,* 13 March 1968. Youthful scepticism extended even to Svitak from time to time; many students questioned his sincerity.

[40] *Rolnicky Noviny,* 29 April 1968, pointed with pride to the mass march of youth commemorating the youth march 123 years earlier led by Slovak nationalist hero Ludovit Stur, noting that today, too, Slovak youth wanted a free Slovak state, i.e., a federated CSSR.

[41] It is in this context that one must see the efforts by students to introduce a second candidate into the Presidential election of the spring of 1968. Student leader Ivan Hartel has said privately that he suggested the candidacy first of Smrkovsky and then of Cisar not out of any opposition to Svoboda, but in the interests of democracy.

be said that the youth accepted Svitak's advice, for whatever their inner reservations about almost all the country's leaders, liberal or otherwise, they did their utmost to support them in the democratization struggle, serving as a rallying point for people of all ages, speaking out and agitating for mass participation in and support of the process.

However, they did not intend to lose their identity as a specific stratum; they operated as a pressure group, maintaining and indeed demanding enough independence to be an effective force. This was perhaps the greatest difference between their role in the pre-revival liberalization struggle, and in the revival period itself. So long as the struggle remained within the party, they joined in, for outside it they could not play a part of any importance. The best they could do, and this they did with varying degrees of success, was to attempt to awaken their own ranks and make sure that their own demands (for changes in the CSM or changes in the educational system) were included among those of the party liberals. When the process became a public affair, when the party turned to the public for support and participation, the youth found that they had room within which to operate. As the best informed and best organized group outside the party—one of the few (if not the only) non-party groups to have grasped from the outset the possibilities of the pre-1968 struggle—they were natural leaders of the hitherto uninformed, uninvolved, or unconsulted masses, and a natural bridge between them and the party liberals with whom they had collaborated in the past. In this new capacity the youth were indeed a force, and both they and the new regime had to consider how best this force might be institutionally constituted and exercised.

The party was naturally concerned that the political activism of the young people should not be used *against* the party but rather *for* it, and an editorial in *Rude Pravo* (22 March 1968), urged communists to go among the youth, talk to them, and try to win them over by deeds as well as words in the spirit of the post-January programme of revival. Dubcek had a clear grasp of the problem: "I do not think we can win over the youth simply by constantly telling them or even throwing constantly in their teeth all that has been successfully achieved . . . their enthusiasm and ardour cannot be exhausted by merely praising what has been realized. They want to create themselves, to implement their longings and ideals themselves—precisely as the older generation wanted to do when they were young and when the revolution provided them with the possibility. They must not get ready-made things, gifts, or achievements, but scope for their own initiative, for their ideas, for arranging their own future life so as to accomplish their tasks."[42] He urged that conditions be created to permit the youth to express

[42] *Rude Pravo,* 23 February 1968 (22 February speech).

themselves, and it was to these conditions or, more specifically, the institutional framework within and through which youth could operate, that attention was turned in the effort to cope with this new force.

Thus once again the question of the structure and role of the CSM was raised. At this point, however, the organization was almost disintegrating, for group after group was demanding autonomy. The most important, or at least most controversial, of these groups was the students. After the Mueller and Strahov affairs, and all that had happened in the first few months of 1968, the earlier demands appeared conservative. The students would no longer be content with a federal CSM but demanded independence, and a bitter struggle ensued between them and the CSM. While the CSM met, temporized, argued, introduced personnel changes, and tried to keep things under its control, the students took matters into their own hands. Student Academic Councils, originally started in December 1967 in response to the failure of the CSM to support student demands in the Strahov affair, began to spring up in various faculties with the CSM representatives in many cases resigning in their favour. From this a student union began to emerge which was organized as a federation of separate Slovak and Czech associations, outside the CSM. The new organization's programme was based on the United Nations Declaration of Human Rights and proposed such things as support for the progressive forces in the party, personnel changes in the party, rehabilitation of the victims of past injustices, legal guarantees of civil rights, postponement of the national elections pending amendment of the electoral law, and shorter military service for students. There was even talk of running candidates for the National Assembly. They rejected the idea of any solution or arrangement within the CSM: it was a moribund organization, membership in which had become a mere formality; in any case it had lost the confidence of the students. They wanted student self-government at the lower levels, working up to a national union of students, on a truly voluntary and elective basis.[43]

[43] The course of events can be followed in the reports over Prague radio, and in *Student,* 31 January, 7 February, 6 March, 26 June 1968; *Prace,* 29 February 1968; *Mlada Fronta,* 1, 15 March 1968, *Svobodne Slove,* 1 March 1968. Mueller and Holacek were reinstated by the CSM and re-admitted to the university. Eventually the students submitted the following demands to the National Assembly's education committee: 1. Democratic legislation on civil rights; a. new concept of the political system in the CSSR, b. open debate, c. speedy justice, d. freedom to travel and stay abroad, e. freedom of internal movement, f. right to demonstrate; 2. Strict observance of laws; 3. Acceleration of the federalization of the State; 4. Retirement of persons involved in past errors; 5. Return to the rule of law. *Student,* 24 July 1968.

The regime's reaction to this movement was perhaps influenced by the rapid appearance of similar demands for independence from (or within) the CSM; young workers held a state-wide meeting in Prague to consider the formation of a Union of Working Youth; young Slovak agricultural workers demanded their own organization, the Hungarian minority demanded their own youth and Pioneer organizations, while the Pioneers themselves demanded autonomy. The Junak (Boy Scouts) were rehabilitated, also as an independent organization, and youth groups began splitting off from another mass organization, Svazarm. Young soldiers spoke of forming their own organization and secondary school pupils decided to set up an independent union. With the founding of a preparatory committee for an Association of Socialist Youth there was even the possibility of a direct rival or replacement for whatever would be left of the CSM.[44]

Despite certain sympathetic comments,[45] the party did not look favourably on this involuntary dissolution or undermining of the CSM. While it was ready to concede the need for an independent federated youth movement as an effective component of the National Front, it was not willing to see the CSM lose its monopoly as the only youth organization. While this was in direct contradiction to the party's Action Programme (which called for freedom of association), the party presidium, meeting 21–22 May 1968, declared its opposition to any youth organization independent of the CSM.[46] The democratization process being what it was, however, most groups went on setting up independent organizations in the hope that the law on freedom of association, for which the liberals and youth were together campaigning, would resolve the issue and force the government to license them. Indeed, more than ten different youth associations were founded in the months before the invasion. The youth defied the party on this issue and on many occasions prodded the regime to act more swiftly and resolutely in accordance with the Action Programme, at the same time expressing their solidarity with the party in face of the pressure and threats from the other communist countries.[47]

[44] Prague radio, 1, 24 March 1968; Bratislava radio, 15 January, 23 March 1968; CTK, 26 March 1968; *Uj Szo,* 15 March 1968; *Mlada Fronta,* 3, 5 April 1968. The Association of Socialist Youth was described as designed to appeal to members and non-members of parties to provide "an open dialogue between equal partners and . . . a source of progress and a guarantee of democracy."

[45] Cf. Smrkovsky speech to the April central committee plenum (*Rude Pravo,* 4 April), or Sik at the same plenum (*Rude Pravo,* 7 April).

[46] *Rude Pravo,* 10 April, 24 May 1968. The programme specifically condemned monopoly by one social organization.

[47] E.g. *Student,* 24 July 1968, on the Warsaw letter.

Despite the profusion of youth organizations and the disintegration of the official movement, solidarity among the young enabled them to maintain their leadership role even in the confused days of the invasion. Their reaction was spontaneous rather than organized, but it demonstrated a genuine solidarity, not only among themselves but with their elders, in which the generational gap was temporarily forgotten. At the same time the natural generational differences were reflected in the greater activity of the youth, who assumed in some degree a leadership role among the public second only to the communications media (which actually carried on the role of the legal government). While for the most part they displayed during the invasion the same degree of discipline as did their elders, and at all times proclaimed their complete support for the country's abducted leaders, the situation did produce conflicting feelings among the young and their elders. The young had been raised in an atmosphere of shame and even contempt for the capitulation of 1938, and it was little comfort that the students had heroically resisted the occupation of Czechoslovakia in 1939; in 1968 the young people were intent upon *not* repeating the shameful mistake of the past. Their open and courageous defiance in the days of the invasion may be seen in this light, and indeed many older Czechs felt that the young people's behaviour had restored their pride. In these days the youth did *not* necessarily feel that their elders had voluntarily abandoned the aims and ideas of the "revival"; on the contrary they joined the party in large numbers to demonstrate their continued faith and solidarity. Nonetheless, as the initial shock wore off, more and more of them began to wonder if the country's leaders had been equal to the tasks confronting them, if the conditions agreed to in Moscow were legitimate, and if indeed they, the youth, had in fact acted any differently from their elders. In retrospect 1968 appeared to many of them as a capitulation no less shameful than that of 1938, no matter how it was rationalized. As one of the protest songs written by and circulating among the youth in 1969 put it, this generation was not much better than its predecessors.[48]

The issue of the generation should not, however, be oversimplified, for from the early days of liberalization in 1963 on through the invasion and after, a certain alliance existed which cut across age differences. It was the primary task of the conservatives to break this alliance; their success as far as one can tell has been only partial, and it is not yet clear just how much the youth feel they are now on their own, as the population becomes resigned to its fate, threatening the return of the pre-1968 mood of apathy and alienation. At a two-day plenary session of its central committee 19–20 September 1968, the CSM decided to set up a preparatory committee for a new youth union which would be

[48] "Pasazova revolta" by Karel Kryl.

a loose federation of the independent associations set up before the invasion.[49] This in fact led to the creation, on 19 December, of a new Czech Association of Juvenile and Youth Organizations. The member organizations were to remain independent and autonomous; the Association was to assume only co-ordinating functions, and to act as representative of the member organizations. It did not claim to speak in the name of all youth and did not assume responsibility or jurisdiction for non-members. Nor did it cover Slovakia. The Slovak section of the CSM had decided at its meeting on 22 November to create a separate Slovak Union of Youth for the Slovak organizations. In addition the Czech Student Union itself insisted upon emphasizing its independence (and was therefore banned in June 1969). While in one respect this comprehensive organization (although there were now two) was what the party had all along sought, the new associations and the refusal of at least the Czech union to fulfil the former functions of CSM suggest that the youth were still asserting their independence. More important, the new Czech association demonstrated its intention to stand by the pre-invasion programme by conferring an award on the Czechoslovak radio for its performance during the invasion, to declare Dubcek, Smrkovsky and Cernik Heroes of the CSSR, and to recommend that Svoboda be given the country's highest honour, accorded till then only to T. G. Masaryk.[50] The Czech association also stood by the youth dailies, *Smena* (Slovak) and *Mlada Fronta* (Czech), which had come under attack from the Soviets and the conservatives. These attacks continued throughout 1968 and into 1969, but the papers remained defiant. Both gained popularity outside youth circles and according to the organ of the journalists union (*Reporter,* 6 February 1969), the Slovak youth daily became the most widely read daily in Slovakia.[51] After the invasion the student journals voluntarily ceased publication, refusing to be bound by the Moscow-imposed restrictions. In their place a Czech student weekly, *Studentske Listy,* appeared in January 1969—and a Slovak student fortnightly, *Reflex,* in April 1969. Both journals continued in the liberal spirit of their predecessors and, as a result, *Studentske Listy* was banned on 6 May and *Reflex* suspended.

[49] These included the University Students Union, Pioneers, Junak (Boy Scouts), Military Youth League, Campers Union, Council of Farm and Countryside Youth, Council of Secondary School and Apprentice Youth, Union of Youth Clubs, Union of Working Youth, and the Union of Polish Youth. Prague radio, 21 September.

[50] Prague radio, 21 September, 19 December 1968; Bratislava radio, 22 November 1968.

[51] *Smena* was reprimanded by the Slovak Office for Press and Information for "articles inconsistent with internal and foreign policy." The paper refused to accept the reprimand. *Smena,* 28 November 1968.

By way of action and agitation the youth organized a demonstration on the fiftieth anniversary of the Czechoslovak Republic, which included a sit-in in front of the Soviet Embassy in Prague, as reported in the western press, and a three day strike throughout Czechoslovakia in protest against the party's November central committee decision which in effect placed serious restrictions on the Action Programme.[52] Together with lecturers and instructors, students peacefully occupied university buildings and conducted seminars and meetings on the situation in Czechoslovakia. They were entertained by outside groups such as a chamber orchestra which played on the premises of the Philosophy Faculty of Charles University, and food and cigarettes were brought in by people of all ages. During the strike, regular visits were exchanged between the universities and factories. The students produced a ten-point programme specifically based on the Action Programme. As before, their demands were not limited to student or even youth issues; they included demands for worker self-government and for the civil rights promised in the pre-invasion period. The significance of the strike was summed up by one journal thus: "By their action, which took its course in a peaceful and orderly manner, the students have proved that they are a force which must be taken into consideration both now and in the future, that they are people who have their own views and who can defend them."[53]

If indeed the students were a force, some of them decided that they must make use of this to prevent the greatest threat to the ideals of the revival, that of a general relapse into resignation and indifference. It was to startle the people out of this, as well as to bring pressure on those in the government who still regarded the people's wishes as

[52] *Rude Pravo,* 19 November 1968, carries the text of the controversial resolution.

[53] *Lidove Demokracie,* 21 November 1968. The ten points were: 1. The Action Programme adopted by the April 1968 plenum of the Communist Party of Czechoslovakia is the basis of our policy; 2. There will never be a policy from behind closed doors. In particular, the flow of information in both directions between the citizen and the leadership will be renewed; 3. The introduction of censorship in the mass communication media is temporary and will not last longer than six months; 4. Freedom of association and assembly must not be encroached upon; 5. Freedom of scientific research and of literary and cultural expression will be guaranteed; 6. Personal and legal security of citizens will be guaranteed; 7. Those who have lost the trust placed in them and have never sufficiently explained their attitude will not remain in important posts; 8. The establishment of enterprise councils of the working people as organs of self-administration will continue; 9. Freedom of travel abroad will be guaranteed; 10. In the area of foreign policy, we must never participate in actions which are contrary to the feelings of the Czechoslovak people, the UN Charter, and the general declaration of human rights.

binding, that a small group chose what was an act of desperation: self-immolation. For the orderly, rational Czechs the use of such a symbol—associated with the martyrdom of Jan Hus as well as with the more recent protest over Vietnam—by a young philosophy student was bound to come as a deep and grievous shock. The honour paid throughout the country to the self-immolated student Jan Palach, the massive attendance at his funeral, the spontaneous attempts in Czechoslovakia (and elsewhere in eastern Europe) to emulate his act, and the hesitancy of the regime to take a stand against it, all demonstrated the efficacy of the deed. Whether it had any lasting effects is another question. That it represented a new weapon in the struggle against the increasingly repressive regime was in fact denied by student leaders. Student and youth leaders were not prepared to make such tragic demands on their followers or themselves, and with the passing of the regime from the hands of Dubcek to Husak there seemed to be few left among the country's leaders who would be impressed or influenced by such pressure from below.

Since April 1969 the sense of frustration among all ages has been growing in Czechoslovakia. It would not be true to say that the younger generation has been broken, for it continues to organize protest wherever and however it can. The alliance between young workers and students has held, as has the broader alliance of youth with the liberals in the older generation. Yet today the younger people understand, in a way they may never otherwise have done, the meaning and nature of their elders' failures, particularly those of 1938. Today they are learning the techniques of passive resistance their parents mastered long ago; yet there are signs that they still consider themselves a generation with an important role to play—if, as some have pointed out, they do not permit themselves to be intimidated as were those before them by the overwhelming pressure to accommodate themselves and to compromise.[54]

[54] P. Pithart, "Words, Words, Words . . ." *Listy,* 21 November 1968.

IV

Prospects for the Seventies

THE preceding sections of this volume have demonstrated that as Communist societies modernize, the nature of the policy-making process and policy implementation has of necessity been considerably modified. In virtually all Communist states the most repressive features of the Stalinist era have not been operative for nearly two decades. This section inquires into the future capability of Communist systems to experiment and innovate as they are increasingly confronted with series of very complex problems, along with the persistent difficulties of earlier problems still unresolved. Some Communist parties inherited various culturally imposed or basic societal problems (ethnic conflicts, a truncated state whose division was artificially conceived and maintained by Great Power rivalries, overpopulation, periodic natural disasters, etc.) when they acquired political power, which defy any easy solution. In addition, the process of modernization has unleashed certain problems common to all societies at a similar stage of socioeconomic development, irrespective of political structure. What is of particular interest is whether Communist systems can solve or mitigate these problems more successfully than other types of political systems. Is the ideological, authoritarian, goal-oriented system better suited to focus on, understand, and handle these problems than other systems?

Are Communist-ruled systems able to adapt to the changing nature and needs of their societies? Can they anticipate change and behave accordingly? Can they modify their structure or method of political decision-making in order to govern more effectively? Or are they victims of conservatism and stagnation, able only to tinker with the mechanism they created decades ago and have become accustomed to, but unable to alter it in any basic fashion? Recent years have witnessed the unprecedented removal of many Communist party leaders in a more or less peaceful, if not entirely constitutionally prescribed, manner (e.g., Khrushchev, Novotný, Gomulka, Ulbricht). This development, significant in itself, does not, however, indicate the extent to which the system is amenable to change. If Communist political systems prove incapable of adopting necessary changes, what predictions can be offered regarding their future? The articles in this section seek to provide some tentative answers to these questions, based on the close scrutiny and interpretation of published materials.

Despite success in handling some almost insoluble problems, the question remains whether Communist regimes can adapt to the changing nature of their societies in the years ahead. Hough suggests that, in the Soviet case, changes have occurred and will continue to do so in measured fashion, gradually and incrementally; Robinson foresees a variety of options and potential courses of political development for the Chinese political system on the eve of its first succession crisis. Korbonski concludes, on the basis of investigating change in three East European states, that major systemic modifications have been adopted and implemented since the Stalinist era, and that these political systems will be able to accept and promote reform as changing conditions require. The validity of these assessments remains the ongoing task of Communist studies in the years ahead.

THE SOVIET SYSTEM: PETRIFICATION OR PLURALISM?

Jerry F. Hough

DURING the last years of the Khrushchev era, scholars vigorously debated the nature of the power relationships within the Soviet Communist Party Presidium, but their images of the relationship between the leadership—however defined—and the rest of society were usually quite similar. Whether the scholar spoke of an "administered society," an "organizational society," or an "ideological system," he summarized the Soviet system as "a command-dominated society," as one in which there is "totalitarianism without terror," as one in which the political system is "used by the political leaders to create a new society along the lines of their own beliefs and aspirations."

Even iconoclastic models were not very iconoclastic on this point. The so-called "conflict model" focused almost exclusively upon conflicts within the leadership and, in so doing, created the strong impression that all persons below the very top were acted upon rather than having any impact on the resolution of conflicts. Similarly, Alfred Meyer's "bureaucratic model" presented an image of modern bureaucratic society very similar to that of Herbert Marcuse and Barrington Moore. Such a society, he argued, "is characterized [in all countries] by the prevalence of certain totalitarian features," including "the imposition of ceaseless social change unwanted by the constituents."[1]

Jerry F. Hough, "The Soviet System: Petrification or Pluralism?" *Problems of Communism* (Washington, D.C.), March–April 1972. *Problems of Communism* is a bimonthly publication of the United States Information Agency.

[1] Allen Kassof, "The Administered Society: Totalitarianism without Terror," *World Politics,* July 1964, pp. 558–75; T. H. Rigby, "Traditional, Market, and Organizational Societies and the USSR," ibid., pp. 539–57; Zbigniew Brzezinski and Samuel P. Huntington, *Political Power USA/USSR,* New York, Viking Press, 1964; Carl A. Linden, *Khrushchev and the Soviet*

Since the fall of Khrushchev, the situation has changed drastically. Although thus far there is wide agreement about the collective nature of the leadership within the Politburo, the basic consensus about the nature of the political system as a whole has disappeared. Now there are a number of competing images or models of the system, and scholarly uncertainty is further reflected in the fact that these images themselves are often quite ambiguous.

Three Models

A "Directed Society." One group of scholars still emphasizes the directed nature of Soviet society and the political leaders' "determination . . . to make a 'new man,' without regard for the individual or social costs."[2] Or at least they emphasized this view in 1966–67 when the articles most clearly expressing it were written. A succinct summary of this position is provided by Jeremy Azrael:

> While the ouster of Khrushchev has inevitably resulted in more open access to the political arena for other elite groups, it has not seriously weakened the political-power position of the party *apparat* . . . If the growth of ideological agnosticism is apt to be a relatively slow process among all convinced Communists, it is likely to be particularly slow among the *apparatchiki* . . . It is precisely by stressing the continuing need to remold society and to juxtapose consciousness to spontaneity that the *apparatchiki* can best hope to legitimate their political sovereignty and the hegemony that they exercise over all facets of Soviet life . . . [Even among the] young men [in] the manpower pool from which the apparatus has been and is being replenished . . . [there] is un-

---

Leadership, Baltimore, Johns Hopkins University Press, 1966; Sidney I. Ploss, *Conflict and Decision-Making in Soviet Russia,* Princeton, Princeton University Press, 1965; Alfred G. Meyer, "USSR, Incorporated," in Donald W. Treadgold, Ed., *The Development of the USSR,* Seattle, University of Washington Press, 1964, pp. 21–28.

[2] John A. Armstrong, "Comparative Politics and Communist Systems: Concluding Remarks," *Slavic Review,* March 1967, p. 27. Armstrong's remarks were made in a symposium, and he was supporting a point made earlier by Robert S. Sharlet (ibid., p. 24). See also Paul Hollander, "Observations on Bureaucracy, Totalitarianism, and the Comparative Study of Communism," ibid., June 1967, pp. 302–7; and for a more recent version of the model, Roy D. Laird, *The Soviet Paradigm,* New York, The Free Press, 1970.

> likely to [be] a rapid erosion of the authoritarian-mobilization impulses that their world view implies . . . The final demise of the "permanent revolution" is many years away.[3]

"Oligarchic Petrification." A second group of scholars presents a model that retains much of the traditional image of a directed society: *i.e.*, they emphasize the dominant role of the officials at the top of the hierarchy, the flow of power from the top down, and the continued importance of ideology. In this view, however, the men at the top are not a dynamic political leadership determined to transform society, but rather a "government of clerks" anxious only to preserve their power and perquisites of office.

The word "ideology" is no longer defined as it once was by the theorists of totalitarianism ("a reasonably coherent body of ideas concerning practical means of how to change and reform a society"[4]), but has reverted to the meaning used by Karl Mannheim and many others: the rationalizations that legitimate and support the dominant interests in a society.[5] Since the Soviet Union is still directed from the top and since the top leaders have lost their will to change society, the Soviet system is described as being in a state of stagnation, decay, immobilism, or petrification. To quote Zbigniew Brzezinski:

> Oligarchic petrification would involve the maintenance of the dominant role of the party and the retention of the essentially dogmatic character of the ideology. In effect, more of the same. Neither the party nor the ideology would be in a particularly revolutionary relationship to society; instead, the main thrust of the relationship would be for the party to retain political control over society without attempting to impose major innovations. Strong emphasis would be placed on ideological indoctrination and the confinement of ideological deviations. Political leadership could remain collective, for the absence of deliberately imposed change would not

[3] Jeremy R. Azrael, "The Party and Society," in Allen Kassof, Ed., *Prospects for Soviet Society*, New York, F. A. Praeger, 1968, pp. 70–73. (The order of the sentences has been changed somewhat.) In fairness, it should be noted that Azrael's analysis of the mobilizational nature of Soviet society seems to have changed since this article was written (see his "Varieties of De-Stalinization," in Chalmers Johnson, Ed., *Change in Communist Systems,* Stanford, Stanford University Press, 1970, pp. 135–51).

[4] Carl J. Friedrich and Zbigniew K. Brzezinski, *Totalitarian Dictatorship and Autocracy,* Cambridge, Mass., Harvard University Press, 1956, p. 74.

[5] As Karl Mannheim has argued in his classic book on the subject, "There is implicit in the word 'ideology' the insight that in certain situations the collective unconscious of certain groups obscures the real condition of society both to itself and to others and thereby stabilizes it." *Ideology and Utopia,* New York, Harcourt, Brace & World, 1965, p. 90.

> require major choices. The domestic result would be rule by an ossified bureaucracy that would pursue a conservative policy masked by revolutionary slogans.[6]

Unfortunately, the model of oligarchic petrification can be quite ambiguous. Professor Brzezinski's reference to "the maintenance of the dominant role of the party and the retention of the essentially dogmatic character of the ideology"—which he sums up as "in effect, more of the same"—clearly suggests continuity with the Soviet past; yet, these terms have different meanings than they did in the past. The end of "deliberately imposed change" means that the party is not, in fact, dominant over society and the bureaucracy in the same sense that it was previously depicted to be. In the language of Friedrich and Brzezinski, the Soviet Union has changed from a totalitarian dictatorship into an authoritarian dictatorship or even an oligarchy.

There are several possible variants of the petrification model that would render it less ambiguous. One such variant would specifically identify the party with the party apparatus, depicting the latter as the central bureaucracy in the Soviet system. (Indeed, this is conceivably the meaning Brzezinski had in mind.) This image of a petrified system would be particularly neat if coupled with Leonard Schapiro's view of the policy position of the party apparatus:

> By and large, the views that favor discipline, centralized controls, and absolute priority for heavy industry can be regarded as those of the party apparatus, while the views that look toward greater reliance on material incentives, increased application of market principles, decentralization of industrial controls, and higher priority for consumer goods can be identified with the government apparatus, including the planners and managers.[7]

There is, however, not the slightest evidence to support the hypothesis of a party apparatus united on a conservative policy position—and a great deal of evidence to indicate that the hypothesis is wrong.[8] Nor is

[6] Zbigniew Brzezinski, *Between Two Ages,* New York, Viking Press, 1970, p. 165. As its wording suggests, the model comes in a discussion of alternative paths of future Soviet development, and Brzezinski actually predicts a combination of petrification and technological adaptation in the 1970's. The model does seem, however, to summarize Brzezinski's analysis of the last seven-and-a-half years of Soviet history, and it is cited here for that purpose alone.

[7] Leonard Schapiro, "Keynote—Compromise," *Problems of Communism,* July-August 1971, p. 2. I do not mean to suggest that Brzezinski would accept this interpretation, but only that it would make the model neat.

[8] The view that Soviet politics revolves around conflict between a con-

there any evidence that there is a simple power relationship between the party and state hierarchies.

A second—and, in the author's view, far more defensible—variant of the petrification model would feature rule by an inherently conservative bureaucracy, an "ossified bureaucracy" in Brzezinski's phrase. The party apparatus would certainly be included as an important component of the bureaucratic system, but it would only be one component. One could use the language of Milovan Djilas and speak of rule by a "new class" embracing all "those who have special privileges and economic preference because of the administrative monopoly they hold."[9] Or one could—and perhaps should—emphasize the relative supremacy of the defense and heavy-industry bureaucracies over the others, as evidenced by the fact that men with experience in these two areas have come to occupy a very large number of key positions in the party and state machinery of the Soviet Union.[10]

---

servative party apparatus and a progressive state apparatus is an old and widely-held one whose persistence defies explanation—at least, in this writer's view. Even the most obvious evidence seems to contradict it. For example, the men who in 1952 would have been called the two leading party *apparatchiki* after Stalin were Malenkov and Khrushchev, but they would hardly be regarded as the leading conservative figures of the post-Stalin era. For an examination of the more esoteric evidence on this question, see Jerry F. Hough, "The Party Apparatchiki," in H. Gordon Skilling and Franklyn Griffiths, Eds., *Interest Groups in Soviet Politics,* Princeton, Princeton University Press, 1971, pp. 47–92.

[9] Milovan Djilas, *The New Class,* New York, Praeger, 1957, pp. 39–40. Djilas' definition of "the party" is quite different from that adopted in the previous variant, and it conveys a clearer impression of the meaning of this model. He conceives of the party in the sense of "the compact party, full of initiative," which, he says, "diminishes," "is disappearing," or "grows weaker."

[10] The present General Secretary, Leonid Brezhnev, and the *de facto* second secretary of the Central Committee (Kirilenko) are ferrous metallurgy and aviation industry engineers, respectively, with extensive party work in centers of the defense and heavy industries. The Central Committee secretary handling planning/financial and also (apparently) military affairs (Ustinov) was Minister of Munitions and the Minister of Defense Industry from 1941 to 1957 before becoming the top official coordinating defense industries in the Khrushchev era. The Chairman and two First Deputy Chairmen of the Council of Ministers do not have a heavy-industry background, but the eight Deputy Chairmen are all heavy-industry engineers. Six have been Ministers for Heavy Industry or Defense Industry, and a seventh was a Deputy Minister of Ferrous Metallurgy before becoming a

"Institutional Pluralism." A third group of scholars has been moving —albeit with great tentativeness in most instances—toward a model of the Soviet system that represents a far more drastic break with the traditional images—a model that will be termed "institutional pluralism." Like the adherents of the petrification model, these scholars accept Alfred Meyer's insight that the Soviet Union is a giant bureaucracy, but they have a quite different conception of the nature of bureaucracy. They do not believe that either Soviet society or bureaucracy is inert. Soviet society is viewed as undergoing a series of dynamic changes produced by industrialization, and Soviet professional-administrative personnel are seen more as the sort of functional specialists who are considered to be a major source of innovation in the West than as the conservative bureaucrats of the petrification model.[11] The scholars of this group believe that ideas and power flow up the administrative hierarchies as well as down, and they do not see immobilism in the process of policy formation. In the words of Robert Daniels,

> What appears to be evolving in the Soviet Union is a new kind of politics, participatory bureaucracy. . . . In any complex modern bureaucratic organization, it is impossible to function purely from the top down: all manner of influences—information, advice, recommendations, problems, complaints—must flow upwards. . . . The problems of managing a complex economy and technology have made it abundantly clear to the Soviet leadership that they must allow this reverse stream of influence to flow freely,

---

top planning official with responsibility for that branch. In the three largest republics, the political leaders are former enterprise managers in defense industry (Solomentsev in the RSFSR and Shelest in the Ukraine) or in non-ferrous metallurgy (Kunaev in Kazakhstan). Since the mid-1950's, the obkom first secretaries in over 80 percent of the 25 most industrialized oblasts have been engineers (usually with substantial managerial experience), and nearly all of these men come from heavy rather than light industry. While the percentage of all obkom first secretaries is not too large, they are concentrated in the populous, urbanized oblasts with large numbers of party members. In 1966, 146 units (small republics, oblasts, and the city of Moscow) sent delegates to the 23rd Party Congress. Less than a quarter of these units had first secretaries with a heavy-industry background, but they named over 40 percent of the delegates.

[11] In the words of Alex Inkeles, "In most areas of life the best way to predict the attitudes, values, and orientations of men in the Soviet system is to draw on the general knowledge that we have about men holding comparable positions in Western industrial societies." *Social Change in Soviet Russia,* Cambridge, Mass., Harvard University Press, 1968, p. 427.

and their main concern is that the flow be kept within the organizational structure of the Communist Party.[12]

Daniels heavily qualifies this image by emphasizing "the power of the party and its monopoly position in the Soviet power structure" and by treating the admission of "segments of the administrative and intellectual class into the decision-making and controlling process" as a future possibility rather than as a present fact. In this respect, he seems to have moved only partially away from the earlier image of "policy groups" whose members come from a very narrow elite and who are "careful not to cross the shadowy line between advocacy and pressure."[13] Other scholars, however, have gone further, emphasizing the existence of group activity "outside the formal system of political authority"[14] or the role of "intermediate actors" and "intermediate participation."[15] Still others have been willing to assert that "Soviet interest groupings . . . share political power in the Soviet policy process."[16]

Like the petrification model, this third construct of the Soviet system is not without its ambiguity. No one is yet willing to equate pluralism of the Soviet type with that in the West. If compelled to characterize the Soviet system as either a "dictatorship" or a "democracy," the third group of scholars would vehemently protest the choice but would ultimately join the others in electing the former term. At most, in Skilling's words, the Soviet Union is viewed as "a 'pluralism of elites,' or to borrow Robert Dahl's expressive term, a 'polyarchical' system, but oligarchical rather than democratic in character."[17] One receives the clear impression of far less direction and/or control from above than in other images of the Soviet system, but the degree of direction and/or control remains far greater than in the classic pluralist model. This intermediate stage has not been defined very precisely. One senses what Daniels means when he speaks both of influence flowing upwards and of the "monopoly position" of the party in the "Soviet power structure." But the concepts are by no means clear.

[12] Robert V. Daniels, "Soviet Politics Since Khrushchev," in John W. Strong, Ed., *The Soviet Union under Brezhnev and Kosygin,* New York, Van Nostrand-Reinhold Co., 1971, pp. 22–23.

[13] Brzezinski and Huntington, op. cit. (fn 1), p. 196.

[14] H. Gordon Skilling, "Groups in Soviet Politics: Some Hypotheses," in Skilling and Griffiths, op. cit. (fn 8), p. 42.

[15] Franklyn Griffiths, "A Tendency Analysis of Soviet Policy-Making," ibid., pp. 369–77.

[16] Philip Stewart, "Soviet Interest Groups and the Policy Process," *World Politics,* October 1969, p. 50.

[17] "Interest Groups and Communist Politics: An Introduction," in Skilling and Griffiths, op. cit., p. 17.

Perhaps the difficulty is the absence of a generally-accepted model (or, more precisely, an ideal type) for a political system that is somewhere in between authoritarianism and classical pluralism. Such a model—which the author has chosen to call "institutional pluralism"—would certainly contain a number of the features of the conventional American model of pluralism. These features may be described as follows:

(1) There exists in society a multiplicity of interests: nothing is monolithic about society or the political system, and no single interest dominates either.

(2) The political process revolves around conflict among a complex set of crosscutting and shifting alliances of persons with divergent interests.

(3) Citizens and officials usually treat politics as "the art of the possible" and see it "as a set of give-and-take interactions in which each side bargains for a set of more or less limited objectives."[18] So long as they stay strictly within this framework, they are free to express their views.

(4) Political leaders serve essentially as mediators or brokers in the political process, their "most universal function" being to bring "men together in masses on some middle ground where they can combine to carry out a common policy."[19]

(5) Governmental decisions on various questions are most heavily influenced by those especially affected by them and especially knowledgeable about them. In short, the government process is one of "minorities rule," featuring "the steady appeasement of relatively small groups."[20]

(6) To the extent that accommodation of the demands of some groups requires restrictions upon other groups, the changes are undertaken gradually and in a way that is accommodating to the disadvantaged group. Incrementalism is thus the hallmark of the system.[21]

The differences between institutional pluralism and classical pluralism center on the framework in which the political process takes place and on the types of political behavior that are tolerated. The model of

[18] Gabriel A. Almond and G. Bingham Powell, Jr., *Comparative Politics,* Boston, Little, Brown & Co., 1966, p. 57.

[19] A. Lawrence Lowell, *Public Opinion and Popular Government,* New York, Longmans, Green & Co., 1914, pp. 61–62.

[20] Robert A. Dahl, *A Preface to Democratic Theory,* Chicago, University of Chicago Press, 1956, pp. 27–28, 133, and 146.

[21] Robert A. Dahl and Charles E. Lindblom, *Politics, Economics, and Welfare,* New York, Harper & Row, 1953, pp. 82–88.

classical pluralism features the opportunity for all citizens to choose between the programs of competing elites in elections and to form new organizations (pressure groups or parties) to advance their political interests. Indeed, the contention that a pluralist system is the most equitable possible rests on the assumption that the disadvantaged and the dissatisfied will regularly use such political mechanisms to seek redress of their grievances. In the model of institutional pluralism on the other hand, those who want to effect political change must, with a few exceptions, work within the official institutional framework. Those who fail to do so run the danger of severe repression, especially when they call for nonincremental change in the fundamentals of the system. While any citizen can make appeals or suggestions for incremental change through official channels, the leading political participants will almost always be "establishment" figures—usually civil servants and political figures, but also policy-oriented scholars and educators. However, the model assumes that the institutional forces are at least somewhat responsive to broader societal forces. It includes an image of bureaucratic officials as men who are driven to represent many of the interests of their clientele and low-level subordinates, as well as an image of politicians as men who take the danger of popular unrest into account as they mediate conflicts among the political participants.

To repeat, the model of institutional pluralism is an ideal type that is meant to conform to Inkeles' usage of the term "model"—an abstraction, a set of "ideas or concepts which have a certain unity."[22] No scholar—and certainly not the author—believes that it accurately summarizes the situation in the Soviet Union today; at most, it could be claimed that the Soviet Union is moving in the direction of the model. Indeed, since past Soviet policy has made the specialized elites associated with heavy and defense industry far stronger in numbers, talent, and power than other members of the upper stratum, the model itself suggests that current Soviet policy will reflect this imbalance for some time to come, and that the dominance of heavy industry will disappear only incrementally.

The crucial question is—how are post-Khrushchev developments in the Soviet Union best summarized? Does the Soviet Union still correspond most closely to a model of "a command-dominated society," or has it moved substantially in the direction either of the petrification model or the model of institutional pluralism? Is the Soviet political system one in which power—whether used for change or for the prevention of change—is still concentrated in the party leadership, or has there been a diffusion of power to other elements of Soviet society?

[22] Inkeles, op. cit. (fn 11), p. 431.

Passing of the "Directed Society"

Seven-and-a-half years have passed since the fall of Khrushchev, and a series of recent events—the 24th CPSU Congress and the republic party congresses that preceded it, the new five-year plan, and the elections to the republic supreme soviets and councils of ministers—have combined to provide a wealth of new policy and elite data. The purpose of this article is to explore the relevance of the three models described above in the light of these new data.

Any reasonably relevant model is likely to illuminate at least some aspects of a political system. But while the model drawn by the first group of scholars—that of a political leadership which actively strives to transform society in accordance with its ideological preconceptions—may help to explain a number of Soviet phenomena rooted in an earlier period, it seems of very little use in explaining the dynamics of the last seven years. Indeed, whatever the future may bring, recent events make this model appear as anachronistic as the image of a system based primarily on arbitrary terror came to appear in the Khrushchev era.

One of the key elements of any model of an "ideological system" is a political leadership that has "beliefs and aspirations" on the basis of which it seeks to remold society. Classically, this image of Soviet society has pictured it as a system in which the leadership endeavors to transform society along the lines of the guiding Marxist-Leninist ideology. Increasingly in the post-Stalin period, however, and especially in the post-Khrushchev period, the Soviet leadership has given the impression that it is far from certain about the solution of society's problems. Increasingly, it has been willing to listen to policy advice from "society" and to permit far-ranging public discussion of policy questions.

To be sure, not all Soviet specialists agree that the last seven years have witnessed a freer flow of information in the Soviet Union; indeed, many would speak of a reverse tendency toward greater repression of criticism and iconoclastic thought. For example, Brzezinski speaks of a "movement in the opposite direction" between 1964 and 1969 and predicts that "in the short run, development toward a pluralist, ideologically more tolerant system does not seem likely."[23] In this writer's view, however, there is in the West more misunderstanding on this subject than on any other development in recent Soviet history.

The contention that the present Soviet leadership is less tolerant of critical ideas rests on three pieces of evidence. The first—and foremost

[23] *Between Two Ages,* p. 167.

in terms of the publicity it receives—has been the repression of well-known intellectual dissenters, such as Andrei Amalrik, who have dared to criticize the fundamentals of the system. The second has been the renewed sensitivity of the leadership to criticism of the past, especially of the Stalin era. On this question, censorship clearly has been more repressive under Brezhnev than it was under Khrushchev. The third bit of evidence has been some slight increase in the political weight of the secret police. The Chairman of the KGB, Yuri Andropov, has been elected to candidate membership on the Politburo, while the representation of the KGB in the republic party bureaus has risen from one full member and three candidate members in 1966 to three full members and four candidates in 1971.[24]

None of this evidence, however—and particularly the last—seems conclusive. Even if we accept an increase in the representation of the KGB in the republic party bureaus as a reliable indicator of the degree of repression in the system, that representation in 1971 is still less than it was in 1961 (five full members and two candidate members), and Andropov's election to the Politburo may owe as much to his responsibilities in the foreign policy field as to his police role (he had 14 years of foreign policy experience before becoming KGB chairman). Moreover, KGB representation in the republic party bureaus is largely confined to the least industrialized republics. The republic KGB chairman was named to the party bureau (as either a full or candidate member) in each of the five republics with the lowest level of urbanization, but there is KGB representation on the bureaus of only two of the five republics with medium urbanization and none on the bureaus of the four most urbanized republics. On the surface at least, this pattern suggests less a preoccupation on the part of the leadership with the rise of unorthodox thought in the more "modern" areas than the persistence of more traditional methods of control (and perhaps of a more traditional political culture) in the less modernized regions.

WIDER INFORMATION AND DEBATE

The contents of the published media, which are quick to reflect changes in policy affecting the flow of information, certainly provide little evidence of an increased sway of "police mentality." The republic newspapers, for example, now contain more articles about victims of

[24] Three republic KGB chairmen were elected to full membership in the republic party bureaus, and three to candidate membership, at the republic party congresses in February and March 1971. The fourth candidate member was named to the Belorussian party bureau the following July.

Stalin's purges than they did in late 1965 and early 1966. The press also reflects less official sensitivity on a number of topics that used to be considered security matters. To cite just two of many examples, the large aviation plants in Tashkent, Tbilisi, and Kiev, which were never mentioned in the newspapers before late 1966, are now discussed quite frequently, and press reports identify by name such holders of security-sensitive positions as border-guard officials and directors of titanium and computer plants.

Even more important is the increasing extent to which policy questions are now debated in the newspapers, periodicals, and particularly books. To speak of "the retention of the essentially dogmatic character of the ideology" and to state that the years since 1964 have seen movement away from "an ideologically more tolerant system" is to overlook the crucial fact that on all but the most central questions, party policy is less and less incorporated into clear-cut, undebatable "ideology," with a consequent widening of the areas open to public discussion. In almost every policy sphere, ideology is ambiguous and ill-defined; and in almost every policy sphere, the published debate is now freer and more wide-ranging than it was under Khrushchev.

There has, in fact, been virtually no conceivable proposal for incremental change in party policy in the last five years that has not been aired in the Soviet press.[25] The proposals must sometimes be carefully phrased, and the more radical ones often have to be published in scholarly journals and books rather than in the pages of *Pravda,* but there is virtually no official policy that is immune from questioning. Even in the sensitive areas of foreign and nationalities policy, where advocacy of change is permitted only in the most veiled terms, lively debate still goes on in the guise of discussions on the nature of the prevailing factual situation.[26]

Certainly the party leadership tolerates no direct challenge to the basic legitimacy of one-party rule or to its own ultimate authority. It still restricts the flow of information severely by comparison with Western countries, particularly in the media that reach the largest au-

[25] Documentation of this point is too scattered and voluminous to be compressed into a footnote of reasonable length. However, one need only refer to almost any Western article or book dealing with a specific Soviet policy area. Two such articles published recently in this journal were Aryeh L. Unger, "Polit-informator or Agitator: A Decision Blocked," September-October 1970, pp. 30–43; and Zev Katz, "Sociology in the Soviet Union," May-June 1971, pp. 22–40.

[26] See, e.g., Grey Hodnett, "What's in a Nation?" *Problems of Communism,* September-October 1967, pp. 2–15; and Franklyn Griffiths, "Four Soviet Images of the American Political System," unpublished paper (prepared for delivery at the meetings of the Canadian Political Science Association, June 11, 1971).

diences, and as Brzezinski correctly emphasizes, it remains extremely inflexible in its rejection of "alien" world views and its determination to combat their dissemination. Those dissenters who try to circulate forbidden ideas can testify eloquently that neither the KGB nor the labor camps have withered away.

Yet, even in those areas, the present regime seems, if anything, more tolerant than that of Khrushchev. The myth has arisen that Khrushchev merely "relied on verbal chatisement," whereas "the Brezhnev leadership has put writers and other dissidents in jail or insane asylums."[27] However, a look at the past experiences of such dissenters as Brodsky, Bukovsky, Dobrovolsky, Galanskov, Grigorenko, and Tarsis indicates very clearly that their suppression did not begin with the advent of the present regime, but rather under Khrushchev.[28] One cannot be certain how the late First Secretary would have reacted to the increase in open dissent and the circulation of documents such as the *Khronika tekushchikh sobytii* (Chronicle of Current Events) on the scale seen since 1964—and especially to the transmission of such materials to Western newsmen. There is, however, good reason not only to doubt that Khrushchev would have been more liberal than the present leadership, but also to suspect that dissent, rather than being more rigorously suppressed, is now enjoying increased publicity.

A willingness to tolerate a freer flow of information and to hear advice does not correspond to traditional Western images of the ideological mind, but it is not incompatible with a political leadership that strives to transform society. Indeed, if the party leadership were to act upon some of the advice that has been publicly expressed, it would transform Soviet society as radically as Stalin did in 1928–1929. On the other hand, if the leadership prefers to follow the advice of those who insist upon maintenance of the status quo, there can be little change. The question is: what sort of advice does the present leader-

[27] *The New York Times,* Sept. 13, 1971, p. 35.

[28] For brief biographical notes about the dissenters, see Abraham Brumberg, Ed., *In Quest of Justice,* New York, Frederick A. Praeger, 1970, pp. 464–74. Elsewhere, Brumberg questions Khrushchev's liberalism by listing a number of his policies: "The restoration of the death penalty for economic crimes, and the unsavory 'vigilance campaign' of 1962–1963 with its heavy admixture of anti-semitism; the assault on private property in agriculture; the recurrent attack on the liberal intelligentsia, so reminiscent of Zhdanov's repressions of the late 1940's; the creation of quasi-legal bodies to administer justice outside of the confines of legally constituted bodies, such as the anti-parasite legislation and comrades' courts. Finally, the creation of yet another 'cult of the individual' . . . with a dash of nepotism thrown in for good measure" ("The Fall of Khrushchev—Causes and Repercussions," in Strong, *The Soviet Union under Brezhnev and Kosygin,* pp. 11–12).

ship seem to be following? Or, to put it in broader terms, what is the leadership's relationship to the rest of society?

End of the "Permanent Purge"?

If one looks at the last seven years of Soviet political evolution in historical perspective, the overwhelming impression one receives is that this period has witnessed a major change in the relationship of the leadership to the key segments of the Soviet "establishment." Whereas Stalin in his last years basically ignored the policy suggestions of the institutional centers of power, and whereas Khrushchev challenged the basic interests of almost every one of these centers (and with some success), the present leadership has not done major battle with any important segment of the establishment and seems, on the contrary, to have acceded to the most central desires of each.

One clear-cut piece of evidence is found in the realm of personnel selection. At the end of the Stalin period Brzezinski could speak of a "permanent purge" in the Soviet Union: he saw its purposes as "many and varied" and the need for it as "ever-present" and not diminishing "with the growing stability of the totalitarian regime."[29] Under Khrushchev, indeed, the purge did seem as permanent as ever, but after his fall the turnover rates among top officials—whatever may have been the cause—took a sharp downturn. For certain categories of officials, the turnover for the *ten* years between 1961 and 1971 has proven considerably lower than it was for the *five* years between 1956 and 1961, and in some cases it was unbelievably low between 1966 and 1971 (see Table 1). For example, not one of the 11 first deputy or deputy chairmen of the USSR Council of Ministers was replaced between the last two congresses, and only four of the 57 ministers and state committee chairmen that sat on the Council of Ministers were removed in the same period (another three died).

Khrushchev's successors have seemed especially reluctant to demote anyone who has reached the level of full membership in the Central Committee or higher—or perhaps they have found it especially difficult to do so. In any event, all of the members or candidate members of the Politburo elected in 1966 were renamed to this body in 1971, while 81 percent of the living full members of the 1966 Central Committee retained their membership in 1971 (82 percent, if we exclude the three workers and peasants on the committee, all of whom were replaced). The reelection rate among the voting members of the Central Committee exceeded 87 percent among the living officials who were

[29] *The Permanent Purge,* Cambridge, Mass., Harvard University Press, 1956, pp. 168–70.

Table 1: Turnover of Leading Personnel
(in percent[a])

Position	1956–61	1961–71	1966–71
Full members, Politburo	70	36	0
Full members, Central Committee	50	39	24
Secretaries, Central Committee	75	67	27
Members, USSR Council of Ministers[b]	67	45	10
Republic First Secretaries	79	43	21
Obkom First Secretaries (RSFSR)	86	67	43

[a] The figures in each column are the percentages of officials who were not in the same position in the terminal year of the period specified as they were at the beginning of the period.
[b] Excluding chairmen of the republic Councils of Ministers, who are ex-officio members of the all-Union body.

still 60 years of age or younger in 1971. The fate of the 1966 obkom first secretaries is quite instructive. Twenty-one of the 44 obkom first secretaries with voting membership on the CPSU Central Committee were replaced between congresses, but 15 of these 21 were named to other posts that resulted in their reelection to the 1971 Central Committee, and a 16th had been appointed to such a post and subsequently died.

Deference to the Establishment

The unwillingness or inability of the present leadership to remove or demote the members of the top administrative elite has been matched by its abstention from imposing any major policy change that would seriously diminish the status of any important institutional group. The policy decisions of the last seven years, unlike those of the Khrushchev period, have been such as would be expected from committee decision-making in which the leadership assumes the role not of the major policy initiator but of a broker mediating the competing claims of powerful interests. Khrushchev's unpopular initiatives were quickly reversed by the succeeding leadership, and subsequent Soviet policy in any particular area has remained fairly close to what the relevant segment of the specialized elite could be predicted to favor (at least, given the limitations imposed by the prevailing distribution of funds). Certainly this seems to be true of policy with respect to education, agriculture, military affairs, industrial organization, and party structure. On questions involving the relative priority to be given to the interests of different institutional centers of power, any changes that have occurred have been slow and incremental.

The leadership's deference to the top specialized officials seems so apparent that it need not be documented at length. It should be noted, however, that this deference may now be increasingly extended to the top elite of the major regional centers as well. The evidence is not certain on this point, but there are a number of evidences that seem to point in this direction.

First, the regional representation on the Politburo has been gradually increasing. When the voting membership of this body was increased by four at the 24th Party Congress, three of the added full members were regional representatives: Shcherbitsky (Ukraine), Kunaev (Kazakhstan), and Grishin (Moscow). The five large republics, as well as Georgia in the Transcaucasus, all now have officials on the ruling Politburo, while the Baltic states have *de facto* representation in the person of the Latvian, Arvid Pelshe, Chairman of the Party Control Commission.[30] An analogous development has occurred in the republics. The number of first secretaries of outlying oblasts and cities named to republic party bureaus has risen from none in 1956 to two in 1961, six in 1966 (two full members and four candidates), and seven in 1971 (four full members and three candidates).

Second, there has been a change in the pattern of selection of obkom first secretaries, at least in the Russian Republic. Brezhnev has announced a policy "of promoting local officials [to the post of obkom first secretary],[31] sending people from the center to these posts only in exceptional cases," and this policy has generally been followed in the RSFSR. In the 1957–61 period, only 26 percent of new obkom first secretaries in the republic had worked for more than five years in their respective oblasts before their appointment, while 64 percent came directly from the outside. (In earlier periods the percentage of outsiders seems to have been even higher.) Between the 23rd and 24th Congresses, on the other hand, 75 percent of new obkom first secretaries in the RSFSR had at least five years of past service within their oblasts, and most had spent their entire careers there.[32]

[30] In contrast to the Politburo, however, the Central Committee Secretariat remains overwhelmingly Russian. All the secretaries and all but one of the department heads are Russian.

[31] *Pravda,* March 31, 1971, p. 10.

[32] Twenty-four obkom first secretaries appointed in this period were promoted from lesser positions within the same oblast. Eleven had been oblispolkom chairman; six had been obkom second secretary; five had been gorkom first secretary (a new and perhaps significant source of re-

Since the center has a wide range of choice among officials living in any given oblast, it is possible that the new personnel policy has not appreciably altered the relationship between the party leadership (specifically the General Secretary) and the obkom first secretaries. However, internal promotion is at least consistent with a possible tendency toward allowing local party establishments to determine their own leadership succession.

Third, a few signs have appeared of slightly greater policy autonomy for the republic leaders, at least on a few issues. On one question—the newspaper treatment of local victims of the Stalin purges—the partial autonomy is readily observable. As indicated earlier, biographies of purge victims have generally been published more frequently now than five years ago, but the republics by no means follow a uniform policy in this matter. At one extreme, the Ukraine in 1970 erected monuments to S. V. Kossior and V. Y. Chubar (both "liquidated" in 1937–38),[33] while Uzbekistan has published a biography of Akmal Ikramov and the collected works of Faizulla Khodzhaev, both of whom were major republic leaders purged by Stalin.[34] (Khodzhaev remained under a shadow throughout the Khrushchev period because of his inclusion among the "Right Oppositionists" prosecuted with Bukharin.) At the other extreme, Kazakhstan appears not to have published any biography of a purge victim in the past five years, and certainly not in 1971. Even the 70th birth anniversary of Levon Mirzoian, Kazakhstan's initial party First Secretary after the republic's formation, was not mentioned in *Kazakhstanskaia pravda* in 1967, despite the fact that a commemorative article about him did appear at that time in Azerbaidzhan, where he had previously served as a republic party secretary during the 1920's.[35]

To this author at least, the press in the individual republics today

---

cruitment); and two had held other positions. However, only some 35 percent of the new obkom first secretaries outside the RSFSR were promoted from within the oblast. (This calculation excludes all newly-formed oblasts.) Except in one case, the new first secretaries did come from within the republic in which the oblast was located.

[33] *Pravda Ukrainy,* April 20, 1970, p. 1, and May 19, 1970, p. 1.

[34] I am indebted to Donald Carlisle, Professor of Political Science at Boston College and Associate of the Russian Research Center, for the information about Ikramov and Khodzhaev.

[35] Mirzoian was first secretary of the Kazakhstan kraikom and then of the republic central committee from 1933 to 1938. His name was also not even mentioned in a page-long article on the history of Kazakhstan in the 1930's that appeared in *Kazakhstanskaia pravda,* Oct. 10, 1967, p. 3. The Azerbaidzhan newspaper in which his biography was published was *Bakinskii rabochii,* Dec. 1, 1967, p. 3.

gives an impression of greater variation on other questions as well, but it is possible that this is more a change in the eye of the beholder than in the actual situation. It would require a comprehensive study of economic, educational, and cultural developments in the republics to determine the extent of any trend toward greater autonomy for the regional elite. As John Armstrong has pointed out, however, the treatment of the union republics by the central Soviet authorities has for some time been much more differentiated and subtle than most of our conceptions of the Soviet federal system would suggest.[36] As a rule, the more industrialized republics appear to have been granted somewhat more autonomy than those in Central Asia in particular, and this would logically seem to imply some increase in authority for all republics as they become more industrialized.

The Party as Political Broker

Whatever devolution of authority to the leading regional officials has occurred, it is clear that the Soviet Union remains a country in which the vertical administrative units—the ministries and state committees (together with associated educational-scientific personnel and specialized party officials)—are on the whole much stronger than the horizontal or regional ones. (Comparison with Yugoslavia is instructive on this point.) Rather than the regional political leaders, it seems to be the leading specialized establishments which have been the main beneficiaries of the diffusion of power from the top party leadership.

Even within the regions, the administrative subordinates of the central ministries (particularly the subordinates of the heavy-industry ministries) have often had a key role in local decision-making. As the author has tried to suggest elsewhere in drawing an analogy between Soviet regional party organs and the French prefectural authorities, the leading party officials in the regions have been granted the great legal authority of the prefect but have had their real influence limited by the same factors that have weakened such officials throughout the world.[37]

[36] John Armstrong, "The Ethnic Scene in the Soviet Union: The View of the Dictatorship," in Erich Goldhagen, Ed., *Ethnic Minorities in the Soviet Union,* New York, Praeger, 1968, pp. 3–49.

[37] Philip Stewart, in reviewing this book in the May-June 1971 issue of this journal, mistook my thesis to be that of an all-powerful Soviet regional party first secretary. The confusion may arise from the old problem of distinguishing clearly between legitimate authority and real influence. The conventional Western conception portrayed the local party organs as a vital

The enormous range of responsibilities placed on the shoulders of party officials, the superior knowledge of the specialized administrators, and the latter's ties with powerful central ministries have all combined to bring about a situation in which the local party first secretaries often function more as broker politicians vis-à-vis local specialized officials than as the source of policy guidance for the latter's specialized decisions.

In at least one respect, the developments of recent years may have pushed the local party organs even more strongly toward the broker role. For the first time, party theorists have been strongly emphasizing the coordinating function of the party organs, and the leadership has continued the practice of gradually building up the state apparatus in policy areas where the party organs had previously assumed (or, perhaps, been compelled to assume) a major operational role. The creation of the State Supply Committee and of republic state committees for labor resources (both with offices in the localities) may have reduced the very considerable burdens on the party organs in these realms. Similarly, the resubordination of the raion agricultural administrations to the raion soviets after nearly a decade of independence, together with the new decrees purporting to give the soviets new powers, may conceivably imply the beginnings of a policy of significantly increasing what is now the virtually nonexistent ability of local soviets to engage in meaningful regional and urban planning.[38] In the ideological (*i.e.*, the educational-cultural-publishing) realm, the creation of new governmental committees was largely the product of the last years

---

force in pushing plant managers to technical innovation but considered party intervention to be a quasi-legitimate (and, on many questions, an illegitimate) violation of the chain of command. My own contention is that the situation is the reverse—that the party organs have clear-cut legal authority but not a great deal of influence with respect to technical policy and several other "intra-industry" questions. The evidence which Professor Stewart cites from the book to challenge the thesis that he attributes to me is actually the evidence that I presented to bolster my major thesis.

[38] The resubordination of the raion agricultural administrations to the soviets occurred in the summer of 1970 (see *Pravda,* July 3, 1970, p. 3). The decrees referred to were published in *Pravda,* March 14, 1971, pp. 1–2, and March 20, 1971, p. 1. In evaluating the decrees, two facts should be kept in mind: (1) any improvement in the position of the soviets begins from a very low point; and (2) even after the decrees, there have been complaints by local officials that the city soviets still do not have adequate authority over housing construction and municipal services expenditures to be able to integrate such development into any meaningful city plan.

of the Khrushchev period, but the status of these bodies has risen significantly since 1964.[39] Whereas 31 officials attached to such committees were elected full members of the republic party central committees in 1961, their number rose to 38 in 1966, and 45 in 1971. (This is one of the most noticeable changes to take place in the republic central committees over the past decade.)

In view of all this, the image of an "ideological system" hardly seems appropriate to the Soviet Union of the last seven years. How, then, should we characterize the present Soviet political system? Has it petrified, or has it been evolving towards the model of institutional pluralism? Have the frequent reorganizations, striking policy innovations, and permanent purge of the Khrushchev era been replaced by immobilism or by Western-like incrementalism in policy change?

Change in What Direction?

It should be recognized that these are extremely difficult questions to answer, for there are few clear-cut criteria by which one can easily distinguish between immobilism and institutional pluralism. If either model were firmly linked with the power position of a specific institution, such as the party apparatus, then incremental changes in the status of that institution might provide a reliable indicator.[40] But this

[39] In addition to the republic ministries of education and culture, state committees have been created for publishing (sometimes misleadingly translated "press"), movie-making, and television and radio. Vocational education has also been raised to the state committee level in many republics, and nearly half of the republics have ministries for higher and secondary specialized education.

[40] Even if one were to accept the relative status of the party apparatus as a reliable indicator, the picture is a mixed one. Three of the four new Politburo members are party officials, but the long-term decline in the percentage of party officials among the voting members of the Central Committee has continued: from 56 percent in 1956 to 46 percent in 1961, 42 percent in 1966, and 39 percent in 1971. In the republics, apparatus representation has remained essentially stable. The proportion of party officials among the voting members of the republic party bureaus has only risen from 57.2 percent in 1966 to 57.5 percent in 1971, while the difference in the proportion of party officials among the voting members of the republic central committees is not statistically significant—34.1 percent in 1966 and 33.4 percent in 1971. (The figures do not incude party officials below the level of raikom secretary and are based on identifications of 93 percent of the 1966 republic central committees' members and 92 percent of the members of the 1971 committees. Very, very few party officials will be found among the unidentified.)

is hardly the case. Moreover, the crucial consideration really is the *nature* of the party and the party apparatus, not their continued "dominance."

Nor does the relative degree of freedom to advocate incremental policy change serve as a convincing criterion by which to judge the degree to which Soviet society corresponds to either model. The important thing is not simply the flow of ideas but rather what practical force these ideas have, and—even more—their very nature. Hence, as stated above, the basic problem is the nature of the "new class"—that is, the upper five-to-ten percent of Soviet society in socio-economic terms. Does the fact that almost all its members are employed in bureaucratic institutions of one sort or another and are almost all required to be members of the Communist Party ensure that the ideas flowing from them will be conservative rather than innovative? Does the fact that almost all the major political actors are senior bureaucrats (or civil servants, to use a more neutral term) who supervise state, economic, party, or educational-scientific institutions of one type or another mean that ideas challenging the status quo will be filtered out before they reach the political decision-makers?

Ultimately, the test of the direction in which the Soviet political system is evolving must be the nature of the policies that emerge from the system. But here, too, evaluation is by no means simple. There are elements of both change and continuity in the life of every country, and unless the former are very dramatic, we face great problems when we try to decide which merit greater emphasis. If changes are less than dramatic, are they the kind of incremental changes that, taken individually, appear relatively insignificant but which, over time, cumulatively transform society and the political system in a most fundamental way? Or do they constitute merely the sort of minor tinkering that would not invalidate the judgment that the system is immobilized?

In trying to differentiate between immobilism and incrementalism, we essentially are making a judgment as to whether changes are or are not "important" or "significant." As the debate over the New Left's charge of immobilism in the American political system demonstrates, however, any evaluation of this type rests essentially upon a subjective value judgment and/or on an unprovable assumption about what is "required" at a particular stage of history. In practice, there is a real tendency for such judgments to vary according to one's view of the status quo. If the status quo is considered fundamentally unjust, then no change short of the most drastic transformation of the system will be considered significant. If, on the other hand, the status quo is considered more or less tolerable (given the inevitable imperfections in man and society), then incremental change seems much more important—and, in fact, desirable. Judgments of this type must remain basically "non-scientific" in nature.

EVIDENCES OF IMMOBILISM

Certainly the patterns of change and continuity in the Soviet Union since 1964 have been sufficiently ambiguous to prevent an absolutely definitive choice between incrementalism and immobilism as the proper label to apply to this period. On the one hand, there have been a number of evidences that might be cited in support of the thesis of immobilism in the Soviet political system. One such evidence surely would be the turnover rates in top administrative positions. Not only do these

Table 2: Rates of Personnel Turnover, 1966-71
(Percentages of 1966 officials not in the same positions in 1971[a])

Party Apparatus

Position	Turnover (percent)
Full members, CPSU Politburo	0
Full members, CPSU Central Committee	24
Full members, CPSU Central Committee (party and government officials only[b])	19
CPSU Central Committee Secretaries	27
CPSU Central Committee Department Heads[c]	46
Republic Party First Secretaries	14
Full members, Republic Party Bureaus	37
Full members, Republic Party CC	41
Full members, Republic Party CC (party and government officials only)	33
Republic CC Secretaries (except first sec'ties)	58
Republic CC Department Heads	65
Obkom First Secretaries	44
Obkom Second Secretaries[e]	67
Gorkom First Secretaries (50 largest cities)[e]	61
Raikom First Secretaries (in 10 republics)	57

State Apparatus

Position	Turnover (percent)
Deputy Chairmen, USSR Council of Ministers	0
Ministers and Chairmen of State Committees sitting on the USSR Council of Ministers	12
USSR Deputy Ministers of Defense	55
Commanders, Military Districts	100
USSR Deputy Ministers[d]	35
Chairmen, Republic Councils of Ministers	60
Deputy Chairmen, Republic Councils of Mins.	45
Republic Ministers and Chairmen of State Committees	41
Oblispolkom Chairmen[e]	56
Directors, 170 largest factories[e]	44

[a] The percentages of turnover shown for members of the CPSU Politburo and Central Committee, CPSU and republic Central Committee secretaries, CPSU Central Committee department heads, republic and obkom party first secretaries, deputy chairmen of the USSR Council of Ministers, Ministers and Chairmen of state committees sitting on the USSR Council of Ministers, and factory directors represent turnover between the 23rd (1966) and 24th (1971) CPSU Congresses (excluding several changes that occurred a few days after the 23rd Congress). The percentages given for all other categories of officials represent turnover between September 1, 1966, and September 1, 1971, these dates having been chosen to permit the utilization of data on republic government officials designated during the summer of 1971.

[b] This excludes military officers (except the Minister of Defense), diplomats, scholars, and factory managers who are full CC members.

[c] In the five cases in which a Central Committee secretary heads the department, the first deputy head is included in the calculation in order to avoid duplication.

[d] As complete information is not available for all categories of officials, the turnover percentages given for USSR deputy ministers are only approximate.

[e] The figures given for obkom second secretaries, oblispolkom chairmen, gorkom and raikom first secretaries are based on identification of 95 percent of the total number in each case; and for factory directors, on identification of 67 percent of the total number.

rates tend to suggest that there have been few "losers" such as are often produced by the resolution of great policy conflicts, but they have, in themselves, led to a significant aging of the top elite. The voting members of the first Central Committee elected after the 1917 Revolution averaged 36 years of age, and the average age thereafter rose quite slowly in both the Stalin and Khrushchev periods: it still was under 45 in 1934, dropped perhaps a year or two by 1939, then increased only to 49 in 1952, to 51 in 1956, and to 52 in 1961. In 1966, however, the average age of voting members jumped to 56, and from there it rose to 58 in 1971.[41] These figures are, of course, a reflection of the average age of the categories of officials from whom Central Committee members are usually drawn, and it is easy to argue that the increase in average age is likely associated with an increase in conservatism among these officials.

From many points of view, indeed, the policies of the Soviet leadership have been as conservative as the aging might lead one to expect. If the Soviet system is viewed as one committed to certain ideological goals, then the failure of the leaders to carry on the transformation of society prescribed by the ideology logically suggests a loss of dynamism, a "petrification" of "the system." Or if the system is viewed as one in which the party has played out "its historical role" and the present stage of technological development of Soviet society dictates evolution toward constitutional democracy and market socialism, then the painfully slow pace of change along those lines is equally suggestive of immobilism. Whatever the long-term impact of the Soviet program of economic reform may be, the organization and operating principles of the economy (both in industry and agriculture) remain at present much more similar to those of the Stalin era than to those now in force in Yugoslavia. Similarly, however much public debate may have broadened in the USSR, there is still no evidence of the type of political liberalization that was seen in Czechoslovakia or the kind of devolution of authority from the center to the republics that is found in Yugoslavia. The continued prosecution of dissidents suggests an unwillingness on the part of the Soviet regime to accept ideological deviation that formally challenges the fundamentals of the system.

[41] The lists of Central Committee members elected at each party congress and the biographies of many of the members can be found in Boris Levytsky, *The Soviet Political Elite,* Stanford, Calif., Hoover Institute on War, Revolution, and Peace, 1970. The 1971 figure excludes the worker and peasant members of the Central Committee. Data on the characteristics of the members elected in 1971 can be found in Robert H. Donaldson, "The 1971 CPSU Central Committee: A Preliminary Assessment of the New Elite," paper presented at the Northeastern Slavic Conference, Montreal, 1971, and to be published soon in *World Politics.* (Professor Donaldson was kind enough to assist the author in the identification of hard-to-identify Central Committee members.)

Moreover, despite some signs of change, the highest rewards and prestige are still accorded to those in the heavy-industry and defense sectors. These sectors continue to receive priority in such matters as material deliveries and housing allocations, and last year's party elections revealed little decline in the status accorded them. It is true that agriculture has experienced some increase in its representation both on the all-Union and republic central committees, but no change has occurred within the urban sector.[42] Even the workers named to these bodies come overwhelmingly from heavy industry—*e.g.,* nine of the ten workers on the all-Union Central Committee and 78 of the 115 identified workers on the republic committees.[43]

Signs of Change

But while this evidence does point to a certain immobilism in the system, changes of some significance have occurred. The devolution of power to the major institutional centers is a very important change indeed—especially if it should turn out to be more or less permanent. Of equal importance are the growing ambiguity of Soviet ideology and the increased vitality of public policy debate. In addition, there have been a number of developments that are not consonant with any petrification model, especially one emphasizing bureaucratic ossification and preservation of the privileges and power of a narrow economic-social elite.

First, the bureaucracy itself has undergone a number of changes that do not suggest ossification. While, as pointed out earlier, the turnover rates of top officials have dropped markedly in comparison with the Khrushchev years, those at the middle levels of the bureaucracy remain substantial (see Table 2). Moreover, the age of officials at the intermediate levels is considerably lower than that of their superiors (see

[42] All the agricultural ministries (including, for the first time, reclamation; Selkhoztekhnika, and rural construction) are now represented by full members on the all-Union Central Committee, while the number of agricultural ministers (or chairmen of state committees) on the republican central committees has risen from 43 to 51. On the contrary, not a single light- or food-industry minister is included among the 42 ministers and chairmen of state committees named to the all-Union Central Committee, despite an increase of 15 such state officials on this body since 1966. The number of ministers and state committee chairmen from light industry and the municipal services on the republic central committees has remained virtually unchanged (58 in 1971 compared with 57 in 1966).

[43] The members of republic central committees who are most difficult to identify are those chosen from among workers and collective farmers. The republic statistics must therefore be considered merely approximate.

Table 3). While age is by no means a clear indicator of attitudes, the relative youth of lower party officials is well worth noting, especially in view of the significant role of the party apparatus as a source of policy initiation. If present trends continue, the apparatus will within a few years be staffed predominantly by men whose entire work experience has fallen in the post-Stalin period.

Table 3: Average Ages of Republic and Oblast Officials, 1967 and 1971

Position	20 Oblasts, RSFSR 1967	5 Republics 1971
First Secretaries, republic CCs or obkoms	52	57*
Second Secretaries, republic CCs or obkoms	49	51*
Other Secretaries, republic CCs or obkoms	47	49
Department heads, republic CCs or obkoms	44	46
Gorkom First Secretaries	44	44
Raikom First Secretaries	44	44
Chairmen, republic Councils of Ministers or oblispolkoms	47	52*
Deputy Chairmen, republic COMs or oblispolkoms	50	52
Republic ministers or heads of oblast administrations	49	51

* Based on data for all republics, instead of just five.

SOURCES: The information on the officials of the 20 oblasts in the RSFSR comes from lists of oblast deputies selected in 1967. The oblasts (in four cases, actually krai) were Altai, Cheliabinsk, Gorky, Ivanovo, Krasnodar, Krasnoiarsk, Kuibyshev, Kursk, Lipets, Novosibirsk, Orel, Penza, Primorsk, Rostov, Smolensk, Tula, Ulianovsk, Volgograd, and Yaroslavl. The lists were published in the oblast newspapers and were examined in the Lenin Library in Moscow.

The information on republic officials comes from lists of deputies to the republic supreme soviets elected in 1971. The five republics (the only ones where the lists gave the year of birth) were Estonia, Kirgizia, Latvia, Lithuania, and Tadzhikistan.

Moreover, while it is admittedly difficult to ascertain how a bureaucracy actually operates in practice, such evidence as is available on the functioning of Soviet officialdom does not suggest petrification. One of the major Soviet campaigns of recent years has focused on the "scientific organization of labor" (*nauchnaia organizatsiia truda,* or NOT), which has as its goals not only the rationalization of work at the factory-bench level but also "scientific" administration at the middle levels of the bureaucracy. Moreover, it has been characterized by a preoccupation not so much with structural details (as under Khrushchev) as with the development of sophisticated managerial techniques, improved organization of information flow, and the like. One important by-product of this has been the recent renaissance of sociology in the USSR, with the regime itself now placing special emphasis on applied sociological research of potential use to party and governmental administrators. One cannot be certain about the end results of this new preoccupation with "scientific management," but it does suggest that what Peter Solomon has termed "a new administrative ethos" may be in the making.[44]

A second type of change that has been observable in the last seven years is a very gradual erosion of those forces—surely the dominant forces of recent decades—that emphasize priority for industrial growth over other interests. These forces (except for the military) are no longer exempt from attack in the widening public debate. Many economists have advocated a change in the ratio of investments between Group A (heavy industry) and Group B (light and consumer industry) as well as institutional changes that would increase the sensitivity of the economy to consumer demands. It is also the dominance of heavy industry that is indirectly challenged by the mounting press criticisms of unsatisfactory conditions of life in the countryside, by the growing attention to environmental issues (a pro-conservationist film on Lake Baikal was the most popular Soviet film in 1970), and by repeated appeals for the transfer of housing and municipal services to the complete control of the local soviets. While the results of the challenge to heavy industry have thus far undoubtedly been disappointing from the critics' standpoint, they have not been inconsequential. The Ninth Five-Year Plan (1971–75) is the first long-term plan to call for a higher rate of increase in investments in Group B than in Group A. Moreover, as will be further detailed shortly, the incomes of collective farmers have been rising more rapidly than those of other groups—and will continue to do so under the new Five-Year Plan.

The third type of change—and perhaps the most important of all—has been in the realm of social policy. It is curious that American specialists writing on the Soviet Union, though usually liberal in their domestic politics and inclined to judge American political leaders by their activism on social-welfare issues, seldom consider such issues in

[44] Peter H. Solomon, Jr., "A New Soviet Administrative Ethos—Examples from Crime Prevention," paper prepared for the meetings of the Northeastern Slavic Conference, Montreal, 1971.

evaluating the Soviet leadership. Yet, it must be recognized that the post-Khrushchev leadership has in fact initiated major steps toward greater egalitarianism—steps that amount to a veritable war on poverty affecting millions of low-income citizens.

The most striking evidence of this is the progress made in recent years toward a narrowing of inequalities in income. Although comprehensive wage data are not published in the Soviet Union—a fact which suggests that considerable inequalities still exist—all the available evidence suggests that the pattern of income distribution has been changing quite substantially in the direction of greater equality. Over the last five years, the minimum wage for wage earners (collective farmers excluded) rose 50 percent to 60 rubles a month, and during the 1971–75 Five-Year Plan it will rise to 70 rubles. Since large amounts of persons have been at minimum wage levels, according to an authoritative analyst, "the resulting very substantial reduction in the spread in basic wage rates must have meant a substantial narrowing in differentials in earnings."[45] The minimum pension will also increase.

The assault on inequality of income has resulted in even more significant gains for the nation's collective farmers, who have long been at the bottom of the income ladder. Average kolkhoznik income (excluding income from private plots) rose 42 percent in the 1966–70 plan period compared with 26 percent for all wage earners, and it is scheduled to increase another 30–35 percent during the new Five-Year Plan compared with a 20–22 percent rise for wage earners. The inherent uncertainty of collective farm incomes has also been reduced by the introduction of a guaranteed payment plan. In addition, the collective farmers have for the first time been included in the national pension system, and they will be the main beneficiaries of a new "family supplement" program that provides cash allowances to families whose income is less that 50 rubles per family member (the generally large size of kolkhoz families tends to reduce income per family member to very low levels).[46]

The precise impact of Brezhnev's "war on poverty" will not be clear until Moscow decides to publish fuller income data, but it may well be that the Soviet Union in recent years has seen a shift in income distribution that is quite striking by Western standards, and that the pattern

[45] Janet Chapman, *Wage Variation in Soviet Industry,* Santa Monica, Calif., Rand Corporation Memorandum RM-6076-PR, 1970, p. 126. For a new discussion of Soviet wage policy pointing in the same direction, see Leonard Joel Kirsch, *Soviet Wages* (to be published by Massachusetts Institute of Technology Press in 1972).

[46] *Pravda,* March 31, 1971, pp. 4–5. See also David W. Bronson and Constance B. Krueger, "The Revolution in Soviet Farm Household Income, 1953–1967," in James R. Millar, Ed., *The Soviet Rural Community,* Urbana, Ill., University of Illinois Press, 1971, pp. 214–58.

of income distribution in the Soviet Union today is substantially more egalitarian than it is in the advanced Western countries, particularly if income from property is taken into account. In any case, if it is true, as many contend, that the entrenched ruling elite in the Soviet Union has been gaining in power since Khrushchev's fall, at least its allegedly augmented authority does not appear to be reflected in a larger share of the national income.

Some Comparisons

The types of change observable in the Soviet Union do not, of course, demonstrate conclusively the absence of immobilism in the system, but they should give reason for pause. This is particularly true if we examine the Soviet Union in a comparative framework. In any assessment of what some see as petrification of the Soviet system, it is, for example, worth considering that former US President Lyndon Johnson was considered a dynamic innovator in American domestic policy. Johnson initiated forward-looking legislation in the realms of medical care, education, civil rights, and social welfare. Yet, he was able to produce only minor institutional change, and his education, fair housing, and War on Poverty programs can scarcely be said to have changed American reality in a major way. Probably his most important innovation—the Medicare program—was limited to those over 65 years of age and was financed through the most regressive of US taxes, the social security tax.

Notwithstanding these qualifications, it still seems fair to credit President Johnson with having been a major policy innovator. Then, we may ask, do the programs of the present Soviet leadership really seem like immobilism by comparison? We have already cited evidence showing the results of the steps taken by Brezhnev to reduce inequalities in income in the USSR. Certainly it would seem fair to say that these steps have had a greater impact on the income levels of the poor than has President Johnson's War on Poverty.

A comparative framework may also be of use in analyzing other data that seem to provide clear-cut evidence of petrification. As has already been shown, the rate of turnover among the top Soviet elite has unquestionably declined, and their average age has increased. But does this apparent desuetude of the "permanent purge" mean that its "many and varied" purposes are not being served and that the system has *ipso facto* become immobilized? Or do the new turnover rates mean that the Soviet Union has adopted a pattern of personnel selection that is more normal for an advanced industrial country?

To delve into such questions in a comprehesive way would require a comparative examination going well beyond the scope of this article. However, there is one comparison that is feasible and may also be useful in putting this whole problem in clearer perspective. That is a comparison of the average ages of various categories of Soviet officials with those of their closest American counterparts. At the time of the 24th Congress, the average age of Soviet obkom first secretaries was 52 as compared with 51 for US state governors; industrial ministers in the Soviet Union averaged 60 years of age as compared with 59 for the chief operating officers of the 50 largest American corporations (who are, in fact, the United States' top industrial administrators);[47] the average age of the party first secretaries of the capital cities of 13 out of the 15 Soviet republics (the ages of the other two are not ascertainable) was 47, as compared with 52 for the mayors of the 25 largest American cities.

Moving toward the higher levels, one of course finds no American equivalent of the Soviet Central Committee, but for purposes of comparison one can construct a hypothetical American "Central Committee" of 200 members, composed as follows: the members of the US cabinet, the governors of the states, the Congressional leadership, the chairmen of the Congressional committees, the justices of the Supreme Court, the chief executives of the 50 largest US corporations, the members of the Armed Forces Policy Council, an additional five military officers, and 30 sub-cabinet officials from the White House staff, the executive departments and the independent agencies. Doing this, we arrive at an average age of 58 for this body in the spring of 1971, which interestingly enough is exactly the average age of the membership of the CPSU Central Committee elected at that time.

Similarly, one can compare the average age of the present Soviet Politburo with that of a select group of 15 high officials who might well have been on an American Politburo if one existed. These would be: President Nixon, Secretary of State William Rogers, Secretary of Defense Melvin Laird, Attorney General John Mitchell, Chief Justice Warren Burger, Special Assistant to the President Henry Kissinger, Director of the Office of Management and Budget George Shultz, Senate Majority Leader Mike Mansfield, Senate Minority Leader Hugh Scott, Speaker of the House Carl Albert, House Minority Leader Gerald Ford, Chairman of the House Ways and Means Committee Wilbur

[47] There are a number of criteria by which the list of the top 50 or top 500 American corporations could be chosen. I have used market value of stock, for this methodology produces a list with many of the great growth companies on it. It is worth noting that the 22 growth companies on the list (those with a price/earnings ratio of 25) had chief executives with the same average age as the executives of the other 28 companies. The lists of corporations and chief officers are found in *Forbes* (New York), May 15, 1971, pp. 91–92 and 128–61.

Mills, Chairman of the Senate Finance Committee Russell Long, and the governors of New York and California, Nelson Rockefeller and Ronald Reagan. The average age of this group would have been 59 years in the spring of 1971, and if the chairmen of the Senate and House Appropriations Committees were substituted for the minority leaders (as they probably should be), the average age comes to 61, identical with that of the Soviet Politburo.[48]

Naturally, a comparative perspective—particularly one based on a two-country comparison—provides no final standard for judging petrification. One might argue that the standard of reference (in this case, the United States) is also afflicted with immobilism, that the Soviet system is so anachronistic that it requires more radical change than the American, or that the Soviet leadership must be more innovative to compensate for the weakness of innovative forces in the social and economic systems. However, if we do speak of a petrification of the Soviet system, let us recognize quite frankly the assumptions we are employing.

In the author's opinion, the contention that the Soviet Union has been petrifying over the last seven-and-a-half years must rest on one of two possible lines of argument. One is that a few non-pluralist developments (notably the renewed restrictions on freedom to discuss Stalin's repressive actions) should outweigh all other developments in any assessment of the direction in which the Soviet system is moving. The second is that the Soviet Union has indeed been moving in the direction of institutional pluralism, but that the pace of change is so slow in comparison with societal requirements that the system must be called immobilized. (One might further argue that the impetus for further change is disappearing.)

To this observer at least, the first line of argument is very unconvincing. It seems to reflect no more than the "group bias" of Western social scientists—namely the unspoken and perhaps unconscious belief that a political system should be judged solely on the basis of how it treats intellectuals who share their own values.

The second line of argument is more difficult to either prove or refute. Ultimately, as indicated earlier, the question is not susceptible of a definitive answer, except perhaps by a future historian who will have the advantage of knowing what has occurred during the rest of this century. But if this line of argument is to be made, let it be made

[48] In July 1971, when a political correspondent of a major American newspaper was asked to provide his list of the 15 most influential political-governmental leaders in the United States, he named the following: Hugo Black, Emanuel Celler, John Connally, Allen Ellender, Henry Kissinger, Melvin Laird, George Mahon, Mike Mansfield, Wilbur Mills, John Mitchell, Edmund Muskie, Richard Nixon, Ronald Reagan, George Shultz, and John Stennis. These men averaged 64 years of age.

explicitly. Let the movement in the direction of institutional pluralism be acknowledged, and then let the precise nature of the argument for immobilism be spelled out.

For this purpose, it seems far more illuminating to begin, not with a petrification model that prejudges the analysis, but with an abstract or ideal-type model such as institutional pluralism. Such a model is much easier to use as a model should be used (to "ask how far reality fits" it[49]), and there is less temptation to confuse the model with reality. One can easily and naturally speak of the movement of a system *either* toward the model or away from it. Moreover, with an abstract model that contains elements of similarity to classical pluralism (notably pluralism of elites and some elite representation of mass interests) as well as elements of divergence from it, it is also much easier to go on to raise a series of important comparative questions that tend to be foreclosed by models based on "good-evil" dichotomies.[50]

Future Possibilities

Clearly the operation of the Soviet political system in the seven years since Khrushchev's removal seems significantly different from what it was during the seven years prior to the event, but the interpretation of the differences is not an easy matter. Is the "permanent revolution" really dead, or is it only hibernating? Have the political leaders forever lost the ability or the will to challenge the major institutional centers of power, or are the developments of the last seven years simply the product of a rather protracted succession crisis? In short, will historians of the future look back at 1964 as a major turning point in Soviet history or merely as the beginning point of one of a large number of cycles in a Soviet political tradition characterized by basic continuity?

If movement toward institutional pluralism is to be reversed, four

49 Inkeles, op. cit., p. 431.

50 The relationship of the elite and the disadvantaged in different political systems is, in particular, a problem that deserves very careful empirical consideration. In the September-October 1971 issue of this journal ("The Status of Soviet Women"—review, p. 62), Ellen Mickiewicz expressed the traditional Western view when she asserted that "without a channel through which to influence politics, it is questionable whether Soviet women can assert their right to genuine equality." The model of institutional pluralism—and a good deal of comparative Soviet-American data on social welfare issues (and surely also on the position of women)—suggests that this is not a closed question. This argument is presented at length in a manuscript which the author will soon finish—*Defining Responsive Government: The Implications of the Soviet and the American Experience.*

possible alternatives suggest themselves. First, a strong leader might emerge—either through a military coup or, more likely, through a consolidation of power by the General Secretary—and initiate drastic political action. Second, one might see the emergence of a strong leader who would base his policy almost entirely on the narrow interests of the military/heavy-industrial elite. Third, a stalemate might develop within the leadership if the low rate of turnover among top officials were to continue so long as to result in a leadership old and rigid by anyone's definition. Fourth, institutional pluralism might prove an unsatisfactory compromise, generating inexorable pressures on the system to move toward classic pluralism.

A comprehensive discussion of the various factors that might lead to or foreclose all these alternatives would far exceed the limits of this article. It seems to the author, however, that the burden of proof rests upon those who would prophesy drastic change away from institutional pluralism in any of the alternative directions just indicated.

A prediction of full pluralism, for example, must face the fact that political institutions associated with economic growth, social mobility for the ambitious, representation of the economic elite in the political process, and the achievement of nationalist goals normally are able to defend themselves quite well against frontal attack. Moreover, as Professor Brzezinski emphasizes, such a prediction must also reckon with the multinational nature of the Soviet system.[51] The profound consequences that full or classic pluralism would have for the relationship of the Russians to the other nationalities in the USSR is likely to make that alternative quite unattractive to most Russians, except perhaps as a last resort. Movement toward classic pluralism in the near term would therefore seem unlikely except in the event of major and persistent unrest among the nationalities or a zero-growth kind of crisis in the economic system.

A prediction of clear stalemate, on the other hand, overlooks the fact that the leading party bodies are broadly representative of the different institutional forces in Soviet society, and that the basic political institutions—as will be further elaborated below—are arranged in a way that is quite conducive to the rise of strong leadership. Given these institutional arrangements as well as the historical commitment of the Communist Party to industrial development and to the enhancement of the USSR's position in the world arena, everything that we have learned about the behavior of elite groups and about committee decision-making suggests that a coalition would form to overcome any stalemate that might begin to have obviously harmful consequences in terms of governmental functioning.

Compared to either of these two possibilities (classic pluralism or

[51] Brzezinski, *Between Two Ages*, p. 167.

stalemate), the possibility of a strong leader emerging in the Soviet Union is much greater. Indeed, Myron Rush has argued in this journal that the last seven years have actually been a period of succession crisis,[52] and there are a number of good reasons to suspect that he may be right.

Return to a Dominant Leader?

The basic Western explanation for the dominance of the General Secretary over other members of the Soviet Politburo in the past has been a theory that Robert Daniels calls "the circular flow of power." According to this theory, the General Secretary derives his great power primarily from his responsibility for supervising the party apparatus throughout the country and from his ability to appoint and remove the provincial party secretaries. Since the provincial secretaries in turn control the selection of delegates to the all-Union Party Congress, and since the Congress names (or at least ratifies) the members of the Central Committee, to which both the Politburo and the Secretariat are responsible, "the circuit is closed: The [General] Secretary is confirmed in office by a circular process that ultimately he himself controls—or can control."[53]

Assuming that the provincial party secretaries and the delegates to the all-Union Party Congress are still selected in the ways suggested by the circular-flow-of-power theory, one could well expect Khrushchev's fall to be followed by an especially slow consolidation of power in the hands of the succeeding General Secretary. To an extent that is not fully appreciated by many scholars (and is completely unappreciated by most journalists), the CPSU Congress is the key institution in the process of the circular flow of power. Even when there is no contest at the Congress, the loyalty of the bulk of the delegates to the regional party secretaries and ultimately to the General Secretary is a decisive factor preventing the old Politburo members from challenging the list of new Central Committee members prepared by the General Secretary.

When viewed from this perspective, the fact that the 23rd CPSU Congress came so soon after Khrushchev's removal, and that the next Congress was not held for five years, could have seriously interfered with Brezhnev's ability to undermine the independence of the Central Committee and quickly consolidate his power. By the spring of 1966, when the Congress met, changes of first secretary had taken place in oblasts and small republics accounting for only 13 percent of the delegates to

[52] "Brezhnev and the Succession Issue," *Problems of Communism,* July-August 1971, pp. 9–15.

[53] Daniels, "Soviet Politics Since Khrushchev," loc. cit. supra, p. 20.

the Congress.[54] The 24th Congress, however, should have marked a very important stage in the unfolding of the circular-flow-of-power process, for in the period between the two congresses new first secretaries had been selected in oblasts and small republics commanding 50 percent of the delegates.[55] In all, the proportion of delegates to the 24th Congress politically indebted to post-1964 first secretaries stood at 63 percent, and of course the proportion would be considerably higher if one were to include in it delegates from the small non-Russian republics on the assumption that they owe their party positions wholly or in part to the Russian second secretaries of these republics.[56]

On the basis of the Stalin and Khrushchev experiences, the circular-flow-of-power theory would have predicted that Brezhnev could force through a substantial expansion in the size of the Central Committee elected at the 24th Congress and in the size of the Politburo elected by the new Central Committee; and that he would then be able to remove his major Politburo rivals by the end of 1972. Naturally, it is too early to check the latter prediction, but the 24th Congress did ratify an increase in the number of voting members of the Central Committee from 195 to 241 and in the number of voting members of the Politburo from 11 to 15. While 82 percent of the still-living members of the 1966 Central Committee were reelected in 1971, proponents of the circular-flow-of-power theory would consider it more significant that 38 percent of the 1971 voting members had reached this status since 1966 and 55 percent since Brezhnev's assumption of the party leadership in 1964.

Relationships within the Politburo today may or may not still be shaped by the factors suggested by the circular-flow-of-power theory.[57]

[54] This figure is based on the list of delegates published at the end of the Stenographic Report of the 23rd Congress. The list includes the region from which each delegate comes, and it is a simple matter to add the number of delegates for each region. The unit of analysis is the region specified in the list itself.

[55] Because of the unavailability, at the time of writing, of the list of delegates to the 24th Congress, it was assumed that the relative number of delegates from each oblast and republic was the same in 1971 as in 1966.

[56] For some time it has been the practice to appoint persons of the local nationality to the post of party first secretary in the non-Slavic republics, with a Russian sent in from the outside as second secretary. Many scholars consider the Russian second secretary the key figure in the republic leaderships as the representative of the party center, but his actual relationship to the lower-level obkom, gorkom and raikom first secretaries is at present very unclear. In the author's view, the native first secretary now seems a more dominant figure than the Russian second secretary, and it is quite possible that the lower-level secretaries tend to be beholden to him.

[57] Daniels acknowledges, in fact, that "a fundamental change had occurred in the circuit of power . . . real control does not pass to the top leader, but flows instead from the top collective bodies around through the party

(It is the author's personal view that the theory still has relevance for an understanding of the Soviet political system.) In any case, however, it should not be assumed that a return to "limited personal rule" (to use Professor Rush's phrase) automatically implies a return to the relationships that formerly existed between the political leadership and the societal centers of power. Much, of course, depends on the type of "limited personal rule" that emerges. If one accepts Rush's citation of Lenin between 1917 and 1922 and Stalin between 1928 and 1937 as typical examples of such rule,[58] and if Brezhnev or anyone else were to succeed in acquiring a similar position, then movement toward institutional pluralism would scarcely seem likely. Lenin and Stalin had the most clear-cut ability as well as determination to force through change of enormous magnitude in the periods in question.

Yet it is possible for a leader to have a dominant political position, to have the final say on policy questions if he wishes, and still to fulfill, usually, a broker-like role. In short, there must be some category (or categories) between the "limited personal rule" of a Lenin or an early Stalin on the one hand and pure oligarchy on the other, and the term "political boss" may have the proper connotations for such an intermediate type. (Some term such as "limited dictator" might be applied to a leader in the position of Lenin and the early Stalin, and some term such as "full dictator" to one in the position of the post-1937 Stalin.)

Whatever label is employed for the intermediate category between "limited dictator" and oligarchy, a "political boss" of the type indicated is, in the author's view, not only compatible with the model of institutional pluralism but perhaps a significant component of it. Change in a classic pluralist system often requires political leadership and governmental action to overcome the entrenched resistance of those who benefit from the status quo, and at times very strong leadership may be required in a system of institutional pluralism, particularly in a country where one group has the superior political weight possessed by the elite associated with defense and heavy industry in the Soviet Union.

---

organization" ("Soviet Politics Since Khrushchev," loc. cit., pp. 22–25). Daniels rests his argument largely on the psychological impact of Khrushchev's removal, but it could be hypothesized that the Politburo has been able to limit the General Secretary's source of power in a more direct manner. One possibility is that the responsibility for selecting obkom and republic party secretaries has been divided among several or perhaps many Politburo members. (For example, the fact that Suslov attended a session of the Leningrad Obkom that selected a new first secretary could conceivably denote Suslov's ability to select a man loyal to himself for that position.) Another possibility is that except in cases of major scandal or mismanagement, the regional elite have been given control over the post of local first secretary. As mentioned earlier, a much higher percentage of obkom first secretaries have been selected in recent years from within the oblasts.

[58] Rush, "Brezhnev and the Succession Issue," loc. cit., p. 10.

Forces for Fundamental Change

Compatibility between institutional pluralism and one type of personal rule does not, of course, guarantee that a strong General Secretary would assume such a role. There are, however, many reasons to doubt that any General Secretary in the near future will become more than a "political boss" as defined here. If the last seven years have been a succession crisis, they certainly have been much less dramatic than either 1924–29 or 1953–57, and it is most probable that the movement toward institutional pluralism has been more the product of fundamental, long-term changes in the Soviet political and social system than simply of a temporary configuration of forces in the Politburo.

One change of long-term significance is the background of those from whom the leadership is selected. While Brzezinski's phrase "a government of clerks" seems unnecessarily pejorative, the Soviet leaders now are, in fact, recruited from among persons who have risen through the ranks of bureaucratic organizations rather than from among men with the very different experience and perspectives of the revolutionary. Today 13 of the 15 voting members of the Politburo have been successful republic, obkom, or gorkom first secretaries—positions that require the abilities and frame of mind of the broker politician. Such men, when they reach the top, certainly may have ideas and ambitions of their own, but it would be surprising if the instincts of the broker did not remain.

A second change is the precedent of Khrushchev's removal. As Daniels emphasizes, "This was the first time in the entire history of Russia since Riurik that the established leader of the country was removed by the rules of representative procedure. Since the leader was removed, it follows naturally that he was and had been removable. It follows equally that the successor leadership is removable in the same way."[59] Under the circular-flow-of-power theory, the power of the General Secretary depends upon the same factors that solidify the position of the leader of any political machine—the gratitude, loyalty, and especially the self-interest of subordinates. The memory of Khrushchev's removal will remind any successor that there can be circumstances in which these factors cease to be decisive, and it is hard to believe—barring a major crisis—that a General Secretary will soon choose to challenge the fundamental interests of as many different institutional groups as Khrushchev did.

Most important, however, are the changes of a gradual and subtle

[59] "Soviet Politics Since Khrushchev," loc. cit., pp. 22–25.

nature that have been taking place throughout the Soviet political and social system. Obviously the structure of material and psychological rewards has over time resulted in the flow of a very large number of the most talented people into the "military/heavy-industrial complex" very broadly defined, and just as obviously these people will long remain a powerful political force. Yet, there are many forces at work, both within and outside Soviet society, that are beginning to undermine the dominance of this complex. They are: (1) the creation in large numbers of new types of personnel with perspectives and backgrounds quite different from the production-oriented, heavy-industrial-engineer types who had been the dominating political force in recent years; (2) the tendency of the children of the top and middle elite to enter occupations less clearly associated with the administration and development of heavy industry; (3) the impact of constant press criticism of poverty problems on the legitimacy of heavy-industry and military expenditures; (4) the egalitarian aspects of the ideology, especially those calling for the elimination of urban-rural differences; (5) the assignment of responsibility for health-education-welfare functions (and of seeking appropriations for them) to the "guardians of the ideology"—the ideological party secretaries; (6) elite fear of popular unrest, reinforced by the memory of events in Eastern Europe, most recently in Poland; and (7) developments abroad, such as the reduction of US overseas military commitments under the Nixon Doctrine and evidences of a possible return to more normal conditions in China—both of which might tend to diminish the Soviet inclination to stress defense and heavy industry.

There are also forces at work that tend, more generally, to undermine the authoritarian features of the system: (1) the rising educational level of the Soviet elite; (2) the gradual disappearance of the economic-social forces that generate a propensity toward authoritarianism (as discussed in Erich Fromm's *Escape from Freedom*);[60] (3) the erosion of ideological certainty under the impact of events in the outside world and the expanding scope of sociological research at home; and (4) the tendency for dissenters to come from the upper stratum of Soviet society, in conjunction with the fact it is difficult for an elite to ruthlessly suppress its own.

[60] In *Escape from Freedom,* Erich Fromm suggested that the breakup of feudalism in Western Europe created major psychological disorientation, that the authoritarianism and determinism of early Protestantism provided some relief for these psychological strains, and that the success of the Protestant Reformation is to be explained in significant part by this fact. If the period 1860–1917 is viewed as one of the breakup of feudalism in Russia, then Fromm's analysis would seem to suggest a similar psychological disorientation and propensity in its wake—and there are, in fact, many striking parallels between early Calvinism and Bolshevism, particularly as the latter developed under Stalin.

It is possible to imagine a Soviet political leader or a group of leaders becoming alarmed at these developments and deciding to seek a return either to revolutionary ideological purity or to a more single-minded dedication to building Soviet military strength. But possibilities are not necessarily probabilities. The usual reaction of a political leader attempting to consolidate his position is to adapt himself to major societal forces rather than to try to combat them. If we are inclined to predict that a Soviet leader will behave differently, we should ask ourselves the reasons for such a prediction. Is it based upon our observations of the Soviet experience of the last two decades, upon "our notions of what a political system is and does,"[61] or upon the lingering impact of the totalitarian model upon our thinking about the Soviet Union?

Predicting the future development of any political system is, of course, even more hazardous than trying to describe an existing one in capsule form. If we are to judge by the evidence of both Soviet and Western experience, the Soviet future will be far more "inconsistent" than any theory suggests. There will be developments that indicate movement toward institutional pluralism and others that seem inconsistent with such movement. The mixture of continuity and change will likely continue to be ambiguous enough to provoke countless more arguments about whether the Soviet Union is or is not petrifying. Only a man who is totally committed to some theory of societal development and who believes that the future is predetermined can predict with a sense of complete confidence.

What is needed as we look at the future of the Soviet system—and at its recent past as well—is not certainty in our judgments, but openness in our approach. We must recognize that, even when we have consciously rejected the totalitarian model, it continues to color many of our assumptions about the rationale and dynamics of Soviet behavior. What is needed is a willingness—indeed, a determination—to subject our assumptions to searching examination and to separate our distaste for the Soviet system from our descriptive analysis of it. Nothing will serve these purposes better than a rigorous comparative approach in the choice of the standards that we apply and strict comparability in the definitions of the concepts we employ.

[61] Alfred G. Meyer, "The Comparative Study of Communist Political Systems," *Slavic Review*, March 1967, p. 11. Meyer argues (and with good reason) that such notions are too often suspended in our study of the Soviet Union, and that our analysis of that country is seriously flawed by the use of "concepts and models reserved for it alone or for it and a few other systems considered inimical."

FUTURE DOMESTIC POLICY CHOICES FOR MAINLAND CHINA

Thomas W. Robinson

To write about the future of Chinese domestic politics is similar to writing about its past: the number and complexity of alternatives for China's future match the longevity and richness of her history. This in itself makes any prognosis difficult. Moreover, the sudden twists and turns that comprised the Cultural Revolution and after, combined with the relative lack of "hard" political data on which to base current analysis, render any attempt to peer into the future exceedingly uncertain. Because of the turmoil of recent years, simple predictions as to the character and personages of the successor regime are out of the question; indeed, the range of possibilities could be as wide as the spectrum of possible political regimes itself. In such a situation, it is foolish to think that any single set of reasoned hypotheses stands a good chance of being borne out by subsequent events, just as it is unwise to presume that any straight-line projection of present trends may continue over the long run.

Nonetheless, based on what facts we do have and possessed of a certain "feel" for the situation, we must at least set out the range of archetypical possibilities that could lie ahead. In the present case, we seek a first-order approximation of what future Chinese domestic politics could look like. For purposes of analysis, we make two major and, in the ultimate sense, untrue, assumptions. The first is that the character of domestic politics uniquely determines the kind of foreign policy adopted by a given state, and not the reverse. Thus, we abstract entirely from foreign policy influences upon Chinese domestic developments. We presume, second, that the character of domestic politics itself is a

Adapted from Thomas W. Robinson, "Future Domestic and Foreign Policy Choices for Mainland China," *Journal of International Affairs,* XXVI, 2

dependent variable, fluctuating according to the leadership "style" of the group in power. In fact, of course, these assumptions never hold up in any detailed analysis of the political history of any state, China included. Foreign policy and domestic politics are inextricably intermingled and neither can be said to lead the other. We make these simplifying assumptions anyway, presuming that they will facilitate our analysis and that they can be relaxed at a later stage.

The mode of procedure is as follows. First, we set out a typology of regimes that can be seen as possible candidates for succession to the Maoist regime. Treating these as given, we will then trace their political consequences in two related spheres of Chinese politics: salient domestic policy issues, and the changing nature of important domestic institutions and groups. In each case the results will be analyzed for regularities across regime types and emergent policy and political alternatives.[1] For brevity, and to draw conclusions as to the degree of similarity of one set of policies with another, these various combinations are displayed in matrix diagrams.

Typology of Possible Regime Types on Mainland China Over the Next Decade

During the height of the Cultural Revolution, six more or less distinct types of future Chinese regimes were discernible, each with its own leadership "style" and set of policies. Looking at the types of regimes that might have emerged at that point is helpful because the competition of forces then apparent could have pulled the society in a variety of different directions. Later, when the Maoist group had better control over events, glimpses into possible futures gained by studying contemporary socio-political trends were not so easy to obtain. For that reason, we have chosen the Cultural Revolution as the base for thinking about alternative Chinese political futures. Let us define each of the

---

(1972). Copyright by the Trustees of Columbia University in the City of New York. Permission to reprint is gratefully acknowledged to the Editors of the *Journal*.

[1] For generalizations on this approach, see the author's "Alternative Regime Types: An Approach to Structuring the Background and Playing of Political Games" (Los Angeles: Center for Computer-based Behavioral Studies, January 1972). For an example of its application to the broader international environment, see Wayne A. Wilcox, "Forecasting Asian Strategic Environment for National Security Decisionmaking: A Report and a Method" (Santa Monica, California: The Rand Corporation, RM 6154-PR, June 1970).

six regime types as a preliminary to speculating about foreign and domestic policies of each.[2]

First, there is a continuation of the *Maoist* style, either under Mao himself or under one or more of his successors. Characteristics of such a regime might include: a tendency to radicalize the political situation at home whenever it is thought necessary and possible; the primacy of political fidelity to the ideas of Mao; putting the goals of economic and social development in second place; an unwillingness to allow Chinese society to settle down into any particular mold; an assumption that age-old problems can be overcome overnight if only the correct attitude is adopted; a continued emphasis on military security; and a cautious but nevertheless forward foreign policy based on the idea of China as the center of the modern Marxist-Leninist movement and as the leader of the developing world.

Associated with the Maoist style and possibly developing from its more extreme manifestations is an *ultra-left/Red Guard* regime. Its basic characteristics would more or less be those that marked the more extreme moments of the Cultural Revolution: a tendency to polarize, even more than the Maoists, between friends and enemies (indeed, to see enemies even among the most trusted supporters of the regime); to carry out, therefore, a constant and at times sanguinary purge of all ranks of society; an inclination, again more extreme than in the Maoist case, to put political fidelity ahead of economic and social development; a presumption to believe that mammoth problems can be quickly solved merely through large dosages of spirit and energy; a tendency to make enemies with every foreign state; and, finally, a propensity to see the external world in the same zero-sum light as the domestic scene. Thus the turmoil attendant upon manifestation of these policies domestically would spill over to affect foreign policy.

A third possibility, whose characteristics began to emerge during the Cultural Revolution, is a *military* regime. It must be included as a salient future possibility, for the People's Liberation Army (PLA), hav-

[2] No justification for the characteristics or policies of these six types is given. They are set forth as alternatives seemingly plausible to the author, flowing from the situation in China as it existed in the summer of 1967 when disorders induced by the Cultural Revolution were at their height. What is to the author, however, may not be to the reader. This is the familiar problem of how to deal with divergent opinions, each apparently as good as the other. One answer is to employ a Delphi process, a device found helpful in causing widely scattered opinions to converge toward agreed areas. While that obviously is not being attempted here, since only the author's opinion is being registered, in any extensive utilization of the regime-type method of salient alternative future generation, some such aid would have to be utilized on the Delphi method. See Norman C. Dalkey, "The Delphi Method, I–IV," (Santa Monica, California: The Rand Corporation RM-5888, 5957, 6115, and 6118, 1969 and 1970).

ing "taken over" in 1967, might not turn power back to the Party willingly. A military regime might exhibit the following characteristics: a continued insistence on popular acceptance of the ideals of Mao but modified in those circumstances (increasingly numerous with time) where his ideals do not accord with the militaristic virtues of order, obedience, division of function, and hierarchy of authority; a tendency to bring other institutions back into the political picture to perform those tasks of administration and development with which the military does not wish to involve itself on a daily basis (the army would exert indirect control over those institutions, especially the Party, and reassert direct rule when necessary); an inclination to place industrial development on an equal plane with political stability, with the result that China's rate of economic development would resume a fairly steady upward course; in foreign policy, a tendency to be more cautious than a Red Guard regime, so that the connection between domestic change and overt moves in foreign policy would become less direct; but, at the same time, a propensity to intervene abroad whenever it appeared that state interests were involved and whenever it seemed that the recapture of "lost territory" could be achieved at minimal cost. Obviously, maximum military security for the state would be a primary goal of this kind of regime; thus it would tend to emphasize the production and deployment of modern weapon systems.

Three other types of Chinese regimes seem possible in the coming years, all less radical than the three styles outlined above. First is a regime whose basic feature is *muddling through.* The Maoist regime exhibited some of these characteristics during the post-Great Leap Forward (GLP), pre-Cultural Revolution period. In the future, muddling through may mean the following: an attempt to put back together the pieces that comprised the Chinese political structure on the eve of the Cultural Revolution (this would mean an attempt to reinstate the Party as the center for authoritative decision making); gradually putting the military back into its place as an important, but specialized and restricted, element of society; attempting, by whatever method that seemed workable—and experimenting in a more or less random fashion—to get production and trade going again; pursuing a policy of compromise, as best as possible, with the various extremist groups left over from the Cultural Revolution, but with no particular plan as to how to proceed; a renewed emphasis on expertise, education, and, concomitantly, on incentives, bureaucratization, and specialization, but with no established policy rigidly enforced in any sphere. There would be a basic tendency to treat the problems of the day as sufficient unto themselves and not to set forth longer range national goals and procedures until the more immediate tasks are dealt with; thus, a tendency to be carried along by events and not to deal with—indeed, not to notice—problems until they call out for immediate solution. In foreign policy a muddling-through regime would tend to make friends with former enemies on all sides and to deal, as on the domestic scene, with issues as they arise.

Muddling through is similar, but not identical, to the policies of the next type of regime, whose basic characteristic might be termed *pragmatic*. The difference between the two stems from the tendency of a pragmatic regime to think ahead, to define goals and methods more closely, and to manipulate the events of the day and the competing political groups in an attempt to assert control over an otherwise turbulent situation. Ideology is obviously less important to a pragmatic regime than gaining, and then retaining, control of the situation. High economic growth is a primary goal of such a regime, as is the assurance of political loyalty of every region and group in the country. The form of administration would not be sacrosanct and one could imagine, for instance, a federal (but still Communist) form of government emerging. A pragmatic regime would be no less nationalist than the forms discussed above, but it would probably not find itself in untenable foreign policy situations as often as a muddling-through regime would. While it would, like the former, tend to make enemies into friends, it would not be above using one state as a foil for advancing or defending its interests against the other. Its policy would be more calculating. In military matters, it would probably try to cover all bets by procuring a mixture of modern strategic and traditional conventional weapons and by mixing nuclear deterrence with a fairly high level of general-purpose conventional forces, but also with a mixture of guerrilla strategy thrown in to keep potential invaders off balance. A pragmatic regime is the style of governance in China at the present time.

Finally, we come to the sixth member of our list, *weak government*. This might have been a likely outcome of the Cultural Revolution were a fairly high level of violence at the local and regional levels to have continued for a lengthy period. Warlordism would probably be the chief characteristic of this regime, with the central authorities holding on to what they could but with power more and more slipping into the hands of regional and provincial militarists. Such an alternative type presumes that, having destroyed the authority of all competing groups, PLA factions would then fight among themselves. When the political and ideological boundaries between factions took on geographic form, warlordism would arise.

Having established these six archetypes, can we say anything concerning the relative probability of their appearance? In particular, can we associate any of the types with particular political personalities presently active on the mainland? I believe it would be a mistake to arrange the six archetypes described above in any hierarchial listing, for two reasons. First, archetypes are no more than ideal constructs set forth for analytical purposes. It is possible—indeed probable—that a regime could come to power that would exhibit characteristics of more than one archetype. Archetypes represent points along continua, and it is perfectly possible to imagine regimes occupying intermediate points. Second, it is possible that, during the coming period, more than one regime type will occupy the center of the political stage. That is, a succession of regimes similar to those described above could come to power during the next three to five years, each pursuing policies different from the former. Obviously, it is impossible to predict which ones they might be and which might precede the other. But it is possible to imagine at least some of the six types emerging from the post-Cultural Revolution, late Maoist situation. It is also possible to imagine one regime type merging, bit by bit, into another. Thus, for instance, the military type that seemed to be dominant in 1970–71 seems to have been transformed, gradually, into a pragmatic regime type.[3]

It is also possible to assign names to these types, which reflect, to some extent, the personal characterizations of some presently prominent personalities. Thus, for instance, a military regime could be associated with the pre-September 1971 Lin Piao; a Red Guard, leftist political style with Chiang Ch'ing; and a pragmatic administration with Chou En-lai. But this does not advance the analysis in any large degree. There is more to a regime's style and characterization than the personality of one political figure, and in the post-Maoist era there is no assurance that the present group of powerholders will survive politically, either singly or as a group. If anything, revolutions throw up new sets of leaders who at least share the one characteristic of wishing to dispense with the former rulers. Since the Cultural Revolution was indeed a genuine revolution, whole new groups of political leaders are now appearing on the scene of whose programs and personalities we are as yet only dimly aware.

Influence of Variance in Regime Types on Important Domestic Political Issues and Institutions in Mainland China

Let us consider some political developments on mainland China that seem likely to occur in the next several years. In keeping with our

[3] We seek to consider all reasonable possibilities regardless of their comparative likelihood. And if the history of the post-World War II era is any guide (to say nothing of the history of China in the Communist era) presently unlikely occurrences should be given serious consideration in any forecasting effort. However, it is probably best not to assign relative probabilities of their appearance.

methodology, we presume that the six regime types set forth above are the main variables, that is, that they alone determine the character of domestic politics for that period. The discussion consists of two parts, the first concerning some of the pertinent political issues likely to arise, the second regarding the status of major political institutions. These are displayed in a matrix table form for convenience, and a discussion follows each. The tables are fairly complex. In the discussion, however, we advance several arguments for collapsing some of the regime types and alternative policies and programs into a smaller number of variables. Thus the strategy is to make things as complex as necessary in the first approximation and then to simplify the picture upon further analysis. The range of each category is defined below, using empirical referents whenever possible.[4]

TABLE 1: REGIME TYPES PLOTTED AGAINST DOMESTIC POLITICAL ISSUE

DEFINITIONS:

1) *Investment Direction: Industry vs. Agriculture*—The comparative percentages of the total amount of investment funds annually available going to industry and agriculture. Five points are defined along this dimension: emphasis on industry; balanced, but tipping toward industrial priority; equally balanced; balanced, but tipping toward agricultural priority; agricultural emphasis.

2) *Pace of Industrialization*—The percentage change per year in industrial growth hoped for or expected by a given regime type. There are five points along this dimension: as high as possible; moderate, trending to high; moderate; moderate, trending to low; low.

3) *Agricultural Organization*—The manner in which the regime organizes rural administration. Five points are defined along this dimension: a trend toward re-imposition of the Great Leap Forward-style commune, with no private plots and little or no pri-

[4] Part of this methodology involves the use of the opinion of area experts to define the salient policy categories and then to register opinion on the specific content of each box in the matrix. For agreement among a number of area experts, indices of inter-expert reliability ought to be used and a Delphi process utilized to obtain convergence of opinion. In the present instance only the author's judgments were registered. The "value" of the conclusions reached thus depend on the acceptability to the reader of those judgments.

TABLE 1
Regime Type Plotted Against Domestic Political Issue

Political Issue / Regime Type	Ultra-Left/Red Guard	Maoist	Military	Muddle-Through	Pragmatic	Weak Government/ Warlord
Investment direction: industry vs agriculture	Industry, using forced peasant deliveries.	Balanced.	Balanced, but tipping toward industrial priority.	Balanced, but tipping toward agricultural priority.	Balanced, but tipping toward industrial priority.	Agriculture.
Pace of industrialization	As high as possible.	As high as possible.	As high as possible.	Moderate.	Moderate, tending to high.	Low.
Agricultural organization	Trend back toward 1957-style commune, no private plots, little private ownership.	Trend back toward 1957-style commune, no private plots, some private ownership.	Probably little modification of post-GLF system.	Probably modification on peasant demand toward greater "free enterprise."	Balanced public-private ownership.	Accelerating trend toward private ownership.
Compliance style	Political-ideological plus force (no monetary incentive).	Skinner cycle, (political/ideological incentives, monetary incentives, force).	Skinner cycle but with emphasis on monetary plus political/ideological incentives.	Emphasis on monetary incentives.	Low-amplitude Skinner cycle, with emphasis on monetary incentives.	No cycle; emphasis on monetary incentive plus some political/ ideological incentives.
Maoist man vs specialized man	Maoist man.	Maoist man.	Specialized man.	Specialized man.	Specialized man.	Specialized man.
Permanent revolution vs orderly development	Periodic revolution, with as few relaxations as possible.	Permanent revolution with periodic relaxations.	Orderly development.	Orderly development.	Orderly development.	Neither (not possible).
Regionalization vs centralization	Centralization.	Mixed, but with centralization dominant.	Mixed (possibly dependent on regionalization of army fractions).	Mixed, but with balance changing constantly.	Mixed, but with the possibility of a new federalism developing.	Regionalization (of necessity).
Borderlands policy	Exploitation, Han influx as an aid.	Development, Han influx as an aid.	Exploitation, Han influx for control.	Development, emphasis on indigenous peoples, Han efflux.	Development, Han influx but local rights emphasized.	Stagnation, Han efflux
Minorities policy	Theory: unity-in-diversity, reality: great Han chauvinism.	Theory: unity-in-diversity, reality: great Han chauvinism.	Submerging and, in some cases, dispersal.	Giving in to demands of minorities, but only up to a point.	Unity-in-diversity with admixture of great Han chauvinism.	Minority separatism.

vate ownership; the present (post-Great Leap Forward) system; modification of the present system towards greater allowance of "free enterprise" and private plots; establishing a balance between private and public ownership of the land, perhaps similar to the pre-1957 collectivization system; an accelerating trend toward private ownership.

4) *Compliance Style*—G. William Skinner, Professor of Anthropology at Stanford University, has proposed[5] that Chinese agricultural politics can be better understood as the sum of three separately varying cycles: one denoting the relative degree of force applied to the peasant to make him carry out the regime's policy; the second indicating the degree to which economic incentives are proffered to him; and the third measuring the strength of ideological pressures. These cycles differentially combine to form a sinusoidal wave of varying frequency and amplitude which the regime, since 1949, has used to govern the countryside. The question in the present instance is whether that political style will continue under successive regimes and, if not, what sort of political style will succeed it. The pure Skinner cycle postulates successive emphasis upon ideological motives, monetary incentives, and force. Deviations from this pure type are possible in relative stress on different incentives, intensity of pressure, and absence of such a cycle altogether.

5) *Maoist Man vs. Specialized Man*—The differentiation here is between the all-purpose communist man envisaged, in his extreme form, as one who would literally divide his time between the fields, the military unit, and party cell, the factory, the office, and the artistic studio, on the one hand, and one who would tend to specialize, in the modernization process, in one particular occupation, on the other. The distinction is important in many areas of Chinese Communist life and has caused many past conflicts. It also seems to be important in determining whether, and by what means, China is to modernize.

6) *Permanent Revolution vs. Orderly Development*—The Maoist regime, up to the present, has stressed the necessity and desirability of uninterrupted revolution. Will this continue into the future? Will there be only an occasional revolutionary outburst, and albeit intensive, or will this political style be replaced with a more orderly political process?

[5] See G. William Skinner and Edwin A. Winckler, "Compliance Succession in Rural Communist China: A Cyclical Theory" in Amitai Etzioni, editor, *Complex Organization: A Social Reader,* 2nd edtion (New York: Holt, Rinehart & Winston, 1969), pp. 410–38.

7) *Regionalization vs. Centralization*—This is a major political and economic issue in the development of every modernizing state, particularly in China. It is possible to think of a continuum between the two extremes, but with several discrete points along the way. These are noted in the table.

8) *Borderlands Policy*—This is another way to differentiate regime types. Two sets of variables are noteworthy: development of borderland areas (i.e., investment, for whatever purposes, in those regions themselves) vs. exploitation (i.e., removing the products of the labor of indigenous people without equivalent compensation and little or no attempt to invest in their betterment), and influx or efflux of Han Chinese.

9) *Minorities Policies*—This is sufficiently different from the previous category to warrant separate treatment, since many minorities live in nonborderland areas. The question is first one of comparing the regime type's statements on the subject with its actual policies and, second, of ascertaining what minority people should be able to gain from each regime type.

Table 1 relates regime types to political issues along several dimensions. Political issue categories separate the six regime types, and for no two types are identical nor is there a particularly narrow spread among regimes. Further, there is a certain progression among regime types: as we move from left to right, there is a general movement from radical Communist to less radical to distinctly nonideological (in the case of the weak government type). Finally, there seem to be "regime clusters": the Maoist and Red Guard/ultra-left regimes appear to distinguish themselves generally from the middle group, made up of the military, muddle-through, the pragmatic regime types, while all of the former seem to be very distant, politically, from the weak government/warlord type.

We can also analyze the diagram by looking along the rows to determine which political issues are dependent on, and which are relatively invariable with regard to, regime type. In industrial policy, for instance, our opinion is that almost all the regime types would choose a balanced approach to industry and agriculture. The exceptions again illustrate the extremes in the continuum: an ultra-left regime would exploit agriculture to augment industrial growth, while a warlord government, having little control over the economy, would have to allow agriculture to assume its natural dominance. As to the pace of industrialization, all the regimes (with the sole exception of the warlord type) would press for high, or at least moderately high, rates of industrial growth.

It is also useful to note issues that help differentiate among regime types. Among Chinese domestic political issues, the status of the rural commune seems to do the best job of differentiation, presenting not only a wide separation but a clearly visible trend across the spectrum. The question of revolution versus order also shows a wide spread among regimes and the tripartite division between the Maoist/Red Guard; pragmatic/military, muddle-through; and the warlord clusters is again apparent. That the Red Guard and weak government/warlord regime types are polar extremes is shown also by the question of regionalization versus centralization. Here all but these two would follow some variant of a mixed policy, while a weak government would pursue a policy of regionalization, opposite to that of the Red Guard variants. Our treatment of minorities and borderlands policies, however, deviates from the otherwise fairly conformist typologies: both the Maoist/Red Guard and the pragmatic/military, muddle-through clusters are broken up to recombine in quite different manners. Some of the same variances from the more standardized clusters are also notable in the rating of regimes vis-a-vis the compliance cycle issue. Although a definite continuum is evident, from more to less extreme use for force, the spectrum is evenly spaced from Red Guard to Maoist to military to pragmatic to muddle-through to weak government regime types. While in this case the virtue of clustering is absent, it is still true that the trend conforms to what intuitively can be regarded as a radical-liberal differentiation.

To what conclusions does this analysis lead? First, looking at future political and policy alternatives through a regime-type analysis does help us to think more clearly about some of the specifics of China's political future. Second, it is apparent that if there is to be movement away from a Maoist type regime in the years to come, changes, while vast, may not be so great as to cause us to think of total "de-Maoification." What changes there may be, if the analysis set forth here is accepted, seem to point more toward greater order, direction, and control by a regime than adoption of vastly different policies. This conclusion does not hold, of course, for the warlord variant, which would signify major departures in almost all respects. Third, it seems that, of the six regime types, the pragmatic would be "best" *for China* in terms of pace and direction of "modernization": quick but not disjointed; industrialization, but with proper attention to agriculture; and centralized rule, but with sufficient attention to particular groups and areas. Following the pragmatic type in order of "desirability" would be the military and muddle-through types. Least desirable for China would be a continuation of the Red Guard and Maoist styles or, even worse, the emergence of a number of warlord governments.

Table 2: Regime Type Plotted Against Domestic Institution or Group

Table 2 attempts to forecast the status of each of the major institutions or groups in China as a function of regime-type variation. The table is designed to convey a large amount of detailed information, and one cannot, therefore, expect the kinds of generalizations that were given in Table 1. Nonetheless, it is possible to set forth some general evaluations. With regard to the "spread" among regime types, the same findings as to "clusters" can be reported as in Table 1, but with the significant exception that the "distance" between regime clusters and even within clusters is greater than before. The Maoist and Red Guard types, for example, show important differences with regard to a number of groups, while a military regime would, in our view, tend to differentiate itself from the muddle-through and pragmatic variants. Once again, the warlord case is *sui generis*. It also appears that, as a whole, the domestic groups listed might fare best under the pragmatic and muddle-through varieties, seconded closely by military rule, and followed by the warlord and Maoist alternatives. A Red Guard administration (if it could be called that) might possibly be the worst alternative regime for most groups to live under.

One interesting question is whether the status of particular groups will improve upon change of regime type, taking the Maoist regime types as the standard *away from which* changes would be made. If we rate each group with regard to a choice between improvement and no change of status, and as a function of regime type, it appears that, with very few exceptions, each group might feel itself to be better off, no matter what kind of non-Maoist regime emerges. That is, all groups (with the exception of the Party) would find any regime-type change to their liking unless that change happened to be installation of a Red Guard regime. (In that case, all except the military and the mass organizations would find themselves worse off than under a Maoist regime.) If this prognosis is correct, it could be used as an index of the presumed stability of an emergent regime or regimes. Any change toward a military, muddle-through, pragmatic, or even a pre-Cultural Revolution Maoist regime would probably be welcomed by most of the important interest groups in China. To the extent that the destabilizing effects of interprovincial military operations were not too great, this may even be the case with regard to emergence of a series of warlord regimes. One might look forward, therefore, to a somewhat less turbulent China—in terms of interest group satisfaction if not political policy—in the future.

TABLE 2
Regime Type Plotted Against Domestic Institution or Group

Institution or group / Regime Type	Ultra-Left/Red Guard	Maoist	Military	Muddle-Through	Pragmatic	Weak Government/ Warlord
Party	Party replaced by revolutionary committees; permanent purge; quick parade of personalities.	Reconstructed Party; "democratic centralism"; personality cult.	Theoretically alive actually moribund.	Reconstructed Party but probably only equal to government and military in coalition.	The leader of the Party-government-military triumvirate. Modified democratic centralism.	Alive but dying; no democratic centralism; recruitment down, members leaving.
Government	Controlled by "the masses"; disorganized administration. Paris-commune style administration.	Controlled by Party's parallel hierarchy, but with some interest group trend.	Military units and personnel inside every office, as a parallel hierarchy.	Increased authority and power with each crisis.	Restored authority; administrative efficiency stressed; semi-independent.	Most important group after military, but inefficient; lacking authority outside of Peking.
Military	Dialectical relationship with revoluntionary committees. Constant struggle for power; much factionalism.	Controlled by intra-military party group. but *primus inter pares* in the party-government-military triumvirate.	The central ruling institution, using party and government primarily, but with factionalism likely.	The most important veto group in the triumvirate; more united.	Second to Party in importance;professionalism, nonpolitics stressed, but still a veto group.	The most important group but so faction-ridden as to hold little positive authority.
Workers	Divided between revolutionary rebels and "capitalist roaders"; constant struggle.	In theory, the base of the party; in fact, a low-paid, dissatisfied group, increasingly cynical.	More stress on their well-being; incentive economy.	More stress on their well-being; incentive economy; workers begin to be a genuine interest group.	More stress on their well-being; incentive economy.	Now a powerful independent voice; frequent strikes, takeovers, inflation.
Peasants	Slow trend toward involvement, struggle, but depending for pace on quality of harvest.	Made to shoulder most of burden of development; party-military domination; tied to land.	Made to feel increasingly important; some trend toward private plots allowed; army as peasants' outlet.	Major trend toward "reprivatization"; alternately in and out of political process.	Experimentation to see which system produces the most of the best.	Left to themselves except for military requisitions and recruitment.
Mass organizers	Centrally important in revolutionary committees, yet struggling within and among themselves.	Reconstructed but strictly controlled; transmission belt.	Resurrected but well controlled; no real power, each with military advisory group.	Resurrected, increasingly achieving independent interest group status.	Resurrected but well controlled; no real power, each with party advisors.	Now full-scale interest groups, contributing to disorder.
Students	Half work, half school at best, little higher education	Suspect, but back in school. Maoism the curriculum core.	Back in school; specialization stressed; the budding officer corps.	Back in school; specialization stressed; more freedom.	Back in school; specialization stressed; more freedom but no "rebellions."	Back in school, but organized; intervening in politics, rebelling.
Intellectuals (teachers, artists, writers)	Struggled against, purged, and largely dispersed.	Little freedom, suspect, little creativity possible.	Little freedom or creativity; but more than Maoist case.	Larger areas of freedom and creativity during periods of political quietude.	Larger areas of freedom and creativity but definite limits	Much freedom, creativity; a new "golden age."
Scientists	Their status dependent upon their protector's power (e.g., military); much involvement in politics, little time to create.	Treated carefully for the most part but ultimately not exempt from political process.	Treated carefully and kept out of politics.	Treated carefully, but alternately in and out of politics.	Treated carefully and kept out of politics.	Left alone but find it difficult to work due to insufficient funding.

Conclusion

What conclusions can we draw from our enterprise? First, with regard to the efficacy of the experiment, an analysis based on regime-type variation does seem to do a good job, at least in the Chinese case, of providing a vehicle for thinking more clearly about the political future. This conclusion stands, we think, despite the natural disagreement and objections that China scholars will raise with regard to many specific conclusions and opinions.

It follows, second, that regime-type variation should be considered as one important variable in any analysis of future Chinese political developments. If projected future variations in regime type were not anticipated to be so great, obviously inclusion of this factor would not be crucial. This may in fact be the case with regard to India and Japan and even with regard to the United States, where political changes are not likely to be so extreme, or where the international system and *its* variation influence policy. In the Chinese case, however, developments *within* the Chinese political system stemming from the Cultural Revolution and its aftermath are the most important factors determining the make-up of future politics and policies. Moreover, China is less beholden to external influence than most of the states comprising the contemporary global political system. These two facts make regime-type variation of critical importance.

The set of policies and decisions that comprise the political attitude of a given state can be seen as the product of a number of factors: government type, political "style," ideological outlook, perceived interests, personality, environmental ("systemic") influences, and chance. Of these, the regime-type concept encompasses the first four, and possibly the fifth, and thus provides us with a shorthand notion for several important variables. A regime-type analysis, therefore, can help to reduce to a minimum the uncertainty inherent in political prognostication. That minimum may still be very wide—indeed, possibly still too wide for immediate policy utilization. But at least a beginning can be made which, when combined with personality analysis and efforts to understand the influence of environmental constraints, may lend more confidence to thinking about political futures.

Third, we may summarize some general conclusions from our analysis:

1) There is evident a three-pronged tendency in regard to differentiation of regime types: general separation one from the other (in the sense that each type is analytically distinct in terms of its operation on

policy, area, issue, and group); a left-right trend as one moves from the ultra-left/Red Guard regime type to the warlord/weak government variant; and a tendency for regime types to "cluster" into three similar groups (Mao/Red Guard; pragmatic/military, muddle-through; and warlord). Although we found significant exceptions to this "rule," the pattern as a whole seems visible. In matching regime-type policy variation for two or more states, such clustering would enable us to reduce the number of relevant "boxes" to a manageable size.

2) There are differential amounts of variance across regime types as one goes through the listings of issues, policies, groups, and areas. Surprisingly, however, it would appear that overall the amount of invariance across regime type predominates over the amount of variance. That is to say, there are a large number of issues in regard to which most Chinese regimes might well act in a similar manner. This may reflect a view of the "national interest," relatively unresponsive to regime-type change. There are other issues, however, on which variance is quite pronounced, and it is the still large number of such issues that causes us to be reluctant to collapse the number of regime types to a smaller number. While in two or more state comparisons such collapsing is inevitable and desirable, for the single state case it may be desirable to preserve the richness of the results.

3) Political changes, to the extent that they are away from the Maoist regime type, will undoubtedly be great in many respects. But they may not be excessively so, nor might they be of such magnitude and direction as to constitute a revolution in policy. Instead, with the partial exception of the warlord case, they may tend to bring about greater order, more centralized direction, and increased regularity of rule in the Chinese body politic and in the conduct of Chinese foreign policy. All this would seem to point toward a China reasserting her strength at home and more actively pursuing her interests abroad.

4) Inspecting the effects of each regime type, it would seem that the pragmatic variant is the "best" outcome for China, in the sense that China's interests are best served thereby, that domestic groups are as a whole well treated, and that policies most suited to quick, if not painless, modernization will most likely be adopted. Although such a regime is not necessarily the most likely outcome, it can be said that, other factors being relatively equal or mutually balanced, there may be a stronger than normal pull in this direction in the post-Maoist period.

COMPARING LIBERALIZATION PROCESSES IN EASTERN EUROPE:

A Preliminary Analysis*

Andrzej Korbonski

INTRODUCTION

It is certainly no exaggeration to say that various East European political systems have undergone significant changes in the course of the last fifteen years. Among the most interesting features of this process have been the timing, the extent, and the different patterns of this systemic transformation. After the first decade or so of Communist rule, when every change was synchronized by Moscow, the lack of coordination which resulted in an impressive degree of systemic differentiation testified to the almost total disintegration of the old monolith.

The process of change naturally did not escape the attention of Western scholars. By and large, however, study of the developments in individual countries took priority over the attempts at synthesis or comparisons. Thus the events preceding the Hungarian revolt of 1956, as well as the revolt itself, provided enough material to fill more than a dozen books and monographs, of which Paul Zinner's well-researched study stands head and shoulders above the rest.[1] The developments in Poland were described and analyzed mainly by journalists, among whom Flora Lewis appeared to be the most perceptive.[2] The Czechoslovak liberalization is still awaiting its historian, although Gordon Skilling,

From *Comparative Politics,* IV, 2 (January 1972), pp. 231–50. Reprinted by permission.

* Research for this article was aided by a grant from the University of California at Los Angeles Political Change Committee, the assistance of which is hereby gratefully acknowledged. An early version of the article was read at the meeting of the Far Western Slavic Conference at Stanford University in April 1969. A revised version was presented at the UCLA Security Studies Seminar in June 1970. The author wishes to thank his seminar colleagues Richard Baum, David Cattell, John Sisson, and David Wilkinson for their penetrating criticism which helped to clarify many of his thoughts.

[1] Paul E. Zinner, *Revolution in Hungary* (New York, 1962).

[2] Flora Lewis, *A Case History of Hope* (New York, 1958).

Morton Schwartz, and Richard Lowenthal have been able in combination to present a comprehensive picture of the progress of democratization in that country.[3]

Until recently the only significant departure from this country-by-country approach was undertaken by Zbigniew Brzezinski in his classic, *The Soviet Bloc*. To be sure, Brzezinski dealt separately with Polish and Hungarian events but he attempted, in addition, to explain the different reactions of all individual East European countries to the de-Stalinization campaign decreed by the Kremlin. In his view the response in each country was the outcome of four major factors:

1. The magnitude of internal socioeconomic crisis;
2. The degree of alienation of the working class and the intelligentsia from the regime;
3. The extent to which the local regime had been involved in anti-Tito policies;
4. The availability of alternative leadership.[4]

With the help of this "model," Brzezinski explained the reasons for the dramatic changes in Hungary and Poland in 1956 as contrasted with the absence of significant transformations in the rest of the Soviet bloc.

While there is little doubt that at least three of the four variables listed above played a key role in determining the course of action taken by individual countries, some reservations should be expressed concerning the importance of the anti-Tito commitment. While this fitted neatly with the general tenor of Brzezinski's arguments regarding the role of Tito in the overall process of liberalization in Eastern Europe, it was nevertheless difficult to test. There is also a problem with the other three factors in that they represent the synthesis of a variety of processes taking place at various times. They tell us little about the nature and weight of political, economic, and social crises in each country and, in the final analysis, the overall verdict concerning the outcome of all of them must be somewhat impressionistic and arbitrary.

After a hiatus of several years there was a new outburst of interest in the process of change in Communist societies, associated with the

[3] Gordon Skilling, "Crisis and Change in Czechoslovakia," *International Journal*, XXIII (3/1 1968) and "Czechoslovakia's Interrupted Revolution," *Canadian Slavonic Papers*, X (4/1 1968); Morton Schwartz, "Czechoslovakia: Toward One Party Pluralism?" *Problems of Communism*, XVI (January/February 1967); Richard Lowenthal, "A Sparrow in the Cage," ibid., XVII (November/December 1968).

[4] Zbigniew Brzezinski, *The Soviet Bloc*, rev. ed. (Cambridge [Mass.], 1967), pp. 205–6.

growing belief that the traditional totalitarian model à la Hannah Arendt, Carl Friedrich, and Brzezinski was no longer applicable for the study of Communist systems. This is not the place to discuss the various attempts to replace the totalitarian syndrome with a syndrome of another hue. Suffice it to say that in the last two or three years a number of authorities in the field have been engaged in the two-pronged study of "comparative Communism" and change in Communist systems.[5]

The various efforts assumed, either explicitly or implicitly, a unidirectional aspect of change, the objective of which was liberalization and/or democratization of Communist systems. Thus, definition of the concept of change as applicable to Communist societies presented no major difficulties. The most comprehensive definition was said to include the following:

> 1. Changes in the structure of the political system, generally from a one-party system with an autonomous dictator to collective leadership and toward a party-dominated national front;
> 2. Changes in the reliance on terror to elicit elite-approved social behavior, generally from a high reliance on terror to a medium and toward a low reliance;
> 3. Changes in the structure of the economic system, generally from a centralized command economy to a semicentralized managerial system and toward market socialism;
> 4. In the case of externally imposed Communist regimes, changes from the status of satellite to that of client state and toward independence as a national Communist state.[6]

While this definition appears unambiguous and noncontroversial, the same cannot be said of the concepts of "liberalization" versus "democratization." According to Skilling, for example, the former must be distinguished sharply from the latter. "Liberalization," in other words, is

[5] One reflection of the growing interest in these two problems was the creation by the American Council of Learned Societies of a "Planning Committee for Comparative Communist Studies." The Committee, formed in 1966, staged two conferences in 1967 and 1968, devoted to the questions of comparison of, and change in, Communist nations. The papers resulting from these meetings appeared in Chalmers Johnson, ed. *Political Change in Communist Systems* (Stanford, 1970). Furthermore, both the American Political Science Association at is annual meeting in 1969, and the American Association for the Advancement of Slavic Studies at its convention in 1970, had panels dealing expressly with the problem of change in Communist systems.

[6] Chalmers Johnson, "Comparing Communist Nations," in Chalmers Johnson, ed. *Political Change*, p. 3.

simply another word for de-Stalinization. The essentials of the Communist system remain unchanged; the impulse for the reforms comes from above; the stimulus is often from outside; and the whole process usually meets with strong resistance within the system. On the other hand, "democratization," which may result from or grow out of "liberalization" is a much rarer phenomenon characterized by far more radical changes, by mass pressures from below, and by a much more vigorous resistance.[7]

The distinction drawn by Skilling between the two concepts appears neither convincing nor useful. It can be argued that in Eastern Europe during the last fifteen years we have been witnessing a combination or synthesis of both phenomena, rather than two separate processes. In other words, the features or variables characteristic of both liberalization and democratization appeared simultaneously in different countries at different times and with different intensities. Take, for example, the question of the impulse for the change. Skilling claims that in the case of liberalization the impulse comes from above, whereas in the event of democratization it originates from below. It would seem, however, that in several instances there was pressure from both the top and the bottom. In Poland in 1956, a group within top leadership joined with the masses to bring Wladyslaw Gomulka back. The same was true in Czechoslovakia in 1967–68 when Alexander Dubcek came to power following the ouster of Antonin Novotny. One may also argue that the Hungarian and Yugoslav cases present examples of a similar synthesis. The remaining variables such as outside stimuli and resistance of leadership are also much less clear-cut than suggested above.

One possible way to avoid some of the pitfalls associated with Brzezinski's and Skilling's theses would be to disaggregate their major synthetic variables and to take a closer look at the component parts. The final result may very well be identical to that reached by using the aggregate variables; but in addition to offering a more detailed insight into the workings of the Communist systems, the disaggregated model is likely to lend itself better to research, making possible the use of more advanced techniques and the formulation of more "scientific" hypotheses and predictions.

The suggested approach is not without pitfalls of its own, to be sure. The application of a dozen or so variables instead of three or four may give a more detailed picture of the situation on the eve of a major systemic change, but the final judgment is still not devoid of a certain degree of arbitrariness. The same applies to the selection of the "stra-

[7] Gordon Skilling, "Scope and Limits of 'Liberalization' in Communist East Europe" (Remarks at the panel discussion devoted to the changes in Communist-bloc countries at the Annual Meeting, American Political Science Association, New York, September 1969).

tegic" variables, some of which can hardly be considered independent. Finally, disaggregation alone—without assigning relative weights to particular variables—is not very helpful since the various conditions that obtained in individual countries had an unequal impact on the process of change. As a rough approximation it was assumed that all the variables grouped under the three main headings in Table 1 had equal weights in the three countries under consideration. This ought to be kept in mind when looking at the "model" presented below. The latter should be considered, above all, as a somewhat crude effort at model building and at postulating some tentative hypotheses regarding change in Communist systems.

The model shown in this article borrowed heavily from another model developed a few years ago for an entirely different purpose. In 1964, Ernst Haas and Philippe Schmitter, writing about economic integration in Latin America, presented a nine-variables paradigm for the analysis of politicization of economic unions. The nine variables were said by the authors to play a crucial role in predicting the success or failure of political integration growing out of economic integration. The variables were divided into three major groups: background conditions; conditions at the time the economic union is established; and process conditions following the creation of the union.[8]

The model (which I have named "liberalization paradigm") consists of twelve variables divided into three major categories and applied to three countries—Czechoslovakia, Hungary, and Poland. Some of the variables include a number of subvariables. The first category, "background conditions," lists the conditions and processes present on the eve of a major change in the system. The second group of "changeover conditions" includes various steps which occur in the second stage of the overall liberalization process. These steps can be seen as conditions which cause the appearance of the final stage in the process, that of liberalization itself. The category of "liberalization conditions" attempts to list the key changes in the system which in the final analysis determine whether liberalization has a chance of becoming a more or less permanent feature of the system. In other words, liberalization in this context is treated as a dependent variable with the other twelve variables assumed, at least implicitly, to be independent of each other.

Each variable and subvariable is assigned a rank of "high," "mixed," and "low," and similar rankings are given to each of the three major categories. Finally, an overall judgment is made with regard to the question under investigation—the chances of lasting and successful liberalization. For our purposes the latter is said to include the following three

[8] Ernst B. Haas and Philippe C. Schmitter, "Economics and Differential Patterns of Political Integration," *International Organization*, IV (Autumn 1964).

Table 1
Liberalization Paradigm

	Czechoslovakia	Hungary	Poland
Background Conditions			
1. Alienation of intellectuals and youth	high	high	high
2. Political reforms	mixed	mixed	mixed
3. Economic difficulties	high	high	high
4. Divisions within the party	mixed	high	high
5. Contacts with the West	high	low	low
6. Anti-Soviet attitudes	low	high	high
Total judgment	high-mixed	high-mixed	high-mixed
Changeover Conditions			
7. Changes in the party	high	mixed	mixed
a. First secretary	high	high	high
b. Presidium (Politburo)	high	high	high
c. Central committee	low	low	low
d. Lower party organs	high	low	low
e. Impending party congress	high	low	low
f. Internal party reforms	high	low	low
8. Changes in the government	high	mixed	mixed
a. Head of state	high	low	mixed
b. Council of ministers	high	high	mixed
c. Armed forces command	high	high	high
d. National assembly (Parliament)	mixed	low	mixed
9. Changes in the economy	high	low	low
Total judgment	high	mixed	mixed
Liberalization Conditions			
10. Emergence of pluralism	high	high	mixed
a. Satellite parties	high	high	high
b. Political clubs	high	high	low
c. Labor unions	high	high	low
d. Youth organizations	high	high	high
e. Religious organizations	mixed	mixed	high
11. Abolition of censorship	high	high	mixed
12. Changes in the economy	mixed	mixed	mixed
a. Agriculture	mixed	mixed	high
b. Other sectors	mixed	mixed	low
Total judgment	high	high	mixed
Chances of Lasting Liberalization	**High**	**High-mixed**	**Mixed**

major features: a large dose of intraparty democracy; emergence of pluralism; and far-reaching economic reforms.

One of the major problems connected with the use of the paradigm is the time dimension. For example, in discussing the background conditions, should one consider one, two, or three years? The longer the time span the larger the number of conditions one is bound to find and the greater the divergence or similarity between the developments in each country. It is also clear that the rate of change in different countries was different. In one of them—Czechoslovakia—liberalization conditions spanned several months, while in Hungary and Poland they lasted only a few days or weeks. Consequently, the time dimension assigned to each of the three categories of conditions varies from country to country. The periodization is shown in Table 2.

Table 2
Stages in Liberalization Process

	Czechoslovakia	Hungary	Poland
Background conditions	January 1965–July 1967	October 1954–July 1956	January 1955–July 1956
Changeover conditions	July 1967–March 1968	July 1956–October 1956	July 1956–October 1956
Liberalization conditions	March 1968–August 1968	October 1956–November 1956	October 1956–January 1957

NOTE: *Czechoslovakia,* January 1965—First draft of economic reforms approved by central committee; July 1967—Writers Congress criticizes the regime; March 1968—abolition of censorship; August 1968—Soviet invasion.

Hungary, October 1954—release of political prisoners; July 1956—dismissal of party leader Matyas Rakosi; October 1956—Imre Nagy reappointed prime minister; November 1956—suppression of revolt by Soviet troops.

Poland, January 1955—central committee criticizes and downgrades secret police; July 1956—readmission of Gomulka into the party; October 1956—Gomulka elected party leader; January 1957—parliamentary elections and stabilization of Gomulka regime.

It must be emphasized that the above periodization is highly arbitrary. The arbitrariness is especially visible with regard to the background conditions and, particularly, to the starting point for the various phenomena and processes to come into play. Thus in the case of Hungary, for example, it might have been proper to extend the period back to July 1953, when Imre Nagy assumed the premiership for the first time, inaugurating the first fairly liberal era in that country after World War II. Similar adjustments could easily be made for the other two countries. Since the primary objective of the whole exercise was to focus on relatively few key variables, an enlargement of the time dimension would necessarily result in an increase in the number of variables and an ensuing loss of focus.

The second problem concerns the parameters of the processes under investigation. Here it was assumed that there was only one parameter which remained roughly constant throughout the various stages of changeover and liberalization, namely, the presence of a Soviet regime committed, at least in theory, to the doctrine of "separate roads to socialism." This, in turn, meant a sharp decline in the level of the Moscow-coordinated rule of terror and greater freedom of maneuver for the members of the bloc. The milestones of the process—Lavrenti Beria's demise, reconciliation with Marshal Tito, and Nikita Khrushchev's "secret speech"—are well known and need not be elaborated. It is then in this context that the process of liberalization in three East European countries will be analyzed in this article.

Liberalization in Three East European Countries

Alienation of intellectuals and youth: Intellectual ferment appears to have been high in all three countries under discussion for several months if not years prior to the changeover. In Czechoslovakia the dissatisfaction of intellectuals reached its peak in the summer of 1967 at the Writers Congress, although for some time prior to that crucial meeting the existence of widespread ferment was reflected in demands for a change articulated, above all, by economists and other social scientists. The developments in Poland followed a similar path. Intellectual ferment began there during 1955, as exemplified by the famous "Poem for Adults." The economists and sociologists expressed their demands in the summer and early fall of 1956. The writers joined the ranks of dissenters at roughly the same time. In Hungary, the disgruntled intellectuals centered around the well-known Petofi Circle which began in the spring of 1956 to challenge the party for the leadership of the nation.

In the same way as the intellectuals, the young people in all three countries showed signs of alienation from the regime on the eve of the changeover. The Warsaw International Youth Festival in the summer of 1955 provided an opportunity for the Polish youth to meet thousands of young people from the West for the first time since the end of World War II. The "iron curtain" was lifted for the duration of the festival and the young Poles were able to exchange views and ideas with their contemporaries from non-Communist countries. The Polish Komsomol has never been quite the same since. The feeling of betrayal, compounded by the revelations of the Twentieth Congress of the Communist Party of the Soviet Union (CPSU), resulted in the virtual collapse of the official Communist youth organization several months prior to the changeover.

The Hungarian youth was probably as alienated as the Polish youth, if not more so. In addition, the slowdown in economic expansion and the growing difficulties in finding jobs only strengthened the existing dissatisfaction. Eventually, it was the Hungarian university students who raised the banner of revolt against the regime in October 1956.

The situation in Czechoslovakia was somewhat different, although the final result was the same. There is little doubt that increasing contacts with the West played an important role in the process of gradual disenchantment augmented by the fact that the two neighboring countries, Hungary and Poland, had gone through their periods of liberalization in which the youth had a prominent role. Economic stagnation, growing difficulties in entering universities, and the apparent inability of the Novotny regime to effect major changes resulted in the increasing alienation of Czechoslovak youth.

Frustrated in their efforts to change the existing systems, the intellectuals and youth in all three countries turned their energies to artistic and literary endeavors. The period just preceding the changeover witnessed the appearance of literary works, films, plays, and works of art not encountered during the previous decade. Most of these creative endeavors contained implicit and even explicit criticism of the past and present; they served as catalysts in the general demand for a change. A strong stimulus in that direction was provided in Hungary and Poland by Khrushchev's "secret speech" in February 1956. Mass media, especially the press, were full of denunciations of past practices, and similar criticism appeared in poems, novels, and films. Criticism assumed an artistic form in Czechoslovakia also, although the wholesale condemnation of the past did not begin there until the lifting of the censorship in the spring of 1968. Nevertheless, some of the most telling criticisms of the old regime appeared in books published a year or more before Dubcek's accession to power in January 1968. The novels of Milan Kundera and Ludvik Vaculik are excellent examples. On the whole, however, the Czechoslovak criticism appeared considerably more restrained than its counterparts in Hungary and Poland. The reason for this lies in the gradual elimination in Czechoslovakia of the worst abuses of the system from the late 1950s on, in contrast with the almost explosive breaks with the past which occurred in the other two countries during 1956.

Political reforms: In the political arena, the event which proved to be most important and to have far-reaching repercussions was the release and rehabilitation of political prisoners. In Poland the release of Gomulka and his group, followed by their readmission into the party, paved the way for the eventual takeover of the top party posts. The release of Gustav Husak, Josef Smrkovsky, and a number of others in Czechoslovakia did not result in immediate changes on top but mainly contributed to the strengthening of the anti-Novotny opposition in the party which came to the surface in the closing months of 1967. One of the most interesting features of the mass release of prisoners in Czechoslovakia—apart from their sheer number, which was staggering—was the emergence of potential opposition in the middle and lower echelons of the party.[9]

In Hungary, the political prisoners released in the fall of 1954 included a number of prominent Communists, among them Janos Kadar, the present leader of the party. Even though the subsequent demise of the liberal regime of Imre Nagy prevented a full rehabilitation of Stalinist victims, the released prisoners were permitted to rejoin the party, thus creating a nucleus of potential opposition. In July 1955, Cardinal Mindszenty was let out of prison and placed under house arrest. Several other Catholic clergymen were also freed.

All three countries went through the motions of planning and conducting some mild political reforms prior to the changeover. These consisted by and large of promises to increase the authority of such elective bodies as parliaments and national councils; of closer adherence to the principle of collective leadership in the party; and of some measures of economic decentralization, especially in Czechoslovakia. None of the reforms proved to be of major consequence, however.

Economic difficulties: Insofar as the economic situation was concerned, there were some interesting contrasts among the three countries. Czechoslovakia experienced an economic crisis so severe in 1963–64 that the party leadership was forced to agree to reform the economy. On the eve of the changeover, economic conditions showed some improvement but the memories of the crisis remained quite strong. Hungary and Poland never went through a major depression, but the situation in both countries in the mid-fifties showed little progress in comparison with the earlier years. The standard of living was quite low and the forecasts did not appear promising. Both factors were responsible for the strong attack on Stalinist industrialization policies in Hungary by Imre Nagy in the summer of 1953; they were also behind the first mass political demonstration directed against the Polish regime and staged by the workers of the city of Poznan in June 1956. Relatively speaking, however, the

[9] Apparently the highest number of political prisoners in Czechoslovakia at one time was approximately 127,000. This represented close to 1 percent of the total population. (Personal interviews by the author, Prague, 1968.)

economic difficulties shortly prior to the changeover were no greater than in the preceding years.

The major difference among the three countries had to do with attempts to reform their respective economic systems. As already mentioned, the crisis in Czechoslovakia resulted in the party's approval of a major reform of the economy. Even though past economic policies, especially those concerned with agriculture and industry, came under heavy fire in Hungary and Poland, there was no serious attempt to do anything about them. The suggested economic reforms in Poland did not make their appearance until the middle of 1957, except in the case of agriculture where the collective farms collapsed during the critical days of October 1956. In Hungary, the gestation period of economic reforms was much longer and the first measures did not take place until the second half of the 1960s.

Divisions within the party: All three countries were faced with potentially dangerous splits within the ruling parties. In Czechoslovakia, the growing dislike of the Novotny clique was pretty well camouflaged and known only to the top echelons of the party, not to the rank and file and the general public. The split was much more visible in Hungary and Poland. In the former case, the ouster of Imre Nagy from all his previous posts was resented by a number of his sympathizers in the top organs of the party who were determined to bring him back. The death of the Polish party leader, Boleslaw Bierut, in March 1956 and the election of a new first secretary provided an opportunity for a short-lived, albeit sharp, confrontation between two opposing factions which had to be settled by Khrushchev himself.

Thus, on the eve of the changeover, the previously monolithic leadership was showing signs of disintegration. The Stalinist or conservative factions were finding themselves under increasing pressure from revisionist elements, with the Soviet leadership assuming an essentially neutral stance. As previously indicated, the release of political prisoners and their partial readmission into the party only added fuel to the existing disarray.

The next variable which also shows striking contrasts among the three countries concerns *contacts with the West*. Except for the already mentioned Warsaw Youth Festival of 1955, the "iron curtain" separated Hungary and Poland from the West until October 1956 and it was only partly lifted thereafter. The situation was quite different in the Czechoslovak case. The improvement in East-West relations ever since the mid-fifties resulted, among other things, in a tremendous increase in the number of Western tourists visiting Czechoslovakia, followed by the establishment of cultural and educational exchange programs with several Western countries. More and more Czechs and Slovaks were able to visit the West and the contacts in various fields were growing at an impressive rate. While the impact of the increased contacts is almost impossible to estimate, there is little doubt that the "demonstration effect" did play a role in contributing to the general dissatisfaction with the system. The final variable, *the anti-Soviet attitudes,* also shows a sharp difference between Hungary and Poland, on the one hand, and Czechoslovakia, on the other. The sources of the contrasting attitudes are to be found in the respective paths of historical development of the individual countries over the last two centuries. They have been analyzed thoroughly by historians who seem to agree that the differing attitudes truly reflect the different experiences of the three countries vis-à-vis the Tsarist and Soviet Russias.

The overall verdict regarding "background conditions" in all three countries shows the mark of "high-mixed" for all three countries. This can be interpreted to mean that the chances of a major systemic transformation appeared to be quite good. It should also be added that these chances were probably understated for each country because of the omission of certain variables which played a major role in one but not in the other systems. Thus, in Czechoslovakia the growing dissatisfaction of the Slovaks with the existing setup was one of the key factors in the overthrow of Novotny. The influence of the Twentieth Congress of the CPSU on the Hungarian and Polish developments was probably greater than all the other factors taken together, and it had no equivalent in the Czechoslovak case. In Hungary, the memories of the relatively liberal interval of 1953–55 associated with the premiership of Imre Nagy were still very strong. It would seem, therefore, that if these and some other factors were to be added to the six variables discussed above, the chances of a changeover in all three countries would be overwhelming.

Moving now to the actual changeover, we discover some interesting similarities and differences among the three cases. To begin with, there were significant *changes in the party*. Apart from the changeover in the post of first secretary, the composition of the Presidium (Politburo) was also changed by the ouster of the most discredited members and their replacement by leaders who enjoyed a more or less deserved liberal reputation. The dramatic changes in the highest party organ were not accompanied by changes in the central committee, since only a party congress had the authority to elect a new one.

It is here that we encounter the first major difference among the three countries. For a variety of reasons it took the Gomulka regime almost three years to convene a party congress in Poland; and by the time it took place in 1959 only memories were left of the euphoria of October 1956. In contrast, one of the first acts of the Dubcek leadership was to announce that the Fourteenth Party Congress would meet in September

1968 to elect a new central committee, to approve the new party statutes, and to ratify the reforms undertaken by the new regime. In the eyes of some observers it was the fear of the congress and of the party reforms it was expected to approve that provided one of the major reasons for Soviet intervention in August. In Hungary, there were many demands for a party congress to be convened, but no firm commitment was made by the Nagy leadership.

The announcement of the impending congress went hand in hand with two other measures which gave the changeover in Czechoslovakia a flavor of its own, largely absent in Hungary and Poland. The first one was that the elections to lower party organs throughout the republic resulted in an extraordinary rejuvenation of membership generally committed to the new course. These elections were accompanied by elections of delegates to the forthcoming party congress which ensured its liberal composition. The other important measure was the publication of the new party program in April and the announcement of new party statutes which aimed at the introduction of true inner democracy at all levels. None of the above measures took place in the other two countries.

The drastic changes in the Czechoslovak party were followed by almost equally dramatic *changes in the government*. General Ludvik Svoboda took over the presidency of the republic from Novotny, and Oldrich Cernik replaced Josef Lenart as premier. The new Council of Ministers also included some new faces, among them Ota Sik, the "father of economic reforms," General Bohumir Lomsky, closely identified with the Novotny regime, had to relinquish the Ministry of Defense to the relatively unknown Slovak, Martin Dzur. Finally, Josef Smrkovsky assumed the leadership of the National Assembly among indications that the latter would exercise considerably greater authority than in the past.

Government changes were perhaps most dramatic in Hungary. Imre Nagy resumed the premiership which he had had to relinquish some eighteen months before, and he reorganized the Council of Ministers by filling a number of posts with his closest followers. Almost overnight he assumed the leadership of the whole country, pushing the party leadership into the background. After some delay the Ministry of Defense was taken over by Colonel Pal Maleter, later to be executed together with Nagy for their part in the revolt. Interestingly enough, the government included at least two well-known members of non-Communist parties.

The government changes in Poland had roughly the same character as the changes in the party. Some new faces were added to the Council of State, the collective head of state. The perennial premier (since 1947), Jozef Cyrankiewicz, managed to weather the storm and retain his post. The new government included some ministers belonging to the satellite parties and even to no party at all. General Marian Spychalski, imprisoned during the Stalinist period, assumed the Ministry of Defense following the departure of Soviet Marshal Konstanty Rokossovsky and the speakership of the Parliament was given to Zenon Kliszko, a close friend of Gomulka. This was generally interpreted as a sign that the Parliament would play an increasing role in the affairs of the country, and the elections in January 1957 were proclaimed as an impending vote of confidence in the new regime.

The changes in the party and the government were accompanied by *changes in the economy* only in Czechoslovakia. The economic reforms initiated in 1965 and accelerated in 1966 were being implemented gradually throughout the country. Elsewhere, the dramatic changes in the political arena gave rise to growing criticism of economic institutions and performance but did not evolve into major reforms.

The total judgment on the character and extent of the changeover was marked "high" for Czechoslovakia and "mixed" for Hungary and Poland. The reasons for the divergent rankings were indicated earlier. In Czechoslovakia the liberalization on top was followed by liberalization at the bottom, with only the middle, as reflected in the central committee, escaping change—at least for the time being. The impending congress and the new program and rules were to remedy that particular situation, thus extending democratization throughout the whole party. The same was roughly true for the government and its institutions. In Hungary and Poland, the new party leaders and the reformed Politburos were unable or unwilling to extend liberalization all the way down and continued presiding over a sharply divided party. In Hungary, at least, the relative vacuum left by the divided and disoriented party was filled by Imre Nagy and his ministers who proceeded to steer the country on the course toward greater liberalization. No such attempt was made in Poland and it took a number of years before the party managed to reestablish a modicum of unity there.

The final category, "liberalization conditions," includes three variables and seven subvariables supposed to denote key processes which followed the changeover and which might have been expected to influence the liberalization process as a whole.

Perhaps the most important and also the most interesting phenomenon was the *emergence of pluralism,* which proved to be particularly striking in Czechoslovakia and Hungary. In the former, a number of groups which behaved in the traditional manner of "transmission belts" until the changeover, began to act as genuine interest groups articulating their demands and claiming their share of power and influence. The most significant was the change in the attitudes and behavior of the trade unions, hitherto probably the most obedient tool of the regime. The satellite parties and the youth organizations followed suit. The various religious bodies harshly persecuted prior to the changeover also began to show signs of life.

The most dramatic occurrence was the appearance of two political clubs which came close to representing what one might call the "loyal opposition." The Association of Former Political Prisoners, known as Club K. 231, and the Club of Concerned (*engagé*) Nonparty Members (*KAN*), managed among themselves to attract some of the brightest and most disaffected minds in the country; these eventually became responsible for the famous "Manifesto of 2,000 Words" that challenged some of the most sacred Communist principles.

In Hungary, the end of October and the beginning of November 1956 witnessed a veritable explosion of pluralism. Its most salient manifestation was the virtual reemergence of the multiparty system. Trade unions were also extremely active throughout the country and contributed greatly to the creation of the revolutionary councils and workers' councils which began to mushroom in most of the Hungarian cities. The university students who spearheaded the revolt continued to press for greater democratization. Interestingly enough, Cardinal Mindszenty, whose release from house arrest acquired almost symbolic proportions, kept largely aloof from the process of change and assumed a wait-and-see attitude.

The corresponding revival of pluralism in Poland exhibited both similarities and differences in comparison with the other two cases. The Catholic church, led by the formerly imprisoned Cardinal Wyszynski, quickly established a modus vivendi with the new rulers of Poland and lent them its support in exchange for a number of concessions. Satellite parties began to insist on some form of participation in government and a number of new youth organizations built on the ruins of the old discredited one made it clear that they did not intend to remain passive. In contrast to Czechoslovakia and Hungary the trade unions played no major role in the liberalization process although many workers, individually or in groups, were actively engaged in it. Poland also had no counterpart to the Czechoslovak political clubs unless one considers the group associated with the weekly *Po Prostu* as fulfilling the function of "loyal opposition." In general, however, the revival of group activities in Poland was more subdued and less convincing than in the other two countries.

Probably the most important single facet of Czechoslovak liberalization which had no real equivalent elsewhere was the *abolition of censorship* in the spring of 1968. Time and space do not permit a fuller discussion of this measure, but all observers seem to agree that this act was responsible for the rapid expansion of the democratization process, aided and abetted by the activity of mass media led by press and television. There is little doubt that the remarkable outburst of the freedom of expression, which included not only a sharp condemnation of the past but also a demand for a better future, did more to infuriate the leaders of the Soviet Union, Poland, and East Germany than any other single act during the Prague spring.

Censorship in Poland was not formally abolished; it was only relaxed for a relatively short time. The press took advantage of the lull in governmental controls, but the closing down of the weekly *Po Prostu* in the early fall of 1957 marked the end of the honeymoon. Judging by the character of the many articles, statements, pronouncements, and revelations which made their appearance in Hungary during the revolt, the censorship in that country simply collapsed overnight. Television, which was only then making its debut in both countries, played a much smaller role than in Czechoslovakia some twelve years later.

The final variable in the syndrome concerns *changes in the economy* stemming out of the changeover. Here the major development was the disappearance of the collective farms in Poland and the return of almost all of the land to private owners. The suppression of the revolt prevented a similar process from taking place in Hungary. There were no corresponding changes in the Czechoslovak agriculture. Economic reforms continued to be implemented in Czechoslovakia mainly in the nonagricultural sectors. In both Hungary and Poland preparations were made for the reforms of the economies but none materialized in the course of the liberalization drive.

Total judgment regarding the extent of, and commitment to, liberalization was marked "high" for Czechoslovakia and Hungary and "mixed" for Poland. As indicated, the difference was primarily due to the effects of the abolition of censorship accompanied by a more intense activity of pressure groups in Czechoslovakia and Hungary. The emergence of pluralism in Poland was quite impressive on paper, but it never reached the depth and breadth exhibited in the other two countries.

The analysis of all twelve variables of the liberalization paradigm adds up to a verdict of "high" for Czechoslovakia, "high-mixed" for Hungary, and "mixed" for Poland, insofar as the chances of a lasting, and presumably successful, liberalization were concerned. Looking at the events in all countries in retrospect, this conclusion should occasion no surprise. It may even be argued that the selection of variables was tailored to achieve this particular verdict. While there was no intention to reach the final result in advance, it is also clear that the analysis suffers from a certain degree of arbitrariness which probably cannot be avoided completely.

Two additional comments are in order here. So far we have discussed variables which might be called "domestic" or "internal" since they concerned only the developments within single countries. The attitudes of other Communist countries in the bloc, and especially of the Soviet Union, were considered a parameter and kept constant. The utility of this procedure lies in its permitting us to concentrate on a few key processes, but it is also highly unrealistic. It is a well-known fact that liberalization processes in all three countries were determined to some extent by the reactions from abroad, particulary from the Soviet Union and other East European countries. If we were to add variable No. 13, entitled "foreign opposition," chances of a successful and lasting liberalization in Czechoslovakia and Hungary would be substantially diminished, while those in Poland would most likely remain the same.

Liberalization in Czechoslovakia was resented and critized from the spring of 1968 on by the majority of Soviet bloc countries, led by the USSR. The Polish democratization was briefly criticized and opposed by the Soviet Union, but once the changeover was completed, the Soviet leadership accepted it more or less at its face value. The opposition of the other East European countries lasted longer and it was finally terminated when it became clear that the new regime was not nearly so liberal as it appeared originally. The Hungarian liberalization which became transformed almost overnight into an open revolt threatened the very foundations of the bloc and especially the Soviet leadership. The latter had no option but to suppress it by force, regardless of the views and attitudes of its junior partners.

Whether it is proper to consider this particular variable or not is a matter of opinion. It may be argued, however, that in the final analysis it was this particular factor which proved crucial in the cases of Czechoslovakia and Hungary, rendering all the other variables largely meaningless.

One other possible variable, referred to earlier, might also properly be considered as playing a key role in the whole process of liberalization. Until now, with two significant exceptions, the paradigm relied on "institutional" variables and changes therein. It would appear, however, that attitudes, perceptions, and expectations also played a major part in providing impetus in the direction of democratization. The alienation of the intellectuals and youth from the system was emphasized as a necessary background condition of liberalization. In addition, one might also take into account the expectations of continuing liberalization which heretofore have been ignored if only because they do not lend themselves easily to empirical investigation.

There is little doubt, however, that such expectations were instrumental in transforming what originally began as a group agitation for a change into a national quasi-revolution. This can be illustrated with reference to the behavior of peasant and worker population in all three countries.

In at least two of the countries—Czechoslovakia and Hungary—the industrial working class responded rather slowly to the changeover and began to support it only in its final stages. While one can think of a variety of reasons for this passive behavior (relatively high wages, full employment, distrust of the intellectuals), for example, one can also analyze the attitude of the workers in terms of their expectations. Only after they became convinced that the changeover appeared permanent and that liberalization was making progress, did they jump on the bandwagon and join in the mass demand for additional measures pushing democratization further ahead. Interestingly enough, in both countries it was also the workers who resisted "recompression" long after other groups gave up the fight.

The situation in Poland was somewhat different. Here both peasants and workers stood in the forefront of the movement for a change in the expectation that their demands would be met. Once their demands were granted, however, they no longer attempted to maintain a united front with the rest of the society, thus making "recompression" somewhat easier. It is quite possible that, their expectations having been fulfilled, they no longer believed in further changes.

It can also be argued that the problem of perception played a vital role insofar as the reaction of other countries was concerned. Perception is to a large extent a combination of available information and of the personalities of domestic and foreign decision-makers. There is evidence to suggest, for example, that the Soviet leadership was fed distorted information about the developments in Czechoslovakia which clearly affected its perception of the various events and potential outcomes, and eventually forced it to intervene. On the other hand, after his lengthy conversation with Gomulka in the critical days of October 1956, Khrushchev apparently came to the conclusion that the Polish leader represented no major threat.

CONCLUSION

The final question concerns the utility and legitimacy of the preceding comparison. In general, comparative studies have a twofold aim: to organize data and to explain political or social processes in order to postulate certain hypotheses.

Insofar as the organization of data is concerned, no claim is made here regarding discovery of new and hitherto unknown facts. On the other hand it is suggested that the paradigm (or check list) shown in Table 1 does provide at least a partial explanation of the liberalization processes in Eastern Europe. It does trace the causal path from the earliest, relatively innocuous changes to the stage of a major systemic transformation in the given polities.

To be sure, the sample is much too small to draw any significant conclusions and to postulate major hypotheses with regard to the process of change in Communist societies. It could be argued that the chosen countries were not representative and that they exhibited a number of unique qualities which rendered the comparison somewhat meaningless. On balance, however, it may be said that, despite a number of differences, the three countries had much in common insofar as political, economic, and social variables were concerned. Thus, it is felt that a comparison of liberalization processes in the three systems was legitimate even if the conclusions can hardly be made into hypotheses with wide applicability.

This brings us to the problem of the selection of "key" or "strategic" variable or variables in the paradigm, the impact of which was likely to prove decisive for the success or failure of liberalization. In other words, which was the necessary and sufficient condition of liberalization? Here the answer seems to lie in the emergence of pluralism, which began to replace the single party mobilization regime. Whenever and wherever this particular process took place it did represent a direct challenge to the whole concept of Communist party supremacy which has been laboriously established and nurtured in the area ever since the end of World War II. The other variable which is occasionally cited in the case of Czechoslovakia—the abolition of censorship—can be looked upon as simply another manifestation of the loss of the party's monopoly of power. It was that loss which eventually resulted in the termination of the liberalization process by the Red Army in the case of Czechoslovakia and Hungary—the two countries where the party's authority was successfully challenged by a variety of formal and informal pressure groups.

Selected Comparative Tables and Bibliography

TABLES

TABLE I
Geographic Size of Communist-Ruled States

State	*Area (in square kilometers)*
Albania	28,748
Bulgaria	110,912
China	9,596,961
Cuba	114,524
Czechoslovakia	127,869
East Germany	107,771
Hungary	93,030
Mongolia	1,565,000
North Korea	120,538
North Vietnam	158,750
Poland	312,677
Romania	237,500
Soviet Union	22,402,200
Yugoslavia	255,804

Source: Statistical Office of the United Nations. *Demographic Yearbook, 1971* (New York, 1972).

TABLE II
Population of Communist-Ruled States

State	*Census Date*	*Male*	*Female*	*Total*
Albania	1/1/69	1,068,300*	1,011,500	2,079,800
Bulgaria	12/1/65	4,114,200	4,113,700	8,227,900
China	6/30/53	297,553,500	276,652,400	574,205,900[a]
Cuba	9/6/70	4,374,600	4,178,800	8,553,400
Czechoslovakia	12/1/70	6,997,000	7,365,000	14,362,000
East Germany	1/1/71	7,857,600	9,200,000	17,057,000
Hungary	1/1/70	4,998,300	5,317,300	10,315,600
Mongolia	1/10/69	597,400	600,200	1,197,600
North Korea	7/1/68	6,703,000	6,650,000	13,353,000[b]
North Vietnam	3/1/60	7,687,800	8,229,100	15,917,000[c]
Poland	12/8/70	15,834,500	16,754,700	32,589,200
Romania	7/1/71	10,056,400	10,413,200	20,469,600
Soviet Union	1/15/70	111,399,400	130,320,800	241,720,200[d]
Yugoslavia	3/31/71	10,328,100	10,007,000	20,335,100

* All figures, including totals, have been rounded to nearest 100.

[a] 1970 population estimated at 759,619,000.

[b] 1970 population estimated at 13,892,000.

[c] 1970 population estimated at 21,154,000.

[d] *Pravda,* April 19, 1970, offers the figure as 241,748,000.

Sources:

UN Demographic Yearbook, 1971 (New York, 1972).

The Statesman's Year Book 1972–73 (London, 1972).

1972 Statistical Yearbook of the Socialist Republic of Romania (Bucharest, 1972).

Yearbook on International Communist Affairs 1971, 1972 (Stanford, 1971, 1972).

Sovremennaya Koreya (Moscow, 1971).

The World This Year 1972 [Supplement to *The Political Handbook and Atlas of the World*] (New York, 1972).

Prethodni Rezultati Topisa Stanovništva i Stanova od 31. Marta 1971. Godina (Belgrade, 1971).

Area Handbook for North Korea (Washington, 1969).

TABLE III
Structure of the Economically Active Population (in percentages)

State	*Date*	*Agriculture*[a]	*Industry*[b]	*Other*[c]
Albania	1967	66	25	9
Bulgaria	1967	43	37	20
China	1971 est.	80	15	5
Cuba	1963	42	42	16
Czechoslovakia	1969	16	55	29
East Germany	1970	15	55	30
Hungary	1970	25	61	15
Mongolia	n.a.	n.a.	n.a.	n.a.
North Korea	1963	43	55	2
North Vietnam	1960	78	14	8
Poland	1967	42	35	23
Romania	1971	47	42	12
Soviet Union	1970	20	55	25
Yugoslavia	1971	43	32	25

[a] including forestry, hunting, fishing
[b] including mining, manufacturing, construction, utilities
[c] including services, professions
n.a.—not available

Sources:

Rozwoj gospodarczy krajow RWPG 1950–68 (Warsaw, 1969).
Narodnoe khozyaystvo SSRS v 1970 (Moscow: 1971).
Statistical Yearbook of the Socialist Republic of Romania 1972 (Bucharest, 1972).
Prethodni Rezultati Topisa Stanovništva i Stanova od 31. Marta 1971. Godina (Belgrade, 1971).
Area Handbook for North Vietnam (Washington, 1967).
Area Handbook for the People's Republic of China (Washington, 1972).
Area Handbook for Albania (Washington, 1971).
Area Handbook for Czechoslovakia (Washington, 1972).
Area Handbook for Cuba (Washington, 1971).
ILO Yearbook of Labour Statistics 1972 (Geneva, 1972).

TABLE IV
Communist Party Membership by Occupation

State	*Date*	*Total Membership*	*Agriculture*[a] *(in %)*	*Industry*[b] *(in %)*	*Other*[c] *(in %)*
Albania	1970	75,700	29.0	35.2	35.8
Bulgaria	1970	637,000	29	40	31
China	1956	17,000,000[d]	57.8	10.2	32
Cuba	1971	120,000	n.a.	n.a.	n.a.
Czechoslovakia	1970	1,200,000	n.a.	26.1	n.a.
East Germany	1971	1,910,000	6	56.6	37.5
Hungary	1970	662,400	18.9	41.7	39.4
Mongolia	1971	71,000	24	26	50
North Korea	1961	1,300,000[e]	27	57	16
North Vietnam	1970	1,100,000	n.a.	n.a.	n.a.
Poland	1970	2,296,000	11.6	40.2	48.2
Romania	1972	2,300,000	23.1	46.15	31.4
Soviet Union	1971	14,455,300	15.1	40.1	44.8
Yugoslavia	1971	1,049,200	6.5	30.3	63.2

[a] including forestry, hunting, fishing
[b] including mining, manufacturing, construction, utilities
[c] including services, professions
[d] Rebuilding the party after the Cultural Revolution makes estimating difficult, although the figure offered in recent years is 20 million.
[e] 1971 membership estimated at 1,600,000.
n.a.—not available

Sources:

Yearbook on International Communist Affairs 1971 (Stanford, 1971).
Area Handbook for North Korea (Washington, 1969).
Socijalizam, 7/8 (July–August 1971).
Pravda, March 31, 1971.
Zeri i Popullit, June 28, 1970.
World Strength of the Communist Party Organizations, 1972 (Washington, 1972).
Franz Schurmann, *Ideology and Organization in Communist China,* 2d ed. (Berkeley, 1970).
Scanteia (Bucharest), June 22, 1973.

BIBLIOGRAPHY

THERE is an ever-growing amount of literature on Communist-ruled states considered singly, jointly, topically, and from the perspective of a number of academic disciplines. Therefore, it seems most useful to provide readers of this volume with a selected guide to bibliographies, a listing of useful and reliable translation services, and a listing of the English-language journals (published in the West) that generally offer articles related to the study of Communist systems.

BIBLIOGRAPHIC GUIDES

ABC Political Science. ABC-CLIO, Inc. (Santa Barbara, 1969–).

ABSEES: Soviet and East European Abstract Series (Glasgow, 1970–).

AUFS Reports (American Universities Field Staff) (Hanover, 1952–).

American Bibliography of Russian and East European Studies (Indianapolis and Columbus, 1945–).

Berton, Peter and Wu, Eugene. *Contemporary China: A Research Guide* (Stanford, 1967).

Fischer, George and Schenkel, Walter. *Social Structure and Social Change in Eastern Europe: Guide to Specialized Studies Published in the West Since World War II in English, French, and German.* (New York State Education Department, 1970).

Foreign Area Studies Program, The American University. *Area Handbooks* on Communist-ruled states. A number of these Handbooks have been published since the early 1960s.

Golan, Galia and Shafir, Michael. *Bibliography for the Study of the Communist World* (Jerusalem, 1971).

Halperin, Joel. "Bibliography of English-language Sources on Yugoslavia," 2d ed. (University of Massachusetts, 1969).

Horecky, Paul L. *East Central Europe: A Guide to Basic Publications* (Chicago, 1969).

———, ed. *Russia and the Soviet Union: a Bibliographic Guide to Western-Language Publications* (Chicago, 1965).

———. *Southeastern Europe: A Guide to Basic Publications* (Chicago, 1969).

Kyriak, Theodore E., comp. and ed., *North Korea 1957–1961* (Annapolis, 1964).

Oksenberg, Michel, *et al. A Bibliography of Secondary English Language Literature on Contemporary Chinese Politics* (East Asian Institute, Columbia University, n.d.).

Rupen, Robert A. *Mongols of the Twentieth Century,* II (The Hague, 1964).

Suárez, Andrés, "The Cuban Revolution: The Road to Power," *Latin American Research Review,* VII, 3 (1972).

U. S. Bureau of the Census. *Bibliography of Social Science Periodicals and Monographs Series, North Korea, 1945–61* (Washington, 1962).

U. S. Department of the Army. *Communist China: Ruthless Enemy or Paper Tiger?* (Washington, 1962).

———. *Communist China: A Strategic Survey* (Washington, 1966).

———. *Communist China: A Bibliographic Survey, 1971* (Washington, 1971).

———. *Communist Eastern Europe. Analytic Survey of Literature* (Washington, 1971).

———. *USSR: Strategic Survey, A Bibliography* (Washington, 1969).

U. S. Department of State. Foreign Service Institute. *A Selected Functional and Country Bibliography for Eastern Europe and the USSR* (Washington, 1970).

Valdes, N. P. and Lieuwen, E., comps. *The Cuban Revolution. A Research Study Guide, 1959–1969* (Albuquerque, 1971).

Vigor, P. H., ed. *Books on Communism and the Communist Countries: A Selected Bibliography,* 3d ed. (London, 1971).

World Communism 1964–1969: A Selected Bibliography (Washington, 1971).

Additionally two useful reference volumes, published annually, are:

U. S. Department of State. Bureau of Intelligence and Research. *World Strength of the Communist Party Organizations* (Washington, 1949–).

Yearbook on International Communist Affairs (Stanford, 1966–).

Translation Services

BBC. *Summary of World Broadcasts* (all Communist-ruled states). Five times/week.

Current Background (China). Irregularly.

Current Digest of the Soviet Press (now incorporates *Current Abstracts of the Soviet Press*). Weekly.
Current Soviet Documents. Weekly.
Digest of the Soviet Ukrainian Press. Monthly.
Foreign Broadcast Information Services. *Daily Reports* (all Communist-ruled states). Five times/week.
International Arts and Sciences Press. *Publications* (translations from Soviet, East European, and Chinese journals and newspapers on a variety of topics). Quarterly.
Joint Publications Research Service Reports (includes translations of materials from all Communist-ruled states). Continuous.
Joint Translation Service (Yugoslavia). Daily until 1972.
Reprints from the Soviet Press. Biweekly.
Selections from China Mainland Magazines. Weekly.
Soviet Periodical Abstracts. Quarterly.
Survey of the China Mainland Press. Weekly.

Periodicals

A useful recent guide to relevant periodicals is Harry G. Shaffer, *English-Language Periodic Publications on Communism: An Annotated Index* (Research Institute on Communist Affairs, Columbia University, 1971).

Asian Survey (supersedes *Far Eastern Survey*). Monthly.
Bulletin. Institute for the Study of the USSR. Monthly.
Canadian-American Slavic Studies (supersedes *Canadian Slavic Studies*). Quarterly.
Canadian Slavonic Papers. Quarterly.
The China Quarterly. Quarterly.
Chinese Communist Affairs. Bimonthly.
Newsletter on Comparative Studies of Communism. Two to three times/year.
Cuban Studies Newsletter. Semiannually.
East Europe. Monthly.
East European Quarterly. Quarterly.
East West Digest. Weekly.
Journal of Asian Studies (supersedes *Far Eastern Quarterly*). Quarterly.
Law in Eastern Europe. Irregular.
Mizan (incorporates *Central Asian Review*). Bimonthly.
Problems of Communism. Bimonthly.
Radio Free Europe *Background Papers* and *Situation Reports*. Continuous.
Radio Liberty *Dispatches* and *Research Papers*. Weekly.
The Russian Review. Quarterly.
Slavic and East European Studies. Quarterly.
Slavic Review. Quarterly.
Sociology and Eastern European Newsletter. Irregular.

Soviet Studies. Quarterly.
Studies in Comparative Communism (supersedes *Communist Affairs*). Quarterly.
Studies in Soviet Thought. Quarterly.
Studies on the Soviet Union. Quarterly.
Survey. Quarterly.

P